P9-CRH-409

WINN LIBRARY
GORDON COLLEGE

The Stream of American Education

Robert E. Potter
University of Hawaii

AMERICAN BOOK COMPANY *New York*

EP 10 9 8 7 6 5 4 3 2 1

Copyright Acknowledgments

Grateful acknowledgment is made to the following publishers and individuals for permission to reprint material which is in copyright or of which they are the authorized publishers:

E. P. DUTTON & CO., INC.: For passages from *Education on the Dalton Plan* by Helen Parkhurst. Copyright, 1922, by E. P. Dutton & Co., Inc. Renewal, 1950, by Helen Parkhurst. Reprinted by permission of E. P. Dutton & Co., Inc.

E. P. DUTTON & CO., INC. AND MRS. JOHN DEWEY: For passages from *Schools of To-morrow* by John Dewey and Evelyn Dewey. Copyright, 1915, by E. P. Dutton & Co., Inc. Copyright renewed, 1943, by John Dewey and Evelyn Dewey. Reproduced by permission of the publishers and Mrs. John Dewey.

THE MACMILLAN CO. AND MRS. JOHN DEWEY: For passages from *Democracy and Education* by John Dewey. Copyright 1916 by the Macmillan Co. Copyright renewed 1944 by John Dewey. Reproduced by permission of the Macmillan Co. and Mrs. John Dewey.

THE UNIVERSITY OF CHICAGO PRESS: For passages reprinted from *American Higher Education: A Documentary History* by Richard Hofstadter and Wilson Smith by permission of the University of Chicago Press. Copyright 1961 by the University of Chicago Press. For passages reprinted from *Lay My Burden Down* by B. A. Botkin by permission of the University of Chicago Press. Copyright 1945 by the University of Chicago Press.

Preface

The history of the United States is one of cycles of social revolution—the Age of Enlightenment and the War for Independence, the Age of the Common Man and the Civil War, the Progressive Movement and the War to Make the World Safe for Democracy, the New Deal and the Second War to Make the World Safe for Democracy. Perhaps the civil-rights movement and the "War on Poverty" are the opening stages of another cycle. Our schools—one of the most important institutions in the American culture—have been both a part and a product of the social forces which gave rise to the revolutions. Their story is an integral segment of America's cultural history; they have changed as the rest of society has changed. It is important, therefore, for the professional teacher to see the school—its ideas, movements, intentions, experiments, goals—in the context of other social movements, so that the future teacher may be better able to evaluate current educational problems in their continuity and be better prepared to participate in making educational policies that will further the needs of American society. This text attempts to offer the student such a view—the school in context.

Another major aim of this book is to help the student learn to use historical materials more effectively as analytical and critical tools in understanding educational questions and developing wise educational policies. To this end, the Prologue discusses the purposes of the history of education in the professional preparation of a teacher. It describes the basic techniques of document selection and evaluation. It is not an attempt to teach historiography to the potential research scholar but a primer of suggestions on how to use history more intelligently in everyday life.

Since the problems of the South today are largely the problems of the nation, and since the progress of the nation depends to a great extent on the progress of the South, I have devoted a complete chapter to the attempts of the South after the Civil War to build a system of universal education. I have also given lengthy consideration to Negro education and school desegregation. I have dealt in detail with federal support practices, because the issue of federal aid is one that the future teacher will have to help decide. Since religious issues appear to be potential conflict areas in the future, I have treated the relationship of religion and education throughout the history of America. Similarly, as teaching moves in the direction of greater professionalization, and as the questions of the teacher's freedom in making educational policy and in acting as a citizen promise to be more critical than ever, I have given considerable attention to the issue of academic freedom as it relates to the revolutionary development of the nation.

The text is developed chronologically, with divisions into parts corresponding to the periods of social revolution. Each period has a brief chronology table and introduction to orient the student. For the reader who wishes to delve deeper into the general history of the period, each part introduction concludes with a list of selected readings. The chapters within the parts concentrate specifically on educational developments, rather than on the general history of the period.

Most of the text is expository, but to give a flavor of the time and a tone of the conflict, texts of laws and court decisions, descriptions of schools, statements of philosophers in their own words, autobiographical accounts of teachers, and other primary documents have been incorporated into the text. The presence of these documents also gives the student opportunity to exercise the skills of historical evaluation outlined in the Prologue.

I owe an incalculable debt to several people—to Dean Emeritus James William Norman and Professor Bozidar Muntyan, of the University of Florida, for valuable criticism of parts of the manuscript; to Dr. Forrest L. Shoemaker, of Ohio University, and the late Dr. A. W. Anderson, of the University of Illinois, for their encouragement of my professional interest; to the patient and careful work of the secretaries and typists, the most long-suffering of whom was Mrs. Dorothy Esry; and to my wife, Prudy, who for several years had to tolerate piles of dusty library books and sheafs of papers while I tried to reduce mountains of documents to a coherent story.

ROBERT E. POTTER

Contents

PROLOGUE

History and the Teacher

"The biggest fault with our professional training," complain many beginning teachers, "is that we had too many theory courses and not enough concrete, practical 'helps' for what to do in the classroom."

Those who make this complaint do not understand the basic characteristics of a "profession." They confuse the professional with the technician who is trained to perform more or less routine tasks. A profession is intellectual in character; it applies a body of theoretical knowledge to the solution of the problems which society has delegated to the professional practitioners as their particular responsibility, and it governs the standards of preparation and performance of those practitioners through reference to that body of theory. For teaching to reach professional status, teachers must work with increased energy at achieving the skills, attitudes, and responsibilities characteristic of a profession. The beginning teacher finds himself faced with many new routine tasks that pose a serious threat to his success—filling out class rollbooks, coping with particular pupil misbehaviors, getting inattentive students to listen. When he encounters this profusion of continuing problems, many a teacher would gladly trade his generalized theory courses for a simple, foolproof answer to each immediate question. He would sell his professional "soul" for a release from the threat of the decision-making which is so much a part of the life of a professional person. The more consistently teachers apply tested theoretical knowledge to the solution of their practical problems, the closer teaching will come to the realization of the goals of "professionalism."

Professional Responsibilities

One characteristic of a professional is that he is personally responsible for making and helping make important decisions. These decisions must be made on the basis of a body of knowledge, arrived at through the intelligent analysis of past experience. Experience—success and failure—is examined, hypotheses are suggested and tested, and the validation or rejection of hypotheses leads to statements that are properly called "theory." Theory is not unsubstantiated speculation or wild hunches; it is the intelligent explanation and generalization of actual experience. Furthermore, theory is useful to the professional practitioner because it serves as a guide for future action. The vocations that have made the greatest and most rapid advances are those that have developed the most complete and most reliable bodies of theoretical knowledge. Only as we generalize our experience, formulate hypotheses, test them, refine them into theory, and apply that theory will we improve our work, ourselves, and our society.

Among the decisions for which the professional worker has responsibility are novel and unique problems that he must solve on the basis of his theoretical knowledge. These decisions must be made by the practitioner; they cannot be made during the period of professional preparation. It is not possible for college engineering students to be told how to design every bridge they will ever build. Nor is it possible for prospective teachers to be told how to meet the infinite number of complex situations they will face in the classroom. The professional is one who can think for himself, relying on theory to help solve the constantly changing problems he faces.

In addition to decisions which must be made within the profession, there are others which, although directly affecting the profession, must be made by the general public. Physicians do not determine the law on health insurance plans. However, the medical associations are always ready to express an opinion on "socialized" medicine. Any profession that abdicates the responsibility of helping the public make policies affecting the work of that profession will suffer unsatisfactory conditions for successful practice. Teachers, individually and through their organizations, have failed particularly to meet this professional responsibility. They have traditionally avoided public controversy even where there is no question of job security. They often do not have the professional perspective to take an intelligent stand on bond issues, textbook and library censorship, loyalty oaths for teachers, religion in the schools, and other matters of public policy affecting schools. Although many subtle forms of pressure are brought to bear on the outspoken teacher, his obligation to improve the quality of schooling demands that he have the courage to take stands on issues directly affecting education. Another reason for teachers' failure to speak out is that they have not recognized their responsibility to do so—an outgrowth of the historical non-professional status of teachers in America. Perhaps, also, teachers do not themselves understand the issues, a result of their inadequate theoretical background, particularly in the relationship of education to other social institutions. It is in the development of this professional awareness and competency that a study of the history of education can make its greatest contribution.

History and Problem-Solving

Often we are not aware of our problems and failures until we see our own time and culture contrasted with other times and other cultures. Placing the familiar beliefs and practices of the present in juxtaposition with the quite different ones of the past may help us recognize significant problems we might otherwise overlook.

To deal effectively with any problem it is necessary (1) to see the problem in its total context, (2) to understand past and present trends, (3) to discover possible solutions, (4) to evaluate the alternative solutions and select that one which seems to offer the most satisfactory consequences, and (5) to persevere against difficulties and social inertia in seeking the desired solution. The study of history can be of value as preparation for increased competency in each of these phases of problem solving.

Understanding Context

Understanding the context of problems includes seeing the interrelatedness of social institutions, the continuity of human experience, and the development of the problem itself.

The study of history should develop an awareness of the interrelatedness of social institutions. To understand the schools of colonial New England, one must understand something about the Puritan religious beliefs, the political system, the family, the economic life, the class structure, and the geographical layout of the town. Time removes the mass of irrelevant details that obscure the relations; in studying the New England schools we learn something of a model for use in the study of our own times.

The study of history should also develop recognition of the continuity of human experience; the problems of the present are the result of the past, and the solutions of today are the source of tomorrow's problems. When the Russians launched their first Sputnik in 1957, some hysterical critics blamed our scientific lag on the lack of science being taught in the American elementary schools, contrasting them with the current Soviet schools. But Sputnik was launched, not by Soviet elementary pupils but by scientists who had attended elementary schools two or three decades before. In assessing the fault of our scientific lag, we should look at the schools of twenty or thirty years ago, when our present adult generation was in school. And when it comes to solving the problem, recognition of the continuity of experience should warn that overemphasis on science today may result in a shortage of other essential specialists and broadly educated "generalists" a generation hence.

The context of a problem includes the problem itself—how it arose and what complications have occurred in its development. For example, one thorny problem facing schools today is the relationship of church and state and how much, if any, religion should be taught in the public schools. This problem goes back to our colonial history and beyond, and the patterns with which many communities are now experimenting have grown up as a result of many compromises in the past. Without an understanding of how our present problems began, we impose an unnecessary obstacle to clear thinking.

Recognizing Trends

Part of the analysis of a problem should be a recognition of past and current trends, and the study of history discloses long-range trends as well as more recent ones. Thus it would be folly for any state to overhaul its school finance system without a careful study of the trends of federal financing of education. Recognizing that a trend exists does not necessarily mean that one must move with it, but action without consideration of a trend is like diving into a stream without observing the force and direction of the current. The strength of a trend may indicate that a problem may be easy to solve or that it may even solve itself through the impetus of already acting forces. On the other hand, the current may be so strong, even though in an undesirable direction, that prudence dictates the application of energies and talents to the solution of other problems.

Seeking Solutions

In the search for solutions, history can be used as a rich source of ideas and as a stimulus to the imagination. Although history does not repeat itself, there are often problems in the past analogous to present problems and past solutions significant for the present. In a like fashion, knowledge of past failures may deter us from making some unwise decisions. Anyone who knew of the nineteenth-century failures to arrive at universal education through philanthropy might have anticipated that Southern schools would not successfully evade racial integration through the establishment of "private" school systems.

Furthermore, awareness of the past should be a warning that no solution is perfect, that there are no panaceas. The monitorial schools of the first half of the nineteenth century did not solve all the educational problems of the time, as their supporters claimed they would; radio teaching was not the cure-all that it was promised to be in the 1930's. Armed with this hindsight, modern teachers should perhaps look on such devices as television and programed learning as useful adjuncts to teaching but avoid the over-enthusiasm that often results in disappointment and failure to use imperfect techniques for what they are worth.

Evaluating Alternatives

Often we have a choice among alternative solutions. Our decision should be based on the values that form the foundation of our culture. The study of how the great philosophers dealt with educational problems can help us develop the personal and professional values for judging the adequacy of possible solutions in the total social context of the problem. The long-range view of the development of our educational institutions reveals those values that have been persistent in our educational policy-making. For example, two of the American ideals which go back to colonial days and which have become increasingly important are the concepts of individual worth and universal educational opportunity. Any educational policy that ignores these ideals is inconsistent with the over-all development of American education and American life in general.

Securing and Sustaining Dedication

In carrying out educational policy, teachers often find themselves frustrated to the point of despair. Progress is slow. Materials are inadequate and out of date. School budgets are insufficient. Everyone thinks he knows how to run the schools better and less expensively than the teachers and administrators who have made it their life work. Under these conditions, teachers are frequently discouraged. Progress may seem slight when we see only the short range, but when we compare schools of today with those of a hundred years ago, or even of fifty years ago, we realize that progress has been phenomenal. The problems we face in the present are no more overwhelming than those faced by Horace Mann in 1837 or by the Southern educator during Reconstruction days. When teachers feel that they are people of little importance, they should recall that many great men—Plato, Augustine, Erasmus, Locke, Rousseau, Franklin, Jefferson—considered education a primary concern and that other men were great because they were teachers—Buddha, Socrates, Jesus. That is the proud heritage of the teacher.

Fundamentals of Historical Study

To increase their effectiveness in the use of history, teachers need some understanding of the basic principles of historical study and documentation. To the historian, "document" means any source that reveals evidence about the past. Although documents are frequently written or printed, they may take other forms: phonograph records, tape recordings, interviews, photographs, maps, artifacts from a museum. The teacher using history may find documentation in books, newspapers, minutes of a school board, oral testimony, blueprints, collections of school equipment and books, or school buildings themselves.

Sources of Information

The most common source of historical information is the library. In addition to the general textbook studies of the history of education, there are many specialized research publications that give the background of educational problems. To locate library sources, the novice historian of education should seek the aid of the reference librarian or bibliography-room staff, for there are printed bibliographies on so many subjects that it is sometimes necessary to use bibliographies of bibliographies to find the pertinent lists. Thumbing through the card catalogue and browsing along the shelves in the stacks, where such access is permitted can lead to discovery of useful sources.

Public documents are invaluable sources for the historian of education, particularly in matters concerning the public schools. These sources include the public laws, legislative proceedings, reports of state and county superintendents, minutes of school board meetings, records of tax assessors, and court decisions.

Some of the information gaps in official records can be filled in from newspaper reports of school board meetings or controversies over schools. Feature stories are almost always secondary sources and should be used as leads to more reliable documents, although sometimes it is necessary to judge these stories themselves for whatever evidence they may contain.

Professional journals and general circulation magazines often present background information useful to the researcher trying to understand an educational problem. The United States Office of Education and various State departments of education prepare and publish volumes of data concerning schools and problems of education. Professional organizations publish the results of current research and summarize contemporary issues in education.

In dealing with current problems, it is possible to utilize the oral testimony of the participants of some past events. School personnel, public officials, businessmen, contractors, and other interested persons are often able to give information not included in any written documents.

Evaluating Sources

Using historical sources is somewhat like detective work. As documents show need for further details and suggest other possible sources, the search broadens. Meanwhile, the accumulated information must be evaluated and organized into a pattern, each new item being analyzed to see how it fits with what is already known and whether it confirms or contradicts data already accepted. Any inconsistency requires careful examination, not only of the newly discovered information but also of the previously accepted documents. One of the major problems for the person using historical evidence is to determine which documents to believe and how much of each to believe.

In the evaluation of documents, there are three questions that must be answered. (1) Is the document authentic? (2) Is it reliable? (3) Are the pertinent details credible?

AUTHENTICITY When the historian encounters a document, he must first ascertain whether it is what it purports to be. Is it a forgery, a hoax, or some other kind of fraudulent document? Fortunately for the historian of education, faked documents are not common in issues relating to education, partly because there has been so little general interest in the institution of schooling and partly because education in the United States has been largely a state affair and therefore reported in public papers or newspaper accounts, neither of which is readily susceptible to tampering. When the historian of education has occasion to use other kinds of documents, however, he must be aware of the possibility that they may not be authentic. A few simple checks serve to detect fraudulence of an obvious kind.

The first step in authenticating a document is dating it. Once a date has been determined, the document should be checked to see whether there are any references out of proper time order. If the researcher is dealing with documents of an early enough period, a check of vocabulary, spelling, punctuation, composition style, and similar minutiae can reveal relatively unskilled attempts to simulate older documents.

The more adroitly prepared hoaxes require the special skills of a trained historian who is able to investigate such matters as watermarks in the paper, chemical composition of inks, and detailed items of historical information on which even a cautious author of fraud might slip. The best guard against being taken in by faked documents is independent corroboration.

In judging authenticity, the historian judges the document as a whole. If any part is fraudulent, none of the document can be accepted as historical evidence. Once a document is judged to be authentic, it still must be evaluated for reliability and credibility.

PRIMARY AND SECONDARY SOURCES To evaluate the reliability of a source and the credibility of its details, the historian first attempts to classify it—or more accurately, portions of it—as "primary" or "secondary." A primary document is one produced by someone who was present at the event he reports; a secondary document is one produced by someone who was not a witness of the event he reports or, even if he was present, reports what someone else said about the event. Many documents are a combination of primary and secondary accounts, and in many instances, it is difficult to determine how much is primary and how much secondary. In a school superintendent's report, for example, much of the information may be derived from the reports of individual principals, but the superintendent, with no intention to deceive, may have written the report as if all the facts resulted from his own observation and firsthand knowledge.

In general, primary sources are more reliable than secondary, because of the inevitable distortion that occurs in each retelling of an event. In many secondary accounts the facts are considerably altered to make the retelling more interesting, more favorable to a particular point of view, more damaging to the opposition, or more sensational. Courts of law reject what lawyers call hearsay evidence. The historian too should be wary of accepting hearsay.

Since the historian is concerned really with the credibility of the specific data he needs in his problem, his analysis as to how much of a document is primary and how much secondary should be applied to the particular data he selects to use, as well as to the over-all reliability of the source.

RELIABILITY When the historian discovers some data that are significant for his studies, one of the first questions he must ask is: How reliable is this source? Obviously, a reliable source is more likely to produce credible facts than one which is unreliable. The more biased a source is, the less reliable it is and the less credibility can be attached to any of its "facts."

How is it possible to judge reliability? Professor Louis Gottschalk suggests four general criteria for determining the reliability of a source: (1) the time-lapse, (2) the purpose for which the document was intended, (3) the confidential nature of the document, and (4) the expertness of the witness.[1]

1. The shorter the time-lapse between an event and the recording of the observation by the *primary* source, the more reliable the document is likely to be. Obviously, the longer the delay in making the report, the more time the witness has had to forget details, make judgments about what was important and what should be left out, and even invent, consciously or unconsciously. For this reason, autobiographies and memoirs are far less reliable than diaries and journals.

For *secondary* documents, on the other hand, the longer the time-lapse, the more reliable the account. The interval permits the source to have greater objectivity. For example, an historian writing of the Civil War today could ordinarily exercise much greater impartiality than one writing in 1870. The intervening time also permits the secondary source to make use of earlier scholarship on the subject, with the wealth of primary sources more fully explored, indexed, and analyzed. For these reasons, a secondary document may give a far more complete and reliable account of a controversy than one written by a participant who might be including primary materials of his own. A twentieth-century historical summary of Horace Mann's controversy with the Boston school men in 1845 might be more reliable in most respects than Mann's own account.

2. A record of an event—the transcript of a court case, a sales slip, a contract, a written order or warrant—is more reliable than a report made to others. The directive from a superintendent to his school principals is more reliable than his report to the school board concerning the directive. Not only is there an opportunity for the reporter to forget some of the details, but in preparing an account for others to read he may alter the details, however slightly or unconsciously. A personal memorandum made by an individual to refresh his memory is more reliable than an account intended to impress others. At the

[1] Louis Gottschalk, *Understanding History* (New York: Knopf, 1951), 90–91.

other extreme, obviously biased reports, including propaganda, are highly unreliable.

3. In general, the more restricted the intended body of readers of a report, the more reliable it is. When someone prepares a report to be released to the general public, he is likely to color the account far more than in a report to be given a close friend or submitted to an immediate superior. The confidential report of a principal to the school board is thus more reliable than his account to a Parent-Teacher Association meeting or to a newspaper. A note of caution in this respect: sometimes a report is made as if it were intended for limited circulation when the author knows that it is to be made public. One would be wrong in assuming that Horace Mann's reports to the Board of Education of Massachusetts were intended to be confidential; Mann expected his annual reports to educate the public as well as inform the Board. In evaluating a document, it is necessary to determine how broad a field of readers the author actually expected to address.

4. Because a person is not likely to observe and understand every detail of an event or be able to report even all he has observed, the expert who knows what to look for and understands what he sees is more reliable than the casual observer. A supervisor's report of what happened in a classroom will almost certainly be more reliable than that of a parent after a one-time visit to her child's schoolroom. The non-teaching mother may have seen only what her child did and could not see the day's lesson in the context of the year's work. It is necessary, of course, to view with great caution the qualifications of many "experts." Simply writing on a subject does not make one an "expert." A scientist's expert knowledge of atomic physics or a historian's research in economic utopian communities will not qualify either as an expert in matters concerning education.

When a document has been evaluated for reliability, it is not necessarily accepted or rejected in toto. Unlike authenticity, reliability is a relative matter. A document may be considered highly reliable, fairly reliable, somewhat unreliable, or highly unreliable. The more reliable it is, the more credibility may be attached to the statements included within it. However, it is possible for even a generally reliable document to be somewhat inaccurate in some details and, on the other hand, it is possible for a relatively unreliable document to contain some highly credible statements. Even a liar often includes statements of whose truth he may be quite unaware. No document should be dismissed summarily for unreliability without examination of its details, since a biased or inexpert source may offer some significant and credible data.

CREDIBILITY Credibility, as the term is used here, means the degree of confidence which can be placed in a particular detail of information. As with reliability of the total document, judgments on credibility of details are relative.

According to Gottschalk, single details of testimony, even from relatively unreliable documents, may be considered credible if they meet four tests. (1) Was the primary source able to tell the truth? (2) Was the primary source willing to tell the truth? (3) In secondary statements, have the primary documents been quoted accurately? (4) Is there independent corroboration for the detail in question?[2]

1. The ability of a primary source to tell the truth rests largely on his presence at the event he reports and on his competence in the field. For a secondary source, the author's ability to tell the truth depends on his competence, which will be displayed partly in his judgment of the reliability and credibility of the documents from which he is drawing his information. Obviously one who was not present at a particular event cannot be a primary source for that incident, and one who limits his research to unreliable documents simply lacks competence. Sometimes even witnesses are not able to tell the truth; their own involvement may make it impossible for them to observe the whole incident or to place objectively their role in the event. In many cases, inability to tell the truth borders closely on unwillingness to tell the truth.

2. Even the most reliable witness, knowing the truth about some detail, will on occasion be unwilling to tell the whole truth. His unwillingness may be conscious or unconscious. It is extremely difficult, if not impossible, to be objective about ourselves or those things that intimately affect us, and the lack of objectivity is often hard to detect. To determine the source's degree of willingness to tell the truth involves knowing as much as possible about the source and his relationship to the matter he is reporting.

The most obvious cause of unwillingness to tell the truth is bias. A person propagandizing to promote existing school systems is not likely to report the shortcomings of the schools or the teachers, and someone engaged in adverse criticism of education is frequently inaccurate in the opposite direction. Propaganda issued by a source who is not aware of his bias or who does not admit it exists is particularly misleading because of the apparent objectivity of the source and the document he has produced.

The relationship between a source and the intended audience may

[2] *Ibid.*, p. 150.

also affect willingness to tell the truth. The need to sell books, the desire to win social approval, the conventions of courtesy—all these can lead to unwillingness to tell the truth. Items may be omitted. Unimportant details may be heightened for effect. Completely false details may be included.

There are several circumstances in which willingness to tell the truth can be assumed.[3] If a witness is disinterested or unbiased in relation to the event he is reporting, there is little reason for him to distort the facts, other than through misinterpretation. Consequently, statements concerning matters in which the witness has no vested interest are fairly credible, even if the remainder of the document is unreliable and highly biased. In judging the disinterest of a witness, it is important to distinguish disinterest from lack of interest. A witness who was uninterested may not have observed closely enough to be able to tell the truth.

When a witness with a vested interest makes a statement contrary to his point of view, to his own interests, or to a cause he supports, that statement possesses a high degree of credibility. When a defender of the private schools admits that public school graduates do better than private school graduates in college, that statement is probably accurate—if, of course, he has sufficient information to be able to tell the truth on the issue.

Similarly, if a witness with a bias makes statements contrary to what he anticipated even about matters in which he has no material interest, those statements may have a high degree of credibility.

Many reports of the past contain significant information that was common knowledge at the time the report was written. Such information may be assumed to be credible because it is unlikely that the source would falsify something everyone knew. For instance, a statement in a report of the Reconstruction period saying that most of the freed slaves were illiterate would be credible because the condition of the freedmen was known by too many observers for anyone to lie about their literacy.

Every document contains many details that are incidental to the main idea. These incidental references can be the basis of some highly credible data, even in very biased documents. Imagine a letter of complaint which states that "Mrs. Smith, the chemistry teacher, gets paid more than any of the other teachers in the school." Whether or not Mrs. Smith is paid more than the other teachers is questionable; however, it is highly credible that the school has a number of teachers, that they are paid, that chemistry is included in the curriculum, and that there is a Mrs. Smith on the faculty.

[3] *Ibid.*, pp. 161–165.

In making judgments as to the willingness of a source to tell the truth, it is particularly helpful to know as much as possible about the source and his times. Knowledge of the witness' interests and points of view can be a critical factor in determining what parts of his reports are credible and what parts are suspect.

3. Although the historian prefers primary documents whenever they are available, he finds it necessary from time to time to rely on secondary documents. In the use of secondary documents, it is essential that he evaluate the accuracy of quotations and references taken from primary documents. Were the primary documents quoted in their entirety? Was the secondary source willing to tell the truth? How competent was the secondary source to evaluate his primary documents? How competent was he in his interpretations and paraphrasing? When these questions can be answered in a manner favorable to the source, the secondary statement can be accepted with some credibility. If a competent state school superintendent reports that many children of school age in his state are not enrolled in school, his remark may be assumed to be highly credible, even though he is a secondary source basing his statement on data reported to him by county superintendents. The fact that such an admission is contrary to the most favorable view of his work as a school administrator indicates that he probably has told the truth. If his report contains the full text of all the reports on that subject made to him by the other school officials, the credibility of his generalization is further enhanced. Since most documents are partly secondary and partly primary, this test of reporting primary documents accurately is not limited to research studies or general history books but is equally applicable to documents which are substantially primary in nature but which also draw on the accounts of others.

4. Just as courts of law hesitate to convict on the word of one witness, so should the historian remain skeptical of any detail, even though it meets the other tests of credibility, without independent corroboration. Care must be taken in assuming corroboration, because two sources which appear independent may have derived their data from the same third source, or one of them may have based his information on the other. Confirming the admission of the school superintendent about children not enrolled by referring to the reports of the county superintendents is not independent corroboration, because these reports were probably the source on which his statement was based. However, statistics collected by juvenile courts might provide the independent corroboration needed to confirm the data.

For some facts there can be no corroboration, for there may have been only one witness. In such cases, the historian must rely on judging the credibility on the general reliability of the source and the absence of any contradictory statements.

In the final analysis, it will be the judgment of the individual historian that determines what data he accepts as credible. The usefulness of any historical generalization depends in large measure on how effective the historian has been in determining the credibility of the data on which the generalization is based. In making the generalization, the historian must exercise considerable self-discipline, using only the credible and discarding interesting but doubtful data.

Limitations of History

Because of the nature of historical evidence, there are limitations to the use of history, and the teacher, basing actions partially on historical generalizations, must observe these limitations.

In his collection of data, the historian suffers from several severe disadvantages. Picture a chemist conducting an experiment in his laboratory and being called away just as the crucial reaction is to take place. Some days later he recalls that the janitor was sweeping in the lab when he left, and so he asks the janitor what happened. How much validity would the physical scientist attach to a report made by an incompetent chance observer who has probably forgotten much of what he saw and who does not know how to describe it in terms the chemist can use? Yet that is often the kind of report on which the historian must base his generalizations. To complicate matters, the reports are often filled with bias, ignorance, and faulty observation. It should be obvious, then, that historical generalizations are not of the same kind as those derived by the physical scientist. The historian cannot control variables; he cannot re-run the experiment; he can never be sure he has all the data pertinent to his problem. Consequently, his generalizations are highly tentative.

Because of the incompleteness and possible inaccuracy of data, the historian can neither prove nor predict human affairs with the same degree of confidence with which the physicist or chemist can predict the outcome of certain phenomena under controlled conditions. There have been periods in the past when conditions were somewhat analogous to certain conditions in the present, and there is the temptation to predict the future on the basis of these parallels. However, because of the highly tentative nature of much historical data and because social conditions of another time and place cannot be exactly duplicated and controlled, history can only help anticipate possible consequences which may result from particular behavior. This is a form of prediction, it is true, but it is prediction with a very low level of precision or confidence. For example, we may observe that, until now, increasing the requirements for teacher preparation has resulted in an increase in the number of aspirants to the vocation of teaching. This evidence suggests a direct ratio between increased requirements for teacher certification and an increased number of students preparing to be teachers; it does not *prove* that further raising of certification requirements will again result in greater enrollments in teacher preparation. On the basis of the evidence, however, we may *anticipate* that requiring an extra year of preparation *might* not aggravate the teacher shortage, as it may logically appear it would.

The same complexity of human affairs and unreliability of evidence that makes prediction unsound makes it difficult to attribute cause-and-effect relationships with much confidence. While it may be possible to indicate an immediate, precipitating factor for some historical event, the true causes are probably long-range and difficult to weigh. The historian must be wary of doing more than postulating that certain factors probably had influence in particular directions. For example, to say that the rural organization of the plantation South during the colonial period was *the* cause of Southern failure to develop a public education system as early as New England would be an unwarranted assertion. It was undoubtedly a factor in that failure, but there were others that may have been far more critical in creating the aristocratic tutorial system then prevalent.

These admonitions should not be taken to mean that history is of no value. The physical sciences have many of the same limitations as history. The astronomer cannot control his subjects and must base his generalization on observation. Yet he has developed techniques that enable him to describe stellar and solar phenomena, to predict eclipses with great precision and confidence, and even to plan rocket orbits which will intercept the moon and the planets. Meteorologists cannot control tornadoes or hurricanes, but they are often able to anticipate them and issue warnings to those areas most likely to be struck. These sciences have used observation of the past as the basis for their prediction of the future, developing specific techniques for the interpretation and projection of their observations. As historians evolve better techniques of collecting and evaluating data, they may produce more useful analyses and interpretations of the past and thus increase the probability of anticipating correctly some of the possible consequences of future actions.

The attitudes and techniques of the historian cannot be acquired merely by reading about them. They must be cultivated through continued use. You will be missing an important value to be gained from the use of this book if you do not continually challenge both the quotations and the expository material in the text. Reading history is more than a pleasant pastime; questioning, doubting, analyzing, and confirming statements within documents can become an exciting and profitable way to acquire a better understanding of the present and more control over the future.

QUESTIONS FOR DISCUSSION

1. Suppose you found two letters from a college senior to his mother, one dated in May and describing the conditions of a teaching position he had just been offered and another dated in October of the same year telling her of the differences between what he had been promised and what he actually received.
   a. Which would be a more reliable source of information about the actual teaching conditions, the May or the October letter? Why?
   b. Which would be the more reliable source about what he had been originally promised? Why?
2. Let us suppose you want to check on the improvements in schools in your state in the last fifty years, and you find three sources describing the schools of fifty years ago. The first is a recently written autobiography of a former teacher who has become a famous novelist; the second is a series of letters written fifty years ago from a school teacher to his parents; the third is a diary kept by a school teacher of that time. Which would you consider generally most reliable? Least reliable? Why?
3. In conversation a teacher angrily states that a local newspaper editor who severely criticizes schools and teachers in his editorials had once tried to teach but could not maintain discipline in his classroom, had later resented the fact that his college-graduate daughter could not get a teacher certificate, and now fights school improvements because he wants to keep the school taxes down on rental property which he owns and which is greatly under-assessed. How reliable do you consider the teacher's report? Why? Where might you go to try to find the best corroboration or refutation of his statements?
4. A chemistry teacher with thirty years' teaching experience has just been discharged for incompetency. He makes the following statement in a letter to the editor of the town newspaper: "The School Board fired me because I am the only teacher in the school who has any real standards and expects the pupils to work. I am not incompetent, because no one

has complained at all during the last thirty years. I teach with the same set of notes I have had ever since I started, and I have had lots of experience in putting those facts across to the pupils. I admit that I don't use laboratory demonstrations, but they don't need to see the experiment to learn the formulae and equations. My former students all do well in chemistry in college. I am the victim of political dirty-work." How reliable do you consider his letter? Why? Select at least two particular details you find highly credible. Why would you accept them? Select two you judge to have relatively low credibility. Why do you reject them?

5. Examine some of the quotations in this text. Evaluate them for reliability. Identify several highly credible statements from each and give reasons for your judgment. Identify and criticize several details which you judge to be of low credibility. Explain how you would attempt to corroborate some of the details.

SUGGESTED READINGS

Bailyn, Bernard. *Education in The Forming of American Society*. New York: Vintage Books, 1960.

Brickman, William W. *Guide to Research in Educational History*. New York: New York U. Bookstore, 1949.

Edwards, Newton D. "General Methods: Historical, Comparative, and Documentary," National Society for the Study of Education, *The Scientific Movement in Education, Thirty-seventh Yearbook Part II*, 1938.

Gottschalk, Louis. *Understanding History*. New York: Knopf, 1951. Chapters III, V, VI, and VII.

Johnson, Allen. *The Historian and Historical Evidence*. New York: Scribner's, 1926. Pp. 43–53, 57–59, 61–63, 82–83, 89–100, 145–150.

Kent, Sherman. *Writing History*. New York: Crofts, 1946. Chapter 1.

Nevins, Allan. *The Gateway to History*. New York: Appleton Century, 1938. Pp. 3–6, 138–204, 375–380.

Renier, G. J. *History—Its Purpose and Method*. Boston: Beacon, 1950. Pp. 13–19, 26–27, 102–105, 108–110, 221–225.

PART One

Our Colonial Backgrounds

CHRONOLOGY

1607—Founding of Jamestown Colony
1619—First Negro slaves in Jamestown
1620—Landing of Pilgrims at Plymouth
1626—Founding of New Amsterdam by the Dutch
1629—Founding of Massachusetts Bay Colony
1630–1642—Period of great migration of Puritans to Massachusetts Bay
1634—Founding of St. Mary's in Maryland
1636—Hooker leads settlers to Connecticut.
1636—Roger Williams flees to Rhode Island.
1638—Delaware settled by the Swedes
1642–1646—Civil War in England
1649–1660—Puritan Commonwealth in England
1663—Grant of Carolina to eight proprietors
1664—Surrender of New Amsterdam to British
1679—New Hampshire settled as a separate colony
1681—Pennsylvania settled by Penn
1688—Glorious Revolution in England; William and Mary replace the Stuarts.
1689—Act of Toleration in England
1692—New Charter for Massachusetts
1755–1763—French and Indian War
1765—Stamp Act
1775—Battles at Lexington and Concord

THE FIRST COLONISTS TO COME TO America brought with them more than their tools, furniture, and clothing. They brought their religions, political theories, economic policies, family organization, community arrangements, and social class structure. They also brought their ideas about education and schools. But the conditions of the New World worked changes in Old World patterns, so that from the very beginning, schools in the colonies began to evolve into peculiarily American systems with definite regional differences. These differences appeared clearly in the colonial period, reflecting the regional contrasts in the other institutions of colonial society.

The English colonies that later became the United States can be divided very conveniently by geographical areas—New England, the Middle colonies, and the South—each with distinctive institutional structures and problems. Although there is a danger of oversimplifying in such grouping, since each region had many different patterns within it, it is nevertheless helpful to make some generalizations about each of the regions to illustrate the integral relationship between the fundamental social pattern of a people and the development of their educational systems. In the following three chapters we will see how social differences among the regions resulted in three quite different patterns of schooling.

SUGGESTED READINGS

Miller, Perry, and Johnson, Thomas J. *The Puritans*. New York: American Book, 1938. Introduction.

Perry, Ralph Barton. *Puritanism and Democracy*. New York: Vanguard, 1944. Chapters IV and V.

Schneider, Herbert W. *The Puritan Mind*. Ann Arbor: U. of Michigan Press, 1958.

Townsend, Harvey Gates. *Philosophical Ideas in the United States*. New York: American Book, 1934. Chapters II, III, and IV.

Waller, George M. (ed.). *Puritanism in Early America—Problems in American Civilization*. Boston: Heath, 1950. Vol. 13.

Wertenbaker, Thomas Jefferson. *The Founding of American Civilization—The Middle Colonies*. New York: Scribner's, 1938, Chapters III, IV, V, VI, and VIII.

———. *The Old South*. New York: Scribner's, 1942. Chapter 1.
———. *The Puritan Oligarchy*. New York: Scribner's, 1947. Chapter II.
Wright, Louis B. *The First Gentlemen of Virginia*. San Marino, California: Huntington Library, 1940. Part I and Chapter IV.

I

New England Theocracy and Universal Schooling

The New England colonies of Massachusetts, New Hampshire, and Connecticut were made up of towns with a homogeneous leadership of English Puritans. Although these settlers came partly for political and economic reasons, the interpretation of much of what happened in New England education must take into account the religious zeal of the Puritan leaders. Unable to "purify" the Anglican Church at home, they braved the dangers of a frontier wilderness to be able to worship in their own manner. They were not a tolerant group, and religious freedom was not one of their goals. All settlers in New England had to follow the dictates of the Puritan leaders, for these leaders held to the Calvinist doctrine that the church was God's representative on earth and, therefore, the interpreter of God's law. Moreover, the church was the supreme institution and the state merely the civil arm. The Bible was the ultimate authority for man, and each man must interpret the Scriptures for himself. Thus each man must be able to read, necessitating schools that would teach reading and religion to all children.

The New England version of theocracy—government control by religious authority—invested authority in the congregation instead of in the priesthood. The Congregational Church was supported financially by taxation; suffrage was limited to its membership; and civil government passed laws to administer God's law as determined by the church. This close partnership of church-town was a major factor in the development of schools in New England. Only in that region of the Colonies were there laws requiring parents to teach their children to read and towns to establish schools.

In addition to the religious and political concepts of Calvinism, other factors favored the early development of schools in New England. Many

Puritan leaders were educated men, even university graduates, and were concerned that their children have the same chances for education they would have had in England. Too, a well-educated ministry could be perpetuated only by schooling through the college level. The homogeneity of language and religion was another favoring element, since it made it possible for one school to serve the general population. The community plan of the first villages was still another: built closely around the church-meeting house, the village kept the children within easy walking distance of a center that could be used as a school. It also made possible community pressure, which often expressed itself as law, to see that "backsliding" parents sent their children to school. Later, the development of thriving commercial ventures in New England brought a need for practical education; the result was the formation of private schools and the academy.

The nature of the colonial schools was also conditioned by the class structure. Although not all the classes of England were represented in the new land—few titled Englishmen came to the Colonies except as royal governors—a definite class structure developed very early. Slaves and indentured servants were at the bottom; somewhat higher were apprentices and journeymen artisans, small farmers, fishermen, sailors, and clerks; above them were small merchants, master artisans, farmers, and lawyers; at the top were the clergy of the established church, the landed gentry, the big merchants and ship owners, and the governing officials. In New England the clergy immediately assumed great importance, with merchants coming to prominence toward the end of the seventeenth century. While there was some opportunity for social mobility—an apprentice or even an indentured servant might sometimes become a master artisan or merchant or farmer—there was a distinct gap in social and educational opportunities for children of the lower classes and those of the more privileged classes. This class differential was partly reflected in a two-track educational system that provided vernacular elementary schooling for girls and most boys, and Latin school and college for boys considered eligible to become ministers, lawyers, or social leaders.

Early Legislation

The religious fervor of the first settlers and the strength of the Calvinist theocracy resulted in educational legislation soon after the Puritans landed at Massachusetts Bay. Following the precedent of the Elizabethan Poor Law of 1601, the General Court of Massachusetts in 1642, "taking into consideration the great neglect of many parents and masters in training up their children in learning and labor, and other implyments which may be profitable to the common wealth," ordered the town officials to "take account from time to time of all parents and masters, and of their children, concerning their calling and implyment of their children, especially of their ability to read and understand the principles of religion." When anyone was found "not to be able and fitt to imploy and bring them up," his children were to be put forth as apprentices to someone who would fulfill this responsibility. This law is a very important legal precedent for all compulsory schooling and child welfare legislation. The law also authorized the town officials to "divide the towne amongst them," perhaps a forerunner to the district schools to come much later, and required each town to "give a breife account in writing of their proceedings herein."[1]

This law was succeeded in 1648 by one which made specific provisions for teaching both "children and apprentices . . . to read the english tongue." It removed the possibility that masters might avoid penalty if they did not teach their apprentices to read. However, the 1648 version omitted the provisions for dividing up the town for inspection and the annual written report.[2]

Just as some parents in 1642, by not teaching their children to read, were seen as not meeting their religious obligations, so some of the towns were failing to provide for the schooling of Bible-reading laymen and the education of a ministry. In 1647 the General Court required towns to establish schools, under penalty of fine for neglect. The preamble to this so-called "ould deluder" law reveals the Puritan concern for religion and for learning.

> It being one cheife piect [project] of yt [that] ould deluder, Satan, to keepe men from the knowledge of ye Scriptures, as in formr times by keeping ym [them] in an unknowne tongue, so in these lattr times by pswading [persuading] from ye use of tongues, yt so at least ye true sence & meaning of ye originall might be coulded [clouded] by false glosses of saint seeming deceivers, yt learning may not be buried in ye grave of or [our] fathrs in ye church and commonwealth, the Lord assisting or endeavors,—
>
> It is therefore ordred, yt evry towneship in this iurisdiction, aftr

[1] Nathaniel B. Shurtleff (ed.), *Records of the Governor and Company of the Massachusetts Bay in New England, Vol. II, 1642–1649* (Boston: Press of William White, 1853), pp. 6–7.

[2] Marcus W. Jernigan, *Laboring and Dependent Classes in Colonial America, 1607–1783* (Chicago: U. of Chicago Press, 1931) pp. 90–93.

> ye Lord hath increased ym number to 50 householdrs, shall then forthwth appoint one wth in their towne to teach all such children as shall resort to him to write & reade, whose wages shall be paid eithr by ye parents or mastrs of such children, or by ye inhabitants in genrall, by way of supply, as ye maior pt [major part] of those yt ordr ye prudentials of ye towne shall appoint; pvided [provided] those yt send their children be not oppressed by paying much more yn they can have ym taught for in othr townes; & it is furthr ordered, yt where any towne shall increase to ye numbr of 100 families or householdrs, they shall set up a gramer schoole, ye mr [master] thereof being able to instruct youth so farr as they shall be fited for ye university, pvided yt if any towne neglect ye performance hereof above one yeare, yt every such towne shall pay 5£ to ye next schoole till they shall pforme [perform] this order.[3]

Although this law was very limited in its demands on the towns and did not specify length of school term or other details, apparently a number of towns continued to neglect their duty. Some paid the fine, others found ways of evading the spirit of the law, and others merely ignored it so long as no one tried to secure any enforcement. In 1650 Connecticut passed a similar law, and subsequent legislation in New England followed this pattern.

The Two-Track System

While the laws of New England required that schools be established, there was no guarantee of equality of educational opportunity. Even where provision was made for children of the poor to be educated free, parents were loath to sign the pauper's oath with its stigma of charity. Consequently, many children were kept at home instead of being sent to school. Furthermore, in a society where class membership was taken to be a part of God's design, parents did not encourage children to aspire to places "above their station." Although there was no law prohibiting any boy in New England from getting an education or even going to Harvard, the great majority of New England citizens probably never contemplated any education beyond the rudiments. As a result of class attitudes and economic pressures, colonial education, from New England to Georgia, was essentially a two-track system. Boys of the lower classes and all girls received no more than an elementary schooling in reading and religion. Boys aspiring to upper-class goals went through the upper

[3] Shurtleff, p. 203.

track of Latin grammar school and college. This two-track system approximated the pattern common in Europe which developed after the Reformation leaders urged universal elementary education in the vernacular tongue.

Once the lower-class boy had learned to read, he was ready for work. He probably received his vocational training by helping his father, but if he wanted some special training, the common system was apprenticeship. Apprenticeship papers in America in the seventeenth, eighteenth, and nineteenth centuries were virtually the same as they had been in the Middle Ages or even in the time of Hammurabi in the twentieth century B.C., except that the American master was called on to see that the apprentice learned to read and write. The apprentice's main concern, however, was to learn the trade, and his education was largely what might be called training rather than schooling.

Elementary Schooling

THE DAME SCHOOL The "ould deluder" law permitted teachers of elementary education to be paid either by parents and masters or by the town. Both systems were followed. The earliest education was generally in a "dame school." A housewife or widow would take into her home a number of children and teach them the alphabet and rudimentary reading for a small fee. Often only barely literate herself, she worked her teaching around her household chores, having each child recite briefly once or twice a day. Children often began coming to the dame school at the age of three or four, generally in the pleasant summer months, when they could walk to school without trudging through deep snow or mud. The high rate of child mortality impressed the Puritans with the need for children to read as early as possible so that they might be "saved." Among "Verses for little children" in the famed *New England Primer* was this sobering warning:

> I in the burying place may see
> Graves shorter there than I;
> From Death's arrest no age is free,
> Young children too may die.
> My God, may such an awful sight,
> Awakening be to me!
> Oh! that by early grace I might
> For Death prepared be.

The children in the dame school did not have the aid of textbooks or other school equipment. Believing that children were by nature depraved, most dames felt that frequent punishment was an essential part of education, and switches or paddles were accepted "aids" to learning. Books and paper were scarce, and children learned to read from a home-made visual aid known as the horn book. It was a wooden paddle with a sheet of paper fastened to one side. On the paper were written the alphabet, perhaps the numerals, and sometimes a Bible verse. The child would point to the letters as he recited and, since memorizing was a long task for those tiny beginners, the paper would get badly smudged and worn if it were not protected. "To keep letters faire from fingers damp," the Puritans peeled a thin sheet from a cow horn and tacked it down over the paper like a piece of transparent plastic. For nearly three hundred years of our history, teachers firmly believed that children had to learn the alphabet before they could read words, and preparing the child for "reading school" was the role of the dame.

READING, WRITING, AND GRAMMAR SCHOOLS Once the child had learned his alphabet and perhaps been taught to read a few words in the Bible, he could then enter reading school. In New England, both boys and girls attended reading school. Writing was a more advanced art, not taught in conjunction with reading. Writing school was for those boys who were going into Latin school or into commercial pursuits, although girls attended occasionally. Reading and writing schools were often supported by the town and in many cases were the same school with different classes. As in the dame school, the reading was not only religious in purpose but also in content. In the earliest period, the first textbook after the hornbook was the Psalter or hymn book, to be followed by the New Testament and then the Old Testament. The child would spell through the whole Book, repeating the words, although no one ever gave much thought to whether he understood them. Neither the dame nor the schoolmaster was able to teach much comprehension of material so unsuited to the level of maturity of their pupils. The reading and writing schools were generally held in the late fall months, when the older children were freed from their farming chores and could attend classes.

Except in the dame schools, teaching was done by men. Some were college graduates; others were part-time tradesmen and farmers; many were itinerant schoolmen unable to keep any job or school very long; a few were indentured servants. The schoolroom was sometimes a room in the master's home, sometimes the meeting house or, in the late Colonial period, a small log cabin, unlighted, poorly ventilated, heated (if at all) by a fireplace, and sparsely furnished, with rough log benches in the center of the room for the reading pupils and shelves around the wall for the boys who were learning to write. In addition to religion, reading, and writing, the master taught some arithmetic, but the latter two "R's" were much subordinated to the first two. Considerable time was spent in memorizing the catechism and in prayers and moral admonitions. In rural areas and smaller towns the schoolmaster was responsible for instructing in English reading and writing and for teaching Latin. In larger towns the Latin masters felt such unscholarly activities as teaching English reading and writing beneath their dignity. Where it was not possible to have separate schools for the elementary subjects and the higher work in the classical language, Latin masters sometimes engaged "ushers" to preside over the teaching of reading and writing. In general, all elementary instruction was in the hands of poorly educated, untrained teachers, who often were uninterested in teaching and regarded children as having "corrupt natures . . . bent unto sin, only unto sin, and that continually," as the catechism said.

One of the earliest records of the Puritan concern for schooling appears in the minutes of the town meeting of Boston on April 13, 1635, when it was "generally agreed upon yt or [our] brother Mr Philemon Pormort shalbe intreated to become scholemaster for the teaching and nourtering of children with us."[4] Whether or not this action resulted in a school immediately cannot be determined, but on August 12, 1636, a "general meeting of the richer inhabitants" pledged a sum sufficient to guarantee a first year's salary for "a free school master of the youth." Seybolt has used the *Records of the Town of Boston, 1634–1660* to trace the continuous existence of this free public school throughout the Colonial period. It was generally known as the Free Schoole until the first public writing school was opened in 1684, when it became known as the Latin School or the Free Grammar School. From 1720 until the Revolution there were two public grammar schools in Boston enrolling from 150 to 200 annually, and three public writing schools enrolling from 600 to more than 900 annually. The grammar schools were open only to boys, but the writing schools accepted girls. Entrance requirements were the same for both the grammar and the writing schools, reflecting the two-track nature of colonial schooling. The boys had to be seven years old and able to read the Bible; girls in writing schools were generally somewhat older. The curriculum of the writing schools of Boston included reading, writing, spelling, arithmetic, and catechism, the lower-track subjects useful for the lower and middle social classes. The grammar schools taught Latin, in preparation for college and

[4] Quoted in Robert F. Seybolt, *The Public Schools of Colonial Boston, 1635–1775* (Cambridge: Harvard U. Press, 1935), p. 1.

"higher" social position, and any boys who did not know how to write attended writing lessons in the late morning and afternoon hours.

A survey of legal records of early New England reveals a fairly high literacy rate, at least as judged by the number of individuals who were able to sign their names to deeds, marriage registers, and similar documents as contrasted with those who signed by mark. By this test of literacy, studies have discovered that as high as 90 percent of the men and between 40 and 65 percent of the women could write their names. Since writing was a skill taught after the child had learned to read, these figures indicate that most New England children received at least a rudimentary education. This might lead historians to question whether compulsory attendance laws are as effective as other incentives in securing universal education. The religious and, later, commercial demands for literacy may have been more influential in promoting Puritan education than any form of compulsory attendance law could have been. In the twentieth century, when compulsory attendance laws became general, it again appeared to be economic and social forces, rather than legal provisions, that were most effective in promoting universal education.

THE "NEW ENGLAND PRIMER" The books used in the schools reflected the religious concern of the Puritans in New England. At first the Bible itself was the most important reading book, even for the small child, but near the end of the seventeenth century the *New England Primer* came into common use. Appearing first in the 1680's, it continued in use for over a hundred years. It went through many editions. Printers all over the colonies pirated its contents, sometimes changing the name, sometimes varying the material. Basically, however, all versions were alike.

The book begins with the alphabet and simple two-letter syllables, all the possible combinations of letters. Apparently these syllables were not learned as phonetic equivalents but simply as a logical step between individual letters and words: "ab, eb, ib, ob, ub; ac, ec, ic, oc, uc; . . . ba, be, bi, bo, bu, by." The syllables are followed by three pages of words, progressing from one to six syllables. The words selected do not seem to have any particular reference to the experiences of children. In one edition the four words of one syllable beginning with the letter "a" are "age," "all," "ape," and "are." The same copy includes "heinous" among the thirty-six words of two syllables, and "for-ni-ca-ti-on" and "fer-men-ta-ti-on" among the fourteen words of five syllables. Other words in the lists also reflect the Puritan concern with sin. These enlightening lists are followed by the Lord's Prayer and the Apostles' Creed.

The most famous part of the *Primer* is the rhyming alphabet, illustrated by crude woodcuts. Other parts of the book might vary in differing editions, and some of the rhymes in the alphabet become more secular as the tenor of life moved from religious concerns to more secular interests, but the first rhyme was invariably the same:

In Adam's Fall
We sinned all.

The rhyme with "T" illustrates the fear of early death and the consequent need to be prepared. Illuminated with a picture of a winged figure with a scythe and an hourglass, the rhyme reads:

Time cuts down all,
Both great and small.

"Y" repeats this concern, showing a picture of a child being stabbed by a skeleton holding an hourglass:

Youth forward slips,
Death soonest nips.

Some of the later versions included special materials for the religious edification of the child. One common inclusion was a poem of advice to his children purported to have been written by the martyr John Rogers shortly before his execution. The poem is introduced in some editions by a frightening wood cut, with Rogers' face peering out of flame and smoke while his wife "with nine small children & one at her Breast" stand gazing at Rogers burning at the stake. Most editions contained the Westminster Catechism, and some versions had a short catechism written by John Cotton and titled "Spiritual Milk for American Babes."

The Latin Grammar School

For boys of the intellectual and social elite there was an opportunity for secondary and higher education. The schooling at this higher track of the two-track system might sometimes be fairly good, with teaching done by college graduates interested in teaching or in the ministry. Although Latin school was free in Boston, in many towns there were tuition schools, often operated by the minister or by a private school master. The purpose of the grammar school was to prepare boys for college by teaching them to read, write, and speak Latin and Greek.

As soon as the boys had mastered the English alphabet and could read, the master would "put them into" Latin grammar. Usually the boys would begin Latin at the age of seven or eight, and the course of their studies extended from six to eight years. As the name indicates, the curriculum was largely Latin, with some Greek and perhaps a little Hebrew in the last year of study. The first three years were given to memorizing a Latin "accidence," or grammar, and to parsing Latin sentences. In practice, the boys often spent time on what amounted to "nonsense syllables," for they did not have the vocabulary to understand the rules they were memorizing. By the end of the Latin grammar course, the boys who had stayed with the task had acquired a degree of facility with Latin as a language and an acquaintanceship with some Latin and Greek literature, but in the light of present knowledge about psychology and human learning, the process seems a very inefficient one. Indeed, even at that time the college often found that it had to review the Latin the boys should have learned in the grammar school. The most famous of the grammar schools, the Boston Public Latin School, was probably the best and was the example followed by all the New England Latin schools.

> Gentlemen,—I send you as requested some reminiscences connected with the old Latin School in Boston. . . . I entered the School, July, 1773, being then seven years and nine months old. . . . The probationary exercise was reading a few verses in the Bible. Having passed muster in this, I was admitted as second boy in the lowest form.
>
> The school was divided into seven classes. A separate bench or form was allotted to each, besides a skipping form, appropriated for the few boys who were intended to be pushed forward a year in advance. The books studied the first year were Cheever's Accidence, a small Nomenclature, and Coderius' Colloquies. The second year, Aesop's Fables, and towards the close of it, Eutropius and Ward's Lily's Grammar. The third year Eutropius and Grammar continued, and a book commenced called Clark's Introduction. In the fourth year, the fourth form, as well as the fifth form and the sixth, being furnished with desks, commenced "making Latin," as the phrase was, and to the books used by the third form Caesar's Commentaries were added. After this were read in succession by the three upper classes, Tully's Orations, the first books of the Aeneid, and the highest classes dipped into Xenophon and Homer.
>
> School opened at 7 in the summer and 8 in the winter, A. M., and at 1 P. M. throughout the year. It was ended at 11 A. M. and 5 P. M., at which hours the greater part went to the writing-school

for an hour at a time—but a portion remained and took lessons in writing of "Master James," son of the Preceptor, and some young girls then came into the school.[5]

The Code of Regulations for the New Haven Hopkins Grammar School in 1684 indicates the structure and organization of the school and its religious emphasis. Although the principal purpose of the school was instruction in Latin, apparently it was also concerned with teaching English reading and writing to boys who had mastered the alphabet, so that it was a combined writing and Latin school.

> Orders of ye Committee of trustees for the Grammer Schoole at Newhaven to be observed & attended in ye said Schoole, made, agreed upon & published in ye sd Schoole in ye yeare 1684.
>
> 1st. The Erection of ye sd Schoole being principally for ye Institucion of hopefull youth in ye Latin tongue, & other learned Languages soe far as to prepare such youths for ye Colledge & publiq service of ye Country in Church, & Commonwealth. The Chiefe work of ye Schoole-Mr is to Instruct all such youth as are or may be by theire parents or Frends sent, or Comitted unto him to yt end wth all diligence faithfullness and Constancy out of any of ye townes of this Country of Newhaven upon his sallary accompt only, otherwise Gratis. And if any Boyes are sent to ye Mr of ye said Schoole from any other part of ye Colony, or Country. [sic] Each such boy or youth pay ten shillings to ye Mastr at or upon his entrance into ye said Schoole.
>
> 2. That noe Boyes be admitted into ye sd Schoole for ye learning of English Books, but such as have ben before taught to spell yr letters well & begin to Read, thereby to perfect theire right Spelling, & Reading, or to learne to write, & Cypher for numeracion, & addicion, & noe further, & yt all others either too young & not instructed in letters & spelling, & all Girles be excluded as Improper & inconsistent wth such a Grammer Schoole.
>
> 3. That the Master & Schollars duly attend the Schoole Houres viz. from 6 in ye morning to 11 a Clock in ye forenoone, And from 1 a Clock in the afternoone to 5 a Clock in the afternoone in Summer & 4 in Winter. . . .
>
> 10. That all the Lattin Schollars, & all other of ye Boyes of Competent age and Capacity give the Mr an accompt of one passage or sentence at least of ye sermons the foregoing Saboth on ye 2nd day morning. And that from 1 to 3 in ye afternoone of every last day of ye week be Improved by ye Mr in Cathechizing of his Schollars yt are Capeable.[6]

[5] Quoted in Seybolt, pp. 74–75.

[6] Quoted in Henry Barnard, *American Journal of Education*, 4 (1857): 710.

Higher Education

A great many of the Puritan ministers were college graduates, more than a hundred coming from Oxford and Cambridge before 1650. This has been calculated as one college graduate for every two hundred emigrants, an unusually high concentration of highly educated men.[7] The settlers feared that any lowering of the educational standards of their clergy might result in disaster for their religious belief. Yet they could not send their young men back to England to study as long as the persecution of the dissenters was driving out the Puritans by the thousands each year. "Dreading to leave an illiterate Ministry to the churches, when our present Ministers shall lie in the Dust," the Massachusetts Puritans chartered Harvard College in 1636 with the aid of a gift from John Harvard; others made smaller donations, and "the publique hand of the State added the rest."[8]

The college began actual operations in 1639 and until 1653 it was a three-year institution. All students followed the same course, which was approximately the one to be established in the later colonial colleges. It was arranged so that only one study was being conducted at a time, making it possible for the college president to be the only professor. On Monday and Tuesday for the first three quarters of the year he lectured to the freshmen at eight in the morning on logic; he lectured on physics in the last quarter. These were Aristotelian and not modern physics and logic. At nine o'clock the second-year class received lectures on ethics and politics, again substantially Aristotelian. At ten the third-year class heard lectures on arithmetic, geometry, and astronomy, three of the classical liberal arts which were taught as abstract subjects to discipline the mind, rather than for any practical application in the world of life. In the afternoon each class would "dispute" or defend propositions logically in its subject or "art," the first class at two, the second at three, and the last at four. On Wednesday the subject for all was Greek—in the morning, etymology and syntax for the first-year class, prosodia and dialects (probably analyses of Greek poetry and dialogues) for the second-year class; in the afternoon both classes practiced on their morning lessons. The third class "perfect their *Theory* before noone, and exercise *Style*, Composition, Imitation, Epitome, both in Prose and Verse, afternoone." On Thursday the first-year students took Hebrew grammar in the morning and read the Bible in the afternoon; the second

[7] Jernigan, pp. 64–65.

[8] *New England's First Fruits*, London, 1643. *Massachusetts Historical Collection*, 1792, Vol. 1, pp. 242–246.

year studied Chaldee in the morning and read "*Ezra* and *Danel*" in the afternoon; the third year studied Syriac in the morning and read from Trestius' New Testament in the afternoon. On Friday all classes heard lectures on rhetoric at eight in the morning and had declamations at nine, with each student given the opportunity to declaim once a month; the rest of the day was devoted to rhetoric. On Saturday they studied "*Divinity Catecheticall at the 8th houre.*" On Saturday afternoon in the winter the professor read lectures in history, and in the summer he discussed the nature of plants.

The average age of entering college freshman was sixteen or seventeen. Most had spent some years with a Latin master or tutor. None was expected to have a "diploma" or to have completed a particular number of years of study. If the candidate could read the Latin and Greek books handed him by the college president, he was qualified to begin college study. On the completion of his course, the student demonstrated his college learning at commencement by defense in public of a number of theses ranging over various topics—theology, politics, ethics, natural law, revealed religion, and moral philosophy. At these exercises the student was awarded a baccalaureate degree. He did not go on to any formal graduate school. When he had been a bachelor for from one to three years, he might come back to his college, give a commencement address along with other master's degree candidates, and be awarded the advanced degree.

(a) Entrance Requirements

1. When any Schollar is able to understand Tully, or such like classical Latine Author *extempore*, and make and speake true Latine in Verse and Prose, *suo ut aiunt Marte* [on his own exertions, as the saying goes]; and decline perfectly the Paradigm's of *Nounes* and *Verbes* in the *Greek* tongue: Let him then and not before be capable of admission into the Colledge.

(b) Rules and Precepts

2. Let every Student be plainly instructed, and earnestly pressed to consider well, the maine end of his life and studies is, *to know God and Jesus Christ which is eternal life*, Joh. 17.3. and therefore to lay *Christ* in the bottome, as the only foundation of all sound knowledge and learning. . . .

3. Every one shall so exercise himselfe in reading the Scriptures twice a day, that he shall be ready to give such an account of his proficiency therein, both in *Theoreticall* observations of the Language, and Logick, and in *Practicall* and spirituall truths, as his Tutor shall require. . . .

(d) Requirements for Degrees

> Every Schollar that on proofe is found able to read the Originalls of the *Old* and *New Testament* into the Latine tongue, and to resolve them *Logically;* withall being of godly life and conversation; And at any publick Act hath the Approbation of the Overseers and Master of the Colledge, is fit to be dignified with his first Degree.[9]

While the English and European universities were governed by their faculties, Harvard was placed under the control of a board of trustees certain to safeguard the Puritan doctrine in matters of administration and curriculum. The American Puritans did not trust their college president to make educational policy. Harvard's method of trustee control has remained the pattern in American colleges and universities, although trusteeship, at first limited to the clergy, has become dominated by business and professional leaders.

For more than fifty years Harvard was the only college in the English colonies, and it was a prototype for the later ones. Even though all the colonial colleges had a religious purpose and clergymen as presidents and professors, they were essentially liberal arts colleges. Vocational or professional education was outside their responsibility. Lawyers and even theologians prepared for their careers by private study. A prospective lawyer would work as a clerk in a lawyer's office while he read law books and studied in his spare time. Ministers prepared for their ordination by study and exegesis (critical interpretation of the Bible) under the direction of a minister, sometimes the college president. In spite of the fact that eight of the nine colonial colleges were church colleges and that all were heavily loaded with religious study, none was a theological seminary, and students had a year or more of intensive study after graduation before they could be ordained. Physicians and surgeons also got their training outside of college, and not until 1765 were there any medical lectures at any college; at that time the College of Philadelphia introduced a series of lectures in the fourth year for those students who wished to become physicians.

Decline in Religious Fervor and Educational Zeal

The ambitious beginnings of schooling in New England did not assure continuous, unfaltering educational progress. Before Massachusetts had been in existence twenty years, forces tending to discourage the steady

[9] *New England's First Fruits.*

development of a universal school system were already in operation. Important among them was the rise to power of Oliver Cromwell and the Puritan Commonwealth in England. The period of the 1630's had been one of great Puritan migration to the Colonies, particularly under the persecution of the sect by Archbishop Laud; but when the Puritans took power in England, the migration slackened and many of the clerical leaders of Massachusetts Bay returned to England. Indeed, more than half the graduates of Harvard before 1660 went to England to pursue their professional careers. At the same time, commercial interests were becoming more important in New England, and the combination of a depleted clergy and a growing merchant class began to undermine the power of the theocracy. As leaders returned to England and the theocracy lost some of its effectiveness, backsliding began among the less fervent members of the church and the outsiders who had come to America for other than religious reasons. King William's War (1689–1697) and Queen Anne's War (1701–1713), as with wars anywhere, also had a deleterious effect on activities like religion and education.

Fewer Graduates

Since schooling had been religiously motivated and supported, New England was threatened with a decline in educational interests. In the first decade of the College (1642–1651), Harvard granted fifty-five bachelor's degrees.[10] But between 1661 and 1670, the average graduating class dropped to only seven members, and between 1675 and 1681, the largest graduating class had only six members, with one class numbering only three.[11] Harvard was not graduating enough young men to fill the empty pulpits and certainly not enough for a surplus to serve as schoolmasters. As fewer able ministers were available, religious fervor declined further. In many communities poorer grammar schools resulted, fewer boys went to college, and fewer graduates were available for teaching.

Public Apathy and Denominationalism

The downward spiral did not mean that education was totally neglected, however. Not only did schools continue to exist, but colonial authorities persisted in legislating in favor of education. In 1683, Massachusetts towns of more than five hundred families were required by law

[10] Samuel Eliot Morison, *The Founding of Harvard College* (Cambridge: Harvard U. Press, 1935), p. 312.

[11] Morison, *Three Centuries of Harvard* (Cambridge: Harvard U. Press, 1936), pp. 40, 43.

to maintain two grammar schools and two writing schools. In 1701 the fines for towns neglecting to maintain schools were increased, indicating interest in education on the part of the political authorities and apathy or worse on the part of some of the local town meetings. The preamble to the law claimed that the new penalty was needed because the "wholesome and necessary law is shamefully neglected by divers towns . . . tending greatly to the nourishing of ignorance and irreligion." In 1712, a law entitled "An Act against intemperance, immorality and prophaneness, and for reformation of manners" required that "no person or persons shall . . . keep a school for teaching and instructing of children or youth in reading, writing, or any other science, but such as are of sober and good conversation, and have the allowance and approbation of the selectmen of the town."[12]

The public reluctance to be concerned with schooling, as indicated by the need for these laws and increased penalties, was only one factor in the decline in educational quality in New England. Another was increasing denominationalism after the religious monopoly of the Congregational Church was ended in 1691 by the new charter of Massachusetts. The new charter extended to Massachusetts the provisions of the Toleration Act of 1689, granting religious toleration to all Protestants. The religious unity of the town school was lost as each sect sought to have its own dogma advanced by schools financed partly by the town.

The District School

Still another factor was the dispersal of the population. As long as the settlers were concentrated in one village, the town school could and did serve most of the children. When the people scattered out in numerous villages throughout the town, it soon became impossible for children in outlying sections to get to school. In an effort to make schooling available for all the children, the people of New England adopted early in the eighteenth century what was known as the "moving school." A "moving school" was simply a moving teacher. He would divide his time among the various villages in the town until that year's allotment for schools had been exhausted, and then schooling ended. Since many towns provided money for only a few weeks a year, the moving school meant that no part of the town received much of a school term and that in some years there would be no school at all for some children. Even towns which had school all year long found that the moving school left some precincts with very short terms.

[12] Elsie W. Clews, *Educational Legislation and Administration of the Colonial Governments* (New York: Columbia U. Press, 1899), pp. 64–65.

Since the moving school failed to solve the problems of a decentralized population, a new system of spreading schools out over the town began to appear. The town was divided into districts, each with a separate board of trustees empowered to levy taxes, establish a school, recommend teachers, and supervise the school. In 1716 the town of Springfield voted to create six precincts in the town to provide schools for all the children.

> Voted that every precinct shall pay to their own school. Voted that the precinct which does neglect keeping a school, that money which is raised upon them for the supporting of the schools shall return into the town treasury.[13]

Some towns continued reading and writing schools in the main village and supported dame schools in the outlying settlements.

> Voted at said meeting that the selectmen provide a schoolmaster to keep a school for reading and writing for children and youth until the first day of September next ensuing, and whereas many small children cannot attend the school in the center of the town by reason of the remoteness of their dwellings, and to the extent that all children may have the benefit of education, etc.
>
> Voted that a suitable number of school dames, not exceeding five, be provided by the selectmen at the charge of the town for the teaching of small children, . . . and such gentlewomen to be paid by the pole [poll] as the selectmen and they may agree.[14]

Although these records indicate that the district or precinct school was in existence as early as 1716, it was not until 1759 that legislation was passed by the Massachusetts General Court permitting the inhabitants of the West Wing of Rutland to incorporate themselves into a precinct and to "appoint and pay" a schoolmaster for their children. In 1768 general legislation was passed authorizing precincts to build and support schools and to assess and collect taxes for those purposes. This law was to be in force only until 1770.

The district system is important in the history of American education because it became the typical school unit throughout the United States in the nineteenth century and extended into the twentieth century. It was the famed one-room, rural "little red schoolhouse" in which many

[13] Quoted in Paul Monroe, *The Founding of the American Public School System* (Ann Arbor: University Microfilms, 1940), Vol. II., p. 263.

[14] *Worcester Town Records*, April 13, 1731. As quoted in Monroe, pp. 264–265.

generations of Americans received their elementary—and generally their only—schooling. The district school was the extreme form of local, decentralized control of schools, and efforts at consolidation and establishment of minimum state or national standards have been made difficult and sometimes blocked by this tradition of immediate local responsibility for schools and school policies.

The Great Awakening

The religious history of Western Christianity is marked with cyclic activity—periods of enthusiasm followed by declining interest and then by revivals of zeal and concern. In the American Colonies, the first half of the eighteenth century was one of religious revivalism. In New England the more fervent Congregationalists, concerned with a loss of enthusiasm for rigorous Calvinism at Harvard, founded in 1701 a new Congregational college that was to be known as Yale College. At first it was called the Collegiate School, and it did not have a fixed location until a college building was erected at New Haven, Connecticut, in 1718. Even then some of the students and citizens refused to accept New Haven as the home of their college; the students of tutor Elisha Williams returned to Wethersfield, and the people of Saybrook wrecked the carts carrying the books of the college library from their town to the new building at New Haven.[15] Religious purpose seemed sometimes to be subordinated to political and local interests.

Jonathan Edwards

One of the most famous preachers of the Great Awakening was a product of Yale, Jonathan Edwards. In 1729, at the age of 26, he succeeded his grandfather as pastor at Northampton, Massachusetts. Disturbed over the levity of the young people of the town, who often made Sunday evening church a pleasant social event, he began to preach fiery sermons about the dangers of Hell and damnation. In 1733 he noted in his congregation an increase in religious concern, and this began to spread to other Massachusetts towns in 1735 and thence to Connecticut. In addition to his personal preaching, Edwards wrote and published pamphlets describing the conversions and fervor of the young people of his community and those nearby. These pamphlets, some of which describe behavior that modern psychologists might term psychotic, were

[15] Clews, pp. 120–134.

widely read and set the pattern for the American evangelism of the 1740's and 1750's.

The renewed religious interest sparked a revival of concern for schools and schooling. An act passed in 1735 for employing and providing for the poor of Boston reflected once again the Calvinistic emphasis on reading as essential to a religious community.

> And forasmuch as there is great negligence in sundry persons as to the instruction and education of their children, to the great scandal of the Christian name, and of dangerous consequence to the rising generation:
>
> Be it therefore enacted that where persons bring up their children in such gross ignorance that they do not know or are not able to distinguish the alphabet or twenty-four letters, at the age of six years, in such case, the overseers of the poor are hereby empowered and directed to put or bind out into good families such children, for a decent and Christian education, as when parents are indigent and rated nothing to the public taxes.[16]

"New Lights" and "Old Lights"

With the revivalistic preaching of Jonathan Edwards, splits appeared in some of the orthodoxies. Among the Congregationalists the two major groups were known as the "Old Lights," who stressed the concepts of predestination and election, and the "New Lights," who held to the ideas of repentance and salvation by conversion. The leaders of the New Lights tried to establish schools that would produce ministers who would preach a doctrine different from that being inculcated at Yale; they apparently succeeded well enough that their training school, known as the Shepherd's Tent, was a threat to the Old Lights. In 1742 the Connecticut legislature outlawed any "college, seminary of learning, or any public school whatsoever, for the instruction of young persons, other than such as are erected and established or allowed by the laws of this colony, without special license or liberty first had and obtained of this Assembly."[17] The Shepherd's Tent was forced to close.

The demand for ministers created by the Great Awakening resulted in the establishment of two colleges that were far more lasting in their effects than the Shepherd's Tent. In Rhode Island the Baptists founded the College of Rhode Island in 1764 (renamed Brown University in 1804). The religious toleration of Roger Williams' colony was reflected

[16] *Ibid.*, p. 68.
[17] *Ibid.*, pp. 106–107.

in the composition of the board of trustees: twenty-two Baptists, five Quakers, four Congregationalists, and five Episcopalians.

The renewed zeal of the Congregationalists in New Hampshire gave rise to a proposal in 1758 by a body of ministers for a college for New Hampshire. When the project was rejected by Governor Wentworth, the Congregationalists gave their support to a school for Indians which had been founded by Dr. Eleazar Wheelock in 1754 at Lebanon, Connecticut. In 1769 the school was moved to Hanover, New Hampshire, where it was named Dartmouth College.

Limited Quality of Education

In the other colonies, where New England's early educational progress had not been matched, the effects of the Great Awakening on schooling were more marked, but even in New England, where educational opportunities were the greatest, the quality and amount of formal education was still very limited at the close of the Colonial period. The great textbook author and lexicographer Noah Webster in an 1840 letter described to Henry Barnard his pre-Revolutionary school days:

> When I was young, the books used were chiefly or wholly Dilworth's Spelling Books, the Psalter, Testament, and Bible. No geography was studied before the publication of Dr. Morse's small books on that subject, about the year 1786 or 1787. No history was read, as far as my knowledge extends, for there was no abridged history of the United States. Except the books above mentioned, no book for reading was used before the publication of the Third Part of my Institute, in 1785. . . .
>
> Before the Revolution, and for some years after, no slates were used in common schools: all writing and operations in arithmetic were on paper. The teacher wrote the copies and gave the sums in arithmetic; few or none of the pupils having any books as a guide. Such was the condition of the schools in which I received my early education. . . .
>
> No English grammar was generally taught in common schools when I was young, except that in Dilworth, and that to no good purpose. In short, the instruction in schools was very imperfect, in every branch.[18]

The colleges at the time of the Revolution were not much different

[18] Quoted in Barnard, 26, pp. 195–196.

from Harvard in 1640. Even those created in response to the Great Awakening and intended primarily for the training of ministers followed the humanist tradition, devoting virtually all their curriculum to the study of the language and literature of Greece and Rome. The religious rebirth was a stimulus to renewed interest in collegiate education, but it changed the curriculum and the purposes of education very little.

Financing and Supervising Schools

During the Colonial period many different methods of financing schools and colleges were used. Tuition fees, called "rate bills," were perhaps the most common, and even the "free" schools of Massachusetts charged entrance fees and collected sums for "firing," or firewood. Many towns assessed taxes—poll taxes, estate taxes, and sometimes both—but at no time during the Colonial period was there a special tax in Boston to be used for school purposes only. A number of towns set aside parcels of land the rent from which was used for schools. Various kinds of fines and licenses were earmarked for support of schools. Yale was partially financed by a customs duty on rum; Harvard received the income from a ferry between Boston and Charlestown. Public lotteries were commonly authorized for the support of schools and other public works; in 1772, a lottery was authorized in the town of New Haven for the extension of a wharf, with the provision that profits earned from mooring charges be appropriated to Yale. Public subscriptions, donations, and bequests were non-governmental sources of support.

Both the Latin and the writing schools were under the close supervision of the town selectmen and the ministers. An annual visitation was made at each of the schools by a committee appointed by the town meeting. In addition, the town meeting and the selectmen were very much concerned with the regular operation of the schools. Actually there were even some cases of what might be considered compulsory attendance laws. As early as 1685 and again in 1692, town meetings in Springfield, Massachusetts, levied the rate bill on all children between five and ten years of age, regardless of whether or not the children attended the school.[19] It is possible that the town was as much interested in making the "rate" a form of compulsory tax for all those who had children of school age as it was in forcing all children to attend the town school.

[19] Monroe, p. 268.

Practical Education

Although many of the first settlers had strong religious interests when they came to America, later generations found other concerns more demanding. Even in New England the theocracy gave way in a few decades to a society dominated by the merchant class. The theology of John Calvin permitted Protestants to earn interest on investments, a sort of religious justification of capitalism. The excitement of the Great Awakening was only a minor interruption in the shift to secular matters among the colonists. As commercialism became stronger, secular interests replaced the overriding concern with religion.

Most girls and those boys who were not intended to enter the ministry, teaching, or a legal or political career received their vocational training through actual practice. Most of them learned by assisting their fathers—farm boys did farm chores; girls took care of younger brothers and sisters and helped around the house. Boys who were going to enter the more skilled trades were apprenticed to masters who were to teach them the skills and "mysteries" of the trade. However, growing commercial interests began to require more formally prepared workers in certain fields, such as bookkeeping, surveying, and navigation. To meet this need, there appeared a new kind of educational institution, the practical private school. At first these schools were quite informal in structure. A teacher would advertise his readiness to teach a number of subjects, and young men interested would make arrangements with the master. Students were often instructed individually, sometimes at their homes, sometimes at the lodging of the teacher. The courses were frequently offered in the evening, a fact indicating that many of the students were working men who aspired to improve their economic condition. Payment was from student directly to teacher. The duration of study was decided by the interest of the student, the extent of knowledge of the teacher, the amount of money the student could pay, and so on.

Later the offerings were broadened. Some of the masters were clearly preparing boys for college, and in the Middle and Southern colonies masters occasionally claimed to offer the "opportunity of Learning the same Things which are commonly Taught in Colledges."[20] Other masters offered courses intended for girls, including music, "polite letters," and "fancy stitching." These pioneer schools, with their practical con-

[20] Seybolt, *Source Studies in American Colonial Education: The Private School* (Urbana: U. of Illinois, Bulletin No. 28, Bureau of Educational Research, 1925), p. 99.

cerns and their wide range of studies, were the forerunners of Benjamin Franklin's educational proposals and led directly to the development of the academy, the prevailing secondary school in the United States from the close of the Revolution to the Civil War.

Following are newspaper statements referring to several of the kinds of private schools and schoolmasters in colonial New England. The first indicates the informal arrangements of master and student; the second is obviously aimed at girls, although Brownell was a famous writing teacher in whose school Benjamin Franklin was briefly a student; the third concerns a master who had attended Harvard; the fourth advertises a master who learned his subjects through the college of experience.

From *The Boston News-Letter*, March 14-21, 1708/9.

Opposite to the Mitre Tavern in Fish-street near to Scarlets-Wharff, Boston, are Taught Writing, Arithmetick in all its parts; And also Geometry, Trigonometry, Plain and Sphaerical, Surveying, Dialling, Gauging, Navigation, Astronomy; The Projection of the Sphaere, and the use of Mathematical Instruments: By Owen Harris.

Who Teaches at as easie Rates, and as speedy as may be.

From *The Boston News-Letter*, Feb. 23-Mar. 2, 2-9, 9-16, 1712/13.

At the House of Mr. George Brownell in Wings-Lane Boston, is taught Writing, Cyphering, Dancing, Treble Violin, Flute, Spinnet, &c. Also English and French Quilting, Imbroidery, Florishing, Plain Work, Marking in several sorts of Stiches and several other works, where Scholars may board.

From *The Boston Weekly News-Letter*, March 3, 10, 1742-43.

These may inform the Publick, that Nathan Prince Fellow of Harvard College proposes, on suitable Encouragement, to open a school in this Town for the instructing young Gentlemen in the most useful Parts of the Mathematicks, Natural Philosophy and History. Particularly in the Elements of Geometry and Algebra; in Trigonometry and Navigation: in Geography and Astronomy, with the Use of the Globes and the several Kinds of Projecting the Sphere: In the Arts of Surveying, Gauging and Dialing; and in the General Rules of Fortification and Gunnery. To these will be added Lectures on History and Natural Philosophy.

The Terms, on which the said Nathan Prince would engage to instruct young Gentlemen in the above-mentioned Arts and Sciences, may be seen at his Lodgings at the House of Seth Cushing in Exchange Lane, Boston.

From *The Boston Weekly News-Letter*, Oct. 3, 10, 17, 1754.

At the Widow Robins's at the North-End, near Mr. Gledden's Ship-Yard, is kept a School by John Leach, from London, who teaches the following Branches, viz. Arithmetick, common, vulgar and decimal; Geometry, Trigonometry; Navigation and Journal keeping in a practical Method; either with all kinds of Books and Instruments in use, or without any; from several Years Experience in His Majesty's Service and three Voyages in the Hon. East-India Company's:—Mensuration of Superficies, Solids, Heights and Distances both accessible and inaccessible;—Gauging, either with or without the Callipars;—Surveying, with or without the Theodolite: Also, Drawing, as far as it is useful for a compleat Sea-Artist, as it respects taking Prospects of Land and surveying Harbours, &c. &c. With the Use and Construction of each Instrument us'd in the above Science. N.B. He keeps an Evening School from 6 to 9 P. M. during the Winter Season.—Also, surveys Land, draws Plans, &c.[21]

New England's Influence on American Education

In New England by the opening of the Federal period the basic framework of American education was established. It was tax-supported, locally controlled public education with the aim of providing a minimum amount of schooling for all children, regardless of sex, financial condition, or social class. In the less than two centuries since the close of the Colonial period, the struggle has been to extend the minimum upward, to equalize opportunity through broader bases of financing and control, to secularize schooling in consistency with the separation of church and state, and to expand the curriculum to fit the needs of new times and conditions and the interests of a varied student population. In achieving these goals, the proponents of educational change frequently found themselves frustrated by the religious traditions of schooling established by the Puritans and by the excessively decentralized and often debilitating local control of the district system. That Massachusetts maintained the national leadership in education in the nineteenth century was due in large measure to the success of men like James G. Carter and Horace Mann in their efforts to overcome these barriers. On the other hand, it was because of the Puritans' desire for schooling and their willingness to subsidize it out of the public treasure that a class of educational reformers, including Carter and Mann, did develop in Massa-

[21] Quoted in Seybolt, *Private Schools of Colonial Boston* (Boston: Harvard U. Press, 1935), pp. 11, 12, 30, 37–38.

chusetts. Historical forces are complex and often conflicting, and the effects of the Colonial period of New England upon schools cannot be stated as succinctly and confidently as many lecturers on education have pretended.

QUESTIONS FOR DISCUSSION

1. Summarize the relationship between the schools of colonial New England and the other social institutions, and by analogy relate modern education to the total social context and historical development of the American culture.
2. Identify some problems of modern schools which were evident in colonial New England. Compare and contrast conditions then and now to show why solutions considered appropriate then are no longer appropriate.
3. One very important American educational tradition is that of local control, growing largely out of the district school. Why was the district school an effective solution to problems in the eighteenth and nineteenth centuries? Is it appropriate now? Is our present social setting one which demands extreme localism? How does the present context of American education suggest different means of control and curriculum?
4. Contrast schooling of colonial New England with current schooling in the United States. What progress do you consider most significant? Are there any ways in which we are not doing as well as was done in the Colonial period?
5. Point out some precedents in colonial New England for educational policies today. Show how present social conditions justify or do not justify following these precedents.

SUGGESTED READINGS

Secondary Sources

Brown, Elmer Ellsworth. *The Making of Our Middle Schools.* New York: Longmans, Green, 1902. Chapters III to VII.

Butts, R. Freeman, and Cremin, Lawrence. *A History of Education in American Culture.* New York: Holt, 1953. Chapters 1 to 4.

Drake, William. *The American School in Transition.* Englewood Cliffs: Prentice-Hall, 1955. Chapters I and II.

Edwards, Newton, and Richey, Herman G., *The School in the American Social Order.* Boston: Houghton Mifflin, 1963. Chapters 2 and 3.

Elsbree, Willard. *The American Teacher.* New York: American Book, 1939. Chapters I to X.

Morison, Samuel Eliott. *The Puritan Pronaos: Studies in the Intellectual Life of New England in the Seventeenth Century.* New York: New York U. Press, 1936. Chapters II, III, IV.

Primary Sources

Cubberley, Ellwood P. *Readings in the History of Education.* Boston: Houghton Mifflin, 1920. Readings 183–194, 201, 202 and 230.

———. *Readings in Public Education in the United States.* Boston: Houghton Mifflin, 1934. Readings 5–19, 28–30, 35–43, 53, and 60–62.

Hofstadter, Richard, and Smith, Wilson. *American Higher Education: A Documentary History.* Chicago: U. of Chicago Press, 1961. Vol. 1, pp. 1–32, 49–82, 121–130, 131–136.

Knight, Edgar W., and Hall, Clifton L. *Readings in American Educational History.* New York: Appleton-Century-Crofts, 1951. Pp. 60–67, 71, 72–74, 80–81, 299, 467–469.

Miller, Perry, and Johnson, Thomas H. *The Puritans.* New York: American Book, 1938. Readings following Chapter VIII.

Monroe, Paul. *The Founding of the American Public School System.* Ann Arbor: University Microfilms, 1940. Vol. II, Chapters VII to X.

Seybolt, Robert F. *The Evening School in Colonial America.* Urbana: U. of Illinois, Bureau of Educational Research, Bulletin No. 24, 1925.

———. *The Private Schools of Colonial Boston.* Cambridge: Harvard U. Press, 1935.

———. *The Public Schools of Colonial Boston,* 1635–1775. Cambridge: Harvard U. Press, 1935.

———. *Source Studies in American Colonial Education: The Private School.* Urbana: U. of Illinois, Bureau of Educational Research, Bulletin No. 28, 1925.

2

Middle Colony Parochialism and Private Schools

The manner in which the New Englanders satisfied their religious and economic needs for schools illustrates how a fairly homogeneous community can cooperate in achieving common goals. In the Middle colonies of New York, New Jersey, and Pennsylvania, the same religious desires and economic needs for schools as those in New England did not result in the same educational patterns.

The Middle colonies were settled by people from many religious sects and many nations. They were Dutch, French, English, German, Swedish; they were Dutch Reformed, Presbyterian, Quaker, Hugenot, Anglican, Baptist, Congregational, Lutheran, Calvinist, Roman Catholic, Jewish. This heterogeneity was encouraged by the founders of all three colonies. The Dutch, who founded New Amsterdam in 1626, had not come to America for religious reasons. New Netherland was under the control of the Dutch West India Company, a commercial enterprise. The Company, in its desire to exploit the New World, adhered to the Dutch tradition of religious toleration and opened the colony to anyone who wished to come. While the Dutch Reformed was the established church, all settlers were permitted freedom of conscience. In 1664, when the English seized the colony, which they called New York, a large measure of this toleration was continued. Religious freedom was granted in New Jersey when the Duke of York gave the land to two of his friends, who set up proprietary governments in 1665. In Pennsylvania, where many Quakers lived, the basis for toleration was the Quaker belief that each individual receives an "inner light," that God speaks directly to each. Consequently, each man must be permitted to worship as his conscience directs him.

Each of the national and religious groups dispersed through the Middle colonies hoped to perpetuate its own culture and traditions;

consequently, in the absence of a single, established church and a universal theocracy, there was no establishment of "town" schools suitable to all children, as was the pattern in New England.

Another factor militating against centrally controlled education in the Middle colonies was the climate and topography. The lands were more suited to agriculture than was New England land. The result was an early dispersal of the population in a rural pattern of small villages and farms. A scattered rural population found it easy to neglect schooling.

Despite these facts, some educational progress was made in the Middle colonies. Most of the sects believed that each man must be able to read the Bible. And the very diversity of nationalities was in one way a favorable force, for school was necessary to teach the child to speak, read, and write the mother tongue and to learn the customs and dogma of his ethnic or religious group. The combination of a heterogeneous, scattered population with a desire for rudimentary education resulted in parochial and neighborhood schools in which religious orthodoxy was the primary qualification for schoolmasters.

New Netherland

In its charter the Dutch West India Company, which brought the colonists to New Netherland, was given most of the sovereign rights of government. For the religious and educational welfare of the colonists it shared responsibility with the Dutch Reformed Church, the established church of Holland. Although there are expressions of religious concern in the charter and early laws pertaining to the colony, the major interest of the Company appears to have been profit-making. This attitude may account in large measure for the lack of educational progress until near the end of Dutch control in 1664.

Religious Purpose of Education

The Dutch Reformed Church, like other Calvinist sects, desired religious education and Bible reading. This religious purpose came to the colony in the 1629 charter, which stipulated that the patroons, the big landholders, should "in the speediest manner, endeavor to find out ways and means whereby they may support a minister and school master, that thus the service of God and zeal for religion may not grow cool and be neglected among them."[1] Similar pious sentiments were ex-

[1] Clews, pp. 198–199.

pressed in laws in 1630 and 1635, but none of these expressions of concern were specific enough to prompt any concrete action by the colonists. Even a 1638 article on education drawn up by the West India Company for the colony, calling for an unspecified tax on "each householder and inhabitant" for the "maintenance of clergymen, comforters for the sick, schoolmasters, and such like necessary officers," tempered the shock of taxation by advising the colonial Director and Council that it "be rendered the least onerous and vexatious."

The emphasis on religion as one of the four "R's" is conveyed in the instructions for schoolmasters in Dutch possessions by the Classis of Amsterdam, the governing body of the Dutch Reformed Church.

> He is to instruct the youth on shipboard and on land, in reading, writing, ciphering, and arithmetic, with all zeal and diligence; he is also to implant the fundamental principles of true Christian religion and salvation, by means of catechizing.[2]

Failure to Build Schools

It appears that all such pious concern was not sufficient to result in significant, concrete efforts at schooling. Kilpatrick concludes that the first official school in New Netherland was probably not begun until sometime after April 1, 1638.[3] The neglect of schooling and the resulting juvenile problems were the subject of one of the reforms suggested by Director-General Peter Stuyvesant when he took over management of the colony in 1647.

> Whereas, by want of proper place, no school has been kept in three months, by which the youth is spoiled, so is proposed, where a convenient place may be adapted to keep the youth from the street and under a strict subordination.

The Council ordered a study to determine how "the best means might be employed at the smallest expense of the commonality." Again it appears that economic concerns were more important than the religious and moral needs for schools.

Stuyvesant offered to assist in the building and support of a school.

[2] Quoted in Thomas E. Finegan, *Free Schools: A Documentary History of the Free School Movement in New York State* (Albany: U. of the State of New York, 1921), p. 16.

[3] William H. Kilpatrick, *The Dutch Schools of New Netherland and Colonial New York* (Washington: U.S. Bureau of Education, Bulletin, 1912, No. 12), p. 50.

> We are inclined to bear personally and in behalf of the Company a reasonable proportion, and continue to do so in the future, and promote this glorious work. Meanwhile, it is required to make some previous arrangement to provide a convenient place during next winter, either in one of the out-houses belonging to the Attorney-General's Department . . . or any other convenient place as may be approved by the church wardens.

Even with this promise of financial help, the school seems not to have been built; for two years later the colonists addressed a remonstrance to the Dutch government complaining that they had no school.

> The plate has been a long time passed around for a common school, which has been built with words, for, as yet, the first stone is not laid; some materials have only been provided. However, the money given for the purpose hath all disappeared and is mostly spent, so that it falls somewhat short: and nothing permanent has as yet been effected for this purpose.[4]

The New Netherlanders lacked the strong sense of purpose of the New England Calvinists and the church-state partnership to carry out that religious purpose. The Dutch were only half-heartedly concerned about schools, and their governments, both in Europe and in the colony, were interested primarily in economic exploitation of the colony and its settlers. The lack of financial support from church or state and the failure of voluntary contributions to build a school forced the Dutch schoolmasters to teach in their own dwellings or other non-school buildings throughout the period of Dutch control of New Netherland.

Dutch Schoolmasters

Although there was no school building, school was apparently kept from time to time; for in 1649 the resignation of a schoolmaster was the cause for Stuyvesant's writing to the Classis of Amsterdam for "a pious, well-qualified and diligent schoolmaster." The Company's reply to the request refers presumably to private schoolmasters who "keep school in hired houses, so that the youth are not in want of schools to the extent of the circumstances of the country." The reply admitted that there was no Latin school, but suggested that the inhabitants provide for it themselves.

> In New England . . . every one is assessed by the local government according to his means, and must pay to the extent of his property

[4] Quoted in Clews, pp. 200–201.

> and as the magistrates tax him, for . . . erection of schools and salaries of teachers. If they are such patriots as they appear to be, let them be leaders in generous contributions for such laudable objects, and not complain when the Directors requested a collection toward the erection of a church and school.[5]

The problem of New Netherland has a modern counterpart—everyone acknowledges the importance of schooling but nobody wants to pay for it!

In 1650 the Company sent the colony a schoolmaster named William Verstius, who remained in America as "chorister and schoolmaster" for nearly five years; his appointment specified that he would "also act as comforter of the sick." The records of the colony refer to a number of teachers, some paid by the city of New Amsterdam, some granted permission to keep private school, and at least one who was ordered to cease keeping a school until he had been properly authorized to do so by the Director and the Council. One petitioner who, "through the caprices of unsteady fortune," had been unsuccessful as a tavern keeper, solicited employment as a writer in the service of the Company, or "if your Honor cannot employ him at this time in their service—that then the supplicant might be permitted to keep school, to instruct the youth in reading and writing, etc."[6] This petitioner was granted a license to keep school. The last resort for many failures in the practical world of earning a living was teaching school, lending strong evidence to the old saying "Those who can, do; those who can't, teach."

The low estate of schoolmasters is further evidenced by the salaries paid them. For example, in 1644 the Company budgeted 3,000 florins for the salary of the Director, 1,440 florins for the minister, and 360 florins for the schoolmaster.[7] Schoolmasters could also sometimes collect fees from their pupils: in 1661 the contract for a teacher named Evert Pietersen in New Amsterdam specified as follows:

> Besides his yearly salary he shall be allowed to demand and receive from every pupil quarterly as follows: For each child, whom he teaches the a b c, spelling, and reading 30 st.; for teaching to read and write, 50 st.; for teaching to read, write and cipher, 60 st.; from those who come in the evening and between times pro rata

[5] *Ibid.*, pp. 202–203.
[6] *Ibid.*, pp. 205–210.
[7] Willard S. Elsbree, *The American Teacher* (New York: American Book, 1939), p. 91.

> a fair sum. The poor and needy, who ask to be taught for God's sake, he shall teach for nothing.[8]

This contract indicates that it was apparent practice among the Dutch teachers, as among those of New England, to teach reading as a more elementary subject than writing. Pietersen may also have been teaching older persons in evening classes, a practice which was to become common after the turn of the century.

There may have been a Latin school for a brief time in 1652 in a vacant tavern in New Amsterdam, and the city finally got a regular Latin master in 1659, a professor sent over by the Company. His salary, like that of several other teachers, was defined as being paid in "seawant"—Indian wampum or unstrung shell beads. Kilpatrick estimates that the income of the Latin masters, part of which was paid by the Company, part by the city, and part by tuition, was considerably more than that of elementary teachers and put the Latin masters nearly on a par with the ministers.[9] Unlike the two known Latin masters in New Amsterdam, none of the Dutch elementary schoolmasters seems to have been paid anything by the city except rent-free use of a house.

New Netherland and New England

Throughout the Dutch period, actual provisions for schools were very meager. Not until the last year of Dutch control was there enacted a general educational provision. In 1664, schoolmasters were ordered to take their pupils to church on Wednesday where the pupils would be examined, after the service, "as to what they have committed to memory of the Christian commandments and catechism, and what progress they have made."[10] Apparently there was never a requirement in New Netherland that children be taught to read or that schools be provided by the cities and villages. While there were schools in most of the villages and towns, these schools were often private, charged tuition, and were limited in curriculum to religion and the rudiments of reading and writing, "with but little arithmetic save in the more commercial atmosphere of the capital and at Albany."[11] Perhaps the forging of effective legislation in New England and the presence of a *laissez-faire*

[8] Quoted in Seybolt, *The Evening School in Colonial America* (Urbana: U. of Illinois. Bureau of Educational Research, Bulletin No. 24, 1925), p. 9. A stiver (st.) was worth about two cents.

[9] Kilpatrick, p. 103.

[10] Quoted in Clews, p. 220.

[11] Kilpatrick, pp. 221–222.

attitude in New Netherland may be explained in part by the contrasting fundamental motivations of the two societies. The religious zeal of the Puritans drove them to build "Zion in the wilderness"; the economic interests of the Dutch led them to seek worldly wealth. Schools reflect the dominant interests of the society they serve.

New York

In 1664 Charles II of England granted his brother, the Duke of York, all the land lying between the Connecticut River and Delaware Bay. When the English arrived, the Dutch surrendered peacefully. The English permitted the Dutch to keep their religion and their schools, doing little themselves to promote English schools until after 1700. Shortly after the surrender, Governor Richard Nicolls called a convention of delegates from each town to draw up a body of laws based on those of the other English colonies. The only law dealing with education was a toothless counterpart of the Massachusetts law of 1642.

> The constable and overseers are strictly required frequently to admonish the inhabitants of instructing their children and servants in matters of religion and the laws of the country. And that the parents and masters do bring up their children and apprentices in some honest lawful calling, labor or employment. And if any children or servants become rude, stubborn or unruly . . . the constable and overseers . . . have power upon the complaint of their parents or masters to call before them such an offender, and to inflict such corporal punishment as the merit of their fact in their judgment shall deserve, not exceeding ten stripes, provided that such children and servants be of sixteen years of age.[12]

The penalty in this law fell on the unruly child or apprentice and not, as in New England, on the negligent parent or master.

Dutch Schools Continued

The language problems of a heterogeneous colony appear in the duplication of school efforts. Governor Nicholls licensed both English and Dutch schoolmasters in Albany. Dutch schools apparently continued to exist as long as the Dutch settlers wanted to perpetuate their cultural traditions, for the New York records continue to contain references to Dutch schools.

[12] Quoted in *Ibid.*, p. 223.

One of the contracts of a Dutch schoolmaster in Flatbush in 1682 has been preserved. It indicates the part-time nature of schoolkeeping, as well as something of the curriculum, the organization of the school day, and the diverse duties and remuneration of the teacher.

> *School Service.* I. The School shall begin at eight o'clock, and go out at eleven; and in the afternoon shall begin at one o'clock and end at four. The bell shall be rung when the school commences.
>
> II. When the school begins, one of the children shall read the morning prayer, as it stands in the catechism, and close with the prayer before dinner; in the afternoon it shall begin with the prayer after dinner, and end with the evening prayer. The evening school shall begin with the Lord's prayer, and close by singing a psalm.
>
> III. He shall instruct the children on every Wednesday and Saturday, in the common prayers, and the questions and answers in the catechism. . . .
>
> IV. He shall be required to keep his school nine months in succession, from September to June. . . .
>
> *Church Service.* I. He shall keep the church clean, and ring the bell three times before the people assemble to attend the preaching and catechism. Also before the sermon is commenced, he shall read a chapter out of the Holy Scriptures . . . the ten commandments, and the twelve articles of our faith, and then take the lead in singing. In the afternoon . . . he shall read a short chapter, or one of the Psalms of David, as the congregation are assembling; and before divine service commences, shall introduce it, by the singing of a Psalm or Hymn.
>
> II. When the minister shall preach at Brooklyn . . . he shall be required to read twice before the congregation, from the book commonly used for that purpose. In the afternoon he shall also read a sermon on the explanation of the catechism, according to the usage and practice approved by the minister. The children, as usual, shall recite their questions and answers out of the catechism, on Sunday, and he shall instruct them therein. . . .
>
> III. For the administration of Holy Baptism, he shall provide a basin of water, for which he shall be entitled to receive from the parents, or witnesses, twelve styvers. . . .
>
> IV. He shall give the funeral invitations, dig the grave, and toll the bell, for which service he shall receive for a person of fifteen years and upwards, twelve guilders, and for one under that age, eight guilders. . . .
>
> *School Money.* He shall receive from those who attend the day school, for a speller or reader, three guilders a quarter, and for a writer four guilders. From those who attend evening school, for a

speller or reader, four guilders, and for a writer, six guilders shall be given.

Salary. In addition to the above, his salary shall consist of four hundred guilders, in grain, valued in Seewant, to be delivered at Brooklyn Ferry, and for his services from October to May, as above stated a sum of two hundred and thirty-four guilders, in the same kind, with the dwelling-house, barn, pasture lot and meadows, to the school appertaining.[13]

Government Interest in Schools

While the English government did little to encourage schools, in 1671 the governor ordered that the town of Hempstead make "speedy payment" to schoolmaster Richard Charlton so "that persons of that calling be not discouraged."[14]

In 1685 the Bishop of London proposed that no schoolmaster coming from England be permitted to teach in the West Indies without license granted by the Bishop or from other colonies without receiving a license from the governor. This was applied to New York in 1686, except that schoolmasters from England were required to be licensed by the Archbishop of Canterbury, and no colonist could keep a school without being licensed by the province. In 1702 the General Assembly of the colony passed "An Act for Encouragement of a Grammar Free School in the City of New York." The act required that the grammar schoolmaster be licensed by the Bishop of London or by the governor of the province. This remained more or less the policy until the time of the Revolution.

The Latin grammar school which had been provided for in the 1702 General Assembly apparently was never permanently established, since a later act in 1732 states that the "not rightly applying of a temporary salary heretofore allowed for a free school, has been the chief cause that an encouragement for the like purpose has ever since been neglected."[15] There were, however, private Latin masters who were licensed by the governors from time to time.

Educational Failure

After 1704 the Society for the Propagation of the Gospel in Foreign Parts (S.P.G.), an Anglican missionary effort, assumed the major role in providing education in New York. The provincial government seems

[13] Daniel J. Pratt, *Annals of the Public Education in the State of New York from 1626 to 1746* (Albany: Argus, 1872), pp. 65–67. A guilder was worth approximately two shillings in English currency.

[14] Quoted in Clews, p. 225.

[15] *Ibid.*, p. 240.

to have neglected all educational responsibilities for almost thirty years. Like the other Middle colonies, New York lagged considerably behind New England in the provision of schools supported even partially by the town or provincial government.

New Jersey

The Duke of York granted the southern part of his lands to two friends who, when they set up the proprietary government of New Jersey in 1665, granted religious freedom. Since no church had a position which enabled it to establish a common school system, a pattern of private and parochial schools developed.

In 1682 the Quakers took over New Jersey. Under their leadership, an Assembly at Burlington passed a law for "the encouraging of learning, for the better education of youth." It decreed that the "rents, issues and profits" earned from the land on Matininuck Island be "employed for the maintaining of a school for the education of the youth" of Burlington.[16]

The New Jersey provinces changed back and forth several times from royal to proprietary control, making the creation of a firm educational policy highly difficult. School proposals would be enacted by a legislative body, but before there was much opportunity to turn the sentiments of the proposals into practice, a change of administration would effectively nullify the proposals. As in New York, schooling was apparently left to the churches, and little of significance was accomplished until the effect of the Great Awakening was felt.

Pennsylvania

The Frame of Government drawn up by William Penn in 1682 provided "That the Governor and Provincial Council shall erect and order all public schools, and encourage and reward the authors of useful sciences and laudable inventions in the said province." It also provided that a committee of the Provincial Council be concerned with "manners, education and arts, that all wicked and scandalous living may be prevented, and that youth may be successively trained up in virtue and useful knowledge and arts."

[16] Quoted in Kilpatrick, p. 317.

The Quakers and Education

When the second Provincial Assembly met in March, 1683, it enacted a law carrying out the educational provisions of the Frame of Government. It closely resembled the 1642 law of Massachusetts Bay, requiring that children be taught to read and write and giving the civil authorities the responsibility of seeing that parents and guardians provided such education. The law was vetoed by William and Mary.

In 1683, Enoch Flower, a Philadelphian who had been a schoolmaster for twenty years in England, opened what was probably the first school in Pennsylvania. His fees depended on how many of the 3 R's the pupils studied.

> To learn to read English, 4 s by the quarter, to learn to read and write, 6 s by the quarter, to learn to read, write and cast account, 8 s by the quarter; for boarding a scholar, that is to say, diet, washing, lodging and schooling, ten pounds for one whole year.[17]

The inclusion of accounting is the result, no doubt, of the economic motives of the settlers in Pennsylvania.

Ten years later, when the Provincial Council charged "Thomas Meaking, keeper of the free school in the town of Philadelphia," with keeping a school without a license, he was "ordered to procure a certificate of his ability, learning and diligence, from the inhabitants of note in this town." Presumably he had no difficulty in doing so, for the Quaker school of which he was master had been established in 1689. Apparently the school was supported by denominational, rather than public, funds. First known as Friends' Free School, it became the William Penn Charter School. The first charter was apparently granted in response to a petition made by a Quaker meeting in December, 1697. The petition refers to "public schools." "Public" seems not to have meant tax-supported, but only that the school would be open to "all children and servants, male and female, whose parents, guardians and masters be willing to subject them to the rules and orders of the said school." The petitioners noted that a school was "much desired by many . . . where poor children may be freely maintained, taught and educated in good literature, until they are fit to be put out as apprentices, or capable to be masters or ushers in the said school." They asked the authority to erect buildings and establish a school where instruction might be provided for the "rich at reasonable rates, and the poor to be maintained

[17] Quoted in J. P. Wickersham, *A History of Education in Pennsylvania* (Lancaster: Inquirer Press, 1886), pp. 281–282.

and schooled for nothing." All "costs and charges" were left to "the people of God called Quakers," and nowhere is there a suggestion that it is the duty of government to do anything more than incorporate or charter the "Overseers of the Public School."[18]

The Quakers and some of the other "plain sects" did not have paid clergymen, since God might speak directly to any individual. Consequently, they did not need colleges for the preparation of a highly educated ministry. Many Quakers regarded the study of Latin as ostentatious, for they deemed that men more often used their Latin for social prestige than for religious enlightenment through Bible reading. Their great concern was for learning the vernacular so that the child could begin to learn his Bible. The Quaker schools which did exist, therefore, were generally of an elementary nature, and little schooling beyond the rudiments was available in the Quaker neighborhoods of the Middle colonies before the Great Awakening.

Perhaps because of the elementary nature of the Quaker schools, perhaps because the Quakers did not discriminate as sharply against women as did other sects, the use of women school teachers was encouraged. Since women teachers were generally paid far less than male schoolmasters, possibly the Quaker practicality might also have had something to do with permitting women to be employed as teachers as early as 1699.

In 1701 Penn revisited Pennsylvania and issued a new Frame of Government, which remained in effect until the Revolution. This document illustrates the almost *laissez-faire* attitude of Middle colony governments toward education. It omits even the vague and general reference to education made in the 1682 Frame of Government. Subsequent laws confirm that attitude in Pennsylvania; particularly after 1701, education was considered the concern of private or religious societies. Because the Quakers had granted religious toleration to most Protestant denominations, Pennsylvania had a population of diverse religious and national groups. With religion and schooling so intimately bound together, no single school could satisfy all the sects of the province. Hence schooling was left to parochial efforts. In 1715 the General Assembly enacted a law which granted to "all religious societies or assemblies and congregations of Protestants" the legal right to buy land and erect buildings for worship, schools, and hospitals. Following the Great Awakening, the denominationalism in Pennsylvania was to give considerable impetus to schooling, as it did in the other Middle colonies, which had been lagging far behind the New England provinces.

[18] *Ibid.*, pp. 284–286.

The Great Awakening

The religious revivalism of Jonathan Edwards in New England had its counterpart in each of the many denominations represented in the Middle colonies. In the Middle colonies the Great Awakening was more the result of European influences than native fervor. But that fervor, once stimulated, led to action on the part of the colonists. Each major denomination had its great revivalist leader, and the enthusiasm of the revivalists for the cause of salvation, particularly among the Bible-reading sects of Protestantism, had a definite effect on schools and colleges.

ANGLICANISM: GEORGE WHITEFIELD One of the first waves of revivalism had its inception in the Anglican Church in England. That Church, seeing many of its adherents attracted to dissenting sects, in 1699 founded a home missionary organization called the Society for the Promotion of Christian Knowledge. It quickly went about setting up charity schools in England, and its example led to the creation in 1701 of the Society for the Propagation of the Gospel in Foreign Parts. The S.P.G. was particularly active in the Southern and Middle colonies. Between 1704 and 1732 it was so influential in New York that the provincial government saw no need for assuming any educational responsibility at all. Even in 1732, when the free Latin school was established and partially supported by peddlers' license fees, the school was treated indifferently. Indeed, the master had great difficulty in the ensuing years collecting the salary promised him by the Legislature.[19] In several of the other colonies the efforts of the Society, although limited, were often taken as an excuse by local authorities to do little or nothing for schools.

One of the most famous of the Great Awakening evangelists was George Whitefield, an Anglican preacher and friend of John Wesley. When Whitefield's unorthodox Calvinist theology resulted in conflict with the established clergy in England and the closing of pulpits to him, he turned to preaching in the fields. It was this revivalistic spirit that he brought with him on his trips to the Colonies. His first "mission" was to Georgia in 1738. In other trips his preaching took him the full length of the Colonies. His influence was felt by many denominations. In New England, where his zeal got him into a conflict with Jonathan Edwards, pulpits were closed to him. He was denounced by the faculties of both Harvard and Yale, but that does not seem to have diminished his effectiveness as an evangelist. His preaching, often to

[19] Clews, pp. 238–247.

large groups in the fields and streets, led to the rise of many dissenting sects, some of which soon disappeared, others of which eventually became Methodist and Baptist congregations.

METHODISM: JOHN WESLEY John Wesley, the founder of Methodism, came to the Colonies in 1735 as a missionary of S.P.G. and stayed three years. On his return to England, Methodism became a formal sect, and Wesley sent over Francis Asbury, a lay preacher, who joined the evangelistic movement of the Great Awakening, carrying the Wesley influence throughout the Colonies.

PRESBYTERIANISM: WILLIAM TENNENT Among the Presbyterians, the Tennent family of preachers was very important. In about 1726, William Tennent opened a small school just north of Philadelphia on the banks of the Neshaminy River for the purpose of training Presbyterian ministers. The graduates of this frontier school later founded the first Presbyterian college in America, the College of New Jersey, now Princeton University.

LUTHERANISM: HEINRICH MUHLENBERG The Quakers and the various German sects of Lutheranism and Calvinism also had their revivalistic activities. Among the Lutherans the movement began in western Germany as pietistic reforms. Through the preaching of Heinrich Muhlenberg this pietism had a great effect on the Germans already in Pennsylvania and on those coming to America in the migration that followed Muhlenberg's arrival in 1742. In addition to his preaching, Muhlenberg helped establish Lutheran schools in Pennsylvania and worked closely with Benjamin Franklin to establish an academy in Philadelphia. The sober concerns of the pietists for industry, orderliness, and learning were manifested in a school operated by the Moravian sect in Pennsylvania.

> In one room children between three and four years old, picking cotton, so orderly and still. For any noise they made you might have been in an empty room. The next two [rooms contained children] between five and six years old knitting. . . . In the fifth and last [room children were] employed at their books. Pieces of their writing were fixed on the walls to raise emulation. Fourteen children were in each room.[20]

Christopher Dock

One of the most famous of the Pennsylvania schoolmasters of the Colonial period was the Mennonite Christopher Dock, whose *Schulord-*

[20] Monroe, p. 219.

nung was the first book on education published in America, appearing in 1770. His account of how he "kept school" illustrates the deep religious concern felt by schoolmasters of the Great Awakening, and it also reveals a moderation in discipline, probably more the exception than the rule even among the gentle "plain sects." Dock's use of reward as motivation and shame as punishment was unusual for his time, but his other methods were representative of other schools of the late Colonial period.

> The children arrive as they do because some have a great distance to school, others a short distance, so that the children cannot assemble as punctually as they can in a city. Therefore, when a few children are present, those who can read their Testament sit together on one bench; but the boys and girls occupy separate benches. They are given a chapter which they read at sight consecutively. Meanwhile I write copies for them. Those who have read their passage of Scripture without error take their places at the table and write. Those who fail have to sit at the end of the bench, and each new arrival the same; as each one is thus released in order he takes up his slate. This process continues until they have all assembled. The last one left on the bench is a "lazy pupil."
>
> When all are together, and examined, whether they are washed and combed, they sing a psalm or a morning hymn, and I sing and pray with them. As much as they can understand of the Lord's Prayer and the ten commandments (according to the gift God has given them), I exhort and admonish them accordingly. After these devotional exercises those who can write resume their work. Those who cannot read the Testament have had time during the assemblage to study their lesson. These are heard recite immediately after prayer. Those who know their lessons receive an 0 on the hand, traced with crayon. This is a mark of excellence. Those who fail more than three times are sent back to study their lesson again. When all the little ones have recited, these are asked again, and any one having failed in more than three trials a second time, is called "Lazy" by the entire class and his name is written down. Whether such a child fear the rod or not, I know from experience that this denunciation of the children hurts more than if I were constantly to wield and flourish the rod. If then such a child has friends in school who are able to instruct him and desire to do so, he will visit more frequently than before. For this reason: if the pupil's name has not been erased before dismissal the pupils are at liberty to write down the names of those who have been lazy, and take them along home. But if the child learns his lesson well in the future, his name is again presented to the other pupils, and they are told that he knew his lesson well and failed in no respect. Then

all the pupils call "Diligent" to him. When this has taken place his name is erased from the slate of lazy pupils, and the former transgression is forgiven.

The children who are in the spelling class are daily examined in pronunciation. In spelling, when a word has more than one syllable, they must repeat the whole word, but some, while they can say the letters, cannot pronounce the word, and so cannot be put to reading. For improvement a child must repeat the lesson, and in this way: The child gives me the book, I spell the word and he pronounces it. If he is slow, another pupil pronounces it for him, and in this way he hears how it should be done, and knows that he must follow the letters and not his own fancy.

Concerning A B C pupils, it would be best, having but one child, to let it learn one row of letters at a time, to say forward and backward. But with many, I let them learn the alphabet first, and then ask a child to point out a letter that I name. If a child is backward or ignorant, I ask another, or the whole class, and the first one that points to the right letter, I grasp his finger and hold it until I have put a mark opposite his name. I then ask for another letter, etc. Whichever child has during the day received the greatest number of marks, has pointed out the greatest number of letters. To him I owe something—a flower drawn on paper or a bird. But if several have the same number, we draw lots; this causes less annoyance. . . .

Further I will state that when the little ones have recited for the first time, I give the Testament pupils a verse to learn. Those reading newspapers and letters sit separately, and those doing sums sit separately. But when I find that the little ones are good enough at their reading to be fit to read the Testament, I offer them to good Testament readers for instruction. The willing teacher takes the pupil by the hand and leads him to his seat. I give them two verses to try upon. But if I find that another exercise is necessary after this (such as finding a passage in Scripture, or learning a passage, in which case each reads a verse), I give only one verse, which is not too hard for those trying to read in the Testament. If pupils are diligent and able, they are given a week's trial, in which time they must learn their lesson in the speller with the small pupils and also their lesson with the Testament pupil. If they stand the test they are advanced the next week from the spelling to the Testament class, and they are also allowed to write. But those who fail in the Testament remain a stated time in the A B C class before they are tested again. . . . This done they are reminded of the chapter read them, and asked to consider the teaching therein. As it is the case that this thought is also expressed in other passages of Holy Writ, these are found and read, and then a hymn is given containing the same teaching. If time remains, all are given a short passage of Scripture to learn. This done, they must show their writing exercises. These are examined and numbered, and then the first in turn is given a hard word to spell. If he fails the next must spell it and so on. The one to spell correctly receives his exercise. Then the first is given another hard word, and so each receives his exercise by spelling a word correctly.

As the children carry their dinner, an hour's liberty is given them after dinner. But as they are usually inclined to misapply their time if one is not constantly with them, one or two of them must read a story of the Old Testament (either from Moses and the Prophets, or from Solomon's or Sirach's Proverbs), while I write copies for them. This exercise continues during the noon hour.[21]

Protestant Orthodoxy and Schools

One of the major concerns was that the schoolmaster be an orthodox member of the denomination maintaining the school. This concern arose not only from the religious import of schooling, but also from the need for a man to fulfill part-time religious duties. In Pennsylvania in 1747 John Hoffman, "parochial teacher of the church at Lancaster," a Reformed Church, contracted "to serve as chorister, and as long as we have no pastor, to read sermons on Sunday." He agreed in summer to hold "catechetical instruction with the young, as becomes a faithful teacher, and also to lead them in singing." For these duties, he was to be granted "an annual salary consisting of voluntary offerings from all the members of the church, to be written in a special register and arranged according to the amounts contributed, so that the teacher may be adequately compensated for his labor."[22] Perhaps the public recording of each person's offering acted in some measure to compel the "voluntary" offering, thus making the arrangement a church-sponsored tax levy. In 1750, the Lutheran congregation at New Providence, Pennsylvania, specified that

The school house shall always be in charge of a faithful Evangelical Luthern schoolmaster, whose competency to teach Reading, Writing, Arithmetic, as also to play the organ (*Orgelschlagen*) and to use the English language, has been proved by the pastor; special regard being had at the same time, to the purity of his doctrine and his life.[23]

[21] Christopher Dock, *Schulordnung* (1770). As translated in Martin G. Brumbaugh, *The Life and Works of Christopher Dock* (Philadelphia: J. B. Lippincott, 1908).

[22] Quoted in Wickersham, p. 140.

[23] *Ibid.*, p. 141.

The teacher was also required to "instruct the children of other denominations, and of the neighborhood generally." Apparently there was no objection to having other denominations integrated with those of the church that supported the school, just so long as the teacher remained one of the faithful.

One effect of the increased zeal of dissenting sects in the Middle colonies was the revival of the requirement that schoolmasters in the royal colonies be licensed by the Bishop of London or the governor of the colony. Thus, in 1758, the governor of New Jersey received instructions from England.

> [N]o Schoolmaster be henceforth permitted to come from England and to keep School in the said province without the License of the said Bishop of London, and that no other person now there or that shall come from other parts, shall be admitted to keep School in that Our said province of New Jersey, without your License first obtained.[24]

Even the non-denominational academy that Benjamin Franklin and his friends were to establish in Philadelphia would reflect the religious concerns of the evangelistic Great Awakening. One of the academy's stated purposes was that it would prepare elementary school teachers for the rural schools.

> The Country suffering at present very much for want of good schoolmasters, and obliged to employ in their Schools, vicious imported Servants, or concealed Papists, who by their bad Examples and Instructions often deprave the Morals or corrupt the Principles of the Children under their Care.[25]

Colleges of the Great Awakening

Perhaps even more important than the renewed interest in elementary education was the new concern of several denominations for colleges to train ministers for the growing number of pulpits. Until the time of the Great Awakening, there were no colleges in the Middle colonies.

COLLEGE OF NEW JERSEY In 1746, the Presbyterians in New Jersey received a charter for a college "for the education of youth in the learned languages and in the liberal arts and sciences." At least twelve of the

[24] Quoted in Elsbree, p. 47.

[25] Quoted in F. N. Thorpe, *Benjamin Franklin and the University of Pennsylvania* (Washington: U.S. Bureau of Education, Circular of Information No. 2, 1892), pp. 245–46.

twenty-three members of the original board of trustees were ministers. Although the college was to be a Presbyterian institution, the religious toleration laws of New Jersey made it necessary for the trustees to promise and the charter to specify that "those of every religious denomination may have free and equal liberty and advantages of education in the said college, any different sentiments in religion notwithstanding."

The provincial Assembly, dominated by Quakers who did not advocate college training for religious leadership, provided no financial assistance, and the college had to rely on subscriptions and philanthropy. In 1755 a building named Nassau Hall, in honor of King William the Third, was finally erected in Princeton to house the college. Subsequently it adopted the name of Princeton College. Although it was founded for religious purposes, the college was not denominational in curriculum or method. A description of its curriculum in 1764 indicates primary stress on the Renaissance studies of Latin and Greek, attention to the Reformation study of Hebrew, and rudimentary concern with the medieval liberal arts of rhetoric, logic and mathematics. In 1764 the faculty probably consisted of the president, who taught most of the courses, and two tutors who assisted the younger students with their language work.

> As to the branches of literature taught here, they are the same with those which are made parts of education in the European Colleges. . . . The Freshman year is spent in Latin and Greek languages, particularly in reading *Horace, Cicero's Orations,* the Greek Testament, Lucian's Dialogues, and *Xenophon's Cyropaedia.* In the *Sophomore* year they still prosecute the study of the languages, particularly *Homer, Longinus,* &c., and enter upon the sciences, geography, rhetoric, logic, and the mathematics. They continue their mathematical studies throughout the *Junior* year, and also pass through a course of natural and moral philosophy, metaphysics, chronology, &c.; and the greater number, especially such as are educating for the service of the church, are initiated into the Hebrew. . . . The Senior year is entirely employed in reviews and composition. They now revise the most improving parts of Latin and Greek classics, part of the Hebrew Bible, and all the arts and sciences. The weekly course of disputation is continued, which was also carried on through the preceding year. They discuss two or three theses in a week; some in the syllogistic and others in the forensic manner. . . . A series of questions is also prepared on the principal subjects of natural and revealed religion. . . . There is likewise a monthly oration-day, when harangues, or orations of their own composition, are pronounced before a mixed auditory. All these compositions before mentioned are critically examined with respect to language,

orthography, pointing, capitalizing, with other minutiae, as well as more material properties of accurate writing.

Besides these exercises in writing and speaking, most of which are proper to the *Senior* class, . . . the three inferior classes, in rotation, pronounce declamations of their own composition from the stage. . . . The same classes . . . pronounce . . . such select pieces . . . as are best adapted to display the various passions, and exemplify the graces of utterance and gesture. . . .

The classics are taught, for the first three years, in nearer the usual method of grammar-schools than in the last. The students then revise them, principally as examples of fine composition. They first give a more literal translation of a paragraph, afterwards the sense in a paraphrase of their own, and then criticise upon the beauties of the author. In which work they are assisted by the President. No authors are read more particularly with this view than *Homer, Horace,* and especially *Longinus*. . . .

Each class recites twice a day: and have always free access to their teachers, to solve any difficulties that may occur. The bell rings for morning prayer at six o'clock, when the Senior class read off a chapter from the original into English. The president then proposes a few critical questions upon it, which, after their concise answers, he illustrates more at large. . . .

The usual method of instruction in the sciences is this. The pupils frequently and deliberately read over such a portion of the author they are studying, on a particular science, as it is judged they can be able thoroughly to impress upon their memories. When they attend their recitations, the tutor proposes questions on every particular they have been reading. After they have given, in their turns, such answers as show their general acquaintance with the subject, he explains it more at large; allows them to propose any difficulties; and takes pains to discover whether his explications be fully comprehended. Advantages which are seldom attainable in the usual method of teaching by lecture.

In the instruction of the youth, care is taken to cherish a spirit of liberty and free inquiry; and not only to permit, but even encourage their right of private judgment, without presuming to dictate with an air of infallibility, or demanding an implicit assent to the decision of the preceptor.[26]

KING'S COLLEGE In the same year that Princeton was chartered, the New York legislature created a lottery to raise funds for the founding of a college. That source proving insufficient, several other lotteries were authorized by succeeding legislatures. By 1751 a sum of £3,443 had been

[26] Quoted in John Maclean, *History of the College of New Jersey* (Philadelphia: Lippincott, 1877), Vol. I, pp. 266–268.

raised by the lotteries, and a board of trustees was then appointed to invest it and to receive additional contributions and donations for the college. The trustees were also authorized to receive proposals from the various towns in the province that wanted the college located in their community. To supplement the lottery funds, the legislature in 1753 voted £500 a year for seven years to be paid to the college out of the excise revenue of the colony. In 1754, the trustees reported that they had received only one proposal for the college; Trinity Church in New York had offered land on the condition that the president of the college be a member of the Anglican Church and that the liturgy of that Church be used for morning and evening service. Over the objections of trustee William Livingston, who argued that the proposal would be unjust to members of other denominations, the Assembly accepted the offer, and King's College (now Columbia University) was chartered by King George II in 1754. According to the charter, there were at least forty members of the Board of Governors, the majority Anglicans. Among the others were ministers from the Reformed Protestant Dutch Church, the Lutheran Church, the French Church, and the Presbyterian Congregation. The presence of these dissenters on the Board of Governors has caused some historians to claim that it was non-denominational, but the power of the majority of the board was clearly Anglican, and the specific privileges granted by the charter to the Anglican Church make it clear that the school was no more non-denominational than was the College of New Jersey.

That there was a greater religious toleration in the Middle colonies than in New England is apparent, however, in the creation at King's College in 1755 of a professorship in divinity of the Reformed Protestant Dutch Church. The amended charter based this concession on the toleration granted to the Dutch on their peaceful surrender to the Duke of York in 1664.[27]

Despite its Anglican president and Dutch Reformed professor, the curriculum of King's College was devoted almost entirely to the study of secular books in classical Greek and Latin. The plan of education for the college was outlined in detail by the Board of Governors in 1763. The first year students read Sallusts' *Historiae,* Caesar's *Commentaries,* Ovid's *Metamorphoses* (poetry), Virgil's *Eclogues* (pastoral poems), Aesop's *Fables* in Greek, Lucian's *Dialogues,* the New Testament in Greek, Grotius' *De Veritate Religionis Christianae,* and Latin and Greek grammars; in addition they did translations from Latin into English and from English into Latin and wrote themes in both English and Latin. The second year students read Cicero's *De Officiis* (Stoic philosophy),

[27] Clews, pp. 250–272.

Quintilian, Terence's *Comedies,* Ovid's *Letters,* Virgil's *Aeneid* and *Georgics,* the New Testament in Greek, Epictetus' *Enchiridion* (handbook of philosophical maxims), Xenophon's *Cyropaedia* (book on government) and *Anabasis* (account of Greek retreat from Persia), Thomas Farnaby's annotated editions of Latin authors, Latin and Greek grammar, John Wallis (English mathematician), and the *Noetica, or Things Relating to the Mind or Understanding* of Samuel Johnson (the first president of King's College); besides their reading, the second year students worked at rhetoric and reciting orations to learn public speaking, translated into Latin and English, and wrote Latin themes and Latin and English verses. The third year students read Cicero's *Orations* and the essay *Of Oratory,* Quintilian's *Institutes of Oratory,* Pliny's letters, the poems of Catullus, Tibullus and Propertius, Horace's *Works,* Aristotle's *Ethics* and *Poetica,* Plato's *Dialogues,* Xenophon's *Memorabilia Socratis,* Theocritus' *Idyls* (Greek pastoral poems), Homer's *Iliad,* Samuel Johnson's *Ethica, or Things Relating to the Moral Behavior,* and Francis Hutcheson's *Metaphysics;* they also engaged in syllogistical disputes in Latin, did Latin declensions and themes, and wrote English essays and English and Latin verses. Fourth year students read Cicero's *Tusculan Disputations* (Stoic philosophy), the histories of Livy and Tacitus, the narrative poems of Lucan's *Pharsalis,* the satires of Juvenal and Persius Flaccus, Plautus' *Comedies,* Homer's *Odyssey,* the tragedies of Sophocles, Euripides, and Aeschuylus, the histories of Thucydides and Herodotus, Longinus' essay *On the Sublime,* the orations of Demosthenes, Dionysius of Halicarnassus and Isocrates, Hebrew grammar and the Bible in Hebrew, Grotius' *De Jure Belli et Pacis,* Pufendorf (a writer of law whose books were not specified in the plan), and Francis Hutcheson's *A System of Moral Philosophy and Metaphysics;* the seniors wrote Latin themes and declamations, philosophical essays in English and Latin, and English and Latin verses, as well as engaging in disputations in Latin and repetitions of orations.[28] Notice the absence of any studies in modern languages, science, history (except that of Greece and Rome), and virtually all courses that make up the modern college curriculum. The whole field of mathematics, long recognized as a part of the liberal arts, is represented by only one book.

QUEEN'S COLLEGE The third of the Great Awakening colleges in the Middle colonies was Queen's College (now Rutgers University), founded by the Dutch Reformed Church in 1766 at New Brunswick,

[28] Columbia University, *A History of Columbia University, 1754–1904* (New York: Columbia U. Press, 1904), pp. 450–451.

New Jersey. Although it had barely started when the Revolutionary War interrupted it, it was following the same purpose and curriculum as the rest.

THEOLOGICAL TRAINING Although all these colleges, as well as those of New England, were founded in response to religious needs and denominational fervor, the preparation for the clergy which they offered was not comparable to the work of modern theological seminaries. The colonial colleges provided the general academic background considered necessary for the theological study which would be pursued in private study by the ministerial candidate. The college graduate still had to spend a year or more in intensive study to be able to pass his examinations for ordination into the clergy. Generally this study was done under the direction of a clergyman, sometimes the college president, who during the Colonial period, was selected from the ranks of the clergy. In some cases these students supported themselves as school teachers or private tutors during their period of study, constituting an important source of teachers. Philip Fithian, who upon graduation from Princeton in 1772 began the study of divinity and Hebrew with two Presbyterian ministers, Enoch Green and Andrew Hunter, accepted a job as a tutor in Virginia, where he spent his spare time writing a thesis, preparing trial sermons, engaging in exegesis in Latin, and reading theology. In his diary he reports some of his studies.

> I left the college the last of September 1772. After having settled my business at Home, I entered upon the Study of Divinity with the Rev'd Andrew Hunter; I was with him a Month, and on the first of December I went to Mr. *Green* with a design to acquaint myself with the Hebrew Tongue; he put me to the Grammar, which I learn'd through, and read some Chapters in the Psalter in the Course of the Winter: In Divinity, he advised me to read Ridgeleys body of Divinity for a System; And he gave me several separate treatisses on Repentance, Regeneration, Faith, &c, & towards spring gave me subjects to consider in the Sermon Way.[29]

Effect of the Great Awakening on Education

While the Great Awakening stimulated a renewed interest in learning, resulting in increased philanthropy for schools and colleges, it also revitalized the tradition of church control over education. This theo-

[29] Hunter Dickinson Farish, *Journal & Letters of Philip Vickers Fithian, 1773–1774* (Williamsburg: Colonial Williamsburg, 1943), pp. 61–62.

cratic viewpoint was to prove an exceedingly difficult barrier to the development of universal public education in the United States.

Financing Schools and Colleges

The methods of financing education in the Middle colonies were quite diverse. During the 1730's the Latin school in New York was supported in part by license fees collected from peddlers and by a tax on the inhabitants of the city. Some schools were assisted by the income from lands. For example, the English letters of patent for the town of Newburg specified that certain glebe lands were to be set aside "for the proper use, benefit, and behalf of a minister of the church of England . . . and of a scholemaster to teach and instruct the children."[30] Lotteries apparently were commonplace.

In spite of the varied means of collecting funds, schools were miserably supported. The buildings were bleak and bare and often served other purposes, such as church or home. The teachers were poorly paid, and even that pay was often by no means sure. Perhaps the sporadic pay was one reason many teachers stayed in teaching for only a short time and moved so often. The Middle colonies, in contrast with New England, show few records of individuals with long teaching careers.

Private Venture Schools

The settlers of the Middle colonies, having strong economic as well as religious motivation in their exodus from Europe, developed the practical, private school even more quickly than their New England neighbors. As early as 1661, a Dutch schoolmaster in New Amsterdam was apparently taking in some evening pupils to add to his regular town school teaching. Evert Pietersen was permitted to charge "a fair sum" for those "who come in the evening and between times." In 1690 there was apparently an English evening school in New York, since an apprenticeship indenture in that year specified that the apprentice was to have "the privelege of going to the evening school." Most of the seaport towns in the colonies appear to have had evening schools by the first years of the eighteenth century.

From the fact that these practical schools were often (though not

[30] Quoted in Ellwood P. Cubberley, *Readings in Public Education in the United States* (Boston: Houghton Mifflin, 1934), p. 69.

always) held in the evening, it may be inferred that at least some of the pupils worked during the day and sought to better their social and economic condition by going to school in their free hours.

Some masters apparently taught only one subject, while others advertised many. Some claimed a college education, some long experience in the practical fields they advertised to teach. School terms varied according to the master, with some masters teaching the year around. Students apparently studied individually and took only those studies they desired. Some masters provided boarding accommodations for their scholars or promised to find them for out-of-town pupils. Tuition fees, different from master to master, were paid directly to the teacher and depended on how many subjects the student took. The school was often located in a regular schoolhouse that was used during the day for the town school, but many times it was at the master's lodging house, in rented rooms, or at the home of the pupil. Pupils might come from any class, almost any age group, and either sex. The only thing that seems to have been common to these schools is that they were all private ventures.

Curriculum

The clearest picture of the varied nature of these schools is in their advertisements. Seybolt, for the period from 1723 to 1770, found advertisements for one hundred of these schools, most of them in the Middle colonies. He found nine in Boston, five in Newport, Rhode Island, one in Providence, and three in Charleston, South Carolina; the rest were in the Middle colonies. His list is, of course, not complete, but the great preponderance of such private, practical schools in New York and Philadelphia is probably a reflection of the commercial interests in those cities. Their existence probably indicates, too, a lack of town or public schools of the kind providing the rudiments of education in New England: some of the private evening schools in New York and Philadelphia offered reading, writing, and arithmetic. Some also taught Latin, a subject many New England boys took in the town school. Before the founding of the Middle colony colleges, some private schools offered courses in Greek, Hebrew, metaphysics, ethics, logic, and rhetoric, subjects included in the college curriculum at Harvard. The main body of subjects, however, lay in the practical or vocational fields, and the list was a long one: merchants' accounts, bookkeeping, algebra, astronomy, dialing, French, gauging, geography, geometry, German, gunnery, logarithms, mensuration, navigation, Portuguese, Spanish, stereometry, surveying, trigonometry, conic sections, globes, shorthand, use of charts, fortification, and fluxions. Dialing is the technique of surveying with a miner's compass; stereometry and mensuration are forms of mathematics concerned with the measurement of lengths, volumes, and areas; conic sections and fluxions are also advanced forms of mathematics. The modern languages were needed for trade with other nations, and subjects such as geography and astronomy were taken by those mariners who wanted to become navigators and ship captains. In addition, the private schools advertised a number of subjects that were to become common in the next century in secondary schools and colleges but were not then being taught in the narrow and conservative public institutions: English, chronology, history, spelling, and natural philosophy (which included the whole field of what is now known as science.[31]) Thus the private evening schools anticipated the broad curriculum of the academies, which were to become the predominant secondary schools in the nineteenth century.

Some of these private schools became somewhat formalized even in the eighteenth century in what were called English grammar schools, in contrast with the more narrow Latin grammar schools which prepared boys for college. Probably the name "academy" was first used for the school Franklin helped organize in Philadelphia in 1751, but earlier schools offered much the same course as the one the Philadelphia Academy was to establish as the curriculum of the academies. One of the first of these earlier schools of which there is still a record was established in New York City by John Walton in 1723. It offered college and college preparatory subjects as well as elementary reading and various practical courses. Walton also volunteered to seek places for out-of-town students to live and board—"suitable Entertainment" was his description of those accommodations.

> There is a School in New York, in the Broad Street, near the Exchange where Mr. John Walton, late of Yale-Colledge, Teacheth Reading, Writing, Arethmatick, Whole Numbers and Fractions, Vulgar and Decimal, the Mariners Art, Plain and Mercators Way; Also Geometry, Surveying, the Latin Tongue, and Greek and Hebrew Grammars, Ethicks, Rhetorick, Logick, Natural Philosophy and Metaphysicks, all or any of them for a Reasonable Price. The School from the first of October till the first of March will be tended in the Evening. If any Gentlemen in the Country are disposed to send their Sons to the said School, if they apply themselves to the Master he will immediately procure suitable Entertainment for them, very cheap. Also if any Young Gentlemen of the City will

[31] Seybolt, *Evening School*, pp. 65–68. See pp. 43–44 for examples of these advertisements as they appeared in the New England colonies.

please to come in the Evening and make some Tryal of the Liberal Arts, they may have the opportunity of Learning the same Things which are commonly Taught in Colledges.[32]

Schools for Girls

Educational opportunities for girls, beyond reading and a little writing, were quite limited until some private schoolmasters saw the financial advantages of offering courses for girls. Some of these masters had both boys and girls in the same schools; others apparently had women teachers who taught the girls separately from the boys; others kept schools for girls alone. Girls were offered the traditional courses of reading, writing, and arithmetic, and also a number of courses intended only for them, such as vocal and instrumental music, sewing, drawing, painting, quilting, embroidery, dancing, English grammar, and letter writing. Some schoolmasters taught girls practical courses like bookkeeping. Others included courses boys might be taking at the town school, particularly Latin. Sometimes girls were offered, for general cultural development, courses boys might take for practical reasons: French, history, and geography. Thus, while the Latin grammar schools and other town schools resisted curricular change and denied admission to girls except for the barest rudiments of elementary education, the flexibility of the private schoolmasters prepared the way for the rise of the popular academies and the downfall of the outmoded Latin schools. The academy was to extend the educational opportunities for girls, until by mid-nineteenth century nearly half the secondary school enrollment in the United States was female.

The Philadelphia Academy

Benjamin Franklin

One of the most famous of the academies was founded at the urging of Benjamin Franklin. Born in Boston and almost entirely self-educated, Franklin undoubtedly recognized the need for a new kind of school to provide suitable education for practical men like himself.

> My elder brothers were all put apprentices to different trades. I was put to the grammar-school at eight years of age, my father intending to devote me, as the tithe of his sons, to the service of

[32] Quoted in Seybolt, *Source Studies*, p. 99.

the Church. I continued, however, at the grammar-school not quite one year, though in that time I had risen gradually from the middle of the class of that year to be the head of it, and farther was removed into the next class above it, in order to go with that into the third at the end of the year. But my father, in the meantime, from a view of the expense of a college education which having so large a family he could not well afford, and the mean living many so educated were afterwards able to obtain,—reasons that he gave to his friends in my hearing,—altered his first intention, took me from the grammar-school, and sent me to a school for writing and arithmetic. . . . I acquired fair writing pretty soon, but I failed in the arithmetic, and made no progress in it. At ten years old I was taken home to assist my father in his business, which was that of tallow-chandler and sope-boiler . . . till I was twelve years old.

From a child I was fond of reading, and all the little money that came into my hands was ever laid out in books. . . .

This bookish inclination at length determined my father to make me a printer, though he had already one son (James) of that profession. . . . My father was impatient to have me bound to my brother. I stood out some time, but at last was persuaded, and signed the indentures when I was yet but twelve years old. I was to serve as an apprentice till I was twenty-one years of age, only I was to be allowed journeyman's wages during the last year. In a little time I made great proficiency in the business, and became a useful hand to my brother. I now had access to better books. . . .

About this time I met with an odd volume of the *Spectator*. . . . I bought it, read it over and over, and was much delighted with it. I thought the writing excellent, and wished, if possible, to imitate it. With this view I took some of the papers, and, making short hints of the sentiment in each sentence, laid them by a few days, and then, without looking at the book, try'd to compleat the papers again, by expressing each hinted sentiment at length, and as fully as it had been expressed before, in any suitable words that should come to hand. Then I compared my Spectator with the original, discovered some of my faults, and corrected them.

And now it was that, being on some occasion made asham'd of my ignorance in figures, which I had twice failed in learning when at school, I took Cocker's book of *Arithmetick*, and went through the whole by myself with great ease. I also read Seller's and Shermy's books of *Navigation*, and became acquainted with the little geometry they contain; but never proceeded far in that science. And I read about this time Locke *On Human Understanding*, and the *Art of Thinking*, by Messrs. du Port Royal.

While I was intent on improving my language, I met with an English grammar (I think it was Greenwood's), at the end of

> which there were two little sketches of the arts of rhetoric and logic, the latter finishing with a specimen of a dispute in the Socratic method, and soon after I procur'd Xenophon's *Memorable Things of Socrates,* wherein there are many instances of the same method. I was charm'd with it, adopted it, dropt my abrupt contradiction and positive argumentation, and put on the humble inquirer and doubter.[33]

Plan For a Practical School

When he went to Philadelphia in 1727 Franklin joined with a number of other young men in an informal society for mutual improvement, discussing various topics and exchanging views as well as books. Out of this group, known as the Junto, came the first subscription library in America, founded about 1731. It was incorporated in 1742 as the Library Company of Philadelphia. The Junto later became the American Society, and in 1769 merged with a similar organization to form the American Philosophical Society, the oldest learned society in the United States. The young men in these societies had quite broad interests and at their meetings discussed scientific and practical problems and experiments. The traditional Latin school education was little related to the kinds of questions raised by members of the Junto and the American Philosophical Society; consequently, it is not surprising that Franklin drafted a proposal for a more practical school. Apparently his friends and he discussed his plan before he published it in 1749 under the title *Proposals Relating to the Education of Youth of Pensilvania.* The plan, though radical in comparison with the Latin grammar schools, included many of the courses offered by the private evening schools and the English grammar schools.

Franklin proposed that "some Persons of Leisure and publick Spirit" apply for a charter, with the power "to erect an ACADEMY for the Education of Youth." One modern part of his plan was the suggestion that the schoolhouse be "furnished with a Library . . . with Maps of all Countries, Globes, some mathematical Instruments, and Apparatus for Experiments in Natural Philosophy, and for Mechanics." Few schools were to have any of these aids until the middle of the nineteenth century. The master of the school, said Franklin, should be "learn'd in the Languages and Sciences, and a correct pure Speaker and Writer of the *English* Tongue." Few schools of the time were much concerned about the master's command of English as long as his Latin was good. A

[33] *The Complete Works of Benjamin Franklin* (New York: Putnam's, 1887), pp. 38–39, 43–50.

proposal that went beyond anything in the private schools was that the academy include physical activity—"Running, Leaping, Wrestling, and Swimming." As regards the studies, the ideal would be to teach "*every Thing* that is useful, and *every Thing* that is ornamental"; but since that is impossible, the students should "learn those Things that are likely to be *most useful* and *most ornamental.* Regard being had to the several Professions for which they are intended." The curriculum would particularly stress English reading and writing and the various practical subjects. Although it would be possible for students to take Latin and Greek, no student would be required to do so, and those who did must not neglect their "*English,* Arithmetick, and other Studies." The subjects taught would be writing, arithmetic, accounts, geometry, astronomy, English grammar, history (with Greek and Roman historians in translation), oratory, geography, chronology, morality, French, German, Spanish, natural history, history of commerce, agriculture, mechanics, and logic. The culmination of this education was to be "an *Inclination* join'd with an *Ability* to serve Mankind, one's Country, Friends and Family."[34]

The proposal elicited immediate and favorable response. Individual subscriptions reached £800 a year, pledged for a period of five years. From the subscribers, a board of twenty-four trustees was formed; the trustees rented a building for the school and hired a master.[35] The advertisement for the school, which appeared in the *Pennsylvania Gazette,* December, 1750, reveals how closely Franklin's proposal was followed at first.

> NOTICE is hereby given, That the Trustees of the ACADEMY of Philadelphia, intend (God willing) to open the same on the first Monday of January next; wherein Youth will be taught the Latin, Greek, English, French, and German Languages, together with History, Geography, Chronology, Logic, and Rhetoric; also Writing, Arithmetic, Merchants Accounts, Geometry, Algebra, Surveying, Gauging, Navigation, Astronomy, Drawing in Perspective, and other mathematical Sciences; with natural and mechanical Philosophy, &c. agreeable to the Constitutions heretofore published, at the Rate of Four Pounds per annum, and Twenty Shillings entrance.[36]

[34] Benjamin Franklin, *Proposals Relating to the Education of Youth in Pensilvania* (Philadelphia, 1749), pp. 7–33.

[35] Elmer Ellsworth Brown, *The Making of Our Middle Schools* (New York: Longmans, Green, 1902), p. 182.

[36] Quoted in Seybolt, *Source Studies,* pp. 98–99.

The school was immediately so popular that the building was too small. Ironically, the only important non-denominational school in the Middle colonies had to turn to a building erected as an assembly hall for the evangelistic preaching of George Whitefield. The structure, which was also supposed to house a charity school, was sold to the trustees of the Academy on condition that a charity school for teaching elementary subjects to poor children be part of their enterprise. In 1753 a new charter was granted the Academy and Charitable School. The Academy was divided into three schools, or classes—the Latin, the English, and the mathematical—each with its own master. According to Franklin's plans, the schools would be of equal importance, but from the first the Latin master apparently received a higher salary and was regarded as the rector of the establishment. In a letter dated September 12, 1751, Franklin listed the faculty and their salaries: "Rector, who teaches Latin and Greek, per annum £200; The English master £150; The Mathematical professor, £125; three assistant tutors each £60."[37]

The College of Philadelphia

In 1754 the Reverend William Smith, an Anglican clergyman who had written a novel plan for higher education, A *general idea of the College of Mirania,* became master of a fourth and new school, the philosophical. A new charter was issued, shortly thereafter, changing the Academy's name to The College, Academy, and Charitable School and granting it the right to confer college degrees. The College grew out of the Latin and philosophical schools; the English and mathematical schools became the Academy.

Smith, who favored the Proprietary family, soon got into political conflict with the provincial legislature, made up mainly of Quakers and members of various German sects. In 1758 they had him jailed for three months on a charge of implication in a libellous attack against the legislature. Later the King disciplined the House of Representatives for taking to itself such powers, an act that invaded "both his majesty's royal prerogative and the liberties of the subject." The legislature then attacked the school through a bill to suppress lotteries, which had been the principal form of support of the Academy and College. The report of the Council to the governor, arguing against the bill, gives an account of the work of the institution as well as the practice of financing public works through lotteries.

[37] Jared Sparks, *The Works of Benjamin Franklin* (Boston: Charles Tappen, 1844), Vol. VII, p. 52.

> That eighty poor boys and forty poor girls were instructed gratis in the school to read, write and cast accounts, and the girls to sew and do all sorts of plain needle-work, under two masters and a mistress. That in the schools there were one hundred and thirty boys who were instructed in the Greek, Latin, and English tongues, and were likewise taught at the same time writing and mathematics. And that in the College there were above twenty students who were instructed by able professors in all the higher branches of learning, oratory, Euclid, logic, ethics, natural and experimental philosophy; that the expenses of professors were very great, amounting to thirteen hundred pounds a year. . . . They have of late supported this expense by lotteries, which had been uprightly managed by people of the best credit in the province, and the prizes always paid with the utmost punctuality and honor. That there had been no lotteries carried on in this province other than of the city, the defense of the province in time of war, and the finishing the Episcopal church.[38]

The legislature passed the bill suppressing lotteries in 1758, but the King repealed it a year later, and the lottery continued to be one of the chief sources of financial support for the school. The school became steadily more important, with large subscriptions obtained in England, particularly from the Penn family and from the King.

Although the school remained nominally non-denominational, with several sects represented among the faculty, the Anglicans soon gained control of the board of trustees. They threw their support to Smith, who gave greatest attention to the College, with the result that the Academy faltered. Franklin attempted to have the two institutions separated, with the lower school given some share of the endowment, but he was unsuccessful and resigned as president of the trustees. In 1789 he wrote bitterly of how his English school had finally been subordinated to the traditional Latin education, referring in detail to the original *Proposal* he had circulated as the basis of the Academy. During the Revolution the legislature had its revenge on Smith, revoking the school's charter, but it revived in 1789 during the conservative reaction to the Revolution. In 1791 the state's short-lived university (chartered in 1789) was turned over to the College and a new charter created the private and independent University of Pennsylvania.

Franklin's original scheme was subverted, but his proposal was given life in the thousands of academies that sprang up all over the United States in the decades following the Revolution. Many of these could have used his original *Proposal* as a fairly accurate description of their

[38] Quoted in Clews, pp. 309–310.

curriculum and purpose. More important was the revolutionary new relationship between the literary liberal arts and the practical studies. Drawing on the whole field of knowledge rather than the narrow emphasis on the classics or the equally narrow utilitarianism of apprenticeship, Franklin's philosophy, and the academies which exemplified that philosophy, broke sharply with the European tradition which isolated the classics from the practical studies. This innovation in educational thought is a genuine American development which can be seen at its best in the great American state universities and the comprehensive high school. In an enlightened democracy, the dichotomy between liberal studies and practical studies is not an appropriate one, as the life and thought of Franklin himself clearly demonstrated—free men in an industrial society need both.

The Middle Colonies and New England

The difference between the New England pattern of public-supported town schools and the parochial and private-school pattern of the Middle colonies was not a result of chance or whimsey. Although the Middle colonies shared New England's religious concern for schooling, they were not in agreement as to which religion should control the schools. They also lacked a theocratically oriented government. Moreover, they developed commercial interests which were soon much stronger than their religious concerns. Thus, while they failed to develop a universal elementary school, they led in establishing the kind of practical schooling that was later to dominate American secondary education.

QUESTIONS FOR DISCUSSION

1. If the schools are a product of the social setting in which they exist, how can you account for the differences between the educational patterns of New England and the Middle colonies, both of which were newly settled colonial regions?
2. In what ways were the Middle colonies more like present-day United States than was New England? What developments in American education resulted in part from the social demands of the Middle colonies?
3. Educational historians have tended to stress the influence of New England on American cultural and educational history. It is possible that this emphasis has obscured our understanding of the full range of influences on American education and that the Middle colonies played a very important part. Can you see any parallels to problems of the Middle

colonies in today's educational issues, where overwhelming concern for one part of a problem may be blinding our awareness of other crucial factors?

4. One of the crucial issues in American education has been the relationship of church and state in education. What influence did the Middle colonies play in the beginning of this issue? What lessons can we learn from the experiences of the Middle colonies which might be helpful in understanding and dealing with this issue?

SUGGESTED READINGS

Secondary Sources

Brown, Elmer Ellsworth. *The Making of Our Middle Schools.* New York: Longmans, Green, 1902. Pp. 73–74, 84–90, 103–104, 117–118, 150–151, 179–191.

Butts, R. Freeman, and Cremin, Lawrence. *A History of Education in American Culture.* New York: Holt, 1953. Chapters 1–4.

Edwards, Newton, and Richey, Herman G. *The School in the American Social Order.* Boston: Houghton Mifflin, 1963. Chapter 5.

Elsbree, Willard. *The American Teacher.* New York: American Book, 1939. Chapters 1–10.

Primary Sources

Cubberley, Ellwood P. *Readings in Public Education in the United States.* Boston: Houghton Mifflin, 1920. Readings 195–199.

———. *Readings in Public Education in the United States.* Boston: Houghton Mifflin, 1934. Readings 20–23, 27, 44–50, 55–59.

Hofstadter, Richard, and Smith, Wilson. *American Higher Education: A Documentary History.* Chicago: U. of Chicago Press, 1961. Vol. I, pp. 82–121, 130–131, 137–146.

Knight, Edgar W., and Hall, Clifton L. *Readings in American Educational History.* New York: Appleton-Century-Crofts, 1951. Pp. 13–14, 16–19, 21–43, 69–70, 74–83, and 467–468.

Monroe, Paul. *The Founding of the American Public School System.* Ann Arbor: University Microfilms, 1940. Vol. II, Chapters IV–VI, VIII–X.

Seybolt, Robert F. *The Evening School in Colonial America.* Urbana: U. of Illinois, Bureau of Educational Research, Bulletin No. 24, 1925.

———. *Source Studies in American Colonial Education: The Private School.* Urbana: U. of Illinois, Bureau of Educational Research, Bulletin No. 28, 1925.

3

Aristocracy and Philanthropy in the South

In the South there developed an entirely different set of social conditions from those in New England or the Middle colonies. The most important motivation for settling the Southern colonies was economic rather than religious. English gentlemen—or would-be gentlemen—came to exploit the land—and the lower classes—so that they themselves might live in a style befitting an English gentleman. The lower classes often came to escape indebtedness or poverty, selling themselves into bond slavery. The planters were not dissatisfied with the life of country gentlemen in England; they merely wished to replicate the religious, social, political, and economic institutions of the homeland, with themselves as the landed gentry.

For the children of the aristocracy, there would be the best education their parents could afford. On the other hand, not only would schools for the lower classes be at the expense of the wealthy, but education might make the lower classes dissatisfied with their "station in life," endangering the aristocratic order. The attitude of the aristocrats is revealed in the report of Sir William Berkeley, Governor of Virginia, to the Commissioners of Trade and Plantations in 1671. In response to the question of what was being done "about instructing the people within your government in the christian religion," Berkeley responded:

> The same course that is taken in England out of towns; every man according to his ability instructing his children. . . . But I thank God, *there are no free schools* nor *printing,* and I hope we shall not have these hundred years, for *learning* has brought disobedience, and heresy, and sects into the world, and *printing* has divulged them, and libels against the best government. God keep us from both.[1]

[1] Hening, *Statutes at Large of Virginia,* II, p. 517.

Berkeley probably meant that each father provided what schooling he could afford for his children. The planters hired tutors, enrolled their children in boarding schools, and even sent them to England to complete their preparation for their roles as gentlemen and ladies. The lower classes could afford little or no schooling.

The established church in the Southern colonies was the Anglican, which preached acceptance of clerical authority and did not share the Calvinist zeal for having each man learn to read the Bible. The clergy, not the congregation, was responsible for the interpretation of religious dogma. Thus, not until it felt the threat of dissenting sects did the Anglican Church take much interest in providing schools in the colonies. The attitude of the Anglican Church toward learning is reflected in a 1631 law which required ministers to "examine, catechise, and instruct the youth and ignorant persons of his parrish, in the ten commandments, the articles of the beliefs and in the Lord's prayer." The law did not require that the people be taught to read the Book of Common Prayer or the Bible for themselves. The law specified that those who did not know the catechism go to church every Sunday evening one-half hour before evening prayer, "obedientlie to heare, and to be ordered by the mynister untill they have learned the same."[2] Apparently the text to be memorized was read aloud by the minister to the children.

Apprenticeship offered some opportunity for the children of the lower classes, but even those opportunities were limited in a number of ways. Some scattered efforts at schooling were made through individual philanthropy and organized church missionary work. In the mid-eighteenth century some free schools, with partial public support, were organized, but all these provisions were exceptions to the general practice of encouraging schooling only for the sons and daughters of planters.

Apprenticeship

As in Massachusetts Bay, one of the first educational acts in Virginia provided for the apprenticing of children of the poor. Unlike the Massachusetts law, Virginia's law of 1642 did not specify that the apprentice be taught to read and write. The county commissioners were authorized to select two children, either male or female, whose parents' "poverty extends not to give them breeding," and to send those children to James City to be employed in the public flax houses. An interesting wording in the Virginia law, stressing the responsibility of the state to exercise

[2] *Ibid.*, I, p. 157.

authority on those parents "who by reason of their poverty are disabled to maintaine and educate" their children, gave full power to the commissioners to take the children, even though "the parents, either through fond indulgence or perverse obstinacy, are most averse and unwilling to parte with theire children."[3]

Subsequent legislation, in 1705, provided that any orphan whose estate was so small "that no person will maintain him for the profits thereof" should be apprenticed by the county court to some master until the orphan reached the age of twenty-one. In addition to teaching him the trade, the master was "obliged to teach him to read and write." In 1769, illegitimate children were similarly provided for.

Other colonies followed Virginia's lead, passing laws which required that orphans and illegitimate children be apprenticed. Some of the laws specified that reading be taught; others did not. In Virginia in 1717 a master named George Smyth was summoned to court to answer the complaints of his apprentice, "Rich'd Williams," who said that his master was not teaching him "to read as by Indenture he is oblig'd." When Smyth promised "to put ye said apprentice forthwith to Schoole & to doe his true Endeavour to teach him his trade," the court ordered the apprentice to return to his master and serve out his indenture.[4] The absence of more such records might be taken as evidence that most masters were fulfilling their part of the bargain; on the other hand, it might mean that few apprentices were in a position to complain. From the number of advertisements in colonial newspapers for runaway apprentices, it appears that conditions were not always ideal for the apprentices.

Free Schools

Virginia

In spite of the hopes of Governor Berkeley, the hundred years after his report did see a few free schools established. In fact, there was at least one at the time he made his report. In 1634 Benjamin Syms wrote a will in which he bequeathed two hundred acres of land and "Eight Milch cows" to be used for "the mantayance of an honest & learned man to keep upon the said Ground a free School to Educate & teach the Children of the adjoining Parishes of Elizb City & Poquoton."[5]

[3] *Ibid.*, I, pp. 336–337.

[4] *The Virginia Magazine of History and Biography*, 2 (1895): 345.

[5] Quoted in Edgar W. Knight, *A Documentary History of Education in the South Before 1860* (Chapel Hill: U. of North Carolina Press, 1949), Vol. I, p. 203.

Perhaps it was Syms' example which led another man in the same county to endow a second school by a will dated 1659. Thomas Eaton bequeathed five hundred acres of land, two "negroes," twelve cows, two bulls, twenty hogs, and a collection of household and dairy furnishings "for the maintenance of an able school master [to] educate and teach the children borne within said County of Elizabeth City." Eaton specified that "no free education bee allowed but to such children as shalbe borne within the said county."[6] A hundred years later, in 1759, the Virginia legislature took notice of the fact that "the said foundation hath been abused, by admitting a great number of children into the said school, whose parents are well able to pay for their education," and they fixed the stigma of charity on the school by requiring that "no person shall enjoy the benefit of the said charity-school without consent of the master . . . except such poor children as the said trustees . . . declare to be the proper objects of the pious founder's charity."[7] Such a stigma was enough to discourage many impoverished but proud parents from sending their children to the school. In 1805 the Syms and Eaton funds were merged to form the foundation of Hampton Academy.

Other bequests for the support of schools were made in Virginia and the Carolinas. Some resulted in the founding of schools; some perhaps did not. One William Gordon, in a will in 1684, wrote that if "my Loving wif after my deceise Shall *conteiu* in Virginia and be maried to another man then I giv" a hundred acres of land and "two *kows* for the proper use of a scoull."[8]

Although it was the oldest of the Southern colonies, Virginia made very limited progress compared with that of the Northern colonies. In 1724 the Bishop of London sent a questionnaire to be answered by parish priests in the colonies. One of the questions concerned the existence and endowment of "public schools," and the answers revealed that there were few schools of any kind in Virginia. Bristol Parish reported no public schools, though there were private ones which taught reading, writing, and ciphering. "The children's fathers hire those schools and pay you out of their pockets." Westover Parish reported no public schools and "but two private ones for to teach reading and writing; consisting of about 35 in scholars both and very indifferently attended by the masters." The pastor at Lawn's Creek replied, "There is no parish school that I know of anywhere, but at the College of William and Mary." At Elizabeth City there were two public schools, Syms and

[6] *Ibid.*, pp. 205–206.
[7] Hening, VII, pp. 319–320.
[8] Quoted in Knight, p. 299.

Eaton, "very meanly" endowed. Accomako, on the Eastern Shore, had one endowed school, and Abingdon Parish reported one school endowed with five hundred acres of land, three slaves, cattle, and household goods. Although twelve of the thirty parishes reported mentioned private schools, only four parishes reported any public or endowed schools at all.[9] Free education for the poor did not seem to be a major concern for many planters.

Georgia and the Carolinas

When the evangelist George Whitefield arrived in Savannah in 1737, he opened a school for girls. In 1739 he began an orphanage, for which he solicited funds wherever he preached in the colonies. At the time of the Revolution the Bethesda Orphan House was "the most prominent institution of learning" in the colony of Georgia.[10] Just before his death in 1770, Whitefield was attempting to convert the orphan school into a college, but shortly after his death the Orphan House was destroyed by fire.

In South Carolina in 1753, at a meeting of the Winyaw Parish Indigo Planters Society, one of the members proposed a toast, asking the others to signify their approval by emptying their glasses. His proposal was that the surplus in the treasury be devoted to the establishment of a charity school. According to the account, "The meeting rose to its feet. The glasses were each turned down without soiling the linen.[11] (Boards of education and college trustees might take note of this happy method of securing affirmative votes!) If not the only school, the Winyaw Indigo Society School was the most important one between Charleston and the North Carolina line for more than a century. In 1886 it became one of the public graded schools of South Carolina.

Occasionally bequests, gifts, and other endowments led to the establishment of quasi-public schools. One example was the Free School at Charleston, South Carolina, established in 1712. The legislature appropriated all gifts and legacies given for a free school in South Carolina to a corporate body of commissioners charged with establishing and operating a free school. To encourage further gifts, the charter granted to anyone who would make a contribution of twenty pounds the right to nominate one person to be taught free for a period of five years. Others might be permitted to enroll at a tuition of four pounds per annum, to be paid to the teacher by the parent or guardian of the pupil. The

[9] Monroe, pp. 105–115.
[10] Knight, p. 236.
[11] *Ibid.*, p. 282.

schoolmaster was required to be an Anglican capable of teaching Latin and Greek and to "catechise and instruct the youth in the principles of the Christian religion, as professed in the Church of England." He would receive his home free and be paid "out of the publick treasure of this Province, the full sum of one hundred pounds per annum." In addition, a teacher was to be employed "to teach writing, arithmetick, and merchants' accompts, and also the art of navigation and surveying, and other useful and practical parts of the mathematicks." He would be paid up to fifty pounds a year, and for that he would be required to teach free those students designated by the commissioners or financial donors; for tuition students, he would receive tuition fees according to how many and what subjects they studied with him. Some twenty years later, when inflation had reduced the salaries of the master, the usher, and the writing master (who also taught the mathematical subjects) to "one-fifth part of their original values," the legislature voted them a 400-percent raise. At the same time, it authorized a second free school in Dorchester but, except for appropriating to the school any gifts or legacies made for that school, did not make any financial provisions for it.[12]

North Carolina was even slower at establishing schools. When the people of Newbern petitioned the governor in 1765 to apply to the S.P.G. for a salary for a schoolmaster, they claimed that "there never has been in this Province any regular settled Schoolmaster."[13]

Maryland

In its early years Maryland had difficulty securing school legislation because of a conflict between the Catholic upper house of the legislature and the predominantly Protestant lower house. When the upper house introduced a school bill in 1671, the lower house killed it by adding an amendment to permit Anglicans to be teachers and Protestants to "have liberty to choose their schoolmasters."[14] In 1691 Lord Baltimore lost his charter and Maryland became a royal colony; the next year, Anglicanism became the established religion. With religious dissent ended, the legislature enacted a series of laws for the maintenance of free schools. In 1694 the legislature accepted gifts of money and tobacco from the governor, his secretary, and members of the council for the

[12] *Ibid.*, pp. 681–683, 697–703.

[13] William L. Saunders, *The Colonial Records of North Carolina* (Raleigh: Josephus Daniels, 1890), VII, p. 35.

[14] Bernard C. Steiner, *History of Education in Maryland* (U.S. Bureau of Education, Circular of Information No. 2, 1894), p. 5.

support of free schools, and Annapolis and Oxford were named as suitable locations for the two proposed schools. Other acts in the same session laid duties on liquors, beef, bacon, furs, and other commodities, the income to be used for free schools. In 1696 the first of these schools, King Williams School, was finally established in Annapolis. Following the second, to be established at Oxford on the Eastern Shore, others were to be located in each county as revenue was available.

By 1723 enough money had accumulated so that the lower house thought it time to be more explicit in its "encouragement of learning," and a new law set up boards of visitors in each county, authorizing them to buy land, build schools, and pay a schoolmaster twenty pounds a year. The schoolmasters should be "members of the church of England, and of pious and exemplary lives and conversations, and capable of teaching well the grammar, good writing, and the mathematics, if such can be conveniently got." Although reports reveal that some such schools were established, the difficulty of getting well-qualified teachers minimized the effect of these schools. One critic wrote that the public or county schools were "allowed on all hands to be useless in 1754."[15]

One strictly philanthropic effort was a charity working school founded in Talbot County by the Reverend Thomas Bacon in 1750 for the education of orphans, other children of the poor, and Negroes. Part of the money was raised by private subscription and part by the sale of one of Bacon's sermons giving reasons for the need of charity schools in Maryland.

> God only knows . . . the great necessity of such a work in this province, where education is hardly to be attained at any rate by the children of the poor. . . . Many poor white children are as ignorant as the children of the poor benighted negroes. Yet even negroes ought not to be neglected. They have souls to be saved. . . . If negroes, then, ought not to be neglected, how much more ought we to strive that the children of poor white people like ourselves should be brought up in the fear of God, and so educated as to make them really useful to themselves and the community.[16]

The school was to teach reading, writing, and accounting, as well as the precepts of the Anglican Church. In addition, the pupils were to engage in labor so "that they may be inured to industry as well as trained up in the principles of piety and virtue." The school apparently lasted until about the time of the Revolution, and appears to have been the only such working school in the colony before the Revolution.

[15] *Ibid.*, pp. 25, 37.
[16] *Ibid.*, p. 35.

Charity Stigma of "Free Schools"

One of the problems of the "free school," which was really free only to the children of paupers while others had to pay tuition, was expressed clearly in Georgia as early as 1743. John Dobell, a teacher at the Savannah free school, reported to the Common Council that a "spirit of pride" kept many parents from seeking permission to send their children to school free, choosing to "keep their children in ignorance" rather than be "beholden to the Trustees."[17]

Religion and Education

Although the Anglican Church was established in all the colonies of the South, many of the settlers were dissenters. Some of the former indentured servants professed other creeds. Scotch-Irish Presbyterians came in large numbers to Charleston and moved back into the Piedmont area; others moved southward from Pennsylvania through the valleys of Virginia to North and South Carolina. In 1753 a large Moravian colony was established in the western Carolinas. Baptists, Lutherans, and other denominations were also represented in the Southern colonies. These dissenters had two influences on education. First, they had schools of their own. Second, their presence stimulated the Anglican clergy to combat the spread of dissent through the missionary efforts of the S.P.G.

Schools of the Dissenters

The Presbyterians, with their desire for well-educated ministers, were particularly active in trying to set up schools in their communities. After the Great Awakening, Presbyterian missionaries, often graduates of the College of New Jersey, came down from New York and Pennsylvania. Schools were established alongside churches until almost every Presbyterian congregation in the South had its Latin school. The most famous was that of Dr. David Caldwell. His school, founded in 1766 in northeastern North Carolina, provided a Latin education for an average of fifty to sixty boys a year until Caldwell's retirement in 1822.[18]

The Moravians were also very much concerned with the need for each

[17] Dorothy Orr, A *History of Education in Georgia* (Chapel Hill: U. of North Carolina Press, 1950), pp. 8–10.

[18] Charles Lee Smith, *The History of Education in North Carolina* (U.S. Bureau of Education, Circular of Information No. 2, 1888), pp. 23, 27–30.

man to be able to read the Bible, and they maintained schools for both boys and girls during their stay in North Carolina between 1756 and 1779.

Apparently there was some conflict between these dissenting schoolmasters and the established church. As we pointed out earlier, schoolmasters, in order to teach, had to secure a license from the Bishop of London if they came from England or from the governor of the province if they were from the Colonies. In South Carolina in 1747, a Presbyterian schoolmaster named MacKenzie, "after some Cavils and Objections, has promised in every thing to conform exactly to the Rites of the Establish'd Church."[19]

The S. P. G.

The Anglican Church in America was under the charge of the Bishop of London, and he was represented by an official called a "commissary." In 1696 Bishop Henry Compton appointed as commissary for Maryland the Reverend Thomas Bray, who remained in England until 1699 recruiting missionaries and collecting books to be sent to America for libraries. Through his efforts thirty-nine libraries were founded in the Colonies, from Boston south to Charleston, and he sent more than 34,000 religious books and tracts for these libraries.[20]

After a few months in Maryland, Bray returned to England and organized the Society for the Propagation of the Gospel in Foreign Parts. Chartered in 1702, the S. P. G. sent both preachers and teachers to the Colonies until the close of the Revolution. More than three hundred missionaries came over between 1702 and 1782, many of them to Southern colonies. There they were particularly important from an educational point of view, providing "free" (charity) schooling for poor children, Indians, and Negroes.

According to the Society's instructions in 1706, the clergy was charged, in part, with catechizing the children and "other ignorant Persons," distributing tracts and lending books to those who could read, and encouraging "the setting up of Schools for the teaching of Children; and particularly by the Widows of such Clergymen as shall die in those Countries, if they be found capable of that Employment."[21] Records of such "dame schools" kept by clergymen's widows have apparently been lost, if there ever were such schools.

[19] Edgar W. Knight and Clifton L. Hall, *Readings in American Educational History* (New York: Appleton-Century-Crofts, 1951), p. 29.

[20] Edgar Legare Pennington, *The Reverend Thomas Bray* (Philadelphia: The Church Historical Society, 1934), p. 14.

[21] Knight, pp. 73–75.

Bray's Associates and Slave Education

Closely affiliated with the S.P.G. was a group known as "Dr. Bray's Associates." Financed by money raised in England by Bray for the education of Negroes and Indians in the Colonies, the Associates were formally organized in 1730. Schools for slaves were founded in New York, Rhode Island, and Pennsylvania, as well as in all the Southern colonies except, ironically, Maryland, the province for which Bray had been commissary. The schools taught the Anglican catechism, reading, some writing, and sewing and knitting to girls. Many of the schools were kept by schoolmistresses. Some remained in operation for years; others were quite short-lived. The whole movement encountered great difficulties. Many owners were opposed to having their slaves baptized or educated, fearing that conversion and education would make them hard to handle and desirous of freedom. Too, many wanted to work their slaves on Sunday. Some masters contended that slaves were subhuman, having no souls to be saved and thus, logically, needed no conversion. Frequent rumors of impending slave insurrections often halted schools and efforts to get schools started.[22]

Fear of slave uprisings sometimes resulted in laws prohibiting the education of slaves. For example, in South Carolina in 1740 it was ordered that no one might teach a slave to write "or shall use or employ any slave as a scribe in any manner of writing whatsoever."[23] It was not uncommon for some masters to use slaves as clerks, bookkeepers, and overseers, and to give enough education to fit them for these tasks. It was apparently against such practices that the law was in part directed.

Aristocratic Education

Tutors

The limited number of schools in the Southern colonies did not prevent the planter aristocracy from securing an education for their children. As Governor Berkeley reported, each man provided for the education of his family "according to his ability." Among Southern planters this ability was reflected in the practice of hiring family tutors and sending sons to boarding schools or even to schools and colleges in the Northern colonies or back to England.

[22] Pennington, *Thomas Bray's Associates and Their Work Among the Negroes* (Worcester, Mass.: American Antiquarian Society, 1939).

[23] Knight, p. 705.

Some tutors were graduates or students from the colleges in the Middle or New England colonies. Others were indentured servants. Philip Fithian, a graduate of Princeton and future Presbyterian clergyman, spent ten months as tutor to the family of Colonel Robert Carter of Virginia. John Harrower, a former merchant from the Shetland Islands, tried to find work as a clerk or bookkeeper in Scotland and England. Unsuccessful, he indentured himself, was transported to the Colonies, and served as a tutor in Virginia.

Both these tutors had a broad age range among their pupils and were responsible for teaching Latin as well as elementary reading and writing. They lived and had their schoolrooms in outbuildings some distance from the main house. Fithian taught only the Carter children and one nephew of Colonel Carter; Harrower had several other children studying in his school, including children of an overseer on another plantation and those of a "wright," or workman. He also taught others on weekends and evenings and tried catechizing some of the Negroes. Although both tutors had considerable difficulty with English spelling, both used spelling books in their schools and Fithian had a dictionary.

The Diary of Philip Fithian

> Monday August 9 [1773]
>
> Waited on Dr Witherspoon, about nine o Clock, to hear his proposal for my going to *Virginia*—He read me a Letter which he receivd from Col: Carter, & Proposed the following Terms—To teach his Children, five Daughters, & three Sons, who are from five to seventeen years Old—The young Ladies are to be taught the English Language. And the Boys are to study the English Language carefully; & to be instructed in the Latin, & Greek—And he proposes to give thirty five Pounds Sterling, which is about Sixty Pounds currency; Provide all Accommodations; Allow him the undisturbed Use of a Room; And the Use of his own Library; find Provender for a Horse; & a Servant to Wait—By the Advice of the Dr & his Recommendation of the Gentleman, & the Place, I accepted the offer, & agreed to go in the Fall into *Virginia*—
>
> Monday Novemr 1st
>
> We began School—The School consists of eight—Two of Mr Carters Sons—One Nephew—And five Daughters—The eldest Son [Ben] is reading Salust; Gramatical Exercises, and latin Grammer—The second Son [Bob] is reading english Grammar Reading English: Writing, and Cyphering in Subtraction—The Nephew [Harry] is Reading and Writing as above; and Cyphering in Reduction—The eldest daughter [Priscilla] is Reading the Spectator; Writing; & beginning to Cypher—The second [Nancy] is reading next out of the

Spelling-Book, and beginning to write—The next [Frances] is reading in the Spelling-Book—The fourth [Betty] is Spelling in the beginning of the Spelling-Book—And the last [Harriot] is beginning her letters.

Thursday 4.

Busy in School—To day the two eldest Daughters, and second Son attended the Dancing School. [Francis Christian, a peripatetic dancing master, held classes in rotation at a number of neighboring plantations. When he was at the Carters' plantation, students would come in from nearby plantations for two days. On other occasions, Priscilla, Nancy, and Bob would go to other homes to meet Christian.]

Saturday 6. Catechised in School til twelve—the Children. And dismiss'd them.

Wednesday 10. Busy in School—The eldest Daughter taken off by her Teacher in Music; Mr Stadley who is learning her to play the *Forte-piano*. [Stadley appeared at intervals to teach Priscilla the piano and flute. Colonel Carter was teaching Nancy the guitar.]

Wednesday [December] 15. . . . In the morning so soon as it is light a Boy knocks at my Door to make a fire; after the Fire is kindled, I rise which now in the winter is commonly by Seven, or a little after. By the time I am drest the Children commonly enter the School-Room, which is under the Room I sleep in; I hear them round one lesson, when the Bell rings for eight o-Clock (for Mr Carter has a large good Bell of upwards of 60 Lb. which may be heard some miles, & this is always rung at meal Times;) the Children then go out; and at half after eight the Bell rings for Breakfast, we then repair to the Dining-Room; after Breakfast, which is generally about half after nine, we go into School, and sit til twelve, when the Bell rings, & they go out for noon; the dinner-Bell rings commonly about half after two, often at three, but never before two.—After dinner is over, which in common, when we have no Company, is about half after three we go into School, & sit til the Bell rings at five, when they separate til the next morning.

Tuesday [January] 11. . . . This morning I put Ben to construe some Greek, he has yet no Testament, I gave him therefore Esops Fables in Greek, and Latin. I also took out of the Library, and gave him to read Gordon, upon Geography. Ben seem'd scared with his Greek Lesson, he swore, & wished for Homer that he might kick Him, as he had been told Homer invented Greek.

Wednesday [February] 2. . . . *Prissy* This day began Multiplication. We had also a large elegant Writing Table brought to us, so high that the Writers must stand.

Monday [March] 14. Bob this morning begg'd me to learn him lattin; his Reason he tells me is that yesterday Mrs *Taylor* told him he must not have either of her Daughters unless he learn'd Latin he urged me so strong that I put him some Lessons for leasure hours.

Fryday 18. . . . [A]t the North East corner of Carter's "great house", & at 100 yards Distance stands the School-house; . . . the School-House is forty five feet long, from East to West, & twenty-seven from North to South; It has five well-finished, convenient Rooms, three below stairs, & two above; It is built with Brick a Story & a half high with Dormant Windows; In each Room is a fire; In the large Room below-Stairs we keep our School; the other two Rooms below which are smaller are allowed to Mr Randolph the Clerk; The Room above the School-Room Ben and I live in; & the other Room above Stairs belongs to *Harry* & *Bob*.

Thursday [July] 7. . . . What, Harry, do you hesitate at that plain Sum in Arithmetical Profession?—*Bob*, attend to your Business—When I am bedizen'd with these clamorous children, sometimes I silently exclaim—Once I was told, now I know I feel how irksome the Pedagoging Scheme is—Fanny—I say, Fanny, dont you hear me, Fanny, and Betsy, sit down—pray, Sir, must I multiply here by 32—Yes, thick-Scull—But Mr Fithian, I dont know how to divide by 5½—Look, Sir, do you see what Mouth's *Harry Willis* is making?—I can say my Lesson—Buz, Buz—To divide by 5½ you must double both your Dividend & divide.[24]

The Diary and Letters of John Harrower

Freiday, [May] 27th. This morning about 8AM the Colonel delivered his three sons to my charge to teach them to read and figure. his oldest son Edwin 10 years of age, intred into two syllables in the spelling book, Bathourest [Bathurst] his second son six years of age in the Alphabete and William his third son 4 years of age does not know the letters. . . . My school Houres is from 6 to 8 in the morning, in the forenoon from 9 to 12 and from 3 to 6 in the afternoon.

Tuesday, [June] 14th. This morning entred to school William Pattie son to John Pattie wright, and Salley Evens daughter to Thomas Evens Planter.

Sunday, 26th. at night I had a small Congregation of Negroes, learnig their Catechism and hearing me read to them.

[From a letter to his wife, dated 6th December 1774.] I have as yet only ten scollars One of which both Deaff and Dumb and his Father pays me ten shilling per Quarter for him he has been now

[24] Farish, pp. 8, 25–28, 33, 41, 46, 66–67, 72, 83, 85, 99, 103, 106–108, 111–112, 168, 175, 270.

five Mos. with [me] and I have brought him tolerably well and understands it so far, that he can write mostly for anything he wants and understands the value of every figure and can work single addition a little. he is about fourteen years of age. Another of them is a young man a house Carpenter who attends me every night with candle light and every Sunday that I don't go to Church for which he pays me fourty shillings a year. . . .

The Colls. Children comes on pretty well. the Eldest is now reading verry distinctly in the Psalter according to the Church of England and the other two ready to enter into it. . . .

Tuesday, [January] 23d [1776]. This day I entred Edwin into the Latin Gramer.

Tuesday, March 5. This morning Bathurest Daingerfield got don reading through the Bible and the Newtestament, and began to learn to write 15 Ulto.

Tuesday, [April] 23d. Settled with Mr. Porter for teaching his two sons 12 Mos. when he verry genteely allowed me £6 for them, besides a present of two silk vests and two pair of Nankeen Breeches last summer and a Gallon of rum at Christenmass, both he and Mrs. Porter being extreamly well satisfied with what I hade don to them.

Tuesday, [May] 7th. Billie ended reading through his Bible.[25]

Private Schoolmasters

In addition to family tutors, the planter aristocracy attracted numerous private schoolmasters, who set up schools offering reading and writing, Latin grammar, and the broad range of practical and ornamental studies advertised by the private venture schools of the Northern colonies. Knight reports that from 1733 to 1744 "more than 400 advertisements relating to schools and schoolmasters were published in *The South Carolina Gazette* at Charleston; and many scores of similar advertisements appeared in Virginia, North Carolina, and Georgia during the late colonial and early national days."[26]

Reading, Writing in all the Hands us'd in Great Briatain, Arithmetick in whole Numbers, and Fractions vulgar and decimal, Merchants Accompts, . . . are taught . . . by George Brownell and John Pratt

The South Carolina Gazette, Sept. 3, 10, 17, 1744.

[25] "Diary of John Harrower, 1773–1776," *The American Historical Review*, 6 (October, 1900).

[26] *Documentary History*, p. 573.

> Nathaniel and Mary Gittens have open'd a School in King street, where will be taught reading, writing, arithmetic, and several sorts of Needle work. They likewise intend to commence an Evening School. . . .
>
> *The South Carolina Gazette*, Sept. 17, 1744.
>
> MR. SINGLETON . . . proposes to Teach the VIOLIN . . .
>
> *The Virginia Gazette*, June 12, 1752.
>
> THE Rev. W. DUNLAP, . . . having engaged a tutor for his own sons, properly qualified to teach the learned languages, as well as writing and accounts, would have no objection to take in two or three boys to board and educate with them. . . .
>
> *The Virginia Gazette*, June 8, 1769.
>
> WANTED as a tutor, in a private family, a single man, who is master of the languages, and will teach the *English* tongue, and arithmetic. . . .
>
> *The Virginia Gazette*, May 30, 1771.
>
> The Rev. Edw. Lucas has opened in the Parsonage House, A Grammar School, where a number of young Gentlemen, not exceeding twelve, will be taught the Greek and Latin Classics, on the most approved plan. Terms: A Guinea and a Half Entrance and Two Guineas a Quarter.
>
> *The Georgia Gazette* (Savannah), Feb. 2, 1786[27]

Some of the advertisements for schools specified that young "Masters and Misses will also be lodged and boarded." Thomas Jefferson received his schooling in boarding schools from the age of five to seventeen, when he was ready to enter William and Mary.

Old Field Schools

Historians of education in the South generally include mentions of "old field schools." Apparently this name referred to location rather than to a type of school. Schoolhouses were sometimes built in abandoned tobacco fields, giving rise to the name. Some of these appear to have been founded by a community, some by a group of planters. Some were obviously only elementary in curriculum; some grew into academies. Perhaps John Harrower's school qualified under the name "old field school." Careful reading of some of the contemporary references to "old field schools" suggests that historians who have made much over them have been too enthusiastic in describing their influence. Only

[27] Quoted in *Ibid.*, pp. 653, 655, 657, 658, 660.

an apologist for the planter aristocracy could attribute much educational influence to any schools in the Southern colonies.

Schooling Abroad

Southern gentlemen, seeking to set up in America a society modeled on that "at home," wanted their children to have an education as like that in England as possible. Those who could afford it and who had friends and relatives "at home" sent their sons and sometimes their daughters across the ocean to school in England and Scotland. Many boys remained to attend grammar school and the university, and to study law in the English institutions. The stream of boys continued to England until the Revolution and even after.

There is, of course, no complete list of all the people who went to England and Scotland for their schooling, but a number of historians have compiled partial lists from colonial letters and other documents. Knight lists 116 Virginians educated through grammar school or college or both in England and Scotland. Other lists give four additional Virginians at Christ College, Cambridge, and one at Trinity College, Cambridge.[28] Many, including at least three signers of the Declaration of Independence from South Carolina, received their law training at the Inns of Court. Meriwether lists 114 Americans at the Inns of Court between 1759 and 1786, some 46 being marked as from South Carolina, 20 from Virginia, and 15 from Maryland.[29]

Some of the planters' sons went North to Harvard, Princeton, and Philadelphia for their schooling. This educational migration continued even though William and Mary was older than any of the Northern colleges except Harvard. Fithian said that Ben Carter planned to attend Princeton or Philadelphia before going to Cambridge University.

From letters, newspaper articles, and speeches of the times, it appears that more children would have been sent abroad except for fear of the dangerous ocean voyage and epidemics of smallpox in eighteenth-century England. One of the main arguments given for the establishment of a college in Virginia was to make unnecessary the long absence from family and hazardous journey. A later argument was that, on their return, the young men often found life in the Colonies unexciting, and just before the Revolution, when feelings against monarchy began to run high, many parents feared that their sons would return as Tories—if they returned at all. After the Revolution, many of the Southern rebels

[28] *Documentary History*, pp. 554–570.

[29] Colyer Meriwether, *History of Higher Education in South Carolina* (U.S. Bureau of Education Circular of Information No. 3, 1888), pp. 25–26.

attacked the continuing practice of Americans' sending their sons to England. Eventually, Southern colleges and a few colleges in Northern states, particularly Princeton and Dickinson in Carlisle, Pennsylvania, supplanted the English universities as the educational capstones for young Southern gentlemen.

The College of William and Mary

Although the Virginia gentlemen came to America largely for economic reasons, they were not entirely irreligious, nor were they unconcerned about an educated ministry or the conversion of the Indians. The original Virginia Company, under the encouragement of King James I, who authorized the famed translation of the Bible, made an attempt at a university at Henrico. But a massacre of the settlers by the "infidels and savages" whom they had planned to convert to Christianity ended the attempt in 1622. Between 1660 and 1662 the legislature petitioned the Crown in vain for a "free schoole & colledge."

FOUNDING AND FINANCING When the first college in the Southern colonies was actually founded, it was largely the result of the work of Commissary James Blair, chief officer of the Anglican Church in Virginia. Blair had come to America in 1685 and played a prominent part in the establishment of the college. In 1690 a number of Virginia gentlemen presented several proposals to the General Assembly for the "founding a Colledge in this Country to consist of three Schools, Vizt Grammar, Phylosophy, Divinity." In July of that year, Governor Francis Nicholson authorized a committee of gentlemen, headed by Blair, to collect subscriptions and benevolences for the building of the college. A royal charter was granted on February 8, 1693, with the financial support of nearly two thousand pounds from quit-rents, twenty thousand acres of land, and the revenue of a penny a pound on all tobacco shipped from Virginia and Maryland to any other colony. In return the college was to pay the Crown two copies of Latin verses yearly. The college had a peculiar privilege which reveals the close tie of government, religion, and education, even in the South: the faculty had the power to elect a member to the House of Burgesses. The Bishop of London was named Chancellor, giving the college a strong advocate in England. Blair was named President of the college and member of the Board of Trustees.[30]

COLLEGE AUTONOMY AND COLONIAL GOVERNMENT One provision of the charter made William and Mary during its early years unique among

[30] Knight, pp. 374–377, 401–439.

American colleges and universities. The New England colonists did not trust their college president and faculty with the responsibility of making major educational policies and operating the financial affairs of the institution, and so created outside boards to govern the college. That pattern was to be followed by all other American colleges, including William and Mary eventually. But according to its charter, the faculty of William and Mary had an autonomy much like that of the English universities. A Board of Trustees was created at first to administer the funds until the college should be firmly established, at which time the endowments and authority would be transferred to the faculty.

> When the said College shall be so . . . established, . . . the President and Masters, or Professors, of the said College, shall be a Body politic and incorporate, in Deed and Name; and . . . they shall have perpetual succession.[31]

The transfer was made in 1729, but the faculty was in such continuing conflict with the governor and the Board of Visitors that by the 1760's the Board, which had been formed as an "advisory body," had taken over the government of the college, perhaps in large part as an expression of the anti-clericalism which was part of the revolutionary feeling developing by that time. In 1766 the Chancellor of the college, Richard Terrick, Bishop of London, wrote President James Horrocks in opposition to the interference by the Board.

> You know very well my opinion of those powers, which the Visitors claimed to themselves of altering statutes as they please, and of removing professors and masters according to their own whim and humour. A college or a place of education so fundamentally wrong in its first principles can never contribute to the ends the founder proposed, the advancement of religion and learning.[32]

Thus ended the noble experiment in America of a college governed by its own faculty.

SOCIAL LIFE AT WILLIAM AND MARY Academic standards do not seem to have been as high as the social life at the college, according to many, including faculty and students. In 1724 the Reverend Hugh Jones, Professor of Natural Philosophy and Mathematics for several years, wrote:

[31] Quoted in *Ibid.*, p. 411.
[32] Quoted in Richard L. Morton, *Colonial Virginia* (Chapel Hill: U. of North Carolina Press, 1960), pp. 782–783.

> The Nature of the Country scarce yet admits the Possibility of reducing the *Collegians* to the nice Methods of Life and Study observed in *Oxford* and *Cambridge;* tho' by Degrees they may copy from thence many useful Customs and Constitutions. . . .
> For it is now a College without a Chapel, without a Scholarship, and without a Statute.
> There is a Library without Books, comparatively speaking, and a President without a fix'd salary till of late . . . and in fine, there have been disputes and Differences about these and the like Affairs of the College hitherto without End.
> These Things greatly impede the Progress of Sciences and learned Arts.[33]

Thomas Jefferson, who attended William and Mary between 1760 and 1762, spent a great deal of time and money on dress and horses in his first year. His letters reveal more social and political activity than academic work. In 1760, Jefferson's first year at the college, the professor of moral philosophy was discharged for drunkenness and leading the college boys in a riot against the apprentices of the town, even threatening with a pistol two of the Visitors who were trying to break up the fight! An alcoholic professor of humanity was removed at the same time and sent to be parish priest away from Williamsburg.[34] This kind of scandal led the Board of Visitors to exert far more than advisory powers and persuaded parents like Colonel Robert Carter that their sons should attend colleges either in the Northern colonies or in England. In his diary, Fithian reported a conversation with Carter about the college.

> He informed me that it is in such confusion at present, & so badly directed, that he cannot send his Children with propriety there for Improvement & useful Education—That he has known the Professors to play all Night at Cards in publick Houses in the City, and has often seen them drunken in the Street!—That the Charter of the College is vastly Extensive, & the yearly income sufficient to support a University being about 4.000 £ Sterling—That the Necessary Expence for each Scholar yearly is only 15 £ Currency.[35]

Another indication of the great emphasis on social activity at William and Mary is the continuation of music and dancing lessons which many of the young gentlemen had received under the tutorial system on their plantations. In 1716 a dancing master received permission to use a room

[33] Quoted in Knight, pp. 489–490.
[34] Morton, pp. 778–780.
[35] Farish, pp. 86–87.

in the college to teach "the scholars and others to dance." In 1736 a company of "Gentlemen of the College" advertised their staging of Joseph Addison's *The Tragedy of Cato* in the Williamsburg playhouse.[36] Clearly, life at the college of the planters was not the sober affair it was in the colleges in the North. The "gentlemen" were not often disposed to be "scholars" or aspirants for the clergy. Even though the first concern for founding the college had been religious, the planter aristocracy was more interested in parties and sport than in religion, more desirous of learning for ostentation and social graces than for scholarship and theology.

Education in the South and Other Sections

As with other institutions in the Southern colonies, there was a far closer resemblance of Southern educational patterns to English educational patterns than existed in the other colonies. Wherever possible, English traditions were preserved. Berkeley's comparison to England was quite apt: education in the Southern colonies was a private matter. While New England was requiring education for all children, the planter aristocracy was providing for their own children according to their finances and their interest in schooling. Little was done to provide schooling for the poor, but paradoxically what legislation was passed concerning schooling appeared to recognize the responsibility of government only in the case of children whose parents were not able or likely to provide for education themselves. The practices were definitely *laissez faire* as far as the planter class was concerned, and minimum provisions for the lower-class children were intended to make them useful artisans or non-troublesome non-entities. The society and its educational institutions appeared to operate for the benefit of the aristocracy. This attitude was to persist in the South, creating serious problems in the nineteenth and twentieth centuries as reformers sought to introduce the principles and practices of universal education.

QUESTIONS FOR DISCUSSION

1. Education in the South has had somewhat different problems from those in the other parts of the nation. Some have developed directly from slavery and racial conflicts. Others have developed from the aristocratic tradition of the planter society. Consider some of the problems of build-

[36] Morton, pp. 487–488.

ing universal education in the South after 1865 and trace the influence of aristocratic traditions upon that problem.

2. One of the issues in American education is that of vocational education. Should there be one kind of schooling for the intellectual elite and another for those who will be entering "blue collar" vocations? What lessons related to this issue are suggested by the educational practices of the colonial South?

SUGGESTED READINGS

Secondary Sources

Brown, Elmer Ellsworth. *The Making of Our Middle Schools*. New York: Longmans, Green, 1902. Pp. 55–57, 96–104, 119–122, 138–139, and 149–150.

Edwards, Newton, and Richey, Herman G. *The School in the American Social Order*. Boston: Houghton Mifflin, 1963. Chapter 4.

Knight, Edgar W. *Public Education in the South*. New York: Ginn, 1922. Chapters 1–3.

Wertenbaker, Thomas Jefferson. *The Old South*. New York: Scribner's, 1942. Chapters I and II.

Wright, Louis B. *The First Gentlemen of Virginia*. San Marino, California: Huntington Library, 1940. Part One and Chapter IV.

Primary Sources

Cubberley, Elwood P. *Readings in the History of Education*. Boston: Houghton Mifflin, 1920. Pp. 308–310.

———. *Readings in Public Education in the United States*. Boston: Houghton Mifflin, 1934. Readings No. 24–27.

Hofstadter, Richard, and Smith, Wilson. *American Higher Education: A Documentary History*. Chicago: U. of Chicago Press, 1961. Vol. I, pp. 32–49.

Knight, Edgar W. *A Documentary History of Education in the South Before 1860*. Chapel Hill: U. of North Carolina Press, 1949. Vol. 1.

Knight, Edgar W., and Hall, Clifton L. *Readings in American Educational History*. New York: Appleton-Century-Crofts, 1951. Pp. 4–12, 19–30, 36, 41–60, 67–69, 186–191.

Monroe, Paul. *The Founding of the American Public School System*. Ann Arbor: University Microfilms, 1940. Vol. II, Chapter 2, Readings 27–35 (Apprenticeship); Chapter 3 (Education in Virginia); Chapter 8, Readings 254–256, 262 (Secondary Schools); Chapter 9, Readings 271–273, 284 (William and Mary); Chapter 10, Readings 288, 306, (S.P.G.); Chapter 11, Readings 320–346 (Education of Indians and Negroes).

PART Two

Revolutionary Enlightenment and Conservative Federalism

CHRONOLOGY

1776—Declaration of Independence signed
1783—Treaty of Paris ending Revolutionary War
1785—Virginia Statute of Religious Freedom
1787—Constitutional Convention
1789–1797—Administration of George Washington
1790—Population of the United States 3,929,214
1791—Vermont admitted into the Union
1791—Bill of Rights ratified
1792—Kentucky admitted into the Union
1796—Tennessee admitted into the Union
1797–1801—Administration of John Adams
1798—Alien and Sedition Acts passed
1800—Population of the United States 5,308,483
1801–1809—Administration of Thomas Jefferson
1803—Ohio admitted into the Union
1803—Louisiana Purchase
1809–1817—Administration of James Madison
1810—Population of the United States 7,239,881
1812—Louisiana admitted into the Union
1812–1815—War with Great Britain
1816—Indiana admitted into the Union
1817—Mississippi admitted into the Union
1817–1825—Administration of James Monroe
1818—Illinois admitted into the Union
1819—Alabama admitted into the Union
1820—Population of the United States 9,638,453
1820—Maine admitted into the Union
1820—Missouri Compromise
1821—Missouri admitted into the Union
1823—Monroe Doctrine
1825–1829—Administration of John Quincy Adams
1828—Andrew Jackson elected President
1830—Population of the United States 12,866,020

THE HISTORY OF A SOCIETY OFTEN reveals traits that distinguish it from other societies. One such distinguishing feature of American history is the pattern of recurrent revolutions by which our nation has developed. Although the word "revolution" is frowned on by many who regard any kind of change a threat, it must not be overlooked that the United States was born in revolution. Actually, the American Revolution was the crisis period of only the first of a series of revolutionary cycles in the United States. It will be the theme of revolution and reaction that will give continuity to this text in the history of American education, for schools as instruments of society reflect the changes in the rest of the culture.

Social Revolution

A social revolution is more than the mere political overthrow of one regime and the substitution of another. A social revolution is one that brings about changes in the entire social order—in religious practices, economic activities, the hierarchy of social classes, and the purposes and scope of education. A social revolution is a widespread, all-pervading change of attitudes on the part of the great masses of the society and their seeking to make that change effective in the practices of life.

A social revolution takes place over an extended period of time, sometimes over generations. Change is normal and continual in any advanced society, and as these changes accumulate, old institutions and mores often fail to change and thus become unable to meet the demands of the new social conditions. This situation has been termed "cultural lag." Sometimes the cultural lag is intensified by those groups who seek to preserve traditional institutions without significant change, making them even less able to give direction in the changing culture. When this happens, criticisms result, at first individual and vaguely directed. Then unrest becomes more general. Repressions are enforced by the *status quo* groups who hold political or economic power. Eventually a crisis results, and there follows the violence commonly called "revolution."

In addition to the loss of life and property in an armed clash, revolutions have proved an inefficient means of social change because during the concluding stage of the cycle of revolution there occurs a period of reaction and conservatism in which many of the revolutionary gains are lost. Often a new power emerges with new institutional arrangements which set up new systems of repression. The French exchanged King Louis XVI for Emperor Napoleon; the Russians shot Czar Nicholas and set up Lenin and Stalin; the Germans dethroned Kaiser Wilhelm and raised up Hitler; the Cubans ousted Batista and surrendered their revolutionary gains to the Castro dictatorship.

Social Revolutions in the United States

In the history of the United States, we have gone through two complete cycles of revolution. The first was the American Revolution, followed by the conservative reaction of the Constitutional Convention and the Federalist period. The second was the reform movement sometimes called the Age of the Common Man and leading to the American Civil War, with its reaction in the Gilded Age and the "robber barons" of the closing decades of the nineteenth century.

Within the twentieth century, the historical perspective becomes blurred because of the recency of events and the difficulty of gaining sufficient objectivity and breadth of view to give a full analysis. However, it is possible that the United States has experienced two abortive revolutions in this century. The first was the progressive movement, climaxing in the first administration of President Wilson; that "revolution" miscarried when World War I intervened, but it did have its conservative reaction in the 1920's. The Depression brought a renewal of social revolutionary tendencies, highlighted by the New Deal, and then aborted by the outbreak of World War II. This one too apparently had a conservative reaction in the McCarthyism of the late 1940's and 1950's. Whether this reaction is continuing or whether the civil-rights demonstrations and incipient problems with mass unemployment herald a new revolutionary period remains for the future to tell.

The stages of each of these revolutionary cycles can be traced in the educational developments of the United States, and that will be the theme of the remaining parts of this text. By attempting to construct analogies between the historical context of education in these past periods and the events of today, we may perceive some direction for education in what may be another crisis period.

SUGGESTED READINGS

Adams, James Truslow. *The March of Democracy*. New York: Scribner's, 1932. Vol. I, pp. 79–107, 149–165.

Beard, Charles A., and Beard, Mary R. *The Rise of American Civilization*. New York: Macmillan, 1930. Vol. I, pp. 189–240, 289–377, 386–390.

Brinton, Crane. *The Anatomy of Revolution*. New York: Norton, 1938.

Curti, Merle. *The Growth of American Thought*. New York: Harper, 1951. Chapters V–VIII.

———. *The Social Ideas of American Educators*. New York: Scribner's, 1935. Chapter I.

Jameson, J. Franklin. *The American Revolution Considered as a Social Movement*. Princeton: Princeton U. Press, 1940.

Krout, John Allen, and Fox, Dixon Ryan. *The Completion of Independence, 1790–1830*. New York: Macmillan, 1944. Chapters VII, VIII, X, XI.

Nevins, Allan, and Commager, Henry Steele. *A Pocket History of the United States*. New York: Washington Square Press, 1960, pp. 68–85, 93–95, 101–144.

Parrington, Vernon L. *Main Currents in American Thought*. New York: Harcourt, Brace, 1958. Vol. 1, pp. 292–308.

Schlesinger, Arthur Meier. *New Viewpoints in American History*. New York: Macmillan, 1922. Chapter IV, pp. 72–86, and Chapter VIII.

4

The American Revolution and Educational Enlightenment

The British Empire was founded on an economic policy known as the mercantile theory, part of which was the doctrine that colonies were sources of raw materials and markets for products of industries in the homeland. To implement this doctrine, Parliament passed a number of laws restricting trade and commerce in the American Colonies. The rising middle class of colonial merchants and shippers objected to these laws and, when Parliament responded by making them more severe, began to evade them. England sent over enforcing officers, and offenders were tried in admiralty courts. The colonists retaliated by demonstrations such as the Boston Tea Party, and repression was followed by defiance until the effort to discipline the protesting, disobedient colonies became war.

When the Continental Congress met in 1776, its members set forth the reasons for their rebellion in a Declaration of Independence which was, in effect, a political statement of the philosophy of the Enlightenment. The Enlightenment was a new outlook on the universe born of the snowballing effect of scientific discoveries. As men like Copernicus, Galileo, Newton, and Boyle began to discover "laws" of astronomy, physics, chemistry, and other sciences, many philosophers were convinced that the universe was governed by a system of natural laws, that it was man's duty to discover those laws and to learn to live by them, and that as man did learn to live in harmony with the natural laws, both the individual and society would move toward perfection. They believed that the natural law governed not only the material aspect of the universe but human relationships as well. Adam Smith, for example, in *The Wealth of Nations* (1776) stated what he considered a natural law governing economic behavior of men: that if man followed the law of supply and demand, there would be no more overproduction, unemployment, financial distress, poverty, crime, or other social ills rising out of economic causes.

Such progress depended on the flexibility of institutions, which would need to change as the new discoveries demonstrated errors in man's past behavior. Historical experience warned that the institutions of church and state were most inflexible, and Enlightened philosophers were very distrustful of both. In the Declaration of Independence, Jefferson expressed the Enlightened view of government when he wrote, "Whenever any government becomes destructive of these ends, it is the right of the people to alter or to abolish it." He and James Madison also led in the effort to separate church and state. This attitude toward government and organized religion created a problem for the Enlightened philosophers; for they believed that education was the means by which all men would learn of the natural laws and thus improve themselves and society, and the institutions of church and state were the only ones strong enough to support the schools necessary for the dissemination of that education. The dilemma was to result in inconsistencies and contribute to the failure of the educational plans of the Enlightened philosophers.

Revolutionary Constitutions and Ordinances

One of the natural rights enumerated in the Declaration of Independence was equality. Education which discriminated on the basis of ability to pay tuition was contrary to the revolutionary ideal that all men are created equal. In the state constitutions adopted during the early years of the War, provisions were made to facilitate equality of educational opportunity. The Pennsylvania Constitution of 1776 was a model for others in North Carolina (1776), Georgia (1777), and Vermont (1777). Although they did not provide free education for all, these states stipulated that salaries for teachers be paid by the public, making possible low tuition for all children. In the conservative reaction to the revolution, some of these states rewrote their constitutions, omitting the liberal provisions for public support and reverting to pious platitudes or, at most, requiring charity education for paupers.

The Enlightenment ideals of freedom and equality, as those words were used in 1776, contained an inherent contradiction which has caused continuing political conflict in the United States. "Equality" was the abolition of all special privileges; "liberty" was the absence of any arbitrary restraints that would interfere with the natural law of the universe. Any legislation that would restrain individuals from seeking what their abilities might open to them would be a violation of the concept of liberty. Any legislation that gave an advantage to any class or individual would be a violation of the concept of equality. Although it was not apparent at that time, it is logically impossible to have both liberty and equality, as they were defined by the Enlightenment philosophers. To prevent some strong individuals from securing special privileges for themselves, it is necessary for society to impose restraints. Consequently, liberty must be lessened to preserve equality. If full liberty is permitted, then equality will be destroyed. This dilemma posed a serious problem for education in a revolutionary society. To provide equality of educational opportunity, public support of education was necessary. But to levy taxes was a restraint, which was contrary to the right of liberty!

One source of public aid for schools which was attempted under the Articles of Confederation was the granting of land for the support of education, a source of school income which had long been used in many of the colonies. When the Congress outlined how the Northwest Territory was to be surveyed, they provided, in the Ordinance of 1785, that the land was to be laid out in townships six miles square, each divided into thirty-six one-mile-square sections. In each township, section 16 was to be "reserved . . . for the maintenance of public schools, within the said township." The Ordinance of 1787, which set up the procedures and principles of governing the territory, took notice of the responsibility of government for encouraging schools.

> Religion, morality, and knowledge being necessary to good government and the happiness of mankind, schools and the means of education shall be forever encouraged.[1]

An act authorizing the Treasury to sell land in the territory, adopted in 1787, confirmed the 16th section grants and also the grant of the 29th section in each township "to be given perpetually for the purposes of religion." The same act stipulated that not more than two complete townships were to be given perpetually for the purpose of a university.

In succeeding legislation concerning the admission of new territories, similar grants were made, affecting all states admitted between 1803 (Ohio) and 1912 (Arizona and New Mexico) except for Maine, Texas,

[1] B. Perley Poore, *The Federal and State Constitutions, Colonial Charters and Other Organic Laws of the United States* (Washington: Government Printing Office, 1877), Part I, p. 431.

and West Virginia. In some states where the land was arid, two and even four sections per township were reserved. In all, more than 125,000 square miles of land have been granted by the federal government to the states in these grants alone. Because of the relative lack of value of the lands when they were turned over to the states, not enough precautions were taken in the administration of the lands and the funds derived from them, and this potentially wealthy endowment was largely wasted in most states through mismanagement, neglect, and even criminal misappropriation of funds. Even so, these grants have been the foundation for permanent school funds in a number of states and, what is more significant, have served as a precedent for subsequent federal programs to aid education.

Separation of Church and State

Although many of the first settlers had come to America for religious reasons and had created "established" churches, by the middle of the eighteenth century religious diversity was so great that there was strong opposition to the church-state relationship which decreed that all men must pay taxes for the support of a particular church. One of the strongest revolutionary fears was that the Anglican Church might become "established" for all the colonies. The disestablishment of religion is important for the history of education since schools were originally the responsibility of the church, and the increasing separation of church and state has resulted in many educational conflicts and problems.

The first American attack on the intolerances and persecutions resulting from bigotry often associated with established religions came in 1644 in the publication of Roger Williams' *Bloudy Tenent of Persecution.* Williams was banished from Massachusetts Bay for claiming, "It is the will and command of *God,* that . . . a *permission* of the most *Paganish, Jewish, Turkish,* or *Anti*-christian consciences and worships, bee granted to all men."[2]

Although the 1691 Massachusetts charter removed the legal basis for a single established church in that colony, the Congregational majorities in the towns preserved the practice until well into the eighteenth century, each town collecting taxes for the support of a minister of its own choosing. This finally began to break down in 1727, when Anglicans won a share in the religious taxes for the support of their ministers.

[2] Quoted in Louis M. Hacker, *The Shaping of the American Tradition* (New York: Columbia U. Press, 1947), p. 108.

Later, Quakers and Baptists were exempted from religious taxes if they could produce certificates that they were in regular attendance at their own churches. In the revolutionary Massachusetts Constitution of 1780, the disestablishment was extended to give all sects and denominations proportional shares in the taxes collected for public worship and education. The taxpayer, however, had to request that his tax be applied to his church; otherwise it went to the town school.

> And all moneys paid by the subject to the support of public worship, and of the public teachers aforesaid, shall, if he require it, be uniformly applied to the support of the public teacher or teachers of his own religious sect or denomination, provided there be any on whose instructions he attends; otherwise it may be paid toward the support of the teacher or teachers of the parish or precinct in which the said moneys are raised.[3]

A similar proposal precipitated one of the most dramatic climaxes in the struggles to disestablish religion; but that was to occur in Virginia, and Massachusetts was not to disestablish religion completely until 1833. Not until 1854 did Massachusetts pass a constitutional amendment which prohibited the use of tax moneys for sectarian schools.

The Virginia Statute of Religious Freedom

Although tidewater Virginia was controlled by the Anglican planter aristocracy, out in the foothills and valleys there were many independent dissenting farmers. Some were indentured servants who had served their time—or run away—and were ready to assert their rights as free men. Others were Northern yeomen coming down the valleys from Pennsylvania. These non-Anglicans objected to paying a tax on tobacco for the support of the clergy of the Church of England, and in 1762 they succeeded in having the tax abolished by the General Assembly. The clergy appealed to the Crown and had the tax repeal vetoed, and in 1763 they brought suit for their back salary. The farmers retained a young lawyer named Patrick Henry to defend their case. Henry made the most of his case, for although he lost, the jury set the back pay of the ministers at one penny. The dissenters had successfully demonstrated their opposition to the established church.

During the turmoil of the war years, Jefferson and Madison carried the battle against the establishment. In 1776 they sponsored a bill which would exempt all dissenters from paying a religious tax and suspend the

[3] Poore, Part 1, p. 957.

requirement even for members of the Anglican Church. In 1779 Jefferson introduced a Bill for Establishing Religious Freedom, but it was defeated. A compromise was offered in 1784 by Patrick Henry which would have placed a tax "on all taxable property, for support of Teachers of the Christian Religion." Each taxpayer would be permitted to designate the sect to which he wanted his tax applied, and in the case of those who did not specify a recipient, "the tax is to be applied to the maintenance of a school in the County."[4] Madison feared that such a "multiple establishment" of religion would delay the complete disestablishment, and he persuaded the legislature not to take the final vote on the bill until the next year. During the summer he wrote and circulated a broadside called *A Memorial and Remonstrance,* attacking the bill and the principle of establishment. It was printed on a large sheet of paper with space below for signatures. Thousands of names were signed to the copies of the broadside before the assembly met again. Armed with these petitions, Madison prevented the Henry bill from coming to a final vote, and while he had the advantage, he pushed Jefferson's 1779 proposal into law. The law is very specific and unequivocal in asserting that "all men shall be free to profess, and by argument to maintain, their opinions in matters of religion, and . . . the same shall in no wise diminish, enlarge, or affect their civil capacities."[5]

The Federal Bill of Rights and Religious Freedom

When Jefferson returned from France in 1787, he found that the Constitution provided no guarantees for the individual freedoms for which he believed the Revolution had been fought. He refused to support ratification until he was promised that a series of amendments would be offered to protect those "natural rights." The first of those amendments to be adopted made disestablishment a national principle. "Congress shall make no law respecting an establishment of religion, or prohibiting the free exercise thereof." This did not prevent individual states from having established churches or aiding church schools, for not until the Fourteenth Amendment (1868) was the principle ratified that "No State shall make or enforce any law which shall abridge the privileges or immunities of citizens of the United States." By the time of the adoption of the Bill of Rights, only four states had even the legal basis for religious establishment: Massachusetts, Connecticut, Maryland, and

[4] From a letter from Madison to Jefferson, January 9, 1785. James Madison, *Letters and Other Writings* (New York: R. Worthington, 1884), I, 130–131.

[5] Paul Leicester Ford, *The Works of Thomas Jefferson* (New York: Putnam's 1905), Vol. II, p. 441.

New Hampshire. State support of religion in these states was abolished by constitutional provision in Maryland in 1810, Connecticut in 1818, and Massachusetts finally in 1833. New Hampshire achieved the same thing by law in 1819. As new states came into the Union, they entered with constitutional provisions for the separation of church and state, a number using the exact words of the First Amendment.

Many of the new constitutions and laws were very explicit in the prescriptions against established religion. Not only was no denomination to be preferred over others, but in most cases the law stated expressly that no public monies were to go for the support of any place of worship or the maintenance of any ministry. Because of the traditionally close relationship between religion and education and because much of the religious tax money went for schools and teachers as well as for churches and preachers, the widening separation between government and religion raised difficult problems for education, problems which have persisted for nearly two centuries and which constitute critical issues in modern education.

Jefferson's Enlightened Proposals

The greatest of the American Enlightened thinkers—perhaps the greatest and most versatile American intellectual—Thomas Jefferson, expressed his faith in education in a letter written in 1822. In spite of rebuffs and rejections of his far-seeing educational proposals, Jefferson never wavered from his belief that the key to America's future—and that of all mankind—was education.

> I look to the diffusion of light and education as the resource most to be relied on for ameliorating the condition, promoting the virtue and advancing the happiness of man. That every man shall be made virtuous, by any process whatsoever, is indeed no more to be expected, than that every tree shall be made to bear fruit, and every plant nourishment. The briar and bramble can never become the vine and olive; but their asperities may be softened by culture and their properties improved to usefulness in the order and economy of the world. And I do hope, in the present spirit of extending to the great mass of mankind the blessings of instruction, I see a prospect of great advancement in the happiness of the human race; and that this may proceed to an indefinite, altho' not to an infinite degree.[6]

[6] Andrew A. Lipscomb (ed.), *The Writings of Thomas Jefferson* (Washington: Thomas Jefferson Memorial Association, 1903), Vol. XV, pp. 399–400.

From the stress on education for religious purposes—Bible reading and preparation for the clergy—and for the utilitarianism of learning a vocation or acquiring social prestige, the Enlightenment tried to turn educational purposes toward the improvement of all human society. It was indeed one of the loftiest motives ever proposed for education, one befitting a society which had had the courage to break off from old ways and bravely strike out in an effort to secure the "unalienable rights" to "which the laws of nature and of nature's God entitle them." One of the tragedies of the Federalist period is the loss of that social vision and its educational purpose.

Proposal for Universal Education

Some historians have called Jefferson's "Bill for the More General Diffusion of Knowledge" the first proposal by a great statesman for free, publicly controlled schools for all the children of the society. It was not a very radical bill as measured by today's standards. Jefferson proposed to create an aristocracy of talent, similar to that in Plato's *Republic*. In a letter to John Adams in 1813 recalling his efforts to establish public schools, Jefferson wrote, "Worth and genius would thus have been sought out from every condition of life, and completely prepared by education for defeating the competition of wealth and birth for public trust."[7] But his plans would allow for only a tiny group of fortunate geniuses to escape the chains of poverty and compete, on very unequal terms, with the sons of the aristocracy of wealth. Only a select group would be aided beyond the first three years, and the elimination process was such that, as Jefferson himself was to describe it, only "twenty of the best geniuses will be raked from the rubbish annually."[8] The sons of the wealthy would have the tremendous advantage of being able to continue their schooling, regardless of their lack of genius, by paying tuition. Pauper boys of great genius might be easily eliminated after the first three years by the limited scholarship opportunities. Late-developing talent, a common phenomenon among the culturally disadvantaged lower classes, would never be discovered under Jefferson's system. Furthermore, the plan did not require compulsory attendance (perhaps because of Jefferson's adherence to the concept of liberty as absence of restraint), so that poor families who preferred to have their children work might not send their children for even the three years of free schooling. This would have tended to perpetuate the separation of the

[7] Ford, Vol. XI, pp. 346–347.
[8] Lipscomb, *Notes on Virginia*, Vol. II, p. 203.

classes, particularly with the lower-class failure to see the need for the kind of academic education Jefferson proposed as the curriculum of the common schools. Yet, in spite of all these criticisms and the twentieth-century recognition of the failure of Jefferson's proposal to offer a democratic education, it was still radical for its time—after all, it did provide for some scholarships and it did offer a minimum of three years of free schooling for everyone.

According to Jefferson's plan, each county was to be divided into districts (or "hundreds") large enough to provide enough children for a school, yet small enough to permit the children to attend school daily. To this school all free children would be permitted to go for three years without charge. The "hundred" schools were to teach reading, writing, common arithmetic, and history. Beyond the "hundred" school would be the grammar school, of which there would be twenty in the state. Although the grammar schools would be partially state-supported, presumably most of the students there would be paying tuition, with a select group of boys on scholarships. The curriculum of the grammar schools would include "the Latin and Greek languages, English Grammer, geography, and the higher parts of numerical arithmetick, to-wit, vulgar and decimal fractions, and the extrication of the square and cube roots."[9] The capstone of the educational pyramid would be the College of William and Mary, which would have *one* scholarship student each year. The proposal provided for state support and control through the supervision of the "overseers" or "visitors." It set up a curriculum somewhat broader, at both the common and grammar-school levels, than was the custom in many schools at the time, revealing the influence of the academy on Jefferson's thinking.

This bill was defeated when Jefferson offered it to the legislature in 1779. In 1796 a number of the principal features of Jefferson's bill were incorporated in a bill which gave local authorities permission to establish district schools, "if it shall seem expedient." The school would provide reading, writing, and arithmetic for three years to all free children, tuition free. The teacher was to be paid and the school maintained by taxes, and a system of visitation and supervision of the schools was outlined. But apparently only a few schools were actually set up under this act.

In 1810, through the influence of Governor Tyler and friends of Jefferson in the legislature, Virginia established a Literary Fund, which was to be used for the support of schools. Jefferson approved the Fund, but he advocated taxes in addition to support the common schools.

[9] Ford, Vol. II, pp. 414–426.

In 1814 Jefferson received a copy of the Spanish constitution, and from it he took a "fruitful germ of the improvement of everything good." It was a provision that would disfranchise every citizen who could not read and write. That same provision was included in the "Bill for Establishing a System of Public Education" which Jefferson sent to his friends in the legislature in 1817. The new proposal was basically the same as he had offered in 1779, with a few changes in the location and number of grammar schools, except that he included the proviso that no minister of the gospel could be a Visitor for the primary schools and that "no person unborn or under the age of twelve years at the passing of this act . . . shall, after the age of fifteen years, be a citizen of this commonwealth until he or she can read readily in some tongue, native or acquired." This solved Jefferson's dilemma of how to "strengthen parental excitement" for education without actually having "to shock the common feelings and ideas by the forcible . . . education of the infant against the will of the father."[10] That bill also was defeated, and the following year the conservative element compounded the injury by passing a pauper school bill. Until the time of his death, Jefferson fought to remedy the defects of the pauper bill, which he charged was not providing the common education it was supposed to and was a gross waste of the appropriations from the Literary Fund. Five months before his death he was urging friends in the legislature to require an annual report on the primary schools, so that the public would know what was being provided.

Proposal for Reorganizing William and Mary

As part of his 1779 plan for the creation of a public system of education that would advance the happiness of mankind through the sciences, Jefferson proposed a reorganization of the College of William and Mary. The reorganization would be a part of the revolutionary developments American society was undergoing.

> The late change in the form of our government, as well as the contest of arms in which we are at present engaged, calling for extraordinary abilities both in council and field, it becomes the peculiar duty of the Legislature, at this time, to aid and improve that seminary, in which those who are to be the future guardians of the rights and liberties of their country may be endowed with science and virtue.[11]

[10] Lipscomb, Vol. XIV, p. 129; Vol. XVII, pp. 418–424.
[11] Ford, Vol. II, p. 432.

In addition to some change in the government of the college, he urged sweeping changes in curriculum. First, he would have abolished the two professorships of theology, substituting one of ancient languages and one of history; instead of rhetoric, logic, and ethics, he would have a professor of "moral philosophy, and the laws of nature and of nations, and of the fine arts"; the professorship of physics, metaphysics, and mathematics would be divided into two positions, one of natural philosophy and natural history and one of mathematics, eliminating metaphysics; the school of Latin and Greek would become modern languages, leaving the classical languages for the grammar schools; and he would add schools of "law and police" and of "anatomy and medicine." These changes he could not get accepted by legislative action, but a few months later, on his election as governor of Virginia, he became a Visitor of the college and succeeded in having some of the changes effected: more emphasis on moral philosophy and mathematics, substitution of the modern languages for Latin and Greek, and the addition of the professorships of law and police and of anatomy, medicine, and chemistry. He did not succeed, however, in having theology separated from the work of the college.

In his last years Jefferson was to concentrate on the founding of the University of Virginia, where he did succeed in trying many of the reforms he had proposed for William and Mary.

Plans for a National System of Education

The Educational Enlightenment Philosophers

Although Jefferson's plans for schools have become more famous because of his political prominence, a number of his contemporaries had educational proposals that were far more radical and far more detailed than Jefferson's. Among these essayists and pamphleteers were: Benjamin Rush, surgeon-general of the American army during the Revolutionary War, first lecturer on chemistry and medicine at the College of Philadelphia, and signer of the Declaration of Independence; Robert Coram, Delaware political essayist; James Sullivan, revolutionary writer and later governor, attorney-general, and Supreme Court justice of Massachusetts; Nathaniel Chipman, Revolutionary War officer and later legislator and justice of the Vermont Supreme Court and United States Senator; Samuel Knox, Maryland physician, minister, and schoolmaster; Samuel Harrison Smith, Pennsylvania magazine writer; Lafitte du Courteil, Pennsylvania academy professor of French, history, and mathematics; Du Pont de Nemours, French political leader and exile from the French Revolution; and Noah Webster, Massachusetts Revolutionary pamphleteer, magazine editor, and author of textbooks and the famous dictionary. A number of these men, including Rush, Knox, and Smith, were active members of the American Philosophical Society, which offered a prize for "the best system of liberal Education and literary instruction, adapted to the genius of the Government of the United States; comprehending also a plan for instituting and conducting public schools in this country, on principles of the most extensive utility." The contest drew many essays, and the prize was shared in 1797 by Smith and Knox.

OPPOSITION TO FOREIGN SCHOOLING Although all the plans were different, there were basic themes which ran through several of them. Most of them opposed schooling that would take American youth to Europe to complete their education. The Georgia legislature decreed in 1785 that any person under sixteen who went abroad to study for three years or more would lose his right to hold civil or military office in Georgia for a period equal to that he had spent in school abroad.[12] A year later Benjamin Rush, in a treatise entitled "Thoughts upon the Mode of Education proper in a Republic," argued:

> The principle of patriotism stands in need of the reinforcement of *prejudice*, and it is well known that our strongest prejudices in favor of our country are formed in the first one and twenty years of life.[13]

Consequently, an American education would "be preferred to an education in a foreign country." President Washington put it very strongly in several documents, including a 1795 letter to Governor Brooke of Virginia.

> It is with indescribable regret that I have seen the youth of the United States migrating to foreign countries in order to acquire the higher branches of erudition and to obtain a knowledge of the sciences. . . A serious danger is encountered by sending abroad among other political systems those who have not well learned the value of their own.

[12] Knight and Hall, p. 93.
[13] Quoted in Allen Oscar Hansen, *Liberalism and American Education in the Eighteenth Century* (New York: Macmillan, 1926), p. 49.

> The time is therefore come when a plan of universal education ought to be adopted in the United States.[14]

In all the plans there appears the insistence that a new kind of society and government demands a distinctive kind of education. Rush wrote:

> The business of education . . . acquired a new complexion by the independence of our country. . . . It becomes us, therefore, to examine our former habits upon this subject, and in laying the foundations for nurseries of wise and good men, to adapt our modes of teaching to the peculiar form of our government.[15]

Sullivan, reviewing the history of autocratic governments, developed the Enlightenment creed that governments and religions of the past had kept the people in ignorance in order to secure "a passive obedience to the will of the sovereign." In the United States such passive obedience was a crime, not a virtue, for a republic depended on individual responsibility for social progress. Coram tied the economic and political needs of democracy together, thus making economic and political independence interrelated concerns for education. Chipman concluded that since government in America was "of the democratic republic kind," a democratic education was necessary.

> We ought to know their principles [of democratic governments], to study well their tendency, and to be able both in theory and practice, to exclude all foreign principles. . . . To this end, common schools, as well as public seminaries, should be considered as an important object of legislative attention.

In stating the purpose of education, Knox also related it to the revolutionary view that our new government was better than any other.

> In proportion, then as our government is superior . . . to the systems of those which have been instituted for enslaving the minds . . . of their ignorant vassals, so should the most general means of diffusing and promoting knowledge, be adopted.

Lafitte du Courteil maintained that ancient republics had flourished or fallen according to the degree of attention they gave to education, and

[14] John C. Fitzpatrick (ed.), *The Writings of George Washington* (Washington: Government Printing Office, 1939), Vol. 34, pp. 149–150.

[15] Hansen is the source for this and all the following quotations on the plans for a national system of education.

he pointed out that the United States had an additional cause to develop a national system of education. Where the ancient republics had had a large measure of homogeneity among their population, the United States was made up of many elements. "National education . . . is absolutely necessary to make and arouse principles of patriotism . . . ; to strengthen the bonds of a union . . . in an immense republic, composed of divers peculiar states."

SCHOOLS MUST BE PUBLIC IN A REPUBLIC A system of education that would serve the needs of a republic could not be achieved by a system of private schools. It would be necessary for the schools to be controlled and supported by the state. Knox, admitting that private schools had provided the leadership of the Revolution, listed seven objections to such schools. First, they did not offer equal opportunity, and genius and leadership talents were not limited to the children of the wealthy. Second, they isolated the educated leaders from those who made up the body of the public, limiting the growth of mutual understanding and sympathy. Third, since they often stood for luxury, they offered a greater chance of moral corruption. Fourth, they tended to make education the concern of the few rather than "an object of national patronage." Fifth, they tended to promote divisions among the classes instead of creating unity. Sixth, public schools would stimulate emulation, thus furnishing the means for "distinguishing literary genius and merit; and consequently pointing out to public view such talents as are best fitted to fill the various stations and offices . . . of the state." And seventh, if the schools were supported by the public, they would all have better "means and apparatus for acquiring a competent knowledge of the arts and sciences." Smith opposed private schools because of the "narrowness of parental solicitude, the general weakness of parents, the lack of competition in private education, and the overwhelming biases of parents; whereas in public education there is the constant stimulation of competition, the unbiased, objective attitude, and the possibility of bringing into play upon education all the available resources of the nation."

COMPULSORY ATTENDANCE Not only must there be a national system of education, but it must be open to all. Coram was particularly bitter in his denunciation of education which favored the wealthy over the rest of society.

> The education of children should be provided for in the constitution of every state. By education, I mean, instruction in arts as well as sciences. Education then ought to be secured by government to every class of citizen, to every child in the state. The citizens

> should be instructed in the sciences by public schools. . . . Education should not be left to the caprice, or negligence of parents, to chance, or confined to the children of wealthy parents. . . . It is a shame, a scandal to civilized society, that part only of the citizens should be sent to colleges and universities to learn to cheat the rest of their liberties.

One of the liberties for which the Revolutionary War had been fought was the right of equal representation, and Coram argued that equal representation could never be achieved until there was an "equal mode of education for all citizens." Until farmers, for example, could get an education equal to that of lawyers, they would never secure places of leadership and hence never be properly represented in government. Lafitte du Courteil warned that the individualism of the Americans made it necessary to convince parents that children were children of the state as well as of their parents and that the state had a right to direct their education. Smith also claimed that society had the right to educate children and that any institution "so momentously important, must not be left to the negligence of individuals." He recommended that "it be made punishable by law in a parent to neglect offering his child to the preceptor for instruction." This was a much stronger stand than any state was to put into practice for more than half a century.

SCHOOLS FOR GIRLS The new republic had new responsibilities for women, and they needed an education to fit them for those new tasks. Lafitte du Courteil's plan of liberal education included both sexes, and Smith apologized for omitting a discussion of female education, saying that he did not want to lose potential support for his plan by introducing such a controversial matter into his scheme. Rush was not so hesitant. In a 1787 lecture at the Young Ladies Academy in Philadelphia, he pointed out that American women, because of economic conditions and early marriages, needed a utilitarian schooling, in contrast with the "ornamental" education of the English lady. American wives "must be the stewards and guardians of their husbands' property," and upon them fell the "principal share of the instruction of children." Not only did they need an education in the rudiments of reading, writing, and arithmetic for economic reasons, but "our ladies should be qualified to a certain degree by a peculiar and suitable education, to concur in instructing their sons in the principles of liberty and government."

TAX SUPPORT A system of schools such as these plans proposed would necessitate tax support. To the objection that some men would have to pay for the schooling of others' children, Coram replied that the "solidarity of interests . . . made each person dependent upon every other person," and if democracy failed to provide adequate education, all citizens would suffer. Smith recommended that there be a national tax "raised from the citizens in the ratio of their property." In addition to such a general tax, Lafitte du Courteil suggested taxes on commodities which were not necessities, such as tea and coffee, and if that did not produce sufficient revenue for the schools, he suggested the establishment of lotteries. Rush contended that the taxes needed for the support of education would not be a burden, for the advancements in agriculture and industry resulting from education would "*lessen* our taxes."

SEPARATION OF RELIGION AND EDUCATION Samuel Knox, the clergyman-author, hailed the separation of church and state in educational affairs as removing the conflict of interest which had retarded the progress of science and "tended to enslave the human mind."

> It is a happy circumstance peculiarly favorable to an uniform plan of public education, that this country hath excluded ecclesiastical from civil policy, and emancipated the human mind from the tyranny of church authority; and church establishments.

CURRICULUM Some of the plans did not suggest many changes in curriculum, but others made radical curriculum proposals, and most of them emphasized science and utilitarian study. Rush was so concerned about the continuation of past errors in education that he wished for a school devoted to the "art of forgetting" where "three-fourths of all our school-masters, divines, and legislators would profit very much, by spending two or three years." Because of their adherence to tradition, Rush said that to oppose the study of Latin and Greek would require "the recollection of escape from a lion and a bear." But oppose the study of those languages he did, calling them "improper in the present state of society and government in the United States." As long as those languages were the only avenues to learning, "education will always be confined to a few people." The study of those languages, he contended, was sheer waste of time, and the habits and biases which they inculcated were "prejudicial to the study of science."

> Under these circumstances, to spend four or five years in learning two dead languages, is to turn our backs upon a gold mine, in order to amuse ourselves catching butterflies. . . .
> The rejection of the Latin and Greek languages from our schools, would produce a revolution in science, and in human affairs.

Coram went even further in abolishing the traditional academic subjects from his plan. "No modes of faith, systems of manners, or foreign or dead languages should be taught in those schools."

In the 1798 essay in which Rush attacked the study of Latin and Greek, he outlined a curriculum in detail. Beginning with reading, writing, speaking, and spelling in English, Rush emphasized those subjects which would be most practical: arithmetic, natural history, geography, French and German (but to be learned "only by ear" for purposes of commerce or law), grammar, oratory, criticism, the higher branches of mathematics, philosophy, chemistry, logic, metaphysics, history, government, the principles of agriculture and manufactures, and "everything else that is necessary to qualify him for public usefulness or private happiness." In place of moral philosophy, which he felt taught pagan or anti-Christian morals, he advocated a series of lectures on "the evidences, doctrines and precepts of the Christian religion."

Rush urged special attention to "the history of the ancient republics, and the progress of liberty and tyranny in the different states of Europe." This would lead young men to a better understanding of progress toward greater enlightenment and "Practical Legislation." The study of American history, particularly the development of the republic, would help "convert men into republican machines." Although this sounds like using history for a new kind of authoritarian indoctrination, he repeatedly stressed the importance of learning what factors tended to liberate and what factors tended to repress. Smith proposed much the same curriculum, and he too had a special role for history, which alone would liberate man from "Fanaticism and superstition." A "liberal acquaintance with history" would reveal the factors which caused mankind to progress or deteriorate, thus enabling the youth to become an intelligent critic of the movements in his own time. Neither science nor geography could teach that kind of lesson. In addition to the study of "General History, and a more detailed acquaintance with the history of our own country," Smith would have the boys in secondary school memorize and frequently repeat the Constitution and the fundamental laws of the United States. Knox also would give considerable attention to modern geography and history, as contrasted with the customary practice of dealing almost exclusively with the classical world, and he would put greatest emphasis on the geography and history of the United States. When Americans began to develop strong feelings of nationalism in the era following the War of 1812, both history and geography were deliberately used to create chauvinistic attitudes among young Americans, a new authoritarianism which was quite different from the "liberating" influence these Enlightened philosophers seem to have been seeking from the study of history.

The scientific attitude towards the study of history as providing the means for the social and political progress of mankind was related to the attitude toward the study of the natural and physical sciences. Knox recognized that education in science was not merely learning facts. Students should be taught in such a way as "to habituate them to call forth their own exertions" and so as "not to discourage, or check the ardour of their pursuit" of knowledge. Anticipating Herbert Spencer's thesis of nearly a century later, Smith contended, "All science ought to derive its rank from utility . . . the real good which it actually does, or is capable of doing." Schools, according to Smith, should inspire youth "with a taste for, and an attachment to, science, so firm, that it should be almost impossible to eradicate it." This interest would be achieved by having the student do projects in science, for "the addition of practical to theoretical knowledge would add to its charms." The plan of Du Pont de Nemours, drawn up at the request of Jefferson, applied the scientific and mathematical studies to practical areas. Geometry would be related to astronomy and engineering for navigation and shipbuilding. Botany, chemistry, and anatomy would be taught in connection with medicine and surgery. Mineralogy would be studied for the purposes of developing underground resources. There should be no clash between scholarship and practicality.

In short, these eighteenth-century writers seemed to have a better understanding of the function of scientific education than did many late nineteenth-century advocates of science in the curriculum who divorced the study of the sciences from the experiences of the child and tried to make science another abstract study suitable for mental discipline.

Knox included in his proposal two aspects that were somewhat unusual. Obviously influenced by Locke's "sound mind in a sound body," he urged that attention be given to the education of the body. Partly for this reason, he included the "Manual of military exercise" for secondary school; another reason was, of course, preparation for military service. The teacher should also teach physical activities that would conform to the principles of the new society and the needs of the individual, "the proper diversions, exercises and amusements suited to those of their years, and views of life."

A NATIONAL UNIVERSITY The capstone of a national system of education would be a national university, which would serve as a research facility as well as a teaching institution. Knox said it would be "the fountain head of science, that centre to which all literary genius of the commonwealth would tend, and from which, when matured by its instructive influence, would diffuse the rays of knowledge and science to the remotest situations of the united government." Smith recommended that a select number of students be sent to such a university where each of them would be supported "at public expense . . . remaining so long as he please, . . . devoting his time to the cultivation of science or literature." Du Pont de Nemours specified that the university be located at Washington City and that it be made up of four schools: medicine, mines, social science and legislation, and geometry and "the sciences that it explains." Affiliated with the university would be the public library, museum, botanical garden, and the home of the philosophical society.

Of all the ideas of these educational revolutionists, the national university proposal attracted the greatest support during the period immediately following the birth of the new nation. But like most of the rest of the proposals, the growing conservatism of the period militated against many significant educational changes. It would take two more revolutions in American society to bring any of the kinds of educational systems these philosophers proposed in the two decades following the Revolutionary War.

Efforts To Found a National University

Although none of the revolutionary proposals for education was adopted during the Federalist period, one did create great interest among the political leaders of the young nation. Even at the Constitutional Convention, according to James Madison's journal, there was some discussion of a national university. Madison and Charles C. Pinckney three times submitted a section which would have given Congress power to establish a university "at the seat of government of the United States." The only line of debate which Madison reported was that Gouverneur Morris said, "It is not necessary. The exclusive power at the Seat of Government, will reach the object."[16] The proposal lost, four states to six, with Connecticut casting a split vote.

Although the Convention did not take any positive action, five of the first six Presidents of the United States advocated federal participation in a national university. Even before the writing of the Declaration of

[16] Gaillard Hunt (ed.), *The Journal of the Debates in the Convention which Framed the Constitution of the United States, May-September, 1787, as Recorded by James Madison* (New York: Putnam's, 1908), Vol. 11, p. 374.

Independence, General Washington, at Cambridge with the Continental army, supposedly received a complaint on the damage caused by the soldiers quartered in Harvard, and he expressed the hope that after the war there would be a union of North America, with a central government which would have a national university. Whether or not this account is true, it is clear that Washington was very much interested in such an institution. In his first message to Congress, January 8, 1790, he called on Congress, in legislating on matters of internal improvements to deliberate on the "institution of a national university."[17] He missed an opportunity to do something concrete about the creation of such a university in 1794. John Adams, in Europe, was approached by a member of the faculty of the College of Geneva with the proposal that the entire college faculty migrate to America. When Adams sent word to the President, Washington responded neutrally. He feared that such a body would not "get assimilated to our customs." Jefferson, minister at Paris, was also approached, and he attempted to have the Virginia legislature provide the necessary funds to transplant the College, but the scheme was dropped for lack of support in America.[18]

In 1785 the legislature of Virginia voted Washington, as a testimonial for his public services, 50 shares of stock in the Potomac River Company and 100 shares in the James River Company. Embarrassed by the gift, Washington requested the legislature to appropriate his shares in the James River Company for the support of an academy in Virginia and the Potomac River Company shares for a national university. The academy designated was Liberty Hall Academy, later Washington College, and now Washington and Lee University. The two gifts were confirmed by Washington's will, but Congress took no action, and there is no record that the Potomac River Company shares were ever transferred to the federal government.

In his inaugural address President John Adams lauded the importance of education and schools, but this former schoolmaster failed to ask the Congress to take any specific action on education. His successor, however, was as enthusiastic about the idea of a national university as he was about other educational projects. In 1806 Jefferson, placing a stricter interpretation on the constitutional powers of Congress than Washington apparently did, suggested a constitutional amendment to specify education as a particular responsibility of Congress. He anticipated a surplus in the federal treasury, which he thought should be spent on internal improvements, and he wanted education to be added to the

[17] Fitzpatrick, Vol. 30, p. 494.

[18] B. A. Hinsdale, "Documents Illustrative of American Educational History," *U.S. Office of Education Report*, 1892–93, Part 2, pp. 1300–1301.

constitutional list of projects for which Congress could spend money.

James Madison did not share Jefferson's strict interpretation of the limitations of the constitutional powers of the federal government. In his second, seventh, and last annual messages to Congress, President Madison recommended that "existing powers" of the Congress be utilized for internal improvements, including "the establishment of a university within the District." On two of these occasions his proposals received favorable committee action within the House of Representatives, but no further action was taken.

President James Monroe shared Jefferson's view of the Constitution, and like Jefferson he called for an amendment to permit greater federal participation in internal improvements. The amendment he sought would grant Congress the right to institute "seminaries of learning for the all-important purpose of diffusing knowledge among our fellow-citizens throughout the United States."

The last of the early Presidents to advocate a national university was John Quincy Adams, whose first annual message pointed out the need for encouraging scientific research, and his plan for a national university included an astronomical observatory. He referred to the observatory as "light-houses of the skies," a figure which brought derisive laughter from the hostile Congress, and the noble Enlightenment idea of an educational capstone for a republican system of schools died an ignominious death.[19]

The excitement of these early leaders in advocating federal participation in educational projects is particularly significant today when the issue of federal aid to education brings so many inaccurate statements about what the "founding fathers" believed about government and education. It appears that a number of them, including Washington and Madison, believed that the federal government had the responsibility and the constitutional authority to aid education. Even the more reluctant, like Jefferson and Monroe, recognized the need and sought to meet it by constitutional amendment.

Noah Webster—Weathercock of Federalism

Perhaps Noah Webster should be part of the next chapter, as a Federalist and conservative, but in the beginning of his public career, he shared some of the ideas of the Enlightened revolutionists. Near the end of the century he became more and more conservative, very much

[19] *Ibid.*, pp. 1309–1311.

like the general national mood, and as such he is a good transition from the radical revolutionary period of public interest in universal tax-supported education to the conservative era when schools were more or less neglected, except for tuition- or charity-supported institutions.

Enlightened Revolutionist

In the 1780's Webster was almost as radical as Jefferson or Paine. In his *Sketches of American Policy* he pointed out that the American republic was the first and only government on earth "founded on the true principles of equal liberty."[20] Two years later, writing on the principles of the proposed Constitution, he maintained, "A general and tolerably equal distribution of landed property is the whole basis of national freedom."[21] During this radical period he expressed distrust of religion as superstitution used to keep people in ignorance and subjection. He criticized Americans for the prevalence of "a blind imitation" of English customs, and to help offset the continuing dependence on England, he advocated language reforms to create an American language.

> A *national language* is a band of *national union.* Every engine should be employed to render the people of this country *national;* to call their attachments home to their own country; and to inspire them with the pride of national character.[22]

With Rush, Coram, and the other intellectuals of his time, Webster insisted in many articles that the success of the republic depended on education, which would be both practical and national in spirit.

> Systems of Education should be adapted and pursued, which may not only diffuse a knowledge of the sciences, but may implant, in the minds of the American youth, the principles of virtue and of liberty; and inspire them with just and liberal ideas of government, and with an inviolable attachment to their own country.[23]

In the American republic, where good government and justice depended on intelligent voters and citizens, "no Legislature can be justified in

[20] Noah Webster, "Plan for the Union of the American States," *Old South Leaflets,* No. 197 (Boston: Old South Meeting House), p. 9.

[21] Quoted in Hansen, pp. 210–211.

[22] "The Reforming of Spelling," *Old South Leaflets,* No. 196 (Boston: Old South Meeting House), pp. 5–6.

[23] "On the Education of Youth in America," *A Collection of Essays and Fugitiv* [sic] *Writings, on Moral, Historical, Political and Literary Subjects* (Boston, 1790), p. 3.

neglecting" schools where "knowledge should be universally diffused."

Like Rush, he saw the importance of women, who were to be the wives of citizens and the mothers of the youth. Since American mothers were "not generally above the care of educating their own children," they should be given an education that would "enable them to implant in the tender mind, such sentiments of virtue, propriety and dignity, as are suited to the freedom of our government."[24] American youth should be schooled in America by American schoolmasters using American textbooks containing materials emphasizing America. It was to this end that Webster made his greatest contribution to American education—his textbooks.

Affluent Textbook Author

Even before the peace treaty was signed, the young schoolmaster was writing his first textbooks.

> In the year 1782, . . . I kept a classical school in . . . New York. I there compiled two small elementary books for teaching the English language. The country was then impoverished, intercourse with Great Britain was interrupted, school-books were scarce and hardly attainable, and there was no certain prospect of peace.[25]

The books to which he referred were probably the first two parts of A *Grammatical Institute of the English Language, comprising an Easy, Concise, and Systematic Method of Education, designed for the Use of English Schools in America.* Part I, the speller, was published in 1783; Part II, the grammar, in 1784; Part III, the reader, in 1785. Although all three parts had the patriotic purpose of creating a distinctive American character through a national language and national literature, the Revolutionary sentiment is perhaps most clearly seen in Part III. A "Greatly Enlarged" third edition, published in 1787, reveals in a portion of its long title its contents and purposes: *An American Selection of Lessons in Reading and Speaking; calculated to improve the Minds and refine the Taste of Youth, and also to instruct them in the Geography, History, and Politics of the United States.* The very title of the revised Part III—*An American Selection*—emphasizes its contents, approximately a third of the more than sixty selections being American patriotic selections: Revolutionary orations, the Declaration of Independence, praises of General Washington. The motto on the title page reads: "Begin with the infant in his cradle; let the first word he lisps be Washington."

[24] *Ibid.*, pp. 24, 27.
[25] *Old South Leaflets*, No. 198, p. 21.

In 1790 Webster published another reader entitled *The Little Reader's Assistant; Containing: I. A Number of Stories Mostly Taken from the History of America, and Adorned with Cuts. II. Rudiments of English Grammar. III. A Federal Catechism, Being a Short and Easy Explanation of the Constitution of the United States. IV. The Farmer's Catechism, Containing Plain Rules of Husbandry—and Calculated for the Use of Schools. V. General Principles of Government and Commerce. All Adapted to the Capacities of Children.* Again the selections were liberally sprinkled with historical references to the young nation and its Revolution. The "Federal Catechism," in a question and answer form, demonstrated the superiority of republican government to other forms. Not only did Webster stress American history in his own readers, but he wrote a historical chapter for the first geography text to be published in America, that of Jedidiah Morse (1789). Although Webster was the first to publish readers in the new nation, his reading books were never as popular as his spelling books. His readers were superseded by those of other writers, especially Lindley Murray, in the 1790's and early 1800's, but he had set what was to be the pattern of organization and content through most of the nineteenth century.

Part I, the spelling book, was by far the most famous of his books and the most enduring. Based on two English texts by Fenning and Dilworth, the speller incorporated some of the reforms Webster agitated for—simplified spelling and Americanized pronunciation. In 1786 the title was changed to the more patriotic *The American Spelling Book,* and in 1829 to *The Elementary Spelling Book,* but it was almost universally known as "Webster's Spelling Book" or "The Blue-back Speller," from its blue-papered cardboard covers. It continued to be widely used into the twentieth century, the longest period of usefulness of any American textbook. At a royalty of half a cent a copy, it supported Webster and his family. In 1807 he estimated the annual sale at 200,000 copies, and in 1843, the year of his death, he estimated it had sold a total of 19 million copies and was still going at the rate of half a million a year. By 1889 the publisher estimated that a total of 62 million had been sold, with the peak year coming in 1880, when a million and a half were sold.[26] The book can still be purchased from the American Book Company, which is continuing to print the 1880 edition. The spelling lessons begin with the alphabet, then two-letter syllables (ba, be, bi, bo, bu; ca, ce, ci, co, cu, etc., followed by ab, eb, ib, ob, ub, etc.), then three-letter syllables (bla, ble, bli, blo, blu) and

[26] Ervin C. Shoemaker, *Noah Webster, Pioneer of Learning* (New York: Columbia U. Press, 1936), pp. 88–89.

four-letter syllables (splu, etc.) before the child ever gets to even the simple one-syllable words in Lesson 12 on page 20. In a very logical fashion the lessons proceed to longer words until Lesson 121, which includes "Words of eight syllables, accented on the sixth," where the two words are most appropriate: "unintelligibility" and "incomprehensibility." Beginning with the 1792 edition Webster's speller included reading lessons and fables as well as spelling words. For many nineteenth-century American children, this composite reader and speller was the only schoolbook.

In some of his prefaces to his textbooks, Webster touched on teaching methods. He believed that the master should be strict, not permitting the pupils "to whisper or play or be idle a single moment," but on the other hand he should be agreeable, pleasant, and good-natured. "Respect for an instructor" should replace the "rod of correction," so that school should be a pleasure to children.[27] Although he was a radical in his reforms of spelling, he was traditional in his ideas about how to teach reading and spelling. Until his death, he defended the alphabet-syllable method of teaching reading. Even after Horace Mann urged that American schoolmasters adopt the successful European system of teaching reading by words, nineteenth-century teachers were almost completely loyal to the traditional pattern so reinforced by the popularity of Webster's speller.

Conservative Federalist

Shocked by the excesses of the French Revolution, Webster, like most other Americans, forgot the excesses of our own Revolutionary War, our own brutal treatment of tax collectors and persecution of American Tories, and he followed the pattern of increasing conservatism of Federalist United States. He repudiated some of his early political views as erroneous. Of his *Sketches of American Policy*, he wrote in 1800, "The sentiments of that pamphlet are too democratic for the author. . . . We grow wiser with age."[28] He ceased to propagandize for reforms—political, educational, or literary. His time was devoted to lexicography and to revising his textbooks, stressing orthodox morality and religious sentiments more than "republican principles." Characteristic of the period, Noah Webster had lost the revolutionary fervor and had become conservative. The final stage of the revolutionary cycle had arrived; Federalist America was in a period of educational as well as political conservatism.

[27] Shoemaker, pp. 35–36.
[28] Quoted in Hansen, pp. 207–208.

The Close of the Revolutionary Period

The great social revolution which characterized the English settlements in America in the 1760's, 1770's, and 1780's had its educational aspects. Unfortunately, few of the revolutionary educational proposals were to be implemented during this brief period of turmoil, and in the conservative period which followed, as the next two chapters will show, the general tendency was away from democracy in education. However, because the conservatism was tempered more in America than in other societies which have undergone social revolutions, the dialogue between the Enlightened philosophers and the conservatives was never completely silenced. Thomas Jefferson, among others, remained an important intellectual figure until the opening stages of the second American social revolution, and many of the Enlightenment ideas were to be revived and reasserted until they became accepted as part of our modern public education.

QUESTIONS FOR DISCUSSION

1. Many of the ideals of American education had their first clear statement in the Enlightenment era. How closely have we come to realizing those ideals? Have the Enlightenment concepts changed in meaning? Are they still significant statements for today?
2. Some of the issues debated by the Enlightened leaders are still problems today. We often include the "founding fathers" in our arguments without really knowing what they did say and believe. Summarize the statements of some of the Revolutionary leaders and early Presidents on the following issues: federal aid to education, separation of church and state in education, public support of schools; universal education. How might their ideas be developed within the context of modern American society?
3. Although many modern intellectuals are critical of present-day schools, educators often defend present practices without listening to the criticism. In much the same way, the early American teacher ignored the suggestions of the Enlightenment leaders. What might we do today to profit from the experience of the late eighteenth century with respect to accepting criticism effectively?

SUGGESTED READINGS

Secondary Sources

Arrowood, Charles Flinn. *Thomas Jefferson and Education in a Republic.* New York: McGraw-Hill, 1930.

Butts, R. Freeman. *The American Tradition in Religion and Education.* Boston: Beacon Press, 1950. Chapters 3 and 4 and pp. 119–122.
Carpenter, Charles. *History of American Schoolbooks.* Philadelphia: U. of Pennsylvania Press, 1963. Chapter V. Also portions of later chapters.
Curti, Merle. *The Social Ideas of American Educators.* New York: Scribner's, 1935. Chapter I.
Dabney, Charles William. *Universal Education in the South.* Chapel Hill: U. of North Carolina Press, 1936. Vol. 1, Chapter I.
Drake, William. *The American School in Transition.* Englewood Cliffs: Prentice-Hall, 1955. Chapters III and IV.
Honeywell, Roy J. *The Educational Work of Thomas Jefferson.* Cambridge: Harvard U., 1931.

Primary Sources

Cubberley, Ellwood P. *Readings in the History of Education.* Boston: Houghton Mifflin, 1920. Readings 259–263.
———. *Readings in Public Education in the United States.* Boston: Houghton Mifflin, 1934, Readings 67–71, 173–175.
Fried, Albert (ed.). *The Essential Jefferson.* New York: Collier Books, 1963. Pp. 146–160, 207–210, 232–235, 389–390, 464–465, 519–520, 527–532.
Knight, Edgar W., A *Documentary History of Education in the South Before 1860.* Chapel Hill: U. of North Carolina Press, 1949. Vol. II, Chapters I–III, VI–IX, and XI.
Knight, Edgar W., and Hall, Clifton L. *Readings in American Educational History.* New York: Appleton-Century-Crofts, 1951. Pp. 91–116.
Monroe, Paul. *The Founding of the American Public School System.* Ann Arbor: University Microfilms, 1940. Vol. II, Chapter XII.

5

Federalist Conservatism and Charity Education

The end of the Revolutionary War left America with a collection of very loosely united states. The intentionally weak central government was unable to bring order out of the chaos of armed rebellion, and within a few years after the signing of the peace treaty, influential men were looking for means of giving the federal government greater authority. These influential and conservative men of property seized the initiative in Philadelphia in 1787, writing the Constitution which marked the beginning of the reaction to the Revolution. Until the rise of Jacksonian democracy, the United States was a limited republic dominated by an aristocracy of wealth and education. During this period, schooling was a matter of great inequality, the children of the wealthy having ample educational opportunity and those of the poor receiving only the most meager schooling or none at all.

The Constitution and Education

It was not through oversight that education was not mentioned in the Constitution of the United States. There were too many educated men present and too many men concerned about schools for no one to have thought about schooling in the months that they argued over the powers and responsibilities of the federal government. The omission can probably be explained by considering the interests of the men who made up the Convention. The minority faction—those who tended toward attitudes of democracy and favored a "general diffusion of knowledge"—feared a central government strong enough to support a school system which could have made universal education a reality. Had Jefferson been present, he might have desired general education greatly enough to overcome the Enlightenment distrust of government, but the champion of schooling was in Paris. The majority faction, the Federalists, wanted a strong central government, but they had no desire to create a "mobocracy." The lower classes did not need an education since the responsibilities of citizenship in the Federalists' limited republic would fall to the gentlemen of property. In general, they apparently subscribed to the belief that schooling might be dangerous for the lower classes, leading to pretensions disruptive of "good" social order. So, by an apparent consensus, education was not enumerated as a responsibility of the Congress.

What, then, is the Constitutional basis for the continuing conflicts over federal participation in education? Programs to aid schools and colleges with federal grants of land and money have been justified on two constitutional grounds. First, the powers granted to Congress (Article I, Section 8, Paragraph 1) include providing for the "general welfare of the United States." The eighteenth paragraph of the same section gives Congress the authority to "make all laws which shall be necessary and proper for carrying into execution the foregoing powers." Under these "elastic" clauses a large portion of Congressional action is taken, and defenders of federal aid argue that education is necessary for the general welfare of the nation. A second ground for federal aid is found in Article IV, Section 3, Paragraph 2, which gives Congress the power "to dispose of and make all needful rules and regulations respecting the territory or other property belonging to the United States." Under this authority the federal government, on several occasions to be discussed later, has granted lands or income from the sale of lands to the individual states to be used for educational purposes. On the other side of the argument, the constitutional basis is found in the Tenth Amendment to the Constitution (adopted in 1791 as part of the Bill of Rights): "The powers not delegated to the United States by the Constitution, nor prohibited by it to the States, are reserved to the States respectively, or to the people." This "states' rights" clause, which has been the ultimate argument of those who have opposed federal aid to education, was ironically demanded by the liberal republican who was so devoted to education that he later called for a constitutional amendment to give Congress the authority to provide a national institution of education—Thomas Jefferson.

State Constitutions

In the heat of the Revolution the rebelling colonies hurriedly wrote constitutions which were generally consistent with the radical creeds expressed in the Declaration of Independence. After the Revolutionary War, several states wrote new constitutions generally reflecting more conservative attitudes. Many of these new constitutions failed to mention schools or education at all. Some of them included pious but unspecific references to education. The New Hampshire constitution of 1784, following closely the words of the Massachusetts constitution of 1780, admonished the legislature "to cherish the interest of literature and the sciences, and all seminaries and public schools."[1] The Vermont constitution of 1787 recognized the need for schools, but relegated the major role to religious and philanthropic efforts. Pennsylvania, whose 1776 constitution required the legislature to provide schools supported by the public treasury, in 1790 returned to a provision for pauper education.

> The legislature shall, as soon as conveniently may be, provide, by law, for the establishment of schools throughout the State, in such manner that the poor may be taught gratis.[2]

Not only did this provision limit free education to those who would sign a pauper's oath that they could not afford to send their children to school, but even that provision was left to the discretion of the legislature. The first constitution of Georgia (1777) required that "Schools shall be erected in each county, and supported at the general expense of the State"; the second (1789) made no reference to education or schools; the third (1798) merely called for "seminaries," probably interpreted as secondary institutions, supported by endowments and philanthropy.

Permanent School Funds

One solution to the problem of how to have free schools without paying taxes was to build up a permanent fund from the sale of lands or licenses or from some other relatively "painless" source of revenue and then use the interest earned by the invested fund. Since tuition was charged to those who could afford to pay and the schools were "free" only to paupers, it was possible to finance a minimal school system through the aid of such funds in some states.

Connecticut

The first state to establish a permanent school fund was Connecticut, which used the proceeds from the sale of lands that it claimed in the Western Reserve, territory to the west of Pennsylvania. A 1786 law had

[1] Hinsdale, Part 2, p. 1317.
[2] Poore, Part II, p. 1553.

authorized the sale of a portion of the lands for the support of "the gospel ministry," and a 1793 law applied the fund to schools as well as churches. There was great controversy over the state support of the clergy, and in 1795 the general assembly passed a law which reserved the fund for school purposes. The lands were sold for $1,200,000, and the interest was permitted to accumulate until 1799 without any dividend being distributed. In 1800, $23,651 was distributed to the schools. Not all the interest was paid out in dividends, so that the fund continued to grow until it amounted to over $2 million in 1890. Between 1799 and 1859 the income of the fund was nearly $5 million.[3]

Although this fund gave Connecticut a dependable source of support for its schools, the tendency to rely so heavily on the income from the fund instead of on a tax base, which would increase with the population and the prosperity of the state, was in the long run detrimental to the schools of the state. In 1821 the legislature abolished the small school tax, and the citizens of Connecticut became so accustomed to paying little or no school tax that they let their schools deteriorate. It took Herculean work by Henry Barnard in the 1840's and 1850's to give the schools of Connecticut a new start.

New York

New York gave state support to the common schools briefly between 1795 and 1800, appropriating £20,000 annually "for the purpose of encouraging and maintaining schools in the several cities and towns in this State." The same act required city and county authorities to raise by local taxes an amount equal to half the sum allotted to the town. It also authorized New York City to use the money for the support of charity schools "whether the children taught in such charity school shall be the children of white parents or descended from Africans or Indians." Outside the city of New York, local freeholders were to elect a board of three to seven men to supervise the schools and disburse the funds.[4] As reflection of the conservative trend, this law was allowed to lapse at the end of its five-year term, and in 1805 New York created a Literature Fund, specifying that there could be no distribution of funds until the accumulated interest totaled $50,000. De Witt Clinton, president of the New York Free School Society, reported in 1809:

> The fund consists, at present, of nearly four hundred thousand dollars in bank-stock, mortgages, and bonds, and produces an annual interest of upwards of twenty-four thousand dollars. The capital

[3] Hinsdale, pp. 1256–1261.
[4] Finegan, pp. 26–30.

> will be augmented by the accumulating interest, and the sale of three hundred and thirty-six thousand acres of land.[5]

In 1812 New York set up a comprehensive district system of common schools, to be supported largely through the income of the Fund, but the high hopes were not realized. The conservatives in the legislature emphasized the inequality of schooling in 1814 with the passage of a pauper-school bill, placing the burden of school support on those families who could afford to pay by levying a rate-bill or tuition fee.

Virginia

A third state to create a Literary Fund was Virginia. In 1809 the legislature appropriated all escheats, confiscations, fines, penalties, forfeitures, and abandoned properties to a Literary Fund to be used for the "sole benefit of a school or schools, to be kept in each and every county within this commonwealth." The income from the Fund was not enough to provide adequate schools, and Jefferson advocated an additional tax for primary schools, but he did recognize the Fund as a "solid provision." In 1817 the legislature directed that $45,000 be appropriated annually from the Fund for the education of pauper children and $15,000 for the University of Virginia, which Jefferson was attempting to found. In 1820 Jefferson, seeking to have the full appropriation dedicated to the university, argued that the use of the Fund for pauper education was inefficient and wasteful and that local taxation was the appropriate method of support for primary schools.

Many other states have developed permanent school funds, most of them relying on the income from land grants made to the states by the federal government. While they have provided an important source of income for some states, in other states mismanagement of the funds resulted in the dissipation of the potentially large endowment. In those states which did manage the funds most effectively, there was a tendency to rely on those funds instead of building up tax support sufficient to finance adequate schools.

District Schools

Massachusetts School Law of 1789

Before the Revolutionary War all the colonies had recognized some public responsibility for the schooling of poor children. In New England this obligation was manifested in the town and district school. The 1647

[5] William Oland Bourne, *History of the Public School Society of the City of New York* (New York: Wm. Wood, 1870), p. 16.

Ould Deluder law of Massachusetts had required towns of one hundred families to have a grammar schoolmaster and towns of fifty families to support a school where children would be taught to read and write. In the conservative reaction following the war, Massachusetts passed a new school law which weakened the provisions of the colonial laws. This 1789 law did continue the requirement that towns of fifty families provide a common school "to teach children to read and write and to instruct them in the English language, as well as in arithmetic, orthography, and decent behavior"; however, the requirement was limited to six months of school a year. Towns of a hundred families had to provide the equivalent of twelve months of common school a year, but no Latin school. Towns of one hundred and fifty families were required, in addition to the twelve-month common school, to have a six-month school, presumably a Latin school, although the law did not specify. Only towns of two hundred families or more were required to employ a Latin master. The weaker provisions permitted many towns to escape the educational responsibilities they had previously had.

The 1789 law confirmed many existing practices, including the district system which had been operating for nearly a hundred years without legislative sanction. Furthermore, it took note of some of the revolutionary ideals and the Puritan religious concern for good character. Schoolmasters were instructed "to impress upon the minds of the children and youth . . . the principles of piety, justice, and a sacred regard to truth, love to their country, humanity, and universal benevolence, sobriety, industry, and frugality, chastity, moderation, and temperance" in order to "preserve and perfect a republican constitution, and to secure the blessings of liberty, as well as to promote their future happiness."

To assure that teachers were properly qualified, they were required by this law to have proof of attendance at some college or to demonstrate their skill to the local minister and be certified by him. Teachers from out of town had to bring a certificate from their home minister certifying that they were of "good moral character." No "settled minister" himself might be employed as a schoolmaster. This last provision was one of the first steps in making teaching a full-time, instead of a part-time, job. The ministers and the selectmen were charged with the duty of visiting and inspecting the schools and pupils at least once every six months. Schools other than those required by law—for example, dame schools—were required to have their teachers certified by the selectmen of the district and by a "learned minister" as being qualified to teach and of good character.

The 1789 law authorized the districts to levy and collect taxes "for the support and maintenance of a schoolmaster to teach their children to read, write, and cipher."[6] This extreme form of local control and support was the pattern that was to prevail throughout the United States in the nineteenth century.

Connecticut "School Societies"

In 1794 school districts were authorized in Connecticut, with the term "school societies" used as the political unit for administering schools. On the basis of early Connecticut laws, a school code was drawn for the "society of Farmington." The code referred to primary school districts within the "society," and specified what the curriculum would be. It also created a higher school of English. Interestingly, Farmington solved the problem of crowded schools by limiting enrollment and rotating pupils in attendance. Apparently limiting educational opportunity was preferable to raising taxes in order to provide adequate schooling.

> The overseers will introduce into schools, besides Webster's Institute in all its parts, as great a variety of reading, both in prose and verse, as the circumstances of the people will admit; among these Dwight's Geography, by question and answer, for its cheapness and simplicity, would be highly proper . . . and common newspapers would be of great use; also see that the Bible is statedly read by those forms who are capable of it, at least as the closing exercise in the afternoon . . . and that the master . . . close the whole at night with prayer. . . .
>
> In addition to the separate districts . . . the society shall be one entire district, for the purpose of maintaining and supporting a school for the further instruction of those children and youth of both sexes who have passed through the ordinary course of a learning in the common schools. . . . The object of the said school shall be to perfect the youth admitted therein in reading and in the grammar of the English tongue, and to instruct them in geography, arithmetic, composition, and speaking. . . .
>
> No youth shall be admitted as a pupil in the said school unless such youth is accurate in a good degree in spelling and reading the English tongue and has acquired a good handwriting. . . . And if a greater number of pupils shall be admitted than can well be accommodated or instructed, in the judgment of the overseers, in such case they shall limit the number who shall attend at a time, and direct all the pupils in a certain order of rotation, by them appointed, to attend the school.[7]

[6] See Hinsdale, pp. 1234–1236.
[7] *Ibid.*, pp. 1254–1255.

Financing the District School

The district school was supervised by a committee or board elected by the inhabitants of the district. In practice the number of directors or trustees varied from one to nine, according to the state. They were responsible for seeing that the school was kept, a teacher hired, taxes levied and collected, and the pupils examined once or twice a year. In addition, they decided which parents would be permitted to take the pauper's oath and send their children free. The rest paid a form of tuition known as the rate. Parents were billed according to the number of children they had in school and the number of days each child attended. The rate was very low by today's standards, often only a penny a day. However, the large families common at that time and the limited circulation of cash made even a moderate rate more than many families could afford. Because of the stigma of charity felt by those children who were "free scholars," many children were sent to school very irregularly to reduce the rate bill. The rate bill and the pauper's oath were thus the cause of inequalities of educational opportunity, a discrimination based on the economic condition of individual families. It was the favoritism of "wealth and birth" against which Jefferson and the other Enlightened leaders had campaigned and which was to be sharply attacked again in the second American social revolution in the mid-nineteenth century.

When New York set up its comprehensive district system in 1812, it created the first state superintendency of common schools. Gideon Hawley was appointed to fill the office at an annual salary of $300. His diligent fight against the conservative legislature for the promotion of public education made him one of the early martyrs of American education. In 1821 the legislature decided it had been irritated long enough by Hawley's insistent demands for more adequate provision for common schools and abolished his office. The supervision of common schools was made an ex-officio responsibility of the secretary of state, and not until 1854 did New York again have a state superintendent of schools.

District Schools in New England

Meager financial support, irregular attendance, low standards for teachers, a narrow curriculum, crude schoolhouses, unprofessional supervision, and public neglect rendered the district schools ineffective in most communities. Of the many accounts of the district schools of our early national period, one of the most interesting and reliable is from the autobiography of Samuel G. Goodrich, who was born in Connecticut in 1793 and educated in the district schools near his home. In the nineteenth century, Goodrich became one of the most popular textbook writers, publishing histories, geographies, and readers under the name of Peter Parley.

> The school-house itself consisted of rough, unpainted clapboards, upon a wooden frame. It was plastered within, and contained two apartments—a little entry, taken out of a corner for a wardrobe, and the school-room proper. . . . The fireplace was six feet wide and four feet deep. The flue was so ample and so perpendicular, that the rain, sleet, and snow fell direct to the hearth. In winter, the battle for life with green fizzling fuel, which was brought in sled lengths and cut up by the scholars, was a stern one. Not infrequently, the wood, gushing with sap as it was, chanced to be out, and . . . the school was dismissed, whereat all the scholars rejoiced aloud, not having the fear of the schoolmaster before their eyes.
>
> It was the custom at this place, to have a woman's school in the summer months, and this was attended only by young children. . . . In winter, a man was employed as teacher, and then the girls and boys of the neighborhood, up to the age of eighteen, or even twenty, were among the pupils. It was not uncommon, at this season, to have forty scholars crowded into this little building.
>
> I was about six years old when I first went to school. My teacher was Aunt Delight, that is, Delight Benedict, a maiden lady of fifty.
>
> I think we had seventeen scholars—boys and girls—mostly of my own age.
>
> The school being organized, we were all seated upon benches, made of what were called *slabs*—that is, boards having the exterior or rounded part of the log on one side: as they were useless for other purposes, these were converted into school-benches, the rounded part down. They had each four supports, consisting of straddling wooden legs, set into augur-holes. Our own legs swayed in the air, for they were too short to touch the floor. Oh, what an awe fell over me, when we were all seated and silence reigned around!
>
> The children were called up, one by one, to Aunt Delight, who sat on a low chair, and required each, as a preliminary, to make his manners, consisting of a small sudden nod or jerk of the head. She then placed the spelling-book—which was Dilworth's—before the pupil, and with a buck-handled penknife pointed, one by one, to the letters of the alphabet, saying, "What's that?" If the child knew his letters, the "what's that?" very soon ran on thus:
>
> "What's that?"
>
> "A."
>
> " 'Stha-a-t?"
>
> "B."

"Sna-a-a-t?"

"C."

I believe I achieved the alphabet that summer. . . . Two years later I went to the winter-school at the same place, kept by Lewis Olmstead—a man who had a call for plowing, mowing, carting manure, &c., in summer, and for teaching school in the winter. . . . All I remember of his person is his hand, which seemed to me as big as Goliah's, judging by the claps of thunder it made in my ears on one or two occasions.

The next step of my progress which is marked in my memory, is the spelling of words of two syllables. I did not go very regularly to school, but by the time I was ten years old I had learned to write, and had made a little progress in arithmetic. There was not a grammar, a geography, or a history of any kind in the school. Reading, writing, and arithmetic were the only things taught, and these very indifferently—not wholly from the stupidity of the teacher, but because he had forty scholars, and the standards of the age required no more than he performed.

About the middle of the main street, was the Up-town school. . . . At the age of ten years I was sent here, the institution being then, and many years after, under the charge of Master Stebbins.

This seminary of learning for the rising aristocracy of Ridgefield was a wooden edifice, thirty by twenty feet, covered with brown clapboards, and except an entry, consisted of a single room. Around, and against the walls ran a continuous line of seats, fronted by a continuous writing-desk. Beneath, were depositories for books and writing materials. The center was occupied by slab seats, similar to those of West Lane. The larger scholars were ranged on the outer sides, at the desks; the smaller fry of a-b-c-darians were seated in the center. The master was enshrined on the east side of the room. . . .

According to the Catechism—which, by the way, we learned and recited on Saturday—the chief end of man was to glorify God and keep his commandments: according to the routine of this school, one would have thought it to be reading, writing, and arithmetic, to which we may add spelling. . . .

Beyond these simple elements, the Up-town school made few pretensions. When I was there, two Webster's Grammars and one or two Dwight's Geographies were in use. The latter was without maps or illustrations, and was in fact little more than an expanded table of contents, taken from Morse's Universal Geography—the mammoth monument of American learning and genius of that age and generation. The grammar was a clever book; but I have an idea that neither Master Stebbins nor his pupils ever fathomed its depths. They floundered about in it, as if in a quagmire, and after some time came out pretty nearly where they went in, though perhaps a little obfuscated by the dim and dusky atmosphere of these labyrinths.

The fact undoubtedly is, that the art of teaching, as now understood, beyond the simplest elements, was neither known nor deemed necessary in our country schools in their day of small things. Repetition, drilling, line upon line, and precept upon precept, with here and there a little of the birch—constituted the entire system.[8]

District Schools in the South and West

In the South the aristocratic opposition to free schools continued as it had before the Revolution. Comprehensive systems were not established, even by law on paper, until near the outbreak of the Civil War. The attitude there was well characterized by a Kentucky legislative report of 1882, which referred to the Southern aristocrats' reluctance to establish the kind of public education the committee was recommending for Kentucky.

> It cannot be denied, that the holder of wide domains, cultivated by numerous slaves, wallowing in luxury and stimulated by the pride of authority, is not calculated to submit with cheerfulness to those neighborhood regulations, which, in the establishment of free schools, place his children on a level with those of the humblest cottager. But happily, there is not in Kentucky, that great inequality of wealth which can form any serious objection to the proposed system.[9]

The Western frontier had the Kentucky advantage of no "great inequality of wealth," and public education there advanced without as much discrimination as in the older states. Before public financing was available, itinerant schoolmasters would "get up" a school by persuading the settlers of a neighborhood to subscribe for it. An 1891 account drew upon some still living primary sources to describe the frontier school practices of the early century.

> The method of "getting up" a school in the period preceding the mode by taxation and the appropriation of public funds, was this: The applicant for a school would draw an article of agreement, stating what branches he was able to teach, and for what rate of compensation. This paper was passed around from house to house

[8] *Recollections of a Lifetime* (New York: Miller, Orton, and Mulligan, 1856), Vol. I, pp. 33–38, 139–144.

[9] Quoted in Moses Edward Ligon, *A History of Public Education in Kentucky* (Lexington: U. of Kentucky, 1942), p. 61.

> for signatures, and subscriptions payable partly in money and partly in "produce." The tuition of the children of the poor was paid customarily by public-spirited individuals of comfortable fortune. The school terms were usually short, from ten to fifteen weeks of six days each; but the daily sessions were very long, extending over eight and even ten hours. . . .
>
> In the work of the school-room, not much system was used in management or method in instruction. The pupils brought to the school such books as they could obtain, or no books at all. A county judge in Warsaw, Kentucky, told me that his father learned the alphabet from a shingle upon which the letters were scrawled with charcoal. I find no reference to the use of the horn-book in the Ohio Valley. The slate superseded that ancient device. Classification and grading were next to impossible; the scholars studied in their own way, with irregular and incidental help from the teacher. . . . At an uncertain hour, all hands engaged in scribbling copies which the master had "set" in advance, beginning with "pot-hooks," and ending with moral sentences in "round hand." With penknife sharpened to the keenest edge, the master skillfully fashioned into pens the goose-quills brought to his desk. But the culminating exercise was the spelling-match, which usually closed the duties of the day. The scholars, ranged in order along the walls, spelled or "missed" the words pronounced with syllabic precision by the master who stood with ferule in one hand, and Dillworth's Spelling Book in the other, like the genius of education holding up the emblems of power and knowledge.[10]

Philanthropy and Educational Panaceas

Most of the leaders of the United States, conservative as well as liberal, recognized a need for some education for future citizens of a republic, but there was an almost universal reluctance to accept taxation for schooling. Many parents could not afford to pay the tuition or rate bills, and the income from permanent school funds and other limited public sources was not enough to fill the needs. To provide some rudiments of schooling for those children who were denied educational opportunity because of the poverty of their parents and the absence of free, tax-supported schools, public-spirited men and women frequently banded together in societies for the establishment and support of charity

[10] Quoted in W. H. Venable, *Beginnings of Literary Culture in the Ohio Valley* (New York: Peter Smith), 1949, pp. 192–193.

schools. Since there were many children who needed the attention of such schools and the funds available for hiring teachers were limited, the societies were quick to seize on schemes that promised to provide mass education at a cheap price. Three popular schemes during this period were the Sunday school, the monitorial or Lancastrian school, and the infant school.

The Sunday-School Movement

The popularization of the Sunday school is generally attributed to Robert Raikes, a printer in Gloucester, England. In 1780 Raikes hired four women to take a number of urchins into schools on Sunday to teach them to read and to learn the catechism. He publicized his venture in a pamphlet which was apparently read in America, for Sunday schools were established as early as 1786 in Virginia and 1787 in Charleston, South Carolina. The one in Charleston was a school "for African children." Quakers in Philadelphia organized a First-Day School Society in 1791, and similar organizations were soon to be found in many cities, particularly in the Middle and Southern states. Although at first they were non-denominational and attempted to provide lessons in reading, writing, and arithmetic, the Sunday schools quickly came under the control of the churches. By 1820 most of the denominations had Sunday schools of their own. In spite of the fact that Sunday schools were church-related, Jefferson's home state gave aid to Episcopalian and Presbyterian Sunday schools through the Literary Fund. In 1825 Sunday schools in Richmond were given thirty cents for each pupil enrolled and $30 for books and supplies.[11] In some cities Sunday schools were used to teach Negro adults, both free and slave.

Although a major part of the one day's study was religious, it appears that in many communities the Sunday school was the only formal education received by many children. The New York Public School Society reported in 1828 that six hundred children in the City attended no other schools than those on Sunday. But in New York City alone there were still "*twenty-four thousand two hundred* children, within the ages of 5 and 15, who attend no school whatsoever."[12] Although the Sunday schools provided an important service, they were obviously not successful in providing universal education; the enthusiasm of charitable ladies and gentlemen was still exceeded by their fear of paying school taxes

[11] Roy J. Honeywell, *The Educational Work of Thomas Jefferson* (Cambridge: Harvard U. Press), p. 154.

[12] Bourne, p. 111.

The Monitorial School

Perhaps the most notable of the educational panaceas of the first half of the nineteenth century was the mechanical system known as the monitorial or Lancastrian school. Shortly after 1790 an Anglican clergyman named Andrew Bell invented some inexpensive ways of schooling the boys of his orphan asylum near Madras, India. In 1797, having returned to England, he published a description of his experience, and the book was read by a Quaker schoolmaster named Joseph Lancaster. The two had a temporary association, broken up by religious jealousies, but it was Lancaster who popularized the system in England and in the United States. It had great vogue in the United States, Lancaster himself coming to America in 1818 and remaining until his death in 1838.

The essence of the Lancastrian system was the use of student monitors to teach other children. The pupils were organized into "draughts" of ten or more children of the same age. One of each draught joined monitors of other draughts of the same age in being instructed by the master. The monitor then returned to his group to instruct them in what he had just been taught. Meanwhile the master instructed another group of monitors. Other pupils were appointed monitors in charge of checking attendance, maintaining discipline, evaluating progress of the members of their draught, and awarding prizes, which Lancaster advocated as motivation instead of threat and corporal punishment. There were even monitors of monitors and a monitor-general to supervise the whole schoolroom. With this arrangement, it was possible for one master to instruct several hundred, or even a thousand pupils. To help the youthful monitors, Lancaster developed many teaching aids which he believed improved the quality of schooling and had the added virtue of being inexpensive. Since the main cost of schools was the salary of the teacher, the monitorial system together with its cheap materials, had great appeal for American philanthropic school societies.

> A monitorial school, divided into classes of ten, though perfectly orderly, must have been very noisy when in full work. . . . Round the room were six hundred or seven hundred boys in little drafts, singing '*L-e-a-p, leap, to jump.*' The babel was such that I remember on one occasion trying if I should be heard singing 'Black-eyed Susan.' I sang and no one noticed me. . . . I was Monitor of Order at the time. . . .
>
> Lancaster prided himself on having discovered the *best* system of education, but the discovery had been accidental. What he had set out to discover was a *cheap* system; and, whenever he boasted that the article he produced was better than any other, he never forgot

to boast that it also cost less. . . . "By an intire [sic] *new system* of education one thousand children may be taught in one school-room, under the care of one master, and a great proportion of these may begin and finish their education in twelve months; *that* education comprising the art of reading, writing, and arithmetic. . . . The whole expense not exceeding seven shillings each child for twelve months, and probably may be reduced by the perseverance of the inventor under *unmerited opposition* to four."

The same desire to economise, which was the first motive for the use of monitors, was also the first motive for changes in methods of instruction. It was to avoid the cost of reading-books that Lancaster introduced reading-sheets; it was to avoid the cost of paper, pens, and ink that he introduced slates; it was to avoid to cost of arithmetic text-books and the "cyphering"-books into which it was the custom to copy all worked "sums" that he introduced his wonderful "plan whereby any child who can read may teach arithmetic with the utmost certainty."

According to this plan, the monitor was provided with a book of examples and a key, not merely showing the complete solution, but also describing, step by step, the processes by which the "answer" was obtained. If the question were one in simple addition, for instance, the monitor might read from the key—"First column: 7 and 9 are 16, and 3 are 19, and 5 are 24. Set down 4 under the 7 and carry 2 to the next column"; and the class would thereupon set down the 4 as told. It is doubtful whether monitor or pupils would understand these steps, and it is certain that neither would understand the reasons for them. . . .

He introduced one practice which seems almost an inspiration; he combined the lessons in reading, writing and spelling; even the beginners of the alphabet class traced in sand the letters which they were learning to name. . . .[13]

When the New York Free School Society opened its first school in 1806, it utilized the monitorial system. De Witt Clinton, president of the Society, called it "the first scion of the Lancaster stock in the United States," and his praise of the system in an 1809 speech emphasized the cheapness of the system, which he compared to the effect of machinery in saving labor and expense in industry.

It comprehends reading, writing, arithmetic, and the knowledge of the Holy Scriptures. It arrives at its object with the least possible

[13] David Salmon, *Joseph Lancaster* (London: British and Foreign School Society, 1904), pp. 9–10, 11–13.

> trouble and at the least possible expense. Its distinguishing characters are economy, facility, and expedition, and its peculiar improvements are cheapness, activity, order, and emulation.[14]

There did not seem to be any concern expressed by members of the Society for the quality of schooling, but it seems certain that none of the gentlemen who supported the Lancastrian schools in New York sent their own sons and daughters to them.

Lancaster came to the United States in 1818, speaking in a number of cities, visiting legislatures and Congress, and training teachers. Monitorial schools were organized as far south as Savannah and as far west as Texas. Maryland provided for a state system of monitorial schools in 1826 but soon abandoned the project. The will of Stephen Girard, 1831, specified that his legacy of $10,000 was "for the use of the schools upon the Lancaster system" in Philadelphia. About the only area not to adopt the monitorial system was New England, where a system of town schools already existed and where the monitorial schools were characterized as fit to provide only a "very limited degree of instruction, at the least possible expense, to those entirely ignorant."[15]

The major shortcoming of the monitorial system was, of course, the lack of immediate contact between the master and the pupil. Monitors could at best learn only faultily the material they were to teach, and they passed on their ignorance with their knowledge. Successful teaching requires that the teacher know more of his subject than he will attempt to impart to his pupils; it also requires some knowledge about how learning takes place and experience in using that knowledge. It is likely, too, that the masters were not prepared to do a very good job in instructing the monitors, and it is certain that the monitors were quite incapable of doing more than have other pupils repeat imperfectly what they themselves had memorized. The questions of confused children could not be answered and the bright could be challenged only if they had an opportunity to serve as monitors—and that would be a very slight challenge! In addition to the obvious weakness in teaching, the monitorial system must have presented considerable problems in discipline; little children are hardly in a position to discipline their peers with consistency and justice.

As a mechanical device, the system did provide some semblance of

[14] Bourne, p. 18.

[15] Newton Edwards and Herman G. Richey, *The School in the American Social Order* (Boston: Houghton Mifflin, 1947), p. 268.

schooling for many children who would otherwise have had none. What is more important, the large enrollments gave the lie to the conservatives' claim that the lower classes did not want schooling for their children and that public support was not needed for schools. Like the Sunday schools, the Lancastrian schools helped build up a tradition of going to school. People with no schooling often do not see the need for their children to go to school, but those with even a small amount of schooling usually want more of it for their own children. Perhaps it is not an exaggeration to say that the taste of school that many lower class workers got in the Sunday and Lancastrian schools was a primary cause of the working men's agitation for free public schools in the period of the "Common School Revival" of the second American revolution.

The Infant School

A third educational experiment was the infant school. Begun as a humanitarian concern in a radical attempt to create a socialist community, the infant school attracted the attention of the economic conservatives as a means of providing some education to children before they were old enough to go to work in the factories and mills. As with the Sunday school and monitorial school, the infant school was English in origin. In 1815, Robert Owen, the radical socialist and cotton manufacturer of Scotland, assembled about a hundred workers' children between the ages of one and six, hired a man as teacher and a seventeen-year-old girl as assistant, and started a school. Owen's school was more like a modern nursery school or kindergarten than a primary school, for he was more concerned with the "formation of the infant and child character" than with reading or other traditional disciplines.

The school attracted the attention of a schoolmaster named Samuel Wilderspin, who changed the curriculum to attempt to use those early years to provide the rudiments of primary education: reading, writing, arithmetic, a smattering of geography and history, and memorizing parts of the New Testament. It was Wilderspin's version that was copied in the United States in the 1820's. In Philadelphia three infant-school societies were established in 1827–1828; within two years their schools were incorporated into the public school system. In New York a group of ladies organized an infant school in 1827, taking in children between eighteen months and six years of age. The Public School Society assumed the responsibility for the infant schools in New York about a year later, staffing them with women teachers. In 1828 the Society reported on the infant school under its jurisdiction.

The Committee on the Infant School and Junior Department System

REPORT:

. . . .

That the infant mind is capable of receiving instruction at the early age of two or three years; that the inculcation of moral, ideal, and literal knowledge cannot be commenced at too early a period after the faculty of speech is developed; that the formation of good habits is of immense importance even with children of the age in question; that the providing a place in which the younger children of the poor may pass the day comfortably, whilst their parents are engaged in their usual avocations, instead of wandering the streets, exposed to the contamination of vice, is an object worthy the regard of the benevolent. . . .

The infant school in Canal street has on register one hundred and seventy children of both sexes, and from about two to six years of age, the latter being the limit at which any was received. The number in attendance varies from fifty to one hundred. There are two female teachers, a principal, and one assistant, employed at salaries of $200 each. The children are allowed to come early in the morning, and to remain till near dark, bring their dinners with them, or to attend during the usual school hours only. The essence of the system pursued in the school appears to be a judicious combination of instruction and amusement, and that both shall be calculated to form and elicit *ideas*, rather than mere literal knowledge, though this is by no means neglected.[16]

When the other schools of the Society were turned over to the New York Board of Education in 1853, the infant schools, numbering 58 by that time, were included.

Because of the short life of the infant-school movement, it is difficult to determine what effect it had. It was not related to the kindergarten later brought over by German political refugees, but even in its American form, it apparently had some of the non-academic goals which later characterized the kindergarten. Perhaps if the pressure for free public schools had not already become so strong before the infant schools were well under way, they might have played a larger role in the effort to provide "a limited degree of instruction" by philanthropy, thus rationalizing away the need for school taxes.

[16] Bourne, p. 660.

The Public School Society of New York

The most famous of the philanthropic societies for the promotion of schools was the Public School Society of New York. Chartered in 1805 as the Free School Society of New York by about a hundred "opulent and charitable" men of property who viewed with alarm the "torrent of irreligion and vice" among the lower classes, it established charity schools which gradually became more and more dependent on tax support and which ironically helped promote the democratic revolution in education in the 1830's and 1840's until they became a part of the New York public school system in 1853.

In 1795 the legislature appropriated twenty thousand pounds annually for five years "for the purpose of encouraging and maintaining schools in the several cities and towns in this State." The law required the local authorities to match the state contribution with money raised from local taxes. Outside the city this had given rise to district schools partially supported by taxes. The same law authorized New York City to use its share of the annual appropriation for charity schools. Consequently, education in the city had been left to private and denominational schools. Families who could afford it sent their children to private schools and paid tuition. Churches maintained "charity schools" for the children of their denomination who could not afford to pay the tuition of the private schools. But many children were receiving no schooling.

A group of Quaker ladies established a "free" school for girls in 1802. Its success inspired the organization of the Free School Society in 1805. The Society addressed a plea to the general public for contributions to aid in the erection of a school building and in paying the general operating costs of the school. The "Address" reveals clearly the social attitudes of the gentlemen of the Society.

> While the various religious and benevolent societies in this city . . . amply provide for the education of such poor children as belong to their respective associations, there still remains a large number living in total neglect of religious and moral instruction, and unacquainted with the common rudiments of learning, essentially requisite for the due management of the ordinary business of life. This neglect may be imputed either to the extreme indigence of the parents of such children, their intemperance and vice, or to a blind indifference to the best interests of their offspring. . . . Children thus brought up, . . . instead of being useful members of the community, will become the burden and pests of society. Early instruction and fixed habits of industry, decency, and order, are the surest

> safeguards of virtuous conduct. . . . It is in vain that laws are made for the punishment of crimes, or that good men attempt to stem the torrent of irreligion and vice, if the evil is not checked at its source.[17]

More than $5,600 was subscribed, and the school was opened on May 6, 1806, using the Lancastrian system. Enrollment was so large that the Society applied to both the city and the state for assistance. In February, 1807, the legislature appropriated $4,000 for the erection of a building and "every year thereafter, the sum of one thousand dollars, for the purpose of promoting the benevolent objects of the Society." The city provided a larger building to be used temporarily, land for the erection of a permanent school, and $2,000 to be used partly for the repair of the temporary school and partly for the erection of the new school. The new building, completed in 1809, was a two-story structure, with a large schoolroom on the second floor and, on the first, a smaller one to be used for the free school for girls operated by the Quaker ladies and for quarters for the family of the teacher. The large schoolroom could contain "nearly six hundred scholars" and the girls' school a hundred.

The Attempt to Charge Tuition

The monitorial system was copied by the schools of the Dutch Reformed, Episcopalian, Methodist, and Presbyterian Churches and by the Manumission Society's school for "people of color." The use of monitors made it possible to increase the enrollment of these schools, that of the Manumission Society school going from 70 to 130 children.[18] In spite of the efforts of these philanthropies to help more children, there were still thousands who received no schooling. The Free School Society therefore built more schools, until there were more than twenty-six thousand pupils enrolled in the Society's fifty schools by 1851. In 1825 the trustees applied to the legislature for permission to reorganize, charging tuition of those who could afford to pay and giving the Free School Society the full share of money from the school fund which was due all the charitable schools in the city. The trustees of the Society argued that this would assure a more efficient expenditure of funds and provide a better quality of schooling for children of the poor. Permitting parents to pay a small tuition would, the trustees said, remove the stigma of charity attached to the schools of the Society.

[17] *Ibid.*, p. 6.
[18] *Ibid.*, p. 22.

Some of the defects in the present system of elementary education among the lower and poorer classes of society may be stated as follows:

1st. *Of the private pay schools.*

Of the four hundred schools which have been ascertained to be in operation in this city, a large number are kept in small rooms, without sufficient light or ventilation, or a due regard to cleanliness—requisites so essential to the health and comfort of youth—and which schools are, in numerous instances, taught by persons without the necessary qualifications for the discharge of their important trusts, and, in some cases, even of doubtful morals. On such teachers is the hard-earned money of our industrious citizens too often wasted, and—what is of much greater consequence—in such schools is the invaluable time of their offspring irretrievably lost.

The great variety of plans pursued in the different schools, and the various and dissimilar school-books used in them, retards the progress of, and increases the expense to, children removed from one to another. . . .

2d. *Of the free and charity schools.*

The school fund, by being divided and distributed through so many channels, is rendered incapable of as economical management, and of producing so great an amount of good, as would be the case were it under the control and applied to its intended purposes by a single society having but the alone object in view of general education.

A fund designed for the civil education of the youth of this State is in part placed at the disposal of religious societies.

Most of the parents of children in the free and charity schools, though unable to pay for their instruction the prices usually charged in pay schools, could probably afford to make some compensation for the education of their children; and, if so, the propriety of their entirely gratuitous instruction is questionable. . . .

In consequence of the poor condition of many of the minor pay schools, and of the very superior instruction and accommodation in our free schools, applications are sometimes made to the trustees of the latter for the admission of children of poor but industrious citizens, provided they may be allowed to pay a small sum annually for that which they are unwilling to receive as a gratuity. . . .[19]

Legislative permission was granted in 1826 to change the name of the Society and to charge tuition, provided that "no child shall be denied the benefits of the said institution, merely on the ground of inability to pay for the same, but shall at all times be freely received and educated

[19] *Ibid.*, pp. 86–87.

by the said trustees."[20] Contrary to the expectations of the trustees, enrollments did not rise when the Society was permitted to charge tuition. Perhaps parents felt there was a greater stigma attached to being "charity" students in a pay school than being "charity" students in a school where everyone else was also attending free. At any rate, enrollments dropped significantly for the first time in the history of the Society, from 4,384 in 1824 to 3,739 in 1826.

Return to Free Schools and Tax Support

Alarmed at the decrease in enrollment, the trustees in 1828 published a public address advocating that more tax support be given the schools so that all children, regardless of financial condition, might be permitted to attend free, thus removing the stigma of charity for everyone. The fact that the trustees in 1828 would advocate a property tax, even though a small one, is evidence that public sentiment was beginning to change, that a new revolution was developing. The changed attitudes toward the working man were more characteristic of Jacksonian democracy than of aristocratic federalism. The proposals anticipated the development of schools supported and controlled by public agencies, instead of by the quasi-public School Society. Some of the phrases are haunting echoes of the old Enlightenment proposals.

> The laboring classes have been justly called the backbone and sinews of the republic. It is not enough that they know how to read, write, and cast accounts. We wish to provide for them better excitements than they now have. We wish them to enjoy the pleasures, as well as other advantages, of intellectual occupation. We wish them to be able to understand and admire the beneficence of the Creator in the works of His hands. We wish them to feel that virtue is the first distinction among men, and knowledge the second, and to be themselves the great exemplar of these truths. . . .
>
> We hold that . . . our schools are the very foundation upon which rest the peace, good order, and prosperity of society. . . .
>
> [S]chools should be supported from the public revenue, should be public property, and should be open to all, not as a charity, but as a matter of common right.
>
> We propose that infant schools should be established throughout the city, to receive children from three to six years of age. . . .
>
> In the next place, we would greatly enlarge the number of schools in which a common English education is taught. A very great majority of the scholars will leave these schools at the age of 15,

[20] *Ibid.*, pp. 101–102.

or at an earlier period. These schools should be provided with such means of instruction as are best calculated to fit their pupils for the various departments of mechanic, mercantile, and agricultural industry. . . .

Next in importance to this object is the establishment of one or more high schools, in which should be taught practical mathematics, natural philosophy, bookkeeping, and, in short, all those branches which are desirable for the active business of life in any of its departments, the learned professions excepted.

We would also recommend, if the means to be provided should be sufficient for that purpose, a classical school, in which the ancient and modern languages should be thoroughly taught.

To all these should be added a seminary for the education of at least such teachers as are required for common schools. . . .

To effect this object, the trustees would recommend a tax of half a mill upon the dollar on the amount of property in the city, according to its valuation in the present estimates of assessment. The fund thus to be raised should be forever kept separate from all other taxes, and sacred to the purposes for which it was created. . . .

We submit to the liberal consideration of the rich, whether their proportion of this money, expended for the purpose of disseminating wholesome knowledge and pure morals, would not be a profitable investment for their children? . . .

[I]t will be perceived that, with regard to a great portion of them, and particularly the children of emigrants, we must choose between the expenses of their education and the cost of their maintenance in our almshouses and penitentiaries. It is proof enough of this, that, small as is the proportion of those who cannot read and write to our whole population, they constitute the majority of our convicts and paupers.

The more the community is enlightened, the more equally will its burdens be borne. It has not, perhaps, been sufficiently considered by political economists, that national wealth chiefly proceeds from the activity of mind, and must, therefore, be proportioned to the extent and universality of its development.[21]

The legislature was not ready to go as far as the Society trustees suggested, but in 1829 they did grant the Society the income from a tax of 1/80 of 1 percent on real and personal property in the city, far less than the 1/20 of 1 percent proposed by the Society. Two years later the tax was increased to the one-half mill requested, and the following year all tuitions were abolished for the schools of the Society. The fully articulated system outlined in the 1828 proposal did not come into

[21] *Ibid.*, pp. 113–117.

being until after the Board of Education was established in 1842, the result of a conflict over the separation of church and state in religion. When New York City's first truly public schools appeared in 1843, the enrollment of the schools of the Society dropped steadily until they were merged in 1853 with those operated by the Board of Education, which was receiving all the public moneys. During the period from 1807 to 1852, the Society had enrolled nearly half a million pupils in its schools, spending something over $3.5 millions. As an effort to secure cheap education, the Society could point with pride to its average annual per capita cost of only $4.29, which had reached a low point of $1.37 in 1822. The life of the Society had spanned the period from the time when protection of property rights was supreme to the time when the human rights of the common man were the great concern of the political and social leaders as well as of the common man himself.

The activities of the Society covered another important aspect of the development of the modern school—the increasing secularization of public education. The role of the Public School Society in the conflict over the support of denominational schools with tax money will be discussed in detail in a later chapter.

Private Schools

All the schools discussed above were intended for children of parents who could not afford to pay tuition or who would not make the necessary sacrifice to do so. For the more affluent or more ambitious, private schools existed, particularly in the Eastern cities. However, it must be admitted that even these institutions did not go very far in providing quality education. The schools of Boston were among the best, but one account of them between 1805 and 1815 is quite critical of the content included in the lessons and of the ineffective teaching methods used, as well as of the continual use of corporal punishment. The following account was written by Henry K. Oliver, son of a prominent Boston clergyman; Oliver later graduated from Dartmouth and Harvard, taught at Salem Latin School and the English High School in Boston, and was a private schoolmaster from 1830–1844, before going into business and politics. His account was written in 1871.

> In the year 1805, or thereabouts, being then something under five years of age, I was first placed under educational influence, consigned to the care of one Mr. Hayslop, who, with his wife and widowed daughter, . . . kept school in an old building . . . on the

second floor, where ruled and feruled the good old master. . . . By him I was taught my A,B,C,D,E,F,G, my a,b, abs, and my e,b, ebs, after the old, old way . . . the old gentleman holding an old book in his old hand, and pointing, with an old pin, to the old letters on the old page, and making each of us chicks repeat their several names, till we could tell them at sight, though we did not know what it was all for. We must have been bright set, excellent of memory, for by this excellent old method, and with the excellent old books of the old times, and the excellent old teacher, and our own excellent young wits, we were not more than four or five weeks in acquiring complete knowledge of the twenty-six arbitrary marks constituting the English Alphabet. To be sure, I learnt the names, family and Christian, of all my fellow scholars, and they were quite a host, in a week; but that was, as it were, naturally . . . while to learn the letters, must only be done after the good old fashion of the ancestral teaching. . . .

From this school I was removed to another, Madam Tileston's . . . of the same nature, where I was taught elementary reading and spelling, after the same ancestral fashion; that is, I received about twenty minutes of instruction each half day, and as school was kept three hundred and sixty minutes daily, I had the privilege of forty minutes' worth of teaching, and three hundred and twenty minutes' worth of sitting still, (if I could), which I could not,—playing, whispering, and general waste of time, though occasionally a picture book relieved the dreary monotony.

My nervous temperament, dislike of confinement at busy nothingness, want of affection for books,—slates then we had none,—love of mischief, and general habit of fidgetiness, often entitled me to Madam Tileston's customary punishment of sundry smart taps on the head, with the middle finger of her right hand;—said finger being armed, for its own defense, with a large and rough steel thimble. . . . Both of these teachers taught as well as they knew how. . . . Nobody taught any better, as far as I have learnt. Nor was there anything like the philosophy of teaching known or thought of, so far as I can now judge on retrospection, by any teacher into whose hands I fell. . . .

There were no schools systematically graded; there were no blackboards; there were no globes, nor other ordinary school apparatus in schools I attended. I never saw a full-sized map, nor illustrative picture of any sort suspended against the school walls. . . . The method of teaching the science of numbers was utterly unscientific. . . . Geography was studied but sparingly, and from very defective books, and mostly without maps. School-houses, school-rooms, and school furniture, were all at the lowest point of inconvenience. . . . Children were huddled together in small, close, unventilated apart-

> ments, regardless of both health and comfort, and of those proper surroundings of seclusion and stillness, that render study a success, and successful teaching practicable. . . .
>
> Corporal chastisement was in full tide of successful experiment. Of the eight different teachers under whose care I fell before I entered college, but one of them possessed any bowels of mercy. He hit me, but in a single instance, and that was for the crime of having left my leg a little out in the passageway between the desks. This was done with a stoutish piece of rattan, though the flogging instruments mostly in use were the cowhide and the ferule. . . .
>
> Reaching the age of nine years, it was deemed to be time for me to commence my '*Singulariter Nominativo, hic, haec, hoc,*' and this I did under . . . Master Ebenezer Pemberton . . . who taught a few pupils at his private school. . . .
>
> This grim and melancholy work was only relieved by an occasional lesson in spelling . . . and a weekly exercise in declamation.
>
> Thus toiling on, I reached the age of ten years, and all I knew, was how to read pretty well, how to write and spell pretty ill, how to declaim pretty well, and the orthography, etymology, and syntax of . . . Latin grammar pretty ill. . . .
>
> Of geography and arithmetic I literally knew nothing, and less than nothing of the grammar of my own language.[22]

The continued reliance on the "excellent old method" and the "excellent old books" long after Enlightenment leaders had called for significant changes in schooling to meet the new needs of a new nation is evidence of the conservatism of the period. It would take a new revolution in education to make any great change.

Perspective on Conservatism

The conservative reaction to the American Revolution gave birth to educational practices far short of those which had been called for by the Enlightenment leaders. Meager district schools, permanent school funds, rate bills, and philanthropy were all attempts to avoid having to pay for the degree of schooling necessary in a successful democracy. Even with novel educational arrangements, such as the monitorial school, it became apparent that society must assume a greater responsibility for the education of all children if equality were to be achieved. As the "common man" rose to more importance—economic, social, and politi-

[22] "Schools as They Were in the United States," *Barnard's American Journal of Education,* 26, pp. 209–215.

cal—in the Jacksonian era, America was to experience a new revolution in educational opportunity.

The failures of this period can be instructive for times when economy or class privilege seems more important than the full educational development of all the children of the society. Education for democracy is not inexpensive, and "cheapness" may perhaps best be achieved by providing the adequate schooling that will help produce capable citizens and productive workers for the myriad economic tasks of society. The shortcomings of the monitorial, Sunday, and infant schools should be a warning against the ready acceptance of panaceas; no solution is so perfect that it does not create its own problems.

QUESTIONS FOR DISCUSSION

1. There is some suggestion in present-day political and social developments that the United States may be in a period of conservative reaction. What educational practices in the Federalist period can you see paralleled in some current educational practices in the United States? What dangers do you anticipate on the basis of what occurred in the Federalist period?
2. One current experiment in mass education is the use of television. There are some educational television proposals that somewhat resemble the Lancastrian monitorial system. What pitfalls might be avoided by a study of the failure of the monitorial schools? What are some ways in which some of the monitorial techniques might be successfully adapted for effective television teaching?
3. Many Americans complain about the cost of public schooling and suggest that the schools be financed in part by fees and public gifts. What consequences for education might be anticipated on the basis of experiences in the period from 1789 to 1828?

SUGGESTED READINGS

Cubberley, Ellwood P. *Readings in the History of Education.* Boston: Houghton Mifflin, 1920. Pp. 417–423, 425–427.

———. *Readings in Public Education in the United States.* Boston: Houghton Mifflin, 1934. Pp. 130–145.

Knight, Edgar W. *A Documentary History of Education in the South Before 1860.* Chapel Hill: U. of North Carolina Press, 1950. Vol. II, pp. 156–158; Vol. V, pp. 4–5, 21–35, 317–334.

Knight, Edgar W., and Hall, Clifton L. *Readings in American Educational History.* New York: Appleton-Century-Crofts, 1951. Pp. 135–145, 150–151.

Monroe, Paul. *The Founding of the American Public School System.* Ann Arbor: University Microfilms, 1940. Vol. II, pp. 972–1028.

6

Secondary and Higher Education —Revolution and Reaction

The social revolution which culminated in the Colonies' winning their independence had developed over several decades. One of the earliest changes in colonial institutions was in the education which followed the common school. The Latin grammar school did not meet the needs of the new society struggling to be born, and long before political and economic protests began to be heard, a new form of secondary schooling was becoming popular—the practical, private evening school. Its most revolutionary form was Franklin's Academy in Philadelphia. In the new republic the academy was to replace the Latin school, but with the conservative reaction to the Revolution, the democratic characteristics of secondary education were very limited; the academy was far from the "people's college" many historians have called it.

The revolution in higher education came late in the revolutionary cycle. Jefferson's attempts to reform William and Mary, the attempt of New York to take over Columbia College, and the first state universities were all consistent with the Enlightenment's concern for an educational system that would include the highest as well as the lowest educational institutions. But before any of the radical Enlightenment proposals could be developed into radically new institutions, they were defeated, compromised, or weakened by the conservative attitudes of the Federalist period. Even near the end of the conservative period, the Dartmouth College case and the founding of the University of Virginia brought sharp conservative reactions.

The Academy Movement

Between the Revolutionary and Civil Wars, the academy supplanted the Latin school as the common form of secondary school. Many of the earliest academies developed out of private schools. For example, in Maryland, where the county schools had been sadly neglected before the Revolutionary War, an old field school founded in Somerset County by "several gentlemen of different religious persuasion" in 1767, accepted a few outside children from time to time, until in 1779 it was incorporated as Washington Academy.[1] The private academy was very popular among the Southern aristocrats, and academies rapidly increased in number. Although many of them were little more than elementary schools, they assumed the function of preparing the sons of gentlemen for the colleges and universities. As with Franklin's school in Philadelphia, the radical ideal of the academy as a practical school useful to all citizens in a republic was subordinated, and the academies of the South and New England were soon favoring the class-oriented goals of the plantation and commercial aristocracies of the two regions.

New England's Academies

Two famous New England academies were those founded by the Phillips family, the first in Andover, Massachusetts, chartered in 1780, and the other at Exeter, New Hampshire, chartered in 1781. Gifts from the Phillips family in 1778 started the school with a "constitution" which proposed

> to lay the foundation of a public free SCHOOL or ACADEMY for the purpose of instructing Youth, not only in English and Latin Grammar, Writing, Arithmetic, and those Sciences wherein they are commonly taught; but more especially to learn them the GREAT END AND REAL BUSINESS OF LIVING. . . . the *first* and *principal* object of this institution is the promotion of true PIETY and VIRTUE; the *second*, instruction in the English, Latin, and Greek Languages, together with Writing, Arithmetic, Music, and the Art of Speaking; the *third*, practical Geometry, Logic, and Geography; and the *fourth*, such other of the liberal Arts and Sciences or languages, as opportunity and ability may hereafter admit.[2]

DECLINE OF THE PUBLIC GRAMMAR SCHOOLS The academies had a much broader curriculum than the old Latin schools, and they fitted the needs of the new republic better. They multiplied in the years following the chartering of the Phillips schools, and in 1789 the Massachusetts

[1] Steiner, p. 39 fn.
[2] Quoted in Brown, p. 195.

school law, perhaps in recognition of the spread of the private academy, lowered the requirement for town support of Latin schools. Under the old grammar school law, which required towns of one hundred families to support a Latin master, there were 230 towns in 1789 which were required to have a grammar school. Under the new law, which put the obligation of supporting a grammar school only on towns of two hundred families, 120 towns were relieved of the responsibility. In 1824 the requirement was further changed, specifying that towns of five thousand inhabitants were to have a school of secondary grade, and this left only seven towns in the whole of Massachusetts required to have a town secondary school. Furthermore, the state, which had granted public lands to seven academies, including four in Maine, changed its policy in 1797 to support only those academies that had substantial private endowments.

> [N]o State lands ought to be granted to any academy, but in aid of permanent funds, secured by towns or individual donors; and therefore, previous to any such grant of State lands, evidence ought to be produced that such funds are legally secured, at least adequate to erect and repair the necessary buildings, to support the corporation, to procure and preserve such apparatus and books as may be necessary, and to pay a part of the salaries of the preceptors.[3]

This was clearly a departure from the Puritan tradition of government responsibility for free secondary education for all those boys who could profit from it, and the old revolutionary firebrand Samuel Adams took notice of that fact in his inaugural address as governor in 1795.

> It is with satisfaction that I have observed the patriotic exertions of worthy citizens to establish academies in various parts of the Commonwealth. . . . But while it is acknowledged that great advantages have been derived from these institutions, perhaps it may be justly apprehended that multiplying them may have a tendency to injure the ancient and beneficial mode of education in town grammar schools.
>
> The peculiar advantages of such schools is that the poor and the rich may derive equal benefit from them; but none excepting the more wealthy, generally speaking, can avail themselves of the benefit of the academies. Should these institutions detach the attention and influence of the wealthy from the generous support of the town schools, is it not to be feared that useful learning, instruction, and

[3] *Ibid.*, pp. 216–217.

> social feelings in the early parts of life may cease to be so equally and universally disseminated as it has heretofore been?[4]

Adams' fears were realized, and public secondary education virtually disappeared in Massachusetts until the rise of the public high school.

State Help Outside of New England

By 1800 all the states had some academies. In the middle seaboard states there was some effort toward state support and control. New York, under the supervision of the University of the State of New York, gave support through land grants, special appropriations and, after 1813, the interest of the Literature Fund. Pennsylvania made appropriations to academies at irregular intervals. Maryland set up a system of county academies, replacing the pre-Revolutionary county grammar schools, and by 1812 there was state support for academies in each county. On the frontier, public support was common. Tennessee, while it was still part of North Carolina, established its first academy at Nashville in 1785 and endowed it with a grant of land. In 1806 Congress extended to Tennessee a land grant of 100,000 acres for the support of two colleges, 100,000 acres for the support of an academy in each county, and 640 acres in each township for the support of common schools. The Tennessee legislature promptly set up boards of trustees for academies in twenty-seven counties. While still a part of Virginia, settlers in Kentucky took advantage of the permissive legislation of Virginia to establish two academies, both endowed by land grants. In 1798 the Kentucky legislature chartered twenty-five academies and seminaries and endowed each with 6,000 acres of land. By 1820 Kentucky had established forty-seven county academies, with land grant endowments of 6,000 to 12,000 acres.[5]

In all these states, problems developed from the land grants. Land was cheap, and the endowments were rarely properly managed. The schools were often inaccessible to many children, and since no tax appropriations were made for most of these institutions, tuition was a major source of income. The expense prevented many children from attending unless they were among the small number of "charity scholars" or "free scholars" at some of the state-aided academies. As a consequence, the academies tended to be patronized by the children of the more-or-less well-to-do. In some states, such as Kentucky, the public academies soon failed financially and were replaced by private academies and short-term public common schools. Thus the aristocratic, conservative pattern of the old South prevailed in the old Southwest.

[4] Cubberley, p. 216.
[5] Brown, pp. 219–220.

Girls and Normal Courses

In addition to the broadened curriculum, the academies furthered two other important aspects of American education: extension to girls of educational opportunity beyond the common school, and the beginning of special preparation for those who were to be teachers in the common schools. During the Colonial period, very few girls received any schooling beyond the rudiments of reading and writing. The exceptions were those who attended the private venture or evening schools. The academy movement included many schools expressly founded for girls, and in the West many academies were co-educational. One particular attraction for girls in the academy was the "normal" or teacher-training course, since it was not uncommon for women to teach the summer term or serve as assistants to men in large schools during the winter term of the common school. One of the purposes of Franklin's academy had been to qualify "a number of the poorer Sort . . . to act as Schoolmasters in the Country." Although there were more opportunities for girls to teach, most of the teachers, even of the common schools, were men, and the normal departments of the academies were intended for schoolmasters as well as schoolmistresses.

One of the earliest attempts (1823–1830) to provide special training for teachers was the seminary of the Reverend Samuel Read Hall at Concord Corners, New Hampshire. In 1829 he published the first important book on pedagogy written in English and published in the United States, *Lectures on Schoolkeeping*, which became one of the most common texts used in normal schools and normal departments of academies until after the Civil War. The program he established at Phillips Andover in 1830 was a model for other institutions. He provided for terms that would not coincide with the winter term of the common schools, since his older students would generally be teaching during those terms to finance their academy education.

> In the TEACHER'S DEPARTMENT are *three classes*. The course of study can be accomplished in three years. . . . Candidates for admission to the junior class must be prepared to pass a satisfactory examination on the sounds of English letters, rules of spelling, reading, geography, first principles of etymology and syntax, intellectual arithmetic, history of the United States, ground rules of written arithmetic, and fractions. The year is divided into *three* terms, and the following studies are pursued at each:
>
> JUNIOR CLASS
>
> First Term.—English, Grammar; Intellectual Arithmetic, *reviewed;* History of the United States, *reviewed.*

Second Term.—Written Arithmetic; Geography, ancient and modern; History of England.

Third Term.—Written Arithmetic, *finished;* Linear Drawing; Construction of Maps; Use of Globes; Book-keeping.

MIDDLE CLASS

First Term.—Algebra; Euclid; Rhetoric.

Second Term.—Algebra, *finished;* Trigonometry; Chemistry.

Third Term.—Chemistry, *finished;* Surveying; Spherical Geometry. Conic Sections.

SENIOR CLASS

First Term.—Natural Philosophy; Logic; Civil Engineering.

Second Term.—Natural Theology; Evidences of Christianity; Moral Philosophy; Astronomy.

Third Term.—Political Economy; Intellectual Philosophy; Art of Teaching.

All the members of the junior class attend to the "*Political Class Book*" on Saturdays, and declamation and composition on Wednesdays, throughout the year. The middle and senior classes write compositions on subjects connected with the art of teaching.

Lectures are given, accompanied with illustrations and experiments, on the most important studies; particularly, natural philosophy, chemistry, and school keeping. Each one who finishes the course will have attended more than fifty lectures on the latter subject.[6]

The practice of using academies to train teachers for the common schools became general in the United States. The Regents of New York urged in the *Annual Report* for 1826 that "Teachers for the common schools must generally be derived from the academies." Two years later the legislature increased the appropriation from the Literature Fund to the incorporated academies "to promote the education of teachers."[7]

Academies Numerous but Often Transitory

A great many of the academies were small, having only one or two teachers. Although some were the ancestors of still existing high schools and colleges, others were very short-lived and changed their location from time to time. It is difficult to determine just how many academies there were during this period. According to an article published in 1833, Maine had 32 academies, with about 1,200 students and property value and endowments totalling $250,000. New Hampshire had 30 "academies

[6] *Barnard's American Journal of Education*, Vol. V, p. 379.
[7] Cubberley, p. 331.

and other public schools"; Vermont "about thirty-five academies and high schools, but not all in actual operation." Massachusetts had 83 academies and private secondary schools, 21 of which had received land and endowment from the state. Rhode Island had one boarding school and one "English and classical seminary"; Connecticut had 14 of academy grade. New York was reported as having 57 academies with buildings and endowments amounting to $400,000 and a $10,000 annual appropriation from the state. Pennsylvania had 92 academies and high schools, with endowments ranging from $500 to $10,000. Delaware had one academy "lately established," and in Maryland "There are several academies, which receive $800 a year from the state treasury." In Virginia 55 academies were reported, in Georgia 4, and in South Carolina 32 were listed as in existence in 1826. The number in North Carolina was not "ascertained." Twelve were mentioned in Kentucky, but as for Ohio, "We are not aware that there are any flourishing incorporated academies in that State."[8]

The academy continued as the dominant secondary school until after the Civil War, when it was replaced by the high school, which was eventually to become the democratic extension of the universal schooling advocated by the more radical Enlightened philosophers of the Revolutionary era.

The First High Schools

Boston's English High School

The first public high school was founded in Boston, where the famed Latin School had been the public secondary school for almost two centuries. In 1818 Boston extended its free schools downward to include primary education, which traditionally had been limited to private and charity schools, and in 1820 the school committee recommended to the town meeting the establishment of an "English Classical School" for those primary-school students not interested in a classical secondary education. The proposal was opposed by the Boston *Advertiser*, which warned that the new school would "degrade" the "English Grammar Schools" and "withdraw a portion of the patronage which is now bestowed on the Latin School."

In spite of this opposition, the town meeting, on January 15, 1821, adopted a report establishing the English Classical School, later named the English High School.

[8] Quoted in Brown, pp. 224–225.

> Till recently, our system [of public education] occupied a middle station: it neither commenced with the rudiments of Education, nor extended to the higher branches of knowledge. This system was supported by the Town at a very great expense, and to be admitted to its advantages, certain preliminary qualifications were required at individual cost, which have the effect of excluding many children of the poor . . . from the benefits of a public education. The Town . . . removed the defect by providing Schools in which the children of the poor can be fitted for admission into the public seminaries.
>
> The studies that are pursued at the English grammar schools are merely elementary. . . . A scholar is admitted at seven, and is dismissed at fourteen years of age; thus, seven years are expended in the acquisition of a degree of knowledge, which with ordinary diligence and a common capacity, may be easily and perfectly acquired in five. . . . This evil . . . should be removed, by enlarging the present system. . . .
>
> The branches of knowledge that are taught at our English grammar schools, are not sufficiently extensive nor otherwise calculated to bring the powers of the mind into operation nor to qualify a youth to fill usefully and respectfully many of those stations, both public and private, in which he may be placed. A parent who wishes to give a child an education that shall fit him for active life, and shall serve as a foundation for eminence in his profession, whether Mercantile or Mechanical, is under the necessity of giving him a different education from any which our public schools can now furnish. Hence, many children are separated from their parents and sent to private academies in this vicinity, to acquire that instruction which cannot be obtained at the public seminaries. . . .
>
> The Committee . . . recommend the founding of a seminary which shall be called the English Classical School, and submit the following general outline of a plan for its organization and of the course of studies to be pursued.[9]

The plan provided for a three-year course for boys; entrants had to be at least twelve years old and qualified in reading, writing, English grammar, and arithmetic "as far as simple proportion." Candidates would be admitted on the basis of examination in these subjects. The studies in the first year were "Composition. Reading from the most approved authors. Exercises in Criticism; comprising critical analyses of the language, grammar, and style of the best English authors, their errors & Beauties. Declamation. Geography. Arithmetic continued." The second year continued composition, reading, exercises in criticism, declamation,

[9] *Ibid.*, pp. 298–300.

and algebra, and added "Ancient and Modern History and Chronology. Logic. Geometry. Plane Trigonometry; and its application to mensuration of Heights and Distances. Navigation. Surveying. Mensuration of Superfices & Solids. Forensic Discussion." In the third year the boys continued composition, exercises in criticism, declamation, mathematics, logic, and history, "particularly that of the United States," and they added "Natural Philosophy, including Astronomy; Moral and Political Philosophy." The school actually opened in May, 1821, with approximately a hundred pupils.[10]

High Schools Slow in Appearing

Although the Boston school was not known as a "high school" until 1824, the term had apparently been used earlier in the American colonies. Among the German settlers in Pennsylvania there were, as far back as the 1760's, schools known as "high schools." Possibly they were schools which taught the more advanced levels of reading and writing and perhaps Latin and Greek. Possibly the name was derived from the German *Hochschule*, but the Scots had used the term "high school" for some time, and John Harrower's diary referred to the school in Fredericksburg, Virginia, in 1775 as a "high school."[11]

When John Griscom, a New York Quaker, returned from a visit to Europe, he published a two-volume account of his travels, a portion of which was reproduced in the January, 1824, number of the *North American Review*. The article included Griscom's observations of the Edinburgh High School, which was teaching the classical languages on the monitorial system. The article reported that the city of Boston paid "at least twice as much for the instruction of a boy in its admirable Latin School, as is paid for the instruction of a boy at the High School, in the more expensive city of Edinburgh" and recommended that the monitorial system be used in America for secondary education. Griscom himself organized a "High School Society" in New York, which opened a "High School for Boys" in 1825 and a "Female High School" in 1826. Both of these used the monitorial system, and the boys' school opened with more than six hundred pupils. The subjects included spelling, writing, arithmetic, geography, elocution, composition, drawing, philosophy, natural history, and bookkeeping. Apparently the monitorial system was somewhat modified for these high schools: the first report of the Society states that "Philosophy and Natural History are taught chiefly by lectures and by questions."[12]

[10] *Ibid.*, pp. 300–301.
[11] *The American Historical Review*, 6 (October, 1900): 98.
[12] Quoted in Brown, pp. 306–307.

Not even the introduction of the inexpensive monitorial techniques could make the public high school popular in that period of social, economic, and political conservatism. Very few cities were to follow the lead of Boston in offering limited public secondary schooling, nor were many to emulate the still more conservative New York monitorial high schools. Even in Massachusetts the early high-school movement was to suffer serious setbacks. One was the short life of the girls' high school in Boston, and another was the failure of the law requiring certain towns to have public high schools.

Girls' High School in Boston

Before 1826 girls in Boston were permitted to attend grammar schools between the months of April and October, but that was the limit of their opportunity for schooling in the public schools. The School Committee in 1825 began consideration of a "public school for the instruction of girls in the higher departments of science and literature," partly as an experiment in the use of the monitorial system for the Boston grammar schools. The success of the English High School for boys prompted the Committee to go ahead with the girls' school, which opened in February, 1826. Candidates had to be between the ages of eleven and fifteen and pass an examination on the studies taught in the public grammar (elementary) schools. The three-year course consisted of required subjects and electives. The required subjects included reading, spelling, writing words and sentences from dictation, English grammar, composition, modern and ancient geography, intellectual and written arithmetic, rhetoric, history of the United States, bookkeeping, geometry, natural philosophy, general history, history of England, natural theology, astronomy, treatise on the globes, chemistry, history of Greece and Rome, moral philosophy, and evidences of Christianity. First-year students were "allowed" to take logic or botany; second-year students logic, botany, demonstrative geometry, algebra, Latin, or French; and third-year students logic, algebra, principles of perspective, projection of maps, botany, Latin, or French.

On the day of the first entrance examination, 286 girls applied for admission, more than twice as many as could be accommodated in the large schoolroom which had been provided. A committee selected 130 girls from those who scored highest on the examination. The following year it appeared that there would be over four hundred applications, and so the School Committee raised the age level from eleven to fourteen, increased the entrance requirements, and reduced the length of the course to one year. In 1828, facing the prospect of between 800 and 1200 candidates, the School Committee solved the problem by abolishing the school! Girls were then permitted to remain in the English grammar schools for the full year, instead of the six months from April to October, and the studies taught in the high school for girls were to be included in the grammar and writing schools. The final conservative blow came in the recommendation to put the monitorial system into "all our public Grammar and Writing schools, as soon as it is practicable" and "also into our Primary Schools." Up to that time, Boston had resisted the monitorial system in the public schools. Not until 1854 did Boston again have a high school for girls.[13]

Massachusetts' High-School Law

Massachusetts had required towns of a certain size to maintain secondary schools ever since the "Ould Deluder" law of 1647, but successive reenactments had raised the population limits, thus exempting more cities from the requirement. The low point was the 1824 version, which permitted towns of less than five thousand to substitute elementary schools for grammar schools. Against this relaxation of legislative requirements, James G. Carter maintained a continuing crusade, resulting in improved legislation in 1827. The 1827 law did not give names to the schools it required but instead defined them by the subjects they were to teach. Towns of fifty householders were required to provide a school that would teach elementary subjects. Towns or districts of at least five hundred families were required, in addition, to have a master "competent to instruct . . . the history of the United States, Bookkeeping by single entry, geometry, surveying, algebra." And towns of four thousand inhabitants were required to have a master to teach Latin, Greek, history, rhetoric, and logic.[14] Although the term "high school" does not appear in the law and the tradition of requiring Latin in school had been followed for nearly two centuries in Massachusetts, this law is often described as the first to make the creation of high schools mandatory. In any event, it is clear that the secondary curriculum specified by this law is much broader than those set up by earlier laws. From the small number of high schools established in Massachusetts after passage of this law, however, it is apparent that it was neither strictly adhered to nor enforced with any rigor.[15]

[13] Brown, "Secondary Education in the United States," *The School Review* (January, 1899): 286–294.

[14] *Laws of Massachusetts,* 1826, Chapter 143:1.

[15] One textbook in the history of education states that two years after the enactment of the 1827 law "all its force was lost when its provisions were made permissive instead of mandatory." (Adolphe E. Meyer, *An Educational History of the American*

High schools did not rapidly increase in number following the pioneer efforts in Massachusetts and New York. Even in the period leading up to the Civil War, secondary education was dominated by the academy, and the development of the high school was not to come until after the Civil War.

Public Higher Education—Trials and Failures

Columbia College

The traditional close association of secondary schooling with colleges was illustrated by the events leading to the creation of the University of the State of New York. When King's College was projected in 1753, William Livingston proposed legislation to provide two grammar schools in every county in New York and put the college under the control of the provincial government. In a bitter conflict between the Tories and Anglicans on one side and dissenters and liberal republicans, who favored more power for the legislature, on the other, the Tories and Anglicans won; and King's College was created as an Anglican institution with certain concessions to other denominations, particularly the Dutch Reformed Church.

In 1784, within six months after the British had evacuated New York, the liberals renewed their efforts to have the college put under state control. The legislature created a new corporation called the "Regents of the University of the State of New York" and vested it with "full power and authority to ordain and make ordinances and bye laws for the government of the several Colleges which may or shall compose the said University," to found "Schools and Colleges in any such part of the State as may seem expedient to them and to endow" them, granting the colleges the right to confer bachelor of arts degrees and to "visit and examine into the state of literature in such College." The Regents were directed to elect a president and professors of King's College, the name of which was to be changed to Columbia College. The board was to include representatives of the "respective religious denominations in this State," but "no Professor shall in any way whatsoever be accounted

---

People, McGraw-Hill, 1957, p. 191.) There is no reference in *The Annotated Laws of Massachusetts* to support such a statement. In 1836, when the Massachusetts statutes were revised, an act was passed "To Repeal Expressly All the Acts Which Are Consolidated in the Revised Statutes," and among those "expressly repealed" was the "act to provide for the instruction of youth" which had been passed in the 1826–1827 session of the legislature. *Revised Statutes*, Chapter 146, 1836.

ineligible, for or by reason of any religious tenet or tenets that he may or shall profess, or be compelled by any bye law or otherwise to take any religious test-oath whatseover."[16]

There was considerable conflict between the supporters of Columbia College and those from "up-state" who wanted to concentrate on building academies. In the fall of 1784, the number of regents was increased to give a majority to "Columbia men," and for the next three years the emphasis was placed on putting the college in good shape while the needs of the rest of the state were somewhat neglected. Antagonism increased throughout the state toward the college and the regents until 1787, when the 1784 laws were repealed, a new charter was issued to Columbia College as a private college, and the University of the State of New York was reestablished as a board charged with the responsibility of visiting and inspecting—but not founding and endowing, as the 1784 law had specified—colleges, academies, and schools.[17] In effect, it became a state agency for the supervision of secondary schools. Thus the attempt to create a state system of schools and colleges was watered down, and the result was a board with considerably limited powers over schools and colleges, which were to be essentially privately controlled.

The University of Pennsylvania

The College of Philadelphia experienced a similar conflict. During the years preceding the outbreak of the war, the Pennsylvania legislature and the college carried on a continuing quarrel, and in 1779, when the British were driven out of Philadelphia, the legislature revoked the charter of the college. During the immediate post-war period, the Pennsylvania legislature attempted to implement the 1776 constitutional provision that "all useful learning shall be duly encouraged and promoted in one or more universities." A state university was created in 1789 with a broadened curriculum, considerable emphasis on science, and opportunity for students to elect from among four parallel courses, all of which were innovations consistent with the principles of Enlightened philosophy. But the new college had hardly got started when, in response to the conservative reaction, the College of Philadelphia was rechartered and its assets returned to it. Two years later, Pennsylvania abandoned its attempt to have a state university, turned over the assets of the state institution to the old College of Philadelphia, and rechartered it as the privately controlled University of Pennsylvania.

[16] A *History of Columbia University*, pp. 60–61.

[17] Elsie Garland Hobson, *Educational Legislation and Administration in the State of New York from 1777 to 1850* (Chicago: The U. of Chicago, 1918), pp. 18–25.

The Dartmouth College Case

Perhaps the most significant attempt of a state to take over an existing institution and make it into a public university occurred in New Hampshire. Eleazer Wheelock, the founder of Dartmouth, named his son John as his successor. Although he was neither a scholar nor particularly suited to the academic life, John Wheelock completely dominated the institution. As the old trustees died, their younger replacements resisted his domination, and in 1815 open conflict began with a pamphlet by Wheelock accusing the trustees of many misdeeds. The trustees retaliated by voting to remove Wheelock and appointing another president. In the elections of 1816 the Democrats—the Jeffersonians—made Wheelock a campaign martyr and won the governorship and a majority of the legislature. Under the leadership of Governor William Plumer and with the accord of Jefferson, who wrote that it was "truly republican" for the nation to modify "institutions established for the use of the nation,"[18] the legislature converted Dartmouth into a state university, increasing the number of trustees and providing that they be appointed by the governor and his council. The new trustees seized the buildings, but most of the students remained loyal to the College. For a period of time Dartmouth University occupied the buildings with a few students, and Dartmouth College met in other quarters. The old trustees brought suit to recover the charter, but the New Hampshire Superior Court decided in favor of the University and against the College trustees. In 1818 the case reached the United States Supreme Court, with Daniel Webster representing the College. Webster's major legal argument was that the charter was a contract, which might not be violated by the legislature. He argued that the principle which involved Dartmouth was actually "the case of every College in the land . . . the case of every Eleemosynary Institution throughout our country."

> Shall our State Legislatures be allowed to take *that* which is not their own, to turn it from its original use, and apply it to such ends and purposes as they, in their discretion, shall see fit![19]

The decision, delayed for eleven months, was written by Chief Justice John Marshall, the Federalist whose decisions did much to sustain the conservatism of the revolutionary reaction long after the revolution of the nineteenth century had started. The majority opinion supported the

[18] Knight, Vol. III, pp. 128–129.
[19] Quoted in Richard Hofstadter and Wilson Smith, *American Higher Education: A Documentary History* (Chicago: U. of Chicago Press, 1961), Vol. I, p. 212.

College and used Webster's argument as its main point. Admitting that "education is an object of national concern, and a proper subject of legislation," and that state universities are themselves constitutional, Marshall ruled that education was not a monopoly of government, that Dartmouth was a chartered private institution, and that the New Hampshire legislation had violated the rights of the College and trustees in reorganizing the College so that it became a state university.

This decision secured the rights of donors to grant gifts for the support of schools and colleges without fear that those gifts would be used for some purpose other than that intended by the donor. Too, it clearly set forth the legal status of public educational institutions at a time when there were few public schools or colleges, but when a new revolution, which would include a crusade for school improvement, was in the making.

The First State Universities

Although the attempts in this period to convert existing colleges into state universities were not successful, the years between the close of the war and the turn of the century was the birth era of the first state universities. In each case they appeared in states where there was no established institution of higher learning: the University of Georgia, chartered in 1785 (although it did not begin admitting students until after 1800); the University of North Carolina, chartered in 1789 (and opened in 1795); the University of Vermont, chartered in 1791; Blount College (later the University of Tennessee), chartered in 1794; and South Carolina College (later the University of South Carolina), chartered in 1801.

The charters of these first universities generally reflected the concern of the Enlightenment for education to achieve social progress, individual happiness, and stability of government. They also reflected the fear of strong governmental control. The North Carolina constitution of 1776 charged the legislature with the duty of establishing "one or more universities," and the preamble of the charter of the University of North Carolina referred to the "duty of every Legislature to consult the happiness of a rising generation, and endeavour to fit them for an honorable discharge of the social duties of life, by paying the strictest attention to their education." The University of Georgia charter, after stating that to insure "free government" it is necessary "early to place the youth under the forming hand of society, that by instruction they may be moulded to the love of virtue and good order," concluded that "sending them abroad to other countries for their education . . . will always be the cause of so great foreign attachments, that upon principles of policy it is not admissible." The University of Georgia was also forbidden by its charter from excluding "any person of any religious denomination whatsoever, from free and equal liberty and advantages of education . . . on account of his . . . sentiments in religion." One other provision of the Georgia charter which was consistent with many of the plans to be published by American leaders of the Enlightenment was that defining the university as including "All public schools, instituted or to be supported by funds or public monies in the State."[20]

Private Control and Little Public Aid

While these institutions have been considered state universities, all were originally founded with self-perpetuating bodies of trustees, so that they were not under the control of the state. Too, they received very little support from public funds. The University of Georgia was partially supported by land grants which the legislature had allotted "for the great purpose of internal education" in 1783 and 1784; but no additional sources of support seem to have been provided in the founding of the institution. The University of North Carolina apparently was expected to operate largely on philanthropic subscriptions; according to its charter, any donor who subscribed ten pounds to the university might name one student to be educated "free from any expence of tuition," and the six persons making the largest contributions would have buildings named in their honor. A separate legislative act, however, gave the university some state support by setting aside all escheated property for its "use and benefit."

When the legislature repealed this grant in 1800 and decreed that all the escheated properties should revert to the state, the trustees brought suit. In 1805 the suit reached the North Carolina Supreme Court where the repealing act was declared void as contrary to the state constitution. In its decision the Court pointed out that the constitution required the legislature to establish a university, thus giving the people "a right highly esteemed in all civilized nations, that of educating their youth at moderate expense." It further declared that the legislature did not have the authority to abolish the university or public schools indirectly through cutting off support to those institutions.

[20] Knight, Vol. III, pp. 5–6, 8–10.

> It would not be competent for the Legislature to declare that there should be no public schools in the State, because such an act would directly oppose . . . the Constitution. . . . But if the Legislature can deprive the university of the appropriated and vested funds, they can do that which will produce the same consequences; for, deprive the institution of funds already vested and refuse to make any additional appropriations, and there never can exist in the State a public school or schools.[21]

One other reason given for declaring the act void anticipated the famed Dartmouth College Case. The North Carolina decision ruled that corporations were as fully protected in their rights as were individuals by the "law of the land," and that "the Legislature are as much restrained from affecting the property of corporations as they are that of a private individual."[22] Within the year, the legislature restored the escheated property to the university by repealing the "repeal act."[23] It is hard to understand how this very moderate financial support could have gone very far in providing many youths, particularly of poorer families, with much education "at moderate expense," but with the Enlightenment distrust of a government strong enough to levy and collect taxes, it was a compromise solution to a difficult dilemma of how to have public education without direct taxation.

Enlightenment Curriculum

The curricula of these colleges also reflect the influence of Enlightenment thought. At the University of North Carolina, freshmen studied English grammar as well as Roman antiquities, Latin classical literature, and the Greek Testament. Sophomores studied arithmetic, bookkeeping, geography "including the use of the Globe," as well as Grecian antiquities and Greek classics. Juniors took mathematics, geometry, surveying, navigation, algebra, natural philosophy, and astronomy. Seniors studied logic, moral philosophy, civil government, chronology, "history antient [sic] & Modern," and "the Bell lettre." In addition, there were weekly lectures on agriculture, botany, mineralogy, or commerce. Some election of studies was apparently possible, for a special class was to be formed of those who "only choose to study the sciences & the english Language."[24]

[21] *Ibid.*, pp. 77–78.
[22] Daniel Webster was to cite this decision in his arguments on the Dartmouth College case before the United States Supreme Court.
[23] Knight, Vol. III, pp. 13–15, 43, 76–80.
[24] *Ibid.*, pp. 27–28.

The courses at the University of Georgia were substantially the same and, to aid in teaching them, the president was ordered by the trustees to purchase a number of specified books covering the fields of mathematics, the sciences, French, Italian, and Latin and to procure a thermometer and a barometer. The sciences and mathematics had become very much a part of the college curriculum.

Conservative Acceptance

These state institutions grew slowly and served primarily the sons of the aristocracy. Perhaps the colleges managed to secure some state support during the period of social conservatism because they served the conservatives who held political and economic power in the Federalist period.

The University of Virginia

The most famous of the early state universities was the University of Virginia. Chronologically it clearly belongs in the period of conservatism; in spirit it is a part of the Enlightenment and Revolution. This paradox can be explained by the dynamic perseverance and forceful personality of Thomas Jefferson.

For years Jefferson had been developing plans for a university similar to his proposed 1779 reforms for William and Mary. In 1814 he was elected trustee to Albemarle Academy, a school which never existed except as a charter. He had the name changed to Central College, a tactical move which later facilitated his arguments that the university should be located at Charlottesville, the "center" of the state. A start was made on buildings at Central College in 1817, giving additional support to Jefferson's cause. Vigorous work by Jefferson's friends, particularly Joseph C. Cabell, led to the creation of "The Board of Commissioners for the University of Virginia" by the legislature in 1818. The Commissioners were charged with locating the university, outlining its curriculum and professorships, and drawing up the laws for its operation. Jefferson apparently dominated the meeting of the Commissioners, and he wrote the report to the legislature. When the legislature chartered the university in 1819, it followed almost exactly the basic ideas of Jefferson.

In the actual construction of the university, Jefferson took a leading role, actually designing the campus, its buildings, and even the landscaping. Recognizing that the $15,000 annual appropriation from the Literary Fund would be grossly inadequate for the institution he visual-ized, Jefferson borrowed money to erect buildings and provide books for the library. He reasoned that if students were admitted to half-finished buildings incompletely furnished, the public would be satisfied that it had done its part and no more funds would be forthcoming. On the other hand, if he did not admit students until the buildings were completed, the legislature would appropriate more to complete the buildings and hire the faculty. Jefferson did not spare the expense. He was building for the future, and he wanted buildings that would be structurally sound and architecturally pleasing. Despite his advanced age, he was active in directing the workmen. For the library he selected and catalogued the books.

Faculty and Academic Freedom

While the construction was going on, Jefferson tried to recruit the best possible faculty, writing to the top men in the country and finally, unable to persuade the ones he wanted, sending his friend Francis Walker Gilmer to England in 1824 to hire five professors. The employment of the foreigners brought criticism, but Jefferson defended his act on the ground that he would not hire the "leftovers" from the other American universities at the expense of making his school one of poor quality. The Visitors did decide in 1824 that it would be "expedient that professors of law and moral philosophy shall be taken from among the citizens of the United States."[25]

Jefferson promised that the faculty would have a large degree of academic freedom, a radical view reflecting his old Enlightenment principles.

> This institution will be based on the illimitable freedom of the human mind. For here we are not afraid to follow truth wherever it may lead, nor to tolerate any error so long as reason is left free to combat it.[26]

Professors were offered security of position, since they could be removed only by a majority vote of five of the seven Visitors, which included Jefferson, James Madison, and President James Monroe, as well as Jefferson's close friend Joseph C. Cabell, in effect giving professors tenure "for life," as Jefferson described it to Cabell in 1824. Professors were also free to select their own textbooks, although Jefferson wanted to

[25] Lipscomb, Vol. XIX, p. 436.
[26] *Ibid.*, Vol. XV, p. 303.

make an exception of the books in government, fearing the influence of a Federalist.

> But there is one branch in which we are the best judges, in which heresies may be taught, of so interesting a character to our own State, and to the United States, as to make it a duty in us to lay down the principles which shall be taught. It is that of government.[27]

One safeguard of academic freedom was the organization of the faculty administration. Although Jefferson served as Rector during his lifetime, there was to be no president; instead, the members of the faculty took turns serving as chairman of the faculty for a year at a time. This practice was followed at the University of Virginia for about twenty years.

Curriculum

Of greatest interest in the history of American education, perhaps, is the curriculum Jefferson outlined for the university and the principle of permitting students to elect the courses they wished to study. The eight professorships covered a very broad range of sciences, mathematics, and modern languages, as well as the classical literature of Greece and Rome. Latin and Greek grammar were relegated to the preparatory years, and theology was omitted entirely. Students might elect what "schools," or professors, they wished, and they paid fees according to the number they elected.

> In the University of Virginia shall be instituted eight professorships to wit: 1st, of ancient languages; 2d, modern languages; 3d, mathematics; 4th, natural philosophy; 5th, natural history; 6th, anatomy and medicine; 7th, moral philosophy; 8th, law.
>
> In the school of ancient languages shall be taught the higher grade of the Latin and Greek languages, the Hebrew, rhetoric, belles-lettres, ancient history and ancient geography.
>
> In the school of modern languages shall be taught French, Spanish, Italian, German and the English language in its Anglo-Saxon form; also modern history and modern geography.
>
> In the school of mathematics shall be taught mathematics generally including the high branches of numerical arithmetic, algebra, trigonometry, plane and spherical geometry, mensuration, navigation, conic sections, fluxions or differentials, military and civil architecture.

[27] *Ibid.*, Vol. XVI, p. 104.

> In the school of natural philosophy shall be taught the laws and properties of bodies generally, including mechanics, statics, hydrostatics, hydraulics, pneumatics, acoustics, optics, and astronomy.
> In the school of anatomy and medicine shall be taught anatomy, surgery, the history of the progress and theories of medicine, physiology, pathology, materia medica and pharmacy.
> In the school of moral philosophy shall be taught mental science generally, including ideology, general grammar, logic and ethics.
> In the school of law shall be taught the common and statute law, that of the chancery, the laws feudal, civil, mercatorial, maritime and of nature and nations; and also the principles of government and political economy.[28]

Students were required to be at least sixteen years of age and to have sufficient background, particularly in mathematics, natural philosophy, and ancient languages.

The University Opens

The university opened in March of 1825, and by September there were more than a hundred students enrolled. The schools of mathematics and modern languages were largest, with 68 and 64 students respectively, while moral philosophy attracted only 14.[29] In 1825 George Ticknor, Harvard professor of modern languages, described the college in a letter.

> It is a very fine establishment, consisting of ten houses for professors, four eating-houses, a rotunda on the model of the Parthenon, with a magnificent room for a library, and four fine lecture-rooms, with one hundred and eight apartments for students; the whole situated in the midst of two hundred and fifty acres of land. . . . It has cost two hundred and fifty thousand dollars. . . . Each professor receives his house, which . . . would rent for $600, a salary of $1500, and a fee of $20 from every student who attends his instructions, which are to be lectures, three times a week. . . . It is more practical than I feared, but not so practical that I feel satisfied of its success. It is, however, an experiment worth trying.[30]

It was indeed an experiment worth trying, and Ticknor himself was engaged in some significant reforms at Harvard. Jefferson lived to see his college in operation, but he died on July 4, 1826, before the experi-

[28] *Ibid.*, Vol. XIX, pp. 433–435.
[29] Roy J. Honeywell, *The Educational Work of Thomas Jefferson* (Cambridge: Harvard U. Press, 1931), p. 103.
[30] George S. Hillard, *Life, Letters, and Journals of George Ticknor* (London: Sampson Low, Marston, Searle, & Rivington, 1876), Vol. 1, pp. 288–289.

ment could have a full test and before national reaction to his broad curriculum and to the principle of election was at its height.

Ticknor's Reforms at Harvard

One of the strangest paradoxes of this period of revolution and reaction was the effort at education reform at Harvard led by a conservative young Federalist, George Ticknor. Ticknor, a graduate of Dartmouth, went to Europe in 1815 to study at the University of Göttingen. There he was greatly impressed by the breadth of courses offered, the depth of scholarship of the professors and their devotion to teaching, the freedom of the students in the election of what lectures they wished to attend, and the methods of teaching. While there, he was invited to become professor of modern languages at Harvard. After two more years spent in travel in Europe learning languages and collecting books, he returned to America in 1819 to take up his professorship. He immediately proposed to President Kirkland of Harvard some unusual ideas for the conduct of the classes in French and Spanish. In the field of belles lettres, which was also to be his, he was unable to effect the changes he wished since his area overlapped the work of the professors of Greek and rhetoric. In the summer of 1823, following a wild student riot, Ticknor proposed a number of reforms to the faculty. His suggestions were incorporated in the 1825 reforms at the university. Among them were the elimination of the winter vacation (during which many of the students had taught district schools), stricter examinations, an increase in the number of subjects, some opportunity for student election of subjects, division of the college into departments, and changes in methods of teaching so that all students would not be required to progress at the same rate. These reforms were not popular with the Harvard faculty and had little chance of success. Only in Ticknor's own department of modern languages did the reforms in teaching receive serious trials, and in 1835 Ticknor resigned.

Reaction to College Reforms

The failure of Ticknor's reforms was not the result of a conservatism limited to Harvard, for there was general opposition in the nation to the broadened curriculum in secondary and higher education and to the idea of letting students have some choice of subjects they wished to study. In 1813 General Thomas Cadwalader complained in an article in the

Port Folio, a Philadelphia magazine, that "chemistry, astronomy, and declamation" were "crowding Latin and Greek out of the curriculum." Even on the frontier, where conservatism was generally less rampant, the *Western Reserve,* a magazine published in Cincinnati, supported the scholastic *status quo* in 1820.

> Should the time ever come when Latin and Greek should be banished from our universities, and the study of Cicero and Demosthenes, of Homer and Virgil, should be considered as unnecessary for the formation of a scholar, we should regard mankind as fast sinking into absolute barbarism, and the gloom of mental darkness as likely to increase until it should become universal.[31]

The Yale Report

The elimination of theology and the substitution of sciences and modern languages for the previous exclusive concern with the Latin and Greek classics were particularly threatening to the denominational colleges. Two of the strongest citadels of fundamentalist, conservative denominationalism were Yale and Princeton, the seedbeds of colleges in the West and South. In response to reforms like those of Jefferson and Ticknor and to criticism that colleges should give attention to practical studies and minimize the "dead languages," the Yale faculty in 1828 issued a report which served as the often-cited defense of the educational *status quo* and was perhaps the greatest influence in stabilizing the college curriculum during the middle third of the nineteenth century.

The Report admitted that Yale was not perfect and that changes were indeed being made, particularly in the introduction of such subjects as chemistry, geology, mineralogy, and political economy. But these changes should come gradually; no wholesale reform was desirable to make the college "*new-modelled.*" The role of the college was still, as it had always been, "to *lay* the foundations of a *superior education*" at a period of the student's life "when a substitute must be provided for *parental superintendence.*" Quite contrary to the reformers' plans to give students some freedom and responsibility for governing themselves and selecting their courses to study, the Yale faculty denied that the immature young men should be accorded such freedoms. In the daily activities of the students, the faculty should always be "present with them, not only at their meals, and during the business of the day; but in the hours allotted to rest." Thus all student rooms must be "near to the chamber of one

[31] Quoted in Frank Luther Mott, *A History of American Magazines, 1741–1850* (Cambridge: The Belknap Press of Harvard U. Press, 1930), Vol. I, p. 146.

of the officers." This attitude of paternalism pervaded the entire Report.

In its statement of the purpose of education, the Yale Report laid down the doctrine of "mental discipline" as the justification for the traditional prescribed curriculum of the collegiate course and for the use of the classical languages to achieve that purpose.

> The two great points to be gained in intellectual culture, are the *discipline* and the *furniture* of the mind; expanding its powers, and storing it with knowledge. The former of these is, perhaps, the more important of the two. A commanding object, therefore, in a collegiate course, should be, to call into daily and vigorous exercise the faculties of the student. Those branches of study should be prescribed, and those modes of instruction adopted, which are best calculated to teach the art of fixing the attention, directing the train of thought, analyzing a subject proposed for investigation. . . . Familiarity with the Greek and Roman writers is especially adapted to form the taste, and to discipline the mind. . . .
>
> [T]he study of the classics . . . forms the most effectual discipline of the mental faculties. . . . Every faculty of the mind is employed; not only the memory, judgment, and reasoning powers, but the taste and fancy are occupied and improved.

The Report also claimed that "Classical discipline, likewise, forms the best preparation for professional study," including divinity, law, and medicine. No other studies would perform the functions of the classical languages, because only the classical languages had power to discipline the mind, their structure being so different from that of English. The study of other modern languages required only the exercise of memory, and thus, "To suppose the modern languages more practical than the ancient . . . because the former are now spoken . . . is an obvious fallacy."

The reformers were urging new methods of teaching in colleges, substituting the lecture for the textbook recitation. Traditionally, the college tutor assigned some reading to students, and then at the recitation period, his function was to quiz the students orally, the only instruction coming incidentally to his questioning. The Yale Report admitted that lectures might have value in calling forth "the highest efforts of the lecturer" and in awakening "the interest and ardor of the student." But the basic method must still be the "*recitations;* that is, examinations in a text book." Studying the book on his own would provide the student the opportunity of "giving a more commanding direction to his thoughts, than when listening to oral instruction." The book—the ancient classical literature—was still *the* authority.

One view of the reformers was that the program of individual students should be varied according to the goals the students had in mind, and that individualization should be developed through permitting students to elect courses and specialize. The Yale faculty disagreed. To that argument they answered that "our prescribed course contains those subjects only which ought to be understood . . . by every one who aims at a thorough education." This kind of "liberal education" would be useful to "*Merchants, manufacturers* and *farmers,* as well as professional gentlemen." The college would serve them all by providing the "mental discipline" by which they would be able to reduce "the principles of science to their practical application."

The report admitted that there was public clamor for practical education, but held that that kind of education was the responsibility of academies, "commercial high schools, . . . agricultural seminaries, etc." The difference between such institutions and a college is not in the number of studies taught but in the fact that the college directs "its efforts to one uniform course," while the "academy teaches a little of every thing."[32]

The popularity of the Yale Report and the rejection of the reforms attempted at Virginia and Harvard illustrate the conservatism of the period.

Compromises and Precedents for Change

The philosophy of the Enlightenment and the attitudes of the Revolution gave rise to new forms of secondary and higher education—the academy and the public university. But the prevailing conservatism in the reaction against the Revolution resulted in these institutions becoming limited to the few, a privilege of the economically independent. Instead of developing into public institutions providing education free or "at moderate expense," they tended to be privately controlled, tuition-supported, with only the barest minimum of public sharing in the supervision or financing. But that bare minimum was the harbinger of significant public control and support in later periods of American educational history. Even during the conservative years the seeds of future revolution were sown and were beginning to germinate. The dreams of Thomas Jefferson, barely adumbrated in his own lifetime, were to be exceeded in the revolutions that followed.

QUESTIONS FOR DISCUSSION

1. It is easy to over-generalize about the effects of historical movements, for some have influences which may operate in opposing directions. Examine

[32] Hofstadter and Smith, Vol. I, pp. 278–290.

the effect of the academy movement on the development of public secondary education. How did it both facilitate and discourage the growth of the public high school?
2. Contrast the preparation for teaching in the academies with that in a modern teacher-training program. What areas have we made progress in? What progress do you consider most significant?
3. One of the most important perennial issues in education is academic freedom, and it is particularly threatened in times of conservative reaction. How might the controversies at the universities of Virginia, Harvard, and Yale help understand the present problems of academic freedom?

SUGGESTED READINGS

Secondary Sources

Arrowood, Charles Flinn. *Thomas Jefferson and Education in a Republic.* New York: McGraw-Hill, 1930. Pp. 24–48.

Brown, Elmer Ellsworth. *The Making of Our Middle Schools.* London: Longmans, Green, 1903. Chapters X–XIV.

Butts, R. Freeman. *The College Charts Its Course.* New York: McGraw-Hill, 1939. Pp. 58–125.

Primary Sources

Arrowood, Charles Flinn. *Thomas Jefferson and Education in a Republic.* New York: McGraw-Hill, 1930. Pp. 93–106, 132–176.

Conant, James G. *Thomas Jefferson and the Development of American Public Education.* Berkeley: U. of California Press, 1962. Pp. 88–161.

Cubberley, Ellwood P. *Readings in the History of Education.* Boston: Houghton Mifflin, 1920. Readings 325–329.

———. *Readings in Public Education in the United States.* Boston: Houghton Mifflin, 1934. Pp. 123–124, 219–235, 252–255, 323–324.

Hofstadter, Richard, and Smith, Wilson. *American Higher Education: A Documentary History.* Chicago: U. of Chicago Press, 1961. Vol. I, pp. 147–232, 251–291, 395–396.

Honeywell, Roy J. *The Educational Work of Thomas Jefferson.* Cambridge: Harvard U. Press, 1931. Appendices, pp. 205–227, 248–286.

Knight, Edgar W. *A Documentary History of Education in the South Before 1860.* Chapel Hill: U. of North Carolina Press, 1949. Vol. III, pp. 1–239; Vol. IV, pp. 1–36.

Knight, Edgar W., and Hall, Clifton L. *Readings in American Educational History.* New York: Appleton-Century-Crofts, 1951. Pp. 186–237.

Monroe, Paul. *The Founding of the American Public School System.* Ann Arbor: University Microfilms, 1940. Vol. II, Chapters XIX and XX.

Spurlock, Clark. *Education and the Supreme Court.* Urbana: U. of Illinois Press, 1955. Chapter 2.

PART Three

"That All May Share"

CHRONOLOGY

1828—Construction begun on the Baltimore and Ohio Railroad, first in the United States
1829–1837—Administration of Andrew Jackson
1830—Population of United States 12,866,020
1831—William Lloyd Garrison establishes the abolitionist newspaper *Liberator* in Boston.
1832—"Tariff of Abominations" leads to nullification attempt by South Carolina.
1832—Controversy over Second Bank of the United States
1834—Cyrus McCormick patents the reaper.
1836—Texas declares its independence.
1836—Arkansas admitted to the Union
1837–1841—Administration of Martin Van Buren
1837—John Deere perfects the plow which "opened the prairies."
1837—Financial panic; Michigan admitted to the Union
1840—Population of the United States 17,069,453
1841–1845—Administration of W. H. Harrison and John Tyler
1842—Dorr Rebellion in Rhode Island
1845–1849—Administration of James Polk
1845—Florida and Texas admitted to the Union
1846—Samuel Morse sends first telegraphic message from Baltimore to Washington.
1846—Dispute over Oregon Territory settled with England
1846—Iowa admitted to the Union
1846–1848—War with Mexico results in United States expansion in Southwest.
1847—Mormons settle Utah.
1848—Gold discovered in California
1848—Wisconsin admitted to the Union
1849–1853—Administration of Zachary Taylor and Millard Fillmore
1850—California admitted to the Union
1850—Population of the United States 23,191,876
1851—Harriet Beecher Stowe publishes *Uncle Tom's Cabin.*
1853–1857—Administration of Franklin Pierce
1854—Kansas-Nebraska Act upsets slavery truce and opens West to railroads and settlement.
1857–1861—Administration of James Buchanan
1858—Lincoln-Douglas debates in Illinois
1859—Oregon admitted to the Union
1860—Population of the United States 31,443,321
November, 1860—Election of Abraham Lincoln as President
December, 1860—South Carolina secedes from the Union.
April, 1861—Fort Sumter fired upon

THE PERIOD FROM THE ELECTION OF Andrew Jackson to the Civil War has been called the Age of the Common Man. Educational historians sometimes refer to it as the Common School Revival. During these years the American public school system took substantially the form it has continued to develop. The common school became almost universal in the North and West and was concerned with teaching the basic skills and building the social, political, and moral character desirable in a democracy. Secondary education was broadened; it was still oriented toward college preparation, but also performed the task of terminal education. Higher education was taking its first steps toward specialization and professionalization. State support and central control, particularly of the common school, became generally accepted, and the principle of separation of church and state was made more explicit in the area of education. These educational developments reflected the general revolutionary movements in American society during the Age of the Common Man.

In the South, tight control of the aristocracy over social, political, and economic affairs limited the reform movements and the influence of the "common man" in politics. Southern society still operated for the benefit of the planter class, and Negroes and poor whites had few rights or privileges. Only in North Carolina, where plantations were fewer and independent farmers more numerous than in any of the other cotton states, was there much progress toward social and political reform. And only in North Carolina among the Southern states was there a public school system of any consequence before 1860. For, while considerable attention was given to secondary and higher education for the sons and daughters of the aristocracy, education for the masses was generally neglected in the South. Consequently, although much of the general story of schooling during this period concerns developments in public elementary education, in the South the important developments are in the academies and colleges.

The political and economic revolution which brought the common man many political rights and much economic improvement also, in theory if not always in practice, brought him basic educational opportunity. Without the rudiments of education, the political rights would have been virtually meaningless; with education, the rights of the individual have continued to expand to include social and economic rights.

The Common School Revival was the educational aspect of the second social revolution in the history of the United States.

SUGGESTED READINGS

Beard, Charles A., and Beard, Mary R. *The Rise of American Civilization.* New York: Macmillan, 1930. Vol. 1, pp. 542–580, 628–662, 748–752, 809–823; Vol. II, pp. 52–54, 99.

Fish, Carl Russell. *The Rise of the Common Man, 1830–1850.* New York: Macmillan, 1935. Chapters I, IV–X, XII.

Schlesinger, Arthur Meier. *New Viewpoints in American History.* New York: Macmillan, 1922. Chapter IX.

Schlesinger, Arthur M., Jr. *The Age of Jackson.* Boston: Little, Brown, 1945.

Turner, Frederick Jackson. *The Frontier in American History.* New York: Holt, 1947. Chapter I.

Van Deusen, Glyndon G. *The Jacksonian Era, 1828–1848.* New York: Harper, 1959. Chapter I.

7

Awakening Public Interest in Educational Reform

During the period of the Common School Revival, free, tax-supported, state-controlled elementary schooling became a firm commitment in the American value system. Furthermore, the principle became something of a reality in the Eastern and Western states. Achieving that principle in practice required that four major barriers be thrown down: public apathy, private financing through philanthropy and tuition fees, extreme local control, and sectarianism. Before the Civil War these barriers were substantially reduced, and some new attitudes toward education were accepted and translated into law. Philanthropy and the rate bill were giving way to tax-supported schools free to all. The office of the state superintendent and the state board of education were equalizing opportunity throughout the state instead of permitting each district to do as it pleased with promoting—or ignoring—schools. The separation of church and state in education was spelled out further, so that schools tended to be more secular than sectarian. But all these advances depended on the awakening of public interest and concern over schooling.

The Common School Revival did not result from the efforts of teachers alone. Such a major social reform occurs only when great social pressures are exerted. Between 1830 and 1860 these pressures resulted from the rise of cities and the industrial working class, the increased political importance of the working man, the devoted efforts of reformers, problems relating to the Americanization of immigrants, and the awakening of political leaders to the importance of schools.

The Frontier

Many of the significant developments of this second revolutionary period in American history have been traced to the influence of the frontier. On the frontier, every man was considered potentially as good as any other, without regard to family background, wealth, education, or experience. This egalitarianism embraced the political view that any man was entitled to vote and to hold public office. Hence all the frontier states entered the Union with democratic provisions for suffrage, unlike the older states, which had property qualifications for voting. This egalitarian feeling gave rise also to the belief that all children should be entitled to the same educational opportunities and that schools must be free to all without the stigma of pauperism. But though the frontier attitude favored schools for all, the notion that the ignorant were as "good" or as able as the educated minimized the *need* for schooling and reduced the effectiveness the egalitarianism might have had for promoting adequate schools as well as free schools. Added to that was the concept of liberty as absence of regulation, law, or restraint—the frontiersman faced the old Enlightenment dilemma of wanting free schools but hating the taxes that would make them possible. It was easy to rationalize that "book larnin' " was worse than useless to pioneer life, thus avoiding the need for any more than the barest minimum of schooling. In addition to strengthening the reluctance against being taxed for the support of schools, the frontier distrust of the educated man may have contributed to the anti-intellectualism that to this day tinges American attitudes in political and business matters.

Factories and the Growth of Cities

The West was not the only frontier in America. The introduction of the factory system of production brought new styles of life in New England and the Middle Atlantic States. For the first time there came to be a sharp difference between the working classes and the owners, and a permanent "working class" began to develop. The factory often employed both women and children, who would work for far less than men, and whole families were kept in a sort of peonage by the mills, which required that the whole family work or none be hired. Approximately two-fifths of the working force in New England in the 1830's were under sixteen years of age, making school attendance impossible for many children except on Sunday or in the evening. The average working day was thirteen hours, six days a week, and with both parents at work, there was little time for family life or the education that comes from family living.

The factory system combined with the improved transportation provided by canals, steamboats, and railroads made possible the growth of cities. The number of cities of over 8,000 increased fourfold between 1820 and 1850, with the centers of commerce making the greatest gains. Boston jumped from 42,000 to 137,000 and New York from 123,000 to 515,000 in these three decades. Such growth was much greater than the increase in the general population: between 1820 and 1840, when the population of Boston increased 115 percent, that of Massachusetts rose only 40 percent. The rapid growth of cities, with their slums, poverty, and crime, made reform and public education imperative. Even the efforts of the philanthropic societies, such as the Public School Society of New York, were hardly scratching the surface in providing schools for the thousands of city children. And that schooling was stigmatized by charity and so was repugnant to the poor but proud working man.

Political Rights

The alliance of the frontier farmer of the West and the workingman of the East gave a new direction to American political life. Successful politicians had to be candidates of the "common man"—or at least appear to be. An aristocratic background became a political handicap, and office seekers often boasted of their lowly birth and lack of opportunity for schooling. With the common man winning power at the ballot box, his demands were finally to be heard by the office holders, and governors and legislators began to show an interest in public schools.

Immigrants

Until the nineteenth century, immigrants had come in small enough numbers and kept enough in homogeneous groups that they did not create particularly trying problems. After 1820 the flow of immigrants began to increase rapidly, and large numbers of them were from national groups with customs quite different from those of the United States. During the 1820's, 143,439 immigrants entered the United States, increasing to 599,125 in the 1830's and 1,713,251 in the 1840's. In 1845 approximately one-third of the inhabitants of Boston and New York City were foreign-born. Many of these newcomers were from the lower economic classes, uneducated, uninterested in schooling, and unprepared for the democratic responsibilities of citizenship. Public education was demanded by many reformers as the means of acculturating the new immigrants into American life.

> Unless we educate our immigrants they will be our ruin. It is no longer a mere question of benevolence, of duty, or of enlightened self-interest but the intellectual and religious training of our foreign population has become essential to our own safety. . . .
>
> It is not merely from the ignorant and vicious foreigner that danger is to be apprehended. To sustain an extended republic like our own there must be a national feeling, a national assimilation. . . .
>
> The only effectual way to produce this individuality and harmony of national feeling and character, is to bring our children into the same schools and have them educated together.[1]

Workingmen's Societies

In the Eastern cities many factory workers, resenting the conditions that made them feel inferior to other Americans, banded together in workingmen's societies. Taking precedence even over higher wages and better working conditions, universal education and the right to vote were primary in their programs of reform.

The State Must Provide Public Schools

The Workingmen's Society of Philadelphia complained specifically about the failure of Pennsylvania to achieve the school system provided for in the early constitutions of that state. "Thousands are now suffering the consequences of this disregard to the public welfare on the part of our rulers."[2] Some attempts had been made "in two or three districts of the state, but they have proved ineffectual."

> The very spirit in which these provisions have been made not only defeats the object intended, but tends also to draw still broader the line of distinction between the rich and the poor. All who receive the limited knowledge imparted by the present system of public education are looked upon as paupers. . . . The spirit of independence and feeling . . . cause the honest and industrious

[1] Calvin E. Stowe, *Western Literary Institute*, 1836. Quoted in Monroe, pp. 794, 796, 797.

[2] "Address of the City and County Convention to the Working Men of the State," *Mechanics' Free Press*, Philadelphia, July 10, 1830. Quoted in John R. Commons, *et al.*, *A Documentary History of American Industrial Society* (Cleveland: Clark, 1910), Vol. V, p. 115.

> poor to reject a proffered bounty that connects with its reception a seeming disgrace.[3]

To the conservative argument that "the poor, if left to themselves, will use their exertions to educate their children," the societies replied that those without education did not recognize the need for it, a problem which still plagues our schools in their efforts to provide universal education. "It is a lamentable fact that, persons destitute of education are ignorant of the loss they sustain, and hence, fail to avert the evil from their offspring."[4]

As the right of suffrage was extended to all adult men, the workingmen's societies used their new political power in the effort to promote education and other reforms. The platform of the Working Men of Boston included the view that "every representative chosen to declare the sentiments of the people, is bound to obey the popular voice, and to express it." A part of the same platform claimed that "the establishment of a liberal system of education, attainable by all, should be among the first efforts of every lawgiver who desires the continuance of our national independence."[5] The Philadelphia Working Men addressed a questionnaire to the candidates for the legislature in 1829.

> Upon the important subject of Education we wish most distinctly to understand whether you do, or do not consider it essential to the welfare of the rising generation, "That an open school and competent teachers for every child in the state, from the lowest branch of an infant school to the lecture rooms of practical science, should be established, and those who superintend them to be chosen by the people."[6]

Public Schools Must Be Free and Tax Supported

The schools should be free from the stigma of charity which characterized the pauper, or so-called "free," schools of that period. All children should attend as equals. "Public Education ought to be equal, republican, open to all, and the best which can be devised" in order to "regenerate America." It would take such a school system to realize the ideal set out in the Declaration of Independence of making all "American Citizens . . . *free and equal*" by producing "one class out of the

[3] *Ibid.*
[4] *Ibid.*, pp. 115–116.
[5] Quoted in Commons, pp. 188–189.
[6] *Ibid.*, p. 93.

many that now envy and despise each other." The workingmen's societies clearly recognized that it would take more than a few hours a day in school together to equalize the opportunities of the children of the rich and the poor. They advocated schools where the children would be boarded as well as schooled.

> If the children from these State Schools are to go every evening, the one to his wealthy parents' soft carpeted drawing room, the other to his poor father's, or widowed mother's comfortless cabin, will they return the next day as friends and equals? . . . Is that education *the best*, which teaches children the common branches of education during six or seven hours each day, and then leaves them to . . . spend five or six hours . . . learning rudeness, impertinent manners, vulgar language, and vicious habits? . . . State Schools to be republican, efficient and acceptable to all, must receive the children . . . altogether; must feed them, clothe them, lodge them; must direct not their studies only, but their occupations and amusements; must care for them until their education is completed.[7]

Whether the members of the workingmen's societies really believed in such a proposal or whether they offered it merely as a dramatization of the issue is not as important as the problem that their proposal pointed out. Certainly the solution of the conservatives—philanthropic schools—could not remove the kind of inequality that results from poor home and environmental conditions.

To those who asked how a free school system would be financed, the workingmen's societies replied that taxes, not lotteries, were the appropriate source. Some funds might be raised by a tax levied for all children between the ages of two or three to twelve or fourteen, "whether the parents chose to send their children to the State schools or not." The "children's poll tax" would have to be very light, in order that every parent might be able to pay it, and would not take care of the whole bill. It was proposed that the deficiency be made up by a direct income tax. Many conservatives protested that it was unfair to tax one man for the schooling of another's child, but the workingmen's societies argued that education is a social responsibility: the entire society benefits from the education of every child.

> Every citizen ought to contribute his fair share towards the expenses of legislation, and . . . education is a most important branch of legislation; as much more important than the criminal law, as "pre-

[7] *The New York Sentinel and Working Men's Advocate,* 1830. Commons, pp. 165, 166, 168.

> vention is better than cure." . . . Is it not as cheap and much more rational and humane to pay for keeping men and women out of the pentitentiary than to pay for putting them in it?[8]

This argument anticipated a famous speech by Thaddeus Stevens before the Pennsylvania legislature in 1835, when he led the fight to abolish the rate bill and to establish a school system much like that called for by the platforms of the workingmen's societies.

Curriculum Should Be the Same for All

Not only should the public schools be open and free to all and supported by taxes from everyone, but the curriculum should be the same for all children. The "sort of education . . . good enough for the common people" was that which was "good enough for the richest and most favored classes of the land." Any essentially useful subject would be "proper to be taught in all state schools, to every child, rich or poor, patrician or plebian." And some subjects (the classics, perhaps) "which now occupy much time" were considered "unfit for public schools . . . not because they are too good for the people, but too useless for them; not because they are fit only for the rich, but because they are fit for nobody." In their emphasis on the practical, the workingmen reformers advocated that "Children ought to be taught something more than abstract science, and *book learning*," for "An education is but half an education . . . unless it makes its pupils productive members of society as well as well taught school boys."[9]

The concern of the workingmen's societies for education did not mean that all working parents were vitally interested in education. Most of them were apathetic and indifferent. And many, indeed, were hostile to public schools, for they looked on children as an economic asset to be put to work at the earliest possible age. The efforts of the workingmen's societies in educating the lower class parents to the importance of schooling for their children was perhaps the greatest contribution of the societies to the development of the universal common school.

Literary Leaders of School Reform

Agitation for school reform was not limited to representatives of the working classes. Among the New England literati, led by Ralph Waldo Emerson, there developed a new religion known as Transcendentalism,

[8] Quoted in Commons, p. 172.
[9] Quoted in Monroe, pp. 858, 864.

a form of liberal rebellion against the restraints of orthodox Calvinism. The Transcendentalists were agitators for many popular causes, and their influence extended far beyond the limits of New England. In an oration at Harvard in 1837, Emerson idealized the common man and exhorted the literati of the new nation to sing the praises of "common" things and people. Democracy and religious duty demanded that the upper class be concerned about the conditions of the poor, including the labor reforms, abolition of slavery, women's rights, universal manhood suffrage, socialism, world peace, temperance, anti-tobacco, prison reforms, improvements in hospitals and in the treatment of the insane. Among the most important of these interests—and at the heart of many of the others—were the common school revival and adult education, particularly the lyceum. Reformers generally argued that raising the educational level of the people would promote reforms in general. Thus all the other reform movements tended to support reform in education.

James G. Carter

The pioneer among reformers in education was James G. Carter, who had worked his way through Harvard by teaching in the Massachusetts district schools and who opened a private school upon his graduation in 1820. Deeply concerned about the conditions of Massachusetts schools, Carter published a series of letters in the Boston newspapers between 1821 and 1824 and a series of essays on education in the winter of 1824–1825. In these he praised the early founders' concern for education, sharply criticized the failures of his state to preserve their high resolve in practice, and urged a number of reforms. Carter was largely responsible for the passage of the Massachusetts school law in 1827, which provided for public secondary schools. He attempted for many years to have the state establish public normal schools for training common school teachers, and he was one of the most effective legislators involved in the passage of legislation establishing the Massachusetts State Board of Education in 1837.

In his *Essays upon Popular Education,* Carter attacked the anti-democratic character of the schools of the conservative Federalist period, particularly the deleterious effect the academies were having on the public common schools. His arguments echoed the fears of Samuel Adams, who, as governor of Massachusetts in 1795, had warned that as wealthy, influential citizens gave their support to private schools, the public schools would be injured. Carter admitted that there were more common schools in 1825 than in 1789, but pointed out that their number had not improved in proportion to the growth of population and their quality had not kept pace with the increase in knowledge, so that the schools were relatively far poorer in 1825 than in 1789. He warned that, unless the legislature took a renewed interest in schooling, Massachusetts might well be reduced to the use of Lancastrian schools.

> If the policy of the legislature, in regard to free schools . . . be not changed, the institution, which has been the glory of New England will, in twenty years more, be extinct. If the State continue to relieve themselves of the trouble of providing for the instruction of the whole people, and to shift the responsibility upon the towns, and the towns upon the districts, and the districts upon individuals, each will take care of himself and his own family as he is able, and as he appreciates the blessing of a good education. The rich will, as a class, have much better instruction than they now have, and the poor will have much worse or none at all. . . . The public free schools will become stationary or retrograde; till at length, they will be thrown for support upon the gratuitous, and of course capricious and uncertain efforts of individuals; and then . . . they will soon degenerate into mere mechanical establishments . . . not for the rational, moral, and intellectual instruction of human beings, but for training young animals to march, sing, and draw figures in sand—establishments, in which the power of one man is so prodigiously multiplied that he can overlook, direct and control the intellectual exercises of a thousand! And this wretched mockery of education, they must be right glad to accept as a charity, instead of inheriting as their birthright as good instruction as their country affords.[10]

Horace Mann

In securing passage of the bill creating the Massachusetts state board of education, Carter teamed with the president of the Massachusetts Senate, Horace Mann, who resigned from the legislature to become the first secretary of the board. During his twelve years as secretary to the board of education, Mann was a most active partisan for common schools. He made frequent lecture tours, speaking everywhere in the state on the subject. He wrote voluminously—articles, letters, and twelve annual reports in which he not only gave statistical facts but expounded at length on critical educational problems. He edited the *Common School Journal.* A former legislator and able politician, he was quite

[10] James G. Carter, *Essays upon Popular Education Containing a Particular Examination of the Schools of Massachusetts and an Outline of an Institution for the Education of Teachers* (Boston: Bowles & Dearborn, 1826), p. 41.

successful in securing passage of better school laws and appropriations. His fame spread far beyond the borders of his home state, and his annual reports and the *Common School Journal* circulated throughout the nation and even to foreign lands. He frequently received letters from educational reformers in other states asking his advice and seeking his aid for schools outside of Massachusetts. A number of other states followed the example of Massachusetts, setting up boards of education and creating the office of superintendent or secretary of the board.

Henry Barnard

One of those states which followed the lead of Massachusetts was Connecticut, where Henry Barnard played the role that Mann and Carter played. Just as Mann richly deserves the title of America's greatest educational statesman, so Barnard merits being known as America's greatest educational editor. A former teacher in an academy, Barnard visited Europe from 1835 to 1837 where he was attracted to the Pestalozzian methods he observed in the schools there. On his return he was elected to the Connecticut legislature, and in 1838 he sponsored legislation similar to the Massachusetts bill of 1837. After Gallaudet refused the office, Barnard became the first secretary of the board at a salary of $3.00 a day plus expenses. The Connecticut schools were in worse shape than those of Massachusetts, and Barnard set out to stir up interest in education. Within four years he had created so much stir that the legislature, which had unanimously established the board, quieted his agitation by abolishing his office!

Barnard then moved to Rhode Island, where the Roger Williams tradition of opposition to government interference in matters of religion or education was still so strong that the Rhode Island schools were far worse than those in Massachusetts or Connecticut. After a two-year campaign to awaken the citizens of Rhode Island to the need for schools, Barnard succeeded in having the legislature pass a school law (1845), which he administered until 1849 as commissioner of public schools. Connecticut, realizing its error, reenacted its law, created a normal school, and offered Barnard his old position and the principalship of the normal school. Barnard held this double job for his home state until overwork and bad health forced him to resign in 1855. During his years as school commissioner and secretary of the board of education, he had written annual reports, edited the *Connecticut Common School Journal* and the *Rhode Island Institute of Instruction*, written monumental books on *School Architecture*, *Normal Schools*, and *National Education in Europe*, and produced countless letters and articles on educational subjects. On retirement he began his greatest work, the editing of the *American Journal of Education*, thirty-one volumes published between 1855 and 1881.[11] During this period of editorial work, he also served as chancellor of the University of Wisconsin from 1858–1860, as president of St. John's College at Annapolis from 1866–1867, and as the first United States Commissioner of Education, from 1867 to 1870. Like Mann, he found educational journalism not profitable, and in spite of his other sources of income, Barnard died in near poverty, having expended his own fortune as well as his time and talents in the cause of improving schools.

Other Educational Leaders

Other states had their educational heroes, although some, particularly, in the South, did not appear until after the Civil War. Among those who were important in the Common School Revival were Samuel Lewis, Samuel Galloway, and Calvin Stowe in Ohio; Caleb Mills in Indiana; Ninian W. Edwards in Illinois; John D. Pierce and Isaac Crary in Michigan; Robert J. Breckinridge in Kentucky; Calvin Wiley in North Carolina; and John Swett in California.

Educational Journalism

Many of the educational reformers secured public support for schools through journals which circulated among lay persons interested in education. Few of the subscribers were actually teachers, though some journals were designed specifically for teachers and most of them had articles aimed at improving teachers culturally and helping them in their classroom work. Perhaps it was the low level of professionalism among teachers that caused these journals to be generally short-lived. The earliest journal of any consequence was the *Academician*, published in New York between 1818 and 1820 by Albert and John W. Pickett, president and secretary, respectively, of the Incorporated Society of New York Teachers. *The American Journal of Education*, published between 1826

[11] Many textbooks credit Barnard with thirty-two volumes, but the last, which is dated 1882, was not produced until 1902, two years after Barnard's death, by a publisher who assembled some of Barnard's unpublished materials. In addition, Vol. XXV is the 1879 report of the U.S. Commissioner and Vol. XXIX the 1877 report. For an analysis of the contents and dates of the full set, see Richard Emmons Thursfield, *Henry Barnard's American Journal of Education* (Baltimore: Johns Hopkins Press, 1945), pp. 317–320.

and 1831 by William Russell, and its successor, the *American Annals of Education,* edited by William Woodbridge from 1831 to 1839, were connected with the lyceum movement. J. Orville Taylor's *Common School Assistant* (1836–1840) was intended for teachers, as the title indicates. Of the twenty or more educational periodicals started before 1840, only two of them were still in existence after 1842: Mann's *Common School Journal* and the *District School Journal of the State of New York.*[12]

With the rise of the office of state superintendent of education (or its equivalent under other names), there came a number of official or quasi-official journals in education. The first were the *Ohio Common School Director* and the *Michigan Journal of Education,* circulated by the legislatures of those states beginning in 1838. The journals of Mann and Barnard followed shortly after, as did the *District School Journal of the State of New York.* A number of states gave aid to journals published by independent groups or teachers' associations. Between 1841 and 1860, nineteen journals were founded by state teachers' associations, and most of them were still alive in 1865. Even though there were soon many journals, their circulation was quite limited. Between 1840 and 1844 the average annual circulation of all educational periodicals was only 13,400, and the highest five-year average before the Civil War, between 1855 and 1859, was only 31,700.

Although the circulation of the journals was limited, they did reach readers influential in community life and school reform, including "school officers, ministers, persons prominent in various other professions, and . . . teachers holding the more important positions." As Sheldon Davis wrote, "there can be do doubt of their having exercised considerable influence in creating and shaping school systems, and in diffusing liberal views of what public education should become."[13]

The Lyceum Movement

One of the most important agencies in the campaign against the inertia of ignorance was the American lyceum. The first lyceums were organized by Josiah Holbrook in Massachusetts in 1826; they soon spread to every state in the nation. In 1831 the *American Annals of*

[12] Sheldon Emmor Davis, *Educational Periodicals During the Nineteenth Century,* U.S. Bureau of Education Bulletin, 1919, No. 28, pp. 11–13.
[13] *Ibid.,* pp. 23, 36–37, 79, 82, 89.

Education reported more than nine hundred towns with local lyceums, in addition to county and state lyceums. On May 4, 1832, the National Lyceum was organized in New York and thereafter held nine annual meetings. During these years the lyceum constitutions stated the purposes of the lyceum as "the improvement of its members in useful knowledge, and the advancement of popular education, by introducing uniformity and improvements in common schools."[14] The annual meetings of the National Lyceum voted in favor of many resolutions supporting education, urged "the establishment of seminaries for the education of teachers," especially female teachers, invited teachers to participate in the meetings of the local and county lyceums to improve themselves, and proposed that "fellow citizens . . . act without delay in visiting and improving common schools by addressing public assemblies, forming lyceums, or by other means to excite and direct general cooperation" in support of education.[15] After 1839 the lyceums tended to become programs more for entertainment than for education, but they had lobbied for legislation resulting in the creation of state boards of education, notably in Massachusetts and Connecticut.

In the West the non sectarian character of the lyceum provided common ground for religious groups to build the understandings necessary to promote public education, and there the lyceums were supplemented by the Western Literary Institute and College of Professional Teachers, organized in 1831 by Albert and John W. Pickett. Its "mission was to create a public opinion in favor of the free school system."[16] The organization published transactions of its annual meetings for a number of years and held meetings until at least 1844, with delegates attending from Pennsylvania, Ohio, Kentucky, Tennessee, Virginia, Indiana, Illinois, Missouri, Michigan, Mississippi, Louisiana, Georgia, North Carolina, South Carolina, Florida, and the Territories of Iowa and Wisconsin. At the fifth annual meeting, held in 1836, the delegates voted to return to their homes and petition their various legislatures "in behalf of universal education." Their petitions were to be accompanied by a short address containing "the general outline of the best and most approved present system of popular education," thus informing the legislatures of the "experience and most approved measures in behalf of education in the Eastern states and in Europe."[17]

[14] Cecil B. Hayes, *The American Lyceum, Its History and Contribution to Education*, U.S. Office of Education, Bulletin, 1932, No. 12, p. 3.
[15] *Ibid.*, pp. 59–64.
[16] Venable, p. 421.
[17] Monroe, pp. 810–811.

Political Leaders

Under the pressures of the workingmen's societies, the reformers, and other agencies, some political leaders began to awaken to the need for legislation to promote education. In the late 1820's and early 1830's a number of governors began sending messages to their legislatures urging the enactment of school laws. In 1831 the *American Annals of Education* reported that the governors of Maine, New York, Pennsylvania, Delaware, South Carolina, Ohio, and Illinois had "adverted to common education" in recent messages to their legislatures. Even in the aristocratic South, Governor Hamilton of South Carolina recommended legislation to provide education for the poor, saying that "the only safe and effective Agrarian system is the scheme of public education. This alone will secure to the poor their just rights."[18] Governor Wolf, of Pennsylvania, charged in 1833 that his state had not met the provisions required in the 1790 constitution of providing schools in which "the poor may be taught gratis."

> Our apathy and indifference in reference to this subject becomes the more conspicuous when we reflect that whilst we are expending millions for the improvement of the physical condition of the State, we have not hitherto appropriated a single dollar that is available for the intellectual improvement of the youth. . . .
>
> [W]ith all this numerous youthful population growing up around us, who in a few years are to be our rulers and law-givers, the defenders of our country . . . and upon whose education will depend in great measure the preservation of our liberties and the safety of the republic, we have neither schools established for their instruction, nor provisions made by law for establishing them as enjoined by the Constitution.[19]

Wolf's leadership, along with that of Thaddeus Stevens, was to put Pennsylvania in the forefront in the fight for free schools.

There was still much to be done to persuade many political leaders that the pious platitudes and half-way measures of the conservative period were not enough. Apparently some of the governors mentioned in the report of the *American Annals of Education* were still only lukewarm. The governor of Delaware urged consideration of the "claims of primary education" but told the legislature that Delaware had already

[18] *American Annals of Education,* I, p. 131.
[19] Quoted in Wickersham, pp. 308–309.

gone far enough with legislation, that "an attempt to give further aid to the cause, by extending the system of taxation, would defeat the object intended."[20]

Although the forces promoting the cause of common education had much to do to bring the political leaders to the point of effective legislation, a start had obviously been made. The implementation of these pressures into law will be discussed in the next chapter.

Foreign Influences

Not all the influences on the development of the common school were American. Many ideas from Europe were adapted to the purposes of a republic. Most significant of these educational imports were the various forms of Pestalozzianism, the kindergarten, and the Prussian state school system.

Pestalozzian Developments in American Education

One of the greatest modern educators was the Swiss teacher Johann Heinrich Pestalozzi (1746–1827), whose schools at Burgdorf and Yverdun aroused enthusiasm among educators all over Europe and in America. Basing his ideas on suggestions in Rousseau's *Emile*, Pestalozzi developed a theory which used love, respect for discipline, motivating through interest, observation of nature, and practical experience as the fundamental method of teaching. He set forth his theories in several books, including *The Evening Hour of a Hermit* (1780), *Leonard and Gertrude* (four volumes, 1781 to 1785), and *How Gertrude Teaches Her Children* (1801). In 1859 Barnard translated *The Evening Hour of a Hermit*, much of *Leonard and Gertrude*, and parts of *How Gertrude Teaches Her Children* in Volumes VI and VII of the *American Journal of Education*. Other journals throughout the period of the Common School Revival included numerous articles on Pestalozzi and his methods.

An American industrialist, William Maclure, was very much impressed by Pestalozzi's schools, which he visited in 1804, and he attempted to persuade the Swiss educator to come to America. Pestalozzi declined but recommended a former pupil, Joseph Neef, who was teaching in a Paris orphanage. Neef accepted Maclure's invitation and came to Philadelphia. Later he taught at Chester, Pennsylvania, and in Indiana and

[20] *American Annals of Education*, I, p. 131.

Kentucky. He wrote two books on educational theory which were reviewed and often referred to in the educational journals. In some of his letters Thomas Jefferson mentions Neef. One of Neef's students at Chester was young David Farragut, who later recalled Neef's teaching methods.

> I was put to school to a queer old individual named Neif. His method of instruction was simple in the extreme; he had no books, but taught orally on such subjects as he desired us to understand. The scholars took notes, and were afterward examined on these lectures. In the afternoon it was customary for us to take long walks, accompanied by our instructor. On these occasions Mr. Neif would make collections of minerals and plants, and talk to us about mineralogy and botany. The course of studies was not regular, but we certainly had an opportunity of gaining a great deal of useful information and worldly knowledge.[21]

The emphasis on observation and the oral teaching instead of almost complete reliance on books were revolutionary in American teaching methods, and it would take many more efforts before the average schoolmaster would change his techniques significantly.

When James Carter attempted to reform Massachusetts education in the 1820's, he praised the Pestalozzian methods. In criticizing textbooks in use as being generally deplorable, he made an exception of Warren Colburn's *First Lessons in Arithmetic upon the plan of Pestalozzi* (published in 1821) and his *Arithmetic, being a Sequel to First Lessons.* Colburn's books were based on Pestalozzi's object teaching, relating number to objects instead of treating number as abstraction; his new approach led to bringing mathematics from the secondary school down into the primary grades. Barnard reported that "about two million copies" were sold between 1821 and 1856 and that they were then selling at the rate of "about one hundred thousand per annum" in the United States, plus additional sales in England.[22]

Perhaps the success of Colburn's textbooks led other writers to follow his example. Two of the most popular English grammar books in the 1830's and 1840's were by Roswell Smith: *Intellectual and Practical Grammar on the Inductive System* (1829) and *English Grammar on the Productive System* (1831). In stating the Pestalozzian principle on which his texts were based, Smith wrote in his preface, "The child

[21] Loyal Farragut, *Life and Letters of David Farragut*, p. 49. Quoted in Monroe, pp. 1240–1241.

[22] *American Journal of Education*, Vol. II (1856), p. 302.

should be regarded not as the mere recipient of the ideas of others, but as an agent capable of collecting, and originating, and producing most of those ideas which are necessary for its education."[23]

One of the most famous Pestalozzian innovations was the method of teaching music developed by Lowell Mason. In 1830 William C. Woodbridge, who had visited European schools and had seen Johann George Naegeli applying the principles of Pestalozzi to the teaching of music, introduced some of the works of Naegeli to the United States and persuaded Mason to incorporate Pestalozzian principles in his *Manual of Instruction*. Again it was the inductive approach, having the children learn to sing before they learned to read notes and to draw out the theory from the experience. Mason's success was such that music was made an official part of the Boston school curriculum in 1838, and Mason was in charge of the program of music until 1850.

Between 1819 and 1822 the Reverend Charles Mayo and his sister Elizabeth assisted Pestalozzi, and on their return to England Miss Mayo wrote a textbook on object teaching. Josiah Holbrook tried to promote the use of Miss Mayo's object lessons, and Horace Mann recommended them in his *Eleventh Annual Report*. Unfortunately, few teachers adopted them because they were not trained to use them, and it was not until after 1870 that the object lesson was widely adopted through the influence of the Oswego Normal School.

Although the object lessons did not win wide acceptance during the Common School Revival, one of the most popular vogues was a form of Pestalozzianism. In 1806 Emanuel von Fellenberg, a friend of Pestalozzi, started a school on Pestalozzian principles at Hofwyl, Switzerland, which included agricultural and other manual activities. All students, rich and poor, had to engage in the work. This practicality made the Fellenberg system attractive to Americans. The workingmen's societies urged the adoption of the manual-labor school, arguing that boys should learn to be productive workers as well as "well-schooled boys." Conservatives saw the manual-labor activities of the schools as a means to help defray the cost of education. During the 1830's and 1840's many of the academies and colleges included manual-labor activities, particularly on the frontier, though there were many "Fellenberg Institutes" in the East and South. The vogue soon passed, partly perhaps because many of the programs lost money. The manual-labor school was not directly related to the much later industrial arts program in schools.

[23] Rollo La Verne Lyman, *English Grammar in American Schools Before 1850* (Chicago: U. of Chicago Libraries, 1922), p. 132.

The Kindergarten Movement

The unsuccessful revolutions in Prussia in 1836 and 1848 forced many German intellectuals to emigrate to America, where they settled in the Ohio and upper Mississippi River valleys. As a means of keeping their language and customs alive among their children, they established "kindergartens." This German institution had been invented by a former assistant of Pestalozzi, Friedrich Froebel, on the theory that the earliest years of a child are the most important in his development. During those years children had to be permitted to "grow in accordance with God's plan," thus the name "kindergarten."

One of the first kindergartens in the United States was started in 1855 by the wife of the German liberal and exile Carl Schurz. She had been a pupil of Froebel, and her school was a German-language kindergarten in Watertown, Wisconsin. Wherever there was a large community of German exiles, kindergartens appeared.

In 1860, after a visit to Europe, Miss Elizabeth Peabody, one of the foremost women in the history of American education and sister-in-law of Horace Mann, established the first English-speaking kindergarten in Boston. The development of the kindergarten will be treated in Chapter 10.

The Influence of Prussian Example

To assure the unquestioning loyalty of their subjects, the Prussian rulers had established the most effective and universal school system in the world in the early nineteenth century. Barnard reported that in Prussia "only two young men in every one hundred between the ages of twenty and twenty-two, . . . could not read, write, and cipher, and had not a knowledge of Scripture history."[24] American visitors were much impressed by the Prussian schools and methods of the Prussian teachers. A report to the French government by Victor Cousin in 1831, translated into English and widely read in the United States, caught the imagination of American educational reformers. When Calvin Stowe, husband of Harriet Beecher Stowe and leader of educational movements in Ohio, was preparing to go to Europe to purchase books for the library of Lane Theological Seminary in Cincinnati, the Ohio legislature commissioned him to report on the European schools, especially those in Prussia. His 1837 report was printed and distributed to every school district in Ohio by the legislature. It was reprinted and distributed by state legislatures

[24] *National Education in Europe* (Hartford: Case, Tiffany, 1854), p. 89.

in Massachusetts, Michigan, North Carolina, Pennsylvania, and Virginia. Barnard reprinted it in 1839 in his *Connecticut Common School Journal.* In Pennsylvania, Alexander Dallas Bache, after a tour of European orphanages and schools, in 1839 published a long and enthusiastic account of Prussian schools. On the invitation of Governor David Campbell, Dr. Benjamin H. Smith, who had been a student in Germany, made a report to the Virginia legislature in 1839 on Prussian schools. Barnard had visited Prussia and published a number of articles on Prussian schools in various sources; later he collected them in *National Education in Europe*, published in 1854.

HORACE MANN'S SEVENTH ANNUAL REPORT The most famous report on Prussian schools was by Horace Mann, and because of the controversy which it occasioned, it was probably the most influential. Mann spent the summer of 1843 visiting schools all over Europe. He included in his report for that year a long discussion of educational conditions he had observed, particularly those in Prussia. He disapproved of the purposes of Prussian education, but he admired their methods, their universality, and the preparation of their teachers. These things he commented on in his report, to the great displeasure of the Boston schoolmasters, who took the report as an attack on their methods. He did criticize some American methods of teaching and of maintaining discipline, but he did not refer to them or to any American teachers specifically.

Mann also praised the Prussian system of grouping or classing students by age and giving each teacher a single grade. The Prussian practice of compulsory attendance Mann believed appropriate to a republic if children were to learn to preserve their freedom. The report led to the first graded schools in Quincy, Massachusetts, in 1847, and to the first compulsory attendance law in 1852.

> If the Prussian schoolmaster has better methods of teaching reading, writing, grammar, geography, arithmetic, &c., so that, in half the time, he produces greater and better results, surely, we may copy his modes of teaching these elements, without adopting his notions of passive obedience to government, or of blind adherence to the articles of a church. . . .
>
> I entered a classroom of sixty children, of about six years of age. . . . The teacher took his station before them, and after making a playful remark which excited a light titter around the room, and effectually arrested attention, he gave a signal for silence. . . .
>
> The teacher first drew a house upon the blackboard. . . . By the side of the drawing and under it, he wrote the word *house* in the German script hand, and printed it in the German letter. . . .

In the single exercise above described, there were the elements of reading, spelling, writing, grammar and drawing, interspersed with anecdotes and not a little general information. . . .

Compare the above method with that of calling up a class of abecedarians,—or, what is more common, a single child, and while the teacher holds a book or a card before him, and with a pointer in his hand, says, *a*, and he echoes *a*; then *b*, and he echoes *b*; and so on until the vertical row of lifeless and ill-favored characters is completed, and then of remanding him to his seat, to sit still and look at vacancy. . . . As a general rule, six months are spent before the twenty-six letters are mastered, though the same child would learn the names of twenty-six playmates or twenty-six playthings in one or two days. . . .

It struck me that the main differences between their mode of teaching arithmetic and ours, consist in their beginning earlier, continuing the practice in the elements much longer, requiring a more thorough analysis of all questions, and in not separating the processes, or rules, so much as we do from each other. The pupils proceed less by rule, more by an understanding of the subject. . . .

1. During all this time, I never saw a teacher hearing a lesson of any kind, (excepting a reading or spelling lesson,) *with a book in his hand.*

2. I never saw a teacher *sitting,* while hearing a recitation.

3. Though I saw hundreds of schools, and thousands,—I think I may say, within bounds, tens of thousands of pupils,—*I never saw one child undergoing punishment, or arraigned for misconduct. I never saw one child in tears from having been punished, or from fear of being punished.* . . .

Parents are not obliged to send their children to a *public* school; if they prefer it, the children may be sent to a *private* school; but they *must* be sent to some one. All teachers, however, of private as well as of public schools, must submit to an examination, and have a certificate of qualification from the government officer.

A very erroneous idea prevails with us, that this enforcement of school attendance is the prerogative of despotism alone. I believe it is generally supposed here that such compulsion is not merely incompatible with, but impossible in, a free or elective government. This is a great error.[25]

When the conservative and orthodox Boston schoolmasters replied to Mann's *Seventh Annual Report,* he engaged in a bitter battle with them through the newspapers and pamphlets. In a series of letters to a friend in England, Mann described the conflict.

[25] *Seventh Annual Report of the Board of Education* (Boston: Dutton and Wentworth, 1844), pp. 22–23, 86, 89–90, 104, 132–133, 149.

> The Boston grammar-school masters saw their own condemnation in this description of their European contemporaries, and resolved, as a matter of self-preservation, to keep out the infection of so fatal an example as was afforded by the Prussian schools. . . . I wrote a "Reply to the Boston Masters."
>
> I think the Reply is doing something in Boston. All except the ultra-orthodox papers are earnest, I may almost say vehement, against the masters. . . .
>
> Our municipal election for mayor, school-committee men, &c., comes on a week from Monday; and, in some of the wards, a change has already been made in nominating school-committee men, the voters being determined to have better schools and less flogging.[26]

When the masters came back with a rejoinder to his "Reply," Mann had a chance to create more public interest through the controversy.

> My doughty assailants, the Boston schoolmasters . . . came out with a Rejoinder to my Reply. Our controversy was taking so obvious a turn in favor of improvement in the schools, that my regret at being called into the field again was very much modified: accordingly, on the first of August, I gave them an answer.

In spite of the strength of the thirty masters and their public support in Boston, Mann succeeded in awakening Massachusetts to such a degree that in the election of schoolmasters during the controversy "*four* of the masters have been turned out; a work which, twelve months ago, would have been deemed as impossible as to turn four peers out of the British House of Lords." Furthermore, Mann reported, community pressure for improvement was already being felt in the schools.

> The change already effected in the public mind, and even in the schools themselves under the old heads, is immense. It is estimated that corporal punishment has fallen off twenty-five per cent; and the masters have gone to work this year with the idea that they are *to make their calling and election sure*. . . . But the old notion of perfection in the Boston grammar and writing schools is destroyed; the prescription by which the masters held their office, and appointed indirectly their successors, is at an end. There is a strong revulsion of feeling in the public mind, and the masters are hereafter to stand upon their good behavior rather than on the self-complacency of their employers.[27]

[26] Mary Peabody Mann, *Life of Horace Mann* (Boston: Walker, Fuller, 1865), pp. 231–232.

[27] *Ibid.*, pp. 240–242.

The reports on Prussian education were very effective in the struggle to substitute state supervision for local district control of schools and in the efforts to improve teacher training through the establishment of normal schools, as well as in suggesting new methods of teaching and conducting schools.

QUESTIONS FOR DISCUSSION

1. The advancement of public education depends on the support of the public. How might some of the efforts to awaken public interest in the period of the Common School Revival be adapted to improve public relations for education today?
2. In our current attempts to view and improve American education by comparing it with schooling in other nations, how might we learn from the nineteenth-century enthusiasm for Prussian education in our utilization of modern educational ideas from abroad?
3. The Common School Revival was a period when many of our educational "heroes" made their contributions. Read the biographies of some of these educators and compare the difficulties under which they worked with those facing educators today. Do their lives and work suggest we might be optimistic or pessimistic about the solution of today's problems?
4. Select some educational figure from your own state and report on what you can find out about his life work and efforts to improve schooling.

SUGGESTED READINGS

Secondary Sources

Butts, R. Freemen, and Cremin, Lawrence A. *A History of Education in American Culture.* New York: Henry Holt, 1953. Chapters 5, 6, and 7.

Drake, William. *The American School in Transition.* Englewood Cliffs: Prentice-Hall, 1955. Chapter VI.

Hinsdale, B. A. *Horace Mann and the Common School Revival in the United States.* New York: Scribner's, 1898.

Mann, Mary Peabody. *Life of Horace Mann.* Washington: National Education Association of the United States, 1937.

Meyer, Adolphe E. *An Educational History of the American People.* New York: McGraw-Hill, 1957. Chapter 8.

Primary Sources

Commons, John R., *et al.* *A Documentary History of American Industrial Society.* Cleveland: Arthur H. Clark, 1910. Vol. V, pp. 93–123, 157–158, 161, 165–177, 188–189, 195–199.

Cubberley, Ellwood P. *Readings in the History of Education.* Boston: Houghton Mifflin, 1920. Readings 310, 315–320.

———. *Readings in Public Education in the United States*. Boston: Houghton Mifflin, 1934. Readings 93–104, 109–113, 116–118, 125, 127–133.

Knight, Edgar W. *A Documentary History of Education in the South Before 1860*. Chapel Hill: U. of North Carolina Press, 1949. Vol. II, Chapters IX, XII, XIII, and XIV; Vol. IV, Chapter II; Vol. V, pp. 228–230.

Knight, Edgar W., and Hall, Clifton L. *Readings in American Educational History*. New York: Appleton-Century-Crofts, 1951. Pp. 143–149, 151–177, 330–346, 362–365.

Monroe, Paul. *Founding of the American Public School System*. Ann Arbor: University Microfilms, 1940. Vol. II, Chapters XIII and XIV.

8

The Common School Revival

At the beginning of the Age of the Common Man, schools for the average child were poor in quality and few in number. Many children were receiving no schooling at all; in 1828 the New York Public School Society estimated that 24,200 of New York City's 52,300 children "attend no school whatever."[1] In many areas, schools met for short terms, perhaps three months in the summer for small children and an even briefer time in the cold weather for older children. Although some children may have attended both terms, there would be opportunity for only five or six months of school at most.

> The "Summer Free Schools" . . . are, generally, taught in the country towns for a few months in the warm part of the year by females; and . . . the "Winter Free Schools," which are taught by men, commonly, for a shorter period, during the cold season. Children of both sexes of from four to ten or twelve years, usually attend these primary summer schools, and females often to much later age.[2]

Even for those who did go to school, the curriculum was very limited.

> Another radical and glaring defect in the existing public school system is the very limited amount of instruction it affords, even to the comparatively small number of youth, who enjoy its benefits. It extends, in no case, further than a tolerable proficiency in reading, writing, and arithmetic, and sometimes to a slight acquaintance with geography.[3]

[1] Bourne, p. 111.

[2] Carter, p. 34.

[3] *Working Man's Advocate* (New York), March 6, 1830. Quoted in Commons, p. 97.

Changes would be very difficult, because teachers were generally poorly qualified, and there was little or no supervision. Perhaps conditions were best in Massachusetts, but even there, as Carter pointed out in his letters and essays, the situation was far from good.

> The teachers of the summer primary schools have rarely had any education beyond what they have acquired in the very schools where they begin to teach. Their attainments, therefore, to say the least, are usually *very moderate*. But this is not the worst of it. They are often very young; they are constantly changing their employment, and consequently they can have but little experience; and what is worst of all, they never have had any direct preparation for their profession. . . .
>
> [A]ny one *keeps* school, which is a very different thing from *teaching* school, who wishes to do it, and can persuade . . . a small district to employ her. And this is not a very difficult matter, especially when the remuneration for the employment is so very trifling. The farce of an examination and a certificate from the minister of the town, for it is a perfect farce, amounts to no efficient check upon the obtrusions of ignorance and inexperience. . . .
>
> Many of the above remarks upon . . . the summer schools apply with equal force to the young men, who undertake the instruction of the primary winter schools, which now constitute the highest class of schools, to which the whole population of the state have free access.[4]

In other states, lacking even the bare minimum of legal structure that Massachusetts had, the condition was worse. In New York some districts had no schools; others granted public money to private schools to meet the requirement of the law to provide instruction "at the most convenient schools."

> From a parsimonious desire to saving the county funds, the cheapest, and consequently the most inefficient schools have been usually selected by the commissioners of the several counties.
>
> The elementary schools throughout the state are irresponsible institutions, established by individuals, from mere motives of private speculation or gain, who are sometimes destitute of character, and frequently, of the requisite attainments and abilities. From the circumstance of the schools being the absolute property of individuals, no supervision or effectual control can be exercised over them; hence, ignorance, inattention, and even immorality, prevail to a lamentable extent among their teachers.
>
> In some districts, no schools whatever exist![5]

[4] Carter, pp. 36–38.
[5] *Working Man's Advocate*, p. 96.

A revolution in education was called for to bring the changes needed for the industrial democracy that was appearing in the United States. And as the attacks on public apathy proceeded, substantial changes were made in the common school. Public financial support increased and the use of the rate bill, paupers' oaths, and philanthropy declined. Local control gave way to several forms of centralization of supervision. Denominational dominance of schools decreased: separation of church and state resulted in a more secular curriculum and government control. Schools multiplied in number, and attendance jumped; school terms were lengthened; the curriculum was expanded; textbooks were improved; better school buildings were built and equipped with new apparatus; and teachers began taking special preparation for their tasks. Few changes of this revolutionary period were more extensive than those in the common schools.

Tax Support

Campaign for Tax Support

As the public demand for universal education increased, even the conservatives realized the necessity for tax support of schools. In New York the Public School Society fought to preserve its share of tax money and to secure a greater portion. In 1828 they urged an increase in the taxes for the support of schools. The use of permanent school funds to support common education had proved harmful. In Connecticut, where the fund was the largest of all the state funds and where it had been used as effectively as anywhere, the Connecticut *Courant* complained in 1830 that complete reliance on the fund had kept the state from having adequate schools.

> The prevailing mode of managing our common schools renders them comparatively useless. Exclusive reliance is placed upon the avails of the fund, and in a great majority of instances, no addition is made to the amount obtained from this source, by tax or otherwise, and consequently adequate means are not provided for employing competent instructors. . . . A cheap instructor is employed for a few months, and the remainder of the year the school-house is closed.[6]

The workingmen's societies and other groups objected strenuously to the charity stigma attached to those schools where parents had to take a

[6] Quoted in Commons, p. 109.

pauper's oath to send their children as "free scholars." The disgrace kept many parents from sending their children to school, preferring "to starve the intellect of their offspring, than submit to become objects of public charity."[7]

The Free-School Law in Pennsylvania

The first state to make a major breakthrough in the elimination of the pauper school was Pennsylvania. Since 1802, Pennsylvania school laws, carrying out the provision of the 1790 Constitution, had provided for the education of the children of the poor only, and the Act of 1809, which was still a pauper school law, had continued in effect until 1834, except for a brief attempt at partial repeal between 1824 and 1826. The Public School Law of 1834 permitted districts to tax themselves for the support of schools which would be free to all children. In spite of the fact that the law *required* no district to tax itself, 52 percent of the school districts voted in the next election to set up the necessary tax levies. The opposition to the tax and the free schools was bitter, particularly among the wealthy farmers and among the German religious sects and Catholics, who maintained their own parochial schools and objected to "double taxation." Many of the legislators who had voted for the law were defeated, and many who were elected or re-elected made campaign promises to vote for the repeal of the law. In addition, the House of Representatives was flooded with petitions containing 31,988 signatures favoring repeal; only a few petitions, with 2,575 signatures, urged its continuance. When the legislature met, the Senate voted, with only eight dissenting votes, to repeal the law and return to the 1809 pauper school provisions. There was every indication that the House of Representatives would do the same, with many of the supporters of the 1834 provision voting for the repeal.

In this situation came a man who must rightly be considered a hero of education, however he may be judged for his later national policies during Reconstruction. Thaddeus Stevens, who had been re-elected by a very slim margin and whose constituents had voted three to one *against* the free school referendum, was the only man in the legislature with the courage to stand up for his conviction that free public schools were essential for democracy. Stevens was a long-time partisan for schools, having been a school teacher in Vermont during his college days and having served on the district board of trustees in his home of Gettysburg. As early as 1825 he had attempted unsuccessfully to get free schools in his home district under the short-lived 1824 law. Whenever he had occa-

[7] *Ibid.*, p. 97.

sion to offer a public toast, it was "Education—May the film be removed from the eyes of Pennsylvania and she learn to dread ignorance more than taxation." To the end of his life he maintained his concern for education, his last substantial writing being a draft for a bill to provide free schools for the District of Columbia, written just a month before he died.

As the House of Representatives prepared to vote on the repeal of the 1834 law, Stevens was in Philadelphia on legislative business. Legislators, faced with the problem of voting for a bill contrary to the expressed opinions of a majority of their constituents, customarily avail themselves of the convenient excuse of being absent at the time of the vote. But Stevens did not dodge the issue. Instead he announced his intention to fight the repeal. Before a packed chamber, with the gallery filled with visitors, newsmen, and Senators, he offered his own substitute bill, which would strengthen the 1834 act rather than repeal it. Speaking from sketchy notes, he criticized sharply those who were willing to compromise their principles for political expediency and predicted that in the long run those who had been defeated on principle would be returned to favor in the eyes of the people. He demonstrated how public schools would be less costly than a system of private schools, and would reach children who were getting no schooling. Finally, he attacked the undemocratic provisions of pauper education.

> The amendment which is now proposed as a substitute for the school law of last session, is, in my opinion, of a most hateful and degrading character. It is a reenactment of the pauper law of 1809. It proposes that the assessors shall take a census, and make a record of the poor. This shall be revised, and a new record made by the county commissioners, so that the names of those who have the misfortune to be poor men's children shall be forever preserved, as a distinct class, in the archives of the country! The teacher, too, is to keep in his school a pauper book, and register the names and attendance of poor scholars; thus pointing out and recording their poverty in the midst of their companions. Sir, hereditary distinctions of rank are sufficiently odious; but that which is founded on poverty is infinitely more so. Such a law should be entitled "An act for branding and marking the poor, so that they may be known from the rich and proud." Many complain of this tax, not so much on account of its amount, as because it is for the benefit of others and not themselves. This is a mistake; it is for their own benefit, inasmuch as it perpetuates the Government and insures the due administration of the laws under which they live, and by which their lives and property are protected. Why do they not urge the same objec-

> tion against all other taxes? The industrious, thrifty, rich farmer pays a heavy county tax to support criminal courts, build jails, and pay sheriffs and jail keepers, and yet probably he never has, and never will have, any personal use of either. He never gets the worth of his money by being tried for a crime before the court, by being allowed the privilege of the jail on conviction, or receiving an equivalent from the sheriff or his hangman officers! He cheerfully pays the tax which is necessary to support and punish convicts, but loudly complains of that which goes to prevent his fellow-being from becoming a criminal, and to obviate the necessity of those humiliating institutions.
>
> This law is often objected to, because its benefits are shared by the children of the profligate spendthrift equally with those of the most industrious and economical habits. It ought to be remembered that the benefit is bestowed, not upon the erring parents, but the innocent children. Carry out this objection and you punish children for the crimes or misfortunes of their parents. You virtually establish castes and grades founded on no merit of the particular generation, but on the demerits of their ancestors; an aristocracy of the most odious and insolent kind—the aristocracy of wealth and pride.[8]

The point of his argument was not wasted on politicians living in the "Age of the Common Man." The House of Representatives immediately voted for his substitute bill by a two-thirds majority, and the next day the Senate rescinded its vote on the repeal and joined the House in passing Stevens' bill.

Although no actual record of the speech was made at that time, Stevens, under the urging of Governor Wolf and other friends of education, wrote a draft of his remarks which were printed widely outside of Pennsylvania as well as within the state. It had tremendous influence in reversing public opinion in the state. In 1834 there were about 800 free schools in Pennsylvania; by 1837 this number had increased to some 3,400.

Legislation in Other States

Following the example of Pennsylvania, other states in the North and West removed the pauper's oath and the rate bill, although New York and Connecticut did not abolish them until 1868 and Michigan not until 1869. In the South the rate bill was to remain even longer. Until the beginning of the twentieth century some taint of charity was attached to the public schools, and those parents who had pretensions

[8] Quoted in Finegan, pp. 59–61.

to higher social standing sent their children to private schools to avoid the suggestion that they were unable to pay for the schooling of their children.

In general, the struggle to provide tax support for schools went through three stages. The first was that represented by the Pennsylvania 1834 law—permissive legislation, granting districts the right to tax themselves. The second was incentive legislation, granting state moneys to districts which did tax themselves. The last was mandatory legislation, requiring districts to tax themselves. In some states it was possible to by-pass one or even two of the stages, and some of the states to enter the Union later did so with constitutional provisions or early laws requiring all districts to levy taxes for the support of schools.

Federal Aid

In addition to state and local tax support, the period of the Common School Revival was a time when federal aid to schools was continued in the tradition of the Northwest Ordinance of 1785. Tennessee had been granted land under a special act of Congress. All the states that had been territories received grants of land for the support of schools under provisions like those in the Northwest Territories. States not participating in the land grants were Maine, which had been a part of Massachusetts until the Missouri Compromise; Texas, which had been an independent nation; and West Virginia, which broke away from Virginia when the rest of that state seceded from the Union. States entering the Union after 1850 received two sections in every township, and three states, which were very arid and where land sold at a low price, received four sections per township. Under this land grant tradition alone the federal government gave the states over an eighth of a million square miles of land, an area greater than that of any of the states except Alaska or Texas and greater than the combined area of all of New England, New York, and New Jersey. In addition to the section grants for the support of schools, many states were granted two whole townships or even more for the support of higher education, an amount totalling more than 5,000 square miles. If these huge endowments had been used wisely by the states, both schools and colleges would have had a much better start and fewer financial difficulties in keeping up with the demands of a growing society—but there were not enough provisions for control over the disposal of the lands and the spending of the funds to assure fiscal integrity.

There were other federal grants to the states during the period from 1820 to 1860. States containing salt springs, swamp lands, and certain

TABLE 1: SECTION GRANTS FOR THE SUPPORT OF COMMON SCHOOLS[9]

States, In Order of Admission	Date of Admission	Sections Received	Total Grant in Acres
Tennessee	1796	one, in part	400,000
Ohio	1802	16th	704,488
Louisiana	1812	16th	786,044
Indiana	1816	16th	650,317
Mississippi	1817	16th	837,584
Illinois	1818	16th	985,066
Alabama	1819	16th	902,744
Maine	1820	none	none
Missouri	1821	16th	1,199,139
Arkansas	1836	16th	886,460
Michigan	1837	16th	1,067,397
Florida	1845	16th	908,503
Texas	1845	none	none
Iowa	1846	16th	905,144
Wisconsin	1848	16th	958,649
California	1850	16th, 36th	6,719,324
Minnesota	1858	16th, 36th	2,969,990
Oregon	1859	16th, 36th	3,329,706
Kansas	1861	16th, 36th	2,801,306
West Virginia	1863	none	none
Nevada	1864	16th, 36th	3,985,428
Nebraska	1867	16th, 36th	2,702,044
Colorado	1876	16th, 36th	3,715,555
North Dakota	1889	16th, 36th	2,542,940
South Dakota	1889	16th, 36th	2,539,175
Montana	1889	16th, 36th	5,112,035
Washington	1889	16th, 36th	2,488,675
Idaho	1890	16th, 36th	3,068,231
Wyoming	1890	16th, 36th	3,480,281
Utah	1896	16th, 36th, 2d, 32d	6,007,226
Oklahoma	1907	16th, 36th	1,413,083
Arizona	1911	16th, 36th, 2d, 32d	8,100,694
New Mexico	1911	16th, 36th, 2d, 32d	8,618,736
			80,785,964

other geographic problems making the land of little value were granted those lands. Nine states used the "salt lands" for educational purposes: Ohio, Indiana, Missouri, Arkansas, Michigan, Iowa, Wisconsin, Kansas, and Nebraska. Approximately 370,000 acres of federal land was involved. Further, any state that did not tax federal lands within its border received from the national government 5 percent of the proceeds of the

[9] Ellwood P. Cubberley and Edward C. Elliott, *State and County School Administration, Vol. II, Source Book* (New York: Macmillan, 1915), p. 33.

sale of those lands. Beginning with Illinois in 1818, at least a part of this money was dedicated to schools and colleges. By 1913, this source had yielded $16,093,417.43.[10]

In 1836 Congress, embarrassed by a large surplus in the national treasury accumulated from the high tariff, passed the Surplus Revenue Act, distributing nearly $28,000,000 among the twenty-six states. At least twenty-one of the states used some part of the revenue, or the interest from it, for education. In 1841 Congress passed the Internal Improvement Act, making actual cash grants to the states. Court decisions ruled that schools were an internal improvement, and Tennessee's share of $29,703.48 and the District of Columbia's share of $1,643.72 went for schools. In addition to money, land grants totaling nine million acres were given to the various states in half-million acre grants. Ten states put all or part of their lands into the common school funds, approximately four million acres.

Tragically, most of these great bounties of federal aid to education were lost, partly through carelessness and lack of recognition of the importance of education and land, partly through political malfeasance. The history of these grants suggests that federal aid without some federal control has little long-lasting benefits to schools. Certainly there is no support in the *ante-bellum* period for the claim that federal aid is inevitably accompanied by controls that will interfere with local control of schools and school funds.

Centralization of Control and Support

The District System

In the nineteenth century, the basic administrative unit of schools was the district. Appearing during the Colonial period, it was first legally recognized in the Massachusetts school law of 1789, which authorized towns to divide their territory into districts small enough to permit all children to get to school. In Massachusetts by 1840, the 307 towns had been divided into at least 2,500 school districts.[11] The districts were administered by "prudential committees" of one or three men. (In other states they were known by other names, the most common being "school trustees.") The prudential committee was to "provide a suitable place in which the school may be kept," "keep it in good repair, at the expense

[10] *Ibid.*, pp. 46–48.

[11] Horace Mann, *Fourth Annual Report of the Board of Education* (Boston: Dutton and Wentworth, 1841), p. 17.

of the district," recommend teachers to the town school committee, and generally oversee the activities of the school.[12] In many districts the committees could not decide on where to locate the schools or who should teach the school, and so the district would be sub-divided. The result was that many schools were very small and many districts did not have enough funds to operate effective schools. In 1840 in Massachusetts, 14 schools had fewer than 10 pupils, 194 had between 10 and 20, and 426 had between 20 and 30.[13]

Quite apart from these problems of the district system, leaving the charge of education up to towns was far from satisfactory. The 1827 Massachusetts school law required towns of five hundred families to maintain a school "'*For the benefit of all the inhabitants of the town,*' ten months, at least, exclusive of vacations, in each year" where children would be taught history of the United States, bookkeeping, surveying, geometry, and algebra, in addition to "the branches of learning to be taught in the district schools." The law also required towns of four thousand inhabitants to employ a master competent in Latin and Greek languages, general history, rhetoric, and logic. Mann reported that of the forty-three towns in Massachusetts which fell into those classifications, only fourteen met the requirements of the school law and the remaining twenty-nine "wholly disregarded" that provision of the law. Furthermore, the law required that the town authorities supervise their schools by visitation, but "not in more than fifty or sixty towns, out of the three hundred and five, has there been any pretence of compliance with the law."[14]

Need for State Control and Support

Since local authorities neglected their educational responsibilities so flagrantly, it appeared necessary to delegate the task of overseeing schools to a more central authority. The states had been granting tax money for the support of schools, and there was a long tradition of state legislation requiring local authorities and parents to see to the education of the children. New York had a state superintendent of common schools from 1812 to 1821. Although he was to manage the common school fund of the state and to advise the legislature on matters relating to the schools, he had little control over local district authorities or teachers. Gideon Hawley filled this office until it was abolished in 1821 and the duties made an *ex officio* responsibility of the secretary of state. In spite of the

[12] Mann, *Tenth Annual Report*, pp. 149–151.
[13] Mann, *Fourth Annual Report*, p. 18.
[14] Mann, *First Annual Report*, pp. 41, 51–52.

lack of power, Hawley was an effective agent for promoting the development of common schools in New York, and during his term of office over five thousand schools were established, with an enrollment of more than three hundred thousand pupils. Although the office was eliminated in a political struggle, Hawley's effectiveness no doubt contributed to the creation of similar posts in other states, where the need for central authority was becoming apparent.

Financial support as well as control had to be centralized to give more equality of educational opportunity. Horace Mann warned that the school could not be left up to the option of the counties, for "it will be rejected by the counties that most require it." He urged that support be based on "*state*, rather than *county* taxation."[15]

Horace Mann and the Massachusetts Board of Education

In Massachusetts the law of 1837 created the state board of education, charged with administering school funds or lands, reporting annually to the legislature on the conditions of the common schools, and suggesting "the most practicable means for improving and extending" public, or "popular education."

Horace Mann was appointed first secretary to the Massachusetts board. Since neither the board nor its secretary had the power to control schools, the office would have had little effect in the hands of a weak leader, but Mann was not a weak leader. With constant persuasion, he induced Massachusetts legislators, town meetings, schoolmasters, taxpayers, and parents to improve the schools of the state. His efforts, in the twelve years he served as secretary, brought rapid improvement in the common schools, not only in Massachusetts, but by example in many other states as well.

State School Superintendents

By the outbreak of the Civil War, twenty-eight of the thirty-four states had some form of state school officer, although nine of them were *ex officio*. Of the six which did not have a state school officer in 1860, Maryland had had a superintendent of public instruction from 1826–1828, New Hampshire a state school commissioner from 1846–1850, and Mississippi the secretary of state as *ex officio* school commissioner from 1846 to 1851; thus only Delaware, Georgia, and Virginia had not had some state school officer prior to the War.[16] The titles of the chief state

[15] Knight, Vol. V, p. 340.
[16] Cubberley and Elliott, pp. 283–287.

school officers varied greatly; some were appointed by the governor or the state board of education, but most of them were elected. In general they were charged with the responsibility of collecting and disseminating information, holding teachers' institutes, visiting schools, and exercising "general superintendence" over the schools. They had little or no executive authority. As a consequence, unless the office was filled with a dynamic leader, little was achieved in the improvement of schools. But a start was made, and after the Civil War these precedents were the foundation for the development of state school systems.

City and County Superintendents

Meanwhile, the existence of many independent school districts within the same city was confusing and almost impossible to administer, so that some cities were beginning to unify their schools under a city superintendent. In 1837 Buffalo created the first superintendent of city schools in the United States and unified its seven one-teacher districts under one control, expanding the number of schools to fifteen in addition to a central school to teach the "higher English branches." In 1842 the Michigan legislature unified the Detroit schools under a city board of education. By 1861, at least twenty-five cities had city superintendents.

In New England, the town (the counterpart of townships or counties in other states) was responsible for supervising schools but, as Mann reported, most of them were not fulfilling that obligation because of the great number of schools and the fact that the town school committee members were unpaid citizens whose private business concerns did not leave them time for the "public duty of visitation." To solve that difficulty, the town of Springfield appropriated $1,000 in 1840 to be used as a salary for a superintendent of schools. In other states the office of county superintendent was created, and by 1861, ten states had county school systems.

Although schools remained largely a local concern and responsibility, the trend was thus definitely toward some form of central control and support. As Mann had pointed out, equality of opportunity appeared to depend on a broader base of control and support than the local community.

Secularization of Schools

Throughout the history of Western civilization there have been close ties between education and religion and, as we have seen, in the American Colonies, schools were the responsibility of the church or a church-state.

One of the Enlightenment fears was the domination by a church and particularly of a church-state, and an issue in the Revolutionary War was the threat of an established Anglican Church for all the colonies. In the years following the War, state constitutions and laws and the federal Constitution provided for separation of church and state with some degree of religious freedom for individual citizens.

In spite of the disestablishment of churches and the granting of religious freedom, schools remained essentially religious institutions. During the Federalist period, schools were often sponsored by religious-oriented philanthropy. The town schools of New England were under the supervision of the clergy, who continued to issue the certificates to those who sought teaching positions. Schools generally favored Protestant Christianity, and in some areas they indoctrinated all children with a particular sectarian creed, regardless of what religious preference the children or their parents might have.

Horace Mann's View of "Non-sectarian" Schools

Until the establishment of the state board of education, the Massachusetts schools had been predominantly Congregational, but Horace Mann began to lead them in the direction of fulfilling the American doctrine that "no one sect shall obtain any advantage over other sects by means of the school system."[17] The Revised Statutes of Massachusetts (1836) required that school committees "shall never direct to be purchased or used, in any of the town schools, any school books which are calculated to favor any tenets of any particular sect of Christians." The fact that Christianity was specified reveals the limited religious freedom in Massachusetts. To that end, the Bible was urged by Mann "either as a devotional or as a reading book," and in 1845 he reported that only three towns out of the 308 in the state did not use the Bible—the schools in 258 towns using it as a reading book and in 38 as either a reading or a devotional book. The Board of Education had directed that the Bible also be used in the state normal schools, and Mann reported that it was used in all the academies. The use of the Bible was justified on the ground that it favored no sect.

> But the Bible has nothing in it of a sectarian character. All Christian sects regard it as the text-book of their faith. . . .
>
> [W]hile our Legislatures have guarded . . . our Common Schools,

[17] Mann, *The Bible, the Rod, and Religion, in the Common Schools* (Boston, 1847). Quoted in Cubberley, *Readings in Public Education in the United States* (Boston: Houghton Mifflin, 1934), p. 209.

> from becoming places for sectarian instruction, they have, at the same time, provided for the instruction of the youth, both in the schools and in the other institutions of learning, in a knowledge of the principles of the Christian religion. The . . . Revised Statutes, enjoins it, as a duty upon all the instructors of youth, that they shall impress upon their minds, "the principles of piety"—and those other virtues, which are the basis, upon which a republican constitution is founded. . . .
>
> It is difficult to perceive, how these results can be accomplished, without a frequent reference to the pages of the sacred volume.[18]

Although he urged the use of the Bible as a "non-sectarian" schoolbook, Mann objected to other books in the schools which were being used at the time he assumed his duties as secretary to the board of education.

> I found books in the schools, as strictly and exclusively *doctrinal* as any on the shelves of a theological library. I heard teachers giving oral instruction, as strictly and purely *doctrinal*, as any ever heard from the pulpit. . . . I have now in my possession, printed directions, given by committee men to teachers, enjoining upon them the use of a catechism, in school, which is wholly devoted to an exposition of the doctrines of one of the denominations.[19]

It was this kind of denominationalism that Mann sought to eliminate from the common schools, but in so doing he aroused the animosity of the religious orthodoxy, particularly the Episcopalians and the more strict Congregationalists. In 1844 the *Christian Witness* and *Christian Advocate*, Episcopalian papers in Boston, attacked Mann and the board for promoting non-sectarian instruction. The public newspapers came to the defense of the board and accused the *Christian Witness* of attempting to "lead the unwary into error, because speciously proposing to reform and improve institutions that would never have been founded, probably, had it depended upon their sect." Mann replied to the *Witness*, demonstrating, according to the Salem *Observer*, that the charges "are utterly destitute of foundation."

But that did not end the conflict. In 1846 the Reverend Matthew Hale Smith blamed an increase in crime, intemperance, and juvenile "depravity" on the "Godless schools" and the reduction of corporal punishment in schools. He charged that the board of education was

[18] Mann, *Eighth Annual Report*, pp. 14–17.
[19] Mann, *Twelfth Annual Report*, p. 113.

working to get out of the common schools "the Bible and all religious instruction" and to "abolish the use of the rod, and all correction, but a little talk." This was the result of allowing Mann "to disseminate through the land crude and destructive principles, principles believed to be at war with the Bible and with the best interests of the young" and by the school library "which excludes books as sectarian that inculcate truths, which *nine-tenths of professed Christians of all names believe,* while it accepts others that inculcate the most deadly heresy." Smith and Mann engaged in a heated exchange of letters and pamphlets over the issue. Mann warned that the indoctrination of a particular faith through the public common schools would eventually destroy religious freedom and bring back the age-old forms of religious persecution.

> If the question, "What theology shall be taught in school?" is to be decided by districts or towns, then all the prudential and superintending school committees must be chosen with express reference to their faith; the creed of every candidate for teaching must be investigated; and when litigations arise—and such a system will breed them in swarms—an ecclesiastical tribunal, some star chamber, or high commission court must be created to decide them. . . . The establishment of the true faith will not stop with the schoolroom. Its grasping jurisdiction will extend over all schools, over all private faith and public worship, until at last, after all our centuries of struggle and of suffering, it will come back to the inquisition, the faggot, and the rack.[20]

The Catholic Campaign for School Funds in New York City

The controversy over religion in the schools came to a legislative climax in New York. Ironically, increased separation of education and religion resulted from an attempt of Roman Catholics to get state money to support schools to teach a religious dogma acceptable to Catholics. In New York City, public education had been left to philanthropic agencies and churches, and the Public School Society had the largest system of schools, receiving a major share of the appropriations from the common school fund. Others which participated in the common school fund moneys allotted to the city were a number of orphanages, including those of the Roman Catholic Benevolent Society and the Bethel Baptist Church. In 1822 the Baptists received permission to use money for schools, and the Public School Society objected that such an appropriation would weaken their own "non-sectarian" schools. Upon the urging of

[20] Cubberley, pp. 208–209. See also pp. 203–205.

the trustees of the Public School Society, the legislature in 1824 gave the New York City Common Council the authority to determine every three years which schools would share in the money from the common school fund, and the Council limited the participating schools to four "non-sectarian" school societies—the Free-School Society (later the Public School Society), the Mechanics' Society, the Orphan Asylum Society, and the trustees of the African free schools.[21]

The controversy was revived in 1831 when the Catholics applied for a share of the school moneys to be used for a charity school for Catholic orphans. The new waves of immigrants from Ireland and Germany were the first heavy influx of Catholics, and since many were of the lower class and had to avail themselves of charity schools for the education of their children, they objected to the strong Protestant orientation of the existing schools. The non-sectarian character of the schools was certainly not non-religious, and school textbooks used such anti-Catholic expressions as "Romish plot," "despised papist," and "popery." The Catholics, aside from this Protestant hostility, believed that no education was complete without religious teaching consistent with their doctrine, and they argued that, since they were paying taxes for the support of public schools, they should have a share of the public funds for schools acceptable to their beliefs. Two weeks after the Catholics applied for a share of the fund, the trustees of the Methodist Charity School, which had formerly been given a share of the fund moneys but had been cut out as a result of the Bethel Baptist Church controversy, also applied for a share of the funds. The Common Council, on a tie vote broken by the vote of the president of the Board of Aldermen, granted a share to the Catholics but turned down the Methodists by a vote of eight to three.[22] The trustees of the Public School Society warned that granting either application would open the door to every imaginable denomination asking for state money for schools, thus dividing the community instead of uniting it and rendering ineffective the meager fund for supporting schools.

The warning of the Public School Society became a serious threat to unity within a decade. When William H. Seward became governor of New York, he made a careful study of the educational problems in New York City and discovered that some thirty thousand children in the city were not attending school. Many were children of foreign-born parents, and although the lack of a tradition of schooling was probably a factor in their failure to attend school, Seward blamed religious and language

[21] Bourne, pp. 48–50, 68–69, 73–75, 97.
[22] *Ibid.*, pp. 124–125, 132–133, 148.

differences. Recognizing that the existing schools in the city were essentially sectarian, Seward proposed in his annual message in 1840 that the common school system which existed outside the city be extended to the city children and that separate schools be set up to meet the religious interests of each religious and national group.

> The children of foreigners, found in great numbers in our populous cities and towns . . . are too often deprived of the advantages of our system of public education, in consequence of prejudices arising from difference of language or religion. . . . I do not hesitate, therefore, to recommend the establishment of schools in which they may be instructed by teachers speaking the same language with themselves and professing the same faith.[23]

Encouraged by the governor's recommendation and by their success in 1831, the Catholics in New York, led by Bishop John Hughes, applied for an apportionment of the school moneys to be used for charity schools. Soon a Hebrew congregation and a Scotch Presbyterian Church also applied for school funds. The Catholics organized thoroughly, creating a special association and establishing a weekly newspaper to press their claims. They charged that the Public School Society was a sectarian body and that its schools were sectarian in nature since reading was required in the Protestant Bible and many teachings were objectionable to Catholics, even though the Society claimed to be impartial to all Christians. The Public School Society led the general opposition to the applications to divide the school fund moneys among the various denominational schools, and the city refused all the 1840 applications on the ground that the fund had been created for the support of "free and common secular education" which would "place all mankind upon a common footing of equality."[24]

Blocked at the city level, the Catholics carried their fight to the legislature, and in 1842 the legislature, expressing the fear that concessions to one religious body would result in every sect's requesting schools of its own, passed a law extending the state common school system to the city, setting up a board of education in the city and authorizing it to establish and maintain ward schools throughout the city.

> No school . . . in which any religious sectarian doctrine or tenet shall be taught, inculcated, or practised, shall receive any portion of the school moneys to be distributed by this act.[25]

[23] Charles Z. Lincoln (ed.), *Messages from the Governors* (Albany: State of New York, 1909), Vol. III, p. 768.
[24] Bourne, pp. 734, 730.
[25] *Ibid.*, pp. 523–524.

In addition to providing free, tax-supported, secular public education for New York City, the law helped bring an end to the philanthropic tradition. Finally, in 1853 the schools of the Public School Society were absorbed into the publicly controlled city system.

Controversy Continues over Religion in Education

Even though the 1842 New York laws, and similar ones in other states, spelled out very clearly the role of schools in the separation of church and state, the matter of religion in education continued to be one of great controversy and even bloodshed in the United States.

Many Catholic children attended the public schools, partly for economic reasons, partly because there were no parochial schools available in their neighborhood. Preferring secular schools to those which inculcated Protestant teachings, the Catholics urged greater separation of religion and education in the public schools. In 1842 Bishop Francis Patrick Kendrick urged that Catholic children be excused from Bible readings in the public schools when the King James version was used, and when the school commissioners granted the request, religious riots broke out between members of the Native American party and Catholics. Philadelphia riots in 1844 resulted in the death of perhaps a dozen people, the injury of many more, the burning of two Catholic churches, a seminary, and over forty other buildings valued at a quarter of a million dollars.[26] Similar violence threatened in New York, and Bishop John Hughes placed groups of armed men in the Catholic churches to protect them from mob action. Political campaigns turned on the issue of Bible reading in school, and in Massachusetts the Know-Nothing majority in the legislature passed (1855) a number of anti-Catholic bills, including one requiring Bible reading in schools.

In many areas Catholic children suffered expulsion, flogging, and threats for refusing to read the King James version of the Bible or engage in other Protestant religious exercises, and court decisions upheld the right of the schools to require students to engage in such exercises and to punish those children who rebelled.[27] It was because of this intolerance and the failure of government agencies to carry out the principle of the separation of church and state in education that the Catholic parochial system was developed.

[26] Peter H. Binzen, "Riots Long Have Raged Over Bible Reading in School," *The Sunday Bulletin*, Philadelphia, Sunday, October 14, 1962.

[27] Leo Pfeffer, *Church, State, and Freedom* (Boston: Beacon Press, 1953), pp. 376–378.

Developments in the Common School

The struggles to reform the common school, making it free, tax-supported, state controlled, and non-denominational, were the major theme in the Common School Revival, but within the schools there were a number of important developments. By 1860 all states had made a start on public elementary schooling, although the ideal of universal education was far from realized. Enrollment increased, terms were lengthened, the curriculum was broadened, new textbooks were published, one-room schools began to give way to "graded" schools, and efforts were made at training teachers for the common schools.

Enrollments

The "common schools" of the mid-nineteenth century were not standardized throughout the nation, and no amount of description could give a complete picture of all the variations. In general, however, they were elementary and open to all children in common. They received financial support from the local and state governments, although many collected fees through a rate bill. They frequently had two terms, one in summer for the smaller children and one in winter for the older boys and girls. Sometimes, particularly in rural areas, the winter term included courses that might be considered secondary-school work. As public concern for schooling was aroused and as the separation of church and state reduced the effectiveness of churches as educational agencies, the common school became the institution which fulfilled the state's educational obligation to the children and to the republic.

The census of 1850 reported common schools in every state and territory, though most of the Southern and Western states were far behind the East and North. A comparison of the number of teachers and pupils reported indicates that most of the schools must have been of the one-room variety. (See Table 2.) The reports do not give percentages of school-age children enrolled, but an approximation can be computed by dividing the number of pupils reported by the number of free white children between the ages of five and fifteen enumerated in each state. These percentages reveal sharp regional differences in the provision of public educational opportunities. The common man of the North and East was winning his right to have common schools, but the hardships of the Far West and the opposition of the planter oligarchy in the South were formidable obstacles to the establishment of common schools in those regions. A notable exception in the South was North Carolina, where the independent piedmont farmers supported the educational reforms of Calvin Wiley; in that state, where the terrain was not favorable to the development of large plantations, social and political institu-

TABLE 2: PUBLIC SCHOOLS, PUPILS, AND TEACHERS REPORTED IN 1850[28]

State	Number of Public Schools	Number of Teachers	Number of Pupils	Number of Pupils as a Percentage of Total White Pop. Age 5–15*
Alabama	1,152	1,195	28,380	22
Arkansas	353	355	8,493	17
California	2	2	49	1
Connecticut	1,656	1,787	71,269	93
Delaware	194	214	8,970	48
D. Columbia	22	34	2,169	23
Florida	69	73	1,878	14
Georgia	1,251	1,265	32,705	21
Illinois	4,052	4,248	125,725	51
Indiana	4,822	4,860	161,500	56
Iowa	740	828	29,556	53
Kentucky	2,234	2,306	71,429	33
Louisiana	664	822	25,046	41
Maine	4,042	5,540	192,815	132
Maryland	898	986	33,111	32
Massachusetts	3,679	4,443	176,475	89
Michigan	2,714	3,231	110,455	102
Mississippi	782	826	18,746	21
Missouri	1,570	1,620	51,754	30
New Hampshire	2,381	3,013	75,643	110
New Jersey	1,473	1,574	77,930	67
New York	11,580	13,965	675,221	95
North Carolina	2,657	2,730	104,095	68
Ohio	11,661	12,886	484,153	90
Pennsylvania	9,061	10,024	413,706	71
Rhode Island	416	518	23,130	77
South Carolina	724	739	17,838	23
Tennessee	2,680	2,819	104,117	46
Texas	349	360	7,946	18
Vermont	2,731	4,175	93,457	126
Virginia	2,930	2,997	67,353	27
Wisconsin	1,423	1,529	58,817	77
Total	80,978	91,966	3,354,011	66

* The percentages of over one hundred result from the fact that some children were reported twice, once during the summer term and again during the winter term, and to the fact that a portion of the enrollments were of children under five and over fifteen.

[28] Adapted from tables in the U.S. Census Bureau *Compendium of Seventh Census* (Washington, 1854), Table CXLV, p. 142, and Table XXX, p. 52.

tions were far more liberal than in other Southern states, and North Carolina had a system of public schools in 1850 which compared favorably with those of many Northern states.

Graded Schools

Although most of the schools had only one teacher, in some of the larger communities the enrollment warranted assistant teachers. The school was then divided so that the principal teacher taught the more advanced subjects, such as arithmetic and writing, and the assistant, often a woman, helped the smaller children with their alphabet and beginning reading. But there was no clear division of children into grades or classes according to their achievements even in such a school. Horace Mann's *Seventh Annual Report* discussed how the Prussian teachers divided children into groups on the basis of their progress and taught groups of pupils at once instead of having each child recite separately. The 1845 report of the Boston school visitation committee suggested dividing the schools up "horizonally" by ages or achievement, instead of vertically under one writing master and one reading master, each working independently of the other and often at cross-purposes. Of course, there had been some "grading" of pupils earlier in the Lancastrian schools under the monitors, but the complete division of children into separate classes, each with its own teacher, did not come until John Philbrick reorganized the Quincy, Massachusetts, grammar school in 1847. The new building had several classrooms and permitted the adoption of the class organization.

The combination of small district schools into "union" schools encouraged the spread of the graded school, so that by 1855 the state commissioner of common schools in Ohio reported that "within the last two years, graded or union schools have been established in nearly one hundred and fifty towns and villages of this State, and . . . most of them are now in vigorous and successful operation."[29]

Compulsory Attendance

Although Massachusetts had had laws as early as 1642 requiring that parents teach their children how to read, it was more than two centuries before it had laws requiring children to attend school. In his *Seventh Annual Report* Horace Mann urged that the United States follow the example of Prussia and pass compulsory attendance laws, arguing that such legislation was consistent with democracy. He and other educa-

[29] Barnard, *American Journal of Education,* Vol. 2 (1856), p. 538.

tional reformers continued to agitate for compulsory attendance laws, and their efforts finally bore fruit in 1852, when the Massachusetts legislature passed the first compulsory school attendance law in the United States. The law required that every child between eight and fourteen years attend school at least twelve weeks a year, of which six weeks must be consecutive. Parents of children who failed to do so would be subject to a fine of twenty dollars, except that any parent not able "by reason of poverty" to send his child to school would not be fined.[30] Even though the provisions of this law were minimal, no other state or territory followed the example of Massachusetts until after the Civil War.

Broadened Curriculum and Traditional Methods

As the common schools multiplied to meet the needs of the common man, the curriculum was greatly expanded to satisfy the practical demands of a society with growing interests. The 4 R's of religion, reading, 'riting, and 'rithmetic were still very much present, though sectarian catechism had given way to nondenominational Protestantism and secular readers had largely replaced the Bible as a reading text. The Massachusetts law required the common schools to teach "orthography, reading, writing, English grammar, geography and arithmetic," but Horace Mann found that many schools were going beyond those subjects and including secondary courses which he thought inappropriate for the elementary level.

> Latin and French are sometimes pursued by those who cannot write, grammatically, a sentence of English. Algebra and the extraction of roots are studied by scholars who cannot carry an item even through a set of books kept by single entry. The heights of astonomy are scaled by those who know almost nothing of the earth they inhabit; and ancient mythology and the history of the antediluvians are studied by pupils who are wholly ignorant of the history of their own country.[31]

Among other studies Mann lists as taught in the common schools of Massachusetts were United States history, general history, algebra, bookkeeping, Latin, Greek, rhetoric, geometry, physiology, logic, surveying, botany, chemistry, natural history, astronomy, intellectual philosophy, and French. Perhaps many of these higher studies were offered in towns

[30] Knight and Hall, p. 365.
[31] Mann, *Sixth Annual Report*, p. 54.

where pupils had no secondary school to follow their common schooling—the law requiring towns to maintain high schools was not very effectively enforced.

Reading was usually taught from reading books instead of the Bible or prayer books, although the selections tended to be religious or moral in content. Writing was more or less mechanical, following set copy rather than composition. Spelling was taught orally, with the spelling bee one of the highlights of the school week. Much of the work in arithmetic was done "mentally," with the pupils struggling to work out long problems in multiplication or division in their heads. Grammar was the memorization of rules based on Latin grammar, correcting false syntax, and parsing words in literary selections; not until some grammarians near mid-century began to apply Pestalozzian rules to grammar was there any effort to use grammar to understand the construction of English sentences or to try to compose sentences or themes in English. History and geography were taught almost as a catechism, with students memorizing set answers to lists of questions which followed each chapter of the textbook.

Apparently these methods did not achieve all the success some patrons of the schools expected: the visitation committee for the schools of Boston in 1845 was very critical of the performance of the pupils on the written examinations they gave. The questions were based on the textbooks in the required subjects of the common schools, and the 530 pupils who took the tests were in the oldest class of the schools, averaging thirteen years and six months in age. If all the children examined had answered all the questions on the tests, the total number of answers would have been 57,873; "but there were only 31,159, of which only 17,216 were correct in sense, leaving unanswered 26,714. The 31,159 answers contained 2,801 errors in grammar; 3,733 errors in spelling; and 35,947 errors in punctuation."

> These results are surprising, when it is considered that the answers were very short—some merely an affirmation or a negation in one word. . . .
>
> The verbal examination which followed in geography, confirmed the opinion which would be drawn from the answers to the printed questions. In a few schools, the children seem to have been taught orally, and upon correct principles; but generally they were lost when taken out of the common routine of questions. They could bound states and countries; name capitals, capes, and mountains; enumerate rivers, lakes, and bays . . . but questioned as to the drainage of countries, their capacities for commerce, the causes which

> direct streams and determine the force of water,—their want of comprehension of these and similar subjects, showed plainly, in almost every school, that they had learned geography as if it were only a catalogue of names of all the divisions of water, from ponds up to oceans; of land, from towns to empires.
>
> In reviewing the answers to the questions upon History, the same conclusion presses upon us as on examining the questions on the other subjects. The scholars have, for the most part, learned to recite the words of the text-book, without having had its spirit illustrated, and without having been accustomed to think about the meaning of what they had learned. . . .
>
> One general inference to be drawn from an examination of these answers is that it is difficult for our scholars to learn to spell correctly, without being more in the habit of writing than they now are. Scores and hundreds of errors, of the most palpable kind, have been committed in their written answers, by children who would spell the very same words correctly, if they were called up in the usual way, and had the words pronounced aloud to them.[32]

The pupils had memorized facts without understanding their significance. They had learned to spell orally without building a useful vocabulary. In short, the committee concluded, the Boston schools "have not the excellence and usefulness they should possess."

The schools of Boston were perhaps among the best in the United States. In the South and on the frontier the curriculum was generally more restricted and teaching methods even less effective. For example, in Ohio in 1847 English grammar was taught only in the intermediate and higher grades; only 19 percent of the students in winter schools and less than 13 percent of those in summer schools were studying English grammar. Few teachers anywhere in the country knew enough about English grammar to teach it.[33] The same criticism could generally be applied to teachers' knowledge of the other subjects of the common school curriculum.

Textbooks

With the new interest in schooling and the increased number of subjects taught in the common schools, the market for textbooks attracted many authors, and textbooks were published in considerable numbers.

[32] *Reports of the Annual Visiting Committees of the Public Schools of the City of Boston, 1845.* Quoted in Otis W. Caldwell and Stuart A. Courtis, *Then & Now in Education, 1845–1923* (Yonkers-on-Hudson: World Book, 1923), pp. 171–174, 178.

[33] Lyman, pp. 88–89.

Webster's "old blue-back" almost monopolized the field of spelling and was widely used to teach reading as well. In no other subject did any one book so completely dominate the field throughout the nation. In other subjects, each teacher might find every one of his pupils using a different book, since each child brought the books he had at home and there was no standardization of texts. In some subjects, however, certain textbooks were used in many parts of the country and had a significant influence on the period and on the books that followed.

Readers

In New England the Lindley Murray, Caleb Bingham, and Worcester readers were the most popular of a number of texts. Perhaps for the reason that they contained selections which were outspoken on slavery, they were not as popular in other parts of the nation. Outside New England the most widely used series of readers after 1840 was the famed McGuffey set, compiled by William Holmes McGuffey and his brother Alexander. The *First* and *Second Readers* were published in 1836; the *Third* and *Fourth* in 1837; the *Fifth* in 1841; and the *Sixth* in 1851. In addition there were a *Primer* and a *Speller*. The set went through five revisions, continuing in wide use until well after 1900. Estimates of the total number of copies sold run upwards of a hundred million.

The McGuffey series was graded, with the authors actually testing their selections with children. The stress was on oral reading, and all the readers beginning with the *Second* contained an introductory section giving rules for articulation, inflection, punctuation, and similar elocutionary aids. The selections in the beginning readers had a strong didactic quality, with easily discovered moral lessons. The more advanced readers included literary selections of some substance. The *Second Reader*, for example, had stories titled "Afraid in the Dark," "At Work," "What a Bird Taught," "If I Were a Sunbeam," "God is Great and Good," "The Greedy Girl," and "Cheerfulness." The *Fifth Reader* included such authors as Whittier, Leigh Hunt, Louisa M. Alcott, Southey, Longfellow, Tennyson, Thoreau, Shakespeare, and Charles Lamb; the *Sixth Reader* included Disraeli, Samuel Johnson, Dickens, Thomas Gray, Patrick Henry, Lyman Beecher, Washington Irving, Jefferson, and Emerson.

The success of the McGuffey readers reinforced the old stress on oral reading, put new stress on phonics as part of reading, and set the tone for literary selections in readers. Cubberley claims that probably half the school children of America between 1836 and 1900 "formulated their code of morals and conduct" from the McGuffey readers,[34] but while the readers were highly moralistic about such questions as honesty, hard work, kindness to animals, drunkenness, and smoking, they did not make reference, even indirectly, to the major social issues of the day—slavery, economic exploitation, or any of the other great problems crucial to the peaceful progress of the United States. Perhaps it was the absence of controversy that helped make them widely acceptable in both North and South and has made them nostalgically attractive to certain conservative critics of modern schools.

History and Geography Textbooks

With the growing concern for nationalism and commerce, the subjects of American history and geography became more important. Chapters in history books were generally organized around wars or Presidential administrations. Geographies were divided into separate chapters on each state. In both kinds of texts, the emphasis was on facts and memorization. A common practice was to list a number of questions at the back of the book—sometimes at the foot of each page—on the facts in the book, numbering the questions to indicate which paragraph would give the answer to be committed to memory. This was the method of one of the most successful authors of history and geography texts, Samuel G. Goodrich, many of whose books were written under the name of "Peter Parley." Goodrich's brother Charles also wrote textbooks, and his *History of the United States for Schools* provides a good example of the question and answer method. In the chapter on the Compromise of 1850, the following paragraph appears:

> For months before the death of General Taylor the discussion of these questions in Congress had given birth to exciting and even angry debate between members from the northern and southern sections of the Union. The former, being generally opposed to slavery, were also opposed to all measures designed to foster and extend it. The latter, on the contrary, were anxious to perpetuate it, and enlarge its area. The people of the United States themselves were similarly divided on the subject, according as they inhabited free or slave states.

The questions based on this paragraph were

> What is said of the discussion of these questions prior to the death of Gen. Taylor? To what were northern members opposed?

[34] *Public Education in the United States* (Boston: Houghton Mifflin, 1947), p. 294.

> For what were southern members anxious? How were the people of the United States divided?[35]

Notice that the questions use the same phrases as the sentences in which the pupil will find the answers; there is no attempt to stimulate thinking on the part of the students.

Women Teachers

From the very earliest periods of our colonial history, women taught the youngest children their a-b-c's in the dame schools and the summer terms of the district schools, but the winter term, when the older students attended, was under a male teacher. During the period of the Common School Revival, many educational reformers favored more women teachers in the common schools. One argument was that, since women would teach for less pay than men, districts could use women and lengthen the term without increasing the cost. Another argument was that women were better suited than men to be teachers of the young.

Horace Mann was pleased to report in 1843 that "the proportion of Female Teachers in our Public Schools, as compared with Males, is rapidly increasing." In a five-year period the increase in number of male teachers was 131 while that of women teachers was 691. Mann was enthusiastic about women teachers because he thought the female personality ideally suited to the task.

While Mann recognized the economy of employing women teachers and encouraged the practice on that ground, he protested against such low salaries that women teachers could not afford to attend normal schools. In Massachusetts in 1842, the average monthly pay for male teachers was $32.22, while women teachers received only $12.78, with the school term four months in the summer and another four months in the winter.

> This disparity . . . is followed . . . inevitably by a deterioration in the quality of the instruction given. There is a pernicious error on this subject which rules no inconsiderable portion of the public mind, and misleads it. It is supposed that a meager supply of literary attainments will suffice for the education of young children, as

[35] Charles A. Goodrich, A *History of the United States for Schools* (Boston: Hickling, Swan and Brewer, 1859), pp. 264, 416.

> though errors were not far more baneful at the beginning than at any subsequent stage of their progress. If earliest impressions are most lasting, we should be most solicitous to have them correct. Over everything which *grows,* those who exert the first influences have the greatest power. . . . And hence, if any difference is allowed, the first teachers of children should be the best,—the most critically accurate in what they are to teach, the most scrupulously exemplary in conduct, the most religiously faithful in the discharge of duty.[36]

Mann continued to agitate for better salaries for teachers to make it possible to attract and retain better teachers in the schools. In his *Eleventh Report,* he complained, "Many a lady, in what is called fashionable life, expends as much, oftentimes far more, on a single article of dress . . . than a devoted female teacher receives for a whole year of laborious service." Appropriate pay for teachers, both male and female, would "reimburse the expense of attending a Normal School," where the prospective teacher "might be qualified to meet these wants of the young."

> In that case, our school committees, when they go abroad in quest of fit endowments and qualifications to cultivate the immortal capacities of the young, would escape the mortification which they now sometimes suffer, of being overbid by a capitalist who wants them for his factory, and who can afford to pay them more for superintending a loom or a spinning-frame, than the people feel willing to give for weaving the infinitely precious tissue of character. And were the same policy adopted in reference to those young men whom Nature has preadapted for school-keeping, they would not be lured away from this employment, as some of them now are, by the temptation of more liberal pay, to become head servants in gentlemen's families, or to superintend the affairs of the kitchen in expensive hotels.[37]

Obviously, the reluctance of the public to pay enough to keep good teachers in the classroom is not merely a recent phenomenon! The willingness of the young woman teacher to teach for small sums was one important factor in creating the notion that teachers need not be paid competitive salaries.

[36] Mann, *Sixth Annual Report,* pp. 32–35.
[37] Mann, *Eleventh Annual Report,* pp. 27, 30–31.

Negro Education Before 1861

While educational opportunities for white children increased during the Common School Revival, there were few advances for free Negroes, and the chances of schooling for slaves actually decreased. During the Colonial and early national periods, many slave owners as a Christian duty taught their slaves to read or at least permitted them to learn. Some owners taught their household slaves to read so that their own children might not be contaminated by close contact with gross ignorance. Some slaves learned by "accident" in accompanying their young masters to the schoolroom; Booker T. Washington reported that his desire for education grew from those occasions when he "went as far as the schoolhouse door with one of my young mistresses to carry her books for her."[38] Undoubtedly the schooled white child sometimes played school with his slave playmate, imitating the lessons he had got from his own teacher. On occasion a very promising young slave would be schooled by his master to become his bookkeeper, store clerk, tally man, overseer, or even schoolmaster. Negroes who acquired some learning tried to pass it on to others, some becoming successful teachers. One of the most famous Negro teachers was John Chavis, who was licensed as a Presbyterian preacher in 1800 and taught until 1832, when North Carolina passed a law forbidding Negroes to preach or teach. Chavis' schools enrolled white boys as well as Negroes, and according to some accounts, he taught the sons of some prominent Raleigh families.[39]

Slaves Denied Education

After the slave rebellions on the island of Haiti at the turn of the century, many Southern whites feared that the United States would become the scene of bloody conflicts. Their fears seemed realized on August 21, 1831, when a Negro preacher named Nat Turner, who had read in his Bible that "the last shall be first," led a rebellion in Southampton, Virginia, murdering some fifty-five or sixty whites, mostly women and children. Turner, who considered himself something of a Negro Messiah, was captured and executed, ironically enough, at Jerusalem, Virginia.

Reasoning that such insurrections were led by educated Negroes, Southern legislatures quickly passed laws forbidding the teaching of

[38] Booker T. Washington, *Up From Slavery, An Autobiography* (New York: Doubleday, Doran, 1938), pp. 4–5.

[39] Knight and Hall, pp. 661–663.

Negroes, free or slave. Although these laws were not always strictly enforced, they apparently did discourage many who would have been willing to teach Negroes to read. Teachers like John Chavis were forced to quit or carry on their teaching surreptitiously. Occasionally some individual would brave public sentiment and legal consequences and try to hold school for Negroes. In 1853 in Norfolk, Virginia, Mrs. Margaret Douglass, a white lady who had been teaching a Negro Sunday school, was arrested for teaching a number of free Negroes to read in her home. When the jury set her fine at one dollar, the judge overruled them and sentenced her to a month in the city jail, in addition to a fine and costs.

The accounts of ex-slaves of their attempts to get an education reveal some of the determination of the slaves and their friends and some of the terrible limitations on their opportunities. In 1936 and 1937, the Federal Writers' Project of the WPA interviewed surviving ex-slaves about their lives before the Civil War. Their reminiscences, often expressed in illiterate language and perhaps marked with exaggeration, include accounts of their attempts to learn to read. A former Louisiana slave named Ellen Betts, born around 1853, reported that the only time a Negro had any writing was when the master put his name down in the "big book," possibly the family Bible but more likely the plantation account book or ledger. Her master permitted his Negroes no "book learning." Jenny Proctor, who was born a slave in Alabama in 1850, described how Negroes had learned to read secretly by studying "that Webster's old blue-back speller . . . way in the night" by the light of a "little pine torch." Others were more fortunate. One reported, "Us house servants was taught to read by the white folks." A former Kentucky slave, born around 1840, said that his master had a "special slave who didn't have nothing to do but teach the rest of us . . . to read and write and figure." But another told of a white man who came to teach her father to read the Bible.

> Papa said, "Ain't you 'fraid they'll kill you if they see you?" The old man said, "No, they don't know what I'm doing, and don't you tell 'em. If you do, they will kill me."[40]

The failure to provide for the slaves or even the free Negroes presented the South with a tremendous educational problem after the Civil War, with the millions of illiterate freedmen all clamoring for a chance to learn to read.

[40] B. A. Botkin (ed.), *Lay My Burden Down* (Chicago: U. of Chicago Press, 1945), pp. 50, 91, 126, 185.

Northern Schools Closed to Negroes

Although there were schools for Negroes in the North, there was opposition to Negroes and whites attending the same schools, and where separate schools did not exist, Negroes were not much better off than those in the South. In Connecticut in 1833, a Quaker named Prudence Crandall admitted a Negro girl named Sarah Harris to her boarding school. White parents withdrew their children, and Miss Crandall advertised in the *Liberator* that she would accept "young ladies and little misses of color." At a town meeting a resolution was adopted calling for Miss Crandall to give up her project. Andrew Judson, an advocate of the resolution and later member of Congress and United States District Court Justice, declared "that the colored people could never rise from their menial condition, . . . ought not to be permitted to rise," and "were an inferior race and should not be recognized as the equals of the whites."[41] When Miss Crandall persisted and enrolled a number of Negro girls, her school was attacked and her pupils insulted on the streets. An obsolete vagrancy law was enforced against the girls who were from out of the state. Finally the legislature enacted a law against establishing a school for Negroes from out of state, and Miss Crandall was arrested and put in jail. A question of constitutionality of the law was raised at her trial and while the appeal was pending, she returned to her school. Someone attempted to set the school on fire, and a few nights later a mob attacked the schoolhouse with clubs and broke the windows. For the safety of her pupils, Miss Crandall decided to give up her school.

The first court case over separate facilities came in Boston. By 1846 Negro children were admitted into town schools in all of Massachusetts except Boston, where two of the 160 primary schools were set aside for Negro children. In 1846 a number of Negro parents petitioned the school committee to abolish the Negro schools and permit Negro children to attend the other schools. The committee denied the petition, stating that "separate schools for colored children" were "not only legal and just, but . . . best adapted to promote the education of that class of our population." When Benjamin Roberts was refused permission to enroll his five-year-old daughter in a white school a fifth of a mile nearer his home than the Negro school, he sued the city. The Massachusetts Supreme Court ruled (1849) that the school committee had the authority to place children in separate schools since the teachers all had "the

[41] George W. Williams, *History of the Negro Race in America* (New York: Putnam's, 1882), Vol. II, p. 151.

same compensation and qualifications." The decision also raised the question of whether law could change public opinion.

> It is urged, that this maintenance of separate schools tends to deepen and perpetuate the odious distinction of caste, founded in a deep-rooted prejudice in public opinion. This prejudice, if it exists, is not created by law, and probably cannot be changed by law. Whether this distinction and prejudice, existing in the opinion and feelings of the community, would not be as effectually fostered by compelling colored and white children to associate together in the same schools, may well be doubted.[42]

Not until 1857 did Massachusetts, the center of abolitionism, pass legislation prohibiting school committees from discriminating against school children on the basis of "race, creed, or previous condition of servitude."

On the "democratic" frontier, conditions for the Negro were no better. The Indiana school law of 1850 provided schooling for children of all taxpayers, but Negroes and mulattoes were expressly omitted from the lists for school taxes. When Negroes applied for the right to be taxed or to send their children to the schools as tuition pupils, they were denied on the basis of social inequality. An Indiana court decision in 1850 ruled that the exclusion of the Negro children

> has not been done because they do not need education, nor because their wealth was such as to render aid undesirable, but because black children were deemed unfit associates of white, as school companions. Now, surely this reason operated with equal force against such children attending the schools at their own, as at the public expense.[43]

A similar decision was rendered by a court in Ohio at about the same time. Clearly, educational opportunities for Negroes were not opening at the same rate as for children of white parents.

The Common School in 1860

Although much remained to be done in equalizing educational opportunity and improving the quality of common education, the American

[42] Quoted in Gilbert T. Stephenson, *Race Distinctions in American Law* (New York: Appleton, 1910), pp. 167–169.

[43] *Ibid.*, p. 167.

elementary school took its basic form as a free, tax-supported, publically controlled, secular school during the period from 1830 to 1860. In a revolutionary age a new and unique school had developed to match the new and unique democratic society arising. The common man had his common school, at least in principle, in all the states, although the South and West lagged behind the North and East in the actual implementation of the ideal. In some regions there was even progress toward improving the quality of the common school, through expansion of the curriculum, dividing the pupils into grades, consolidating small schools, and seeking better teachers.

QUESTIONS FOR DISCUSSION

1. What analogies can you draw between the movement from local district control to state and county supervision in the Common School Revival and the issue of federal aid and control today?
2. What would the early nineteenth-century attempts at federal grants to schools lead you to anticipate as possible problems in present-day federal aid to schools?
3. What possible warnings can you see for the church-state issue in education which are suggested by the problems in the movement to secularize the schools in the Common School Revival?
4. One of the paradoxes of this period is the adoption of the first compulsory attendance law during a time when freedom was exalted. How can the inconsistency between freedom and compulsory attendance be resolved?

SUGGESTED READINGS

Secondary Sources

Bond, Horace Mann. *The Education of the Negro in the American Social Order*. New York: Prentice-Hall, 1934. Pp. 367–383.

Carpenter, Charles. *History of American Schoolbooks*. Philadelphia: U. of Philadelphia Press, 1963.

Cremin, Lawrence. *The American Common School*. New York: Teachers College Bureau of Publications, 1951.

Curti, Merle. *The Social Ideas of American Educators*. New York: Scribner's, 1935. Chapters II–IV.

Drake, William. *The American School in Transition*. Englewood Cliffs: Prentice-Hall, 1955. Chapters VI, VII, VIII, and X.

Edwards, Newton, and Richey, Herman G. *The School in the American Social Order*. Boston: Houghton Mifflin, 1963. Pp. 291–356, 375–383.

Good, Harry. A *History of American Education*. New York: Macmillan, 1956. Chapters VI and VII.
Hinsdale, B. A. *Horace Mann and the Common School Revival in the United States*. New York: Scribner's, 1898.
Mosier, Richard D. *Making the American Mind*. New York: King's Crown Press, 1947.
Noble, Stuart G. A *History of American Education*. New York: Rinehart, 1954. Chapters VIII to XIII.
Pfeffer, Leo. *Church, State and Freedom*. Boston: Beacon, 1953. Pp. 281–286, 374–382, and 442–444.
Woodson, Carter G. *The Education of the Negro Prior to 1861*. New York: Putnam's, 1915. Chapters V–X, XIII.

Primary Sources

Caldwell, Otis W., and Courtis, Stuart T. *Then and Now in Education: 1845–1923*. New York: World Book, 1923. Pp. 163–344, 375–392.
Cubberley, Ellwood P. *Readings in the History of Education*. Boston: Houghton Mifflin, 1920. Readings 316–324.
———. *Readings in Public Education in the United States*. Boston: Houghton Mifflin, 1934. Pp. 178–211, 264–298.
Gross, Carl H., and Chandler, Charles C. *The History of American Education Through Readings*. Boston: Heath, 1964. Pp. 94–101, 111–119, 128–138.
Knight, Edgar W. A *Documentary History of Education in the South Before 1860*. Chapel Hill: U. of North Carolina Press, 1949. Vol. V, pp. 42–209, 223–228, 231–236, 239–244, 257–259.
Knight, Edgar W., and Hall, Clifton L. *Readings in American Educational History*. New York: Appleton-Century-Crofts, 1951. Pp. 346–366, 414–415, 418–420, 488–516, 664–673.
Monroe, Paul. *The Founding of the American Public School System*. Ann Arbor: University Microfilms, 1940. Vol. II, Quotations 484–523, 538–545, 557–562.
Sellers, Horace B. *The Constitution and Religious Education*. Boston: Christopher Publishing House, 1950. Pp. 20–33.

9

Secondary and Higher Education for the Middle Classes

Until the educational revolution of the nineteenth century, secondary and higher education had been virtually an exclusive privilege of the upper socioeconomic classes. Even in colonial Massachusetts, where the town Latin school was free for any boy who wished to attend, few boys of the lower or middle classes went beyond the rudiments of English reading and writing. During the Age of the Common Man, the reforms in education were the most democratic at the elementary level—the common school. Still, there were changes in secondary and higher education that were the result of the second American social revolution. Academies began to offer practical as well as college preparatory courses and were opened to girls as well as boys. Public high schools began to include scientific and technical courses in their curriculum. One of the culminating educational events of the period was the Morrill Act, the foundation stone of the vocationally oriented state universities.

The Academy Movement

The academy played a paradoxical role in the history of American secondary education. Though most academies were private, they were a transition from the classical language orientation of the Latin grammar school, which was public in New England, to the broad curriculum of the public high school. When the academies first appeared, they were intended to give practical terminal education, but later they became largely college preparatory. Often endowed by philanthropy, their struggles to operate on tuition fees made apparent the need for tax support for secondary schools. Before 1820, most of the academies were for boys, but between 1830 and 1860, academies for girls outnumbered those for boys, and the large number of coeducational academies set the pattern for the American high school.

Academies Numerous and Widespread

Although some academies had been incorporated even before the Revolution, and though their numbers increased each year, rapid growth did not come until the period from 1825 to 1860. After the Civil War, the number dropped sharply. In Massachusetts between 1780 and 1825, 40 academies were incorporated, but between 1826 and 1855, 109 were incorporated, 60 of them appearing in the decade from 1826 to 1835. By 1856, high schools were already becoming important in Massachusetts, and between 1856 and 1875 only 20 academies were incorporated. The story was much the same in New York. There from 1787 to 1825, 61 academies were chartered, but from 1826 to 1853, 254 were incorporated. Six of those incorporated between 1847 and 1853 were actually high schools. In Ohio between 1803 and 1850, the legislature incorporated 172 academies. In Virginia, 200 academies had been incorporated by 1850.[1]

Many academies lasted only a few months. Some of them were actually only elementary schools, having no pupils enrolled in courses beyond reading, writing, and arithmetic. A few were almost college level institutions. Because of the variations in type of school and the brief existence of so many of them, it is difficult to find any reliable reckoning of the exact number at any one time. The 1850 Census enumerated academies and private schools together, and reported 6,085 with 12,260 teachers and 263,096 pupils enrolled. There was at least one such school in every state and territory except Utah. Minnesota and New Mexico had only one one-teacher academy each. At the other extreme, New York had 887 academies, with 3,136 teachers. From a comparison of the numbers of schools and teachers, most of the academies must have been one- and two-teacher institutions. All the states and territories, except California (170), Minnesota (12), New Mexico (40), and Oregon (842), were reported as having at least a thousand pupils in academies and private schools; the only states having more than 10,000 were New York (49,328), Pennsylvania (23,751), Ohio (15,052), Massachusetts (13,436), Kentucky (12,712), and Maryland (10,787).[2] Although they were obviously

[1] I. L. Kandel, *History of Secondary Education* (Boston: Houghton Mifflin, 1930), pp. 397–416.

[2] U.S. Census Bureau, *Compendium of Seventh Census* (Washington: 1854), Table CXLV, p. 142.

not serving a very large percentage of the secondary-school-age children, it would appear that most of the well-settled parts of the nation had at least a pretense of secondary education through the private academies.

Financial Support

Most of the nineteenth-century academies were private institutions operated for profit. The schoolmaster owned and operated the school as his livelihood. Consequently, one of the most important sources of income for the academy was tuition fees. The amount charged varied widely according to the school and the locality; in some schools, too, charges varied according to the subjects taken. The 1839 statement of Mercer Academy in Pennsylvania is an example.

TERMS OF TUITION PER QUARTER

Languages, higher Mathematics, Chemistry, Botany and Mineralogy	$5.00
Natural Philosophy, Logic, Moral and Intellectual Science	4.00
Woodbridge's large Geography, Grammar, Smith's 2d part	3.00
Olney's Geography, Smith's Grammar 1st Part	2.50
Reading, Writing, Arithmetic	2.00

Extra—French $3.00, Music $10.00.[3]

Some eighteenth-century academies had been partially supported by state-authorized lotteries, but this method of financing was generally discontinued after 1800. A few academies in some states received grants of money from the state on condition that they provide free schooling for pauper children, generally only four and rarely more than ten. York County Academy in Pennsylvania received a grant of $2,000 on condition that it admit "any number of poor students, who may at any time be offered, in order to be taught gratis, Provided the number so admitted shall at no time be greater than seven, and that none of the said students shall continue longer than two years if others should offer."

Such cash grants extended the earlier precedents of land grants and shares of the interest from permanent school funds as means of state support. As the revolutionary forces in the Age of the Common Man pressed for free secondary education without the stigma of the pauper provisions, the academies gave way to the tax-supported public high schools.

[3] Quoted in James Mulhern, *A History of Secondary Education in Pennsylvania* (Philadelphia: Published by the Author, 1933), p. 330.

Academies for Girls

One of the major social reform efforts of the mid-nineteenth century was the women's rights movement, and perhaps the greatest advance in gaining equality for females came in the increase in educational opportunity. Among the many dedicated pioneers in the campaign to open secondary education to girls were Mrs. Emma Willard, Mary Lyon, Mrs. Almira Phelps, and Catherine Beecher. Mrs. Willard, in addition to founding Troy Female Seminary (New York, 1821), wrote many articles on education for girls, was active in the Western Literary Institute, and made an 8,000-mile tour through the South and West promoting female education. Mary Lyon founded Mount Holyoke Female Seminary (Massachusetts, 1837) for middle class girls, keeping costs as low as possible by having the girls do all the domestic work at the school. Mrs. Phelps wrote *Lectures to Young Ladies* on almost every subject, from ancient languages and mythology to physical training and mineralogy; these became popular textbooks in the female seminaries. Catherine Beecher was the female counterpart of Horace Mann, writing, speaking, organizing schools for girls from Hartford, Connecticut, to Burlington, Iowa, founding the American Women's Education Association, and promoting the study of "domestic economy," which she declared as necessary for women as professional study for men.[4]

Although the most famous academies for girls were in New York and New England, the female seminary was also popular in the South. In the states of Louisiana, Kentucky, Maryland, North Carolina, Mississippi, and Alabama, the number of schools for girls chartered between 1820 and 1860 outnumbered those for boys by about two and one-half to one. In the Western states, particularly in the rural areas, academies were often coeducational, partly because of the difficulty of attracting enough students for separate schools and partly because of the frontier willingness to recognize the capabilities and responsibilities of girls and women.

Not only was there an increase in the number of schools open to girls during the period from 1830 to 1860, but the quality of education available improved markedly. The early female seminaries were little more than elementary schools, with a little sewing added to reading and writing. Later, as girls acquired the basic subjects in the common schools, the seminaries expanded their course offerings to include the classical and modern languages, mathematics, and science. Thomas Woody com-

[4] Thomas Woody, *A History of Women's Education in the United States* (New York: Science Press, 1929), Vol. I, Chapter VIII.

pared the curricula of 55 seminaries between 1749 and 1829 with those of 107 between 1830 and 1871. In the earlier period 89 percent of the schools taught reading, compared with only 65 percent in the later period. The study of writing declined from 76 percent to 41 percent; arithmetic from 86 to 79; plain needlework from 42 to 5; ornamental needlework from 43 to 12. On the other hand, Latin grammar went from 24 to 59; algebra from 15 to 83; geometry from 27 to 79; trigonometry from 2 to 40; chemistry from 30 to 90; geology from 2 to 30; United States history from 16 to 45; political science from 2 to 34. Courses in the "cultural refinements" increased slightly—painting from 25 to 43, drawing from 49 to 50, and music from 21 to 30. Altogether, Woody found 180 different subjects taught in these 162 schools, an indication of the breadth of the curriculum and the confusion as to the purpose of female education.[5]

One part of the academy program particularly attractive to young ladies was the preparation of common-school teachers. The academies continued to be the main source of the comparatively few teachers with any training for their schoolkeeping duties.

Although many men ridiculed the idea of girls studying Latin and having other "academic pretensions," the female seminaries and the coeducational academies demonstrated movement away from the notion that the female intellect was greatly inferior to that of the male.

From Academy to High School

Although the academy did not reach as wide a range of the population as the public common school, its expanded curriculum served the needs of a far broader spectrum of the young people than the old Latin grammar school. Though the academy was designed to appeal to the average farmer and the small business man, tuition fees were a major barrier to many children, and in the industrial East and frontier West, opposition began to develop against the academy as a select, exclusive, aristocratic school. The free public high school was the logical outgrowth.

The Public High School

The high schools followed the pattern of the academies except for one major difference: the high schools were public—tax supported and state controlled. The academies were essentially private in ownership and con-

[5] *Ibid.*, pp. 418, 563–565.

trol, even though they might be chartered by the state or local government and might occasionally receive small grants from the government. Both had a relatively broad curriculum. Both offered practical courses as well as preparation for college. Both generally included normal courses, training teachers for the common schools. In the East, both tended to be segregated by sex, while in the West both were often coeducational. Among both high schools and academies there were many institutions that were more nearly upper elementary schools than clearly secondary schools. Until well after the Civil War, high-school pupils came from the same middle-class background as academy pupils had.

A Proposal for High Schools

An 1838 article, written perhaps by Henry Barnard, reflects the democratic nature of the high schools at a time "when there was not a single institution of the kind out of Massachusetts."

> By a Public or Common High School, is intended a public or common school for the older and more advanced scholars of the community in which the same is located, in a course of instruction adapted to their age, and intellectual and moral wants, and, to some extent, to their future pursuits in life. . . . It is open to all the children of the community. . . . It must make a good education common in the highest and best sense of the word common—common because it is good enough for the best, and cheap enough for the poorest family in the community. . . . To be cheap, its support must be provided for wholly or mainly out of a fund, or by public tax.[6]

Just as the academy movement accorded recognition to the girls, so did the high schools. The above proposal urged that "the advantages of a High School should not be confined to the Male sex."

> The great influence of the female sex, as daughters, sisters, wives, mothers, companions, and teachers, in determining the manners, morals, and intelligence of the whole community, leaves no room to question the necessity of providing for the girls the best means of intellectual and moral culture.

Although this still seems to imply a masculine dominance over society, the recognition of the importance of the feminine role in society and the social need for educating girls was a concession that was necessary before

[6] Barnard, *American Journal of Education*, Vol. 3 (1857), p. 185.

the high school could become a "common" school at the secondary level. Progress was slow until after the Civil War, but the principle of public secondary education for girls was clearly established by 1860, in both separate high schools for girls and coeducational high schools.

The Founding of High Schools

The first high school in the United States was the English High School in Boston (See Chapter 6). It was followed by a few in the cities of the Northeast and Midwest. It is difficult to determine how many high schools there were before 1860, because many schools that used the name were merely the upper grades of a graded elementary school. In 1900 the United States Office of Education sent a questionnaire to city school superintendents and asked when the first high school had been established in their cities. Twenty-eight cities claimed to have had high schools before 1850; 41 claimed to have established high schools between 1851 and 1860.[7] However, at about the time this report was published, the commissioner himself, W. T. Harris, told a meeting of the National Education Association that there were only 40 high schools in the United States in 1860.[8] Perhaps Harris was screening out some of those schools of lower grade. Perhaps also some of those which had been claimed as being founded earlier had not maintained a continuous existence. At any rate, the number of high schools was quite small compared with the number of private and semi-private academies operating in 1860.

The High School Curriculum

The curriculum of the high school, like that of the academy, was designed to meet practical needs as well as prepare for college, but the orientation was still toward "books" rather than trade or vocational courses, which were to be added after the Civil War. College preparation was still dominated by the study of Latin and Greek. A typical curriculum was that of the coeducational public high school of Chicago, founded in 1856. Students were admitted on the basis of an examination on the common school subjects: reading, writing, spelling, grammar, geography, arithmetic, and United States history. Presumably the course was four years in length. Of the 151 who completed the first year of the school, fifty were in the college preparatory course of the Classical De-

[7] *Report of the U.S. Commissioner of Education*, 1900–1901, Vol. 2, p. 1912.
[8] W. T. Harris, "Recent Growth of Public High Schools in the United States as Affecting the Attendance of Colleges," *National Education Association Journal of Proceedings and Addresses, 1901*, p. 175.

partment, seventy-nine in the general course of the English Department, and twenty-two in the Normal Department. The average age of the pupils was fifteen years and seven months. The one elective, beyond the choice of course, appears to have been the choice of German or French, either being optional in the Normal course; forty-seven students elected German and forty chose French.

ENGLISH DEPARTMENT

1. Preparatory studies reviewed, using the text-books authorized in the Grammar Schools. 2. Warren's Physical Geography. 3. Weber's Universal History. 4. Ancient Geography. 5. Greenleaf's National Arithmetic. 6. Greenleaf's Algebra. 7. Davie's Legendre. 8. Plane and Spherical Trigonometry. 9. Mensuration. 10. Gillespie's Surveying. 11. Navigation. 12. Crittenden's Elementary Book-Keeping. 13. Botany. 14. Burritt's Geography of the Heavens. 15. Higher Astronomy. 16. Cutter's Physiology. 17. Tate's Natural Philosophy. 18. Youman's Chemistry. 19. Geology and Mineralogy. 20. Rhetoric. 21. Logic. 22. Wayland's Political Economy. 23. Principles of Government. 24. Wayland's Mental Philosophy. 25. Wayland's Moral Science. 26. Etymology. 27. English Literature. 28. Hillard's First Class Reader. 29. Drawing. 30. Vocal Music. 31. German or French. Woodbury's German Series. Fasquelle's French Course. 32. Recitations and Compositions.

NORMAL DEPARTMENT

Nos. 1, 2, 3, 4, 5, 6, 7, 12, 13, 14, 16, 17, 18, 19, 20, 23, 24, 25, 26, 27, 28, 29, 30, 32. Theory and Practice of Teaching, German and French; both optional.

CLASSICAL DEPARTMENT

Nos. 1, 2, 3, 4, 5, 6, 7, 14, 16, 17, 26, 28, 30, 32. Andrews' and Zumpt's Latin Grammars. Harkness's Arnold's First and Second Latin Lessons. Arnold's Latin Prose Composition. Andrew's Caesar. Johnson's Cicero. Bowen's Virgil. Andrew's Latin Lexicon. Anthon's Classical Dictionary. Crosby's Greek Grammar. Crosby's Greek Lessons. Arnold's Greek Prose Composition. Felton's Greek Reader. Boise's Xenophon's Anabasis. Owen's Homer's Iliad. Lidell and Scott's Greek Lexicon.[9]

As the Civil War approached, the high schools were definitely in the ascendancy and the academies had passed their zenith. The new industrial plutocracy which developed after the War was to encourage the democratic high school to turn out technicians, stenographers, bookkeepers, and candidates for the new technical schools and science-oriented colleges.

[9] Barnard, *American Journal*, Vol. 3, pp. 535–536.

Normal Schools

Massachusetts

The Prussian school system had been a source of inspiration and innovation for many American educational reformers, including Mann, Barnard, and Stowe, and one whose imagination was caught by the Prussian system of training common-school teachers was the Reverend Charles Brooks, who considered himself a "Missionary Agency, in Massachusetts, of the State Normal Schools of Prussia." From 1835 to 1838 he campaigned for public normal schools. He began his campaign with a sermon from his own pulpit on Thanksgiving Day, 1835: "AS IS THE TEACHER, SO IS THE SCHOOL, and therefore we *must* have seminaries for the preparation of teachers." Expressing "grave objections to *private* Normal Schools," he called for "*State* Normal schools, owned, supported, and governed by the State for the State's service."[10] He recruited many prominent citizens to press for the establishment of public normal schools; two of the most effective orators for normal schools were Daniel Webster and John Quincy Adams. When the Massachusetts legislature set up the state board of education in 1837, the groundwork was laid for bringing Brooks' campaign to fruition.

In 1838 Edmund Dwight, a wealthy Boston industrialist and member of the state board of education, offered $10,000 to be used for teacher education if the state would match it. The offer was quickly taken, and the $20,000 was used for salaries and operating expenses for three normal schools for a three-year experiment. The schools were located in Lexington (1839), Barre (1839), and Bridgewater (1840). Even without provision for books or equipment or buildings of their own, the schools survived, and the legislature extended them for three more years with an appropriation of $6,000. Some Boston philanthropists gave $5,000 for a building, and the first state normal school building was erected in Bridgewater in 1846.

The normal schools reviewed the common school subjects and spent some time in lectures on keeping school. In each school there was a model school where the "normalites" observed as the principal taught the common school subjects. The school term was short. Many normal pupils stayed only a few weeks. The low quality of the work and the short term resulted in the opposition and contempt of many educated people.

[10] Vernon Lamar Mangun, *The American Normal School* (Baltimore: Warwick and York, 1928), p. 46. Although Prussian schools were the model for the American institution, the name apparently came from the French *école normale*.

There was apparently an early doubt that teaching could or should ever become a profession. In 1840 the Committee on Education of the Massachusetts legislature recommended that the House of Representatives abolish the normal schools. The committee reported:

> Academies and high schools cost the Commonwealth nothing; and they are fully adequate to furnish a competent supply of teachers. . . . Considering that our district schools are kept, on an average, for only three or four months in the year, it is obviously impossible, and perhaps it is not desirable, that the business of keeping these schools should become a distinct and separate profession, which the establishment of Normal Schools seems to anticipate.[11]

The proposal was defeated 246–184, and the Massachusetts normal schools weathered the storm.

One of the most famous teachers in the normal schools was the Reverend Cyrus Peirce, the first principal of the Lexington school. He was the total faculty, not only of the normal pupils but of the model school as well. Peirce described his curriculum and methods of preparing teachers in a letter published in the *Connecticut Common School Journal* in 1841.

> The branches that have been actually taken up are the following, viz: all the common branches *particularly* and *fully;* together with Composition, Geometry, Algebra, Physiology; Natural, Intellectual, and Moral Philosophy; Natural History, Botany, Political Economy, Book-keeping, Vocal Music, and the *art of Teaching*. . . . Sometimes, instead of reciting the lesson directly to me, I ask them to imagine themselves, for the time, acting in the *capacity* of *teachers,* to a class of young pupils, and to adopt a style suitable for such a purpose. At many of our recitations, more than half the time is spent with reference to teaching *"the art of teaching."* Besides delivering to the school a written *Formal Lecture* once a week, in which I speak of the qualifications, motives, and duties of teachers, the discipline, management, and instruction of schools, and the *manner* in which the various branches should be taught, I am every day, in conversations, or a familiar sort of lectures, taking up and discussing more *particularly* and *minutely,* some point or points suggested by the exercises or occurrences, it may be, of the day, relating to the *internal operations* of the schoolroom, or to physical, moral, or intellectual education:—I say much about the views and

[11] Charles A. Harper, *A Century of Public Teacher Education* (Washington: American Association of Teachers Colleges, 1939), pp 35–36.

motives of teachers, and the motives by which they should attempt to stimulate their pupils. . . . *Annexed school, or model school.*—This school consists of thirty pupils, of both sexes, from the age of six to ten, inclusive. . . . It was committed to the immediate care of the pupils of the Normal School, one acting as superintendent, and two assistants, for one month in rotation, for all who are thought *prepared* to take a part in its instruction. In this experimental school, the teachers are expected to apply the principles and methods which they have been taught in the Normal School, with liberty to suggest any improvements, which may occur to them. Twice every day the Principal of the Normal School goes into the model school for general observation and direction, spending from one half to one hour each visit. In these visits I either sit and watch the general operations of the school, or listen attentively to a particular teacher and her class, or take a class myself, and let the teacher be a listener and observer. After the exercises have closed, I comment upon what I have seen and heard before the teachers, telling them what I deem good, and what faulty, either in their doctrine or their practice, their theory or their manner. Once or twice each term, I take the whole Normal School with me into the model schoolroom, and teach the model school myself, in the presence of the pupils of the Normal School, they being listeners and observers. In these several ways, I attempt to combine, as well as I can, theory and practice, precept and example. . . . From the model school we exclude all appeals to fear, premiums, or emulation; and yet we have had good order, and a fair amount of study.[12]

Other States

Other states were slow to follow Massachusetts' example. New York had experimented with subsidizing academies that would include normal courses, but in 1844 the legislature established a normal school at Albany, with David P. Page as its first principal. Page's *Theory and Practice of Teaching* (1847) was the foremost textbook for preparing teachers throughout the nineteenth century. Before 1860 there were only twelve state normal schools in the United States: four in Massachusetts and one each in New York, Connecticut, Michigan, Rhode Island, New Jersey, Illinois, Pennsylvania, and Minnesota. There were a few private and municipal normal schools in addition to those supported by state governments.

The willingness of many school districts to hire completely untrained adolescents as teachers and the competition of the much broader acad-

[12] Arthur O. Norton, *The First State Normal School in America* (Cambridge: Harvard U. Press, 1926), pp. xlix, li, liii–liv.

emy for the comparative few who did seek some preparation beyond their own common schooling limited the expansion of the normal schools until after the Civil War.

Teacher Institutes

Another effort to improve the quality of common-school teaching was the "teacher institute," short-termed courses which reviewed the common-school subjects and demonstrated teaching techniques to teachers and prospective teachers. Perhaps the first was a "Teachers' or Normal Class" held in 1839 by Henry Barnard in Hartford, Connecticut, paid for out of Barnard's own pocket. By 1845 there were institutes held in "more than half the counties of the state of New York, and in the states of Ohio, Pennsylvania, New Hampshire, Rhode Island and Massachusetts." The six institutes held in Massachusetts in 1846 enrolled between four and five hundred participants.

The institutes met for varying periods, ranging from one week to two months. In Massachusetts they were held for two weeks between the summer and winter terms. The object was to improve both the "art," or practical techniques, and the "science," or theory, of teaching; however, "on account of the shortness of their duration, the art rather than the science is attended to."[13]

When Barnard became chancellor and professor of normal instruction at the University of Wisconsin in 1858, he organized a series of teacher institutes in that state the following spring. In Wisconsin, as in some other states, the institutes were forerunners of a system of normal schools.

The teacher institute has survived, largely as in-service training. In some states—for example, Florida—where teacher institutes were held on university campuses during the summer, the institutes eventually became summer sessions and a part of the university program.

Higher Education

The thirty years immediately preceding the Civil War saw the establishment of many colleges. One study has traced 182 colleges in the United States founded prior to the Civil War; only 49 of them had been

[13] Mann, *Ninth Annual Report*, p. 45.

founded before 1830. A sample of sixteen states revealed that approximately 80 percent of the colleges founded before 1860 were no longer in existence in 1927. A great many of them, particularly on the frontier, were colleges only in name; although they were empowered to confer degrees, they actually offered only secondary school work.[14]

Most of the colleges were denominational, but one of the significant developments in the democratic Age of the Common Man was the founding of the state universities in the Midwestern states. Other innovations in higher education during this period were colleges for women and for Negroes, coeducational colleges, expansion of curriculum, and technical colleges.

Denominational Colleges

A Second Great Awakening in religion in the United States, coupled with the effects of the Dartmouth College decision, led to the founding of church-related colleges, particularly in the Midwest. Bands of Eastern missionaries carried their culture with messianic zeal to Ohio, Indiana, Illinois, and other states of the old Northwest Territory. Methodists, Presbyterians, and Congregationalists led in establishing colleges. Finally these efforts were so diffuse and demands for support so confusing that the Society for the Promotion of Collegiate and Theological Education at the West was founded in 1843 to coordinate the various denominational efforts. The "Yale Bands" carried the stream of Congregational orthodoxy westward, while Princeton men claimed credit for twenty-five colleges to the South and West. Of the 182 colleges in Tewksbury's list of permanent colleges, 49 were Presbyterian, 34 Methodist, 25 Baptist, 21 Congregational, 14 Roman Catholic, 11 Episcopal, and 26 others were scattered in lesser numbers among 9 other denominations.[15] Some of these colleges were reported under two or three denominations, because some of them were joint ventures and some changed their relationships after their original founding.

State Universities

A more important indication of democracy in higher education was the founding of the state universities in the Midwest. The first state universities, particularly in the South, were more closely related to the interests of the aristocracy than to those of the common man. The

[14] Donald G. Tewksbury, *The Founding of American Colleges and Universities Before the Civil War* (New York: Teachers College, 1932), pp. 5fn., 27, 32–54, 70.
[15] *Ibid.*, pp. 14, 90.

aristocracy which controlled the society for its own benefit saw the advantage to themselves in state-supported colleges. On the Western frontier between 1828 and 1860, the motivation and development was very much different. In a 1910 commencement address at Indiana University, founded in 1828, the historian Frederick Jackson Turner summarized the relationship of the frontier colleges to the democractic spirit of the West.

> An essential characteristic of the State University is its democracy in the largest sense. The provision in the Constitution of Indiana of 1816 . . . for a "general system of education ascending in regular gradations from township schools to a State University, wherein tuition shall be gratis and equally open to all," expresses the Middle Western conception born in the days of pioneer society and doubtless deeply influenced by Jeffersonian democracy. . . .
>
> Nothing in our educational history is more striking than the steady pressure of democracy upon its universities to adapt them to the requirements of all the people. From the State Universities of the Middle West, shaped under pioneer ideals, have come the fuller recognition of scientific studies, and especially those of applied science devoted to the conquest of nature; the breaking down of the traditional required curriculum; the union of vocational and college work in the same institution; the development of agricultural and engineering colleges and business courses; the training of lawyers, administrators, public men, and journalists.[16]

In Indiana and Michigan the concept of a state university was considerably broader than that of an institution of higher learning. The university was the entire public school system, from the common school to the university, all free and tax-supported and open to all classes.

THE UNIVERSITY OF MICHIGAN In 1817 territorial Judge Augustus B. Woodward set up a complex educational system which he called "The Catholepistemiad, or University of Michigania." Complete with thirteen departments or *didaxiim*, the scheme resembled the plans of Jefferson for Virginia. The Catholepistemiad never actually taught any university courses, and the building which was built for it was used by a private academy for a number of years. The only service performed by the University of Michigania was to charter and supervise a few academies before the institution was dropped in 1821. But when the newly admitted state

[16] *The Frontier in American History* (New York: Holt), pp. 282–283. Copyright 1920, 1948.

passed legislation establishing the University of Michigan in 1837, it included many of the broad concepts of the Catholepistemiad without all the high-flown Greek terms.

The university became a pattern for other state universities in the Midwest, opening the way for a broad curriculum, practical studies, teacher training, and education for women. According to the 1837 law, the curriculum was to include many scientific and practical subjects in addition to the traditional literary courses. The university was to be divided into three departments: literature, science, and the arts; law; and medicine. The department of literature, science, and the arts was to have thirteen professorships: ancient languages; modern languages; rhetoric and oratory; philosophy of history, logic and philosophy of the human mind; moral philosophy and natural theology, including history of all religions; political economy; mathematics; natural philosophy; chemistry and pharmacy; geology and mineralogy; botany and zoology; fine arts; and civil engineering and architecture. Six professorships were specified for the department of medicine and three for law.[17]

The effort to minimize the effects of wealth in keeping "the avenues of promotion to the highest offices, the highest honors, open to the humblest and most obscure lad who has the natural gifts"[18] resulted in low fees and no tuition charge in the university.

The regents were ordered to cooperate with the superintendent of public instruction in establishing branches, apparently secondary schools, in different parts of the state. "In connection with every such branch of the university, there shall be established an institution for the education of females in the higher branches of knowledge" whenever suitable buildings could be built. In each of the branches there was to be a "department of agriculture, with competent instructors in the theory of agriculture, including vegetable physiology and agricultural chemistry, and experimental and practical farming and agriculture." The branches were also directed to have a department for "the education of teachers for the primary schools."[19]

THE FRONTIER STATE UNIVERSITIES The frontier states had several advantages over the older regions of the country in establishing democratic state universities with curricula to fit the needs of the farmer, engineer and primary-school teacher. First, there was not the competition of older, denominational colleges. Second, there was a greater spirit of democracy

[17] Lucius L. Hubbard, *University of Michigan: Its Origin, Growth and Principles of Government* (Ann Arbor: [U. of Michigan], 1923), p. 10.
[18] Turner, p. 283.
[19] Hubbard, pp. 12–13.

and equality of opportunity for all. Third, there was a greater need for the education of the practical man rather than the scholar, who dominated the Eastern colleges. The first president of the University of Michigan, Henry P. Tappan, took note of these advantages in his 1856 report to the regents of the university.

> The field is not occupied by old institutions, all alike governed by ancient prescriptions, and conflicting with each other on theological and other grounds. We have indeed a few denominational institutions, but these neither in plan, purpose, nor interest can come into collision with a State university. . . . We have an open field for our University standing on the natural and necessary culminating point of our whole educational system.[20]

According to Tewksbury's tables, ten modern state universities trace their founding to charter dates of 1821 and earlier. Eleven claim to have been founded between 1828 and 1855, all except Delaware being located in the "new" states west of the mountains. Beginning with Indiana in 1828, the frontier state universities were Kentucky (1837), Michigan (1837), Missouri (1839), Mississippi (1844), Iowa (1847), Wisconsin (1848), Minnesota (1851), Louisiana (1853), and California (1855). A number of these actually trace their charter to antecedent institutions, sometimes an academy. For example, the University of Florida, which in 1930 claimed 1905 as a founding date, a few years later decided to claim the chartering of East Florida Seminary in 1853 as a more impressive date. As a matter of fact, East Florida Seminary was founded partially on the township grant from Congress for a seminary of higher learning, though it offered only elementary school subjects during most of its history and never was more than a secondary school.[21] Thus the founding dates of pre-Civil War universities must sometimes be taken with a grain of salt. Few of them were really universities or even colleges, and most of them were concentrating on secondary work, preparing students for college-level courses. For example, "as late as 1865, only 41 out of 331 registered students" at the University of Wisconsin were in "regular" classes, the rest being registered in preparatory classes, the normal department, or classified as "special students."[22]

[20] University of Michigan, *Regents' Proceedings, 1837–1864* (Ann Arbor: U. of Michigan, 1915), pp. 664–665.

[21] From a conversation with Prof. H. P. Constans, University of Florida, who helped plan the Silver Anniversary celebration in 1930 and the Centennial in 1953.

[22] John S. Brubacher and Willis Rudy, *Higher Education in Transition* (New York: Harper & Row, 1958), p. 152.

Technical Institutes

The increasing industrialization of the American economy called for technicians and engineers, but the older colleges clung to the traditional literary studies rather than condescending to serve the bourgeois requests for scientific and mathematical subjects. The United States Military Academy at West Point, founded in 1802, was the first institution of higher education to train engineers. The most important innovator in technical education was The Rensselaer School, founded at Troy, New York, in 1824. Its founder, Stephen Van Rensselaer, described its purpose as "the application of science to the common purposes of life."

> My principal object is to qualify teachers for instructing sons and daughters of farmers and mechanics, by lectures or otherwise, on the application of experimental chemistry, philosophy, and natural history to agriculture, domestic economy, the arts, and manufactures.[23]

In 1832 the name was changed to Rensselaer Polytechnic Institute, and a year later "the trustees were empowered to establish a department of mathematical arts, for the purpose of giving instruction in engineering and technology." R.P.I. became famous for its teaching methods as well as its curriculum. All students were required to recite daily in every subject, class sections being kept small to make such individual participation possible. The students not only answered orally but had to make blackboard demonstrations. At the end of each term students reviewed all the subjects and took examinations over all the subjects.

When Eliphalet Nott, the president of Rensselaer from 1828 to 1845, assumed the presidency of Union College in Schenectady, he introduced a department of civil engineering. Two years later, Harvard and Yale compromised with industry and established, respectively, the Lawrence Scientific School and the Sheffield Scientific School, thus offering scientific and technical subjects without sullying the academic traditions of the old, original arts colleges of the universities. In 1852 Dartmouth made a similar compromise in its Chandler Scientific School, and the same year Brown organized a department of practical science. In 1855 the University of Pennsylvania created the Department of Mines, Arts, and Manufacturers. In some of these schools, the technical and scientific courses were considered much easier than the classical studies, and in general the graduates of the scientific schools did not receive degrees. The Lawrence and Chandler schools required only a common-school education for admission, so that they were reduced to the level of secondary schools.

[23] *Report of the U.S. Commissioner of Education,* 1892, Part II, p. 757.

Morrill Act

The most important event in higher education during this second American revolution occurred during the Civil War itself, although it is a clear illustration of the democratic pressure of the revolutionary period preceding the War. In December, 1857, Congressman Justin S. Morrill, of Vermont, introduced a bill to grant public lands for the establishment of colleges of agriculture and mechanical arts. He argued that Congress had the constitutional right to dispose of federal lands, pointing to the more than 25 million acres granted the railroads, and to land grants for "general education in all the new States."

Up to June 30, 1857, the federal government had granted 67,736,572 acres of land to the states and territories for schools and universities. Although no one questioned the constitutionality of these grants, "all direct encouragement to agriculture has been rigidly withheld." Morrill claimed that the advance of the nation depended on "encouraging useful knowledge among farmers and mechanics in order to enlarge our productive powers."

> There is no class of our community of whom we may be so justly proud as our mechanics. . . . But they snatch their education, such as it is, from the crevices between labor and sleep. . . . Our country relies upon them to do the handiwork of the nation. Let us, then, furnish the means . . . to acquire culture, skill, and efficiency.
>
> We have schools to teach the art of manslaying and to make masters of "deep-throated engines" of war; and shall we not have schools to teach men the way to feed, clothe, and enlighten the great brotherhood of man?[24]

After considerable debate over amendments, a substitute bill which Morrill had presented for the one which came from the Committee on Public Lands was passed by a close 105 to 100 vote.

The Senate Committee on Public Lands reported the bill with no recommendation, and action was delayed on it until the spring of 1859. When it did come up for debate, the sectional interests were well illustrated by the arguments on the bill. Senator Henry M. Rice, of Minnesota, an independent, "stand-on-our-own-feet" type of Westerner, argued the constitutional issue and warned that giving one state income from the sale of lands in another would "disturb the harmony now existing between them"—a tragically amusing statement considering the strife

[24] *The Congressional Globe,* Vol. 27, Part 2 (1858), pp. 1692–1697.

that was already tearing the nation apart! Ignoring the fact that the federal government was already giving land for "seminaries of higher learning" to new states, including his own, Rice asked:

> If we give lands to States for colleges . . . how long will it be before they will ask aid for every object, and come to rely entirely upon the General Government even for the expenses of their own, until they have become so dependent upon the national Treasury that they will have but a shadow of sovereignty left? . . . If you wish to establish agricultural colleges, give to each man a college of his own in the shape of one hundred and sixty acres of land, where he and his children can learn to make it yield . . . but do not give lands to the States to enable them to educate the sons of the wealthy at the expense of the public. We want no fancy farmers; we want no fancy mechanics.[25]

Rice, like many a frontiersman, apparently distrusted "book learning" as impractical.

Senator James M. Mason, of Virginia, took the aristocrat's view that public money as aid would corrupt the morals of those who received "alms" from the federal government. He presented the traditional states' rights position, saying that the bill proposed

> using the public lands as a means of controlling the policy of the State Legislatures. It is misusing the property of the country in such a mode as to bring the appropriate functions of the State . . . under the discretion of Congress by a controlling power; and it is doing it in the worst and most insidious form—by bribery.

Mason then predicted that the logic of the bill could eventually lead to the federal government's legislating what kind of schools states must have.

> If you have the right to use the public property . . . to establish agricultural colleges, cannot you establish a school system in each State for general purposes of education? Would it not be in the power of a majority in Congress to fasten upon the Southern States that peculiar system of free schools in the New England States which I believe would tend, I will not say to demoralize, but to destroy that peculiar character which I am happy to believe belongs to the great mass of the southern people.[26]

[25] *Ibid.*, Vol. 28, Part 1 (1859), pp. 717–718.
[26] *Ibid.*, p. 720.

Mason's praise of Virginia's inadequate school system was immediately challenged by Iowa Senator James Harlan.

> It may be that it is a blessing to Virginia that she is now more largely represented by adult white people who are unable to read and write, in proportion to her population, than any other State of the Union; it is a blessing, however, that the people of my State do not covet.

He went on to give a Jacksonian version of Robert Coram's Enlightenment creed that there would be no equal representation until farmers could get an education equal to that of lawyers and thus have the chance to be represented in government by farmers. Finally, he reminded the Virginia Senator that the proposed law did not require Virginia to take advantage of the land grants if they did not wish to do so.

The bill finally passed the Senate by a vote of 25–22, eighteen of the nays coming from Southern senators. President Buchanan vetoed it, largely on constitutional grounds, and Morrill was unable to get Congress to overrule the veto.

After the election of Lincoln, Morrill re-introduced his bill. This time it was discussed in the Senate first, with Senator Harlan's Committee on Public Lands giving it the only favorable committee report it ever received in either house. Although most of the arguments were on constitutionality, the issue of land speculation was raised by Senators from Western states. Harlan pointed out that more than a billion acres of land were in the public domain, and that the grants proposed for agricultural and mechanical arts colleges would be only ten million, less than 1 percent of the total. One of Harlan's speeches particularly exemplified the common-man spirit, when he challenged the consciences of the Senators.

> This body is a body of lawyers. There are very few gentlemen here who are not professional lawyers. Heretofore appropriations of land have been made for State universities. The proceeds of the sales of these lands have usually gone to educate the children of professional men—men who are able to defray the expense of the education of their children away from home, in classical studies and in the learned professions. Here . . . a proposition is made to make an appropriation of lands for the education of the children of the agriculturists of the nation, and it meets with strenuous opposition from a body of lawyers.[27]

[27] *Ibid.*, Vol. 32, Part 3 (1862), p. 2629.

The Senate passed the bill 32 to 7. In the House, the Committee on Public Lands brought an unfavorable report, but with very little debate, and with the favorable action of the Senate as an example, the bill was passed, 90 to 25. On July 2, 1862, President Lincoln signed it into law.

Perhaps one reason the bill passed was that many of the Southern opponents were no longer in Congress. Another reason, perhaps, was that the new version provided for the schools to teach military tactics, and the Union needed military officers badly. But undoubtedly one factor involved in the passage, even in the consideration of the bill, was the political force of the farmer and industrial worker in a social revolutionary age.

According to the Morrill Act of 1862, the federal government granted to the states 30,000 acres of land for each member of Congress, the income from the sale of which was to be invested in such manner as to

> constitute a perpetual fund, the capital of which shall remain forever undiminished . . . and the interest of which shall be inviolably appropriated . . . to the endowment, support, and maintenance of at least one college where the leading object shall be, without excluding other scientific and classical studies, and including military tactics, to teach such branches of learning as are related to agriculture and the mechanic arts in such a manner as the Legislatures of the States may respectively prescribe, in order to promote the liberal and practical education of the industrial classes in the several pursuits and professions in life.[28]

This significant step in federal aid to education leaves virtually all control to the state, requiring only that the interest on the fund be used to teach, in part, courses in agriculture, mechanical arts, and military tactics. The law expressly assigns the details of the colleges to the legislatures of the states.

From the way in which these grants were administered, it appears that the danger of federal aid may be not too much control but too little, for many of the colleges which utilized the funds from these grants met only the letter of the law and not its spirit. Where money was used by already existing colleges, the practical courses were limited as much as possible and denied places of importance in the college. In some colleges a single professorship covered all the agricultural, mechanical, and scientific studies. In others a single summer course met the technical requirements of the law. In some states the fund was mis-

[28] *Ibid.*, p. 2770.

managed, so that little interest accrued and what did was sometimes misappropriated. The generally poor handling of the income resulted in these colleges soon being in such financial distress that Morrill, in 1890, had to have Congress make supplementary cash grants, a step that was itself a significant precedent in the practice of federal aid to education.

Because of the unsettled conditions during the War, the development of the "land grant" colleges did not begin until later, the law giving encouragement to the growth of state universities and the expansion of the curriculum in the direction of the practical and scientific courses in the period of conservative reaction which followed the War.

Academic Freedom

In times of developing social crisis, professors and presidents often are attacked because of their political preferences, religious beliefs, or other controversial opinions. During the social revolution of the mid-nineteenth century, a number of outstanding leaders in higher education were harassed over matters other than their competence as teachers or administrators.

One celebrated case was that of Thomas Cooper, professor of chemistry and later president of South Carolina College. Cooper had the anti-clerical views of an Enlightenment philosopher and was bitterly opposed by the Presbyterian clergy of the state. Similarly, his "out-of-date" Enlightenment attitudes toward centralized government and nullification offended unionists. In a public hearing held by the trustees in 1832, Cooper defended himself against the charges leveled at him and made an eloquent case for intellectual freedom. He pointed out that many great teachers and thinkers, including Socrates, Jesus, Wickliffe, Galileo, and Locke, had been silenced, not because they were wrong, but because they held unpopular views.

> Let me now suppose a case: that you have a President of the College, of known talents and extensive acquirements; who possesses the difficult art of communicating knowledge to others; whose literary reputation is established; whose manners are conciliatory; whose morals are unexceptionable, and his long tried course of conduct, unimpeachable—would you reject these qualifications, because some of his speculative opinions were unpopular to a portion, and that not a large one of his fellow citizens? . . .
>
> It savors of unfair dealing with the Students of the College, to conceal from them, differences of opinion which they are sure to

meet, when they leave it; and prohibit all insight into views and arguments, which are necessary to be known and considered, before any man can honestly determine, where truth is to be found.[29]

Cooper also argued on the grounds of freedom of speech guaranteed by the First Amendment to the Constitution.

> I claim . . . the right of entertaining in private, and professing and defending in public, peaceably, by all fair and reasonable argument, any opinion whatever on any subject whatever without exception, within the illimitable extent of human inquiry. I claim it as one of the *rights of man,* before political constitutions were invented or proposed. I claim it as a right clearly and fully guaranteed by the Constitution of the United States, and of this State in particular.[30]

Two days after Cooper made his defense, the board of trustees dismissed the charges against him as unsubstantiated.

As the crisis period heightened and political, social, and religious aspects of the revolution became more controversial and conflicts more bitter, other college professors and presidents were not as fortunate as Cooper. In 1851 the regents of the University of Michigan dismissed Daniel D. Whedon, professor of logic and history, and John H. Agnew, professor of Greek and Latin, because they "talked too much anti-slavery." The nomination of Oliver Wolcott Gibbs as professor of chemistry at Columbia College (now Columbia University) was rejected by the conservative Episcopal majority of the board in 1854 because he was a Unitarian. Francis Lieber, distinguished professor of history and political economy at South Carolina College from 1835 to 1855, was "passed over" at a time of electing a president because, as he complained to a friend, he was an Episcopalian and a suspect abolitionist, although he owned slaves himself. Disappointed at his failure to be made president, Lieber resigned his professorship. The trustees of the University of North Carolina dismissed Benjamin S. Hedrick, professor of chemistry, in 1854 because he favored the election of John C. Frémont. A newspaper editorial states the issue unmistakably: "*That man is neither a fit nor a safe instructor of our young men, who even inclines to Frémont and black Republicanism.*[31]

Nathan Lord, president of Dartmouth from 1828 to 1863, was a strong supporter of slavery. When the Congregational Church complained of

[29] Hofstadter and Smith, Vol. I, pp. 405–406.
[30] *Ibid.*, p. 416.
[31] North Carolina *Standard,* Sept. 29, 1856.

his position, the trustees did not dismiss him, but they expressed such strong disapproval that he resigned. In his resignation he took his stand on his right of academic freedom, saying that he refused "to surrender my moral and constitutional right and Christian liberty." He claimed that the trustees had no "right to impose any religious, ethical or political test upon any member of their own body or any member of the College Faculty, beyond what is recognized by the Charter of the Institution."[32] But the "excited passions of the hour" in a time of revolution unfortunately overrule reason and law at times, and these institutions lost valuable leaders and teachers at a time when higher education was struggling to come of age.

An Educational Legacy

The basic principles and organization of American education are a product of the Age of the Common Man. Between 1830 and 1860 the free, tax-supported, state-controlled, secular common school became firmly established as the foundation of the school system. The public high school had its first struggle in the contest with the private academy as the truly American secondary school. And the state university as the capstone of a public education that would equalize opportunities of all classes made its first appearance. Much of what has transpired since 1865 in the history of American education has been the slow struggle to realize in practice what was accepted in principle during this great revolutionary age.

QUESTIONS FOR DISCUSSION

1. Until the appearance of the academy, girls had little opportunity for secondary education. Examine the influence of the private academy on the development of the public high schools. What relationships can you point to between the opportunity for education and the women's rights movement in general?
2. Contrast the preparation of teachers in the normal schools and teacher institutes of the Jacksonian period with teacher training today. Where has our progress been most praiseworthy? In what ways have we advanced very little?
3. The appearance of the state universities and the passage of the Morrill Act brought almost revolutionary changes in secondary and higher education. Discuss these changes in relation to the spirit of the Jacksonian era.

[32] Hofstadter and Smith, p. 473.

4. Compare the attacks on academic freedom during the Jacksonian period of social controversy with similar attacks in the twentieth century. Did the firing and harassment of professors then prevent the Civil War or help solve any of the social issues of the time? Or may those attacks have helped make peaceful solutions of the problem impossible?

SUGGESTED READINGS

Secondary Sources

Brubacher, John S., and Rudy, Willis. *Higher Education in Transition.* New York: Harper & Row, 1958. Chapters 4, 5, and 8.

Harper, Charles A. *A Century of Public Teacher Education.* Washington: American Association of Teachers Colleges, 1939. Chapters I–III.

Kandel, I. L. *History of Secondary Education.* Boston: Houghton Mifflin, 1930. Chapter IX.

Thwing, Charles F. *A History of Higher Education in America.* New York: Appleton, 1906. Chapters IX–XII.

Woody, Thomas. *A History of Women's Education in the United States.* New York: The Science Press, 1929. Vol. I, Chapters VII–XI.

Primary Sources

Cubberley, Ellwood P. *Readings in the History of Education.* Boston: Houghton Mifflin, 1920. Readings 329, 331, 332, 349, 350.

———. *Readings in Public Education in the United States.* Boston: Houghton Mifflin, 1934. Readings 150, 151, 157, 158, 169–171, 212–223.

Gross, Carl H., and Chandler, Charles C. *The History of American Education Through Readings.* Boston: Heath, 1964. Pp. 139–143, 153–192.

Hillway, Tyrus. *American Education: An Introduction Through Readings.* Boston: Houghton Mifflin, 1964. Readings 5 and 8.

Hofstadter, Richard, and Smith, Wilson. *American Higher Education: A Documentary History.* Chicago: U. of Chicago Press, 1961. Vol. I, pp. 232–250, 292–391, 396–474; Vol. II, pp. 478–549.

Knight, Edgar W. *A Documentary History of Education in the South Before 1860.* Chapel Hill: U. of North Carolina Press, 1949. Vol. III, Chapters V–VIII; Vol. IV, Chapters III and IV; Vol. V, pp. 236–239, 244–246, 251–257, 259–277, 387–458, 459–515.

Knight, Edgar W., and Hall, Clifton L. *Readings in American Educational History.* New York: Appleton-Century-Crofts, 1951. Pp. 237–296, 415–417.

Monroe, Paul. *The Founding of the American Public School System.* Ann Arbor: University Microfilm, 1940. Vol. II, Chapter XVII, Quotes 547–551; Chapter XVIII, Quotes 568, 569, 571; Chapter XIX, Quotes 576, 581–587, 589, 590, 599, 600; Chapter XX, Quotes 606, 613–619.

PART Four

"Behold Them Everywhere"

CHRONOLOGY

1859—Charles Darwin publishes *Origin of Species.*
1861–1865—Administration of Abraham Lincoln
1861–1865—Civil War
1864—Nevada admitted to the Union
1865–1869—Administration of Andrew Johnson
1865—Thirteenth Amendment abolishes slavery.
1866—Fourteenth Amendment prevents states from depriving persons of life, liberty, or property without due process of law.
1867—Reconstruction Act passed
1867—Alaska purchased
1867—Nebraska admitted to the Union
1869—Fifteenth Amendment guarantees civil rights to all individuals.
1869–1877—Administration of U. S. Grant
1869—Union Pacific and Central Pacific Railways joined, making the first transcontinental railroad
1870—Population of the United States 38,558,371
1873—Financial panic caused by over-expansion of business and speculation
1877–1881—Administration of Rutherford B. Hayes
1880—Population of the United States 50,155,783
1881–1885—Administration of James A. Garfield and Chester A. Arthur
1885–1889—Administration of Grover Cleveland
1889–1893—Administration of Benjamin Harrison
1889—North Dakota, South Dakota, Washington, and Montana admitted to the Union
1890—Population of the United States 62,947,714
1890—Wyoming and Idaho admitted to the Union
1890—Sherman Anti-Trust Law enacted
1892—Army of Pinkerton detectives and state troops used against strikers at Homestead plant of Carnegie Steel Company
1893–1897—Second administration of Grover Cleveland
1893—Financial panic
1894—President Cleveland uses federal troops against strikers at Pullman Company.
1896—Utah admitted to the Union
1897–1901—Administration of William McKinley
1898—Spanish-American War
1900—Population of the United States 75,994,575

THE ELECTION OF ABRAHAM LINCOLN was the climax of the revolution which had been building up through the preceding decades; the plantation aristocracy of the South had lost their political, social, and economic control of the nation. The Civil War and the social chaos of the Reconstruction period were the bitter stages of violence in that great social revolution. As with other social revolutions, there was a time of reaction; in the Gilded Age a new industrial plutocracy captured control of the nation, supplanting the planter aristocracy and aborting the agrarian democracy for which the common man had struggled for half a century.

The period between 1860 and 1900 was a time of sudden increase in the personal wealth of industrial and financial leaders, public corruption at all levels of government, rapid expansion of industrial technology and science, and the closing of the frontier as caravans of settlers moved west and drove the Indians from the scene. This was all justified through the religion and ethics of social Darwinism, while the victorious North inflicted punitive Reconstruction policies on the suffering South.

SUGGESTED READINGS

Beard, Charles A., and Beard, Mary R. *The Rise of American Civilization.* New York: Macmillan, 1930. Vol. II, pp. 52–77, 98–121, 170–210, 227–236, 261–263, 269–271, 301–311, 335–337, 383–393, 406–419, 467–477.

Commager, Henry Steele. *The American Mind.* New Haven: Yale Press, 1950. Chapters IV and V.

Coulter, Morton. *The South During Reconstruction, 1865–1877.* Baton Rouge: Louisiana State U. Press, 1947.

Gabriel, Ralph Henry. *The Course of American Democratic Thought.* New York: Ronald Press, 1956. Chapters 13, 14, 24.

Hofstadter, Richard. *Social Darwinism in American Thought, 1860–1915.* Philadelphia: U. of Penn. Press, 1944. Chapters I, II, VII.

Nevins, Allan. *The Emergence of Modern America, 1865–1878.* New York: Macmillan, 1927. Chapters 1, 2, 4, 6, 7, 10.

Schlesinger, Arthur M. *The Rise of the City, 1878–1898.* New York: Macmillan, 1933. Chapters 1, 2, 3.

Schlesinger, Arthur M., Jr. *The Age of Jackson.* Boston: Little, Brown, 1945, Pp. 505–510.

Woodward, C. Vann. *Origins of the New South, 1877–1913.* Baton Rouge: Louisiana State U. Press, 1951. Chapters I–X.

10

Toward Professionalization of Teaching

Vocations generally considered professions[1] have several characteristics which distinguish them from non-professional vocations. Foremost is the fact that professional workers base their practice on theoretical knowledge. This theory and its application are acquired through a relatively long period of training. Further, there are definite standards for admission to practice, and these standards are enforced by the profession itself through a professional association. Although it may be concerned with the pay and working conditions of its members, the professional association has broader aims than those of a labor union; much of its concern is with raising the level of performance of the practitioners in the field through professional journalism and meetings.

Before the Civil War teaching had few of these characteristics. It is true that college professors were well educated and had a body of knowledge related to their subject and that most academy teachers were academy graduates, many of them having attended college. But the mass of the teachers in the common schools were graduates only of the very schools in which they were to teach for a very brief career. They knew little about their subject matter and less about how to teach. It was a rare teacher indeed who belonged to any teacher organization or subscribed to an educational journal.

[1] We should note two common meanings of the word *profession* that have nothing to do with the meaning discussed in this chapter. One is the very loose use of the term to mean almost any white-collar job, as when one speaks of barbering as his "professon." The other distinguishes those who engage in activity as a means of livelihood from those who participate for other reasons: *professional* baseball players, and so on.

Beginnings of Educational Theory

Most of the pedagogical theories of the late nineteenth century were derived from European philosophers—Pestalozzi, Herbart, Froebel, Hegel, Wundt, Ritter, Spencer, Huxley. The Prussian schools were still looked on as the best in the world, and German educational philosophies were logical sources for the foundations of pedagogical theory, though some of these philosophies arrived very indirectly. The emphasis on science by Spencer and Huxley and their influence on the curriculum will be discussed in the next chapter.

The Oswego Movement: Object Lesson

The revolutionary ideas of the great Swiss educator Pestalozzi have influenced American schools ever since Joseph Neef came to the United States around 1805. The most effective injection of Pestalozzianism came through the work of Edward Sheldon. Sheldon, who was superintendent of schools in Oswego, New York, visited other towns in hopes of finding ways to improve his schools, and on a tour of inspection of the Toronto, Ontario, schools in 1859 observed a collection of materials for teaching produced by the Home and Colonial Training Institution of London. The Institution had been founded forty years earlier by the Reverend Charles Mayo and his sister Elizabeth after they had spent three years teaching with Pestalozzi. Horace Mann had recommended the use of Miss Mayo's object lessons in his *Eleventh Annual Report* in 1848. But not until Sheldon brought the object lesson concept to Oswego did it "catch on" in the United States.

Sheldon bought three hundred dollars' worth of "collections of objects, pictures, charts of colors, form, reading charts, books for teachers, giving full directions as to the use of this material." He trained his teachers in its use, beginning with the first grade.

> I met the teachers every Saturday, laid out work for the coming week, discussed principles and methods with them and then gave my whole time, the following week, to seeing that the work was properly carried out in their rooms. The second year I did the same thing for the second grade.

He discovered that as soon as he had trained a group of teachers, other cities lured them away with higher salaries. He proposed that the school board set up a city school for the training of primary teachers. To teach this school he hired Miss Margaret E. M. Jones, who had been a teacher with the London Home and Colonial Training Institution for eighteen years. From May, 1861, through the summer of 1862, she demonstrated the use of the object lessons during the regular school day and held classes for teachers after 3:30 on afternoons and on Saturday mornings. To pay her salary of $1,000 and all living expenses required a certain amount of business acumen:

> In the first place I charged a tuition of fifty dollars to all persons not residents of Oswego who joined the class. In the second place I persuaded a number of the more progressive teachers to contribute one-half of their salary for the year, in view of the benefit that would come to them from the instructions. . . . In the third place, by converting one of the schools into a school of practice, I saved the salary of one teacher.[2]

Miss Jones taught the "school of practice."

From this one experimental year came a permanent normal school, which for a time was the most famous teacher-training institution in the nation. Sheldon intended that it be open only to high school graduates and offer "one year of strictly professional training." Apparently, however, academic courses, including a classical department, were added over Sheldon's objections. Not until 1891 was he successful in getting the classical department dropped, thus gaining an additional year for "work in history, science, psychology and teaching, and in higher English."[3] By 1900, Oswego graduates had carried the enthusiasm for object lessons to every state and territory in the United States.

The basic principle of the object lessons was to start with something familiar to the pupils and proceed to the abstractions of language. In teaching geography, for example, Sheldon adopted the practice of Pestalozzi of having the child begin with "a consideration of that part of the earth which he sees in his daily walks . . . as a preparation for the consideration of what lies beyond his own neighborhood." In all lessons, "the cultivation of language should be one of the leading points," from oral expression, to written words, to compositions.[4]

As with any other "system," object lessons soon lost much of their original meaning and became highly formalized drill-type activities with which teacher-trainees in normal schools and summer institutes were indoctrinated. This departure from the original spirit of Pestalozzi was

[2] Edward A. Sheldon, *Autobiography* (New York: Ives-Butler, 1911), pp. 117; 133–136.

[3] *Ibid.*, p. 177–178.

[4] *Proceedings of the National Teachers' Association for 1863*, pp. 362–363.

partly the result of the opportunistic practices of publishers who, to capitalize on the wave of popularity of object teaching, changed title pages of old books to include the words "object lessons" without altering the contents of the books. In addition to this fraudulent practice, about which Sheldon complained in his papers at N.T.A. meetings, the terribly mechanical process of training teachers in the normal schools contributed largely to the loss of vitality in the method of object teaching. Instead of teachers learning general principles on which they could build their own techniques and lessons suited to the lives and experiences of their pupils, they were given specific lesson plans and objects, some of them undoubtedly inappropriate for the children they were later to teach. Thus, instead of the lessons growing out of the lives of the children, they became just as contrived as were the old formal book lessons. This story is unfortunately a familiar one in the history of teacher training.

William T. Harris—Traditionalist

Just as the career of Horace Mann epitomizes the educational developments of the Age of the Common Man, that of William T. Harris characterizes the spirit of educators of the Gilded Age. Superintendent of schools in St. Louis from 1867 to 1880, Harris was a leading figure in American schools for over forty years. In 1880 he resigned his post in St. Louis to devote full time to editing *The Journal of Speculative Philosophy*, which he had founded in 1867 when he could not find a publisher for articles he had written in criticism of Spencer. From 1889 to 1906 he served as United States Commissioner of Education, leaving his imprint on American schools almost as effectively as Mann had left his on those of Massachusetts. In the 1890's Harris was a leader in both the National Herbart Society and the National Education Association. He was a member of the Committee of Ten on secondary curriculum and the Committee of Fifteen on elementary curriculum.

Harris was an opponent of the materialism of science. He believed that the school should develop the mental powers needed to let the individual withdraw from the material world and its confusion of sense experiences and concentrate on logical principles. For such an education he recommended the classics and literary masterpieces. He made only moderate compromises with science and utilitarian courses, and even then he seemed motivated by a concern for conservative economic interests. He defended the factory system for the benefits it had brought to labor, ignoring the poverty, unemployment, and urban slums created by industrialism. He believed that education in the cultural subjects would not only bring students into greater consonance with God's order but would enable the masses to use wisely the leisure that machines made possible. He minimized the importance of manual training, denying that it had any great intellectual value and relegating it to the kindergarten years. His educational theory stressed the "five windows of the soul," through which even elementary schooling should prepare the youth for life in an industrial nation.

> There are five windows of the soul, which open out upon five great divisions of the life of man. . . . Arithmetic furnishes the survey of whatever has the form of time. . . . Through the geographic window of the soul the survey extends to organic and inorganic nature. . . .
> The study of the history of one's native country in the elementary school opens the window of the soul which looks out upon the spectacle of the will power of his nation. In the language of a people are revealed the . . . intellect and the conscious realization of the mind of the race. . . . Grammar opens to the child his view of the inner workings of the mind of the race, and helps him in so far to a comprehension of his own spiritual self. Literature, finally, is the most accessible, as well as the fullest and completest expression of the sentiments, opinions, and convictions of a people.[5]

Harris based his arguments on introspective psychology, rejecting the "new" physiological psychology.

> Our appartus for observing material objects can not perceive feelings or thoughts. This being so, it is evident that physiological psychology can make no progress whatever without introspection.[6]

His absolutist philosophy was firmly rooted in the educational traditions of the past, and during his long term of office as United States Commissioner of Education, he used his position and personal influence to fasten the dead hand of the past on the schools of the nation.

Herbartianism

Johann Friedrich Herbart (1776–1841) was a German philosopher ranking in importance with Kant and Hegel during his own lifetime. His psychological and pedagogical theories provided one of the bases for modern educational theories. His concept of mind as an organic whole was ultimately to replace the view of mind as made up of specific "faculties"

[5] William T. Harris, *Psychological Foundations of Education* (New York: Appleton, 1898), p. 322.
[6] *Ibid.*, p. 5.

of reason, memory, appreciation, love, and so on. His theory of learning was that knowledge came through sense perceptions, that these perceptions were interpretations of raw experience made on the basis of previous perceptions, and that the mind was a storehouse of all past perceptions. This storehouse, or "apperceptive mass," was a sub-conscious part of the mind, and only a few perceptions could be called into the conscious mind at any one time. "Interest" was the force which tended to bring perceptions to the conscious awareness when they were needed to solve a problem. In order to develop the moral man—the educational aim of Herbart—the schools should utilize subject matter as "presentations" from which pupils would get "perceptions" to be used later in life, and should invest these perceptions with a high degree of "interest," so that they would be recalled when appropriate.

From Herbart's philosophy of learning, German schoolmen developed a very complex pedagogical theory. The leading American Herbartians—Charles DeGarmo and Charles and Frank McMurry—based their work on those German schoolmasters, including Tuiskon Ziller, Karl Stoy, Otto Frick, William Rein, and Karl Lange. DeGarmo and the McMurry brothers published several books on Herbartian theory, taught collectively or individually in some half dozen American colleges, and generally promoted Herbartianism in several educational associations. In 1895 they founded The Herbart Society for the Scientific Study of Education. During its brief commitment to Herbartianism, it was known generally as the National Herbart Society. In 1900 it was apparently inactive, and following its reorganization in 1901, the reference to Herbart in its title was dropped and a few years later the word "Scientific" was omitted. It is now The National Society for the Study of Education, one of the leading professional associations in promoting educational theory.

To the Herberatians, "The ultimate aim of the school is the development of good character."[7] The focus of the Herbartian educational program was on the individual child, "his understanding, his sympathies, his interests, his feelings and mental stages, his natural ways of living."[8] This emphasis on the child, in contrast with the customary complete concern for subject matter, was one of the legacies of the Herbartians to twentieth-century educational theory.

The Herbartians did not overlook the problems of subject matter,

[7] Charles McMurry, "Concentration," *The First Yearbook of the National Herbart Society* (1895), p. 61.

[8] Charles DeGarmo, "Most Pressing Problems," *The First Yearbook of the National Herbart Society* (1895), p. 9.

however. Many of the discussions of their meetings dealt with the organization of the material to be studied by the child. Although they admitted a number of courses to the curriculum, they stressed the moral value of the study of history and literature, which were to be the "center about which all others as far as possible are grouped." The organization of the curriculum around one subject was called the "principle of concentration," and relating other subjects to the central study was "correlation." In considering "what truths of the desired kind will prove the most interesting to children at different ages," the Herbartians relied on the "cultural epoch" theory. "The child, on the whole, passes through the same great stages of development through which all races pass," and the kind of literature appropriate to children depends on what "epoch" the child is passing through in his development.[9]

The longest-lasting direct influence of Herbartianism was the methodology developed to facilitate the presentation of material and to build "interest." Herbart believed that there were two factors which contributed to interest: association with related perceptions, and repetition of the presentation. From this he and Ziller proposed four steps in a method of teaching; Rein and the American Herbartians expanded them into the "Five Formal Steps." Different Herbartians called these five steps by various names; Charles McMurray, in *The Method of the Recitation* (1892), called them Preparation, Presentation, Association or Comparison, Generalization or Abstraction, and Application.

> It is first necessary to bring vividly into consciousness all the experiences the child has had which pertain to the subject at hand. After they have been thus reproduced, the new ideas should be presented, to be explained by the light of the old and thoroughly apperceived ones.
>
> We pass from percepts to concepts by a careful comparison of the percepts and abstraction of the essential characteristics. . . . Here, also, there are two important steps: first, the act of comparison; and second, the separation of the essential from the non-essential, the mind dwelling upon and formulating the general notion. The comprehension of this notion is to be followed by its application. . . . This is the fifth necessary step in learning. . . . So the Herbartians have named these the five formal steps.[10]

Long after Herbartian theories were discarded, normal-school students learned to make out their daily lesson plans in accord with the Five Formal Steps. At a time when schools were expanding rapidly and

[9] Frank McMurry, "Value of Herbartian Pedagogy for Normal Schools," N.E.A. *Proceedings*, 1892, pp. 428–430.
[10] Frank McMurry, pp. 431–432.

teachers were in short supply, some effectiveness in teaching could be achieved by having prospective teachers follow the mechanical organization of the Herbartian method.

From its beginning, Herbartianism had sharp critics, even from within the Herbart Society itself. W. T. Harris attacked the emphasis on interest, holding that it would not provide the mental discipline he favored. John Dewey opposed the concentration on literature and history, arguing that children are interested in their immediate pursuits, not in the dead past.

Psychology

Herbart's philosophy gave rise to the scientific study of psychology, and the work of the Germans in experimental psychology, beginning with Wilhelm Wundt of Leipzig in 1879, attracted many Americans, including G. Stanley Hall and James McKeen Cattell. The foremost American psychologist prior to 1900 was William James, who was instructor in anatomy and physiology at Harvard and began teaching psychology in 1875. In 1890 James published a two-volume *Principles of Psychology* and later a very popular simplification of psychology for educators, entitled *Talks to Teachers.* Many of the leaders in education, such as W. T. Harris, clung tenaciously to the traditional mental disciplinary theories of mind, minimizing the effect of the new psychology in educational theory.[11]

Teacher Training

Before the Civil War, secondary teachers had often had some college work, and many had degrees, but virtually none had had courses in pedagogy. Teachers in the common schools generally had very little schooling of any kind beyond their own common-school training. A few normal schools had appeared between 1830 and 1860, and normal courses were part of the program of most academies and high schools, but they graduated far fewer teachers than were needed. By the end of the century, normal schools and colleges were trying to raise the standards of preparation of secondary- as well as elementary-school teachers.

Normal Schools

Following the lead of Massachusetts and Horace Mann, a number of states established normal schools for training common-school teachers. By 1874 there were 134 normal schools in the United States, enrolling

[11] Since the influence of psychology has been a twentieth-century development, James, Hall, and other psychologists will be discussed later, in Chapter 14.

24,405 students. Of these at least 67 received "appropriations from States, four from counties, and nine from cities." The remaining 54 either failed to report or were supported by private endowment and fees.[12] Most of the normal schools were apparently a sort of secondary school, with only common-school prerequisites. The length of the course ranged from two to four years.

In less than a quarter of a century, the number of normal schools had more than doubled and the number of students had almost tripled. In 1897–1898 there were 345 normal schools, 167 public and 178 private. The public normal schools enrolled 46,245 pupils; the private, 21,293. In the public normal schools, female students outnumbered males 33,667 to 12,578; in the private schools, boys and girls were about even: 10,696 girls to 10,597 boys. In 1898 these institutions graduated only 11,255, of whom over 8,000 were from the public schools and over 8,000 were females. The public normal schools were fairly well scattered over the nation; by 1910 New York had 12, Pennsylvania 13, Massachusetts 9, West Virginia, North Carolina, Missouri, and Wisconsin 7 each. Ohio was "the only great state that has no state normal school."[13]

Many of the normal schools were still secondary schools by the end of the century, offering only two years of review of elementary school studies and a few lectures on pedagogical matters. But some were moving in the direction of becoming colleges. Although the Massachusetts normal schools still offered two-year courses for elementary school teachers, they were requiring graduation from high school for admission.

> The general two years' course designed for intending teachers below the high school comprises, (1) psychology, history of education, principles of education, methods of instruction and discipline, school organization, and the laws of Massachusetts; (2) methods of teaching English, mathematics, science, vocal music, physical culture, and manual training; (3) observation in the model school and in other public schools. The Bridgewater school has a regular four years' course embracing, in addition to the foregoing studies, work of a more academic character, as instruction in Latin and French, Greek and German, English literature, history, etc. This course looks to the preparation of grammar school principals and a grade of high school teachers. Bridgewater also offers a three years' course, a cross between the other two, while provision is also made for

[12] N.E.A. *Proceedings*, 1876, p. 51.

[13] Nicholas Murray Butler, *Education in the United States* (New York: American Book, 1910), pp. 370, 377.

> advanced instruction for college graduates and other approved candidates in all the schools. Diplomas are given to graduates from all courses.[14]

The normal schools, in spite of their growth, still fell "very far short of supplying the common schools with a sufficient number of professionally trained teachers." Massachusetts led the rest of the nation in trained teachers, but only 38.5 percent of the public-school teachers in 1897–1898 had received normal instruction and only 33.5 percent were normal graduates. According to one estimate in the above source, only 15 percent of the teachers in 1891–1892 had "passed through a normal school."

To supplement the work of the normal schools, some cities established training schools for teachers. Requiring high school graduation for admission, these offered a one- to two-year course in the principles of education and methods of instruction. In 1895 the New York legislature authorized cities to maintain training schools, for not less than thirty-eight weeks a year; such schools received state funds and followed a course outlined by the state superintendent of public instruction. But in 1898 these schools enrolled fewer than two thousand students.

Another important source of teachers for the common schools were the high-school and academy normal courses. At the turn of the century there were over 16,000 pupils in the high-school and academy normal training classes.[15]

All these sources combined produced considerably fewer than half the 50,000 trained persons needed to replace teachers leaving the schools and provide the new personnel called for by the constantly expanding schools. The critical shortage helped induce the universities to train teachers, but they too graduated only a small proportion of the needed number. Consequently, at the turn of the century most of the beginning teachers in the nation's schools started their duties with no more schooling than could be acquired in the same common schools in which they taught.

Pedagogy in the Universities

Until the Civil War the traditionalists managed to keep the higher academic cloisters virtually untainted by courses in education. One crack in the dike was Antioch College, where Horace Mann introduced an elective course in the theory and practice of teaching in 1853. At the

[14] *Ibid.*, p. 371.
[15] *Ibid.*, pp. 372–382.

University of Iowa there was a normal department from 1856 to 1873, when it was incorporated into the university as a chair of "didactics." In 1879 the University of Michigan established a chair of the science and art of teaching. President Angell had recommended the course to prepare graduates for "the higher positions in the public school service." By 1899 Michigan offered ten courses in education: the art of teaching, the science of teaching, school supervision, comparative study of educational systems, child study, sociological aspects of education, and four courses in various phases of the history of education. In addition, other departments of the university offered special courses for teachers, in methods as well as subject matter.

At first most universities appointed only one professor of pedagogy or didactics. The next step was to broaden this single professorship into a college of education. In his annual reports of 1881 and 1882, President F. A. P. Barnard of Columbia proposed the creation of a department of history, theory and practice of education. When the idea was rejected by the trustees, he assigned Nicholas Murray Butler, a young assistant in psychology and philosophy, to give a series of four Saturday morning lectures. Over 2,000 teachers applied for these lectures, and over 200 requested copies of a supplementary bibliography. On this show of interest, Butler suggested that a senior elective on "pedagogics" be instituted, but the trustees voted against it on the grounds that it would introduce coeducation to Columbia. Butler then (1889) organized the New York College for the Training of Teachers, while still holding his position on the faculty of Columbia. In 1892 the trustees accepted the Teachers College as an affiliate of Columbia, and in 1898 the college became an integral part of the university.[16]

Other universities introduced courses in pedagogy and colleges of education, and by 1897 more than half of the 432 colleges and universities reported by the United States Bureau of Education were giving courses for the special training of teachers.[17]

The colleges of education and pedagogical professors were often treated with the same contempt and derision directed toward the normal schools. The academicians considered the preparation of public-school teachers beneath their dignity. When asked to give some assistance in the solution of the problem of staffing the schools, they merely scoffed, but then "viewed with alarm" when public school graduates came to college poorly prepared for success in the academic disciplines.

[16] *Ibid.*, p. 396. See also Nicholas Murray Butler, *Across the Busy Years* (New York: Scribner's, 1935), pp. 176–177.

[17] Knight, "The Story of Teacher Training," *High School Journal*, 10 (Dec., 1927): 240.

In-Service Training

Since many teachers began teaching with little or no preparation, leaders in education tried several ways to improve the quality of instruction. One of the most common was the teacher institutes, which had been popularized by Henry Barnard. Sponsoring agencies included states, counties, and districts. Some institutes were held for only a day or two; others extended for several weeks in the summer. Some had regular classes, with textbooks and recitations; others were merely a series of lectures. The range of subjects was very broad, including review of the subjects of the common schools, study of professional subjects, and general cultural activities. In 1867 the Pennsylvania legislature enacted a law requiring teachers to attend their respective institutes, and other states soon had similar laws. In 1886–1887 the United States Commissioner of Education reported 2,003 institutes enrolling 138,986 teachers, about half the total number of teachers in the nation.[18]

Another important agency for in-service training was the summer schools sponsored by the colleges and universities. The first summer session for teachers was a course in instruction in natural history held by Harvard scientist Louis Agassiz at Buzzards Bay, Massachusetts, in 1872. The University of North Carolina held summer schools for eight years beginning in 1877 and revived them in 1894. The University of Wisconsin began summer schools in 1887 under the auspices of the teacher associations of the state.[19]

The Chautauqua movement, started in 1874 as a summer program of adult enlightenment and entertainment, provided not only cultural and ethical programs but occasionally professional education for teachers. The success of the Chautauqua movement inspired the formation of teachers' reading circles in Ohio, sponsored by the State Teacher Association. Started in 1882, the Ohio teachers' reading circle had more than 2,000 members within two years. Each year certain books were recommended for "professional and literary reading," and teachers were awarded certificates if they passed examinations on the books. Teachers who earned certificates in four successive years were granted a diploma. In the late years of the century, the Indiana reading circle had a membership of about 15,000, of whom 12,000 were in service and 3,000 were preparing to teach. The list of books read by the Indiana circles between 1884 and 1899 included Parker's *Talks on Teaching*, Green's *History of the English People*, Carlyle's *Heroes and Hero Worship*, Compayre's *History of Education* and *Lecture on Teaching*, Page's *Theory and Prac-*

[18] Butler, *Education*, pp. 384–385.
[19] Knight, "Teacher Training," pp. 242–243.

tice of Teaching, Holme's *Autocrat of the Breakfast Table,* DeGarmo's *Essentials of Method, Select Letters and Essays of Ruskin,* McMurry's *General Method,* Shakespeare, and Plato's *Republic.* Each year two or three books were listed, at least one dealing with professional matters and one a general cultural book.[20] Reading circles were particularly popular in the Midwest where cultural opportunities were limited. Though better than nothing, they were a poor substitute for thorough professional training.

In the twentieth century the trend toward professional preparation was to become very much accelerated. Colleges of education became important units of universities, and normal schools gradually raised their entrance requirements and lengthened their course until they became four-year teachers colleges.

Teacher Certification

Closely related to the training of teachers is teacher certification. From early colonial days, teachers generally had to secure a certificate proclaiming their proficiency and their religious orthodoxy. Even after the separation of church and state, certification of teachers was often the responsibility of the local clergyman. As schools came more and more under the control of government, the trend in examination and certification was toward the district or county board. With many of these board members poorly schooled, even illiterate, the teacher examination was often a farce, a requirement to be evaded when the trustees wished to hire a particular candidate or to be invoked when a superior candidate challenged a privileged friend or relative of a board member. Educational leaders sought a way by which the state could establish a uniform method of examining and licensing teachers. In California, John Swett, who complained that the New England examinations he had suffered were "as great an absurdity as it would be for a green-grocer to examine JOHN STUART MILL in Political Economy," resented the annual examinations he had to undergo during his eight years as a teacher on the West Coast. On his election as State Superintendent of Public Instruction he "abolished the New-England annual-examination farce" in California and "placed the examination of teachers throughout the state exclusively in the hands of experienced teachers." Teachers who passed the examination received life diplomas. A normal school diploma from any state normal school in the United States, a life diploma from any state, or a certificate granted by any state was recognized as valid in California.

[20] Butler, *Education,* pp. 388–391.

No other state gave such recognition to the diplomas of normal schools. Swett recommended to the N.E.A. in 1872 that other states follow California's lead in granting certification on the basis of normal school graduation, in recognizing the certification of other states, and in having the state board of examiners made up of professional teachers.

> These boards . . . ought to be made up exclusively of practical teachers, for the same reason that only lawyers can legally examine law students applying for admission to the bar, that only physicians examine medical students, and that only clergymen pass on the fitness of theological students to enter the clergy.[21]

In spite of the success in California of Swett's reforms, other states were very slow to adopt his recommendations. Indeed, only now are a few states beginning to delegate to the teacher-training institutions the responsibility of certifying teachers by recommendation to the state's department of education; reciprocity of certificates among states is still limited; and as yet no state has granted teachers the authority to examine and certify teachers. As a matter of fact, most state certification regulations prohibit teachers from serving on certification boards. Denial of the professional privilege and responsibility of defining and enforcing standards of admission to the vocation is one serious barrier to the further professionalization of teaching.

Professional Organizations

One characteristic of those vocations called professions is that they have associations which attempt to set minimum standards of training, admission, and performance for practitioners; to secure working conditions that will facilitate the success of the practitioners; and to raise the level of performance through encouraging research and the dissemination of professional information. Until the Civil War, education associations were made up largely of non-educators, laymen interested in educational reform. Organizations for teachers, such as the Western Literary Institute and College of Professional Teachers, usually lasted only a few years. But in the period following the Civil War, the number of learned associations and professional organizations grew rapidly. Some of these associations represented special interests, and although they were certainly not limited to professors or teachers, they strove to encourage

[21] N.E.A. *Proceedings*, 1872, pp. 72, 78–79.

the growth and spread of knowledge in their discipline. The American Chemical Society (organized in 1876), Modern Language Association (1883), American Historical Association (1884), and American Mathematical Society (1888) are examples of this kind of organization.

By 1857 there were at least twenty-three educational associations in the United States, with memberships made up of teachers, administrators, editors, and the general public. In that year a meeting was called in Philadelphia by the presidents of ten of the state educational associations, and the National Teachers' Association (N.T.A.) was organized. Its name was misleading, for it was not limited to teachers; indeed, teachers probably made up a minority of its membership. In 1870 the N.T.A. was combined with the American Normal School Association (which had been organized in 1858 and had met annually with the N.T.A. after 1866) and the National Association of School Superintendents (which had been organized at the N.T.A. meeting in 1865 and had met annually with the N.T.A.). The new organization was named the National Educational Association. Originally the N.E.A. was made up of four departments: School Superintendence, Normal Schools, Elementary Schools, and Higher Education. Other departments were added as new interests developed: Industrial Education (1875; changed to Manual Training in 1899); Art Education (1883); Kindergarten Instruction and Music Education (1892); Child-Study (1894); Physical Education, Natural Science Instruction, and School Administration (all in 1895); Library (1896); Education of the Deaf, Blind, and Feebleminded (1897; changed to Special Education in 1902); Indian Education (1899); and Technical Education (1905). Each of these departments held annual meetings in conjunction with the general meetings.

The membership of the N.E.A. fluctuated greatly and was made up largely of persons from the locality surrounding the convention city, who paid dues in order to be permitted to hear the speeches and often failed to continue membership in subsequent years. The average membership between 1884 and 1894 was only 3,986; the high point was the 9,115 who registered and paid dues at the 1887 Chicago meetings, and one of the low points was in the same city six years later, when only 1,465 persons registered. However, the Association was able to employ a full-time, salaried, permanent secretary in 1898, an office which has become the administrative branch of the N.E.A.

One important part of the N.E.A. was the National Council of Education, which was added through a constitutional amendment in 1880 and was discontinued in 1947. This Council, limited to sixty members, met just before the annual convention of the N.E.A. and gave direction to the Association. Because of the fluctuating and generally disinterested membership of the Association, the Council determined what the various departments would discuss at the conventions and to a great extent defined what the "correct thinking on educational questions" should be. It was the Council which stipulated the appointment of the Committee of Ten. The basic conservatism of the Council colored the work of the N.E.A. for years. While they are undoubtedly due much credit for building the Association, they probably also deserve considerable blame for the failure of the N.E.A. to become a truly professional organization and remaining to our own day little more than a polite debating society, unwilling to grapple seriously with major professional problems and exert the kinds of influence upon its membership and the general public that the American Medical Association or the American Bar Association have exerted to facilitate improved standards in their professions.

Women Teachers

One definite handicap to the professionalization of teaching has been the great number of temporary workers in the field. Many men have taken up teaching as a means of financing their further education or as a stop-gap until a better job comes along. The vast number of elementary-school teachers have been young women who have taught only a year or two before marriage. Those who make a life-time of teaching often have been the social misfits who could succeed at nothing else, timid, unwilling to speak out for themselves or their pupils, avoiding controversy at any cost. No vocation can become professional when such a bulk of its membership is either uninterested or pusillanimous.

By the turn of the century, many of the more courageous leaders in education were aware of the problem and spoke with great concern of the "woman peril" in the schools. In 1896–1897 there were 131,386 male teachers and 271,947 female teachers in the American public schools.[22] In some communities women teachers almost monopolized the educational field.

> In Minneapolis, Minn. . . . all the 605 teachers are women, excepting 4 principalships of high schools, 6 special teachers and 6 instructors of manual training. Substantially the same thing is true of several other cities, most of them being located in the West.[23]

[22] *U.S. Commissioner of Education Report for 1896–97*, p. LXV.
[23] *U.S. Commissioner of Education Report for 1891–92, Part II*, p. 669.

In addition to women as teachers and principals, in 1899–1900 there were two women state superintendents (Colorado and Idaho), twelve city superintendents, and 284 county superintendents.

The preponderance of women teachers was attributed to "the conviction that women are naturally better fitted than men to be teachers of young children, and also by the lower price at which women may be employed." As school teaching came more and more "to be considered a woman's business," it offered "less attraction to young men than formerly," and the "low salaries also operate to repel them." As a consequence, fewer young men were teaching in the "subordinate positions" which had been "the training schools for principals." Thus even the administrative positions fell to women by default.

The "increasing femininity of the schools" threatened "serious results." Of particular danger was the effect on boys of too much feminine influence in the schools, especially in the secondary schools.

> The already noticeable decrease in the proportion of boys in the higher grades is ascribed by many to this cause, and with some show of plausibility. . . .
>
> It is necessary that the more sturdy character of men should be allowed to have an influence upon our growing generation. . . .
>
> A man . . . will inspire the children with more respect, after they have advanced to a certain age, than a woman, and they therefore will be more ready to listen to the teachings of the man and pursue their studies more diligently than if they are in the hands of a woman.[24]

The opinions about the dangers of the psychological influence of women teachers have never been adequately substantiated, but a greater danger to the hope of improving the standards of teachers and teaching was the brief tenure of most of the teachers, male as well as female. Despite their hard work in the classroom and even their devotion to the children in their own school, the transient young "schoolmar'ms" who have made up the body of the teaching corps are nevertheless one of the most serious barriers to the professionalization of teaching.

QUESTIONS FOR DISCUSSION

1. Perhaps a great deal of the conflict between academic professors in colleges of arts and sciences and education professors over the preparation of teachers can be traced to the reluctance of academicians of the nineteenth century to undertake the preparation of teachers. What historical

[24] *U.S. Commissioner of Education Report for 1891–92, Part II*, pp. 669–671.

background for this problem can you find in the period from 1870 to 1900?
2. Select one professional education organization and trace its history, noting particularly the changes in its program and membership as the social context has changed.
3. What are some of the historical antecedents of the predominance of women in present-day schools? Do you view this predominance with the same concern as did some of the educators of the 1890's? What problems are created in the professionalization of teaching with such a large body of female teachers who often teach for only a few years?
4. Compare the progress in professionalization of physicians with that of teachers in the past hundred years. Why has medicine advanced more rapidly than education? What have been some of the problems delaying the professionalization of teaching? What are some of the historical barriers to making teaching more professional in character? What hopes do you see for education? What recent trends substantiate your hopes and fears?

SUGGESTED READINGS

Secondary Sources

Brauner, Charles J. *American Educational Theory*. Englewood Cliffs: Prentice-Hall, 1964. Chapters 3 and 4.

Curti, Merle. *The Social Ideas of American Educators*. New York: Scribner's, 1935. Chapters IV, VI–XIII.

Drake, William. *The American School in Transition*. Englewood Cliffs: Prentice-Hall, 1955. Chapter XI.

Good, Harry G. *A History of American Education*. New York: Macmillan, 1962. Chapter XI.

Meyer, Adolphe E. *An Educational History of the American People*. New York: McGraw-Hill, 1957. Chapter XII.

Moulton, Gerald L. "The American Herbartian: A Portrait from His Yearbooks," *History of Education Quarterly*, 3 (Sept. and Dec. 1963): 134–143, 187–197.

Parker, Samuel Chester. *A Textbook in the History of Modern Elementary Education*. Boston: Ginn, 1912. Chapters XIII–XVIII.

Primary Sources

Cubberley, Ellwood P. *Readings in Public Education in the United States*. Boston: Houghton Mifflin, 1934. Readings 224–228, 243–252, 315, 323–324.

Gross, Carl H., and Chandler, Charles C. *The History of American Education Through Readings*. Boston: Heath, 1964. Pp. 292–299.

Knight, Edgar W., and Hall, Clifton L. *Readings in American Educational History*. New York: Appleton-Century-Crofts, 1951. Pp. 423–436, 736–739.

11

Education in an Industrial Plutocracy

One of the revolutionary dreams of the Age of the Common Man was of a universal system of education, free to all who wished to attend and with enough schools so that every child could attend. In the North and East that dream was near reality before the Civil War; in the South and West it was still largely an ideal. An even more revolutionary dream was secondary and higher education free to all and suited to the needs of the common man, but high schools and technical colleges were still few in number in 1860. Those dreams were to move closer to realization during the Gilded Age, perhaps because the schools and colleges could be used to suit the purposes of the new class which dominated American society, the industrial and financial plutocracy.

Perhaps never before in history have so many men become so fabulously wealthy in so short a time as between the Civil War and 1900. Some of these fortunes were begun in war profiteering; others developed during the Gilded Age itself. In virtually every case, the sudden rise to wealth was without any ethical principles except that the acquisition of wealth was a positive good in itself, a material proof of the survival of the fittest. Fraud, bribery, corruption of public officials, deceit, physical violence, embezzlement of public funds—all these and many other forms of crime accompanied the acquisition of wealth. Cornelius Vanderbilt boasted that he cared nothing for the law as long as he had the power. Railroad pioneer Collis P. Huntington openly admitted that he bought whole Congresses for half a million dollars a session, which was cheaper than trying to buy elections. The railroads, which were being built with the aid of federal land grants and sometimes with government credit, commonly issued stock valued at many times the worth of the physical assets of the line. The Credit Mobilier scandal, which became public in 1873, disclosed that Congressional leaders and members of Grant's administration were involved in the corruption, but the Union Pacific and its triply inflated stock were undamaged, even though investigation detailed by whom and how the fraud was carried out.

The new rich were acquiring wealth much faster than they could spend it, even with the most blatant conspicuous consumption. They built huge mansions, maintained palatial yachts, gave lavish parties, and engaged in pretentious philanthropy. Preachers in the conservative, fashionable churches sermonized on the stewardship of wealth, how God intended the fittest to administer the worldly goods for the welfare of everyone, the justification of philanthropy and the "trickle-down" theory of economics.

The working class, bitter at such things as the Belmont horses stabled in better quarters than those the workers lived in, attempted to organize in protest, but unions and strikes were countered with federal troops, police, and armies of Pinkerton detectives. Unlettered aliens were imported as strikebreakers. Labor leaders were imprisoned, often on trumped up charges or rigged trials. Social reform was dead in the churches, and in missions set up in the slums, subsidized exhorters told the socially undesirable masses to be content with their station in life. It was no longer an age of the common man.

Class Distinction in Education

Although there were great advances in public education between 1865 and 1900, there was still the lasting stigma of charity attached to public schools, and the "better" families did not send their children to the public schools with the children of the poor. Families with social standing sent their children to the polite private schools, particularly in the older cities of the East, where the distinctions were carried down into the middle classes as well as among the very wealthy. In his autobiography Henry Seidel Canby speaks of the strong class feelings, even as late as the 1890's, in Wilmington, Delaware, about attendance at public schools—feelings subtly communicated to the children.

> No parent among us ever spoke of classes in society to her children—she merely let them be felt. . . . Yet we all knew children who belonged to Us had standards of conduct . . . far more rigorous than the creed of the hated "micks." . . .
>
> A "mick" was a tough boy from the slums or near slums. He went to public school, which, in our town, none of Us . . . ever did, except as a result of a disaster.[1]

[1] Henry Seidel Canby, *The Age of Confidence, Life in the Nineties* (New York: Farrar & Rinehart), pp. 40–41. Copyright 1934, 1962.

There was strong reactionary sentiment that advocated rolling back the progress of the free school and returning to a system which would have placed all schools on a tuition basis. One of the most articulate proposals from this point of view was made in 1893 by a University of California professor, G. H. Howison, who argued that the "prevalent theory of public education" was "downright communism." Tax support for schools "lay upon the diligent and capable not only their own burdens, but those of the incapable and shiftless besides." No agency of government, he wrote, can

> take measures that would compel the parents to submit to one mingled contagion, children of every grade of morality and immorality, coarseness and refinement, uncleanliness and cleanliness, high social development and low.
>
> By the former reasoning it seems to follow that schools universally and entirely free are unsound, or at any rate dangerous schools.[2]

Education for Productivity and Morality

But reactionaries such as Howison were not in the majority, even among the wealthy upper classes. The demands of business and industry called for more education, not less. Leaders among educators were responsive to these demands, urging that the schools support the new industrial society not only through teaching the practical subjects needed for success in commerce and industry but also through inducting the pupils with social attitudes of patriotism, order, thrift, respect for property, and diligence. The United States Commissioner of Education John Eaton urged teachers to inculcate the attitudes in the masses which would "avert" such socially undesirable issues as "conflict between the producing and capitalist classes."

> It is clear that the worth of a common school education to the common laboring man is universally conceded, with the single exception of those speaking of colored laborers; that his value to the community at large is positively increased and his power as a producer, of adding to the common stock of wealth, is materially enhanced by the education given him as a child in the common school. . . . That this increase of value arises, 1st from the fact of his being more readily instructed in the duties of his work; 2d, that he needs less supervision; 3d, that he does his work to better advan-

[2] "Real Ground for State Control of Schools," *Educational Review*, 5 (May 1893): 425–433.

> tage and therefore produces more in a given time; 4th, that he is less liable to join in unreasonable and unseasonable strikes; 5th, is more industrious; 6th, less dissipated; and, lastly, is less liable to become an expense to the commonwealth through poverty or crime.[3]

He concluded that appropriate education for "all citizens of the state" would result in the "successful solution of every question arising between capital and labor," for it would demonstrate that "there is no necessary antagonism between these fellow workers."

At a time when strikes and other demonstrations by the workingmen were equated with Marxism, leaders in education claimed that the public schools were not responsible for the strikes and riots; rather, "had it not been for the public schools, the results of the strike would have been still more disastrous." But the schools had not gone far enough, in the view of National Education Association president M. A. Newell, who asked, "Would such an outbreak have been possible if the workingmen engaged in it had been men accustomed and trained to think as well as to toil?" The public schools must do more to help the youth "to become intelligent, moral and industrious citizens." Part of the problem was that many of the children who needed the schooling most, those of the lowest classes, were not "welcomed" at the public schools, and he urged the passage of compulsory attendance laws to bring "the very classes that need it most" into the public schools.[4]

The school superintendents and college professors who dominated the N.E.A. demonstrated that they were in favor of obedience to duly constituted law and respect for property rights when their 1894 convention unanimously adopted a resolution commending President Cleveland's use of federal troops in suppressing the Pullman strike and accepting for the schools "the duty of preparing the rising generation for intelligent and patriotic citizenship, by inculcating the principles of public and private morality."[5]

History is a subject which has often been used to teach values of patriotism. In Prussia an imperial order of 1799 directed that the study of history in the schools should "have no other purpose than to awaken patriotic love and affection, pride in the deeds of our forefathers, and the desire to emulate them."[6] Almost exactly a century later an American

[3] *Report of the U.S. Commissioner of Education for 1870*, pp. 51–53.

[4] M. A. Newell, "The President's Address," N.E.A. *Addresses and Journal of Proceedings*, 1877, pp. 6, 9.

[5] N.E.A. *Proceedings*, 1894, pp. 34–35.

[6] Thomas Alexander, *The Prussian Elementary Schools* (New York: Macmillan, 1918), pp. 32–33.

educator proposed virtually the same role for history in a speech at the 1898 meeting of the National Herbart Society.

> We are a people animated by the highest and noblest ideals of humanity, of the rights of man, and no history of our country is rightly taught which does not set this forth. Above all, it should be so taught as to destroy that baneful belief that we have degenerated from our forefathers. There is no land where the people are so prosperous, so happy, so intelligent, so bent on doing what is just and right as the people of the United States.[7]

There were many Americans, including those who most "needed" these lessons, who were not so convinced of the justice of American society.

Education for Utility

One of the most important developments in the curriculum of all levels of American education during the Gilded Age was the emphasis on subjects that were practically useful. This trend was supported both by the interests of business and the theories of the evolutionists.

The new industrial forces were stimulated by discoveries in science and, even more, by the attitude of science. Applied chemistry developed new products and improved old ones; it contributed to agriculture through soil analysis, fertilizers, and animal nutrition. Geologists helped in the search for mineral resources. Chemical analyses of newly found petroleum led to its commercial development. The biological sciences were applied to improving plant and animal varieties and combating insects and diseases which attacked farm and grove products. "Practical" men and tinkerers found ways of applying the discoveries of science in many ways to benefit large-scale industry and agriculture. The invention of the self-binding reaper and the chilled steel plow made possible the huge wheat farms of the West, while barbed wire enclosed the prairie, halting the long cattle drives from the Southwest to Kansas. New technical schools and agricultural colleges sprang up to prepare the many scientists, engineers, and technicians needed by industry and agriculture.

New Scientific Emphasis

Science was becoming the religion of the age. Materialism was justified and rationalized by the brutal law of the jungle, the survival of the

[7] John Bach McMaster, "The Social Function of United States History," *The Fourth Yearbook of the National Herbart Society* (1898), p. 30.

fittest. Wealth and its acquisition were positive goods; poverty was immoral and the fault of the individual. Horatio Alger, Jr., a Unitarian clergyman, sang the "rags-to-riches" song in 119 "inspiring" books for boys, helping build the legend that even the poorest boy, if he works hard, is polite to the right people, and has the other humble virtues, can become wealthy and a great philanthropist. Henry Ward Beecher, the leading preacher of the age, pointed out that "where there is the most religion, there is the most worldly possessions."

The intellectual religion and philosophical justifications of the Gilded Age were founded on a scientific theory diametrically opposed to the evangelistic religions of the preceding era. The publication of Charles Darwin's *Origin of Species* in 1859 was important not because it was a sudden innovation in scientific thought but because intellectuals were ready to accept a new scientific view of the universe and of life itself. In 1809 Jean Baptiste Lamarck (1744–1829) had published his *Philosophie Zoologique,* advancing evolutionary ideas about the change in species and the appearance of new forms. Darwin's grandfather, Erasmus Darwin, had anticipated some of Lamarck's theories, though he probably had little direct influence on his grandson. Sir Charles Lyell (1797–1875) cast grave doubts on the generally accepted date of Creation as 4004 B.C. in his *Principles of Geology* (1830–1833) in which he suggested a much greater age of the earth. Herbert Spencer and Thomas Huxley, who were to become most famous as popularizers of "Darwinism," actually ante-dated Darwin's publication in their own statements of evolutionary theory, and indeed it was Spencer who must be credited with the principle of the "survival of the fittest."

The American enthusiasm for Darwinism began soon after the close of the Civil War. John Fiske (1842–1901) was threatened with expulsion from Harvard for publishing two articles on evolution in the *North American Review,* but within six years after his graduation he was lecturing on evolution at Harvard. These lectures, printed in the *New York World,* led to bitter denunciation of Harvard by religious leaders and newspapers but were supported by the college's new scientist-president, Charles W. Eliot. Later the articles were incorporated in Fiske's *Outlines of Cosmic Philosophy* (1874). Edward L. Youmans, publisher of *Popular Science Monthly,* who had arranged for the publication of Fiske's lectures in the *World* and had collected seven thousand dollars in 1865 to enable Spencer to publish his *Synthetic Philosophy,* gave the writings of Spencer wide circulation in his magazine. Thomas Huxley visited the United States on a speaking tour in 1876, and the *New York Tribune* issued an extra number containing all his

American addresses, taking the evolutionary theories to an estimated hundred thousand readers.

It was from these popularizers, rather than from Darwin himself, that Americans received the scientific ideas that threatened evangelistic religion and the essentially religious orthodoxy of American schools and colleges. Their efforts led to the inclusion of more scientific courses in schools and colleges, as well as new emphases in the disciplines of history and the newly emerging social "sciences."

"What Knowledge Is of Most Worth?"

Herbert Spencer provided the philosophical argument for the inclusion of scientific and practical subjects in the curriculum in his lengthy essay, "What Knowledge Is Of Most Worth?" In answering the question, Spencer classified human activities into five categories: (1) those which minister directly to self-preservation; (2) those which indirectly minister to self-preservation by securing the necessities of life; (3) those concerned with the rearing and discipline of offspring; (4) those involved in the maintenance of proper social and political relations; and (5) those used for leisure. The ideal of education, said Spencer, is to achieve a balance among these divisions, but the attention should be "greatest where the value is greatest, less where the value is less, least where the value is least."[8]

Activities were listed in order from what he considered most valuable to least valuable. Knowledge which leads directly to self-preservation "preventing . . . loss of health, is of primary importance." Therefore, he considered physiology "an all-essential part of a rational education." Science and mathematics, in addition to reading, writing and arithmetic, should be studied as knowledge which "aids indirect self-preservation by facilitating the gaining of a livelihood." "Industrial success" demands knowledge of "the Science of Society." "Without knowing it, men who daily look at the state of the money-market . . . are students of social science." Passing to the next level of activity, Spencer said, "Some acquaintance with the first principles of physiology and the elementary truths of psychology is indispensable for the right bringing up of children." Next come the functions of the citizen, for which Spencer prescribed the study of "Descriptive Sociology" and "Comparative Sociology," rather than the traditional history, which was made up merely of the "biographies of monarchs" and gave no "clue to the right prin-

[8] *Education: Intellectual, Moral, and Physical* (New York: Appleton, 1860), pp. 32–70.

ciples of political action." The bulk of what then made up secondary and higher education Spencer relegated to the place of least importance.

> Accomplishments, the fine arts, *belles lettres,* and all those things which, as we say, constitute, the efflorescence of civilization, should be wholly subordinate to that knowledge and discipline in which civilization rests. *As they occupy the leisure part of life, so should they occupy the leisure part of education.*[9]

Spencer's essay was widely read and was used as major ammunition in the battle with the classicists over the college and secondary curriculum.

When teachers and school administrators who agreed with the Spencerian position found themselves in conflict with academicians who believed that if a subject "has practical value it is besmirched" and was not appropriate for schools, they submitted a questionnaire to businessmen for opinions about what the curriculum should include.

> It is comforting to feel that business men may be deferred to in matters of educational policy without danger. . . . Latin was thought to be of little practical value and Greek none at all. German and French were recognized as of slight value. . . . Mathematics was placed high by all who answered these questions. Chemistry and biology were thought to be of special value only in definite lines of activity. That business-men comprehend the more liberal aspects of education, is shown by the answers to the inquiry concerning the values of histories and language. In both these cases these were placed high. . . . Those who answered the requests favored political economy in the high school and opposed psychology, except that there was some favor shown to ethics. Stenography, type-writing, and book-keeping were generally recommended.[10]

Apparently the "language" considered important was English, since the foreign and "dead" languages were rated very low.

The supporters of "commercial education" preached that "the only hope of success is in having men of affairs and educators come to a better agreement as to what education is, and how subjects having a practical value can be utilized in obtaining it."[11] Actually, by 1899 educators were well along the road to accepting the dictates of the "men of affairs."

[9] *Ibid.,* pp. 74–75.

[10] Chessman Herrick, *Commercial Education, Supplement to the Fifth Yearbook of the National Herbart Society for 1899,* pp. 199, 206.

[11] *Ibid.,* p. 206.

Higher Education

The influence of "men of affairs" on education in the Gilded Age was seen most dramatically in the institutions of higher learning. The land grant colleges and new technical schools led the older institutions to curricular expansion, and greater concern with expanded curriculum led to the elective system and graduate work. Professional schools developed, and colleges became universities. Even the social life on campus reflected the interests of the new upper classes of society. Higher education was transformed from little colleges limited largely to literary and classical subjects of the age-old liberal arts to complex universities closely related to the market place and factory.

Land Grant Colleges

The Morrill Act of 1862, which provided federal lands for the support of colleges teaching agriculture and mechanical arts, helped stimulate the trend toward vocational and scientific subjects in colleges and universities. By 1900, sixty-five institutions had been established under the Morrill Acts. Twenty-seven of these were separate colleges of agriculture and mechanic arts, and nineteen were universities with departments of agriculture and engineering. Assisted primarily by the 1890 cash grants of the second Morrill Act, eight Southern states established separate institutions for Negro students, although instruction in them was limited largely to secondary work and training in industrial and agricultural skills.[12]

Although sixty-one of the sixty-five institutions offered regular courses in agriculture, some technical schools also benefited from the Morrill Act grants. For example, the Massachusetts Institute of Technology, which was chartered in 1861 but did not begin instruction until 1865, received a third of Massachusett's share of the funds accruing from the land grants. Purdue University was originally organized under the Morrill Act grants as the Indiana Institute of Technology, and the University of Illinois, another Morrill Act land grant college, was first named Illinois Industrial University. Most of the great state universities of the twentieth century either were founded as land-grant colleges or used the land grants to develop from insignificant schools to major institutions of higher learning.

[12] Butler, *Education*, pp. 619–620.

Philanthropy and Private Technical Schools

Philanthropy was a primary virtue among the wealthy of the Gilded Age, and one form of giving that combined business with public virtue was the endowment of schools to provide the engineers and technicians for the expanding industrial society. In 1865 Worcester Polytechnic Institute was incorporated and received a grant of $100,000 from a Massachusetts merchant named John Boynton and another from a steel and wire factory which paid for the erection and equipping of workshops for the training of mechanical engineers. Lehigh University was incorporated in 1866 with a donation of $500,000 and 115 acres of land from Asa Packer, a Pennsylvania coal mine and railroad owner; later Packer bequeathed nearly $2,000,000 to the college, which stressed mining and engineering. The Stevens Institute of Technology opened in Hoboken, New Jersey, in 1871, having benefited from $650,000 plus a parcel of land in Hoboken, all granted by the Stevens family of railroad and shipbuilding engineers. Between 1892 and 1900 Philip D. Armour gave over $2.5 million to the Armour Institute of Technology in Chicago. Gifts to already-existing institutions resulted in the Towne Scientific School at the University of Pennsylvania and the John C. Green School of Science at Princeton.[13]

The new schools, having none of the academic traditions of the liberal arts institutions, did not hesitate to offer the kinds of courses that would prepare young men to enter the industrial world. Relatively independent financially, they blazed the trail toward practicality and applied science in higher education.

Business Control of Other Higher Education

Two ways of influencing the policies of an institution are to control its sources of income and to capture its system of government. Before 1900 the business community had begun to influence the policies of higher education in both ways.

In addition to having much political "pull" with the legislators who appropriated money to the state universities, the tycoons of the Gilded Age could impress their interests on the colleges by granting or withholding substantial gifts. Philanthropy affected some of the liberal arts colleges and universities as well as the strictly technical schools. Ezra Cornell gave $500,000 to the institution which now bears his name. Cornelius Vanderbilt revitalized a failing Methodist institution with a

[13] *Ibid.*, pp. 562–568, 572, 581.

million dollars, and it was gratefully re-named for him. Johns Hopkins left $3,500,000 to start America's first graduate school. Railroad magnate Leland Stanford in 1885 began a memorial for his deceased son with $20,000,000, and followed with other gifts. John D. Rockefeller revived the defunct University of Chicago in 1890 with a gift of $600,000; later gifts raised the total to over $30,000,000. Not all these gifts were accepted without opposition. When Rockefeller offered Wellesley $100,000, for instance, a number of professors demanded an investigation of Rockefeller's business ethics. But the gift was accepted without any such embarrassing investigation. Money "talked," and struggling college presidents had ears.

Coinciding with these lavish gifts was a trend toward the domination of college boards of trustees by businessmen. Up to the time of the Civil War, most of the colleges were denominational institutions under the control of ministers, and college presidents were chosen almost exclusively from the ranks of the clergy. By the twentieth century, the situation was quite changed. Thorstein Veblen, commenting in 1918 on the control of higher education, noted that there had been "a widespreading substitution of laymen in the place of clergymen on the governing boards."

> This secularization is entirely consonant with the prevailing drift of sentiment in the community at large. . . . The substitution is a substitution of businessmen and politicians; which amounts to saying that it is a substitution of businessmen. So that the discretionary control in matters of university policy now rests finally in the hands of business.[14]

A study by Earl J. McGrath in 1930 confirmed Veblen's observations.

> Even as early as 1910 more than four-fifths of the trustees in these state universities were selected from the fields of business, banking and law. . . .
>
> The control of higher education in America, both public and private, has been placed in the hands of a small group of the population, namely financiers and business men.[15]

In addition to the changes in the boards of trustees, there was a marked change in the background of the college presidents. After the

[14] *The Higher Learning in America* (New York: Sagamore Press, 1957), pp 46–47.

[15] "The Control of Higher Education in America," *The Educational Record*, 13: 266.

Civil War, the presidents were generally selected from some field of scholarship other than theology. Charles W. Eliot, for example, was a mathematics and chemistry professor before his administration as president of Harvard from 1869 to 1909. Not a few college presidents were chosen from among the political, business, and military leaders of the nation. The practical world did not trust the college presidency to men whose greatest concern was the "heavenly world."

Curriculum Expansion and the Elective System

With the leadership of the land-grant colleges and the technical institutes and the pressure of business interests, colleges began to expand their curricular offerings, though often with great reluctance and against faculty resistance. As new subjects were added, old ones lost their privileged positions. It was soon impossible for any student to study all the subjects offered, and it was necessary to permit students some choice.

As early as 1825 Harvard, prodded by George Ticknor, experimented with an elective system, but between 1846 and 1860, it was almost dropped, getting down to where electives were limited to one subject for three hours for juniors and seniors. Between 1860 and 1869 the number of electives at Harvard was increased, but the real development of the elective system came under the presidency of Charles W. Eliot. In 1872 all course requirements for seniors were abolished; in 1879 for juniors; and in 1884 for sophomores. In 1885 requirements for freshmen were reduced, and after 1894 the only required courses for Harvard students were English composition, French or German, and some lectures in chemistry and physics. The old liberal arts and the classical languages had been ousted from their secure center of the Harvard curriculum and had to compete with other subjects for students.

Eliot justified the Harvard curriculum on the grounds that the "general growth of knowledge and the rise of new literatures, arts, and sciences . . . have made it necessary to define anew liberal education." In a speech at Johns Hopkins University in 1884 he traced the history of the liberal arts curriculum, pointing out how the classical seven liberal arts of rhetoric, grammar, logic, arithmetic, geometry, astronomy, and music had been replaced by scholastic theology in the Middle Ages and how that in turn gave way to Latin and Greek in the Renaissance. Those studies had been appropriate to the knowledge and social circumstances of earlier times, but a new culture called for the program leading to the Bachelor of Arts degree "to be fundamentally and openly changed." He urged the inclusion of English language and literature, French, German, history, political economy, and natural science. English, French, and

German should be studied not only for their utilitarian value but for the sake of "the magnitude and worth of the literatures. . . . Indeed, the advanced student of our day can dispense with Latin better than French, German, or English." To add to that academic heresy, Eliot claimed:

> If any study is liberal and liberalizing, it is the modern study of history—the study of the passions, opinions, beliefs, arts, laws, and institutions of different races and communities.[16]

The kind of history he outlined was quite different from what was generally taught under that name, coming closer to Spencer's "Descriptive Sociology."

This expanded curriculum created the problem of which subjects the students would take. In 1884 the eighty Harvard faculty members taught "about four hundred and twenty-five hours of public instruction a week without any repetitions." In four years an undergraduate could not take more than a tenth of what was then being offered.

Educational conservatives attacked the elective system bitterly, insisting that the classics were the only appropriate study for colleges or high schools. In 1884 Dartmouth still had no professor of history and even "in so excellent an institution as Princeton there is only one professor of history against three of Greek, and this single professor includes poltical science with history in his teaching."[17]

In spite of the opposition, even the conservative strongholds had to follow Harvard's example to some extent. The American leader of the opposition to the elective system was Noah Porter, president of Yale, but in 1888 Yale had 22 electives in the classics, 10 in mathematics, 4 in English, 4 in modern languages, 5 in philosophy, 2 in chemistry, one in physics, 3 in biology, 3 in geology, and 12 in history and political economy.[18]

At Columbia, President Frederick A. P. Barnard, though he opposed the elective system and believed in the "disciplinary" value of the classics, reported to the trustees that those colleges which had adopted the elective system were growing, while those which stuck to the old required curriculum grew little, if at all. Cornell had a plan under which the practical and scientific subjects were of equal status, and students could choose one of five plans, ranging from the traditional classical

[16] *Educational Reform* (New York: Century, 1898), pp. 89, 101–102, 104.
[17] *Ibid.*, pp. 105–106.
[18] *Report of the U.S. Commissioner of Education for 1888–1889*, Part 2, pp. 1228–1231.

course to one of free election. Michigan also had a plan of elective courses and advanced research. Barnard contrasted the growth of these universities with the stagnation of Yale.

> Cornell University, in the third year of its existence, outnumbers any three of those colleges of the state which have been in existence half a century. The University of Michigan . . . numbers at present nearly five hundred students in its undergraduate department. . . . Harvard . . . when compared with Yale . . . is exhibiting at the present time a growth more vigorous than has marked any former period in her history, the second [Yale] is nearly stationary.[19]

To compromise between the belief that students needed the disciplinary studies and the practical consideration that students would not enroll unless there was an opportunity to have some electives, Columbia permitted juniors and seniors free election after 1881 and introduced some electives in the underclass years. Other colleges followed the Columbia pattern, few having as complete freedom of electives as was permitted at Harvard and Cornell.

At Indiana University, President David Starr Jordan introduced a plan of specialization within electives. In 1886 he instituted the "major subject" system, requiring students in their junior and senior years to choose a specialty or major. A "major professor" was appointed to counsel the student in planning his program so that there would be some coherence in the courses taken and yet be "best fitted to his tastes and capacity."[20] In addition, students might have minors or elective studies. Some form of compromise between free election and required subjects was the rule among the American universities at the turn of the century.

Professional Schools

Before the Civil War most practitioners in the "professional" vocations acquired their training outside of colleges. Theologians studied privately under the guidance of clergymen in their church. Lawyers prepared by "reading law" as clerks for practicing attorneys. Physicians and dentists learned their skills as apprentices to established practitioners. In the post-Civil War period, this situation changed rapidly, the emphasis on practicality resulting in the mushroom growth of professional schools in many fields. Of the 532 professional schools in 1899, 257

[19] *American Journal of Education*, Vol. 22 (1871), p. 436.
[20] David Starr Jordan, *The Days of a Man* (New York: World Book, 1922), Vol. I, p. 293.

TABLE 3: GROWTH OF PROFESSIONAL SCHOOLS[21]

	1860	1899
Theology	72	165
Law	22	86
Medicine	48	156
Dentistry	4	56
Pharmacy	7	52
Veterinary Medicine	1	17
	154	532

were separate institutions and 275 were departments of colleges and universities. By contrast, in 1961 there were only 97 medical schools and 47 dental schools in the United States. Even though many of these nineteenth-century schools granted degrees, their low entrance requirements and short terms indicate that they fell far short of "professional" standards. "Low standards in many professional schools are due to a failure to subject the degree-conferring power to strict state supervision."

Entrance requirements ranged from nothing at all to college graduation. In 1899 only one medical school, Johns Hopkins, required college graduation for admission:

> In 2 medical schools the requirements are indefinite; 29 demand a grammar school education; 97, 12, 3, and 12 require respectively one, two, three and four years of high school work.

Of the professional fields, only theology generally required a bachelor's degree for admission, a requirement in 71 of the theological schools. In 1898, 54 percent of the students in theological schools had degrees, compared with 29 percent of the law students and 21 percent of the medical students.

The length of the professional course varied greatly among the schools. In 1899, seventeen theological schools required more than four years for graduation, 24 required four years, 116 three years, 7 two years, and 1 required only one year. It is important to recall that perhaps some of those which had low entrance requirements might have made up some of the general background by requiring several years for graduation; there are, however, no figures to prove that. Of the law schools, 44 required three years, 37 two years, and 4 one year. Medical schools had courses which ranged from four years in 141 schools and three years in 10 schools to two years in two schools and one year in two more. Fifty-

[21] Butler, *Education*, pp. 466–468.

five of the dental schools required three years and the remaining one required four. Most of the pharmacy schools had two-year courses, and most of the veterinary medicine schools required three years for graduation.

Except for the theological schools, the length of the school term was fairly short. For example, 74 of the medical schools had terms of only six to seven months of the year, and only six had terms which extended to as long as nine months. However, that was reported to be "a much greater part of the year" than had formerly been the case.

During the last quarter of the century, the number of students enrolled in the professional schools rose rapidly. In 1898 there were 24,119 medical students, an increase of 142 percent over 1878. In law there were 11,883, an increase of 294 percent, in the same period. For theology there were 8,093, an increase of 87 percent. For dentistry, 7,633 and 988 percent. For pharmacy, 3,563 and 200 percent. For veterinary medicine, 378 and 17 percent.[22]

Graduate Schools

American colleges offered degrees beyond the bachelor's from the very first days of Harvard, but for a long time they were substantially honorary. The only graduate study in America before 1872 was in the form of private study with individual professors; Americans wanting academic specialization had to go to Europe.

American scholars finally did recognize the need for graduate study in the United States. At Harvard, Eliot expanded an informal series of "university lectures" into a Graduate Department in 1872, but the first real graduate school was Johns Hopkins University, founded in 1876. The first president, Daniel Coit Gilman, assembled the finest scholars he could employ and invited a number of outstanding young college graduates to do advanced study with these scholars. Hopkins became a major source for professors for other universities in the United States, and within twenty years, "over sixty American colleges or universities had three or more professors holding Hopkins degrees on their staff."[23] Harvard had 10, Columbia 13, Wisconsin 19, Chicago 23.

The University Ideal

Although many American institutions had long dignified themselves by the name of "university," most of them were no more than liberal arts colleges, some with more students in their secondary or preparatory

[22] *Ibid.*, pp. 465–485.
[23] Richard H. Shryock, *The Unique Influence of Johns Hopkins University and American Medicine* (Copenhagen: Ejnar Munksgaard, 1953), p. 10.

department than in the college course. At the opening of Johns Hopkins University in 1876 Thomas Huxley spoke on his concepts of a university education, stressing breadth of curriculum and the importance of research for truth rather than the indoctrination of a particular set of ideas.

With the appearance of graduate departments and professional schools, American colleges began to develop into "universities." In 1888–1889 there were 12 private universities, of which 9 had graduate departments, and 25 state universities, of which at least 17 had graduate departments. These universities did not include the 384 liberal arts colleges and 32 schools of science endowed by the Morrill Act and not part of state universities. In addition to the universities and liberal arts colleges in 1889, there were also 233 business and commercial colleges in the United States.[24] The form which the American university took—organization along lines of specialization and the fact that the number of schools and colleges in a university vary considerably—was largely a result of the demands of business, science, and industry on higher education.

Higher Education for Women

Colleges for girls in the Gilded Age were of three types: coeducational colleges, separate colleges for women, and colleges for women affiliated with men's schools. In the West and among some of the newer schools of the East and South, particularly the land-grant state colleges, coeducation was common. In the frontier states coeducation was general in the academies, and the extension to higher education created little controversy compared with the storm raised by coeducation in the East and South. The first coeducational college was established at Oberlin in 1833. Horace Mann's Antioch was next in 1852. When the state university in Iowa opened in 1856 it immediately admitted women. By 1879 more than half the colleges of the United States were coeducational.[25]

In the East and the South, the independent women's college was the most common means of providing higher education for girls. Many of these colleges grew out of the "female seminaries," as did Mount Holyoke, which received a college charter in 1888. Most of them were little more than academies even when they granted degrees to their graduates.

The first women's college to approach the standards of men's colleges was Vassar, and even so, many of its 30 faculty and 353 students were

[24] *Report of the U.S. Commissioner of Education for 1888–1889,* pp. 1090–1095, 1140, 1368.

[25] F. A. P. Barnard, in *The Rise of a University* (New York: Columbia U. Press, 1937), p. 251.

in the preparatory department. In spite of the large endowment left by Matthew Vassar of Poughkeepsie, there were too few qualified girls to maintain entrance requirements equal to those of the colleges for men. According to Woody, the first women's colleges to match institutions for men in their entrance requirements were Smith and Wellesley, both of which opened in 1875.[26] Bryn Mawr opened in 1885 with the goal of providing graduate study for women equivalent to Hopkins' courses for men, an ambition not at all realistic in the light of the current undergraduate work for women.

A third kind of higher education for women was the "coordinate" or affiliated college. Radciffe at Harvard was the first such college. In 1874 Harvard began giving examinations for women in the college subjects, and four years later thirty-seven of the professors at Harvard began repeating their lectures for women under the sponsorship of The Society for the Collegiate Instruction for Women. In 1893 the name of the society was changed to Radcliffe College, which granted degress to women. Columbia University had created Barnard College in 1889, staffed largely by Columbia professors and with senior year electives in Columbia open to Barnard students. Other coordinate colleges included Sophie Newcomb Memorial College for Women, established in 1887 as a department of Tulane University with a grant of $100,000 by Mrs. Josephine Louise Newcomb of New York. In 1891 Brown opened a Women's College, which later became Pembroke College.

In addition to the study of liberal arts, many women took courses in various professional fields. In 1898 there were 1397 women students in medicine, 174 in pharmacy, 198 in theology, 162 in dentistry, and 147 in law.[27] Some of these were in coeducational institutions, others in "female" colleges.

The only vocational field that admitted women in any number was teaching, and by the end of the century some educators were disturbed about the preponderance of women in that profession. For most of them, it was only a brief career—the woman's place was still the home.

Social Life on the Campus

The broadened curriculum and the developing concept that college should lead to practical efficiency brought changes in the character of the student bodies in American colleges. The budding theologian and serious academician were out-numbered by the ambitious young men

[26] Woody, Vol. II, pp. 179, 182.
[27] Butler, p. 353.

of the world who were going to become the wealthy, popular community leaders and to whom the social life in college was at least as important as the classroom or library.

Social fraternities, which had begun to be a part of campus life before the Civil War, multiplied in the post-war period. Attempts by faculty members, presidents, boards of trustees, and even political groups such as the Populist party were unable to check alumni and undergraduate devotion to the Greek letter organizations and secret societies. Along with social organizations, though of less influence, were musical groups, student publications, dramatic and debating clubs, academic interest clubs, eating clubs, religious groups, and the YMCA. Newspaperman William Allen White has described his days at Kansas State University (now the University of Kansas) in the last years of the 1880's.

> Into university politics I plunged with Christian zeal. But I found quickly that unless I expected to be a leader of the nonfraternity world, known as the Barbs, I was barred from leadership in the college activities. . . .
>
> My extracurricular activities should have given me a Phi Beta Kappa pin, for I poked my nose into everything on the Hill except athletics. . . . As I look back at it, classroom pictures blur in my memory of the university. Fraternity meetings are clear; political excursions are etched deeply; parties, little dances, picnics, and what, in the student nomenclature of the time, was called "girling," I recall vividly.[28]

Most important of the extra-curricular activities was varsity athletics. In the decade before the Civil War, rowing and baseball had made their appearance as inter-collegiate sports. In the years immediately after the war, track and field became popular, but football was soon to become the mania of American collegiate life. Perhaps no aspect of college life has been so widely accepted in so short a time and so controversial over so long a time as football. It has been excessively praised as the source of almost all the advantages of college attendance, and bitterly condemned as the underlying cause of virtually all the evils of "town" as well as "gown."

The first intercollegiate football game was actually a soccer game between Rutgers and Princeton in 1869. Within the next ten years, the game had become "big time," controlled by the alumni, employing paid coaches and players and providing "circuses for the populace." In 1876,

[28] *Autobiography* (New York: Macmillan, 1946), pp. 142–147.

representatives of a number of Eastern colleges met in New York and organized an intercollegiate football association, adopting a set of modified Rugby rules which gradually developed into the American variety of football. By 1884, football was so engaging student attention and opening the campus to gambling that the Harvard faculty voted to abolish the sport at Cambridge. Few institutions were able to exert such control, having let the athletic program be run entirely by the alumni and students; and even Harvard was able to maintain its prohibition for only two years. All the academicians and moralists could do was rail against overemphasis on football and promote minor reforms which removed some of the greatest physical danger to students. The demands of the students, alumni, and the general public in the Gilded Age successfully superimposed the extracurricular program on the expanded curriculum.

Influence of the College on the High School

As the colleges and universities began to broaden their curriculum and provide opportunities for more young men and women, the high schools which prepared the students for entrance to higher education were necessarily affected. Instead of the high schools continuing their development primarily as an extension of the ideal of universal education, the college-preparatory function became the major concern of educators both in the colleges and in the high schools.

High Schools

In 1875 the public high school was still not of major importance as an institution in the United States. In 1877 the United States Commissioner of Education reported only 24,925 high-school students enrolled in the United States, almost half of them in New York, Massachusetts, and Ohio. By 1900 there were more than 6,000 public high schools, enrolling over half a million students.

Accompanying this sudden growth in high schools and high-school enrollment were sharp conflicts over the purpose of secondary education, the responsibility of the public for financing it, the curriculum, and coeducation. The matter of finance was settled by court decision and general public acceptance. The chaotic curriculum was structured by committee work. Coeducation, both supported and attacked on the basis of crude medical and psychological opinions, was settled on the basis of financial expediency and social pressure. By the close of the century, the high school had become a public, coeducational institution, ostensibly serving several purposes but dominated by a college-preparatory curriculum.

Purpose of High Schools

When the high school first appeared in the Age of the Comman Man it was considered an extension of the common school, leaving to the private academy the responsibility of preparing students for college entrance. As the high school replaced the academy in the last quarter of the nineteenth century, it took on the dual purpose of providing "semi-technical education" for "the masses who are destined to fill the ranks of common laborers," and a "purely disciplinary" or "liberal" education for those who were preparing for college.[29] The tendency was in the direction of emphasizing the college-preparatory studies, and one result was some public dissatisfaction.

> From . . . the habit, on the part of school authorities and high school teachers, of looking upward to the colleges for close links of connection and sympathy, instead of downward to the elementary schools . . . a gulf of separation has been created between the two classes of schools. . . .
>
> Many of the studies pursued in most high schools have been of a purely disciplinary or preparatory character. . . . Many a parent who has maintained his boy in the high school for a year or two . . . finds that the practical interests of his life have not been taken into account, and that he has little or nothing in that direction to show for the time he has spent in the school.[30]

Although the high-school curriculum continued to expand with the inclusion of practical and scientific subjects, the basic structure was built around the college-preparatory course, particularly after 1894.

Tax Support for High Schools

The dual purpose of the high schools led to controversy about tax support. Except for some private-school defenders in the South, there was little opposition to tax support for elementary schools, but in many communities of the East and West, as well as the South, there was considerable objection to public-financed secondary schools.

[29] William T. Harris, "A Course of Study from Primary School to University," N.E.A. *Proceedings*, 1876, pp. 61–62.

[30] *Report of the U.S. Commissioner of Education for 1877*, p. LXXXI.

> The arguments of those who hold that the State has no right to provide education beyond the rudiments may be briefly summarized as follows:
> 1. The State has the right to educate its citizens just so far as will enable them to understand their duties and exercise their rights as citizens. . . . A primary education is sufficient for this. . . .
> 2. The high school being patronized by but few and the majority deriving no benefit from it, it is unjust to level a general tax for its support.
> 3. "Instead of educating the masses of children so as to prepare them for the pursuits and industries upon which they must depend for a living, high schools educate them in such a way as to make them discontent with their condition." . . .
> 4. Our common school system has been enlarged and extended beyond the original purpose of its founders. . . .[31]

State superintendents of public schools defended public support for high schools. In 1877 Ezra S. Carr of California argued, "The right of the State . . . to maintain high schools is not legally distinguishable from the right to maintain elementary schools." That point had been clarified in Michigan by the Kalamazoo case (see below). James H. Smart of Indiana, in his 1876 report, summarized several of the arguments for the public high school.

> Good citizenship requires intelligence enough to make good laws. . . . A primary education, a mere ability to read and to write one's name, is not sufficient to qualify one to exercise this high function. The fact that a man sends no children to school does not justify the claim that he ought not be called upon to pay for its support. . . . This principle would limit the schools all over the State to four months, because a majority of the children do not attend the schools more than four months. . . . It would be as logical to maintain that the insane asylum should not be supported because a majority of the people do not patronize it. . . . The argument of "original design" is one that is used as a last resort. . . . Experience has shown that . . . the Federal constitution, as originally constructed, was not adequate to meet the wants of a growing and progressive people. . . . Adherence to "original design" turns us back upon the perfecting future to embrace the prejudices of a dead past. . . .
>
> The term "high school" is, possibly, an unfortunate one, inasmuch as it leads many to suppose that the grade is one above the

[31] *Ibid.*

common school. This is not the case. The high school is an advanced elementary school. It is an integral part of the common school system.

H. F. Harrington, superintendent of the New Bedford public schools, harked back to an argument from the period of the common man.

> 1. High schools are important because they give increased efficiency to all the schools below them.
> 2. High schools are important because they are the best seminaries from which competent recruits can be obtained for the great army of public school teachers.
> 3. More than all, high schools are important as a branch of the public school system, because they constitute the only trustworthy agency to perform the essential service of bringing worthy representatives of the lower classes into the councils of the state and the organism of society. Abolish the high schools, and at once you draw a broad line or separation between the rich and the poor. You limit the higher education to the children of the well to do, for only the well to do would have the means to pay for it.[32]

The position of these educational leaders was confirmed by important court decisions in the 1870's, and the public high schools multiplied rapidly.

The Kalamazoo Case

One of the important court descisions on public support of high schools came in Michigan. The town of Kalamazoo established a high school in 1858, "where a course of study similar to, if not identical with, the present course was established, and has ever since been maintained."[33] Thirteen years later, three taxpayers brought suit "to restrain the collection of . . . school taxes . . . for the support of the high school in that village, and for the payment of the salary of the superintendent."

The complainants argued that the district had no authority to tax for high schools in which dead or foreign languages were taught, since such study was intended for those who were going to attend college and was thus not a part of "common" education. The case finally reached the Supreme Court of Michigan, where the opinion was written by Justice Thomas M. Cooley. In sustaining the right of the school authorities to

[32] *Ibid.*, pp. LXXXIV–LXXXV.
[33] *Thirty-Seventh Annual Report of the Superintendent of Public Instruction of the State of Michigan*, 1873, p. 399.

levy taxes for high schools "and by such taxation to make free the instruction of children in other languages than the English," Justice Cooley took note of the fact that the Michigan system was capped by a state university and that the purpose of the high school was "to constitute a connecting link between the ordinary common school and the state university." Thus the high schools were not an aid to the privileged upper classes alone, but to any young men who wished to avail themselves of the education in the university. The absence of high schools would be a discrimination in favor of the wealthy, for they could afford private schooling outside the state to prepare their sons for study at the university.[34] A second argument in favor of tax support for high schools was the legal ground that the school had had *de facto* existence for thirteen years without being challenged.

Similar cases were tried in other states, but the Kalamazoo decision was the important precedent. The *Report of the United States Commissioner of Education for 1874–1875* predicted accurately, "It may be supposed that the status of the high school is settled for the States at large."[35]

Growth of High Schools

With the legality of the high school established, public secondary education grew rapidly. Between 1889 and 1899 the number of public high schools and students more than doubled. In the scholastic year 1889–1890 there were 2,526 public high schools with 202,963 students; in 1899–1900 there were 6,005 schools and 519,251 students. The Midwestern and Northeastern states had by far the greatest concentration of high schools and students.

> Of the total number of students in the public high schools of the United States, 254,816 or nearly 50 per cent, are found in the 3,163 schools of the North Central Division. The 1,448 public high schools of the North Atlantic Division had 169,405 secondary students, the 675 schools of the South Central had 39,669, the 449 schools of the South Atlantic had 27,013, and the 270 schools of the Western Division had 28,348 secondary students.
>
> In the total number of students reported, there were included 8,395 colored secondary students. Of this number only 4,393 were in the colored high schools of the two Southern divisions.[36]

[34] *Reports of Cases Determined in the Supreme Court of Michigan, 1874–1875*, vol. 30, pp. 69, 70, 82–84.

[35] p. 211.

[36] *Report of the U.S. Commissioner of Education for 1899–1900*, pp. 2121–2122.

The growth in the number of high schools and students was to continue into the twentieth century, until most of the youths of secondary-school age were enrolled in school. After 1940, high-school enrollments increased only a little more rapidly than the actual growth in population.

Coeducation

One factor in the great increase in high-school enrollments was the admission of girls to public secondary schools. In the scholastic year 1899–1900, girls enrolled in high schools outnumbered boys 303,044 to 216,207; over 58 percent of the total enrollment was female.[37] Most of the girls were in coeducational high schools, which constituted 98 percent of the number of high schools and enrolled 93.6 percent of all pupils in high schools.[38]

Coeducation in the common schools had been the general practice everywhere in the United States and in the academies and high schools in the West. But in the East and South proposals to mix boys and girls in the same school at the secondary and higher levels raised heated quarrels, both sides arguing largely from *a priori* opinion and neither having much evidence to support their arguments. Even where there was any experience behind an argument, the combatants often generalized on the basis of a single example.

In general the arguments against coeducation were that it would damage the health of the female, lower the academic standards, destroy morality, lead to promiscuity and early marriage, and create an over-familiarity which would destroy the desire to marry, so that the United States would have a lessened birth-rate and eventually be populated only by immigration—obviously these last two arguments were not advanced by the same persons! The main arguments for coeducation were that it was more economical, would inspire both sexes to do their best, would create a better background for successful marriage, would refine the boys by the presence of girls, would strengthen the intellectual qualities of girls, and would fit the woman for her new role in a modern civilization.

Even though they used "scientific" terms and claimed that "physiology teaches," many of the medical men opposing coeducation viewed the problems of the menstrual cycle with as much ignorance and mysterious superstition as might have been expected from a medieval physician. Dr. Edward H. Clarke, a Boston physician, contended in 1874 that requiring a girl to attend classes during her menstrual period "by de-

[37] *Ibid.*, p. 2121.

[38] *Report of the U.S. Commissioner of Education for 1901*, vol. II, p. 1227.

ranging the tides of her organization, may add to her piety at the expense of her blood." Study would "divert blood from the reproductive apparatus to the head," thus causing girls to "lose health, strength, blood and nerve."[39] G. Stanley Hall, the leading psychologist of the period and author of the classic study *Adolescence,* opposed coeducation on both physiological and psychological grounds.

> We should ask . . . whether for a girl in the early teens, when her health for her whole life depends upon normalizing the lunar month, there is not something unhygenic, unnatural, not to say a little monstrous, in school associations with boys when she must suppress and conceal her instincts, feelings, and instinctive promptings, and these times which suggest withdrawing . . . from . . . mental effort in the school.

Hall feared that education for women and their emancipation from the home would eventually result in "a female sex without a female character." For boys the opposite would be true, because of the preponderance of women in the schools "at an age when strong men should be in control more than at any other period in life." "The feminization of the school spirit, discipline, and personnel is bad for boys." Finally, he blamed coeducation for the "decreasing percentage of marriage among educated young men and women."

> There is a little charm and bloom rubbed off the ideal of girlhood by close contact, and boyhood seems less ideal to the girls at close range. In place of the mystic attraction of the other sex that has inspired so much that is best in the world, familiar comradery brings a little disenchantment.[40]

Among the very few serious attempts to determine the effects of coeducation was a survey made of the health of women college graduates, conducted in 1885 by the Massachusetts Bureau of Statistics and Labor in cooperation with the Association of Collegiate Alumnae. The conclusion was that a college education did not harm the health of women. Aside from this one study, the proponents of coeducation depended largely on opinions of teachers and parents for their arguments. In the end, the most telling argument was economic, the cost of maintaining two separate schools. Indeed, the degree of ignorance and prejudice apparent in the entire controversy and the lack of any concerted effort to

[39] *Ibid.,* pp. 1276–1277.
[40] N.E.A. *Proceedings,* 1903, pp. 447–449.

find objective facts regarding the effects of both systems were of the same kind of irrationality that has characterized the mid-twentieth century conflict over the desegregation and coeducation of the races.

Curriculum

The curriculum of the high schools did not undergo any great or radical changes between 1860 and 1900. The range of courses was fairly broad, including both traditional and practical subjects, but the college preparatory subjects increasingly dominated the offerings. Only 10 percent of the high-school students and 30 percent of the graduates in 1900 were preparing for college. Yet over half of them took Latin, an increase from approximately 35 percent in 1890. About 56 percent of the students took algebra, the most popular single subject. Fewer than 3 percent studied Greek.[41] In general, mathematics, Latin, and English were commonly studied, with history and civics on the rise at the end of the century. Commercial subjects began to appear in considerable numbers by the end of the century, particularly bookkeeping, which had been one of the most common practical courses throughout the period.

While most high schools offered more subjects than any student could take in four years, it was not general practice to permit free election. Instead the student chose a course in which the subjects were specified. Most high schools had a course designed to prepare students for college, sometimes called the "classical" course or the "college-preparatory" course, but occurring under a variety of other names. Many high schools had another college-preparatory course intended for those who wished to get more science and less Latin and Greek; it was usually called by some variation of "scientific course." For the non-college-bound student, there would be an "English course" or perhaps a special course, such as the normal course for those who wanted to be elementary-school teachers or the commercial course or manual training course. In a study of 60 schools in the period from 1896 to 1900, 25 had only one course, 12 had two, 8 had four, 2 had six, and 1 had seven. Of 20 schools surveyed between 1860 and 1865, 12 had one course, 6 had two, and 2 had three.[42]

There was little general agreement on how long any subject in the curriculum should be studied. Some schools spent three or four years on a subject that other schools disposed of in only half or a third of a

[41] *Report of the U.S. Commissioner of Education for 1899–1900*, pp. 2122–2123.

[42] John Elbert Stout, *The Development of High-School Curricula in the North Central States from 1860 to 1918* (Chicago: U. of Chicago, 1921), pp. 46, 49, 62, 67–70.

year. Nor was there agreement on the length of the recitation period or the number of days a week a subject should be pursued. The result was almost complete confusion, particularly to college administrators trying to evaluate an applicant's high-school background.

In addition to the academic and practical subjects, music, drawing, and physical training had also appeared. The physical training movement, stimulated largely in the 1880's by exercise systems from Sweden and Germany, grew out of physiology and concern over body conditioning. It stressed formal exercises rather than games or free play. Extra-curricular activities in the high school of 1900 did not take up a fraction of the time given them in the modern high school, nor nearly as much as was devoted to them in the colleges of that era.

Conflict Between Classicists and Modernists

The most controversial issue in curriculum matters concerned the time to be allotted the study of Latin and Greek as compared with the rest of the curriculum. In a period of utilitarianism and science, teachers of the classics were fighting a desperate rear-guard action to prevent the total eclipse of their courses. Their chief argument was that Latin and Greek were the best means for disciplining the faculties of the mind which, properly exercised over the difficult dead languages, would then better serve the needs of practicality.

> Put . . . pupils into the study of Latin grammar, and the slow but gradual dissection of a Latin sentence . . . will open the intellect, develop the powers of discrimination and adaption, multiply the instruments of labor, enlarge the vocabulary, until when they have studied Latin one-half of the time that they have studied English . . . they will know more of their own language, write a better English essay . . . than if they should spend double, aye, quintuple the time in a continuance of the study of English grammar. And all this . . . because we more naturally dissect the dead than the living, . . . because strength of intellect comes more from solving the difficult than the easy.[43]

Herbert Spencer and Thomas Huxley led the forces for science. Spencer advanced science as the knowledge of "most worth," not only on practical grounds, but also on the grounds of its possessing "a great superiority over language as a means of discipline," for it "cultivates the

[43] A. F. Nightingale, "The Claims of the Classics," N.E.A. *Proceedings*, 1887, p. 408.

judgment" and provided for "*moral* discipline." The study of languages, argued Spencer, would do just the opposite.[44] In a speech in 1880, Huxley charged that

> neither the discipline nor the subject-matter of classical education is of such direct value to the student of physical science as to justify the expenditure of valuable time upon either; and . . . for the purpose of attaining real culture, an exclusively scientific education is at least as effective as an exclusively literary education.[45]

At the N.E.A. convention in 1887, Samuel Thurber, master of the girls' high school in Boston, contested the right of the classicists to the name of "Humanists."

> Humanism meant at first, education in the best thought of the human race as this best thought took form in the most beautiful literary productions. But humanism means to-day education in what was the best thought of the human race five hundred years ago. . . . The humanist ignores modern times, ignores modern literature, ignores Europe and America. . . . The early humanist learned Latin as the absolutely necessary medium through which to come into relation with the thought of his contemporaries. He never thought of Latin as a precious discipline. . . . The mediaeval man had no literature about him to respond to the stirrings of his mind except the literatures of Greece and Rome. . . . There were to him no modern languages and literatures. . . . Not to know Latin was to lack the fundamental condition of all culture. . . .
>
> The ancient literatures still exist, but they do not exist alone. . . . I need only mention the immense modern literatures of England, France, and Germany. . . . No modern scholar speaks Latin outside monastic or ecclesiastic precincts; or writes Latin, except as an indoor school gymnastic. . . .
>
> The conditions, in short, are all changed. Yet the studies which the elder humanists pursued because there were no others to answer their desires, we pursue because the elder humanists pursued them. . . . Wholly unintelligible to them would have been the argument that the ancient languages should be studied because they exhibit the etymologies of words in modern languages. Strange would have seemed to them the practice of studying a language which there would never be an opportunity to speak, or to hear, or to write, and which, for lack of interest, would practically never, in the course of

[44] Spencer, p. 88.
[45] Thomas Huxley, *Science and Education* (New York: Appleton, 1898), p. 141.

> a lifetime, be read. In short, the renaissance impulse has died out, but the renaissance forms remain.[46]

Thurber outlined a high-school course in a modern humanist form, centered around "the English language and its literature" as "the truly humanistic group." At the close of the meeting, a resolution was passed calling for English to be given an equal place with the classics and science in high school courses of study.

One of the participants in the N.E.A. discussion was almost pitifully prophetic when he warned that the "abrogation of Greek from our high-school courses" would be the "entering wedge" in "the subordination of Latin to make room for the claims of practicability involved in the study of the sciences, and a more extended knowledge of English literature."[47] Despite all the dire threats of the classicists that only the study of Latin would preserve the "continuity of civilization," English, modern languages, history, science, and the practical studies gradually secured a greater proportion of the high school curriculum.

The Committee of Ten

The lack of uniformity in high-school curricula presented college administrators with the difficult task of trying to determine which high-school graduates to admit. Although the generally confused situation in high-school curriculum and organization created many problems, it was the issue of college admission that precipitated an effort to bring order out of chaos. In 1892 the National Education Association appointed a ten-man committee to arrange a series of conferences of school and college teachers in the college preparatory subjects to study the proper content, time allotments, methods of teaching, and testing procedures for the academic high-school subjects. This Committee of Ten included Charles W. Eliot, president of Harvard, William T. Harris, United States Commissioner of Education, four other college presidents, a college professor, the headmaster of a private school, the headmaster of the girls' high school and girls' Latin school in Boston, and the principal of the high school in Albany, New York. The committee, whose report was to do much to standardize the American public high school, was dominated by college men and contained only two public high-school administrators and no public-school teachers.

The committee set up nine sub-committees or conferences on the

[46] N.E.A. *Proceedings*, 1887, pp. 437–438.
[47] Nightingale, p. 408.

various academic subjects: (1) Latin; (2) Greek; (3) English; (4) other modern languages; (5) mathematics; (6) physics, astronomy, and chemistry; (7) natural history (biology, including botany, zoology, and physiology); (8) history, civil government, and political economy; and (9) geography (physical geography, geology, and meteorology). Each conference was made up of ten members, and of the ninety appointed to serve, more than half were from college faculties. Most of the others were headmasters and teachers in private schools and academies stressing college preparation. For example, the conference on mathematics was made up of six college professors, three private schoolmasters, and only one public high-school principal. Each conference chose its own chairman and secretary; six of the chairmen and two of the secretaries were college professors. Clearly, the colleges dominated the conferences as well as the parent committee.

After the conferences met in December, 1892, they submitted reports to the Committee of Ten, recommending how much of their subject ought to be included in the high-school program. The final committee report said, "The spirit of the conferences was distinctly conservative and moderate, although many of their recommendations are of a radical nature." The two science conferences and those on history and geography "ardently desired to have their respective subjects made equal to Latin, Greek, and mathematics in weight and influence in the schools; but they knew that educational tradition was adverse to this desire."

None of the conferences "demanded for its subject a larger proportion of time than is now commonly assigned to it in primary and secondary schools," and the committee report particularly praised the "moderation in this respect" of the "old and well-established subjects" of Latin, Greek, and mathematics. However, it must be recognized that these subjects already claimed a major portion of the time of the secondary-school curriculum, and even the classicists realized that they were fighting from a defensive position which might best be maintained by the magnanimous acceptance of the very favorable status quo. When the committee tried to organize the conference recommendations into programs which could be included in a student's four years in high school, they had to reduce the number of periods requested for several of the subjects. The members of the committee all accepted a "disciplinary" psychology and the chairman, President Eliot, was an enthusiast for electives; consequently, it is not surprising that the committee solved the time problem by equating all the subjects as suitable for general education. Since all the subjects would "be used for training the powers of observation, memory, expression, and reasoning," colleges ought to admit "any youth who has passed creditably through a good secondary school course, no matter to what group of subjects he may have mainly devoted himself in the secondary school."

All the conferences recommended that their subjects be introduced at an earlier age; all but the Greek conference suggested changes in the elementary schools that would have tied even those schools closer to the colleges and oriented them in the direction of the "insignificant percentage of the graduates" of the high schools who "go to college or scientific schools." This was justified on the grounds that waiting until high school is too late to build the kind of mental habits needed for secondary school and college work. Nowhere does the committee show awareness that the assumption of a mental disciplinary psychology was being challenged by psychologists.

In emphasizing the mental discipline of the high-school subjects, the conferences and the committee refused to admit that individual students might learn differently from the same subject or might profit from different teaching methods. All the conferences and the committee

> unanimously declare that every subject which is taught at all in a secondary school should be taught in the same way and to the same extent to every pupil so long as he pursues it, no matter what the probable destination of the pupil may be, or at what point his education is to cease. . . . Not that all the pupils should pursue every subject for the same number of years; but so long as they do pursue it, they should all be treated alike.[48]

The committee outlined four parallel programs that students might elect. All were made up of five or six courses each year and were divided to make twenty periods a week. All included four years of English, three or four years of mathematics, two to four years of history, and a year each of physical geography, physics, and chemistry. All but the classical course required a year of botany or zoology, a year of astronomy and meteorology, a year of geology or physiography, and a year of anatomy, physiology, and hygiene. The main difference among the four was in the amount of foreign language. The classical course required four years of Latin, three years of French or German, and two years of Greek. The Latin-scientific required four years of Latin and three of French or German, the modern language four years of either French or German and three years of the other, and the English four years of a foreign language

[48] *Report of the U.S. Commissioner of Education for 1892–1893*, Part II, pp. 1416–1423.

—Latin, French or German. "The two programmes called respectively modern language and English must in practice be distinctly inferior to the other two." The only concessions to utilitarian or vocational subjects were the option of bookkeeping and commercial arithmetic for algebra and of "subjects thought to have practical importance in trade or the useful arts" for "some of the sciences contained in the third and fourth years of the 'English' programme."[49]

The report of the Committee of Ten was a monument of educational conservatism. It was based on a psychological theory already largely discredited. It ignored the educational problems of the 90 percent of elementary-school students not attracted to secondary education, and it assumed that the kind of schooling appropriate to the 10 percent of the high-school students preparing for college should be given all high-school pupils. In short, the committee structured a program suited to the needs of less than 1 percent of the high-school aged population.

The report was vigorously attacked at educational meetings, where it was discussed at great length. C. M. Woodward of Washington University complained that the committee erred "in omitting the manual and art elements from the programs of the literary high schools" and "in ignoring that vast army of youths who do not go to the literary high schools at all." G. Stanley Hall assailed "the doctrine of equivalence of subjects" as "very highly pernicious." He criticized the report for stating that "all pupils may be taught in the same way."[50]

In spite of criticism, the report was widely accepted by practicing schoolmen, who seized upon it as a framework for bringing some kind of order out of the chaos of the high-school curriculum. Consequently, when the progressive revolution of the 1890's and early twentieth century was trying to free American society and American education from the autocratic domination of the Gilded Age, the high schools were saddled with the dead weight of the academic conservatism of the Committee of Ten.

Committee on College Entrance Requirements

Following discussions on how the Committee of Ten report might be introduced in practice, the N.E.A. appointed a committee (sometimes known as the Committee of Thirteen) to consider college entrance requirements. The regional accrediting associations and the various

[49] *Ibid.*, pp. 1441–1443.
[50] N.E.A. *Proceedings*, 1894, pp. 661–666.

learned societies were requested to make reports to the Committee of Thirteen on what colleges were requiring for admission and what the specialists in particular fields felt was necessary as preparation for college. The "Partial List of Those Who Have Assisted in the Preparation of this Report" included 137 names, of which 84 were college presidents or professors; most of the rest were on the faculties of private academies and college preparatory schools. Again the public high schools had a very small representation. The chairman of the committee was A. F. Nightingale, a city superintendent of schools in Chicago, but a strong supporter of the classics.

The final committee report was submitted in 1899, and it recommended limited election in high schools.

> The committee . . . especially emphasizes the importance of a certain number of constants in all secondary schools and in all requirements for admission to college. . . .
>
> [T]he committee recommends that the number of constants be . . . four units in foreign languages (no language accepted in less than two units), two units in mathematics, two in English, one in history, and one in science.[51]

A unit was a subject studied for at least a year of four periods a week.

The effect of this report and of those from the committees of the learned societies associated with it was to compound the conservatism of the Committee of Ten report. The increasing conservatism of educators of the Gilded Age is clear when the educational reports and discussions of the 1890's are contrasted with those of the 1860's and 1870's, when the leaders were men who had come to prominence during the revolutionary Age of the Common Man.

The New England Prep School

While the leaders of the business and financial world encouraged a more "practical" secondary education for the middle class in public high schools, they developed a new form of exclusive school for their own sons and daughters. The ostensible purpose of these schools was to prepare the young men for college—hence the name "prep" schools. In addition to the highly traditional academic curriculum, the prep schools had a carefully planned program of preparation of the young men for

[51] N.E.A. *Proceedings*, 1899, pp. 656–671.

their upper-class social positions. In essence they did for the young men what the female academies—or "finishing" schools—did for the young ladies of those families.

Although there were a few prep schools in New York, Pennsylvania, and Virginia, they clustered in New England. They attracted the sons of the wealthy from all over the land, and the fact that they were boarding schools enabled them to maintain an exclusiveness impossible in day schools drawing from only a limited geographical region. A few of the prep schools, notably Phillips Andover (1778) and Phillips Exeter (1781), were descendants of the early academies, but most of the socially prominent ones were founded in the Gilded Age. St. Paul's (New Hampshire) was founded in 1856, St. Mark's (Massachusetts) in 1865, Groton (Massachusetts) in 1884, The Taft School (Connecticut) in 1890, Hotchkiss (Connecticut) in 1892, St. George's (Rhode Island) and Choate (Connecticut) in 1896, Middlesex (Massachusetts) in 1901, and Kent School (Connecticut) in 1906. Deerfield Academy, dating back to 1797 as a local Massachusetts academy, was reorganized as a boys' boarding school in 1902.

All these schools have been closely associated with the wealthy industrial and financial families—the J. P. Morgans, Vanderbilts, Tafts, Mellons, du Ponts—as benefactors, trustees, patrons, and alumni. Although they have accepted a limited number of scholarship students, they are still predominantly upper- and upper-middle-class institutions—expensive, exclusive, and academically, socially, and politically conservative.

Elementary Education

The influence of the conservatism of the Gilded Age was not as apparent on elementary schools as on secondary and higher education, although it was reflected to some extent in the shifts in emphasis in the curriculum. The principle of universal elementary education was so firmly established that only in the South was there any open opposition to it. Indeed, the *post-bellum* period brought considerable strengthening of the "common school" through better supervision, consolidation of small schools, longer terms, compulsory attendance, elimination of the rate bill, and free textbooks.

By 1900 public schools were available to almost all children whose parents wanted to enroll them. The percentage of children between the ages of 5 and 18 who were in school rose from 61 in 1870–1871 to a little over 70 in 1897–1898. First in 1897–1898 was the state of Washington with 91 percent; lowest was New Mexico with 52 percent.[52] Since the upper ages of the range of 5 to 18 included many children who had completed the elementary grades, the percentage of children of elementary-school age enrolled was much higher than the over-all figure.

Curriculum

The elementary-school curriculum continued to be devoted largely to the basic skills of reading, writing, and arithmetic. However, under the stimuli of the Darwinists and the popularity of the Pestalozzian object lesson, science and nature study became more important. There was also a greater interest in the social studies, especially civics, perhaps because of the information-giving aims of Spencer and the moral goals urged by the Herbartians. More emphasis was placed on literature and somewhat less on spelling, again perhaps a result of the Herbartian theories. The appearance of manual training in the elementary school was one consequence of practicality of the era, although it was also defended on the mental disciplinary ground that it "exercised the executive faculty."

An 1888 Bureau of Education survey of elementary schools in eighty-two cities found over twenty subjects being taught, including reading, writing, spelling, drawing, music, English grammar, United States history, geography, arithmetic, physical culture, physiology, morals and manners, natural sciences, civil government, algebra, geometry, German, woodworking, sewing, and cooking. Some were taught in only a few cities; several were taught only in the upper grades and for short periods of time each week; some, such as morals and manners, were covered primarily through "oral lessons."

One of the clearest influences of the conservative forces in society and American education was the enthusiastic public support of two systems of manual training. One was stimulated by an exhibit of a Russian school at the Philadelphia Centennial Exposition in 1876; the other was a Swedish system called "sloyd," introduced in 1886. Both were instruction in wood-working. Neither aimed at teaching trades, only the "principles which underlie all trades."

> The supreme purpose of manual training is to quicken and develop the mental powers, to cultivate the moral instincts, to awaken and stimulate the aesthetic tastes, to lead up towards the good, the beautiful and the true.

[52] *Report of the U.S. Commissioner of Education for 1898*, p. LXVII.

The sloyd system was construction of "small wooden articles used in the house and garden." The Russian system emphasized making the fittings and joints used by carpenters and cabinet-makers. Although educational reformers urged manual training "as a potent moral force, as an aid in securing respect for labor, as an important civilizing agent, and as a possible remedy for some of the evils which menace modern society," the obvious practicality of the subject had much to do with its popularity.

> As a practical and economic measure, as a means of raising the skill of the American workingman . . . utilitarians have eagerly caught up the novel idea of something practical in education. . . .
>
> And the utilitarian idea (however much we may depreciate that phase of the question) is really what has captured the people,—the people who furnish the funds.[53]

The "people who furnish the funds" apparently had political influence, for by 1900 a number of state legislatures had begun to require that manual training be taught in all elementary schools. The widespread acceptance of relating education to occupations to counteract the overly verbalized approach of traditional education awaited the progressive revolution in education led by John Dewey.

In 1893 the Department of Superintendence of the N.E.A. appointed a Committee of Fifteen to "investigate the organization of school systems, the co-ordination of studies in primary and grammar schools, and the training of teachers." This committee was made up of twelve city superintendents, one state superintendent, United States Commissioner of Education W. T. Harris (who had earlier been the city superintendent in St. Louis), President of the University of Illinois Andrew S. Draper, who had been state superintendent in New York and city superintendent for Cleveland. The committee was made up entirely of administrators and is an indication of the centralization of administration of the schools by the 1890's. The committee made its report in 1895, and although there was very little new in any of the recommendations, the effect tended to standardize the curriculum of the elementary schools. The report contains strong traces of Herbartian theory and was consistent in several ways with the recommendations of the Committee of Ten.

> Language, as a subject of study, has a distinct and definite relation to the introduction of the child into the civilization of his time,

[53] N.E.A. *Proceedings*, 1894, pp. 261–266.

> and . . . [forms] the true basis of correlating the elementary studies.
>
> In correlating geography and history, the former should be subordinate to the latter.
>
> Instruction in the elements of physics and chemistry . . . should be given in all grades in connection with topics in physiology and physical geography. . . .
>
> The use of good English, including the correct use of technical terms, should be required in all studies. . . .
>
> The study of English grammar should be made subordinate and auxiliary to the study of English Literature.
>
> Writing, as a special branch, should be taught only through the sixth year of the course.
>
> Manual training in wood and metals should be made a part of the course for boys during the seventh and eighth years; and sewing and cooking should be taught to girls. . . .
>
> Music should be taught throughout the elementary course. . . .
>
> Latin should be studied during the eighth year instead of English grammar. . . .
>
> United States history should be studied for one and a half years.[54]

Rural Schools

This report by the Committee of Fifteen described the curriculum substantially as it existed in the larger city schools, but in many of the rural schools, the courses were more restricted. Manual training, sewing, cooking, and other practical subjects were learned by the farm child doing his chores at home. School was "book larnin'." For rural schools the curriculum was the three R's, spelling, some history and geography, perhaps a bit of science through nature study or physiology, and for older children too remote from high schools a little of the secondary subjects of algebra, geometry, and Latin, provided the teacher knew anything about these subjects.

In the nineteenth century the United States was still very much a rural society, though the "drift of population into the cities" was already accelerating. In 1880, only 38 percent of the pupils in Illinois schools were enrolled in graded schools; the remaining 62 percent were in ungraded rural schools. By 1890, 51 percent were in graded schools, but ungraded schools still provided the education for 378,160 children in the state. The average term of the ungraded schools in 1890 was 7.2 months, compared with 8.6 in the graded schools. The inequality of educational opportunity afforded the rural child was described to the N.E.A. in 1892 by Henry Raab, State Superintendent of Schools in Illinois.

[54] N.E.A. *Proceedings*, 1895, pp. 235–236.

> In many instances the school grounds are bare, the fences torn down and neglected, no shade trees nor flowering shrubs, coal bin open to the depredations of the tramps, outhouses unclean and offensive, no walks nor well, a rectangular, tasteless house, looking more like a barn than a building for human beings to live in. . . . The provisions for healthy light, one of the first requisites of a schoolhouse, are totally ignored. . . . Without sound blackboards, without maps and charts, without globe, reference books or supplies, the teacher is compelled to "make bricks without straw."
>
> Now, all this would not be so bad if care were taken to procure good teachers. . . . But what is the practice? The school-year is divided into a fall, a winter, and a spring term. During the winter term, when the work on the farm does not require their presence at home and the larger boys can attend school, a strong, experienced (?) teacher, sometimes a man, is hired; in fall and spring, when only younger children attend, a young, cheap teacher of little experience, generally a woman, is considered good enough for that primary work. . . . When a boy or girl, mostly the latter, has "fagged through" the country school as it is, and has imbibed sufficient textbook knowledge to pass the county superintendent's examination and is of the minimum age at which she is by law permitted to engage in teaching, she goes out in search of a school, and hires to the district at the closest salary they can agree upon.[55]

CONSOLIDATION AND TRANSPORTATION As the rural areas became more densely settled and roads better, it was possible to transport children by wagon or horse to a rural school large enough to have the advantages of a village graded school. As early as 1874 Quincy, Massachusetts, began transporting pupils from a small dilapidated school to a large graded school at a financial savings as well as to the improvement of the educational opportunities of the children. In 1892, transportation of pupils was tried in Kingsville township, Ohio. The success of the "Kingsville system" led the Ohio legislature to broaden the experiment to three counties, and in 1898 a general law was passed covering the whole state. By 1900, eighteen states, from Maine to Florida and as far west as the Dakotas, were transporting some pupils to schools.[56]

In 1897 the N.E.A. heard a report of the Committee of Twelve on Rural Schools. In addition to summarizing the arguments for consolidation, the report included a sample notice to "bidders for transportation of pupils." The bidders were required to "furnish a suitable vehicle with sufficient seating capacity to convey all the pupils belonging to their route," as well as "to furnish all necessary robes, blankets, etc., to

[55] N.E.A. *Proceedings*, 1892, pp. 572–575.
[56] *Report of the U.S. Commissioner of Education for 1899–1900*, p. 2581.

keep the children comfortable; and in severe weather the conveyance must be properly heated by oil stoves or soap stones."[57] The idea of an oil stove in a straw-strewn wagon filled with little children would be enough to discourage modern safety experts from transporting pupils, but such were the conditions under which the consolidation of the rural school proceeded before the invention of the motor bus.

Compulsory Attendance Laws

Even where schools were available, many parents were lax in their responsibility of sending their children to school. In addition to not enrolling youngsters at all, many parents who had their children's names on the roll books had them attend very irregularly. In 1898 the average length of the school term in the United States was 143 days, but the average days of attendance per pupil was only 98. Ever since the 1642 apprenticeship law of Massachusetts, there had been the legal precedent for civil authorities to compel parents to educate their children. In 1852 Massachusetts had enacted a compulsory attendance law, the first in the United States. By 1900 thirty states, one territory, and the District of Columbia had compulsory attendance laws. In most cases, the law specified the ages of compulsory attendance as seven to twelve; Wisconsin required attendance from seven to thirteen; three other states extended the upper limit to fifteen, and seven more to sixteen. In many states, the child was required to attend only a certain percentage of the total term, ranging down to eight weeks a year in Kentucky.[58]

In 1918 the principle became accepted in all the states when Mississippi finally enacted a compulsory attendance law, but some Southern states have weakened their compulsory attendance laws in their attempt to circumvent the 1954 desegregation decision of the Supreme Court. South Carolina and Mississippi have repealed their compulsory attendance laws.

Opponents of compulsory attendance argued that the laws were contrary to the principle of liberty and that they interfered with the parental prerogative to act as they chose about bringing up their children. Such arguments, educators charged, were based on "erroneous notions" about "the nature and just powers of a government" founded for "the protection of their persons and property."

> The education of the mass of the people of a State has never been done by individual enterprise, and perhaps never can be; and so

[57] N.E.A. *Proceedings*, 1897, pp. 510–516.
[58] *Butler*, pp. 79, 97–99.

> long as this remains a fact, such education will remain one of the proper functions of that State. . . .
>
> If, then, all the things a State may properly do . . . can only be effectually done through the means of education, . . . why should it hesitate to . . . demand, when it has provided the means for the education of all, that every one of its children shall have an opportunity to enjoy these advantages? . . . No parent has such a paramount right over his child, as to be entitled to deny him through obstinacy or caprice, that education necessary to his highest good as an individual and his usefulness as a citizen.[59]

In most states, compulsory attendance laws were made more effective by passage of child labor laws which prohibited the employment of children below certain ages, generally twelve to fourteen. Several states, however, limited child employment only in mines, and none of them appear to have limited their use in farm labor, where there was probably the greatest employment of children. Thus in the rural areas, where school attendance was poorest and terms shortest, compulsory attendance laws had their least effect.

Free Textbooks

Even though the schools were public, education was not without cost to many parents. In some states of the South and Far West, the old specter of the rate bill remained. For many parents there was the cost of school books, and reformers in education continued to fight for equalizing opportunity by having school authorities provide the books. The practice of having each child bring to school whatever books his family happened to have obviously prevented dividing children into grades for group instruction. The compromise of having free books given to those whose parents were indigents raised the same objections as the old pauper oaths in the charity schools.

By 1900 twenty-five states and the District of Columbia either required school authorities to provide textbooks or permitted local authorities to provide them for all students. At least seven more states had provisions for free books for indigent children.[60]

Kindergartens

Before the Civil War the only kindergartens in the United States were German-language schools supported by the middle-class intellectual exiles from the German revolutions. As institutions to preserve German

[59] N.E.A. *Proceedings,* 1871, pp. 220–221.
[60] Butler, *Education,* pp. 135–138.

traditions in the German communities, they had little direct influence on American educational practices. The kindergarten movement in America was more an outgrowth of the work of two native Americans, Elizabeth Peabody and W. T. Harris. In 1860 Miss Peabody and her sister Mary, the widow of Horace Mann, founded the first English-speaking kindergarten in the United States in Boston. In 1867 Elizabeth Peabody went to Germany to study the kindergarten system, and from 1868 until her death in 1894 was the leading apostle of Froebelianism in the United States. She urged philanthropists to endow charity kindergartens, persuaded the Boston school board to experiment for four years with a public-school kindergarten, and founded a periodical which disseminated the ideas of Froebel.

William T. Harris, the city superintendent of St. Louis, was very much interested in the kindergarten, and in 1873 he opened the first permanent public-school kindergarten in the United States. When Harris resigned his office in 1880 there were 7,828 children enrolled in the St. Louis kindergartens. Other cities followed the example of St. Louis, and in 1897–1898 kindergartens were part of the public-school systems of 189 cities. The total number of public kindergartens was 1,365, with 95,867 children enrolled. In addition, there were nearly 100,000 children enrolled in 3,000 private kindergartens in the United States.[61]

The purpose of the kindergarten, as Harris saw it, was to provide moral and physical education, leaving the primary and secondary years free to concentrate on subject matter. In addition to training the child's hands and muscles to useful employment, Harris believed that the moral instruction of the kindergarten would be good for rich and poor alike; the child would learn to be law-abiding, well-behaved, productive, and hard-working and avoid the evils of "crime," "vicious habits," "arbitrariness and self-will," and "self-indulgence."[62]

Though Harris was one of the most conservative of the American educators in both his social philosophy and his educational ideas, the kindergarten which he championed was one of the levels of schooling least affected by the conservative forces of the day. Perhaps the devotion of the practicing kindergartners to the liberal ideals of Froebel accounts for the freedom and creativity which characterized the kindergartens in their early years. The theories of the Froebelians were to have great influence in the twentieth-century progressive revolution in education, particularly among the experimental private schools which made up the founding group of the Progressive Education Association.

[61] *Ibid.*, pp. 35–42.
[62] *Ibid.*, p. 41.

QUESTIONS FOR DISCUSSION

1. Summarize the relationships between the development of industrial and commercial interests in the United States during the Gilded Age and the changes in secondary and higher education. What parallel situations can you point to today between current national interests and changing emphases in education?
2. Review the arguments over the coeducation of the sexes and compare them with modern arguments over the coeducation of the races. How might the former controversy help in analyzing the conflict over school integration?
3. What actual experimental evidence can you find on the educational advantages or disadvantages of coeducation? Does it support the views of either side in the coeducation controversy at the turn of the century?
4. One of the most bitter controversies in education is over the curriculum and the content of courses. Discuss the effects of the curriculum expansion during the Gilded Age and the Report of the Committee of Ten on the present issue.

SUGGESTED READINGS

Secondary Sources

Brown, Elmer Ellsworth. *The Making of Our Middle Schools*. New York: Longmans, Green, 1902. Chapters XVI–XIX.

Brubacher, John S., and Rudy, Willis. *Higher Education in Transition*. New York: Harper & Row, 1958. Chapters 6–10.

Butts, R. Freeman. *The College Charts Its Course*. New York: McGraw-Hill, 1939. Chapters IX–XIII.

Handlin, Oscar. *John Dewey's Challenge to Education*. New York: Harper, 1959. Pp. 15–39.

Thwing, Charles F. A *History of Higher Education in America*. New York: Appleton-Century, 1906. Chapters XVIII, XX, XXI.

Woody, Thomas. *A History of Women's Education in the United States*. New York: The Science Press, 1929. Vol. II.

Primary Sources

Cubberley, Ellwood P. *Readings in Public Education in the United States*. Boston: Houghton Mifflin, 1934. Readings 159, 248–250, 266, 277.

Gross, Carl H., and Chandler, Charles C. *The History of American Education Through Readings*. Boston: Heath, 1964. Pp. 195–199, 221–241, 286–292, 306–317.

Hillway, Tyrus. *American Education: An Introduction Through Readings*. Boston: Houghton Mifflin, 1964. Readings 9, 24.

Hofstadter, Richard, and Smith, Wilson. *American Higher Education: A*

Documentary History. Chicago: U. of Chicago Press, 1961. Vol. II, pp. 549–761, 841–860.

Knight, Edgar W., and Hall, Clifton L. *Readings in American Educational History*. New York: Appleton-Century-Crofts, 1951. Pp. 367, 516–520, 544–560, 718–723, 727–728.

Monroe, Paul. *The Founding of the American Public School System*. Ann Arbor: University Microfilms, 1940. Vol. II. Quotes 600–603, 616, 620–623.

12

Southern Schools and Federal Interest in Education

While the East and West were experiencing great financial gains during the Gilded Age and expanding their schools rapidly, the South was having terrible difficulties. The leaders and many of the people of the region suffered the despair and dejection of a defeated nation. Two hundred and fifty thousand men had died in the armies; many thousands more were crippled and diseased. Over two billion dollars' worth of property, in the form of slaves, had been wiped out by emancipation. Land values were low, particularly without field hands to work. Property had been destroyed. Perhaps half the draft animals and most of the livestock had been destroyed during the war. The sudden release of the completely unschooled slaves, who had not the vaguest notion of how to use independence and citizenship, contributed to political as well as economic chaos. Northern "carpetbaggers" and Southern "scalawags" teamed with the illiterate Negroes to make a mockery of government, and mismanagement and embezzlement of public funds were almost unbelievable. Gangs of freedmen and poor whites who had learned violence during the war continued their "bushwhacking" activities. Ku Klux Klan violence aggravated the situation. Many Reconstruction policies were harsh, punitive, inept, and corrupt. Southern financial institutions, which had converted to Confederate currency, were bankrupt. The very poverty of the region made recovery a monumental task, and the struggle of Southern educators to build a school system in the South is a story of almost heroic proportions.

Educational Reconstruction in the South

Since most of the states of the Confederacy had had only the rudiments of school systems before the War, the problem of the South after the War was not so much one of "reconstruction" as it was of erecting a complex structure on unfavorable ground. Most rural areas had had no schools whatever. Many of the relatively few schools that had existed had been destroyed or damaged by war and neglect. To compound the difficulty, the South had no tradition of schooling for the people. There was only a small educated class to draw on for teachers and administrators. Communities had to be convinced of the importance of schooling. Parents had to be convinced that "book larnin' " was essential for their children. Taxpayers had to be persuaded that schools were a necessary and worthwhile investment for democracy. In a culture which had avoided creating a public school system, developing public sentiment for education was a difficult task, vastly greater than that which had confronted Horace Mann in Massachusetts.

During slave days, few Negroes—slave or free—had been given any schooling, and emancipation burdened the South with about four million illiterate freedmen. The educational needs of the poor whites had been almost as completely ignored by the planter aristocracy; consequently, there were nearly as many illiterate whites as freedmen. Many adults as well as children wanted to learn to read, particularly among the Negroes, who saw ability to read as a symbol of freedom. The task of providing schooling for this mass of humanity was indeed formidable.

Even a wealthy society would have had difficulty coping with these educational problems, and the South was deeply impoverished, facing tremendous burdens of rebuilding all its institutions with a shattered economy and almost no tax base to finance its tasks.

Tentative Efforts: 1865–1867

The aim of Presidents Lincoln and Johnson were to restore law and government to the South with provisional governments of native whites. New constitutions and *post-bellum* legislation contained provisions and laws which authorized schools in much the same language as that of the laws in effect just before the War. Edgar W. Knight, North Carolina educational historian and apologist for the South, has described these efforts in over-enthusiastic terms. For instance, the Arkansas legislature of 1866–1867 passed a school law requiring schools "to be maintained by public taxation for three months in the year." Knight describes the law as "advanced and modern in respect to its provisions for educational administration and support," and he writes of "some schools" opened under the law as "the basis of public school education in Arkansas." Knight claims that the taxation provisions of the law—resulting in some $65,000, which "served as handy pocket change for the reconstructionists"—"provided resources which made possible later establishment of schools in that State." Even Knight, however, can point to no more concrete developments than "unusual interest" in Mississippi, Georgia, and North Carolina. In Tennessee, where an 1866 law "provided for an adequate administrative organization and for the maintenance of schools for not less than five months in the year, with separate schools for colored children," little was accomplished because "the popular mind was confused, and distrust prevailed everywhere." In addition, there was "considerable trouble over the Bank of Tennessee, in which the antebellum literary fund was invested and through it was eventually lost."

These meager provisions came to an end in March, 1867, with the passage in Congress of the Reconstruction Act. Edgar Knight, a proud and "unreconstructed" conservative in his social, political, and educational views, praises the Southern leaders during the period of the Presidential Reconstruction:

> [T]he leaders of the period recognized the changes which the result of the war had produced and courageously set themselves to the task of readjustment; and but for the inauguration of the congressional plan of restoring the South, the educational needs of both white and colored children would have been more properly cared for during the years following the war.[1]

Although the military occupation of the South and the political ineptness and dishonesty of Reconstruction legislatures complicated the educational tasks of the South, there is room for considerable difference of opinion with Knight as to whether the "unreconstructed" Southerner would have done much more for schools after the War than he had before.

Reconstruction Legislatures and Mixed Schools

Congressional attitudes toward the South were far more bitter than those of Lincoln or Johnson, and in 1865 both the Senate and the House refused to seat the Southerners who came to take their place in Congress. Led by Senator Charles Sumner and Congressman Thaddeus Stevens, Congress set out to punish the South. The Fourteenth Amendment and the 1866 Civil Rights Law granted Negroes citizenship, and the Fourteenth Amendment also denied political office to anyone who had taken an oath to support the United States Constitution and had "engaged in insurrection or rebellion against the same." Until the Southern states ratified this amendment, Congress refused to seat their representatives.

[1] *Public Education in the South* (Boston: Ginn, 1922), pp. 314–317.

Over the veto of President Johnson, Congress passed the Reconstruction Acts in March, 1867, placing the South under military government and disfranchising all men who had violated their oath to the Union or had voluntarily fought in the Confederate forces. This left government in the South in the hands of the virtually illiterate freedmen, the almost equally illiterate poor whites, and Northern "carpetbaggers." During the congressional Reconstruction period (1867–1876), little of lasting value was achieved in the South, and tremendous debts were accumulated by all the Southern states, further handicapping progress when some degree of normalcy could be restored.

One educational issue raised in most of the legislatures of the Reconstruction period was the "mixed school." The Reconstruction constitution of South Carolina authorized schools in which white and Negro children would be educated together. In Mississippi the school law of 1870 opened schools to all youth of school age without distinction, but apparently, as in South Carolina, no attempt was made to enforce the law. In Louisiana, the constitution of 1868 required a school system in which "all children should be admitted without distinction of race, color, or previous condition," but the one recorded attempt of Negro children trying to attend a white school in New Orleans was by the children of the Negro Lieutenant-Governor of the state, P. B. S. Pinchbeck. A mob of white children drove the Negroes from the school.[2] The effect of the provision prohibiting any "separate school or institution of learning . . . exclusively for any race" was apparently to keep white children out of schools where Negroes attended.[3] The 1868 Florida constitution also provided for free schools "for the education of all the children . . . without distinction or preference," but public opposition prevented the establishment or successful operation of more than an isolated few such schools in the state.

Northern Educational Missionaries

Many Northerners and even foreigners were concerned about the plight of the South and particularly the Negroes of the South. In the early years of the War, Northern churches organized missionary societies to work among the freedmen. In addition to religious effort, a great many benevolent societies for the aid of the freedmen were organized and engaged in educational activity between 1862 and 1874. The United States

[2] Horace Mann Bond, *The Education of the Negro in the American Social Order* (New York: Prentice-Hall, 1934), pp. 51–52.

[3] Charles William Dabney, *Universal Education in the South* (Chapel Hill: U. of North Carolina Press, 1936), Vol. I, p. 370.

Bureau of Education listed seventy-nine religious and benevolent societies engaged in freedmen's aid during the Reconstruction era.[4]

The American Missionary Association, which had carried on antislavery work in the South before the War, was one of the most important religious agencies. Supported by the Congregational, Free-Will Baptist, Wesleyan Methodist, and Dutch Reformed Churches, it concentrated on sending teachers to the South to establish common and normal schools for Negroes. In 1868 it supported 532 teachers and missionaries in the South. Methodists, Presbyterians, and Baptists also had denominational societies supporting teachers and missionaries in the South among the freedmen. In spite of the earnestness of these churches, they were unable to provide schooling for more than a tiny fraction, perhaps less than one percent, of the freedmen, and they did almost nothing for the Southern whites.

The first society to be established primarily for the aid of the freed slaves was the Boston Educational Commission, later known as the New England Freedmen's Aid Society. Organized in 1862, it held its final meeting in 1874, the last of the benevolent societies for freedmen still in operation. During its twelve years of operation, it supported an average of 82 teachers. The high point of its career was in 1866, when it supported 182 teachers in 79 schools enrolling a total of 9,649 pupils, scattered in the Carolinas, the District of Columbia, Virginia, and Maryland. At other times it also had schools in Georgia and Florida. Yet, including possible duplications in different years, the total enrollment supported by this largest of the aid societies was only about 40,000.

In the twelve years in which the freedmen's aid societies carried on their work, they expended about $6 million and provided schooling for some half a million pupils. Although the constitutions of most of the freedmen's societies specified that no pupil would be excluded because of race, most of the pupils were Negro, the whites generally refusing to attend schools with Negroes. In 1867 the schools of the Northern societies supervised by the Freedmen's Bureau enrolled 111,442 students, and only one percent of them were white. Not only did these schools fail to attract the white children, but they reached only about 10 percent of the Negro children, and the adult illiterates not at all. Those children who did enroll attended very irregularly, limiting the effectiveness of the schools.[5]

The most important lasting effect of the religious and benevolent societies was the establishment of schools which have become colleges

[4] *Bulletin, 1916*, No. 38, pp. 299–301.
[5] *Ibid.*, pp. 269–298.

and teacher-training institutions. Fisk University and Berea College were started by missionaries from the American Missionary Society. Between 1861 and 1890, thirty-three denominational "higher schools for Negroes" were established.[6] Some of these have since become state colleges or have occasionally received state assistance.

Philanthropic Educational Funds

The educational problems and developments of the South were different from those of the rest of the nation in many ways, but one phenomenon the South shared with the North was private philanthropy, the great social virtue of the Gilded Age. As with the introduction of technical education in the North, philanthropy in the South served largely as incentive. The great funds were the carrot dangled before the nose of the Southern political mule. When Southern legislatures balked at the educational tasks facing them, the promise of a grant of cash was often enough to entice local and state action. Even with the munificence of the philanthropists, the Southern need for schools was so great that outside gifts could do little for solving educational problems without determined efforts by state and local governments.

One of the most famous gifts was that of George F. Peabody, a Massachusetts native who made a fortune as a merchant and banker in Washington, Baltimore, Philadelphia, New York, and London. In 1867 he established the Peabody Education Fund with an initial gift of $1 million, to be administered by a board of trustees including some of the leaders of the South as well as the North. The principal and income from the fund were to be used in those states which had "suffered from the destructive ravages and the not less disastrous consequences of Civil War."[7] Two years later he added another $1 million, as well as nearly $1.5 million in Mississippi and Florida bonds, which were repudiated by those states. As a consequence of this repudiation, Mississippi and Florida did not share in the distribution of the fund until 1892. Unlike most funds, which specify that the principal may not be spent, Peabody authorized the spending of the principal itself and the closing out of the fund after thirty years, an indication of his intention that the fund be an incentive to public financing of education rather than a substitute for it.

The first agent of the fund was Barnas Sears, who served from 1867 until his death in 1880. Under his leadership, the basic policies of the

[6] Ullin Whitney Leavell, *Philanthropy in Negro Education* (Nashville: George Peabody College for Teachers, 1930), pp. 33–54.
[7] *Ibid.*, p. 59.

fund were established. Aid was to be given only to public schools and state normal schools, with preference for those places that would "exert the widest influence." The training of women teachers for the primary schools was to be emphasized, rather than collegiate education for men. The fund was to "favor the appointment of superintendents, the formation of associations of teachers and the publication of journals for their improvement." In no case would the fund "meet the entire expense of a school or institute," limiting its participation to "only a small portion of the amount, usually one-fourth."[8] In 1870 the Peabody Board detailed new rules, limiting the shares to "Well Regulated Public Free Schools" and requiring that the "people are to pay for current expenses at least twice and usually three times as much as they receive from the Fund," that the schools be graded, and that a teacher be provided for every fifty pupils. Negro schools would receive grants two-thirds of the rates specified for white schools, since Negro teachers were paid less than white teachers.[9]

Sears' successor was Jabez Lamar Monroe Curry, a former Congressman from Alabama and Confederate army officer. As a law student at Harvard in 1845, he had acquired an interest in education and greatly admired Horace Mann. From 1881 to 1903, Curry was the Horace Mann of the South. Speaking before teachers' associations and public groups, addressing legislatures, starting schools, encouraging communities to tax themselves, discovering and training other educational leaders, Curry dedicated his talents and energies to the promotion of universal education in the South. Because of his political experience and Southern background, he had far more influence than others might have had with the limited funds at his disposal. In spite of his belief that whites were biologically and intellectually superior to Negroes, he worked diligently for Negro schools as well as for white. In his last years he helped organize the Conference for Education in the South and was a leader in the first Southern Education Board and director of its field work. In his devotion to education he declined a cabinet post offered him by President Hayes, and he accepted a post as ambassador to Spain for three years (1885–1888) only after President Cleveland argued that the appointment of a Southerner would demonstrate that the Union was fully reunited.

The annual income of the fund was rarely more than $90,000, though it did go as high as $130,000. From 1868 to 1914 the total amount ex-

[8] Dabney, Vol. 1, pp. 111–112.

[9] Jesse Pearl Rice, *J. L. M. Curry* (New York: King's Crown Press, 1949), pp. 91–92. Leavell, p. 86.

pended was $3,650,556. Beginning with Curry's administration, the stress was put on aiding teacher training, and during the decade from 1883 to 1892 over 86 percent of the moneys granted went for that purpose.[10] In 1905 the board appropriated $1 million to endow the George Peabody College for Teachers at Nashville, thus expanding the Peabody Normal School, which had been receiving grants from the fund since 1875. By the time the endowment was available in 1910, it had been increased to $1,700,000. Other contributions to the college included $260,000 from the Carnegie Foundation, $250,000 from J. P. Morgan's estate, $2,700,000 from the General Education Board (a Rockefeller foundation), $300,000 from Rockefeller, and nearly $5 million from other sources.[11] Scholarships were granted to students from other states to bring them to Peabody for training as teachers of teachers and as school administrators.

When the Fund was closed out in 1914, the $350,000 remaining was placed with the Slater Fund for assisting Negro schools. Impressed by the success of the Peabody Fund, John F. Slater, a New England cotton manufacturer, had set up a fund in 1882 of $1 million, the "income of which was to be used to assist in the education of the Negro people of the South." The first agent of the Slater Fund was Dr. Atticus Haygood, president of Emory College. On Haygood's resignation in 1890 Curry took over the duties of agent of the Slater Fund along with the administration of the Peabody Fund. The main use of the Slater Fund grants under Haygood and Curry was for vocational ("industrial") education. Unlike the Peabody Fund, Slater moneys were not restricted to public schools, and of the over $3 million expended between 1882 and 1929, about 70 percent was granted to private and church institutions.[12]

By far the largest of the educational philanthropies was the fund set up by John D. Rockefeller and ministered by the General Education Board. Beginning in 1902 with an initial gift of $1 million, it was supplemented by grants of $10 million in 1905, $32 million in 1907, and $10 million in 1909. By 1920 the total endowment of the Board was $126,788,094. The General Education Board was concerned with education of both Negroes and whites throughout the nation and with a number of non-school problems relating to the welfare of all the United States, but its grants were concentrated in the South. Between 1920 and 1928 the Board granted nearly $3 million to public education for Negroes, and from 1924 to 1929 nearly $12 million for Negro education,

[10] Leavell, p. 93.
[11] Dabney, Vol. II, pp. 116–121.
[12] *Ibid.*, pp. 433, 439.

public and private, in the fourteen Southern states.[13] Most of the grants were made on condition that additional funds be raised locally or that the receiving institution take steps to improve its teaching staff.

Another large educational fund in the twentieth century was established by Julius Rosenwald. In 1911 Rosenwald met Booker T. Washington and became interested in Tuskegee and the problems of Negro education in the South. Appalled by the condition of the Negro schools he observed on his trips to Tuskegee, he donated $25,000 for the construction of Negro schools. The grant was made on condition that the state, local Negroes, and white citizens all contribute toward the erection of the building. The first such school was in Lee County, Alabama; of the total cost of $943, "$150 was raised from the local people and labor was volunteered to the amount of $133; Negro and white citizens donated a sum of $360 in cash, and Mr. Rosenwald's share was $300."[14] Pleased with the results of his experiment, Rosenwald incorporated the Julius Rosenwald Fund in 1917, and by 1928 he had given about $22 million to the fund.[15] Although the fund aided colleges and granted fellowships to 999 Negro and 538 Southern white college scholars, its original purpose was to build Negro schools. Between 1917 and 1948, when the fund was liquidated, $22,249,624 was expended. Of that total, over $13 million was spent for educational activities, with over $5.3 million for school buildings.[16]

To encourage lengthening the usual school term of four months, after 1920 grants were made only to those communities that would guarantee a five-month term; and if a community would set up a minimum term of eight months the fund would build a teacher's home, share in bus transportation costs, and pay part of the cost of the extended time. By 1932, when the school building program ended, the fund had assisted in building 4,977 schoolhouses, 217 teachers' homes, and 163 shops. As an indication of the success of the incentive principle, only about 15 percent of the money expended for all these buildings was contributed by the fund. A slightly larger amount was raised by local Negroes—often at great sacrifice, for their incomes were miserably low. Approximately 4 percent was donated by local white friends, and the remaining 64 percent was raised by taxation.[17]

Other philanthropies benefitted the South. One was the Carnegie Foundation, although its grants have been very diffused and often

[13] Leavell, pp. 69–70, 179–180.
[14] Dabney, Vol. II, pp. 465–466.
[15] Leavell, pp. 81–82.
[16] Edwin R. Embree and Julia Waxman, *Investment in People: The Story of the Julius Rosenwald Fund* (New York: Harper, 1949), pp. 155, 262.
[17] *Ibid.*, pp. 41, 50–53.

made through other funds. The Daniel Hand Fund was begun by a Connecticut donor in 1888 with a gift of $1 million and increased by a bequest of $500,000 in 1891. Administered by the American Missionary Association, its income was to be used "for the purpose of educating needy and indigent people of African descent residing . . . in the recent slave States."[18] In 1907 Miss Anna T. Jeannes of Philadelphia gave $1 million to help rural Negro schools. Much of the income of this fund went for supporting county supervisors of home economics, whose main duties were encouraging better nutrition, home industries, sanitation, personal cleanliness, and home gardens. In 1909 Miss Caroline Phelps Stokes left nearly $1 million for the endowment of the Phelps-Stokes Fund. Among its projects were financing studies of Negro education, research fellowships at the Universities of Virginia and Georgia in the sociological study of the Negro, and a fund at George Peabody College for Teachers to subsidize visitations to Negro schools and otherwise improve Negro education.

The usefulness of these philanthropies in stimulating public action was demonstrated very early. In 1871 only 57 percent of the funds spent for public education in the South was derived from tax sources. Ten years later, 85 percent was derived from taxes.[19] In short, the financial carrot roused the energies of the South until substantial progress was made toward the creation of a tax-supported school system.

Hampton and Tuskegee Institutes

One of the most heroic struggles to achieve an education in the face of adversity was that of Booker T. Washington. As a slave Washington acquired a desire for education while carrying his young mistress' books to school for her. After emancipation, he got a copy of Webster's "blue-back" speller and taught himself to read. When an educated Negro from Ohio came to Washington's West Virginia village and became teacher in a subscription school, young Booker could not go because he had to work in a salt-furnace. He arranged with the teacher to take classes at night and later convinced his stepfather to let him attend school during the day, working at the furnace for a few hours before nine in the morning and again after school. Then he heard of Hampton Normal and Agricultural Institute and set out to walk from Charleston, West Virginia, to Hampton.[20]

Hampton Institute, which set an important pattern for Negro school-

[18] U.S. Bureau of Education, *Bulletin*, 1916, No. 38, p. 167.
[19] Leavell, p. 89.
[20] Booker T. Washington, *Up From Slavery, An Autobiography* (New York: Doubleday, Doran, 1938).

ing in the late nineteenth century, was the product of the insight and leadership of Samuel C. Armstrong. Armstrong was born in Hawaii in 1839, the son of a missionary who was minister of public instruction for Hawaii from 1847 to 1860. As assistant to his father, Samuel Armstrong learned many of the principles that were to be the foundation of Hampton Institute. During the Civil War he commanded Negro troops in the Union Army, and at the close of the War was assigned to the Freedmen's Bureau and charged with the care of thousands of refugee freedmen gathered at Hampton. There he found a school being operated under the sponsorship of the American Missionary Association. A missionary at heart, he urged the Association to purchase a large estate on Hampton Roads and establish a permanent school. As its first principal, Armstrong opened Hampton Institute with two teachers and sixteen pupils in April, 1868. His purpose was

> to train selected negro youth who should go out to teach and lead their people, first by example, by cultivating land and making homes; to give them not a dollar that they could not earn themselves; to teach respect for labor; to replace stupid drudgery with skilled work; and to these ends to build up an industrial system, for the sake not only of self-respect and efficient labor, but also for the schooling of character.[21]

The combination of academic and vocational work resulted in such productive and effective graduates that Hampton won almost immediate fame. In 1878 a number of Indians, including "several of the worst specimens, then in banishment in Florida," were sent to Hampton, and the success of the experiment led Congress to grant $20,000 a year to the Institute for the education of 120 Indians a year. In 1879 Congress authorized an Indian training school at Carlisle, Pennsylvania, patterned after the program at Hampton.

Armstrong raised money from many sources and utilized student labor to stretch his limited finances. Students learned trades by erecting buildings and raising their food on the school farm. Girls learned domestic skills by doing the housekeeping and making clothing. By the time of Armstrong's death in 1893, Hampton had 650 boarding students, averaging 18 years of age.

Throughout Armstrong's administration, Hampton was a primary and secondary school, making no pretense at offering collegiate work. Pupils learned the basic skills of reading, writing, and arithmetic. Beyond that

[21] Quoted in *Report of the U.S. Commissioner of Education for 1901*, p. 477.

the main concerns were character education and vocational proficiency. This was the kind of schooling Booker T. Washington sought. He was apparently not a very promising prospect when he arrived at Hampton. "Having been so long without proper food, a bath and change of clothing, I did not, of course, make a very favourable impression," and the admitting teacher dismissed him by sending him to sweep an adjoining class room. She was satisfied with his "entrance examination," for after he had swept the room "three times" and dusted it "four times," she could find no dirt. He earned part of his expenses doing janitorial work, and the annual tuition of $70 was paid by a Massachusetts donor, S. Griffitts Morgan.

> Life at Hampton was a constant revelation to me; was constantly taking me into a new world. The matter of having meals at regular hours, of eating on a table cloth, using a napkin, the use of the bathtub and of the toothbrush, as well as the use of sheets upon the bed, were all new to me. . . .
>
> The education that I received at Hampton out of the text-books was but a small part of what I learned there. . . .
>
> I also learned a valuable lesson at Hampton by coming into contact with the best breeds of live stock and fowls. . . .
>
> Perhaps the most valuable thing that I got out of my second year was an understanding of the use and value of the Bible . . . not only for the spiritual help which it gives, but on account of it as literature. . . .
>
> At Hampton I not only learned that it was not a disgrace to labour, but learned to love labour, not alone for its financial value, but for labour's own sake and for the independence and self-reliance which the ability to do something which the world wants done brings.[22]

He was graduated in 1875 and returned to teach in his home town, Malden, West Virginia.

In 1881 Armstrong recommended Washington as a teacher for a proposed Negro normal school in Tuskegee, Alabama. This school opened in "a rather dilapidated shanty" and "the coloured Methodist church." The thirty students admitted to the first class were all over fifteen years of age and had previous schooling. Most of them were public-school teachers. Additional students arrived, until at the end of the first month, Washington had nearly fifty. He proposed to follow the program of Hampton, concentrating on vocational and moral education rather than an academic program.

[22] Washington, pp. 51–62, 66–68, 72–74.

> From the very beginning, at Tuskegee, I was determined to have the students do not only the agricultural and domestic work, but to have them erect their own buildings. My plan was to have them, while performing this service, taught the latest and best methods of labour, so that the school would not only get the benefit of their efforts, but the students themselves would be taught to see not only utility in labour, but beauty and dignity would be taught, in fact, how to lift labour up from mere drudgery and toil, and would learn to love work for its own sake.[23]

By 1900 Tuskegee Normal and Industrial Institute owned 2,300 acres of land, "one thousand of which are under cultivation each year, entirely by student labour." The grounds contained sixty-six buildings, all but four of which had "been almost wholly erected by the labour of our students."

> While the students are at work upon the land and in erecting buildings, they are taught, by competent instructors, the latest methods of agriculture and the trades connected with building.
>
> There are in constant operation at the school, in connection with thorough academic and religious training, thirty industrial departments. All of these teach industries at which our men and women can find immediate employment as soon as they leave the institution.

The daily schedule of Tuskegee Institute is evidence of the moral virtues of hard work, cleanliness, and religious observances.

> 5 A. M., rising bell . . . 6 A. M., breakfast bell; 6:20 to 6:50 A. M., rooms are cleaned; 6:50, work bell; 7:30, morning study hour; 8:20, morning school bell; 8:25, inspection of young men's toilet in ranks; 8:40, devotional exercises in chapel; 8:55, "five minutes with the daily news"; 9 A. M., class work begins; 12, class work closes; 12:15 P. M., dinner; 1 P. M., work bell; 1:30 P. M., class work begins; 3:30 P. M., class work ends; 5:30 P. M., bell to "knock off" work; 6 P. M., supper; 7:10 P. M., evening prayers; 7:30 P. M., evening study hour; 8:45 P. M., evening study hour closes . . . 9:30 P. M., retiring bell.[24]

Washington's emphasis on the role of the Negro as worker won the support of the Southern white leaders. Not only did they assist Tuskegee in its program, but wherever Negro schools were established in the

[23] *Ibid.*, p. 148. See also pp. 110, 121–132.
[24] *Ibid.*, pp. 311, 314.

South, Tuskegee was held up as the model. Washington's fame was national. He received an honorary degree from Harvard. He even spoke from the lecture platform to white audiences in the South. Perhaps his avoidance of any statements about social or political equality caused the whites to see him as a tool for their purposes. Certainly he was more highly respected by whites than by many Negroes who had hopes of securing greater equality than Washington envisioned. Time has demonstrated a certain logic to his argument, of course, for political and social equality appear to be integrally related to economic opportunity. Where the Negro has been able to make the most progress vocationally, he has made the greatest advances in other aspects of life; where he has suffered economic discrimination, he has also been denied social, political, and educational opportunities.

Segregated Schools

Except for the unsuccessful attempts of the Reconstruction legislatures and the early freedmen's aid societies, the South struggled to overcome its educational handicap, not by establishing one system of schools but by trying to maintain two separate systems. As soon as the Reconstruction period ended and the troops were withdrawn, white "supremacy" was restored, and the chances for Negro schooling were as restricted as were Negro opportunities in political and social activities. Immediately after the War, Negro schools were taught largely by white teachers, and these teachers, having some influence in the community, "were able to secure more favorable attention" for their schools than Negro teachers could have. After Reconstruction it was less socially acceptable for whites to teach in Negro schools, and those jobs fell to the poorly trained and politically voiceless Negro teacher.

> An unfortunate consequence of giving up the Negro schools to Negro teachers was a diminished interest in them on the part of the influential people of the community. . . . The schools under Negro teachers had no effective advocates, and so they were constant losers. They became the prey of unscrupulous politicians and the mark of bitter prejudice. They were discriminated against in the distribution of school funds; their schoolhouses were given no proper attention, so that they became shabby and unfit to occupy; and, worst of all, corruption entered into the appointment of the Negro teachers. The amazing contrast between the public schools for white children and those provided for Negroes in nearly all parts of the South tells the story of this misfortune.[25]

[25] U.S. Bureau of Education, *Bulletin*, 1916, No. 38, p. 262.

Fourteen Southern states and the District of Columbia had laws requiring separate schools for white and Negro children. Florida made it a penal offense to conduct "any school of any grade, public, private, or parochial, wherein white persons and negroes shall be instructed or boarded within the same building, or taught in the same class, or at the same time by the same teacher." A number of the states softened the separation by requiring that facilities be equalized "in respect to attainments and abilities of teachers and length of term time."[26]

Even in the states where the law required "impartial provisions" for both races, separate schools resulted in gross inequalities. In the sixteen former slave states and the District of Columbia between 1870 and 1898, the per capita expense for the education of a Negro child was only a fraction of that spent for a white child. In 1870–1871 the per capita expenditure for white children was $2.97, for Negroes $.49. In 1897–1898 the proportion was somewhat less unequal, with $4.25 spent for each white child and $2.27 for each Negro. In the latter year North Carolina had almost equalized the per capita cost, $1.17 for whites and $1.03 for Negroes, but Florida was spending $5.92 for each white and $2.27 for each Negro. In 1897–1898 the District of Columbia spent $14.82 for each white and $10.64 for each Negro student.[27]

Although some progress was made during this period, the South remained far below the national average in such matters as length of school term and per capita expense for schools. In 1876–1877 the average length of school term for the nation was 132.1 days; but the South Atlantic Division (Delaware, Maryland, West Virginia, District of Columbia and the states to the south bordered by the Atlantic Ocean) averaged only 91.4, and the South Central Division (Kentucky, Tennessee, and Alabama westward to Texas and Oklahoma) only 80.3. By 1900–1901 the national average was 144.2, the South Atlantic 112.1, and the South Central 96.4. The total expenditure for schools per capita of the total population was $1.56 for the nation in 1879–1880 and $2.93 in 1900–1901. For the South Atlantic Division, it was $.68 and $1.28 and for the South Central $.55 and $1.06. An important part of the Southern lag was due to the fiscal strain of two school systems in a society which would have been economically unable to match the rest of the nation if it had tried to maintain only one set of schools.

> Primary education is the duty of the State. . . . The Southern States are too poor to do their full duty in this regard. The effort

[26] *Report of the U.S. Commissioner of Education for 1901*, pp. 749–750.
[27] *Ibid.*, pp. 752–753.

> which they put forth, however, is commendable in the highest degree. No other community in this country lays such heavy proportional taxes upon itself for school purposes as the South.[28]

The financial hardships of separate systems were not unnoticed, and the plight of the South in trying to build two school systems under the many adversities of the time suggested the importance of Federal assistance. Throughout the period, the matter of Federal aid was much discussed, and many educational leaders felt it imperative.

> It is well known that a dual scheme of schools covering a sparsely settled territory practically duplicates the expense of a unified system. Although race prejudice proves to be very expensive, yet the white South is pledged to its maintenance at any cost. The wisdom of this policy is not a profitable subject of discussion. The policy emphasizes the necessity of outside aid for the education of both classes of children.[29]

Private philanthropy, even in huge sums, was proving unequal to meeting the needs. The struggles of the South, under the encouragement of outside grants, were at times heroic but also woefully inadequate. The nation had been reunited politically, and the educational problems of the South were the educational problems of the nation. The failure of the federal government to provide massive assistance in rebuilding—actually *building*—a Southern school system caused the educational reconstruction of the South to be tragically slow and inadequate.

The Federal Government and Educational Reconstruction

Although federal land grants for schools were authorized as far back as 1785 and both land and cash grants were made from time to time in the first half of the nineteenth century, federal activity in educational matters was far greater in the forty years from 1860 to 1900 than it had been in the seventy-five years from 1785 to 1860. Much of the new federal interest was a result of the problems of the South. Congress considered many measures intended to help the South though most of them died in debate. The Supreme Court was called on to decide many issues which bore directly or indirectly on the Southern practice of

[28] *Ibid.*, p. 833.
[29] *Ibid.*, p. 750.

racially segregated schools. The arguments in Congress and before the Court are significant and relevant to similar problems under discussion in the present.

The Freedmen's Bureau

Whenever Union armies invaded the South, they were faced with the problem of caring for the many Negroes who ran away from their masters. In October, 1861, a naval landing at Port Royal, South Carolina, freed some 40,000 slaves, who were placed under the charge of General Rufus Saxton. Some of the men were mobilized into four regiments of troops. Work battalions were organized to harvest the cotton and other crops. And with the help of Northern benevolent and religious societies, schools were established for nearly two thousand children. A year later as Grant moved down the Mississippi Valley, he too was flooded with Negro refugees; he delegated Chaplain John Eaton to "take charge of the contrabands." Eaton had been a school teacher in Ohio and Superintendent of Common Schools in Toledo before the War. For his new task, Grant commissioned Eaton a colonel, and by the end of the War he was a brigadier-general. He later served two years as State Superintendent of Public Instruction in Tennessee during the Reconstruction, and then from 1870 to 1886 was United States Commissioner of Education. Like Saxton, Eaton tried to organize the Negroes for work and to set up schools where teachers from the North could begin educating the children of the freedmen. In 1862 General N. P. Banks, in command of the Union forces in New Orleans, encouraged the return of Louisiana to the Union, and the new state government established a system of common schools. Banks had been the first general agent of the State Board of Education of Massachusetts under the secretaryship of Barnas Sears, Mann's successor, and was dedicated to the principle of universal education. In spite of local white opposition, Banks succeeded in having some industrial schools opened for the freedmen.[30]

The efforts of Saxton, Eaton, and Banks and the diffused zeal of the missionary and benevolent societies called for some agency to coordinate the aid intended for the freedmen. To this end, Congress created the Bureau of Refugees, Freedmen, and Abandoned Lands in March, 1865. It was a branch of the War Department, and General O. O. Howard was named Commissioner. The bureau was to continue for a year after the end of the War, but it was later extended, and when the bureau's other activities were ended by Congress on January 1, 1869, an exception

[30] *Ibid.*, pp. 417–418, 428, 431–433, 435–436.

was made of the school work, which was permitted to continue for another year. The Freedmen's Bureau spent $3,512,927 for schools, much of it going for school construction. The teachers in the Freedmen's Bureau schools were sent by the Northern aid societies. By 1870 there were 150,000 children in the schools supervised by the Freedmen's Bureau, virtually all of them Negro.

Although any educational effort under such conditions was praiseworthy, the few millions spent by the Freedmen's Bureau was little more than a drop in the deep bucket of educational need of the South.

Howard University

Howard University is unique among American colleges in that it is supported directly by the federal government. Founded by act of Congress in 1867, Howard continued to receive federal appropriations after its founding organization, the Freedmen's Bureau, passed out of existence. For many years Howard offered secondary work as well as teacher training and collegiate courses. Although many of the Negro colleges of the period were "for the most part huge primary schools with the college course attached for ornament and style," Howard had entrance requirements "nearly equal to the smaller New England colleges."[31] It was the source of many Negro leaders in all the professions.

United States Office of Education

When Horace Mann resigned as secretary to the Massachusetts Board of Education and accepted an appointment to Congress in 1848, one of his dreams was to have Congress create a national educational officer who might do for the nation what he had done for Massachusetts. Henry Barnard had earlier attempted to get the federal government to collect information concerning education, with the result that the 1840 census included questions about illiteracy and schools. In the 1866 meetings of the National Association of School Superintendents, Emerson E. White, State Commissioner of Common Schools for Ohio, advocated a federal agency that would encourage individual states "to maintain an efficient school system." The proposal was aimed particularly at the Southern states, which had failed in that respect before the War and were now at the mercy of the federal government. Four days after the Association sent a resolution to Congress asking for such an agency, Representative James A. Garfield of Ohio introduced a bill, actually

[31] *Ibid.*, pp. 833–834.

drafted by White, to establish a "Department of Education." There was much opposition to the bill, largely out of fear that it would lead to federal control of schools, and it was not until 1867 that it was passed and signed into law. The duties of the new department were limited to

> collecting such statistics and facts as shall show the condition and progress of education in the several States and Territories, and . . . diffusing such information respecting the organization and management of schools and school systems, and methods of teaching, as shall aid the people of the United States in the establishment and maintenance of efficient school systems, and otherwise promote the cause of education throughout the country.[32]

The first Commissioner was Henry Barnard, but hopes for an effective department were dashed by a hostile Secretary of the Interior, who recommended to Congress that the Department of Education be abolished. Two years later an appropriations bill ended the independent existence of the department and made it a bureau under the Department of the Interior. The Commissioner's salary was reduced from $4,000 to $3,000, and his staff from three to two clerks. Under these circumstances, Barnard resigned. He was succeeded by General John Eaton, who served until 1886. During Eaton's term the bureau was expanded, appropriations were increased, additional clerks and specialists were employed until the staff numbered thirty-eight, and the library was increased from a hundred volumes to eighteen thousand volumes and forty-seven thousand pamphlets.

In one of his first speeches, Eaton clearly defined the role of the national government in education, a role which the Office of Education and the federal government have followed closely for nearly a century. Although the federal government should do nothing "calculated to decrease local or individual effort for education," it "may fitly stimulate the whole to a higher emulation, and seek that the excellencies of one may be attained by all." On the other hand, it "may not suffer either the local or general prevalence of ignorance." It was responsible for education in the territories and the District of Columbia and among the Indians. The major role of the Bureau of Education would be the collection and dissemination of information about education, both in the United States and abroad. Eaton pointed out that early national grants had not been wisely spent and advocated that the states account for federal aid granted for educational purposes.

[32] *14 Statutes at Large*, p. 434.

> Had the national government, from the first donation or aid, simply required a report of the management of all grants bestowed and deposits made, there would have been much better use made of them and vastly greater benefits accrued to her youth and citizens.

In the tradition of federal aid in the past, "The National Government may use either the public domain or the money received from its sale for the benefit of education." Finally he left a big "loophole" category of federal responsibility.

> The Government may take . . . such exceptional action as exceptional circumstances may require, (*a*) for the public welfare, (*b*) for the assurance of a Republican form of government, . . . (*f*) for the equality of all men before the law, and (*g*) for the fitting of any citizen for any responsibility the nation may impose on him.[33]

The bureau was removed from the Department of the Interior to a separate and independent Office in 1930, then to a bureau in the Federal Security Agency in 1939, and finally into the newly organized Department of Health, Education, and Welfare in 1953. It has rendered valuable service in collecting information and advising school officials, and it has never developed into the monster of control that many of its opponents predicted it would, although large grants authorized by various acts, beginning with those of 1965, are enticing universities and school systems to move in directions approved by the United States Office of Education.

Proposals for Federal Financing of Public Schools

The educational problems of the South were the subject of speeches at virtually every education meeting in the nation during the period from 1865 to 1890, and resolutions to Congress calling for federal assistance to Southern schools were sent by Southern state legislatures as well as educational associations. Some cold, hard facts supporting these resolutions were the poverty of the South, the high ratio of children to adults in the South, and the great number of illiterates throughout the nation but especially in the South. In the 1880's the per capita taxable wealth in the Northern and Western states was $2,225, while in the South it was only $851. In the South in 1880 there were 1,242 persons under 21 years of age for every thousand adults; in the North there

[33] "The Relation of the National Government to Public Education," *Proceedings of the National Teachers Association*, 1857–1870, pp. 778–782, 785–789.

were only 909 minors per thousand adults. In the nation in 1870 there were over five and a half million illiterates, and over four million of them were in the South. Among the former slave states, over 42 percent of the population were illiterate, compared with less than 8 percent in the Northern states and 15 percent in the Pacific states. By 1880 the percentage of illiterates in the South had decreased by 5 percent, but population growth resulted in an increase of over half a million illiterates in the decade.[34]

The closing of the Freedmen's Bureau in 1870 ended direct federal participation in the educational problems of the South. The National Association of School Superintendents that year passed a resolution calling on Congress to extend the life of the Freedmen's Bureau and to equalize in some manner the educational funds of the states. In 1870–1871 Congress received thirty-two petitions, all from the South, requesting federal aid for "the establishment of common schools in the southern States."

In a speech before the National Teachers' Association in 1870, United States Commissioner of Education John Eaton detailed some of the educational problems of the nation, and while there were some failures in the North, it was in the South that he found the least progress. Delaware had no state supervision and no provision for education of Negroes. Maryland was "educating colored children only in Baltimore." Virginia was "just putting a free school law on her statute book." West Virginia was "upon the point of striking from her system its right arm, county supervision." Kentucky's new school law had no provision for Negro children. Tennessee provided only "the most inefficient county action, outside her largest cities." North Carolina had a school law but "not a school in the country districts, directly under the auspices of the state law," and South Carolina was only "slightly in advance." Georgia was just where it had been before the War. Alabama's schools were "so connected with the old order of private schools, as to rob it of much of its freedom of action, and prevent its highest usefulness." Florida's legislature had not provided for a levy of school tax. Mississippi was just writing a school law. Arkansas had a system of schools, but it was only partly organized. Louisiana had only seventy-five schools outside of New Orleans. Texas had no school legislation, "the Senate refusing to confirm the Superintendent nominated by the Governor." "All over this southern section," there was "not only lack of educational sentiment, but positive hostility to instruction and instructors." Even though this

[34] Gordon Canfield Lee, *The Struggle for Federal Aid: First Phase* (New York: Teachers College, Columbia U. Press, 1949), pp. 30–32.

may not have been a fair and objective appraisal of the facts, it is an indication of the widespread feeling in 1870 that education should "no longer be excluded from the topics of congressional discussion."[35]

In response to this public pressure, Representative George F. Hoar, Massachusetts Republican, introduced a bill in 1870 designed "to establish a national system of education." Unlike almost all other bills, before and since, regarding federal participation in public education, this bill would have created stringent federal controls. Under Hoar's proposal the President would appoint a "State superintendent of national schools" in each state. The state superintendent would divide the state into divisions generally corresponding to Congressional districts and administered by a "division inspector of national schools" appointed by the Secretary of the Interior and districts of "convenient size" administered by a local superintendent of national schools appointed by the Secretary of the Interior. Every child would have the opportunity to attend school six months in each year. Schoolbooks would be prescribed by the state superintendent under the direction of the Commissioner of Education, and any child whose parents could not pay for his books would have them supplied by the system. "No books shall be used in any of the national schools, nor shall any instruction be given therein calculated to favor the peculiar tenets of any religious sect." The national schools would be financed by a direct tax levied by the federal government, provided that "all sums of money assessed and raised in each State by virtue of this act shall be expended therein for the purposes of education." If in the judgment of the President "there is established in said State a system of common schools which provides reasonably, for all the children therein," "no further steps should be taken for the appointment of officers or the assessing of the tax therein."[36]

The bill was almost universally opposed. Southerners viewed it as another Reconstruction imposition. Educators feared its consequences, and the National Education Association, which favored federal aid for the common schools, but without controls, took a strong stand against it. During the debates no vote was ever taken on the bill, and it died. Perhaps Hoar never intended that his bill should pass. From his speeches it appears that he may simply have been goading the states into doing something about the school situation. The threat scared more than the South, and the immediate and almost universal opposition to any kind of control over schools imposed from Washington is noteworthy. No subsequent proposal for federal aid attempted to institute similar con-

[35] Eaton, pp. 793–794.
[36] Knight and Hall, pp. 728–732.

trols, and even the prospect of federal aid has usually generated concern about the controls. Hoar may have been indirectly responsible for the failure of subsequent federal aid legislation, for the opponents of such aid always conjure up the spectre of Hoar's controls.

In spite of the failure of the Hoar Bill, President Grant sent a message to Congress in 1875 calling for a constitutional amendment which would have required the states "to afford the opportunity of a good common school education for every child within their limits." The proposed amendment provided that "no sectarian tenets shall ever be taught in any school supported in whole or in part by the State, nation, or by proceeds of any tax levied upon any community." It made attendance virtually compulsory by depriving "all persons who can not read and write from becoming voters after the year 1890, disfranchising none, however, on the grounds of illiteracy, who may be voters at the time this amendment takes effect." Congressman James G. Blaine introduced a resolution proposing an amendment making clear the separation of church and state in tax-supported schools. The resolution omitted any reference to the literacy standard proposed by Grant. It passed the House August 4, 1876, by a vote of 180 yeas to 7 nays. Three days later the Senate voted 28 to 16 in favor of a similar resolution, but since this was not the required two-thirds majority, the resolution failed to be adopted.[37]

The problem of education in the South still vexed the nation, and in 1872 Congressman Legrand W. Perce, Mississippi Republican, introduced a bill to establish an educational fund endowed by the sale of public lands, the proceeds to be used for the free education of children between the ages of six and sixteen. For the first ten years, the money was to be apportioned on the basis of relative illiteracy. The money could be used for teachers' "wages," except that a certain amount might be used for maintaining institutions for the training of common-school teachers. An important amendment specified that money could *not* be withheld from states which provided separate schools for different races or prohibited "mixed" schools. This was a recognition, even in the period of Radical Reconstruction, of the practice of school segregation. Opposition to the bill was based on fiscal arguments and the fear of controls, particularly by the South, which suspected a scheme to bring "mixed" schools eventually. Although the bill passed the House, it never came to a vote in the Senate.

In 1879 Senator Ambrose E. Burnside, Rhode Island Republican, introduced a bill to establish an educational fund from the proceeds of

[37] *Report of the U.S. Commissioner of Education for 1892–1893*, p. 1294.

public lands and surplus revenues from the Patent Office. The interest from this fund was to be applied to public education and colleges for the advancement of scientific and industrial education. Like the Perce bill, it encountered opposition. It did attract the support of the forces of industry, and with their backing, it passed the Senate by a vote of 41 to 6. However, because of opposition by the leadership of the House, it never reached the floor of that body.

Even if the Perce and Burnside bills had passed, they would have provided only a fraction of the financial aid the Southern schools needed, and educators and Southern leaders continued to urge Congress to provide federal aid. The National Education Association held its 1881 meeting in Atlanta, and Georgia's Senator Joseph E. Brown's brief speech of welcome included a plea for federal aid.

> At the close of the war we had turned from slavery into freedom four million colored people. . . . Now they are citizens, and it is our interest, our wish, and our duty to make the best citizens in our power of them. . . . But you see we were too poor to do much for them. The interest of the union requires their education, and now I ask the whole union to come up and help us to educate them. . . .
>
> We in Georgia have adopted a system that has met the approbation of our colored friends. By a compromise between the white and colored people it was agreed that the colored people should not send any pupils to the State university at Athens. . . . In our constitution we have pledged one colored university in the State. We have the white and colored separate in our city schools, and soon we will give the colored schools colored teachers, and we shall make the experiment of giving them a colored superintendent. The only trouble is we have not the money to do what both races desire to do.[38]

Brown's speech led to a resolution calling for federal aid not unlike that proposed by the Perce bill in 1872. The resolution was adopted unanimously by the convention.

The high point in the efforts to secure federal aid for common schools came during the 1880's. Senator Logan of Illinois introduced a bill specifying that all revenue from taxes on distilled spirits be used for education and requiring states to enact compulsory attendance laws to qualify for the aid. Two proposals in the House of Representatives, the Updegraff bill in 1882 and the Sherwin bill in 1883,

[38] N.E.A. *Proceedings*, 1881, pp. 158–159.

provided a temporary appropriation of $10,000,000 for five years to be made from the national treasury for the support of free common schools. But none of these bills received more than cursory consideration.

The real champion of federal aid was Senator Henry W. Blair, of New Hampshire, who introduced a bill providing for temporary federal aid to schools in each Congress from 1882 to 1890. His bills proposed that the aid be divided among the states in proportion to the number of known illiterates in each state. He recognized the practice of racial segregation, requiring that states which maintained separate schools must apportion their share of federal money according to the ratio of Negro to white children. While the grants were to be administered by state and local authorities, the bills required that the money be spent for non-sectarian common schools which must teach certain subjects, for training of teachers, and, for the first year only, for buildings. Although there were some differences among the various bills, particularly in the form of amendments, they were substantially the same.

There was considerable public support for the bills. Between 1881 and 1888, no fewer than 1,419 petitions were registered in Congress supporting federal aid to common schools, 620 of them from the South. They included statements from business, religious groups, labor organizations, and state governments, as well as educational associations. Many newspapers, particularly in the South and in New England, were outspoken in favor of Blair's bills, which passed the Senate three times: in 1884 by a vote of 33-11; in 1886 by 36-11; and in 1888 by 39-29. But each bill was blocked in the House of Representatives by an unfriendly Committee on Education.[39]

The Senate debates on the Blair bills included the traditional arguments for and against federal aid. Among the arguments in favor were the following: (1) a democracy requires a literate electorate; (2) federal aid is constitutional under the "general welfare" clause; (3) there was ample precedent for such aid; (4) it was the logical consequence of the War and of the federal government's freeing the slaves and making them citizens; (5) it would help reduce illiteracy throughout the nation; (6) it would aid states and as they become better able to help themselves, the aid would be reduced; and (7) since states could refuse the grants, federal controls would not be imposed unless the states accepted them. The opposition argued that such legislation would (1) undermine the foundations of democratic government by making the states dependent on the national government; (2) be unconstitutional; (3) have no precedents, for land grants were different from the proposed direct appropri-

[39] Lee, pp. 89–95, 157.

ations; (4) introduce party politics and racial issues into the public schools; (5) lead to all sorts of other demands on the federal government, including labor organizations seeking government charity for unemployed men; (6) not be needed because the South was already slowly improving its educational facilities; (7) be unjust, for it would tax states with good school systems to help support schools in states that were less advanced; (8) destroy local initiative; (9) be diverted to other purposes because there were *not sufficient controls* in the bill; (10) demand that states relinquish their power over schools because the bill had *too many controls;* and (11) create difficult problems for the states by establishing school systems beyond the means of states when the temporary aid ceased.[40] It is somewhat ironic that whenever the issue of federal aid arises so much time is spent in quarrelling over unsupported opinions and so little attention is given to a reasonable discussion of the needs and related past experiences.

Two successful bills which were related to education were the second Morrill Act of 1890 and the Hatch Act, which established agricultural experiment stations in 1887. These served only a very specialized educational purpose, and the federal government did nothing substantive about the common schools and the great blight of illiteracy in the nation. By the 1890's the conservatives were firmly entrenched in the Congressional halls, and the hope of federal participation in the education of the children of America was ended temporarily.

The Supreme Court and School Segregation

The Fourteenth Amendment, which gave rise to Reconstruction policies, has been the source of much conflict as the courts have attempted to interpret the "equal protection" clause. After defining all persons born in the United States as citizens, the first section of the Amendment states:

> No State shall make or enforce any law which shall abridge the privileges or immunities of citizens of the United States . . . nor deny any person within its jurisdiction the equal protection of the laws.

The first cases based on "equal protection" came in 1873. One was a suit brought by New Orleans butchers against an exclusive privilege granted one company to slaughter animals in and around the city. The

[40] *Ibid.*, pp. 149–155.

Supreme Court ruled that the amendment was solely for the purpose of protecting freedmen from discrimination on the basis of color, applied only to Negroes as individuals and not as a class, and applied only to matters related to national citizenship.[41]

Within the year the Supreme Court ruled on a case of individual discrimination in transportation. Catherine Brown, a Negro woman, had been ejected from the "white car" of a two-car railroad train in Virginia. The cars were identical; actually, the one used for whites when the train was going in one direction was used for Negroes when it returned. The Court decided that separate facilities, even though identical, could not be construed as equal.[42] But in 1878, the Court reversed itself on the matter of separate accommodations. A Mississippi River steamboat passenger was denied use of a cabin designated for whites, thereby violating a Louisiana Reconstruction law prohibiting segregation by races. The Supreme Court ruled that such state laws were a handicap to interstate commerce, and the Mississippi was used for interstate commerce. In the decision, the Court took note of an Ohio Supreme Court decision regarding segregation of schools by Ohio law.

> Substantial equality of right is the law of the State and of the United States but equality does not mean identity. . . .
>
> Under that law, colored children were not admitted . . . into the schools for white children. . . . The Supreme Court of the State held that it worked no substantial inequality of school privileges . . . that equality of rights does not involve the necessity of educating white and colored persons in the same school . . . that any classification which preserved substantially equal school advantages is not prohibited by either State or Federal Constitution, nor would it contravene the provisions of either.[43]

The Court seemed to go out of its way in that decision to put the stamp of approval on the concept of separate schools.

The most famous of the nineteenth-century cases on "separate but equal" facilities also involved transportation. In Louisiana in 1892, Homer Plessy, of one-eighth African descent, attempted to board a coach reserved for white passengers. He was forcibly ejected and jailed, and his suit reached the Supreme Court in 1896. The Court, in affirming the principle of separate but equal facilities, made particular note of schools.

[41] *Slaughter-House Cases,* 16 Wallace 36 (1873).
[42] *Railroad Company v. Brown,* 17 Wallace 451–453 (1873).
[43] *Hall v. De Cuir,* 5 Otto 503, 504.

> The object of the amendment was undoubtedly to enforce the absolute equality of the two races before the law, but in the nature of things it could not have been intended to abolish distinctions based upon color, or to enforce social, as distinguished from political equality, or a commingling of the two races upon terms unsatisfactory to either. Laws permitting, and even requiring, their separation in places where they are liable to be brought into contact do not necessarily imply the inferiority of either race to the other. . . . The most common instance of this is connected with the establishment of separate schools for white and colored children, which has been held to be a valid exercise of the legislative power.[44]

The decision was clearly a legal justification for segregated schools, and the dissenting opinion of Justice John Marshall Harlan reflected the only tinge of liberalism in a Court predominantly conservative in a conservative age.

> I deny that any legislative body or judicial tribunal may have regard to the race of citizens when the civil rights of those citizens are involved. . . .
>
> The white race deems itself to be the dominant race in this country. . . . But in view of the Constitution, in the eye of the law, there is in this country no superior, dominant, ruling class of citizens. There is no caste here. Our Constitution is color-blind, and neither knows nor tolerates classes among citizens. . . .
>
> The arbitrary separation of citizens, on the basis of race, while they are on a public highway, is a badge of servitude wholly inconsistent with the civil freedom and the equality before the law established by the Constitution. It cannot be justified upon any legal grounds. . . .
>
> We boast of the freedom enjoyed by our people above all other peoples. But it is difficult to reconcile that boast with a state of the law which, practically, puts the brand of servitude and degradation upon a large class of our fellow-citizens, our equals before the law. The thin disguise of "equal" accommodations . . . will not mislead any one, nor atone for the wrong this day done.[45]

Prophetically Harlan warned that segregation by law would "arouse race hate" and "certainly create and perpetuate a feeling of distrust between the races." But separate schools became the national pattern. Seventeen states and the District of Columbia required schools segre-

[44] *Plessy v. Ferguson,* 163 U.S. 544 (1896).
[45] *Ibid.,* 555, 559, 562.

gated by race, four more states made school segregation optional, and many Northern states with large Negro populations operated segregated schools through careful districting. Virtually nowhere, South or North, was there much more than a pretense at equality in the separate schools.

Richmond County, Georgia, had approximately four hundred Negro children in 1897 who could not be accommodated in the existing elementary school for Negroes. Instead of building additional classrooms, the county board of education closed the Negro high school, which it had been assisting since 1880, and in place of the sixty high school pupils who had been attending, two hundred elementary children were enrolled. County assistance was continued for the white high school. (Both Negro and white high schools had charged tuition to help support the schools.) Negro parents sought an injunction preventing the board from using tax money to assist the white high school while no corresponding school existed for Negroes. The Supreme Court ruled in 1899 that the board's decision as to how to spend what money it had was one which seemed to favor the larger number of Negro children, that the injunction would serve only to harm the white children without securing better schooling for the Negroes, and that education was a state matter except where there was a clear and unmistakable violation of federal law. Justice Harlan, who wrote the decision, seemed disappointed that the plaintiffs sought relief in a manner which could not be justified by federal powers.

> If, in some appropriate proceeding instituted directly for that purpose, the plaintiffs had sought to compel the Board . . . to establish and maintain a high school for colored children, and if it appeared that the Board's refusal to maintain such a school was in fact an abuse of its discretion and in hostility to the colored population because of their race, different questions might have arisen.[46]

For a combination of reasons, the "appropriate" proceedings seem not to have been initiated, and the legal foundations of the separate but obviously unequal school system were not undermined until 1954.

Consequences of Southern Success and Failure

In many ways the South made progress in developing public education by the end of the century, providing more than a mere token of schooling even for the suppressed Nego population. Although there

[46] *175 U.S.* 543–544 (1899).

was the incentive of outside aid, most of the advances of the South resulted from the efforts of local and state governments. The accomplishments prove what can be done by a people who sincerely desire schooling, even when financing, staffing, and building schools seem virtually impossible.

On the other hand, the failure bred out of racial feelings is one of the greatest tragedies of American intellectual history. It is impossible to calculate the loss of human potential, white and Negro, resulting from the two separate, unequal, and inadequate school systems.

Given the quality of Southern schools, it was not surprising that Southern World War I draftees, both white and Negro, fell far below the national average as measured by Army intelligence tests. Indeed, the cumulative effects of the attempt to maintain separate schools will be felt for many generations. The results of the conservative reaction to the revolution of the common man were observable throughout the nation; but in the South, where the reaction was most intense, the educational damage was the greatest.

QUESTIONS FOR DISCUSSION

1. Compare and contrast the federal government's educational policies during the Reconstruction period with those of the American government in Germany and Japan following World War II. Which provides the better model should there be a future situation similar to these? Why?
2. How did the social, political, and educational policies during the Reconstruction period intensify the problems of developing a universal educational system in the South? How did they promote universal education?
3. Compare Booker T. Washington's educational policies with those of modern Negro integration leaders. Were Washington's policies appropriate for his time? Would they be today? Why or why not?
4. What historical backgrounds for the modern problems of school integration are derived from the period of Reconstruction?
5. There is an obvious current trend toward federal aid to education. What arguments and issues from the 1870's and 1880's might be relevant to the problems of federal aid today?
6. Relatively small sums of money from philanthropic funds did much to influence the development of education in the South after the Civil War. What analogies might be made with the similarly proportionately small federal grants and philanthropic gifts offered to schools and universities today? What warnings might be suggested?

SUGGESTED READINGS

Secondary Sources

Bond, Horace Mann. *The Education of the Negro in the American Social Order*. New York: Prentice-Hall, 1934. Chapters I–VIII.

Dabney, Charles William. *Universal Education in the South*. Chapel Hill: U. of North Carolina Press, 1936. Vol. I, Chapters VII–XXII; Vol. II, Chapters IX, XXVIII.

Good, Harry G. *A History of American Education*. New York: Macmillan, 1962. Chapter IX.

Knight, Edgar W. *Public Education in the South*. New York: Ginn, 1922. Chapters IX–XII.

Lee, Gordon Canfield. *The Struggle for Federal Aid: First Phase*. New York: Teachers College Bureau of Publication, 1949.

Rice, Jesse Pearl. *J. L. M. Curry*. New York: King's Crown Press, 1949.

Primary Sources

Cubberley, Ellwood P. *Readings in Public Education in the United States*. Boston: Houghton Mifflin, 1934. Readings 239–242.

Fleming, Walter L. *Documentary History of Reconstruction*. Cleveland: Arthur H. Clark, 1907. Vol. II, pp. 165–212.

Gross, Carl H., and Chandler, Charles C. *The History of American Education Through Readings*. Boston: Heath, 1964. Pp. 300–305.

Knight, Edgar W., and Hall, Clifton L. *Readings in American Educational History*. New York: Appleton-Century-Crofts, 1951. Pp. 673–685, 728–736.

Washington, Booker T. *Up From Slavery, An Autobiography*. New York: Doubleday, Doran, 1938.

PART Five

"Soars Upward Still"

CHRONOLOGY

1900—Population of the United States 75,994,575
1901–1909—Administration of Theodore Roosevelt
1903—Wright brothers' flight at Kitty Hawk
1907—Oklahoma admitted to the Union
1907—Lee DeForest patents the vacuum tube.
1909–1913—Administration of William H. Taft
1909—Ford begins mass production of the Model T.
1910—Population of the United States 91,972,266
1912—Arizona and New Mexico admitted to the Union
1913–1921—Administration of Woodrow Wilson
1913—Ratification of the 16th Amendment (income tax) and the 17th Amendment (direct election of Senators)
1917—United States enters World War I.
1918—Armistice declared
1920—Population of the United States 105,710,620
1920—Ratification of 19th Amendment (women's suffrage)
1921–1929—Administrations of Warren Harding and Calvin Coolidge
1929–1933—Administration of Herbert Hoover
1929—Stock market crash
1930—Population of the United States 122,775,046
1933–1945—Administration of Franklin D. Roosevelt
1935—Congress of Industrial Organizations founded
1940—Population of the United States 131,669,275
1941—Attack on Pearl Harbor
1945–1953—Administration of Harry Truman
1945—United Nations Conference at San Francisco
1945—Atomic attack on Japan
1945—End of World War II
1950—Population of the United States 150,697,361
1950—McCarran-Nixon Bill to control "subversives" passed over Truman's veto
1950–1953—Korean War
1953–1960—Administration of Dwight D. Eisenhower
1957—Russian satellite put into orbit
1958—First American satellite in orbit
1959—Alaska and Hawaii admitted to the Union
1960—Population of the United States 179,323,175
1961–1963—Administration of John F. Kennedy
1963– —Administration of Lyndon B. Johnson

THE FIRST TWO REVOLUTIONARY CYCLES in the history of the United States are quite clear: the first culminated in the Revolution of 1776 and was followed by the conservative reaction of Federalism; the second climaxed in the Civil War and was followed by the conservative Gilded Age. Within the present century the perspective becomes blurred and analysis more difficult. Perhaps the United States has undergone two abortive social revolutions, or perhaps it has been only one interrupted by great wars. A definite revolutionary movement developed in the 1890's with the Populist Party and then William Jennings Bryan and the Democratic Party. It reached an accelerated stage in 1912 at the election of Wilson and the first months of his administration. But World War I ended—or set back—that progressive surge, and the administrations of Harding, Coolidge, and Hoover were definitely conservative. During the 1930's the revolutionary aspect of American society disturbed a number of sociologists and economists, who feared that the United States was heading for a revolution not unlike the one Russia underwent in 1917. Then came World War II, perhaps averting revolution where the piecemeal measures were only forestalling it. Once more a period of conservatism followed the War, exemplified in the McCarthyist movements and the "respectability" of groups like the John Birch Society. Threats, insinuations, and loyalty oaths have been used to coerce social conformity and silence new and unconventional ideas.

There is much to suggest that the twentieth century has actually been one revolutionary cycle, interrupted and renewed. The fact that the conservatism of the 1950's may be giving way to a new liberalism in the civil rights movement among the Negroes and many young whites suggests that this latter movement is actually a continuation of the liberalism seen in the earlier part of the century. There are three threads which characterize the progressive surges of the present century: (1) a broadening of the base of political participation; (2) "collectivizing" American social and economic life; and (3) using government as an agent for social progress.

Broadening the Base of Political Participation

Although the common man received the right to vote in the nineteenth century, the political machinery of the nation placed the real power in the hands of a few. Until the adoption of the Australian ballot between 1888 (Massachusetts) and 1910 (when its use was general), there was virtually no secret ballot in America. Bosses also controlled officeholders by determining who would be candidates through the "backroom" caucuses until primary elections, first adopted statewide in Wisconsin in 1903, gave the voters a greater chance to have an effective choice in voting. Demands for more efficient city government, free from the corruption characteristic of many city halls and state houses, led reformers to seek and secure home rule for cities. The Seventeenth Amendment provided for the direct election of Senators by the voters instead of by state legislatures, and the Nineteenth Amendment enfranchized women. The current civil rights movement has continued this broadening of the political process by massive campaigns to persuade Negroes to register and by local and national struggles to remove barriers to Negro voting.

Collectivizing American Life

In a complex industrial culture, Americans have found it necessary to organize into groups to carry on their social functions. The individual has become lost insofar as his social, political, and economic influence is concerned. In place of the individual there is the group or association, often a corporate body, a legal entity designed to produce, distribute, consume, control, entertain, influence, and educate. Private enterprise of the type where the owner controlled and managed his business has given ways to corporate enterprise, where ownership and management are often completely separated. The individual worker is now represented by his labor union and management by the Chamber of Commerce and the National Association of Manufacturers. Every profession has its organization to promote its collective interests. Consumers' cooperatives and credit unions, veterans' organizations, civic clubs, religious societies, vocational interest groups, bowling leagues, golf clubs, bridge clubs, "golden age" clubs, ethnic societies and racial associations—all these and many, many more "collectives" characterize modern American society.

Government as an Agent for Social Progress

Up to the close of the nineteenth century, the generally accepted role of government was as an agency for adjudicating internal disputes and defending the nation against outside aggression. In the twentieth century the American collectives, from the Chamber of Commerce to the American Federation of Labor-Congress of Industrial Organizations and from the National Association of Realtors to the National Association for the Advancement of Colored People, have adopted the political "lobby" and legislation as the primary means of advancing their own goals in seeking the welfare of the society.

The use of federal government for social reform reached its first high point in the opening months of the Wilson administration with the graduated income tax, antitrust legislation, the creation of a Federal Trade Commission to investigate corporations engaged in interstate commerce, and the Federal Reserve Act of 1913. This last reform placed control of the currency of the United States in the hands of the government and away from the private bankers, a step which brought strong protests from the bankers and cries of "socialism." Congress and state legislatures passed laws limiting the length of the work day and work week, setting minimum standards for safety in certain jobs, and restricting the use of child and female labor.

The collapse of the stock market in October, 1929, brought the United States to a new crisis, and even under the administration of Hoover, some radical reforms were begun as measures to relieve the financial depression. Under the Roosevelt New Deal, reforms continued with the national government a principal agent in providing economic security and a better life for the masses of the American people and limiting severely the power and wealth of the few. The outbreak of World War II changed the agencies and the direction of their efforts, but the extension of government as an agent for social progress was accelerated. Opponents called the trend the "welfare state"; proponents spoke of it as "social democracy." Both generally recognized that the promotion of public progress had become one of the most important responsibilities of government, particularly the national government.

Many specialized interest groups in the "collectivized" America sought government assistance toward what they believed to be the "general welfare" of society—highways, tax concessions, industrial subsidies, wage or price controls, research grants, school aid, an almost infinite number of proposals by one group or another for government support.

Effect of the Progressive Revolution on American Education

As there has been an increasing concern with "democratizing" our political system, so has there been much interest in making the American schools more democratic in the content of the curriculum, the methods of presentation, the purposes of schools, and the attitudes toward children. This democratic trend has been observable in both theory and practice, although many times the practice has represented a poor application of the theory.

The social pressures of the "collectives" in securing school programs suited to the particular interests of this or that group have resulted in a curriculum which has been broadened tremendously in attempts to serve all the organizations in our society. The extra-curricular program has also grown in proportion to the encouragement offered by the special interest groups. Each group sees its suggestion for the schools justified and doubts the wisdom of the prescriptions of other groups, leading to bitter conflicts among the critics of the schools. Practical businessmen's associations and labor unions doubt the value of Latin and of literature; academic societies indict the schools for teaching typewriting and auto repair. The WCTU calls for lectures against liquor and tobacco, and churches in some communities expect schools to indoctrinate students with non-denominational religious orthodoxy. Delegations call upon the school board and lobby with the legislatures; objectors go to court to seek injunctions; organizations set up school contests and offer prizes for students who best parrot what the organizations want them to learn; free material propagandizing all kinds of special interests deluge the teachers' mail boxes; teachers, schools, and children are enticed, threatened, cajoled, and pressured in a dozen conflicting directions at once.

Increasingly these groups have relied on indirect pressure through state and national government to attempt to remake the schools in their own image. Laws are passed requiring schools to teach driver training, physical education, or American history; to admit all children regardless of race, sex, social class, or level of intelligence; to encourage teachers to specialize in a particular subject by subsidizing their professional preparation. Governmental controls have become a reality in American education. However, these controls are not the result of some sinister conspiracy, as some of the special interest groups warn; there is no singleness of purpose and direction which might result from the coordinated efforts of a conspiracy. Instead, the controls are a conflicting confusion of *ad hoc* requirements developing from the particular programs of many divergent interest groups in our society. Since American society has so many conflicting purposes, the schools, which are the agents of the society, are also suffering from conflicting goals, methods which are inconsistent with goals, and indecision on many questions of basic educational policy.

SUGGESTED READINGS

Beard, Charles A., and Beard, Mary R. *The Rise of American Civilization.* New York: Macmillan, 1930. Vol. II, pp. 337–341, 543–608, 665–667, 674–680, 692–704, 730–732, 735–740.

Johnson, Gerald W. *Incredible Tale.* New York: Harper, 1950. Pp. 8–14, 38–44, 105–107, 133–137, 144–148, 158–196, 206–212.

Nevins, Allan, and Commager, Henry Steele. *A Pocket History of the United States.* New York: Washington Square Press, 1960. Pp. 341–376, 397–400, 414–437, 490–492, 518–530, 546–550, 553–555, 557–558.

Rugg, Harold. *Foundations of American Education.* New York: World Book, 1947. Part Three.

13

Expansion of Educational Opportunity

Though there have been some minor changes in the organization and structure of American education in the twentieth century—notably the junior high school and the junior college—the basic American educational pattern evolved between 1830 to 1860, a single track from elementary school through secondary school to college. The educational revolution of the present century has been in enrollment, goals and purposes, curriculum, financing, methods, and public attitude toward schooling. Lawrence A. Cremin indicates ten major new developments in American schooling: the extension of educational opportunity downward and upward, the introduction of the junior high school, the expansion of both curricular and extracurricular opportunities, greater flexibility in grouping students, the use of guidance services, more activity and informality in classroom procedure, new and more varied instructional materials, improved school architecture, better teacher preparation, and specialization in school administration.[1] None of these involves a major shift in the concept of American education, but taken together they have resulted in schools and school practices vastly different from those of 1900.

Reorganization of the American School System

While there have been no major changes in the administrative structure of American education, increasing enrollments and new purposes

[1] *The Transformation of the School* (New York: Knopf, 1961), pp. 306–308.

have called for some shifts in the patterns of school organization. Improved means of transportation, particularly the motor bus and the paved highway, have made it possible to consolidate rural schools. The expansion of secondary education to include children with goals other than college preparation has created problems which the junior high school and junior college were organized to solve.

Consolidation of District Schools

In the late nineteenth century, educators began to seek ways of eliminating the ineffective one-room district schools, particularly where there was enough concentration of population to permit the creation of "union" schools. The horse-drawn wagon-omnibus limited the size and extent of these schools outside of towns. The twentieth-century motor bus and improved roads encouraged the trend toward consolidation, especially after 1920. The number of one-room school buildings in the United States was reduced from 189,227 in 1920 to 133,223 in 1936. In 1920 one-room schools made up 70 percent of the number of school buildings in use in the United States; in 1936 one-room schools accounted for only 56 percent of the total. By 1962, the number had dropped to only 13,333 or about 10.5 percent of the total number of public schools.[2]

The Junior High School

Perhaps the most important twentieth-century innovation in school reorganization is the junior high school. In August, 1909, Columbus, Ohio, established a junior high school consisting of the seventh, eighth, and ninth grades. Since then there has been a steady increase in the number of junior high schools, and a marked trend away from the traditional 8-4 or 7-4 organization to a 6-3-3 or 6-6 organization. In 1920 there were 13,421 regular four-year public high schools in the United States, making up 93.7 percent of the total number of public secondary schools; there were 55 junior high schools, or 0.4 percent. In 1930 there were 16,460 regular high schools, 1,842 junior highs, and 3,287 junior-senior highs. In 1952, for the first time, the number of four-year high schools was less than half of the total number. In that year there were 10,168 four-year high schools, making up only 42.8 percent; the 3,227 junior highs (13.6 percent), 1,760 senior highs (7.4 percent), and 8,591 junior-senior highs (36.2 percent) made a total of 57.2 percent.[3] In 1959, there

[2] U.S. Office of Education, *Bulletin,* 1938, No. 10, p. 257. *Statistical Abstract of the United States,* 1965 (Washington: Bureau of the Census, 1965) p. 106.

[3] U.S. Office of Education, *Biennial Survey, 1950–52,* Chapter 5, pp. 22–23.

were 6,044 (24.9 percent) high schools on the 8-4 system, 1,407 (5.8 percent) high schools on the 6-2-4 system, 1,651 (6.8 percent) senior high schools on the 6-3-3 system, 5,027 (20.7 percent) junior high schools on the 6-2-4 and 6-3-3 systems, and 10,155 (41.8 percent) junior-senior high schools on the 6-6 system.[4]

A number of communities in New York, Illinois, Florida, California, and Massachusetts are experimenting with "Middle Schools," the middle grades on a 4-4-4 or a 5-3-4 plan. In New York City this is being tried as a means of reducing *de facto* racial segregation, but in other communities it is defended on the grounds that the elementary school is no longer challenging to many pre-adolescent fifth and sixth graders, and that they need an organization which permits greater flexibility.

The Junior College

When the University of Chicago was reopened in 1892 under the presidency of William Rainey Harper, the freshman and sophomore years were known as the "academic college," with the upper two years called the "university college." In 1896 these names were changed to "junior" and "senior college," and the degree of Associate in Arts was granted students on completion of the junior division. In 1902 Joliet, Illinois, established a public junior college under the leadership of J. Stanley Brown, Joliet Superintendent of Schools and close friend of Harper. When the United States Office of Education began collecting data on junior colleges in 1917, it reported 46, enrolling 4,504 students; 14 were publicly controlled and 32 were private. In the fall of 1964 there were 357 public junior colleges with 555,082 students and 216 private ones with 74,548 students. Approximately 16 percent of the total number of students in higher education were enrolled in junior colleges.[5] In 1965–1966, fifty new junior colleges were opened in the United States, bringing the total to 771. They enrolled 1,292,753 students, an increase of 22.6 percent over 1964–1965.[6]

Goals and Curriculum

The real significance of the reorganized schools lies in the changing purposes and curriculum of the new institutions, made necessary by the expansion of enrollments.

[4] *Statistical Abstract*, 1965, p. 127.

[5] U.S. Office of Education, *Bulletin 1964*, No. 18, pp. 74, 84. See also *Statistical Abstract*, 1965, p. 127.

[6] Garland G. Parker, "Statistics of Attendance in American Universities and Colleges, 1965–66," *School and Society*, 94 (January 8, 1966): 20.

Elementary Education

The changes in elementary schools can be more accurately described as changes in attitudes toward children and in the methods of teaching than changes in content. Children still spend most of their time on the basic tool subjects of reading, writing, and arithmetic, with less time devoted to spelling and increasingly more time to social studies and science or nature study. Music and art or drawing are often taught by visiting teachers, who make the rounds of the schools at weekly or other infrequent intervals. Physical education is generally relegated to the free play at recess time or at noon, though some city systems have specialists in elementary-school physical education.

The relative stability in broad areas of content does not mean that educators have not been greatly concerned about what elementary-school children learn. Particularly after 1920 there was a confusing amount of experimentation in elementary curriculum. Actually, much of this experimentation might be described as "tinkering," for it was not the result of careful and disciplined research and had little or no truly theoretical basis. Almost every teacher-training institution organized a "curriculum laboratory," which cranked out a bewildering array of proposals for reorganizing elementary curriculum. Edgar W. Knight lists no fewer than thirty-six proposals for curriculum changes.[7] Many of the various schemes were internally inconsistent, in sharp conflict with other proposals, and soon went into oblivion, if indeed they ever attracted any serious support among the practicing school people.

Curriculum by Legislation

One reflection of the political influence which organized interest groups of twentieth-century America have had on schools is the practice of legislative prescriptions and proscriptions affecting the curriculum. Through effective lobbying, small but determined and resourceful minorities have secured passage of many laws which require or prohibit schools from teaching certain subjects. One survey revealed that there were at least 564 such legislative commands in 1903, and that they had increased to 926 by 1923. In 1923, 304 of these were classified as "nationalism," the increase of 108 in the preceding decade due undoubtedly to the effect of World War I. Among the "nationalism" laws were requirements that United States history be taught and proscription of the teaching of German. Except for the 216 legal provisions related to the "fundamental subjects," the next most important area of legislative

[7] *Fifty Years of American Education* (New York: Ronald Press, 1952), p. 74.

enactments about elementary schools was "health and prohibition," with 171 curricular prescriptions. While those dealing with alcohol and narcotics and physiology and hygiene were generally the oldest, the greatest expansion after World War I was in requiring physical education. This increase was due primarily to public concern over the number of World War I draftees rejected for military service on physical grounds. New subjects on the lists of prescriptions ranged from fire prevention to cotton grading.[8]

Educators were naturally disturbed by such legislative enactments. The practice of laymen engaging in curriculum revision when they did not understand the development of children or the processes of learning was termed an "inadvisable" procedure which could "impede or actually prevent" achieving the very goals for which the laws were intended.[9]

As the high school developed into a popular institution, legislative enactments determined secondary curriculum in large measure. Over the years a hodge-podge of laws has been built up in each state, some forgotten, many ignored; but potentially, and sometimes actually, these legislative restrictions are a dangerous interference with wise over-all educational policy. An example are the laws prohibiting the teaching of biological evolution and Darwinism which were passed in Southern states during the early 1920's.

Secondary Education

Although high schools had long offered vocational courses, the major emphasis in both purpose and curriculum of nineteenth-century secondary education was college preparation. The general acceptance of the report of the Committee of Ten points up the preoccupation of most educators with the goals and courses suitable to the minority of students bound for college. With the progressive revolution and the democratization of secondary education, the reorganization of secondary education became imperative. As a result of a report at the N. E. A. meeting in 1911 on the articulation of high school and college, a Commission on the Reorganization of Secondary Education was appointed. In contrast with the college-dominated Committee of Ten, the new commission consisted almost entirely of professors of education and public-school administrators. The commission reported its recommendation in a number of bulletins for each subject field and a small pamphlet entitled *Cardinal Principles of Secondary Education*. This brief document (only

[8] Jesse K. Flanders, *Legislative Control of the Elementary Curriculum* (New York: Teachers College, Columbia U. Press, 1925), pp. 8–9, 66–67, 175–176.
[9] *Ibid.*, pp. 180, 184.

26 pages of text) summarized the changing secondary program. After taking note of the changes in society, in secondary-school population, and in educational and psychological theory, it listed the main objectives of democratic education, outlined the curriculum which should achieve these objectives, and recommended the adoption of the junior high school.

> In order to determine the main objectives that should guide education in a democracy it is necessary to analyze the activities of the individual. Normally . . . he is called upon to engage in activities that enrich the family life, to render important vocational services to his fellows, and to promote the common welfare. . . .
>
> [E]very individual should have a margin of time for the cultivation of personal and social interests. This leisure, if worthily used, will re-create his powers and enlarge and enrich life. . . .
>
> To discharge the duties of life and to benefit from leisure, one must have good health. . . .
>
> There are various processes, such as reading, writing, arithmetical computations, and oral and written expression, that are needed as tools in the affairs of life. . . .
>
> And, finally, the realization of the objectives already named is dependent upon ethical character. . . .
>
> This commission, therefore, regards the following as the main objectives of education: 1. Health. 2. Command of fundamental processes. 3. Worthy home-membership. 4. Vocation. 5. Citizenship. 6. Worthy use of leisure. 7. Ethical character.
>
> The six years to be devoted to secondary education may well be divided into two periods. . . . In the junior period emphasis should be placed upon the attempt to help the pupil to explore his own aptitudes and to make at least provisional choice of the kinds of work to which he will devote himself. In the senior period emphasis should be given to training in the fields thus chosen. This distinction lies at the basis of the organization.
>
> The ideal of a democracy . . . involves, on the one hand, specialization whereby individuals and groups of individuals may become effective in the various vocations and other fields of human endeavor, and, on the other hand, unification whereby the members of that democracy may obtain those common ideas, common ideals, and common modes of thought, feeling, and action that make for cooperation, social cohesion, and social solidarity. . . .
>
> Specialization demands the following provisions in secondary education:
>
> (a) *A wide range of subjects*. . . .
>
> (b) *Exploration and guidance*. . . .

> (c) *Adaptation of content and methods* . . . to the capacities, interests, and needs of the pupils concerned. . . .
>
> (d) *Flexibility of organization and administration* . . . by "election" of studies or curriculum. . . .
>
> (e) *Differentiated curriculum*. . . .
>
> The unifying function calls for the following provisions in secondary education:
>
> (a) Studies of direct value for this purpose, especially the social studies and the mother tongue, with its literature.
>
> (b) The social mingling of pupils through the organization and administration of the schools.
>
> (c) The participation of pupils in common activities in which they should have a large measure of responsibility, such as athletic games, social activities, and the government of the school.
>
> The comprehensive . . . high school, embracing all curriculum in one unified organization, should remain the standard type of secondary school in the United States.[10]

In junior high schools, courses are offered in the departmental organization common to the high schools instead of the single-teacher, single-classroom pattern of elementary schools. However, to secure the purposes of exploration for which the junior high school was intended, the departmentalization has been tempered by considerable correlation between courses. Further, it soon became common for a number of subjects to be fused into one general course. Spelling, grammar, literature, and speech became English; history, geography, and civics became social studies; courses in general mathematics, general science, home economics, and general shop were organized from the "isolated, piecemeal elements" of the elementary curriculum. The next step was to integrate the general courses into "broad courses" or "core curriculum courses." The most frequent combination was English-social studies; others included science and social studies or English, science, and social studies. In general, junior high schools have offered many fewer courses than the senior high, and students have not had the option of election, except for perhaps one course a year.

The curriculum of the high school has been quite different, opening up many avenues for specialization. Students can choose from a number of curricular avenues—college preparatory, commercial, general, agriculture, vocational, and many others. Within these programs, there may be elective options, but all students are required to take certain subjects, often spelled out by legislative enactment.

[10] U.S. Bureau of Education, *Bulletin 1918*, No. 35, pp. 9–11, 18, 21–24.

Because of the opportunities for specialization at the high-school level, the curriculum has expanded rapidly. The Office of Education reported data on 16 subjects in high schools in 1895 and 206 in 1934. Of the 206, 111 were offered in virtually every state; others were limited to only a few or even a single school. Many of the new courses were in vocational and commercial fields, but others were in scientific fields, art and music, social studies, and foreign languages, including Bohemian, Czechoslovakian, and Norse.[11]

Higher Education

The curricular expansion in higher education has been even more dramatic than that at the secondary level. Continuing the trends begun during the Gilded Age, colleges have become more utilitarian and vocational in orientation. To the traditional college of liberal arts and the professional schools of law, medicine, and theology have been added many vocational or professional schools—agriculture, architecture, business, commerce, dentistry, education, engineering, forestry, and so on down the alphabet to veterinary medicine. Within the colleges or schools, separate departments have been organized. Every department proliferates courses designed to create specialists in its field. And the vocational and professional schools are not the only "course factories," for the older academic disciplines have often equalled them in the production of narrow courses developed from some scholar's doctoral dissertation. By mid-century, this process had already been well advanced, particularly in the immediate post-war years with the demands of the returning veterans for utilitarian, "down-to-earth" courses that would pay off in better salaries to support their already established families.

The proliferation of courses and the splintering of knowledge by the demands of specialization had begun to generate new attacks on the elective system as early as 1930. Proposals for dealing with over-specialization and "crass utilitarianism" in higher education ranged from the "Great Books" theories of Robert M. Hutchins and the "Essentialism" of William C. Bagley to the development of comprehensive or survey courses for freshmen and sophomores and the creation of junior colleges.

The most common attempt to solve the problem of compartmentalization of knowledge was the reorganization of the freshman and sophomore years into a general college, in which students were required to take a number of survey courses designed to give an introduction to all the broad fields of human learning. Amherst is generally given credit for

[11] U.S. Office of Education, *Bulletin*, 1938, No. 6, pp. 2, 34–96.

developing the first survey course, in 1914, under the leadership of President Alexander Meiklejohn. It was a survey of social and economic institutions. Later, in 1927, Meiklejohn became chairman of the Experimental College of the University of Wisconsin, where he attempted to organize the entire first two years into two broad interdisciplinary courses, surveying all aspects of, first, ancient Athenian civilization and then, in the sophomore year, modern American life.

Other colleges and universities followed with less radical reorganizations, generally requiring freshmen and sophomores to take several comprehensive courses to provide an overview of science, mathematics, social studies, humanities, and literature. Among the leaders were the University of Minnesota, which organized its General College in 1932, and the University of Florida General College, which opened in 1935.[12] Although students might be permitted to elect one or two courses a semester, specialization was delayed until the junior year. Many other universities have since adopted similar organizational arrangements.

Extracurricular Activities

Along with the expansion in courses, there has been a great growth in extracurricular activities. In the secondary schools, expansion of the extracurricular activities came somewhat later than it did in colleges, and elementary schools have felt considerably less effect, keeping many of the activities closely related to class work: assembly or P.T.A. programs, classroom clubs, or the safety patrol.

More Activities and Student Participation

Tracing the history of extracurricular development in secondary schools is difficult because school officials until the 1920's tended to discourage such activities and reports on them are limited. In four Chicago high schools the number of nonathletic extracurricular activities increased from 53 in 1913 to 148 in 1930, most of the gain coming between 1925 and 1930. During the same period, the number of athletic activities increased from 32 to 49. The 1932 National Survey of Secondary Education received reports on non-athletic extracurricular activities from 224 schools, with a range from one activity to more than 50 and a median of 13. Not only were the activities increasing in number, but

[12] National Society for the Study of Education, The 38th Yearbook, Part II, *General Education in the American College* (1939), pp. 139, 153.

they were involving a substantial number of pupils. The 1932 National Survey reported that in 132 secondary schools which did not require participation in extracurricular activities, approximately 60 percent of the pupils were participating in non-athletic extracurricular activities.[13] Many students were active in several organizations, and it was necessary to limit the number of activities in which any one student could participate.

Variety of Activities

The variety of activities makes classification difficult, but several studies have grouped the extracurricular offerings in broad categories. Roughly, these categories include student government and service clubs, social clubs, departmental or subject-matter clubs, publications, dramatic and debating clubs, musical organizations, and athletics. One 1947 textbook on the junior high school listed 498 different kinds of clubs which the authors found in one or more junior high schools; these clubs ranged from kites to bankers and presidents' cabinet, from rag dolls to "junior hustlers" and "little mothers."[14] Supervising the extracurricular activities has become a major responsibility of the school faculty, and some teachers, particularly in music and physical education, are hired on the basis of their reputation for producing quality bands or teams.

Over-emphasis on Spectator Activities

The pressure on schools to serve as an entertainment medium for the general public as well as for the student body has placed a great interest on the spectator aspect of the extracurricular program, particularly in athletics, music, and dramatics. Intramural athletics have been sidelined to give the football and basketball stars the undivided attention of several of the highest paid teachers of the faculty. Music classes often get perfunctory teaching so that the band director can work out fancy drill routines for the weekend game. In some parts of the nation the mania for winning teams and prize bands has extended downward to the elementary schools, where afternoon football and basketball leagues and "development bands" serve as training grounds for the high-school and college "big time." Teachers are expected to excuse their students from classes to "represent the school" without serious regard to the effect of frequent absences from class on the educational development of the

[13] U.S. Office of Education, *Bulletin*, 1932, No. 17, pp. 5, 18–19, 23.
[14] William T. Gruhn and Harl R. Douglass, *The Modern Junior High School* (New York: Ronald Press, 1947), pp. 355–359.

absentees. Worse yet, the desire of local groups to see their school have a winning team or the "classiest" band results in virtually all public interest in education being directed to varsity athletics or marching bands, with little attention to the needs and development of the rest of the school or college program. Dads' Clubs, Quarterback Clubs, and Booster Clubs are organized in town, with a very narrow interest in many cases; they are willing to screen new candidates for football coach or help fire the old one and to raise money to send the band to games away from home, but they rarely give more than lip service to the academic or non-athletic and intramural sports programs of the school. While the extracurricular program often looks very broad on paper, in many schools a few students take active leadership, a few more are the follower-members, and the great majority are watchers of a handful of superior performers.

State and National Associations

In keeping with the national trend toward collectivizing American life, many extracurricular activities have developed state and national organizations, which set up national standards, projects, topics for discussion, and rules of eligibility. Among these groups are the National Honor Society, the Future Farmers of America, the Future Teachers Clubs, the National Forensic League, the Inter-scholastic Athletic Association, and the state organizations affiliated with them. Sometimes these state and national organizations are sponsored and controlled by school-oriented leaders; sometimes they are promotional groups organized by individuals or companies with special interests to be served. In some states an over-all state high-school activities association has been formed to guide school officials in their recognition of those organizations and contests which are legitimately in the interest of schools and students and to standardize and supervise student eligibility and other rules regarding contests and athletic meets and games.

Special School Services

Not only have schools added public entertainment to their educational responsibilities, but they have been forced to take on many other special services to pupils. The school lunch program grew out of Depression problems. The weakening of family ties in American society has placed on the school the responsibility of helping children with their personal problems, their sex education, their physical health, and their vocational future. In many cases it has become crucial for the schools to offer guidance services, even psychiatric therapy, to enable pupils to become well enough adjusted so that they and their classmates can make satisfactory academic progress. Schools conduct health examinations, particularly of eyes and ears and often of teeth. Classes in English and social studies survey vocational possibilities, and full-time counselors assist pupils in making vocational and college choices. In some schools, placement centers have been established for the convenience of employers as well as graduates and students.

The problems of physical health have been recognized longer than those of social and psychological adjustment. Schools have been utilizing the services of county health officers and visiting physicians throughout the century. In 1952, there were 111 physicians employed full time by school systems and 2,409 others working part time. There were also 50 full-time and 850 part-time dentists; 609 full-time and 22 part-time dental hygienists; 4,436 full-time and 906 part-time nurses.[15] Other schools continue to have the services of public health officers and medical volunteers.

By mid-century, special guidance personnel and school psychologists were becoming common in schools, although much of the guidance work was still being done by homeroom teachers, principals, and deans. As the guidance movement has gone from almost exclusive concern with academic advisement and vocational guidance to the problems of counseling in depth, many schools now employ school psychologists and occasionally school psychiatrists. In 1961–1962, 23,561 full-time guidance and counseling specialists were reported in public elementary and secondary schools.[16] The National Defense Education Act appropriated funds for training guidance counselors, and the influence of this program has greatly expanded the number of counselors in secondary schools and has encouraged the preparation of counselors for elementary schools.

Expanding Enrollment

In each succeeding decade in the twentieth century more children have attended school more regularly and for more years than ever before, extending educational opportunity upward to secondary and higher education and downward to the kindergarten. The movement toward universality of attendance which began in the nineteenth century at the

[15] U.S. Office of Education, *Biennial Survey, 1950–52*, Chapter 2, p. 38.
[16] U.S. Office of Education, *Bulletin 1964*, No. 18, p. 35.

elementary-school level was extended upward rapidly after 1900, when elementary grade enrollments grew as the population increased, secondary school enrollments "exploded" in almost geometric progression, and college enrollments increased steadily. According to the United States Office of Education, elementary enrollments between 1890 and 1938 ran about a million higher than the number of children of the ages of five to thirteen years, inclusive. This excess of elementary-school children over those of elementary-school age reflected the children who had been retarded one or more grades. By 1938 there were an estimated 21,049,000 children 5-13 years of age, and there were 22,042,902 enrolled in elementary grades. In 1964, the elementary school enrollment was 31,734,000, with 26,811,000 in public schools. In 1965–1966, the enrollment in public elementary schools was 27,800,000.[17]

The change in secondary school enrollment has been dramatic, as Table 4 shows. Not only are more children going to secondary school,

TABLE 4: GROWTH IN SECONDARY SCHOOL ENROLLMENT

Year	Secondary school enrollment	Percent of total population, aged 14–17
1890	359,949	6.7
1900	699,403	11.4
1910	1,115,398	15.4
1920	2,500,176	32.3
1930	4,484,255	51.4
1940	7,123,009	73.3
1950	6,427,042	77.3
1964	12,813,000	83.3

but a steadily increasing number are staying in for longer periods of time and the number of graduates is increasing, both absolutely and proportionately, except during the years of World War II, when there was a slight decline in the proportion of graduates. In 1965–1966, secondary school enrollment reached 16,100,000, with an expected 2,400,000 graduates, 1.1 percent more than were graduated in 1965.[18] Higher education is now experiencing a similar growth. In 1965–1966, the 1,110

[17] U.S. Office of Education, *Bulletin 1940*, No. 2, p. 10. *Statistical Abstracts of the United States, 1965*, p. 108, for 1964 data. *School and Society*, 94 (April 2, 1966): 174, for 1965–1966 data.

[18] U.S. Office of Education, *Biennial Survey, 1950–52*, Chapter 1, pp. 21–22. *Statistical Abstract, 1965*, p. 108, for 1964 data. *School and Society*, p. 174, for 1965–1966 data.

accredited universities, senior colleges, and four-year colleges enrolled 3,312,703 full-time students and a grand total of 4,618,997—the latter up 10 percent over the grand total of 1964–1965.

> Since 1955, the increase in total enrollments for all accredited institutions reported has been a tremendous 117%, and just since 1960 the increase has been 55.8%. In full-time enrollments, the respective increases have been 104% and 61%.

Very significant has been the increase in freshman enrollment, which was 815,119, an increase of 173 percent, "despite the fact that the 18-year-old population increase this year was no more than 10–12% above 1964."[19]

TABLE 5: GROWTH IN COLLEGE ENROLLMENT [20]

Year	College enrollment	Percent of total population, aged 18–21
1890	156,756	3
1900	237,592	4
1910	355,213	5
1920	597,880	8
1930	1,100,737	12
1940	1,494,203	15
1950	2,659,021	27
1960	3,215,544	31
1964	4,950,173	—

The opportunities for schooling are also being extended to younger children and to adults. In 1963–1964, there were 2,211,000 enrolled in public kindergarten.[21] Part-time schools for adults had become an important activity in many cities by mid-century. In 1950, 889 school systems reported a total of 1,544,829 adults enrolled in adult, Americanization, night, and continuation schools. By 1963, there were 1,908,400 adults enrolled in federally aided vocational programs alone.[22]

[19] Parker, pp. 7, 18.

[20] U.S. Office of Education, *Bulletin 1964*, No. 18, p. 76. *Statistical Abstract, 1965*, p. 132, for 1964 enrollment.

[21] U.S. Office of Education, *Bulletin 1964*, No. 18, p. 6.

[22] U.S. Office of Education, *Biennial Survey, 1950–52*, Chapter 3, p. 10. *Statistical Abstracts, 1965*, p. 138.

Compulsory Attendance

Although no legislation can be effective without the support of public sentiment, undoubtedly important factors in the increase in enrollment and attendance figures were the child labor and compulsory school attendance laws passed in the various states. The last state to enact compulsory attendance legislation was Mississippi, in 1918. By 1945 thirty-six states had raised to sixteen the age at which students were permitted to leave school; three states permitted students to leave schools at fourteen and six required them to remain until eighteen. The child labor laws reinforced the compulsory attendance laws. The strictness of enforcement of attendance laws has varied, but in most states some form of attendance officer, usually designated by some more euphemistic title than "truant officer," is responsible for enforcement. Child labor laws are generally enforced by the state welfare or labor department in cooperation with educational authorities, who issue work permits to youngsters below the minimum age limit.

The extreme of compulsory attendance laws was tried in the period immediately following World War I. Michigan held referendums in 1920 and 1924 to amend the state constitution to abolish all private schools, but the referendum failed each time. In 1922 the voters of Oregon, through the process of initiative, adopted the so-called Compulsory Education Act, requiring all children between the ages of 8 and 16 to attend public schools. Any parent who wanted to teach his own child or send him to a private school had to receive written permission from the county superintendent, and the child had to report to the county superintendent every three months to be examined in the work covered. If the county superintendent decided that the child was not being properly taught, he could order him sent to public school for the rest of the year. The act was to take effect in September, 1926. The private-school cause was defended by a Roman Catholic parochial school and a military academy, which sought injunctions to prevent enforcement. The state appealed to the courts, and the case was decided by the United States Supreme Court in June, 1925. While declaring unconstitutional any law which prevents parents from sending their children to private or parochial schools, the decision did affirm the right of the state to supervise and regulate any non-public schools within their borders.[23] As part of the campaign to circumvent school integration, Mississippi and South Carolina have repealed their compulsory attendance laws.

[23] 268 *U.S.* 534–535.

Financing Education

The nineteenth-century struggle for free, tax-supported schools was virtually won by the turn of the century. It is true that there remain today many financial barriers to equality of educational opportunity. Some states still do not have free textbooks. Fees are generally charged for supplies, lockers, gym towels, and activity cards. Students are required to buy gym suits and supplementary study materials, such as *The Weekly Reader,* work books, and laboratory kits. Some extracurricular activities necessitate the purchase of uniforms, musical instruments, or other items. Graduation often involves renting a cap and gown or getting a new suit or new dress. College, even at the state universities, is very expensive, with fees, book costs, tuition, room and board charges, living expenses, and travel. But the basic financing of the public schools and universities is clearly the tax levy.

The major shift in financing policies in the twentieth century has been toward greater centralization of tax collection and distribution. Traditionally, the local community was responsible for supporting its school system, but the last decades have seen a strong trend in the direction of state and federal financing. In 1920 the total school revenues for public elementary and secondary schools was a little under $1 billion; of that amount, local and county governments raised 83.2 percent, state governments 16.5 percent, and the federal government only 0.3 percent. By 1962 the total receipts had jumped to over $17.5 billion, with local and county governments providing just 56.9 percent, state governments 38.7 percent and the federal contribution up to 4.3 percent. In 1965–1966 the total appropriations for public schools was $24.7 billion, an increase of 13 percent over the preceding year. Of this total, $13.1 billion came from local sources (up 5.8 percent), $9.7 billion from state sources (up 10.9 percent), and $1.9 billion from federal funds (up 130 percent over 1964–1965).[24]

Federal Aid to Education

Except for the early land grants, federal support for education has not been in the form of general aid to schools; instead, each appropriation has been specifically designated—vocational education, school surveys, school lunch programs, veterans' education, aid to federally affected areas.

[24] U.S. Office of Education, *Bulletin 1964,* No. 18, p. 60. *School and Society,* p. 174.

Vocational Education

The Smith-Hughes Act in 1917 marked a revolutionary change in federal participation in educational activities. The bill provided an annual appropriation to be used for salaries, teacher preparation, research, and administration in the fields of agriculture, trades and industries, and home economics. In 1930, additional funds were appropriated for salaries for home economics teachers and supervisors.[25]

The law marked two new departures in federal assistance: states were required to match federal funds in order to receive their share of the appropriations; and a Federal Board of Vocational Education was established, including the Secretaries of Agriculture, Labor, and Commerce, the United States Commissioner of Education, and three citizens representing manufacturing and commerce, labor, and agriculture. Although state departments of vocational education were responsible for the actual administration of the programs, the Federal Board of Vocational Education had to approve all plans for courses, methods, teacher qualifications, and so on. The Board was authorized to withhold monies from any state whose programs did not meet the conditions of the Act.

Later laws expanding federal aid for vocational education include the George-Reed Act of 1929, the George-Ellzey Act of 1934, the George-Deen Act of 1936, and the George-Barden Act of 1946. The George-Barden Act expanded the program to include distributive education and permitted money to be spent for vocational guidance programs and for the purchase of supplies and equipment. In 1951–1952, federal funds allotted for vocational education of "less-than-college" grade totaled $27,127,882.[26] State and local funds in the same programs equalled about $120 million, making the federal share about 18 percent. This is considerably more than the dollar-for-dollar matching called for by the laws. The careful accounting of funds required by the various vocational education laws has been repeated in later federal appropriations, but controls over curriculum or teaching methods have been kept to a minimum.

The National Defense Education Acts have extended vocational education to include training—and retraining—of technicians for scientific and technical fields.

World War I Programs

During the First World War the shortage of trained technicians led to the creation of a War Department Committee on Education and

[25] U.S. Office of Education, *Bulletin 1930*, No. 8, p. 39.
[26] U.S. Office of Education, *Bulletin 1954*, No. 14, p. 42.

Special Training. Under that committee vocation training detachments were operated at more than 150 institutions of higher learning, and units of the Students' Army Training Corps drilled at 525 colleges and universities. The programs lasted only a few months, but some 130,000 technicians were trained and the precedent was set for the more effective programs of World War II.[27]

Depression Programs

SCHOOL LUNCH PROGRAM The economic warfare waged against the Great Depression included several programs that brought benefits for schools and young people. One was the school lunch program. Begun in 1935 as one method of providing an expanding market for agricultural products, it was made permanent in 1946 by the National School Lunch Act. Although the 1935 law did not specifically mention school lunches, the Secretary of Agriculture was authorized to purchase and distribute surplus food commodities "among persons in low-income groups." In the first year of the program approximately $250,000 worth of food was distributed to schools. The surplus food donations increased until the outbreak of World War II created a new demand for agricultural products. In 1940 the federal government instituted cash assistance for the school milk program. The National School Lunch Act of 1946 authorized both cash payments and distribution of surplus foods to schools. The school lunch program has constituted the second largest single program of aid to elementary and secondary schools, totalling over $377,000,000 in 1964.[28]

THE NATIONAL YOUTH ADMINISTRATION Among the temporary depression measures designed to assist young people, the National Youth Administration had as its principal purpose keeping youths in school. Established by executive order of President Roosevelt in 1935, the NYA provided part-time employment for youth between the ages of sixteen and twenty-four, enabling them to earn enough to remain in school. Although payment was made directly to the student, the work was assigned by the school or college which he attended. The school was also responsible for selecting from among the many applicants those who most needed to be included within their limited quota. The maximum any elementary- or high-school student could earn in one month was $6; undergraduate college students could earn an average of $15 a month; graduate students, an average of $30. The work had to be useful and practical, and it could not result in the laying off of regular employees.

[27] Knight, *Fifty Years of American Education*, pp. 339–341.
[28] U.S. Office of Education, *Bulletin 1964*, No. 18, p. 135.

Students worked in kitchens, graded papers, mended books, tended grounds, did construction work, assisted in laboratories, and so on. In March, 1939, the student aid program involved 378,692 students: 266,419 elementary and secondary pupils, 109,413 college undergraduates, and 2,860 graduate students.[29] In that month 27,549 institutions were participating, including 1,651 colleges and universities and 25,898 lower schools. Before the program was terminated in 1943, an estimated 600,000 college students had participated.[30] The NYA not only subsidized individual students, but served to bolster many schools and colleges. The support of the NYA helps explain why college and secondary enrollments continued to climb during the Depression.

CIVILIAN CONSERVATION CORPS Important educational by-products resulted from the creation of the Civilian Conservation Corps, technically the Emergency Conservation Work, approved by Congress in 1933. Young unmarried men between the ages of seventeen and twenty-three were enrolled in the CCC for six-month terms, with re-enlistments permitted up to a total of two years. The camps were under the direction of the War Department and were commanded by reserve army and navy officers. Forty hours a week was spent on the projects, with additional time required for carrying out camp duties. In addition to the on-the-job training in their work, the enrollees were encouraged to continue their schooling in evening and Saturday classes. Many took elementary work in language usage and arithmetic. Others took secondary-school and vocational courses. Through the cooperation of nearby colleges and correspondence courses, some enrollees studied for college degrees. During the month of February, 1939, 91 percent of the total enrollment strength of the CCC participated in some educational activity. During the year 1937–1938 elementary-school certificates were given to 3,517 enrollees, high-school diplomas to 634, and college degrees to 13.[31] Before the war ended the need for the CCC in 1943, the Corps had given employment to over two and a half million young men. In addition to the advancement in learning made possible for those boys who had already attended schools, more than eight thousand illiterates were taught to read in the CCC educational work.[32] The NYA and the CCC were truly "New Deals" for youth.

[29] Educational Policies Commission, *Federal Activities in Education* (Washington: N.E.A., 1939), p. 102.
[30] Alice M. Rivlin, *The Role of the Federal Government in Financing Higher Education* (Washington: Brookings Institution, 1961), p. 64.
[31] Educational Policies Commission, p. 82.
[32] Cremin, p. 321.

WORKS PROGRESS ADMINISTRATION The efforts of the New Deal to combat unemployment resulted in many concrete benefits to education. The Works Progress Administration (WPA), established by executive order in 1935, undertook the construction of public facilities and educational, professional, clerical, recreational, and other non-construction projects. The educational projects included literacy and naturalization classes, workers' education, public affairs education, education for home and family living, vocational education, recreation and leisure time activities (including arts and crafts, music, dramatics, public speaking, and literature), college courses, correspondence courses, and nursery schools. Although the WPA was concerned primarily with employing idle workers, many of its projects consisted of the construction and repair of schools. In those projects the local sponsoring agency provided the materials and supervision and the WPA paid for the labor. The WPA participated in the construction of nearly 6,000 new public school buildings.[33]

PUBLIC WORKS ADMINISTRATION More important in the construction of schools was the Public Works Administration (PWA), which was established in 1933. It made grants and loans for the construction of public buildings and facilities. School systems and state colleges and universities could receive grants covering up to 30 percent (later 45 percent) of the cost of construction, and the PWA would lend some or all of the rest through the purchase of 4 percent interest bonds issued by the school system or college. Although the construction was contracted by the local sponsor, the PWA supervised, to assure that the contractor met his responsibilities. Through 1938, when it became a part of the Federal Works Agency, the PWA participated in the construction of 7,290 school, college, and library buildings, granting local authorities $179,421,227 and lending them $93,916,383.[34]

RECONSTRUCTION FINANCE CORPORATION One other federal agency to participate in aid to schools was the Reconstruction Finance Corporation (RFC), created in 1932. Though its purpose was "to provide emergency financing facilities for financial institutions," the RFC lent money to state and local agencies in the early Depression years for the construction of a number of school and college buildings, totaling about $5 million by 1939. In addition, the RFC made loans to public-school authorities whose bond issues were being defaulted because of inability to collect assessments. Before 1935, payments could be made to public-

[33] *Ibid.*, p. 323.
[34] Educational Policies Commission, p. 106.

school authorities to pay back salaries for teachers. In August, 1934, a loan of $22,300,000 was made to the Chicago Board of Education to pay teachers who had gone without salaries for six months.[35] The RFC was abolished in 1957.

World War II Programs

NATIONAL DEFENSE TRAINING PROGRAM World War II brought new federal programs in education. The industrial lull during the Depression left the United States with a great shortage of the engineers and technicians needed to conduct a modern war. Even before Germany invaded Poland, the United States Office of Education was urging public vocational schools to train workers for the aircraft industry. The program was intensified with the outbreak of the European conflict as the National Defense Training Program was begun in July, 1940, in hundreds of vocational schools all over the country.[36]

Before the program ended on June 30, 1945, over seven and a half million workers had participated, two and two-thirds million in pre-employment courses and nearly five million in supplementary courses. In addition to defense workers, the program trained some 200,000 uniformed service personnel and over 400,000 civilian employees for the military services. Courses which had the greatest enrollments were those for electricians, machinists, aircraft mechanics, welders, riveters, and radio technicians. The total federal cost reached almost $300 million and included the rental of space and purchase of equipment as well as salaries for teachers and supervisors.[37] The equipment purchased by schools with federal funds remained the property of the schools when they completed their programs.

RURAL WAR PRODUCTION TRAINING PROGRAM The National Defense Training Program and its successors were concentrated in the cities, but a similar program was set up for rural areas. The Rural War Production Training Program was designed originally to prepare rural youth to take jobs in defense industies. Later it concentrated on improving farm production through machinery repair and agricultural courses and on con-

[35] *Ibid.*, p. 107.

[36] The federal government specified that no trainee could "be discriminated against because of sex, race, or color, and where separate schools are required by law for separate population groups, . . . equitable provision shall be made for facilities and training of like quality." Ironically, when it was fighting a war against a nation that claimed racial superiority, the United States still recognized the "separate but equal" policies in its educational programs. The same segregationist provisions were applied in the Rural War Production Training Program and the engineering short courses.

[37] U.S. Office of Education, *Bulletin 1946*, No. 10, pp. 19, 196, 156–158, 72, 176.

serving food through home canning courses. As in the NDT program, the RWPT courses were held in schools wherever possible, but it was often necessary to rent space in garages and shops. Federal funds were allocated for the purchase of school equipment needed for the new courses. More than 3,000 school-community canning centers were built by local school authorities to provide space for the food preservation courses. Enrollments in the program totaled over four million before it ended in 1945; the cost to the federal government was almost $50 million.[38]

ENGINEERING SHORT COURSES The two programs just described supplied many of the urgently needed skilled workers, but the rapid expansion of industry for war required engineers, scientists, and management specialists. In October, 1940, Congress appropriated $9,000,000 to finance "short engineering courses of college grade, provided by engineering schools or by universities of which the engineering school is a part." During the five years of the program, over a million and a half persons were enrolled in one or more courses. Federal funds totaled nearly $60 million, and colleges were permitted to retain title to equipment purchased for their courses. Of particular significance was the recommendation of the Council of the Society for the Promotion of Engineering Education in October of 1943. On the basis of the success of the cooperation between the federal government and the colleges, they recommended that the general policies of the program "be used as a prototype for the administration of Federal participation in the postwar education."[39]

STUDENT LOANS During the first years of the War, the federal government urged colleges and universities to accelerate their program and go on a year-around basis. Since this put a financial hardship on many students who lost the opportunity to work part time and during vacations, Congress authorized the Office of Education to make students loans beginning in 1942. The loans were limited to college students in their last two years of college who were majoring in medicine, engineering, dentistry, pharmacy, veterinary medicine, physics, and chemistry. The program lasted only two years, but during that time 11,081 students received loans totalling over $2 million.[40] These loans were an important precedent and pattern for the National Defense Education Act loans of 1958.

[38] *Ibid.*, No. 11, pp. 44, 48, 72, 32.
[39] *Ibid.*, No. 9, pp. 14, 44–45, 36, 65.
[40] *Ibid.*, No. 14, pp 2, 6, 7.

MILITARY TRAINING PROGRAMS ON COLLEGE CAMPUSES As young men left campuses for military service and defense work, enrollments in colleges dropped to levels which threatened to close some institutions of higher learning. The military services, needing additional facilities and training staffs for their purposes, came to the aid of the colleges with a number of special programs. For example, the Navy utilized facilities in a number of large universities for their V-5, or naval aviation, program. In addition to the Pre-flight Schools in the large universities, smaller colleges were granted "pre-preflight schools" to offer some of the basic mathematics and science courses, and other colleges were awarded contracts to participate in Civilian Pilot Training courses for Navy enlistees in the V-5 program. Beginning in 1943 the Navy also used colleges in the V-12 or Navy College Training Program, sending some officer candidates through one or more semesters of regular college work in approximately three hundred colleges and taking over facilities for Midshipman Schools in other universities. The Army Specialized Training Program had a peak enrollment of 215,000 students in 350 colleges in December, 1943.[41] Through programs such as these, in 1943–44 there were 270,034 enlisted men and 7,721 enlisted women taking full-time regular college work, plus 529,364 other military students doing full-time work in short courses of less than a year's duration.[42]

While the primary purpose of these programs was the preparation of military personnel for an all-out war, they also kept many colleges and universities from having to close. For these programs, the federal government paid more than $300 million to institutions of higher learning.[43]

AID TO IMPACTED AREAS Mass migrations of families to locations of defense plants and military establishments created financial hardships on some school districts. Not only was the number of pupils often suddenly increased, but taking large areas of land off tax books for public use, such as airfields or army camps, often removed a sizeable block of school income. To aid these communities, federal money was appropriated to local school authorities for "construction of school buildings and centers for preschool children, for the maintenance and operation of schools, and expense of extended school service in areas affected by war activities." In 1950 Congress extended these programs through two acts: PL 81-815 provides federal assistance for school construction in "federally affected areas," and PL 81-874 provides federal assistance for

[41] Richard G. Axt, *The Federal Government and Financing Higher Education* (New York: Columbia U. Press, 1952), pp. 263–264.

[42] U.S. Office of Education, *Biennial Survey*, 1942–44, p. 20.

[43] Axt, p. 264.

maintenance and operation of schools. Between 1951 and 1963, aid from 815 totaled $1.2 billion and from 874, $1.7 billion. The 88th Congress extended the program for fiscal years 1964 and 1965. In 1964 these federal funds amounted to $382,871,000.[44]

Although President Johnson advocated cutting this program as an economy measure and putting more in general aid to education, Congress seems determined to continue it. On April 28, 1966, the House Appropriations Committee restored the $232.8 million cut recommended by the President, bringing the appropriation to the full authorized total of $416 million for fiscal year 1966. On May 5 the House approved the appropriation.

SURPLUS PROPERTY When the War ended, the federal government possessed a huge stockpile of property which it no longer needed. Legislation permitted the donation or transferral at "public benefit discounts" of this property to tax-supported and tax-exempt nonprofit educational institutions. Between 1946 and 1954, educational institutions were allotted personal property equipment and materials valued at nearly $690 million. Within the same period, over 100,000 acres of land and nearly 30,000 buildings were transferred from federal control to educational institutions. These transfers ranged from fences and furnaces removed for installation at schools and colleges to buildings and entire establishments taken over for temporary quarters for higher education. The value of this real property was set at over $.5 billion.[45] The donations of surplus property appear to be a permanent part of federal assistance to education.

THE "G.I. BILL" Of all the federal programs in education, the most dramatic in its effect and size was the Servicemen's Readjustment Act of 1944 (the "G.I. Bill"). In 1943 a rehabilitation law for disabled veterans had provided educational benefits for veterans with service-connected disabilities. In 1950 and 1952 similar benefits were extended to those veterans who served during the period of the Korean conflict. According to these Acts, disabled veterans were entitled to special educational or on-the-job training privileges. Under the 1944 Act, the federal government contracted with schools and colleges to pay tuition and fees charged non-disabled veterans enrolled as students, paid for the veterans' supplies and books, and gave them a subsistence allowance.

Although the program revolutionized the college campus and provided

[44] *School Life*, 46 (May, 1964): 8–9. U.S. Office of Education, *Bulletin 1964*, No. 18, p. 134.

[45] U.S. Office of Education, *Bulletin 1954*, No. 14, pp. 49, 51.

educational opportunity for many veterans, the lack of adequate controls in the early forms of the Bill resulted in abuses. Colleges profited by charging all veterans out-of-state tuition, regardless of the place of residence. Veterans took unfair advantage of the G.I. Bill by purchasing unnecessary books and supplies, which they later resold. Fly-by-night schools of less-than-college level were set up in every imaginable field, including truck driving, ballroom dancing, and bar tending; in some of these schools, students conspired with fraudulent contractors by accepting "kick-backs" of tuition fees paid for schooling never received. Some veterans tried to make a career of going to college, changing their educational goals each semester. To correct these abuses, Congress and the Veterans Administration instituted more controls. In the Korean veterans' programs, Congress avoided the abuses and minimized the needs for controls by paying the veteran directly and requiring him to meet his tuition costs as well as his living expenses.

Overshadowing the abuses of the relatively few immoral and selfish individuals and institutions involved in such a mass operation, the vast majority of the veterans in each program took their opportunities seriously. Campuses were crowded as never before, and the students were men and women with a new purposiveness which changed the "playboy" atmosphere of many a campus. The veterans surprised college administrations by their superior academic work. They also created new problems, not only in their overwhelming numbers, but also in the fact that many of them were married and had children, imposing demands for housing that no campus was prepared to meet.

The explosion of higher education enrollments dates from the time of the returning veteran. Nearly eight and a half million World War II veterans, or approximately 54 percent of those eligible, received educational benefits from the laws of 1943 and 1944 before the program ended. In the ten years from 1943 to 1953, the federal government expended over $318 million for tuition, equipment, and supplies for the disabled-veteran programs and a billion and a quarter in subsistence payments; in the same period, it expended over $4.25 billion for tuition, supplies, and equipment of the non-disabled student-veterans and paid them nearly $10 billion in subsistence allowances.[46] These programs and those benefiting the veterans of the Korean War have done much to promote the growth of colleges as well as create a national expectancy of higher education as a prime condition of success in the United States. In 1966 Congress enacted a law extending certain benefits to all veterans of the Armed Forces since the Korean War.

[46] *Ibid.*, pp. 91–93.

Education and the Cold War

NATIONAL DEFENSE EDUCATION ACT In keeping with the long-standing precedent of federal aid for specific educational purposes, Congress enacted the National Defense Education Act in 1958. This aid was justified under the argument that the "defense of this Nation depends upon the mastery of modern techniques developed from complex scientific principles." In order to "increase our efforts to identify and educate more of the talent of our Nation," Congress declared that it was necessary that "the Federal Government give assistance to education for programs which are important to our defense," through "substantial assistance . . . to individuals, to States and their subdivisions." The Act prohibited federal control over educational programs or school personnel.

> Nothing contained in this Act shall be construed to authorize any department, agency, officer, or employee of the United States to exercise any direction, supervision, or control over the curriculum, program of instruction, administration, or personnel of any educational institution or school system.[47]

The largest appropriation authorized in the Act is for loans to students in institutions of higher education. To be eligible for the federal money, an institution must set up a student loan fund, contributing to the fund an amount "no less than one-ninth of such Federal capital contributions." Preference is given to students "with a superior academic background who express a desire to teach in elementary or secondary schools" and "students whose academic background indicates a superior capacity or preparation in science, mathematics, engineering, or a modern foreign language." Students can borrow no more than $1,000 each fiscal year nor more than a total of $5,000. The loan can be repaid over a ten-year period at 3 percent interest, but interest does not accrue while the student is in school or serves in the Armed Forces. Up to half of the loan can be cancelled by "service as a full-time teacher in a public elementary or secondary school, . . . at the rate of 10 per centum . . . for each complete academic year of such service."

A second program sponsored under the NDEA is designed to strengthen science, mathematics, and modern foreign language instruction. Annual appropriations are authorized to assist "State educational agencies" in the "acquisition of laboratory and other special equipment, including audio-visual materials and equipment and printed materials" for instruction in "science, mathematics, or modern foreign language, in

[47] *Congressional Record,* Vol. 104, Part 15, August 23, 1958, p. 19598.

public elementary or secondary schools, or both." "Minor remodeling of laboratory or other space for such materials or equipment" was also authorized. In addition to the grants made to public schools, private nonprofit schools are eligible for loans for the same kinds of materials and equipment.

To encourage the training of "persons interested in teaching in institutions of higher learning," the Act authorizes National Defense Fellowships: 1,000 the first year and 1,500 for the next three years. Fellowships are for periods of study not to exceed three academic years and carry stipends. The institution at which the fellow is studying receives up to $2,500 for each academic year for each such fellow. This program, like others in the Act, have been continued through later legislation.

To aid in the "identification and encouragement of able students," the Act also appropriates grants to state educational agencies to "assist them to establish and maintain programs of testing and guidance and counseling." Additional funds allotted for contracts with institutions of higher learning for the operation of counseling and guidance institutes "to improve the qualifications of personnel engaged in counseling and guidance of students in secondary schools." Trainees in these institutes are paid a stipend of $75 a week plus $15 a week for each dependent.

Because "adequate instruction" in modern foreign languages "is not readily available in the United States," the Act authorizes annual appropriations to match contributions from institutions of higher learning in programs for educating teachers, supervisors, or training teachers "of any modern foreign language in a public elementary or secondary school."

The Act establishes in the Office of Education an Advisory Committee on New Educational Media, which "shall (through grants or contracts) conduct, assist, and foster research and experimentation in the development and evaluation of projects involving television, radio, motion pictures, and related media of communication which may prove of value to . . . public elementary or secondary schools, and to institutions of higher learning."

The NDEA also extends the vocational education program of the Smith-Hughes Act (1917) and the George-Barden Act (1946) with annual grants for "technical training and retraining of youths, adults, and older persons . . . designed to fit them for useful employment as technicians or skilled workers in scientific or technical fields."

One issue over which the passage of the bill was threatened was the matter of racial discrimination. When Congressman James Roosevelt of California objected to the omission of the anti-discriminatory provisions, the Department of Health, Education, and Welfare assured Congress that there would be no discrimination on the grounds of sex, race, color, or creed in the award of loans or fellowships.[48] Thus an impasse was avoided and Congress passed a law which may well be a major step in the federalization of educational financing.

Education and the "New Frontier"

In John F. Kennedy, the nation got its first scholar-president since Woodrow Wilson, and Lyndon B. Johnson is a former school teacher. Under the Kennedy and Johnson administrations, education has received tremendous federal support from many different kinds of programs

THE HIGHER EDUCATION FACILITIES ACT OF 1963 The Higher Education Facilities Act of 1963 authorized $835 million in matching grants and $360 million in loan funds over a five-year period to institutions of higher learning (public and private non-profit, two-year, four-year, and graduate) for construction. Excluded are facilities for events to which the public is charged admission, gymnasiums and other athletic or recreational facilities for other than physical education classes, buildings to be used for sectarian instruction or religious worship, or schools of medicine, dentistry, osteopathy, pharmacy, optometry, podiatry, nursing, or public health (the last eight may receive funds for construction under PL 88-129, the Health Professions Act). Although funds may not be used for chapels or divinity schools, church-related colleges may receive grants and loans for construction of other kinds of facilities, raising the bitter issue of the separation of church and state in education. For fiscal year 1966 Congress appropriated $628 million for this act.

THE VOCATIONAL EDUCATION ACT OF 1963 The Vocational Education Act of 1963 extended and expanded all previous vocational programs, including the Smith-Hughes Act of 1917, the George Barden Act of 1946, the vocational provisions of the NDEA Act of 1958, and the Manpower Development and Training Act of 1962. It set up a permanent program of vocational education, authorizing $60 million in 1963–1964, $118.5 million in 1964–1965, $177.5 million in 1965–1966, and $225 million for 1966–1967 and each fiscal year thereafter. The definition of vocational education was broadened to cover any skilled, semiskilled, or technical occupation but not education for "professions" or occupations requiring a college baccalaureate or higher degree. The Act

[48] *Ibid.*, pp. 19596–19605.

also authorized $150 million for a four-year program from 1965 through 1968 for encouraging potential dropouts to stay in school.

EDUCATION OF HANDICAPPED CHILDREN In October, 1963, Congress included in the Mental Retardation Facilities and Community Health Act of 1963 authorization for training of teachers and specialists and for programs of demonstration and research in the education of handicapped students. Title III of the bill authorized $47 million for fiscal years 1964 through 1966, and many communities and universities have set up special programs in education of various kinds of exceptional children under the encouragement of these funds.

Education and the "Great Society"

When President Johnson signed the Higher Education Act of 1965 on November 8, 1965, he said:

> This bill is only one of more than two dozen education measures enacted by the first session of the 89th Congress. And history will forever record that this session . . . did more for the wonderful cause of education in America than all the previous 176 regular sessions of Congress did, put together.[49]

But the President had already indicated his great interest in education in leading the 88th Congress to enact several programs aiding education. Included were the Nurses Training Act of 1964 and the Library Services and Construction Act, which he signed on February 11, 1964, the latter authorizing $45 million for public libraries. Most significant in its potential effect, however, was the Economic Opportunity Act and its educational provisions.

ECONOMIC OPPORTUNITY ACT OF 1964 Some of the most important battles in the "War on Poverty" are being waged with the weapon of education, and Titles I and II of the Economic Opportunity Act open new doors for developing educational policy as well as new doors of opportunity for many of the children and youth of poverty.

Part A of Title I sets up a Job Corps for youth between the ages of 16 and 21, to prepare them for responsible citizenship and employment in conservation camps and residential training centers. It is a modernization of the old CCC program of the Depression years. The Act authorized $190 million for fiscal year 1965 for the program. Part B authorizes a work training program for youth 16 to 21. It is aimed at

[49] United States Senate Committee on Labor and Public Welfare, *Enactments by the 89th Congress Concerning Education and Training*, 1966, p. 126.

the school dropout and was supported by an authorization of $150 million for 1965. Part C is like the old NYA program, providing for work-study programs for needy college students, with funds of $72.5 million for 1965.

Title II, Part A authorized federal support for community anti-poverty programs. The most widely publicized of these have been the various forms of "headstart" for the cultural enrichment of 3 to 5 year olds from culturally disadvantaged families. The funds authorized for these programs totaled $315 million for 1965. This is perhaps one of the most significant of all the programs, because of its implications for future educational policy. If it is important for some children to be in school at age three, why should not all children have that advantage? Perhaps we have delayed school entrance too long and much more emphasis should be placed on kindergarten and nursery schools. The influence of these EOA programs could be to push the age of universal education downward to include younger children.

Title II, Part B authorized $25 million for basic adult education. Although this has not received the attention of the programs for children, its influence could be to extend universal education upward at a time when the community colleges are beginning to serve as extensions of the public high schools.

ELEMENTARY AND SECONDARY EDUCATION ACT OF 1965 The most massive breakthrough which has yet occurred in federal participation in school financing was the Elementary and Secondary Education Act of 1965, which President Johnson signed on April 11, 1965. It provides annual appropriations for educating children from low-income families, beginning with $100 million for 1965–1966 for the purchase of textbooks, library resources, and other published material for use in public and private elementary and secondary schools, and a like amount "to stimulate and assist in the provision of vitally needed educational services." A third appropriation of $100 million was authorized to be spent on "research, surveys, and demonstrations in the field of education." Although the United States Office of Education administers the research and training appropriation, the other money is channeled through the states to local agencies. States are required to assure that "such fiscal control and fund accounting procedures will be adopted as may be necessary to assure proper disbursement of, and accounting for, Federal funds paid to the State," but the law expressly prohibits federal officials from exercising "any direction, supervision, or control over the curriculum program of instruction, administration or personnel of any educational institution or school system, or over the selection of library resources, textbooks, or other printed or published instructional materials."[50]

On May 11, 1966, the House Education sub-committee voted a four-year extension of the Act at a cost of $11.8 billion.

THE HIGHER EDUCATION ACT OF 1965 President Johnson spoke of the Higher Education Act of 1965, "with its companion, the Elementary and Secondary Education Act of 1965," as the "keystones of the great, fabulous 89th Congress." He promised that it would "swing open a new door for the young people of America . . . —the door to education."

Title I of the Act authorized $25 million for 1966 and $50 million for years 1967 and 1968 for assisting in the solution of community problems in such areas as housing, poverty, recreation, youth opportunities, employment, and government. This provision would be carried out through grants to colleges and universities for strengthening their programs of community service, research, extension, and continuing education in community problems.

Title II authorized $50 million annually for three years for grants to institutions of higher learning to assist in the acquisition of books, periodicals, documents, magnetic tapes, phonograph records, audiovisual materials, and other related library materials. An additional $15 million was authorized in annual appropriations for training librarians.

Title III aims at "strengthening developing institutions . . . which for financial and other reasons are struggling for survival and are isolated from the main currents of academic life." An appropriation of $55 million for fiscal year 1966 was authorized to support "cooperative arrangement under which these colleges may draw on the talent and experiences of our finest colleges and universities, and on the education resources of business and industry, in their effort to improve their academic quality." Although theological schools were expressly excluded, other church-related colleges and universities could participate in this as well as other provisions of the Act.

Title IV authorized $70 million for fiscal year 1966 for grants of financial assistance to needy students. Individual grants could range from $200 to $1,000, depending on the need and academic standing of the student. It also set up a fund for insuring low-interest student loans, limiting the total amount of new loans to be insured at $700 million for 1966, $1 billion for 1967, and $1.4 billion for 1968.

A controversial part of the Act was the National Teacher Corps,

[50] 79 Stat. 27, pp. 36, 39, 44, 31, 57.

teams of experienced teachers and college graduate interns who would work in schools in areas having concentrations of children from low-income families. The teams would supplement, not supplant, the work being done by regular teachers. The teacher interns would enroll in colleges to participate in in-service training programs leading to certification and advanced degrees. Although this is one of the President's favored interests, Congress has balked at appropriating the funds to implement the program it has authorized.

In addition to the National Teacher Corps, Title V establishes in the Office of Education an Advisory Council on Quality Teacher Education to review the administration and operation of programs carried out "under this title and of all other Federal programs for complementary purposes." The review "shall include recommendations for the improvement of these programs." This generally overlooked provision can be the lever for considerable federal influence in the realm of teacher training, since institutions may well accede to recommendations in order to receive the large grants which come under other titles of this and other federal education acts.

The Act also provides for 24,500 graduate fellowships over a three-year period for persons pursuing careers in elementary and secondary education. It authorized $170.5 million over a three-year period for purchase of equipment and minor remodeling leading to improvement of undergraduate instruction, and $15 million over three years for faculty development through institutes or workshops on the use of educational media equipment in teaching in institutions of higher learning.

THE PRESIDENT'S PLANS At the annual meeting of the American Association of School Administrators in February 1966, President Johnson listed five "top priority requests" for Congress:

> —to enlarge and extend through 1970 all programs under the Elementary and Secondary Education Act of 1965;
> —to double the funds for Operation Head Start;
> —to give the National Teacher Corps money to get going;
> —to pass a new law providing free school lunches to needy children.
> For the fifth salvo, the President summed up "reams of recommendations in a single sentence—my budget for this year proposes a $10 billion investment in education and training."[51]

Trends and the Future in Federal Aid

The federal government has become a very important junior partner in the financing of public schools, and very likely this junior partnership

[51] *Nation's Schools*, 77 (March, 1966): 29.

will become one of control as well as support. School systems and universities are now designing their programs to attract the maximum amount of federal funds, and other forces are already at work in shaping our educational future. The inclusion of "private non-profit" schools and universities in the provisions of these acts has permitted their passage by glossing over the issue of the separation of church and state, but court cases are already in the making to test the constitutionality of such grants to church-related institutions.

All of these programs have been justified on the basis of national emergency—defense, poverty, health, international problems, and so on. From past experience, we have noticed that "emergencies" have a way of becoming permanent, and in a world which may be unstable for generations, the trend toward federal aid is likely to accelerate rapidly. The provisions of the NDEA and the programs for the war on poverty may be patterns for future programs of general support to schools. Political leaders, as well as educators, recognize the advantages of centralized tax collection, and the need for equalizing opportunity throughout the nation has made the local tax something of an anachronism. The changing social context of a mobile, inter-related population demands new practices.

The big issues to be fought are those of the separation of church and state in this federal aid and of the degree of local control to be exercised over the spending of federal money. The strong tradition of localism in American education is running into conflict with influence exerted by Washington, and some school administrators are beginning to complain, even to turn down federal funds. But the same social context which has made local support obsolescent may begin to turn control from the state to federal agencies, just as in the past one hundred years the states have taken the control from the local districts and counties.

QUESTIONS FOR DISCUSSION

1. What social forces have contributed to the rapid growth in enrollment in secondary and higher education? Why has the "drop-out" problem become serious for modern America? Contrast the present problem with attendance issues in earlier periods.
2. Trace some of the trends in federal aid to education. Notice particularly trends in controls associated with support.
3. In what ways has the "G.I. Bill" revolutionized secondary and higher education in the United States?
4. Criticize recent federal legislation aiding education on the basis of past

experience with federal aid. When has Congress corrected past difficulties? What additional problems do you foresee as possible?

5. Compare and contrast educational legislation passed by Congress with examples enacted by state legislatures. What does the experience of the past suggest about the dangers of educational control by federal legislation as against state control by legislatures?

SUGGESTED READINGS

Secondary Sources

Axt, Richard G. *The Federal Government and Financing Higher Education.* New York: Columbia U. Press, 1952.

Good, Harry S. *A History of American Education.* New York: Macmillan, 1962. Chapters XV–XVII.

Noble, Stuart G. *A History of American Education.* New York: Rinehart, 1954. Chapters 18, 19.

Primary Sources

Cubberley, Ellwood P. *Readings in Public Education in the United States.* Boston: Houghton Mifflin, 1934. Readings 279–280, 297–307, 326–333.

Hillway, Tyrus. *American Education: An Introduction Through Readings.* Boston: Houghton Mifflin, 1964. Pp. 184–205, 227–231.

Knight, Edgar W., and Hall, Clifton L. *Readings in American Educational History.* New York: Appleton-Century-Crofts, 1951. Pp. 373–399, 530–531, 586–590, 598–604, 609–623, 644–654, 744–765.

14

Toward An American Theory of Pedagogy

Before the twentieth century, American education was based largely on European pedagogical theory, but beginning in the last decade of the nineteenth century, native American theories of education began to develop. The new science of psychology contributed significantly to the development of new pedagogical theories. Dewey, Kilpatrick, Bode, and other American educators turned attention to the individual, as psychology made it possible to theorize on human motivation, learning, and personality development. Experiments in psychology led to efforts at measuring individual intelligence and achievement and to the attempt to measure schools through the school survey. From the techniques of the measurement specialists as well as from other psychologists, educational theorists secured the raw material for developing new attitudes toward children, new courses in the school curriculum, new teaching methods, and new means of evaluation. The scientific attitude which stimulated the development of psychology and measurement was also one of the influences in the rise of a new philosophy—pragmatism—which looks at life in the spirit of science. Thus science, psychology, pragmatism, and American democracy gave rise to a distinctively American pedagogical theory and practice. It is entirely consistent with the progressive revolution in the United States that the most influential book on education in the first half of the twentieth century was Dewey's *Democracy and Education*.

Psychology

Philosophers have always been concerned with problems that are now the province of psychology. Plato and Aristotle had theories of mind and how man learned, and so did all other philosophers who developed a complete philosophy. Their speculations were largely, of course, the result of commonsense observations of general experience. The growing interest in science during the latter half of the nineteenth century gave rise to a new approach to psychological problems, and psychology moved from a branch of philosophy to a closer alliance with the sciences of physiology, physics, and chemistry. Beginning with investigations into sensation and perception and extending to the processes of learning and growth, psychological research soon presented many new concepts which called for radical changes in the purposes and practices of schooling.

Faculty Psychology

Until the twentieth century most educational theories were based on faculty psychology and mental discipline. The mind was thought to be made up of separate and distinct faculties—reason, memory, appreciation, judgment, and so on—and certain studies could best discipline each faculty. For example, geometry was the best exercise for developing reason; reading the classical authors developed appreciation; learning Latin improved memory. It was believed, too, that these faculties, once developed, were generally applicable: reason developed through the study of geometry could be applied in *all* areas of life, and so on. The high point of the development of faculty psychology came in the nineteenth century with the popularization of phrenology. In 1796 Franz Joseph Gall listed some thirty faculties of the mind and declared that these faculties resulted in protuberances and depressions in the skull, giving an index to the strength and weakness of an individual's mind. George Combe, an enthusiast of phrenology, persuaded his friend Horace Mann to accept this extreme view of faculty psychology. Mann's endorsement bulwarked the general acceptance of mental disciplinary arguments throughout the nineteenth century.

Faculty psychology died slowly, in spite of the modern theories of knowledge and new scientific work in psychology. As early as the seventeenth century, the British empiricists, particularly John Locke, had proposed a theory of knowledge inherently opposed to faculty psychology. But despite the fact that they argued that all knowledge came through sense impressions and that there were no innate faculties to be developed in the age-old tradition of abstract and literary studies, even Locke wrote of education and learning as involving mental disciplinary values. Herbart's psychological theory dispensed with mental faculties, and the Herbartians considered the mind to be a storehouse of apperceptions. He and his followers were concerned with developing "interest" and not with exercising mental "muscles." But the popularity of Herbartianism did not materially weaken the commitment of many educational leaders to the principles of mental discipline. Huxley and Spencer defended the study of science on the ground of its disciplinary value. The classicists depended on mental discipline as their main argument for the retention of Latin in the curriculum. The report of the Committee of Ten recommended the study of all subjects for "a time allotment sufficient to produce . . . substantial mental training."

Experimental Psychology

While the phrenologists were attempting a crude scientific explanation of the mind, other scientists were beginning investigations that would lead to experimental psychology. In 1834 Ernst Weber, a German physiologist, completed a study of ability to discriminate between different weights. In 1850 Herman von Helmholtz, a German physicist, published a study of the speed of the nerve impulse, and ten years later a theory of color vision. In 1860 another German physicist, Gustav Theodor Fechner, published *Elements of Psychophysics,* giving the fundamental processes for objective psychological research. Wilhelm Wundt in 1873 described the procedures for psychological experimentation in *Principles of Physiological Psychology,* following the model of physiological experimentation rather than philosophical speculation. Finally in 1879 Wundt founded his famous psychological laboratory at Leipzig, and young scholars from all over Europe and America flocked to study with him. A number of them, including the Americans G. Stanley Hall and James McKeen Cattell, became pioneers in the new science.

Edward B. Titchener, a Briton who studied under Wundt, came to Cornell University in 1892 and trained a number of students who devoted their efforts to the examination and description of the structure of organs rather than their function. The "structuralists," as Titchener called them, were closely allied with anatomists and considered that the function of organs and the behavior of individuals was the proper study of physiologists and biologists rather than of psychologists.

Those who studied the function of organs and the behavior of individuals Titchener called "functionalists," and since educational theories have been built more on concepts of function than those merely of structure, various forms of functionalism will be examined in more detail.

William James

The great popularizer of scientific psychology in America was William

James, who began teaching anatomy and physiology at Harvard in 1873. James began experimenting in psychology soon after his appointment, and in 1875 he first offered a course in psychology at the university. In 1890 he published his two-volume *Principles of Psychology*, greatly stimulating subsequent work in the field. His *Talks to Teachers* put psychological principles in a simplified form so that teachers could make practical application of the ideas. His view, that the function and structure of an organ are integrally related, influenced John Dewey and the functionalists in their development of a scientific psychology.

John Dewey and Functionalism

In 1896 John Dewey published an article in the *Psychological Review* entitled "The Reflex Arc Concept in Psychology," the first public statement of the functionalist position. In this article Dewey held that when the structuralists attempted to study conscious processes only as a mechanical structure and not in their function in human life, they created a dualism between structure and function. They also considered stimuli as discrete from the responses they elicited, connected by a neural reaction called the "reflex arc." Dewey rejected the dualism, pointing out that each response becomes in turn a stimulus for new responses, making the process more like a circle than an arc. The continuity of stimulus and response leads to coordinated activity of the entire organism. The functionalist is concerned not merely with the isolated existential facts about the structure of the individual and his organs but with his overall behavior as he seeks to adapt to his environment. Dewey's two major books in psychology, *How We Think* (1910) and *Human Nature and Conduct* (1922), both deal with the individual in interaction with his environment.

Since "function" cannot be directly observed, the functionalists turned from introspection as the method of research to other forms of laboratory research. Dewey's colleagues at the University of Chicago, James Rowland Angell and Harvey Carr, established an animal laboratory to study the processes of adjustment to environment. This laboratory was to make important contributions to theories of learning.

Functionalism was never as clearly defined or limited in its concerns as was Titchener's structuralism, and consequently there is no easily identified "school" of functionalism. However, the general methods and principles of Dewey, Angell, and Carr have been incorporated, to some degree, in other more readily identified "schools," including associationism, connectionism, and behaviorism.

Associationism and Edward Lee Thorndike

The early psychologists, including James, were not as much concerned about learning as about the process of remembering or recalling what had been learned. Learning was generally considered to take place through an association of ideas and past experiences. In 1885 Herman Ebbinghaus attempted to study the formation of associations, experimenting with the memorization of nonsense syllables, three-letter "words" without meaning. His experiments led to the development of "learning curves" and "forgetting curves," records of a subject's learning and forgetting as plotted on a graph.

In the 1890's Wundt and Britain's Lloyd Morgan experimented with animal learning, concluding that animals learned by association or trial and error, rather than by reasoning. Apparently influenced by the studies of Wundt and Morgan, Edward Lee Thorndike, of Columbia University, began a series of animal learning experiments, using puzzle boxes and mazes. A hungry animal would be placed in a box where a particular action would produce food. After some random activity, the animal would chance upon the action that would release food. As the same animal was given further trials in the same box, it would gradually learn to make the proper response sooner. The association of the satisfaction with the desired act Thorndike called the "law of effect." The first statement of the law gave equal weight to the unsatisfactory actions resulting in negative learning and to the positive associations between the successful act and the satisfaction; however, in 1932 and 1933 Thorndike reported on some human learning experiments in which he found a strong effect from reward but less influence from punishment. Thorndike's theory, which he called "connectionism," considered all associations—or learning—to be the result of stimulus-response reactions, which came to be known as S–R bonds.

Stimulus-response theories were elaborated by a chance discovery in 1902 by the Russian physiologist Ivan Pavlov, who noticed that dogs accustomed to being fed at a particular time by a particular handler began to salivate at the appearance of the handler or even at the sound of his footsteps before the food was placed in front of them. The response of salivation which had been stimulated by the food came to be associated with the sight and sound of the handler. The response to the substitute stimulus—the handler—was called the "conditioned reflex." Pavlov continued to carry on learning experiments with animals, demonstrating how conditioned reflexes could be reinforced or inhibited. In the 1920's much of the theory of learning was based on the principles of the conditioned reflex, and much of the experimentation on learning done since has been based on the principles derived by Pavlov.

In the late 1930's B. F. Skinner began a series of experiments in animal learning which linked together the trial-and-error theories of Thorndike and the conditioned-reflex theories of Pavlov. He used a puzzle box which presented the animal with a simplified task, and by a carefully established series of conditioned stimuli, he "taught" the animal a very complex task. On the principles of grading tasks-to-be-learned into small, easy steps and of rewarding success at each step, Skinner refined the "teaching machine" and programed instruction.

John B. Watson and Behaviorism

An extreme form of functionalism was the behaviorism developed by John B. Watson at Johns Hopkins. His earliest article on behaviorism appeared in the *Psychological Review* in 1913; in 1925, after he left Hopkins to enter the advertising business, he published a book titled *Behaviorism,* a semi-popular explanation of his point of view which influenced writers in all the social sciences. Since he reduced all behavior, human as well as animal, to stimulus-response units, Watson placed all the emphasis on environment, denied any importance to heredity, and eliminated choice or free will of individuals. Any individual was what he was because of the stimuli to which he had been subjected. Given a normal child, Watson claimed, he could make him any kind of specialist, regardless of any interests or talents the child might have. "Good" or "bad" children were merely those who had had "good" or "bad" environments.

In the 1920's behaviorism was a fad among educators and social scientists, particularly because it attempted to be scientific in its methods. Perhaps the most important contributions of behaviorism have been objective observation and the study of the environment of the child.

Gestalt and Field Psychologies

In 1911 and 1912 three German psychologists—Max Wertheimer, Wolfgang Kohler, and Kurt Koffka—performed a number of experiments in the apparent motion created at a motion picture by flashing a series of still photographs. This phenomenon occurred, they explained, because human perceptions take a form or pattern—or, as they called it in German, a *Gestalt.* During World War I, when Kohler was interned on the French island of Tenerife, he applied this concept to the problems of learning. Working with chimpanzees, he noticed behaviors he could not explain as simple trial-and-error learning. His ape subjects seemed to demonstrate an insight into problems set up for them, solving a problem on first trial when they could see the problem in its full context. In short, they appeared to put together a number of elements of the problem, forming a Gestalt.

Gestalt psychology has made a number of important contributions to theories of learning, including stress on understanding a problem, seeing it in context, relating all aspects of a problem, considering the consequences of possible solutions before acting, and acting on the basis of reason rather than at random.

Closely related to Gestalt psychology is the "field" theory of Kurt Lewin, developed in the 1930's. The "field" is the "life-space" of an individual, his environment as he perceives and understands it. Lewin was particularly concerned with motivation, and in his analysis of the life-space of an individual, he included "vectors" of attraction and repulsion which describe the individual's relationship to the forces he perceives in his environment. Lewin's stress on motivation and individual perception has been important in modern theories of learning.

Holistic Psychologies

One mid-century cliché in education has been "the child as a whole," a concept which has had its psychological counterpart in theories viewing the organism as a unit or whole. Although there are considerable differences among them, the psychologists who emphasize the "whole" individual can be generally described by the word "holistic." Like the Gestaltists and field theorists, the holistic psychologists have contributed to our awareness that human behavior cannot be fully explained by isolating and studying only the mechanistic processes of learning and behavior. Motivation, needs, feelings, and personality are all factors which, the holistic psychologists point out, must be taken into account.

Psychoanalysis

Although psychoanalysis has been concerned primarily with therapy of the mentally disturbed, psychoanalytic theories have had considerable effect on educational theories, particularly on those held by founders of the private progressive schools.

When Sigmund Freud began treating neurotic patients in Vienna around 1886, he searched the patient's memory to locate the experience that was the source of his disorder. He adapted the Herbartian concept of the mind as made up largely of a subconscious storehouse to explain how repressed childhood experiences, generally related to the sex drive, caused personality disturbances. Later psychoanalysts broadened Freud's concepts, adding to the analytical tools for dealing with personality problems. Alfred Adler considered the most important human drive not sex but the "urge to dominate." He added to the psychologist's arsenal such concepts as "inferiority complex" and "compensation." Carl Jung wrote of personalities as "introverts" and "extroverts."

All psychoanalytic theories placed great emphasis on childhood experiences. In the first three decades of the twentieth century when psychoanalysis first became fashionable among the well-to-do intellectuals in the United States, many parents were concerned lest they inhibit some of the desires of their offspring and so "warp" their personalities and create neuroses. That fear led some parents, particularly upper-middle-class city dwellers, to be very permissive in rearing their children, and they sought schools equally permissive. To satisfy that demand, private schoolmasters set up experimental "progressive" schools, which were extremely "child-centered." These schools minimized social and adult control, giving the children considerable freedom and making much of the "democratic" practices of the school. Actually the "freedom" was more nearly license, and the "democracy" closer to anarchy. In 1919 the teachers of these schools organized the Progressive Education Association, and many of the extreme practices which have been ridiculed by critics of modern education were limited to those schools. The cartoonists, editorial writers, and academic conservatives who have tended to blame John Dewey for those extremes have failed to see the strong influence of Freud and psychoanalysis. Actually, Dewey refused to be associated with the Progressive Education Association until 1928, when many of the founders of the Association had been replaced by educators who did accept the essential social and intellectual principles of Dewey's philosophy.

G. *Stanley Hall and Child Study*

One of the most influential educators at the turn of the century was G. Stanley Hall. A student of Wundt, Hall joined the faculty of Johns Hopkins in 1881, and in 1889 became the first president of Clark University, serving until 1919. Like Hopkins, Clark emphasized graduate study. At Clark, President Hall was also chairman of the psychology department and devoted much of his time to child-study. In 1883 he published *The Contents of Children's Minds on Entering School,* having collected the data by questioning little children, a method others criticized as incapable of producing reliable data. In addition to his own research and his direct inspiration to his students, he promoted the development of the field through his leadership of the American Psychological Association, of which he was one of the founders and first president (1891). Author of many articles and books, his monumental two-volume work *Adolescence* (1904) was the cornerstone of child psychology.

Like the Herbartians, Hall accepted the "recapitulation" theory of evolution: that each individual went through all the stages mankind had undergone in its evolution. Hall believed that childhood play was a recapitulation of the primitive stage of human history; thus if the play activities of a child were inhibited, harmful expression of the primitive tendencies might result later in life. Other child interests represented other stages of human evolution, and teachers must study the child to understand these stages of development and take advantage of them in organizing the learning process.

At the International Congress of Education of the World's Columbian Exposition in 1893, the Congress of Experimental Psychology in Education heard fifteen addresses, at least five of which were in child study. The psychology meetings were chaired by Hall, whose opening address outlined the directions of child study, including the "measurement of children," the study of "exceptional and defective children," and child hygiene. Each of these had important implications for education. The measurement of growth indicated differing rates of growth at different times and for different parts of the body.

> Times of physical growth are also times of mental growth in acquisition, though children then are not able to systematize well. Hence, in time of great acquisition ease up the constraint of methods.

The study of exceptional children led from child study to "Study *this* child." Concern for the health of the child led Hall to doubt the wisdom of the great pressure of school work on children.

> The modern school is a tremendous engine to drive the child organism. . . . Better let children grow up in idyllic ignorance than vitiate their health.[1]

Other papers at the meeting pointed out the importance of child study as a basis for pedagogical practice, drawing on concrete examples from the psychological theory of the day.

The child study pioneering of Hall led to the specialties of child psychology and adolescent psychology. Major contributions to the understanding of children have come from the developmental psychologists,

[1] N.E.A. *Proceedings,* 1893, pp. 717–718.

whose close observations of children are the basis for statistical statements about the stages through which children pass. At Yale, Arnold Gesell established the Clinic of Child Development in 1911, where he and co-workers observed children through one-way screens. By means of observing many children over prolonged periods, Gesell and his associates have described the stages through which a child typically passes as he grows up. The Gesell studies focused particular interest on the pre-school ages and lent strong support to the idea of nursery schools and kindergartens.

Educational Psychology

Most of these psychological schools had implications for education, and just as some psychologists have become specialists in therapy or counseling, others have given their attention to discovering the implications of the various psychological theories for education. Educational psychologists may belong to any one of a number of schools or they may be eclectic; they often develop a particular interest—learning, child development, counseling, testing, and so on. Although no one field or school can yet solve all the psychological problems teachers meet in working with children, together they provide a considerable body of tested theory which teachers may utilize to improve their professional competence. In any program of teacher preparation today, one essential is a solid course in the application of psychology to education.

The Measurement Movement

Closely related to the work in psychology has been the attempt to measure human capacities and accomplishments. Sir Francis Galton, a cousin of Charles Darwin, devised tests to measure the capacities of individuals and developed statistical methods for analyzing the quantitative data gained from the tests. Karl Pearson contributed further statistical tools. James McKeen Cattell, under the influence of Galton's work, published *Mental Tests and Measurement* in 1890 and conducted measurement experiments on entering freshman classes at Columbia University. Two French psychologists, Alfred Binet and Theophile Simon, developed the first intelligence test in 1906, and an American version was produced at Stanford University under the direction of Lewis Terman in 1916. During World War I the United States Army gave intelligence tests to millions of draftees. Not only did the tests provide a mountain of statistics for generalizations about levels of intelligence in the United States, but they were models for other group intelligence tests to be published shortly after the war.

Ironically, it was not a professional educator or psychologist who gave educational measurement its first important popular impetus. In 1892 and 1893 Joseph M. Rice published a series of "muckraking" articles in the *Forum* exposing political interference in schools and the incompetence of many teachers. The articles created great public furor, including an anguished howl from virtually all educational leaders and editors of educational journals. Despite this Rice undertook a survey of methods of teaching spelling. Before his journalistic career he had been a student of pedagogy in Germany for two years, and he knew something of the techniques of objective measurement. In testing some 30,000 pupils, Rice discovered that those who spent fifteen minutes a day on spelling learned just as much as those who spent thirty minutes and more. In reacting against Rice's criticisms, educators tended to reject his methods of objective measurement, claiming that spelling was a mental exercise valued for its discipline as much as for improvement in the ability to spell words.

Feeling was so strong against Rice and other outside critics that the Department of Superintendence of the NEA resolved in 1912 to "encourage all fair and candid investigations" of schools and school policies, but "we condemn and resent all such investigations whose obvious purposes are to debase the systems or exalt the investigators."[2] The sharp words were softened considerably the next year, with the Department recommending "expert surveys" as "helpful and valuable."[3] In 1918 the National Society for the Study of Education published as Part II of its *Seventeenth Yearbook* "The Measurement of Educational Products." There Thorndike, who had become the high priest of measurement, stated the credo of measurement: "Whatever exists at all exists in some amount." Thorndike, Charles H. Judd, and their students set out to quantify and measure every conceivable "educational product." In an age of science, they were attempting to make pedagogy scientific. Thorndike claimed that his credo was the same as

> that of the physicist or chemist or physiologist engaged in quantitative thinking—the same, indeed, as that of modern science in general. And, in general, the nature of educational measurements is the same as that of all scientific measurements.

[2] N.E.A. *Proceedings*, 1912, p. 331.
[3] N.E.A. *Proceedings*, 1913, pp. 102–103.

He had "faith" that the development of new scales of measurement would make possible precise measurement of products which "people now measure crudely by mere descriptive words."[4]

One of Thorndike's students, William A. McCall, expanded the credo of measurement: "Whatever exists at all, exists in some amount. . . . Anything that exists in amount can be measured." In *How to Measure in Education,* McCall included chapters on classifying and placing pupils by "educational age" so that "homogeneous groups will make more satisfactory progress," on diagnosis of "the initial condition and a more detailed diagnosis of the particular defects of classes or pupils," on the use of tests in teaching, particularly in the "fundamental skills" where "it is advisable to teach almost entirely by testing;" on "evaluating the efficiency of instruction;" and on matching individuals and occupations in vocational guidance.[5]

Beginning with Cliff W. Stone, who developed an objective test in arithmetic reasoning in 1908, Thorndike's students began preparing tests for measuring student achievement in almost every subject in the curriculum. The *17th Yearbook* of the NSSE (1918) describes 84 standardized tests for use in elementary schools, covering arithmetic, drawing, geography, handwriting, history, language, music, silent reading, oral reading, and spelling; 25 were listed for high schools, covering algebra, drawing, foreign language, geometry, history, physical training, and physics. These tests received wide acceptance very quickly. In 1917 nearly 900,000 copies of one test were used, and "the annual sale of a few other tests run well over 100,000 copies each."[6]

There were soon attempts to evaluate more than achievement in school subjects. By mid-century, tests had been devised for measuring personality (particularly the Rorschach), physique, temperament, aptitudes, attitudes, interests, and character. Curriculum makers sought objectivity about what subjects ought to be taught and what content should be included by surveying the kinds of arithmetic problems and spelling words used by adults. Guidance workers attempted by "job analysis" to determine the knowledge, skills, and habits needed in certain vocations. State and city school systems, universities, and normal schools organized special bureaus or divisions to carry on quantitative research. In 1917 at least 18 cities, 8 state universities, 2 normal schools, and 3 state departments had bureaus or divisions of research.[7]

[4] National Society for the Study of Education, *17th Yearbook, Part II* (Bloomington, Illinois: Public School Publishing Co., 1918), pp. 16–17.

[5] New York: Macmillan, 1922, pp. 3–4, 19, 67, 112, 149.

[6] National Society for the Study of Education, *17th Yearbook, Part II*, p. 56.

[7] *Ibid.*, pp. 56, 68 69.

In 1897, in an experiment designed to measure intellectual fatigue, Ebbinghaus invented the completion or "fill-in-the-blank" test. Other kinds of short-answer tests that could be scored easily and consistently (hence called "objective") were the multiple choice, matching, identification, and true-false tests. McCall urged that teachers lighten their task by adopting objective tests instead of lengthy essay and oral examinations. He claimed that "these new techniques of scientific testing" would not only "improve certain kinds of examinations," but would also "make examinations a real pleasure instead of an onerous task to both teacher and pupils."[8] That happy millenium has not yet arrived.

The School Survey

A complex application of the measurement movement and testing was the school survey. Like most other innovations, the school survey had a more ancient and distinguished ancestry than is customarily accorded it. Before he published his letters and essays on "popular education" in 1824 and 1826, James Carter had taken a good look at the Massachusetts schools. Henry Barnard, when the Connecticut legislature abolished his office in 1842, made a study of the Rhode Island schools that led to the creation of a state commissioner there in 1845. Joseph Rice's "muckraking" articles in *Forum* in 1892 and 1893 resulted from six months of visiting the nation's schools. While Rice did not use the word "survey" in his articles, his methods of quantitative comparison and analysis of the significance of his findings were characteristic of later "surveys." Also in 1897, the Educational Commission of Chicago, under William R. Harper, president of the University of Chicago, published a report based on a thorough study of the city schools.

Most textbooks accord Boise, Idaho, the honor of having instituted the first full-blown "schools survey." In 1910 Calvin N. Kendall, superintendent of schools in Indianapolis, was invited to spend a week inspecting the schools of Boise. His report, published in the local newspaper, covered the school buildings, teachers, curriculum, organization of the system, and community attitude. A year later, Paul Hanus, of Harvard, and E. C. Moore, of Yale, inspected the schools of Montclair and East Orange, New Jersey, respectively. By 1914 the survey had reached such popularity that the NSSE published as Part II of its *13th Yearbook* "Plans for Organizing School Surveys, with a Summary of Typical School Surveys," and its bibliography listed 36 different school surveys.

[8] McCall, p. 119.

Some of these surveys were very complex. In contrast with Kendall's one-man study in Boise, Baltimore conducted a survey in 1911 with a five-man commission including United States Commissioner of Education E. E. Brown, Professor Elwood P. Cubberely, and Kendall. In 1911 New York City began a three-year survey conducted by Professor Hanus and eleven other educators, together with engineers, accountants, and political scientists. The survey cost $95,139, and the report ran to three volumes totalling over 2,500 pages.[9]

The prevailing practice in these early surveys was to rely entirely on observation and testing by outside experts. The primary method of rating a school system was ranking it against systems of other cities considered comparable. The emphasis on improving the position in the rank-order without considering how well the schools might do if resources were fully utilized was one of the sharpest criticisms of these surveys. Another criticism expressed by school superintendents sprang from the great number of recommendations for change which ordinarily came as a conclusion of the survey. So many recommended changes coming at one time often had the effect of lowering public confidence in the schools and school administrators. The NSSE recommended that local personnal take the lead in conducting surveys, bringing in the experts for assistance, advice, and a fresh point of view.[10]

The NSSE *13th Yearbook*, in an effort to help local leaders conduct surveys, presented two outlines for an "educational survey." The "brief" outline is twenty-seven pages long. Among its headings are "School Plant, and Equipment," "Organization, Administration, and Supervision of Schools," "Course of Study," "The Child," "Teachers," and "Finances." Questions in the long form are quite detailed: height of risers in stairs, dimensions of closets, number and value of "victrola and piano-player" records, salaries of school board members, amount of insurance against earthquake, "pressure back of introduction of each subject" in the curriculum, number of homes having one, two, three, or four children of school age, how often blackboards are cleaned and by whom, freedom of teachers to experiment—literally hundreds of questions.

Detailed surveys have been conducted for accrediting schools, revising curricula, planning for expansion or consolidation, and improving educational opportunities in general. In a society which values quantitative measures and uses polls and questionnaires to determine the bases for collective action, the school survey is an example of the businesslike, "efficient" approach to educational evaluation.

[9] National Society for the Study of Education, *13th Yearbook, Part II* (Chicago: U. of Chicago Press, 1914), pp. 64–66, 73.

[10] *Ibid.*, pp. 22–23.

Pragmatism

The general American acceptance of science and utilitarianism had sharply undermined the traditional philosophies by the end of the nineteenth century, and the newer concepts in psychology and pedagogical theory were at considerable variance with viewpoints developed from the older philosophies. To give coherence to the new theories and new attitudes, a new philosophy was called for. It is not surprising that the seminal expression of a native American philosophy came from a scientist and mathematician, Charles Sanders Peirce. Between 1872 and 1874, Peirce and a number of other brilliant young men, including Chauncey Wright and William James, met in an informal discussion society which Peirce called the Metaphysical Club. From ideas which Wright outlined to the group, Peirce developed the foundations of pragmatism. He presented his new philosophy to the public in a series of articles in Youman's *Popular Science Monthly* in 1877 and 1878, but little attention was given them.

William James: Verification by Experience

In the same month that Peirce published his second article, William James laid down one of the principles of pragmatism: that what we consider the truth is what we can verify from our experience. In human affairs, truth is not something that exists apart from human action.

> The knower is not simply a mirror floating with no foot-hold anywhere, and passively reflecting an order that he comes upon and finds simply existing. The knower is an actor, and . . . he registers the truth which he helps to create. Mental interests, hypotheses, postulates, so far as they are bases for human action . . . help to *make* the truth which they declare.[11]

A central idea of pragmatism is that thought processes are carried on in relation to human purposes.

The term "pragmatism" was reintroduced by James in a lecture at the University of California in 1898, but he gave it a somewhat different interpretation than Peirce had originally used. Through his books and lectures, James' view of pragmatism came to be the one generally accepted. James sought to have pragmatism become a philosophy for human affairs, rather than a speculative exercise for "ivory-tower" academicians.

[11] "Remarks on Spencer's Definition of Mind as Correspondence," *Journal of Speculative Philosophy*, 12 (January 1878): 17.

> A pragmatist turns his back resolutely . . . upon a lot of inveterate habits dear to professional philosophers. He turns away from abstraction and insufficiency, from verbal solutions, from bad *a priori* reasons, from fixed principles, closed systems, and pretended absolutes and origins. He turns towards concreteness and adequacy, toward facts, towards action and towards power. . . . It means the open air and possibilities of nature, as against dogma, artificiality, and the pretense of finality in truth. . . .
>
> Metaphysics has usually followed a very primitive kind of quest. You know what a great part in magic *words* have always played. . . . So the universe has always appeared to the natural mind as a kind of enigma, of which the key must be sought in the shape of some illuminating or power-bringing word or name. That word names the universe's *principle,* and to possess it is . . . to possess the universe itself. "God," "Matter," "Reason," "the Absolute," "Energy," are so many solving names. You can rest when you have them. You are at the end of your metaphysical quest.
>
> But if you follow the pragmatic method, you cannot look on any such word as closing your quest. You must . . . set it at work within the stream of your experience. It appears less as a solution then, than as a program for more work, and more particularly as an indication of the ways in which existing realities may be *changed.*
>
> *Theories thus become instruments, not answers to enigmas.* . . . "Truth" in our ideas and beliefs means the same thing that it means in science. It means . . . *that ideas (which themselves are but parts of our experience) become true just in so far as they help us to get into satisfactory relation with other parts of our experience.* . . . Any idea that will carry us prosperously from any one part of our experience to any other part, linking things satisfactorily, working securely, simplifying, saving labor; is true for just so much, true in so far forth, true *instrumentally.*[12]

John Dewey

It was the pragmatism of James to which John Dewey was converted during the 1890's, although he returned to many of the original ideas of Peirce. Because of the close relationship between Dewey's concepts of pragmatism and his educational philosophy, they will be discussed in a later section of this chapter.

American Pedagogical Theory

Until the close of the nineteenth century, pedagogical theory in the

[12] William James, *Pragmatism* (New York: Longmans, Green, 1907), pp. 51–53, 58.

United States was derived directly from European philosophers and educators. Not until Parker and Dewey did the United States begin to develop a native American theory of education.

Francis W. Parker

Francis Wayland Parker's rise in the Civil War from private to colonel was equalled by his advancement from rural school teacher to the leading educational theorist of his day. His service as teacher and principal in New Hampshire earned him an appointment in 1868 as principal of a normal school in Dayton, Ohio. In 1872 he went to Germany for three year's study, learning the philosophies of Pestalozzi, Herbart, Froebel, and Ritter, parts of which he incorporated into the schools of Quincy, Massachusetts, when he became superintendent there in 1875. Opposition to his innovations led to an investigation by the Massachusetts Board of Education. Although the investigation resulted in praise of his work, Parker resigned to work in Boston as a supervisor. In 1883 he left that position to become principal of the Cook County Normal School in Chicago. There and at the Chicago Normal School until 1899, Parker developed and demonstrated educational theories that were to help revolutionize twentieth-century American education. While there were definite European influences in his theories, the synthesis was a product consistent with American democracy and the newly developing science of psychology.

Characteristic of the educational theories of both Parker and Dewey was a whole-hearted commitment to democracy and to the public schools that could make a democratic society a reality.

> Fighting for four years, as best I could, for the preservation of the democratic ideal, a teacher of little children for nearly forty years, I believe four things as I believe in God—that democracy is the one hope of the world; that democracy without efficient common schools is impossible; that every school in the land should be made a home and a heaven for children; fourth, that when the ideal of the public school is realized, "the blood shed by the blessed martyrs for freedom will not have been shed in vain."[13]

Parker criticized the Herbartians for attempting to make history and literature the center of the curriculum, pointing out that those subjects had been "a prominent means of adjusting the child to the society, to

[13] Francis W. Parker, *Talks on Pedagogics* (New York: E. L. Kellogg, 1894), p. 451.

the state, to the government." He argued instead for a child-centered education. "*We do claim that the child is the center*, that this being, the highest creation of God . . . determines in itself, the very nature and condition of its growth."[14] All educational activity should spring from the child's "spontaneous study and persistent interest." The subjects a child should study are determined by the things about him, "because his environment acts upon him and educates him." His own family life is the beginning of the study of anthropology and history. The school and the community are "the true foundation of civics." Zoology begins with the child's delight in birds, butterflies, and bees; botany with his love of flowers. Interest in physical sciences is manifest in the collections of pebbles and the damming of streams after a rain.[15] The child's life demands a broad curriculum, but the motivation and purpose of the study must be derived from the child's interest, rather than from a slavish acceptance of the formal academic "book lessons" of the past.

Although Parker frequently used traditional theological concepts and terms, such as "the Creator" and "He put into that child Himself, His divinity," he did not picture the universe as complete and unchanging. Like John Dewey, he recognized the evolutionary process: "Everything changes in this universe. . . . Creation is the order of progress."[16] Thus, even with an absolutist view of reality and creation, Parker developed educational principles consistent with a pragmatic philosophy.

In a series of lectures to teachers at the Martha's Vineyard Summer Institute in 1882, Parker anticipated a number of educational principles that were later keystones of the "progressive" theories of Dewey and his associates. He stated, for instance, that it is possible to understand an act only if the motive directing the act is known; for "Every act has a motive, and it is the motive which colors, directs, forms the action." He charged that to determine the quantity of skill and knowledge to be learned by "courses of study and the conventional examinations . . . is a mistake," because it assumed a "false motive of education." "The true motive of education . . . is the harmonious development of the human being, body, mind, and soul." He quoted Comenius: "Let things that have to be done be learned by doing them"; and Pestalozzi: "Education is the generation of power." To achieve these goals and that of Froebel—"the harmonious growth of the whole being"—Parker advocated an instrumental theory of learning: "Knowledge and skill are simply the

[14] *First Supplement to the Year Book of the National Herbart Society*, 1895, pp. 155–156.

[15] Parker, pp. 11–16.

[16] *Ibid.*, pp. 32–33.

means and not the end, and these are to work toward the symmetrical upbuilding of the whole being." Finally, he said that if the teacher understands the child's mind and regards the subjects of the school as means, then "he can work toward the end, which is growth."[17] All of these are key concepts in Dewey's philosophy.

In the conservatism of the Gilded Age when "Many wealthy people . . . look to-day upon the common-school system as a charity, and hold that there should be one education for rich children and another for the poor," Parker found a great threat to democracy. In a democracy the common schools must be truly common, a radical idea for the 1890's that is still too radical for some Americans seventy years later.

> When in American society classes become permanent, and the children of these classes are educated in separate schools, the doom of the Republic is sealed. . . .
>
> No child, no citizen of a republic, can be educated into citizenship outside the common school; *the common school is not a charity; it is the inalienable right of every child, and common education is the imperative duty of every community.*[18]

These revolutionary sentiments were expressed in a chapter bearing a title which John Dewey was later to use for his major educational book —"Democracy and Education." In his theory and in the practice of that theory demonstrated in his own schools, Parker helped stimulate and direct the twentieth-century democratic revolution in American education.

John Dewey

Among the native American pedagogical theorists, none is more important than John Dewey. Born in 1859, Dewey attended the public schools and the University of Vermont before serving briefly as a rural school teacher. At Vermont he studied classical philosophy but was also greatly stimulated by the writing of Huxley. When he went to Johns Hopkins to continue his graduate study, the greatest immediate influence on his thinking was George Sylvester Morris, whose Hegelianism strengthened Dewey's absolute idealism. At Hopkins he met G. Stanley Hall and Charles S. Peirce, who later were to contribute to his conversion to pragmatism. After several years of teaching philosophy at the universities of Minnesota and Michigan, he went to the new University

[17] *Notes on Talks on Teaching* (New York: E. L. Kellogg, 1884), pp. 21–22.
[18] *Talks on Pedagogics*, pp. 437–438.

of Chicago in 1894 as head of the departments of philosophy, psychology, and education. He became an active, though usually dissenting, member of the National Herbart Society. Although his earliest writings were in psychology, at Chicago he turned more and more to philosophy and the pragmatism of William James. As early as his contributions to *Studies in Logical Theory*, published in 1903, Dewey acknowledged his "obligation" to James' philosophy.

Many of the interpreters of Dewey, his followers as well as his critics, have grossly distorted the meaning of pragmatism and experience in Dewey's writings. "Experience" does not mean activity alone, nor does "doing" as a learning process mean merely muscular movement. Nor is it adequate to define the pragmatic test of an act as "Does it work?" Dewey's philosophy stresses intellectual activity, for the processes of thought are essential to effective action and learning. We must observe the relationships between an act and its consequences in order to learn from our experiences, and the recognition of these relationships is what Dewey defines as "thinking." Thinking comes into play when we project anticipated consequences to an act we plan to take, and thereby decide whether to take the action. If we do follow the action and the consequences we predicted result, then and only then can the conclusions we drew be said to be valid or proven. If any other consequences result, regardless of whether or not they are satisfying or favorable, our conclusions have failed to pass the pragmatic test.

> Thinking is the accurate and deliberate instituting of connections between what is done and its consequences. It notes not only that they are connected, but the details of the connection. It makes connecting links explicit in the form of relationships. The stimulus to thinking is found when we wish to determine the significance of some act, performed or to be performed. Then we anticipate consequences. This implies that the situation as it stands is, either in fact or to us, incomplete and hence indeterminate. The projection of consequences means a proposed or tentative solution. To perfect this hypothesis, existing conditions have to be carefully scrutinized and the implications of the hypothesis developed—an operation called reasoning. Then the suggested solution—the idea or theory—has to be tested by acting upon it. If it brings about certain consequences, certain determinate changes, in the world, it is accepted as valid. Otherwise it is modified, and another trial made. Thinking includes all of these steps,—the sense of a problem, the observation of conditions, the formation and rational elaboration of a suggested conclusion, and the active experimental testing. While all thinking results in knowledge, ultimately the value of knowledge is subordi-

> nated to its use in thinking. . . . Knowledge . . . is of value in the solidity, security, and fertility it affords our dealings with the future.[19]

For Dewey, thought was such an essential ingredient of human life that he did not regard education as something restricted to the schoolroom. Every act, if we consider its effects, teaches us something we may be able to use in the future. Thus Dewey did not separate the concerns of philosophy from those of education.

> If we are willing to conceive education as the process of forming fundamental dispositions, intellectual and emotional, toward nature and fellow men, philosophy may even be defined *as the general theory of education.*

Therefore, when the pragmatists argued for a redirection of philosophy toward the practical problems of the actions of men, they were also calling for the reform of education.

> The reconstruction of philosophy, of education, and of social ideals and methods thus go hand in hand. If there is especial need of educational reconstruction at the present time, if this need makes urgent a reconsideration of the basic ideas of traditional philosophic systems, it is because of the thoroughgoing change in social life accompanying the advance of science, the industrial revolution, and the development of democracy.[20]

Dewey's pragmatism was to provide the philosophical foundation for the revolution in educational methods and attitudes he was to lead in the twentieth century. Even before he left the University of Chicago in 1904 to join the faculty of Columbia University, he had already published *My Pedagogical Creed* (1897), but it was at Columbia that he wrote his most influential educational work: *Democracy and Education* (1916). At Columbia he achieved worldwide fame for himself and for Teachers College. There he and a number of the most able professors of education in the country attracted many superior graduate students and turned out many of the nation's top school administrators and professors of education. Retiring from Columbia in 1930, Dewey continued to be active until his death in 1952 at the age of 92.

[19] John Dewey, *Democracy and Education* (New York: Macmillan, 1916), pp. 177–178.
[20] *Ibid.*, pp. 383, 386.

"KNOWING AND DOING" Many of Dewey's critics have accused him of being anti-intellectual, of being concerned only with physical activity. Such a criticism ignores Dewey's abhorence for any kind of dualism. Just as he refused to accept a separation of man into mind and body, or the isolation of the individual from society, or the consideration of ends without relation to means, so he attacked any theory of knowledge or learning that divorced "intellect" from "action." His insistence on the integration of knowing and doing was derived from the analysis of experimental science. "There is no such thing as genuine knowledge and fruitful understanding except as the offspring of *doing*."[21]

On the other hand, doing by itself is not learning. An experience is significant for learning because it provides the basis for an intellectual examination of the event with its consequences.

"EDUCATION AS RECONSTRUCTION" Dewey defined education as the "reconstruction or reorganization of experience which adds to the meaning of experience, and which increases ability to direct the course of subsequent experience."[22] This reflection on experience in order to learn how to act more effectively epitomizes Dewey's concept of the relation of theory and practice: theory is derived from experience and is practical to the extent that it serves as a guide to further experience.

"THE INDIVIDUAL AND THE WORLD" Dewey has been accused of giving children such complete freedom that they learn no social responsibility and, at the other extreme, of destroying individuality by demanding that children conform, "get along with the group." Both charges are far from what Dewey believed, for both imply a dualism of the individual versus society. For Dewey there could be no democratic society without individuality and no opportunity for individuals to develop without the support of society. He spoke of education as "a freeing of individual capacity in a progressive growth directed to social aims."[23]

> A progressive society counts individual variations as precious since it finds in them the means of its own growth. Hence a democratic society must, in consistency with its ideal, allow for intellectual freedom and the play of diverse gifts and interests in its educational measures.[24]

It is in the relationship between the individual and society that Dewey finds the basic function of education. Every individual is "born imma-

[21] *Ibid.*, p. 321.
[22] *Ibid.*, pp. 89–90.
[23] *Ibid.*, p. 115.
[24] *Ibid.*, p. 357.

ture, helpless, without language, beliefs, ideas, or social standards," and he must be "initiated into the interests, purposes, information, skill, and practices of the mature members" if the society is to persist and the individual to develop. This education, when defined in its broadest sense, includes both formal and informal means of maintaining and renewing the continuity of life within the society. "Schools are, indeed, one important method of the transmission which forms the dispositions of the immature; but it is only one means."[25]

"THE PLAN OF FORMAL EDUCATION" Simple societies—"savage groups"—are able to transmit their culture without formal education. Children learn the culture "by sharing in what the elders are doing." This is "learning by doing" reduced to its crudest level, but these learning activities are most meaningful to the child because of the observable direct relation between the learning and the adult life of the culture.

> But as civilization advances, the gap between the capacities of the young and the concerns of adults widens. Learning by direct sharing in the pursuits of grown-ups becomes increasingly difficult. . . . Ability to share effectively in adult activities thus depends upon a prior training given with this end in view. Intentional agencies—schools—and explicit material—studies—are devised.

The establishment of formal education carries a grave danger, however, for it "easily becomes remote and dead—abstract and bookish." The accumulated knowledge of the society becomes preserved in symbols which are "far from translation into familiar acts and objects." Schooling tends to become concerned with learning the symbols and not the real cultural experience for which the symbols stand.

> There is the standing danger that the material of formal instruction will be merely the subject matter of the schools, isolated from the subject matter of life-experience. . . . Thus we reach the ordinary notion of education: the notion which ignores its social necessity and its identity with all human association that affects conscious life, and which identifies it with imparting information about remote matters and the conveying of learning through verbal signs: the acquisition of literacy.[26]

Dewey was not opposed to the acquisition of literacy, but he did object to the assumption that recognizing and pronouncing symbols was

[25] *Ibid.*, pp. 3–5.
[26] *Ibid.*, pp. 9–10.

the same as acquiring knowledge. Words acquire meaning only as they are used in "an action which is participated in by a number of people." When the mother puts a child's hat on and says *hat*, "the sound 'hat' soon gets the same meaning for the child that it has for the parent."

> They acquire the same meaning with the child which they have with the adult because they are used in a common experience by both. The guarantee for the same manner of use is found in the fact that the thing and the sound are first employed in a joint activity. . . . Similar ideas or meanings spring up because both persons are engaged as partners in an action where what each does depends upon and influences what the other does.[27]

It is in this sense that Dewey advocated "activity" in school: "Not that the use of language as an educational resource should lessen; but that its use should be more vital and fruitful by having its normal connection with shared activities."[28]

"THE SCHOOL AS A SPECIAL ENVIRONMENT" Dewey's insistence that learning takes place through shared activity means more than children engaging in just any kind of group work. Knowledge that will be of significance in life is acquired when the shared activity is related to life outside the formal institution of school. "The learning in school should be continuous with that out of school."[29] But even this does not mean that all social activities are appropriate for schools. There is too much in the culture for anyone to learn it all. Much of it, indeed, is not worth learning, and much of it has to be organized in sequences fitted to the development of the learner. All aspects of the child's development need to be balanced. Consequently, the school must be a special environment, selecting, refining, and organizing what the child is to learn, eliminating socially undesirable features of the general environment and incorporating desirable features which the child is unlikely to learn in his life outside school. The learner faces confusion because of the conflicting influences exerted at times by the diverse goals of his family, peer group, neighborhood, church, and work; therefore, the school must help the child integrate his experiences if he is to develop a stable, well-adjusted personality.

[27] *Ibid.*, pp. 17–18.
[28] *Ibid.*, p. 46.
[29] *Ibid.*, p. 416.

"INTEREST AND DISCIPLINE" Dewey recognized that some teachers think that interest means attaching "some feature of seductiveness to material otherwise indifferent; to secure attention and effort by offering a bribe of pleasure." That meaning he rejected as being "properly stigmatized as 'soft' pedagogy."

Interest was, for Dewey, far more than entertaining children or even permitting them to follow a fleeting whim; interest was a whole-hearted involvement, a concern for reaching a goal.

> The word interest . . . expresses (I) the whole state of active development, (II) the objective results that are foreseen and wanted, and (III) the personal emotional inclination. (I) An occupation, employment, pursuit, business is often referred to as an interest. . . . (II) By an interest we also mean the point at which an object touches or engages a man; the point where it influences him. . . . (III) When we speak of a man as interested in this or that the emphasis falls directly upon his personal attitude. To be interested is to be absorbed in, wrapped up in, carried away by, some object. . . . We say of an interested person both that he has lost himself in some affair and that he has found himself it it. Both terms express the engrossment of the self in an object.[30]

Limiting the meaning of interest by failing to see all of these as included leads to "soft" pedagogy or "spoon-feeding" theories of education.

Dewey criticized traditional education for taking seriously the humorist's statement: "It makes no difference what you teach a boy so long as he doesn't like it." That attitude isolated subject matter from the activities of life, from the problems that people really face. Interest, as Dewey defined it, is necessary in teaching, because "learning takes place in connection with the intelligent carrying forward of purposeful activities."[31] The teacher must locate significant interests of the child and help him see the connections between his present knowledge and abilities and his future goals or purposes.

> In learning, the present powers of the pupil are the initial stage; the aim of the teacher represents the remote limit. Between the two lie *means*—that is middle conditions:—acts to be performed; difficulties to be overcome; appliances to be used. Only *through* them . . . will the initial activities reach a satisfactory consummation.
>
> These intermediate conditions are of interest precisely because

[30] *Ibid.*, pp. 148–149.
[31] *Ibid.*, pp. 157, 161.

> the development of existing activities into the foreseen and desired end depends upon them. To be means for the achieving of present tendencies, . . . to be of interest, are different names for the same end. When material has to be made interesting, it signifies that as presented, it lacks connection with purposes and present power: or that if the connection is there it is not perceived. To make it interesting by leading one to realize the connection that exists is simply good sense; to make it interesting by extraneous and artificial inducements deserves all the bad names which have been applied to the doctrine of interest in education.[32]

Dewey's attack on the doctrine of formal discipline has been taken to mean that children should be uninhibited in their activities, but this point of view, which was attempted only by the most extreme of the private experimental schools, was far more a product of Freudian dogma than of Dewey's concepts. Dewey *was* opposed to the negative kind of imposed discipline suitable for an autocratic society, a discipline which sought "to cow the spirit, to subdue inclination, to compel obedience, to mortify the flesh, to make a subordinate perform an uncongenial task." In a democracy, each individual must learn to be responsible for himself. Dewey's concept of discipline stressed the importance of each individual consciously and intelligently determining his own purposes and then striving to carry out those purposes "in spite of difficulties and contrary solicitations."

> A person who is trained to consider his actions, to undertake them deliberately, is in so far forth disciplined. Add to this ability a power to endure in an intelligently chosen course in the face of distraction, confusion, and difficulty, and you have the essence of discipline.[33]

What could be a better definition of intelligent discipline for a citizen of a democracy? This kind of discipline can be developed only when students have an interest in what they are to learn, when the "subject matter of learning is identical with all the objects, ideas, and principles which enter as resources or obstacles into the continuous intentional pursuit of a course of action."[34]

Much of the experimentation and perhaps most of the debate over pedagogical theory between 1920 and the present have been rooted in the philosophy of John Dewey.

[32] *Ibid.*, pp. 149–150.
[33] *Ibid.*, pp. 151–152.
[34] *Ibid.*, p. 162.

William Heard Kilpatrick

One of the most important interpreters of Dewey was William Heard Kilpatrick (1871–1965), who added considerable contributions of his own to theories of pedagogy. Kilpatrick was professor of mathematics and psychology at Mercer College before joining the faculty of Teachers College in 1909. From 1918 to 1938, when he retired, he was professor of philosophy of education at Teachers College, and his classes were so large and attracted so many tuition-paying students that he was known as the "million-dollar professor." Lawrence Cremin has estimated that Kilpatrick "taught some 35,000 students from every state in the Union, at a time when Teachers College was training a substantial percentage of the articulate leaders of American education."[35] Kilpatrick's 1918 article on the project method went into 60,000 reprints, and he was author of several influential books on educational theory, as well as numerous short articles.

Kilpatrick's principal contribution to pedagogical theory was the project method, the educational equivalent of "whole-hearted purposeful activity proceeding in a social environment." Not all purposes could be considered good, but a "worthy life consists of purposive activity and not mere drifting." The moral and practical man in a democratic society "regulates his life with reference to worthy social aims." Slaves or members of a non-democratic society cannot enjoy this worthy life, for they must "be habituated to act with a minimum of their own purposing and with a maximum of servile acceptance of others' purposes."

> As the purposeful act is thus the typical unit of the worthy life in a democratic society, so also should it be made the typical unit of school procedure. . . . If the purposeful act be in reality the typical unit of the worthy life, then it follows that to base education on purposeful acts is exactly to identify the process of education with worthy living itself. . . . If the worthy life of the coming day is to consist of well-chosen purposeful acts, what preparation for that time could promise more than practice now, under discriminating guidance, in forming and executing worthy purposes? To this end must the child have within rather large limits the opportunity to purpose. For the issues of his act he must—in like limits—be held accountable. That the child may properly progress, the total situation—all the factors of life, including comrades, speaking if need be through the teacher—must make clear its selective judgment upon what he does, approving the better, rejecting the worse.[36]

[35] *The Transformation of the School*, p. 220.

[36] William H. Kilpatrick, "The Project Method," *Teachers College Record*, 19 (Sept., 1918): 320, 322–323.

In this statement Kilpatrick affirms Dewey's principles of interest, discipline, activity, and education for present living rather than traditional preparation for an unknown future.

The project must be judged on more than satisfying present needs if it is to be educationally valid. The educational criterion of the value of any activity is whether it can "lead the individual and others whom he touches on to other like fruitful activity" by helping the individual become "modified so that he sees what before he did not see or does what before he could not do."

Similarly, the project method does not mean that the school or teacher should be subordinated "to childish whim," for the child is not always a suitable judge. It may be necessary, therefore, that a child "be forced to act against a purpose which he entertains." However, unless educational planning aims "consciously and insistently at securing and utilizing vigorous purposing on the part of the pupils," it "is founded essentially on an ineffective and unfruitful basis." Dewey had said that purpose is the essence of discipline. By utilizing the interests of the child in teaching him how to discriminate among purposes, select the worthwhile ones, and pursue them effectively, Kilpatrick believed that the teacher could build moral character.

> Moral character is primarily an affair of shared social relationships, the disposition to determine one's conduct and attitudes with reference to the welfare of the group. . . . Under the eye of the skillful teacher the children as an embryonic society will make increasingly finer discriminations as to what is right and proper.[37]

Much of the revolution in twentieth-century educational methods and content came through the efforts of Kilpatrick and his students to apply the theories of Dewey to educational practice.

Boyd H. Bode

Perhaps one reason Dewey's philosophy was so widely accepted was that the United States needed someone to analyze and interpret the problems and needs of a modern industrial democracy and to synthesize a new philosophy out of conflicting and changing values. Had not John Dewey appeared, some other philosopher would have had to produce some similar statement in order for our society to understand and reorient itself. One who might well have filled that role and whose position was somewhat like that of Dewey was Boyd H. Bode.

[37] *Ibid.*, pp. 328–329.

Bode was born in Illinois in 1873 and grew up in the individualistic democratic tradition of the South Dakota prairie. His school experiences and his college study, leading to a doctorate in philosophy at Cornell in 1900, did not help him understand the "gosh awful mess" of his "cultural heritage." It was only through the "unbelievably slow process" of his own intellectual struggles that he was able to "reconstruct" himself, as he phrased it, a process that took place over the years from 1900 to 1921 when he was teaching philosophy at the universities of Wisconsin and Illinois. "I'll never forgive my teacher for letting me flounder without help to which I was entitled." During this period he moved in much the same direction as Dewey had a decade earlier, "from idealism and moral absolutism to pragmatism and an empirical morality."[38] The transformation of the philosophy of these two men is typical of the revolution in American thought from the absolutism and otherworldliness of theological idealism to the practicality of scientific pragmatism.

In 1924 Bode became professor of philosophy of education at Ohio State University and there followed his major contributions to the development of an American theory of pedagogy based on the pragmatic interpretation of American democracy. Among his books are *Fundamentals of Education* (1921), *Modern Educational Theories* (1927), *Conflicting Psychologies of Learning* (1929), and *Progressive Education at the Crossroads* (1938). These readable books are often closer to the spirit of Dewey's philosophy than those written by Dewey's own students and disciples.

Like Dewey, Bode sought to develop an educational theory consistent with the development of individuality in a scientific, industrial society and with the social control appropriate to a democracy. Although he appears to have arrived at his philosophy more or less independently of Dewey, Bode took many of Dewey's basic positions. Both of them rejected any dualism of individual versus society in a democratic system. Bode defined democracy as "*a social organization that aims to promote cooperation among its members and with other groups on the basis of mutual recognition of interests.*"[39] But the concept of a democratic individual *in* a democratic society, if misdirected, could result in dangers from extreme emphasis on either the individual or the society.

> We have faith that education can humanize the social order. But the problem is full of difficulties. On the one hand the democratic movement has meant the liberation of the individual through the

[38] From a letter to John L. Childs, July 9, 1951. Quoted in John L. Childs, *American Pragmatism and Education* (New York: Holt, 1956), p. 249.

[39] *Modern Educational Theories* (New York: Macmillan, 1927), p. 14.

> development of his interests and capacities. In terms of education this has meant emphasis on individual differences, on individual initiative, on freedom and self-expression. But these things are not ends in themselves; they are valuable only in so far as they make for the enrichment of personal and social life. If they are misdirected, they result in "soft pedagogy," in the encouragement of whim and selfishness, or perhaps in a one-sided development of vocational interests. When this happens, the idea of democracy miscarries and the evils of the past are perpetuated. But on the other hand democracy has meant a wider social consciousness, a heightened sense of responsibility for the common weal. This aspect of democracy is reflected in the educational emphasis on "social" values. But this emphasis may easily result in an evil tendency to subordinate the individual to society, to train him in the passive acceptance of ideals and standards. This again means that democracy has been defeated. Teaching in patriotism, when conducted on this level, prepares for intolerance and heresy hunting; just as "freedom" in education may become synonymous with caprice and license. In some sense or other democracy has always meant the right to freedom and self-determination.[40]

Bode criticized many of the current educational movements as being "unfriendly to the ideas of democracy because they center on the ideal of a static rather than a changing social order." Education must become an "agency for progress and reform."[41] A new society demands a new education.

On the other hand, Bode criticized those innovators who let children follow their immediate interests "without a sufficiently counterbalancing emphasis on the need of developing and directing the activities of pupils toward a preconceived end." Children's "felt needs" are not broad enough to assure that "childhood will grow automatically into wisdom and power." There is much in the cultural heritage of which the children are not aware and hence experience no "felt need" for. "It is the duty of the schools to transmit what is really valuable in racial experience so as to insure continuous progress."[42] This necessitates adult planning in the content of schooling.

Bode objected strenuously to curriculum construction through "the selection of material for training in specific duties, as though life consisted in an aggregate of specific duties and tasks." He pointed out that

[40] *Ibid.*, pp. 18–19.
[41] *Ibid.*, pp. 20, 32.
[42] *Ibid.*, p. 34.

it is contrary to the democratic ideal to use the school to "impose our own standards upon the next generation."

> Education must prepare for life, but life is a changing thing. The life of the next generation will be different from ours and it will be different in ways that we cannot foresee. How then can we prepare for it?
>
> Perhaps the simplest answer to this question is that education should enable the individual to educate himself when the time comes. . . . Sound education does not seek to prescribe belief or conduct, but to provide for the creation of new standards in accordance with new conditions and new needs.[43]

This education would mean the end of the "traditional opposition between vocation and culture."

> The type of education which tries to use the practical activities of the workshop and the home for purposes of social insight is in line with this development. So is the attempt to educate children in the art of self-government while they are in the schools. So again are the revisions in the organization of material and in classroom methods which place the stress on initiative and independent thinking. . . . This type of education directs intellectual development toward wider ranges of social understanding and fosters habits and methods of thinking that carry over into later life.[44]

Conflict and Change

In the twentieth century the range of opinions on the role and the content of schools has been tremendous. Traditional points of view have clashed with those derived from the modern philosophers of democracy and pragmatism. Orthodox methodologists have defended their ways of teaching without regard to the principles advanced by contemporary psychology. Although few public schools have incorporated extreme progressive practices, the methods and content of the public schools have changed tremendously since 1900. The society has called for schools which contribute to the creation of effective, democratic citizens. Increased knowledge about child development and the process of learning, as well as deeper understandings of the meaning of democracy, has led

[43] *Ibid.*, pp. 238–239.
[44] *Ibid.*, p. 265.

to these revolutionary changes. Contrary to the critics' complaints, however, many of the proponents of the modern pedagogical theory would claim that the schools have not gone far enough in putting into practice modern principles of psychology in achieving democratic educational goals.

QUESTIONS FOR DISCUSSION

1. How has psychology contributed directly and indirectly to building a body of educational theory? What weaknesses in psychological research have resulted in corresponding weaknesses in educational theory?
2. Select one of the following and read some of his works: William James, Francis W. Parker, John Dewey, Boyd Bode, William H. Kilpatrick. How would you incorporate in your own theory of education some of the ideas you find? How would you apply them in your teaching?
3. What interests are European and Asian educators taking in American educational theories and practices today? How do their efforts to copy American education compare with the current enthusiasm of critics here who urge making American education like that of European countries? Relate these attempts to adapt one system to that in another society to the changing concepts of democracy. As nations become more concerned about being democratic, to which nation do they look as a model? What might this suggest as a basis for evaluating some of the proposals to revise American education to make it follow the model of Russia, England, or France?
4. At the same time that the progressives were turning their greatest attention to methods of teaching, the world was undergoing a tremendous expansion in knowledge. To what extent was this expansion ignored? Review Bode's criticism of basing the curriculum on "felt needs." In permitting curriculum to be dictated largely by pupil interest, how did the progressives fail to prepare them for dealing with an expanding culture?
5. How did the attitudes of the progressives toward the traditional subject-oriented curriculum help broaden the separation between the academic professors and education specialists? What efforts are currently being made to bridge this gap?

SUGGESTED READINGS

Secondary Sources

Atkinson, Carroll, and Maleska, Eugene T. *The Story of Education*. Philadelphia: Chilton, 1962. Part Five, Psychology.

Baker, Melvin C. *Foundations of John Dewey's Educational Theory*. New York: King's Crown Press, 1955.

Butler, J. Donald. *Four Philosophies and Their Practice in Education and Religion.* New York: Harper, 1951. Chapters XVII–XIX.
Chambliss, J. J. *Boyd H. Bode's Philosophy of Education.* Columbus: Ohio State U. Press, 1963.
Childs, John L. *American Pragmatism and Education.* New York: Holt, 1956.
Cremin, Lawrence A. *The Transformation of the School.* New York: Knopf, 1961.
Freeman, Frank N. *Mental Tests: Their History, Principles and Applications.* Boston: Houghton Mifflin, 1939. Chapters II, IV, V, VI, VII, VIII.
Heidbreder, Edna. *Seven Psychologies.* New York: Appleton-Century-Crofts, 1933. Chapters IV to X.
Hilgard, Ernest R. *Theories of Learning.* New York: Appleton-Century-Crofts, 1948.
Meyer, Adolph E. *The Development of Education in the Twentieth Century.* New York: Prentice-Hall, 1949. Pp. 421–488.
Rugg, Harold. *Foundations for American Education.* New York: World Book, 1947. Chapters III–VII, XXIII.
Tenenbaum, Samuel. *William Heard Kilpatrick, Trail Blazer in Education.* New York: Harper, 1951.
Woodworth, Robert S. *Contemporary Schools of Psychology.* New York: Ronald Press, 1948.

Primary Sources

Bode, Boyd. *Modern Educational Theories.* New York: Macmillan, 1927.
———. *Progressive Education at the Crossroads.* New York: Newson, 1938.
Dewey, John. *Democracy and Education.* New York: Macmillan, 1916.
———. *Experience and Education.* New York: Macmillan, 1938.
Gross, Carl H., and Chandler, Charles C. *The History of American Education Through Readings.* Boston: Heath, 1964. Pp. 265–286, 370–420, 456–472.
James, William. *Essays in Pragmatism.* New York: Hafner, 1948. "What Pragmatism Means" and "Pragmatism's Conception of Truth." These essays have been included in many editions of James' works.
Kilpatrick, William H. *Foundations of Method.* New York: Macmillan, 1925.
———. *The Project Method.* New York: Teachers College, 1918.

15

Experiments in School Reform

The proof of any theory is, of course, whether it works. Since 1896 there have been a number of successful efforts to establish schools which embodied in their curriculum and methods the new psychological principles and were manifestations of the new democratic, pragmatic philosophy.

The Dewey School

When John Dewey became head of the departments of psychology, philosophy, and education at the University of Chicago, he had "certain philosophical and psychological ideas which he desired to test in practical application." In January, 1896, the school that was to be the proving ground for these ideas opened in a private dwelling with two teachers and sixteen pupils. It grew rapidly, including kindergarten and secondary work as well as elementary. In 1902 Colonel Francis W. Parker's old Cook County Normal School and two other institutions became the laboratory school for the University of Chicago, and shortly thereafter the Dewey School ended its brief existence. In its last year, it had 140 pupils, 23 full-time teachers, and 10 part-time graduate assistants from the University.[1]

Dewey's description of the school indicates that he had carefully tested the basic educational theories he was to put down in *Democracy and Education* and his other books and articles.

[1] Katherine Camp Mayhew and Anna Camp Edwards, *The Dewey School* (New York: Appleton-Century, 1936), p. 8.

> Because of the idea that human intelligence developed in connection with the needs and opportunities of action, the core of school activity was to be found in occupations, rather than in what are conventionally termed studies. Study in the sense of inquiry and its outcome in gathering and retention of information was to be an outgrowth of the pursuit of certain continuing or consecutive occupational activities. Since the development of the intelligence and knowledge of mankind has been a cooperative matter, and culture, in its broadest sense, a collective creation, occupations were to be selected which related those engaged in them to the basic needs of developing life, and demanded cooperation, division of work, and constant intellectual exchange by means of mutual communication and record. Since the integration of the individual and the social is impossible except when the individual lives in close association with others in the constant free give and take of experiences, it seemed that education could prepare the young for the future social life only when the school was itself a cooperative society on a small scale. . . .
>
> The primary skills, in reading, writing, and numbers, were to grow out of the needs and results of activities. . . . Knowledge was to grow out of the active contact with things and energies inherent in consecutive activities. History, for instance, was to be a deepening and an extension of the process of human invention and integration. The development of character and the management of what is ordinarily called *discipline*, were to be, as far as possible, the outgrowth of a shared community life in which teachers were guides and leaders.[2]

Although Dewey's school lasted for only seven years, its influence—both as example and as source of ideas for Dewey's philosophy—has been beyond measure.

"Schools of To-morrow"

Marietta Johnson's School of Organic Education

In 1915 Dewey and his daughter Evelyn reported on a number of experimental schools in a book called *Schools of To-morrow*. The pioneer of these schools was Mrs. Marietta Johnson's School of Organic Education, founded in 1907 in Fairhope, Alabama, a community of reform-minded single-tax disciples of Henry George. Like many of the Progressive educators, Mrs. Johnson was oriented more toward Rousseau than

[2] Quoted in *Ibid.*, pp. 5–6.

toward James or Dewey. In his educational novel, *Emile,* Rousseau argued that the child was essentially good but was corrupted by society, that proper education came from the child's active association with nature rather than from books or social influences, and that the child must have freedom to follow his interests, being limited only by the natural consequences of his acts. The attitudes, curriculum, and methods of Mrs. Johnson's school appear to have been modeled directly on the plans outlined by Rousseau in *Emile.*

At Fairhope there was no adult structuring of the curriculum through "forced tasks, assignment of lessons to study, and ordinary examinations." The freedom to pursue their interests would not only prevent children from acquiring a dislike for school, but would permit them to develop naturally, as their own "organic" interests developed. It would teach them morality in its most meaningful sense.

> Children in their early years are neither moral nor immoral, but simply unmoral; their sense of right and wrong has not yet begun to develop. Therefore, they should be allowed as much freedom as possible. . . . Give a child plenty of healthy activity. When he must be disciplined, do not appeal to a sense which he has not got, but show him by a little pain if necessary what his naughty act meant to his playmate. If he is to share in fun and good things with his family and friends, he must behave so that they will want his company. This is a motive which a young child can understand.

Mrs. Johnson, like Rousseau, prevented children from "learning to read at too early an age," holding them back until eight or nine, when the child was "well grounded in his experience and knowledge of the larger relations of things."

> He should not begin school life by learning to read and write, nor by learning to handle small playthings or tools. He must continue the natural course he began at home of running from one interesting object to another, of inquiring into the meaning of those objects, and above all of tracing the relation between the different objects. . . .
>
> Following this path of natural growth, the child is led into reading, writing, arithmetic, geography, etc., by his own desire to know.

The Fairhope school covered both elementary and secondary years, and the curriculum included "physical exercise, nature study, music, hand work, field geography, story telling, sense culture, fundamental conceptions of number, dramatizations, and games." Many of the classes were conducted out of doors, particularly nature study and field geography. The classroom was quite different from the traditional school room. "There are no cramping desks, the pupil may sit where or how he pleases, or even move from place to place if he does not disturb his fellows."[3]

Her school attracted enough attention that Mrs. Johnson was asked to conduct summer seminars for teachers in Greenwich, Connecticut, and finally opened a second school there. She was later a founder of the Progressive Education Association.

J. L. Meriam and the University of Missouri Elementary School

A school similar to that in Fairhope was the University of Missouri Elementary School, under the direction of Professor Junius L. Meriam. Believing that the work and play of the school should be what the children enjoy doing outside school, the school day was divided into four periods—play, stories, observation, and handwork. Observation included nature study and community activities, leading to science and social studies. These activities required number work, reading, and writing. Story-telling led to literature, dramatics, music, art, and foreign language. The school had about 120 pupils in seven grades, attending classes in large rooms divided by folding doors. Students had freedom to move about and talk to one another as they worked. Many of the children went on to the University high school, which was a traditional college preparatory school, but they had "no unusual difficulty in keeping up with the regular college preparatory work" in spite of their relatively unstructured elementary schooling. Indeed, it was reported that their college marks "indicate that their elementary training has given them some advantages over the public school pupils in ability to do the hard formal studying."[4]

Principles of Rousseau in "Schools of To-morrow"

The Deweys described a number of other "Schools of To-morrow" which were strongly indebted to the principles of Rousseau. The Little School in the Woods, in Greenwich, Connecticut, built its curriculum around "exercise in the things the woodman does." A boys' school at Interlaken, Indiana, achieved its motto of "To teach boys to live" by abolishing textbooks and providing "an environment which is full of

[3] John Dewey and Evelyn Dewey, *Schools of To-morrow* (New York: Dutton, 1915), pp. 25–26, 21–22, 29, 31.
[4] *Ibid.*, p. 57.

interesting things that need to be done," including constructing their own buildings, running a farm, editing a newspaper, and doing their own housekeeping.

> Most of the boys are preparing for college, but this outdoor and manual work does not mean that they have to take any longer for their preparation than the boy in the city high school.

The Cottage School, in Riverside, Illinois, where all the children came from well-to-do families, centered its educational activities around a garden in which the children raised vegetables to be cooked in class and kept a goat and other school pets. Although most of this experimentalism and Rousseauean influence was in private schools, the public schools of Indianapolis had gardening as a regular activity of the seventh and eighth grades and high school, using it as a basis for other studies. The same was true of some of the public schools in Chicago.[5]

Play was very much a part of some of these experimental schools. The Play School, begun in Greenwich Village, New York City, by Miss Caroline Pratt in 1914, was a kindergarten with its entire program organized around the play activities of the children. These children naturally had little opportunity for the "return to nature" of the other Rousseau devotees, and so their observations of city life were the basis of their constructive play. Dramatization, as used in the Francis Parker School in Chicago, applied play to the study of history and literature. Fourth graders studying Greek history "play Greek games and wear Greek costumes, and are continually acting out stories or incidents which please them."[6]

Dramatization, music activities, and art work related to what the children are learning in other studies is common today, but it was a part of the revolution of educational method of the early twentieth century. When *Schools of To-morrow* was written, plays and recitations were often a part of the school exercises held at the close of the year for the entertainment of the parents, but the use of dramatics or art in the day-to-day learning process was rare.

An Early Community School Project

One of the clearest examples of relating school work to the life of the children was a public school in an Indianapolis slum district. The school enrolled only Negro pupils, and perhaps the principal, a Mr. Valentine,

[5] *Ibid.*, pp. 87–95.
[6] *Ibid.*, pp. 100, 116–119, 123–124.

was influenced by the example of Booker T. Washington's Tuskegee. Because of the "immoral surroundings" of the school, the school board bought the neighboring tenements and a tract of land to clear a space around the school. Valentine, however, secured permission to use the tenements as part of the school, converting them into workshops, a demonstration house for teaching domestic science, and a club house. Much of the work of putting the buildings into condition for use was done by the pupils as part of their learning program; the efforts of the parents and community were enlisted to complete jobs the students could not do, such as plumbing and major plastering. In such a manner, community support for the school was created, and parents who had been hostile to schooling became involved with what their children were doing. The school also became a model for living for the entire community. Evening classes for adults and vacation classes extended educational opportunity. In short, it was what was later called a "community school." With all the vocational and practical activity, the academic was not omitted, for reading, writing, arithmetic, and other skills developed out of the work projects.

Many of our cities have the continuing problem of slum schools, with juvenile delinquency, dropouts, truancy, classroom disorder, and neighborhood hostility. All of these characterized Valentine's school at first. As the program progressed, radical changes developed in the attitudes of the children and their parents. Delinquency dropped. Truancy and school disorder decreased. Children wanted to come to school, and parents began to understand the value of education.

> A visitor when leaving this school can not fail to wish that such ventures might be started in . . . any community where people need to be aroused to a sense of their needs, including . . . how to earn a living, and how to use their resources for themselves and their neighbors both in leisure time and in working hours. Mr. Valentine's school is a school for colored children only in the sense that the work has been arranged in relation to the conditions in the neighborhood; these modify the needs of the particular children who are the pupils.[7]

The relevance of this experiment to today's urban educational problems is obvious.

The "schools of to-morrow" were based on the assumption that "their work ought to prepare children for the life they are to lead in the

[7] *Ibid.*, pp. 207–208.

world." Traditional schools had been providing that kind of education for only the few children "who will pass this life in intellectual pursuits." These experimental schools worked "away from a curriculum adapted to a small and specialized class towards one which shall be truly representative of the needs and conditions of a democratic society." Each of the schools described was different from the others because of "the influence that local conditions must exercise over methods." The vital similarity among all these schools was that of "making the connection between the child and his environment as complete and intelligent as possible, both for the welfare of the child and for the sake of the community."[8]

The Gary Plan

With the building of the steel mills in 1906, Gary, Indiana, underwent rapid and relatively unplanned growth, resulting in congested, near-slum living conditions for most of the city's residents. To deal with the social problems arising out of these conditions, school superintendent William Wirt began a massive reorganization of the Gary schools, with new aims, new programs, and a radically new administrative set-up.

> Its aim is to form, with its well-balanced facilities of work, study, and play, a genuine children's community, where the children's normal healthy interests are centered, and where they learn, in Professor Dewey's phrase, "by doing the things that have meaning to them as children." The Gary school aims to meet the comparative failure of the public school to-day to care for the city child. It tries to take the place of the old household and rural community life which provided for our forefathers the practical education of which the city child in his daily life is deprived to-day.[9]

This broadened purpose he achieved by careful scheduling and intensive utilization of school facilities.

A "Wirt school" had laboratories, workshops, gymnasium, auditorium, playgrounds, and studios as well as classrooms, all essential parts of the school plant. The school day was lengthened to eight hours, keeping the children off the streets and under adult supervision. To accommodate a larger number of children for more hours a day, scheduling of small

[8] *Ibid.*, pp. 288–289.

[9] Randolph S. Bourne, *The Gary Schools* (Boston: Houghton Mifflin, 1916), p. 35.

classes in classrooms, laboratories, and workshops alternated with large group activities in the auditorium, gymnasium, and playground. Thus Wirt doubled the number of children being handled in the school—actually, he treated the student body as two schools. Because of the movement of pupils within the school, the Gary Plan became known as the "platoon system." Classes were also held on Saturdays and during the vacation periods. In the evenings the schools were opened as recreational facilities and for adult classes. To help finance the program, pupils in the workshops, under the direction of skilled workmen as teachers, did the routine maintenance and repair work of the school. Girls in "domestic science" classes prepared the meals served in the cafeteria. Since each school housed grades from kindergarten through high school, there were plenty of children old enough to take care of these services for the children of all ages.

The purpose of the Gary schools was not to prepare workers for the steel mills, "but to keep the natural interests and enthusiasms of childhood, to enable each pupil to gain control of his mind and body, and to insure his being able to do the rest for himself."[10] Wirt recognized the vast range of individual differences among children, and one of the admirable features of his plan was its "greater flexibility in adapting studies to exceptional children of all kinds."[11]

Perhaps because of its revolutionary approach, perhaps because it promised more schooling for proportionately less cost, the Gary plan attracted wide notice. In 1914 the United States Office of Education published a bulletin on the Gary schools. Randolph Bourne popularized the movement in a series of articles in the *New Republic* in 1915. Not all opinion was favorable, and Wirt invited the General Education Board to make a study of the Gary schools. Their report, an eight-volume study, was published in 1919. While the Gary experiment was recognized as interesting and stimulating, the conclusions of the report were not highly favorable. Stuart A. Courtis applied the widely acclaimed measurement techniques to determine the amount of educational progress made by the Gary pupils in handwriting, spelling, arithmetic, composition, and reading.

> The product of classroom teaching of the fundamentals is, at Gary, poor in quality and inadequate in amount; it approximates in character the product of the poorer conventional schools, and reveals in no particular the slightest indication that it has been affected either

[10] Dewey and Dewey, *Schools of To-morrow*, p. 177.
[11] Randolph Bourne, p. 167.

favorably or unfavorably by the enriched curriculum or other special features of the Gary Schools.[12]

In spite of this criticism, the "platoon system" increased in popularity. By 1929 there were over a thousand platoon system schools in 202 cities spread over 39 states, Hawaii, and the District of Columbia. These schools enrolled nearly 730,000 pupils.[13] Some aspects of the Gary schedule, especially the platoon organization, have become accepted parts of most high-school and junior high-school programs, and even some elementary-school activities may be traced in part to innovations begun by Wirt.

The Dalton Laboratory Plan

One of the earliest reversals of the pattern of importing foreign ideas into American education was the "laboratory plan" introduced by Helen Parkhurst in Dalton High School, Dalton, Massachusetts. Beginning her career as a teacher in a rural one-room school, Miss Parkhurst taught in high school and normal school as well as in the primary grades. In 1914 she went to Italy to study with Maria Montessori, and on her return promoted Montessori methods in the United States from 1915 to 1918. During these years of teaching and experimenting, she gradually formulated the laboratory plan, which received its first full-scale trial in 1920. By 1925 it had been adopted by 200 schools in the United States, and there were over 1,500 Dalton schools in England and hundreds more in Holland, Russia, Norway, Germany, Poland, Austria, Spain, Japan, China, and India.[14]

The general principles of the Dalton Laboratory Plan were similar to the views of John Dewey. Indeed, Parkhurst's concepts of freedom, interest, experience, and society were adaptations of Dewey's. Her goal was to find an educational arrangement that would facilitate the growth of the child "into a harmonious, responsible being, able and willing to lend himself consciously to cooperation with his fellows for their common benefit."[15]

[12] Stuart A. Courtis, *The Gary Public Schools: Measurement of Classroom Products* (New York: General Education Board, 1919), p. 384.

[13] Roscoe David Case, *The Platoon School in America* (Stanford: Stanford U. Press, 1931), pp. 27–30.

[14] National Society for the Study of Education, *Adapting the Schools to Individual Difference*, 24th Yearbook, Part II (Bloomington, Illinois: Public School Publishing Co., 1925), p. 83.

[15] Helen Parkhurst, *Education on the Dalton Plan* (New York: E. P. Dutton, 1922), pp. 18–19.

She ridiculed the assumption that all the children in a class would seize simultaneously upon the same interest and then, at the end of an arbitrary period, suddenly put away that interest and acquire a new one, again all at the same time. She pointed out that the child learns more effectively when he is "free to continue his work upon any subject in which he is absorbed without interruption." In her method "there are no bells to tear him away at an appointed hour and chain him pedagogically to another subject and another teacher." She did not try to achieve this freedom by letting children follow their own interests, as did some of the Progressives, but laid out the work of the traditional subjects into month-long "contract-jobs." Each pupil "should progress at his own rate" in meeting his contract, learning to budget his time so that he completed all the contracts for each of the five or six subjects he was taking. Classrooms would be laboratories where students would work at their own projects under the direction of a teacher who became a "subject specialist, or advisor."[16]

While the plan emphasized individualization, it did not separate the child from the social group. One principle of the Dalton Plan was that of "interaction of group life." As students worked on their contracts, others would be working on the same interest, giving rise to small groups "doing intensive work, which stimulates discussion and exercises social influence." This group work and the need to share facilities are the conditions which require the pupil to function "involuntarily" as a "member of a social community." "He is accepted or rejected by his community according as his functioning, or conduct is social or the reverse."[17] Aside from this informal social discipline, the Dalton Plan did not provide opportunity for the "interaction of group life" that Dewey advocated.

The Dalton Plan was a compromise between the traditional subject-oriented curriculum and the concern of the Progressives for pupil interest. It provided for the kind of flexible school facilities and scheduling that is central to more recent proposals for "team teaching."

The Winnetka "Plan"

Beginning in 1912, the San Francisco State Normal School under President Frederic Burk experimented with ways of individualizing assignments so that each child could work at his own speed. Burk's

[16] *Ibid.*, pp. 19, 35–41.
[17] *Ibid.*, pp. 43, 20.

description of the experiments in a monograph called *Remedy for Lock-step Schooling*, came to the attention of a rural school teacher named Carleton Washburne, who had been trying much the same thing in his own schools. From 1914 to 1919 Washburne served as a member of Burk's staff, leaving to try the system in the public elementary and junior high schools of Winnetka, Illinois, where he remained as superintendent until 1943. What developed there has generally been called the Winnetka Plan, though Washburne objected: "It is and was a spirit, a condition, an attitude of teaching, but never a fixed plan."[18] Whatever the terminology, the Winnetka schools have been among those that have most consistently tried to utilize the theories of John Dewey.

Washburne divided the school subjects into (1) the "common essentials"—reading, writing, arithmetic, science, and, to some extent social studies—and (2) the "group and creative activities"—literature, music, art, play, assemblies, handwork, projects as an end in themselves rather than as means for acquiring subject matter, and the background material of history and geography.

In the common essentials each student went at his own rate. The essentials were broken up into units of work, each with specific goals; each pupil was given diagnostic tests to determine whether he had mastered the material and, if not, what his difficulties were; "self-instructive, self-corrective practice materials" were used to teach him the material or skill needed to achieve the goals. The practice materials for the common essentials were in some ways like the more recent programed instruction materials.

> One of the characteristic features of the practice materials is that they are written directly to the child as if they were to constitute a series of correspondence lessons. They lead the child step by step very gradually from the elements he knows to the elements he is to learn. The child practices on each step until he masters it. Then he goes on to the next.[19]

The teacher assisted the pupils as individuals or, occasionally, as a class. Since each child worked on the common essentials at his own speed, there was no repetition of grades by the slow pupil; each pupil

[18] Carleton W. Washburne and Sidney P. Marland, Jr., *Winnetka, the History & Significance of an Educational Experiment* (Englewood Cliffs: Prentice-Hall, 1963), p. 169.

[19] Carleton W. Washburne, Mabel Vogel, and William S. Gray, *A Survey of the Winnetka Public Schools* (Bloomington, Illinois: Public School Publishing Co., 1926), p. 19.

was kept with those approximately his own age and "same general degree of grade advancement." In other words, even if a slow student stayed in the same classroom for two years, he continued to work on new material as he mastered units, and failure to learn some arbitrary amount of work did not force him to repeat a whole year in lock-step fashion with a new group of children.

The group and creative activities occupied "about half of each morning and half of each afternoon." For these activities there were "no set standards; . . . no pre-determined formal preparation; no tests." They usually grew "out of the children's interests or out of their history-geography work."

Students who mastered the work of the elementary grades rapidly used "their saved time for broadening and enriching their education" in the junior high school, where electives and special subjects were offered. "A child is not graduated to the senior high school until he is considered ready not only academically but physically and socially."

The Winnetka children attended a high school outside the town, where they made up about one-fifth of the enrollment. During the freshman year their grades in mathematics, social studies, and Latin were above the average for the school, and in English they fell a little below the students from one of the other two "feeder" schools. A 1926 study by the University of Chicago revealed that the Winnetka children did better than children "under the traditional class method" in the common essentials, except the "ability to spell words not studied." The students apparently made a better social adjustment in high school than did their classmates from other junior high schools.[20]

The Winnetka system produced its own tests and teaching materials, which it published from 1925 to 1952. It had a Graduate Teachers College to prepare teachers to work in the system. Visitors came to observe, and Winnetka teachers were hired to help other school systems incorporate some Washburne ideas. It is difficult to measure the effect of the innovations at Winnetka, partly because other progressive experiments arrived at similar proposals independently, partly because later experiments were influenced by several of these experiments. There are a number of contributions, however, which seem to have been derived directly from Winnetka—ranging from the individualization of instruction through the use of workbooks and "self-instructive" materials to the popularity of the playground "Jungle Gym."[21]

Winnetka has continued its "state of mind" in regard to education.

[20] *Ibid.*, pp. 20–21, 25, 80–83, 132–133.
[21] Washburne and Marland, p. 155.

Under Superintendent Sidney Marland, who assumed office in 1956, new ideas were implemented. Whereas Washburne tended to "defer" the academic disciplines somewhat later than more traditional schools, Marland moved in the opposite direction, "to release and fulfill the intellectual potentials of the child." Washburne was concerned about the "whole child," but Marland regards "as our unique and primary concern the development of the intellect." Under Marland, creative activities at Winnetka were deliberately blended "*with* formal learnings."[22]

Marland became superintendent of schools in Pittsburgh, Pennsylvania, in 1963.

The Lincoln School

In 1916 the General Education Board, a Rockefeller philanthropy, held several meetings on elementary and secondary education, and as the basis for these discussions Charles W. Eliot prepared a paper entitled *Changes Needed in American Secondary Education* and Abraham Flexner one called *A Modern School.* In his paper Eliot criticized American secondary education as being "based chiefly on literature" and allotting "only an insignificant portion of school time to the cultivation of the perceptive power." Both elementary and secondary schools, he charged, were oriented toward the "small percentage of the youth . . . that go to the colleges and higher technical schools" and thus do not serve "the interests of the 95 percent of the children."[23]

Flexner's paper attacked the formal discipline theory of learning as "none too well founded." He also rejected the inclusion of subjects because they have historically been a part of the curriculum; "traditional esteem is an insufficient offset to present and future uselessness." In making up their curriculum, the schools must not be dependent on the past but must look only to the "actual pertinency to genuine need, interest or capacity." The object of schooling is "to give children the knowledge they need, and to develop in them the power to handle themselves in our own world." Even the "progressive curricula" had not achieved that goal, for "their eliminations are altogether too timid." Flexner's curriculum would be built around science, industry, aesthetics, and civics. Formal grammar would be dropped because of its "futility . . . as an aid to correct speaking and writing." Mathematics beyond arithmetic would

[22] *Ibid.*, pp. 207–208.
[23] New York: General Education Board, 1916, pp. 6–7, 17–18.

be taught incidentally to science and industry. Latin and Greek would disappear, since a "positive case can be made out for neither."

Flexner also criticized the traditional school for its failure to integrate the content of various subjects.

> The Modern School would from the first undertake the cultivation of contacts and cross-connections. Every exercise would be a spelling lesson; science, industry, and mathematics would be inseparable; science, industry, history, civics, literature, and geography would to some extent utilize the same material.

Methods would be changed with the content to "suit the spirit and aim of the instruction."

> Children will not be taught merely in order that they may know or be able to do certain things that they do not now know or cannot now do, but material will be presented to them in ways that promote their proper development and growth—individually and socially. For education is not only a matter of what people can do, but also of what they are.[24]

As a result of the discussions of these papers, the General Education Board decided to help finance a laboratory school at Teachers College, Columbia University, and in 1917 the Lincoln School opened. It was intended, as Flexner said, to be to education what Johns Hopkins Hospital was to medicine.[25] Lincoln School was a model for Progressive education. In both elementary and secondary grades, the curriculum was organized around "units of work" rather than traditional subject courses, though special work was available in music, fine and industrial arts, science, home economics, physical education, and (in high school) in English, mathematics, social studies, and foreign languages. The faculty experimented in methods and developed many texts, curriculum guides, workbooks, outlines of teaching units, and achievement tests.

In 1940 Teachers College merged the Lincoln School with the Horace Mann Schools in the interest of economy and administrative efficiency. Finally, over the objection of parents who argued that the college had no legal or ethical right to use the General Education Board Endowment for other than an experimental school, Lincoln was closed in 1948 and its funds transferred to other purposes.

[24] Abraham Flexner, *A Modern School* (New York: General Education Board, 1916), pp. 8–17.

[25] Flexner, *I Remember* (New York: Simon & Schuster, 1940), p. 250.

The Progressive Education Association

One of the most important experiments in American education in the twentieth century has been the Progressive Education Association, (PEA), despite its relatively short life (1919–1955). During the winter of 1918–1919 a group of private-school leaders and laymen held weekly meetings in Washington "for the purpose of furnishing a focus to the then scattered and ununified attempts at educational reform."[26] Led by Mrs. Marietta Johnson, Eugene R. Smith (head of Park School, Baltimore), and Stanwood Cobb (a Naval Academy instructor who had become interested through reading *Schools of To-morrow* and listening to Mrs. Johnson's speeches), they drafted "a minimum set of principles which prove truly descriptive of the various educational experiments."[27]

THE PRINCIPLES OF PROGRESSIVE EDUCATION

I. Freedom to Develop Naturally.
The conduct of the pupil should be governed by himself according to the social needs of his community, rather than by arbitrary laws. Full opportunity for initiative and self-expression should be provided, together with an environment rich in interesting material that is available for the free use of every pupil.

II. Interest, the Motive of All Work.
Interest should be satisfied and developed through: (1) Direct and indirect contact with the world and its activities, and use of the experience thus gained. (2) Application of knowledge gained, and correlation between different subjects. (3) The consciousness of achievement.

III. The Teacher a Guide, Not a Taskmaster.
It is essential that teachers should believe in the aims and general principles of Progressive Education and that they should have latitude for the development of initiative and originality.

Progressive teachers will encourage the use of all the senses, training the pupils in both observation and judgment; and instead of hearing recitations only, will spend most of the time teaching how to use various sources of information, including life activities as well as books; how to reason about the information thus acquired; and how to express forcefully and logically the conclusions reached.

[26] Stanwood Cobb, "Concerning Ourselves," *Progressive Education*, 6 (Jan.-Feb.-March, 1929): 67.
[27] *Ibid.*

Ideal teaching conditions demand that classes be small, especially in the elementary school years.

IV. Scientific Study of Pupil Development.
School records should not be confined to the marks given by the teachers to show the advancement of the pupils in their study of subjects, but should also include both objective and subjective reports on those physical, mental, moral and social characteristics which affect both school and adult life, and which can be influenced by the school and the home. Such records should be used as a guide for the treatment of each pupil, and should also serve to focus the attention of the teacher on the all-important work of development rather than on simply teaching subject-matter.

V. Greater Attention to All That Affects the Child's Physical Development.
One of the first considerations of Progressive Education is the health of the pupils. Much more room in which to move about, better light and air, clean and well ventilated buildings, easier access to the out-of-doors and greater use of it, are all necessary. There should be frequent use of adequate playgrounds. The teachers should observe closely the physical conditions of each pupil and, in co-operation with the home, make abounding health the first objective of childhood.

VI. Co-operation Between School and Home to Meet the Needs of Child Life.
The school should provide, with the home, as much as is possible of all that the natural interests and activities of the child demand, especially during the elementary school years. These conditions can come about only through intelligent co-operation between parents and teachers.

VII. The Progressive School a Leader in Educational Movements.
The Progressive School should be a leader in educational movements. It should be a laboratory where new ideas, if worthy, meet encouragement; where tradition alone does not rule, but the best of the past is leavened with the discoveries of today, and the result is freely added to the sum of educational knowledge.[28]

At an organizational meeting of the Progressive Education Association held on March 15, 1919, in the Washington Public Library, eighty-five founding members adopted these principles. From that modest start, aided by a donation of "several hundred dollars" from a Washington

[28] *Progressive Education,* 1 (April, 1924): 2. Reprinted with permission of the John Dewey Society.

philanthropist, the Association enlisted the support of other parents and educators. Charles W. Eliot consented to become honorary president and lent the prestige of his name until his death in 1926. None of the education professors later to be associated with Progressive Education were among the founders. The first members were chiefly parents and teachers of experimental private schools, such as those founded "as a result of the influence of Francis W. Parker, . . . of Dewey's writings, of Marietta L. Johnson, and some modeled after the Parker School of Baltimore which was founded by Professor Hans Froelicher directly upon the educational principles of Rousseau, Pestalozzi, and Froebel."[29] John Dewey did not join the PEA until 1927.

In 1924 a grant from Mrs. Avery Coonley, of Chicago, subsidized the publishing of the journal *Progressive Education.* The breadth of current experimentation in education was indicated by some of the articles of the first issue: Frederic Burk on individualization of instruction at San Francisco State Teachers College, Carleton Washburne on the Winnetka system, Helen Parkhurst on the Dalton Plan, and Ovide Decroly on a system of individualizing "auto-education" which he had introduced in Belgium. Until its demise in 1957, *Progressive Education* was one of the most stimulating and controversial educational journals in the nation.

After the death of Eliot, Dewey accepted the honorary presidency. By then the Association had attracted many professors from teacher-training institutions, particularly Columbia University, and they were beginning to dominate the thinking of the organization. In his inaugural address as honorary president in 1928, Dewey chided the progressives for their assumption that freedom is only an absence of restraint and not a positive opportunity to improve life.

> All new and reforming movements pass through a stage in which what is most evident is a negative phase, one of protest, of deviation, and innovation. It would be surprising indeed if this were not true of the progressive educational movement. For instance, the formality and fixity of traditional schools seemed oppressive, restrictive. Hence in a school which departs from these ideals and methods, freedom is at first most naturally conceived as removal of artificial and benumbing restrictions. Removal, abolition are, however, negative things, so in time it comes to be seen that such freedom is no end in itself . . . but . . . an opportunity to do something of a positive and constructive sort.

[29] Cobb, pp. 67–68.

To achieve significant value from an education, teachers must "intelligently organize" the work of the school. Flexibility should be permitted to take advantage of unexpected questions and interests but, if freedom is taken as permitting "improvisation to dictate" the course of a child's education, "the result is a jerky, discontinuous movement which works against the possibility of making any important contribution." Freedom and individuality are not "hostile" to organization; "a child's individuality . . . can be found only in the connected course of his actions. . . . Consequently, some organization of subject-matter . . . is the only means which corresponds to real individuality."

Dewey further charged in his address that the progressives tended to misunderstand the meaning of learning by doing.

> Bare doing, no matter how active, is not enough. . . . The test of a good project is whether it is sufficiently full and complex to demand a variety of responses from different children and permit each to go at it and make his contribution in a way which is characteristic of himself. The further test or mark of a good activity, educationally speaking, is that it have a sufficiently long time-span so that a series of endeavors and explorations are involved . . . in such a way that each step opens up a new field, raises new questions, arouses a demand for new knowledge, and suggests what to do next on the basis of what has been accomplished and the knowledge thereby gained.

Instead of letting children seize on every passing whim, it is the "duty" of the teacher, "having the riper and fuller experience and the greater insight into the possibilities of continuous development," to suggest to the pupils the appropriate lines of activity.[30]

With the new leadership of the Teachers College professors and Dewey's urging that social concerns must be integrated with individual development, the PEA took a different direction in the 1930's. The social and economic problems of the Great Depression pressed upon the schools a role for helping reconstruct American society if violent revolution were to be avoided. At the 1932 PEA convention, Professor George S. Counts delivered an address entitled "Dare Progressive Education Be Progressive?" (Later it was incorporated into a pamphlet called *Dare the School Build a New Social Order?*) Counts' answer to his question was that the schools must take an active part in bringing out the new, "pro-

[30] "Progressive Education and the Science of Education," *Progressive Education,* 5 (July-Aug.-Sept., 1928): 200–203.

gressive" America if social injustice was to be relieved. A group of the social and educational liberals among the professors at Teachers College, including Counts, Kilpatrick, John L. Childs, R. Bruce Raup, and Harold Rugg were the nucleus of the John Dewey Society for the Study of Education and Culture, established in 1935. The same men had begun publishing, in 1934, a journal called *Social Frontier*, dedicated to outspoken criticism of the evils of capitalism and to the militant crusade of reconstructing American society. The John Dewey Society took over sponsorship of *Social Frontier* until 1939, when the PEA assumed sponsorship and changed its name to *Frontiers of Democracy*. World War II brought a cessation to much of the liberal criticism in America, and the PEA, already struggling financially, stopped publication of *Frontiers of Democracy* in 1944. Although it lasted only nine years and reached only a few thousand readers, *Social Frontier* definitely colored much of the Progressive theory in the late 1930's. On the other hand, it may have hastened the end of the Progressive Education Association by helping "to discredit progressive education in the eyes of the public" and by splitting the Progressive movement into factions of liberals and moderates on social issues.[31]

In 1955 the PEA was dissolved. For two more years *Progressive Education* continued under the sponsorship of the University of Illinois, and then it too died. The PEA and *Progressive Education* did not bring a complete revolution in American education. Certainly the public schools, taken on the whole, have remained basically traditional in structure and curriculum organization and have rarely attempted the continuous experimentation which characterized the Progressive movement. However, much of the methodology and attitude toward education commonly accepted in contemporary schools is due largely to the influence of Progressive education. Dewey summarized Progressive education's "distinctive contribution to the body of educational theory" in 1928.

> Respect for individual capacities, interests and experience; enough external freedom and informality at least to enable teachers to become acquainted with children as they really are; respect for self-initiated and self-conducted learning; respect for activity as the stimulus and centre of learning; and perhaps above all belief in social contact, communication, and cooperation upon a normal human plane as all-enveloping medium.[32]

[31] C. A. Bowers, "The *Social Frontier* Journal: A Historical Sketch," *History of Education Quarterly*, 4 (Sept. 1964): 179.

[32] "Progressive Education and the Science of Education," p. 198.

The Eight-Year Study

One of the PEA's most significant projects—and unfortunately one of the least known to the general public—was the effort to measure the effect of secondary-school reorganization on students' success in college. Before 1930, efforts at reforming secondary education had generally been thwarted by the pressure of college entrance requirements. In order to explore the possibility of broadening the entrance requirements and thus make possible fundamental reconstruction of secondary schooling, the PEA in 1930 created a Commission on the Relation of School and College. After a two-year preliminary study, the commission secured the permission of more than 300 colleges and universities to release the graduates of thirty selected secondary schools from the usual subject and unit requirements for college admission. The Thirty Schools included public and private schools, some large, some small, scattered from Boston to Los Angeles. Actually, three of the "schools" were the school systems of Des Moines, Tulsa, and Denver.

In the fall of 1933 the Thirty Schools, acting independently, began experimenting with reforms. Two major principles were agreed upon for the attempted reconstruction of secondary education. The first was that "*the general life of the school and methods of teaching should conform to what is now known about the ways in which human beings learn and grow.*" The second was that schools must go beyond the teaching of the traditional subjects and lead American youth "to understand, to appreciate, and to live the kind of life for which we as a people have been striving throughout our history." In short, the development of a democracy demanded that "the school itself should become a demonstration of the kind of life in which this nation believes."

These principles required "radical change in many aspects of the curriculum and ways of teaching." One characteristic of the Thirty Schools must be "*the spirit and practice of experimentation and exploration,*" but the revisions "*should be undertaken only after thoughtful, co-operative reconsideration of the high school's function in the community it serves.*" The curriculum "*should deal with the present concerns of young people as well as with the knowledge, skills, understandings, and appreciations which constitute our cultural heritage.*" There must be "*greater unity and continuity in the curriculum*" instead of the fragmentation of the traditional curriculum into unrelated courses. In order to guide the student "in meeting his personal, educational, and vocational problems," the teacher "*must know each student well.*" The individual differences among students may best be provided for by "basing the secondary school curriculum upon the needs of youth in our society." For pupils to learn the "democratic principle of participation," greater opportunity should be provided "for them to share in school management and curriculum planning."

> Pupils join with the teacher in deciding what goals are to be sought, in selecting the steps to be taken to reach the desired ends, and in setting up tests or measures to find out whether objectives have been reached.[33]

The degree to which these changes were pursued and adopted varied greatly from one school to another among the Thirty. Some instituted "core curriculums"; others tried the "broad fields type of curriculums"; the least radical merely limited their changes to "the content of conventional subjects."[34]

The graduates of these high schools began to enter college in the fall of 1936. Detailed records were kept of their progress in college, and each student was paired with another student in his college from a nonparticipating high school, with matching done on the basis of sex, age, race, scholastic aptitude test scores, home and community background, interests, and probable goals. In this manner 1,475 matched pairs were selected. To these students a large number of tests, questionnaires, and interviews were given, and dossiers were kept of their grades and instructors' reports. Finally, in 1942, a five-volume report on the Eight-Year Study was made public. The general results supported the Progressives' argument that the traditional college preparatory subjects were not necessary for success in college.

In the comparison of the 1,475 matched pairs, the college follow-up staff found that the graduates of the Thirty Schools:

1. earned slightly higher total grade average;
2. earned higher grade averages in all subject fields except foreign language;
3. specialized in the same academic fields as did the comparison students;
4. did not differ from the comparison group in the number of times they were placed on probation;
5. received slightly more academic honors in each year;
6. were more often judged to possess a high degree of intellectual curiosity and drive;

[33] Reproduced by permission from *The Story of the Eight-Year Study* by Wilford M. Aikin. Copyright 1942 by McGraw-Hill, Inc. See pp. 17–23, 42–43.
[34] *Ibid.*, p. 61.

7. were more often judged to be precise, systematic, and objective in their thinking;
8. were more often judged to have developed clear or well-formulated ideas concerning the meaning of education—especially in the first two years in college;
9. more often demonstrated a high degree of resourcefulness in meeting new situations;
10. did not differ from the comparison group in ability to plan their time effectively;
11. had about the same problems of adjustment as the comparison group, but approached their solution with greater effectiveness;
12. participated somewhat more frequently and more often enjoyed appreciative experiences in the arts;
13. participated more in all organized student groups except religious and "service" activities;
14. earned in each college year a higher percentage of non-academic honors (officership in organizations, election to managerial societies, athletic insignia, leading roles in dramatic and musical presentations);
15. did not differ from the comparison group in the quality of adjustment to their contemporaries;
16. differed only slightly from the comparison group in the kinds of judgments about their schooling;
17. had a somewhat better orientation toward the choice of a vocation;
18. demonstrated a more active concern for what was going on in the world.[35]

The more closely the evidence was examined, the more it appeared to support the educational theories of the Progressives. The success of the graduates from the six schools "in which least change had been made" was compared with the success of those from the six schools "in which the most marked departures from the conventional college preparatory courses had been made." Not only had the Thirty Schools' graduates, as a whole, out-performed the students to whom they were compared, but those who had been in the most progressive schools had been "strikingly more successful than their matches" while those from the least experimental schools had shown "no large or consistent differences" from their comparison group. Furthermore, the graduates of two of the most experimental schools "surpassed their comparison groups by wide margins in academic achievement, intellectual curiosity, scientific approach to problems, and interest in contemporary affairs." They showed

[35] *Ibid.*, pp. 110–112.

greater "general resourcefulness," "enjoyment in reading, participation in the arts," and success in winning "non-academic honors," than did their matches. In fact, they excelled their counterparts in the comparison group in "all aspects of college life, except possibly participation in sports and social activities."[36]

In spite of criticisms about the techniques of measurement used in the Eight-Year Study, a committee of college presidents and deans reported to the Association of American Colleges that "the pattern of preparatory school program which concentrates on a preparation for a fixed set of entrance examinations is not the only satisfactory means of fitting a boy or girl for making the most out of the college experience." Contrary to traditional preparation, the "stimulus and the initiative which the less conventional approach to secondary school education affords sends on to college better human material than we have obtained in the past."[37]

Perhaps because the report of the Eight-Year Study was published in the confusion of World War II, its effect was minimized, and even the experimental schools tended to revert to more conventional patterns.

The Community School

The Great Depression of the 1930's gave rise to a number of school experiments very similar to the program at the Indianapolis school described by the Deweys in *Schools of To-morrow*. The "community school" was an attempt to organize the curriculum around the lives of the children and at the same time help the community deal more effectively with their economic, social, and recreational problems. The children studied the problems of the community, and their classroom activities grew out of projects related to those problems. The community used school facilities—shops, home economics equipment, auditorium, library, gymnasium, playground—for community projects and recreation.

The first criterion of a good community school was that it must develop an individual who could take an effective part in the kind of social interaction which Dewey described in *Democracy and Education*. The characteristic which distinguished the community school from other "progressive" innovations was its attempt to deal with the immediate problems of the community.

In the early and mid-1940's, the Alfred P. Sloan Foundation provided grants for three Projects in Applied Economics. Under these grants

[36] *Ibid.*, pp. 112–114.
[37] *Ibid.*, p. 150.

community school materials were developed in food at the University of Kentucky, in clothing at the University of Vermont, and in housing at the University of Florida. In 1943 a small community school in McIntosh, Florida, began using these materials. The McIntosh experiment is representative of the rural community school movement. As early as 1932 the school took on the aspects of a "community school," joining with the McIntosh Civic League to combat malnutrition, hookworm, malaria, and other health problems. In 1942 the community pitched in to continue the school garden which had been started with WPA assistance. Patrons and pupils joined in the gardening and preserving of food which was to supply the bulk of the food for the school lunch room. The more traditional school activities—reading, writing, arithmetic, and so on—were related to the community projects being carried out in and with the school. In such work the community school put into action the principle that "children learn best when they have the opportunity to use what they are learning."[38]

Most of the best examples of the community school were in small rural communities where there already existed a great deal of interdependence and strong community of interest, often centered around the school or church as the only structured institutions in the community. The Highlander Folk School of Monteagle, Tennessee, is one well-known example. Although the community school experiments were sometimes backed with financial grants from foundations and assisted in their planning by university staffs, the movement did not catch on, perhaps because of the problems of a nation at war.

Life Adjustment Education

Very much misunderstood and, in effect, ridiculed out of existence by its detractors was the ill-fated Life Adjustment Movement of the post-World War II period. In 1945, at the close of an eighteen-month study of vocational education made by the United States Office of Education, Dr. Charles A. Prosser charged that secondary schools were not serving the needs of the 60 percent of the youth who were not being trained for a specific vocation. In 1947 Commissioner John W. Studebaker appointed a Commission on Life Adjustment Education for Youth to consider the educational needs of the more than a fifth of the youth who never enter high school, the more than 40 percent who drop out before

[38] Clara M. Olson, A *Community School of Social Action* (Gainesville; Florida Curriculum Laboratory of the U. of Florida, 1944), p. 18.

graduation, and those graduates whose high school activities are "so unrelated to everyday needs of life that when they graduate they are not well adjusted to life."[39] These children often were from families employed in unskilled or semiskilled occupations, from families with low incomes and low cultural attainments; they were retarded in school and began school late, made lower scores on intelligence tests and achievement tests, made lower marks than other pupils, were less emotionally mature, and lacked interest in school. It was for this large body of educationally neglected youth that Life Adjustment Education was developed, but the definition of Life Adjustment Education was broad enough to cover the goals of all children.

As with other movements in the progressive tradition, Life Adjustment Education was defined as "that which better equips all American youth to live democratically with satisfaction to themselves and profit to society." It was concerned with all aspects of the child's development, "with ethical and moral living and with physical, mental, and emotional health." Contrary to the indictments of the critics, it recognized "the importance of the fundamental skills" of arithmetic, reading, writing, listening, and speaking. One aspect greatly over-emphasized in both application and criticism was the concern with "the development of wholesome recreational interests of both an individual and social nature" and with "the present problems of youth as well as their preparation for future living." It took into account the vast range of individual differences and provided that the goals of both general and specialized education "be attained through differentiation both as to subject matter and experience." In considering subject matter, it recognized that "many events of importance happened a long time ago, but . . . the real significance of these events is in their bearing upon life of today." Finally, adjustment was not merely teaching the child to accommodate himself to existing conditions, for "active and creative achievements" were emphasized as to the means for "the appropriate revising of aims and the means of attaining them."[40]

By 1954 twenty-nine states had curriculum revision programs generally associated with the Life Adjustment Education. Even a number of Catholic schools were participating in the movement. One area of considerable attention was the problem of dropouts and the "holding-power" of the secondary school. The Second Commission on Life Adjustment Education for Youth, in summarizing the progress of the movement in 1954, indicated some "unfinished business of secondary educa-

[39] U.S. Office of Education, *Bulletin 1951*, No. 22, p. 42.
[40] *Ibid.*, pp. 9–10.

tion." Included were calls to study youth and especially the dropouts, to establish a fourteen-year sequence of educational experiences that would eliminate the selective character of secondary education, to seek a balance between required and elective courses, to provide for greater individualization in instruction, to provide for more work experience, to develop an adequate program of appraising the educational development of individual pupils, to improve teacher training, to continue to equalize financial support, and to re-examine the whole question of home-community-school responsibility.[41]

This broad expression of the role of secondary education drew considerable fire from those critics of education who insisted that the only responsibility of education is the intellectual development of youth and that this intellectual development be limited to certain narrow fields of traditional subject matter. Whether it was through ignorance or deliberate distortion, these critics, including a number of newspaper and magazine editors, charged that Life Adjustment Education was concerned only with the creation of conformists and intellectual dimwits who were able to ask a girl for a date but knew no dates of history. Perhaps because of this criticism, no new commission was appointed after 1954, and Life Adjustment Education was cast aside.

"Progressive" Colleges

Even excluding the myriad changes in professional and vocational courses in higher education, changes in liberal-arts colleges have been almost innumerable. In 1930 a questionnaire sent to all the liberal-arts colleges on the lists of the American Association of University Women and the Association of American Universities brought 315 responses, describing 1,389 "changes and experiments current in liberal collegiate education along the lines of care and direction of students, curriculum and instruction, organization and administration."[42] And the summary of these changes was published too early to include any of the progressive colleges except Rollins, which received the unique distinction of a whole chapter devoted to it.

In 1931 Rollins College, in Winter Park, Florida, conducted a Curriculum Conference under the chairmanship of John Dewey. Others in

[41] U.S. Office of Education, *Bulletin 1954*, No. 4, *A Look Ahead in Secondary Education*, pp. 84–90.

[42] Kathryn McHale, *Changes and Experiments in Liberal-Arts Education*, National Society for the Study of Education, Thirty-First Yearbook, Part II (Bloomington, Illinois: Public School Publishing Co., 1932), pp. 2, 4, 10, 26–40.

the Conference included the presidents of Antioch and Sarah Lawrence, two other progressive colleges. The final report of the Conference served as a starting point for Rollins' own experiments and as a statement of purposes and curriculum for the progressive colleges. The Conference decided that the "purpose of the college of liberal arts is to discover and achieve the values and significance of life, individual and social." The liberal-arts college had been limited by "its tendency to deny worth to economic and other practical issues and to assume the old classical attitude that usefulness and dignity are in conflict." The "wall between vocational and cultural education" was being "thinned" by the recognition that "study within one's vocational preparation is an important means of freeing and liberalizing the mind." The report included thirteen points for consideration in regard to curriculum. A number of these reflect the influence of the philosophy of John Dewey and progressive education.

1. Less emphasis on the acquisition of mere facts and more emphasis upon generalization, and awareness of gaps in knowledge.
2. Different introductory courses for those who plan further work in a field and for those who do not.
3. More emphasis upon breadth in the first part of the college student's career; more emphasis on specialization in the latter part. . . .
4. More emphasis on the development of the individual, not machine production. . . .
8. It is recognized that the student should understand the relationship to life of each portion of education and to the organized body of the subject matter of which education is a part. . . .
10. So-called "extra-curricular activities" are really part of the educational offerings of the college.
12. Prerequisites for entrance and within the college have been too rigid, too formal, and not fully justified. . . .
13. In general the conference favors the extension of methods of individual guidance through advisors and faculty committees.[43]

In keeping with the principles of the report, Rollins adopted a new program in the fall of 1931. The college was divided into a Lower Division, which stressed "the broad fundamentals of educational outlook and development," and an Upper Division, which offered more special-

[43] *Ibid.*, pp. 223–224, 225–226.

ized work. All grades, points, and credits were abolished, as was classification into freshman, sophomore, junior, and senior years. Students progressed at their own speed, attending classes only if and when they wished. The college course might be completed in two years, or perhaps in six. Although the curriculum or "subject matter" of the program remained substantially the same as in more traditional liberal-arts colleges, student "accomplishment" was carefully guided "under the close personal contact between teacher and student provided by the Rollins Conference Plan of Study."

According to the Conference Plan, both morning and afternoon were divided into two two-hour periods. In the morning the student was scheduled for the more academic subjects; the first period of the afternoon was used for laboratory or field work and the second for athletics, outdoor work, or recreation. In the morning classes students might attend classrooms where the teacher sat at his desk, available generally to assist students who requested help. Occasionally there would be tests, assignments, or a lecture, but most of the time was spent in individual conferences. Promotion to Upper Division and graduation depended on the student's being able to demonstrate to a faculty committee that "the work which he has accomplished is of such character and of sufficient amount to warrant his recommendation for the degree."[44]

Two colleges that were conceived as progressive institutions were the women's colleges Sarah Lawrence and Bennington. Sarah Lawrence opened as a junior college in 1928 and was extended to a four-year institution in 1931. The emphasis was on individualization of instruction, with students following syllabi at their own speed through class work and frequent tutorial consultations. The purpose of liberal education was "the development of social responsibility; a synthesis of work, recreation, social life; a sense of comparative values in use of time." Students were evaluated by written reports from their instructors and advisors; and graduation was at the recommendation of the Faculty Committee on Student Work, so that a girl could progress "from entrance to graduation without the necessity of a single test or arithmetic figure—although these may, in any individual case warranting it, be employed."[45]

Bennington opened in 1932. Its program had been carefully planned for nine years, with W. H. Kilpatrick taking an important role in the early planning. Bennington stressed three themes of the progressive

[44] *Ibid.*, pp. 81–83.

[45] Louis T. Benezet, *General Education in the Progressive College,* Teachers College Contributions to Education, No. 884 (New York: Columbia U., 1943), pp. 56, 70.

education movement. The education for each student should be "continuous with *life*, and especially *her* life." The program for each student should be "literally defined and motivated by her own individual wants, needs, traits, and abilities," and it should "prepare her for intelligent, cooperative living in her society."[46] Bennington permitted students to major in depth, rather than trying to cover all learning superficially. Great emphasis was placed on individual work and conferences between student and instructor.

In 1939 Bennington and its faculty began a self appraisal, assisted by Dr. Alvin C. Eurich of Stanford University. The study concluded, among other things, that Bennington students were low in their knowledge in certain fields and tended to over-specialize. Consequently, in 1942 Bennington introduced a new program of Basic Studies, which students were urged but not required to take. Along with the Basic Studies, students in the Junior Division (the first two years) took Special Studies in two or more fields. In the Senior Division students developed a major, in which they took at least half their work under one tutor. As before 1942, the methods of instruction stressed "experience" and "activity." Degrees were granted on the basis of competence in a major field and "*general education based on the important elements in American civilization.*"[47]

A quite different program was tried at Antioch College, in Yellow Springs, Ohio, beginning in 1929, when the Extramural School was established. At Antioch part-time work was included as part of the "liberal education" of students. The students would spend five weeks in classes and then five weeks at practical economic work somewhere away from the campus.

> Some of the benefits to the students under this cooperative plan are: (1) a ready appreciation of the responsibilities and opportunities of life . . . (3) a maintenance of practical interests simultaneously with theory study enforces the idea that both are continuing processes; (4) job experiences quicken intellectual interests . . . (6) partial self-support . . . (8) learning by doing.

Antioch experimented with other progressive ideas, such as an "Autonomous Plan of Study," comprehensive examinations, and the organized program of "Community Service," all of which helped the college come "nearer to meeting the best of American purpose than do the

[46] *Ibid.*, p. 80.
[47] *Ibid.*, p. 144. (Italics supplied by Benezet.)

highly specialized curricula of our conventional colleges and technical schools."[48]

The Future of Progressive Education

It is something of a paradox that all of the most progressive of the colleges were small, private, liberal-arts schools. The teachers colleges and state universities, which were the centers of Dewey philosophy among educators, have remained essentially traditional in their organization, curriculum, and methods. This phenomenon, however, actually parallels the concentration in private schools of radical progressive experiments at the elementary and secondary level. Public schools, from the first grade to the university, have been very hesitant to adopt the principles of progressive education in any pronounced form. Unmistakably, progressive education has been very much a part of the revolution in twentieth-century American education, but it has been a revolution only partially realized. Whether it will be continued depends very much on the tenor of American society. If the twentieth-century social revolution has already passed its climax, education may become more conservative along with other institutions of our society. If the revolution is still developing, perhaps more of the fifty year-old proposals of John Dewey may yet be accepted by schools in general.

QUESTIONS FOR DISCUSSION

1. To what extent do you consider that the experiments in school reform validated the theories of progressive education? How might you adapt some of these practices to your own teaching? How might they be used to suggest directions for curriculum and school organization?
2. What concepts of the community school, the Gary plan, the Indianapolis school described in *Schools of To-morrow*, and the Life Adjustment Movement could be usefully adapted in schools for culturally disadvantaged children?
3. Read the reports of the Eight-Year Study. How could this study be a model for evaluating other curriculum studies? Look up some of the criticism of the study. How could these criticisms be avoided in future studies?
4. Compare your own college education with the proposals of the "progressive" colleges. What changes do you think could be made in your own college to help make your own education more effective and meaningful?

[48] McHale, pp. 87–90, 188.

5. Contrast educational practices and statements of the founders of the Progressive Education Association with those of John Dewey. Where do they agree and disagree? How would you adapt these ideas in your own educational philosophy?
6. How deep has been the actual influence of the principles and practices of "progressive education" on the schools of America? How do the changes reflect a greater interest in democracy? Where did the early progressives create problems because they took a definition of democracy which was no longer that appropriate to the social context?

SUGGESTED READINGS

Secondary Sources

Cremin, Lawrence A. *The Transformation of the School.* New York: Knopf, 1961.

Meyer, Adolph E. *The Development of Education in the Twentieth Century.* New York: Prentice-Hall, 1949. Pp. 36–107, 147–162, 488–498.

Rugg, Harold. *Foundations for American Education.* New York: World Book, 1947. Chapters XVI–XVIII.

Primary Sources

Bode, Boyd. *Progressive Education at the Crossroads.* New York: Newson, 1938.

Dewey, John. *Experience and Education.* New York: Macmillan, 1938.

Gross, Carl H., and Chandler, Charles C. *The History of American Education Through Readings.* Boston: Heath, 1964. Pp. 409–420, 439–455.

Hillway, Tyrus. *American Education: An Introduction Through Readings.* Boston: Houghton Mifflin, 1964. Pp. 215–220.

16

Critical Issues in Education: I

As American education has expanded in its purposes and scope and as American pedagogical theory has developed, many problems have arisen which affect the direction and effectiveness of American education. Some of these are matters of political debate—racial desegregation, federal aid, separation of church and state. Some are hidden and recognized by only a few voices in the wilderness, including those conflicts which center about the basic philosophical differences of the purposes of education and the nature of man and society. Some are the subject of academic infighting and editorial polemics—particularly the preparation and certification of teachers and the curricula and methods of teaching in the high schools. Some are differences of opinion within the body of teachers—the effectiveness of visual aids and programed learning, the function and nature of teacher organizations, and the organization of the curriculum.

Conflicting Philosophies

Part of the difficulty of securing effective social action in our nation lies in the diversity of our basic beliefs or philosophies. Such is the case with many of the current issues in education. Not only are there fundamental differences in formal philosophical positions, but there are equally serious undefined conflicts among the assumptions implicit in the varied criticisms of the schools and in the arguments for educational reforms. Theodore Brameld has described four major educational philosophies which are related to the prevailing social and economic orientations of our time and which are more useful in analyzing educational issues than the traditional divisions of idealism, realism, and pragmatism.

Corresponding to the conservative position in political, social, and economic theories is the *essentialist* philosophy of education. In the 1930's, as a reaction to the progressive movement, defenders of the educational *status quo* founded the Essentialist Committee for the Advancement of Education. Leaders of the Committee were William Chandler Bagley, a realist in his philosophy, and Michael Demiashkevich, an idealist. The essentialists defend the traditional curriculum as "the tried and tested heritage of skills, facts, and laws of knowledge that have come down to us through modern civilization." Since both idealists and realists accept truth as existing in the nature of the universe, the school and the teacher serve as "mediator between the store of knowledge possessed by the outside world and the mind of the student." The process of learning is thus primarily one of "absorption" of the essential facts.

Brameld classifies the *progressive* as the educational liberal. Recognizing the need for society to continue its growth, the progressive looks to the present rather than the past as the source of authority for the content of education. The primary purpose of education is not the absorption of a body of knowledge, but learning how to think effectively, to make wise decisions, to use the scientific method. The schools thus become "centers of democratic living." Dewey and the Progressive Education Association leaders are the major exemplars of this philosophy.

The remaining two philosophies view the current social situation with grave misgivings and recommend drastic steps to correct the "drift to disaster." One of these positions Brameld calls the *perennialist*. Actually a reactionary philosophy, perennialism looks to the "restoration of the spirit that governed education during the Middle Ages" as the means for training the minds of an intellectual aristocracy that will lead mankind once more to the right life. One major branch of the perennialists is the Catholic or Thomistic scholar; the other is the Great Books school led by Mortimer J. Adler and Robert Maynard Hutchins.

Brameld's own position also stresses the "desperate need for clarity and certainty, for our civilization is fraught with confusion and bewilderment." But he rejects a return to the past and fixes his hopes on the future. His *reconstructionism* is an outgrowth of progressivism and seeks to use cooperative social efforts to "build the widest possible consensus about the supreme ends that should govern man in the reconstruction of his environment." This he considers is the "radical" philosophy which proposes to promote social change and assist in "the birth of a new cultural design."[1]

Since the categories outlined by Brameld are very broad, each includes

[1] Theodore Brameld, *Patterns of Educational Philosophy* (New York: World Book, 1950), pp. 79–82.

a multitude of particular proposals about the purposes and content of education. For example, some essentialists stress the literary and modern foreign language subjects while others would have the schools concentrate on the sciences and mathematics. Businessmen who complain about their employees not being grounded in the basic skills applicable in their work—such as bookkeeping or writing checks—assume that they are in agreement with Robert M. Hutchins, unaware that the Great Books program is anything but vocationally oriented. With such controversy and confusion as to the basic philosophy appropriate to a democratic school system, it is no surprise that teachers and school administrators are frequently inconsistent in developing school policies.

Curriculum

The conflict over school curriculum has been most bitter between the essentialists and the progressives. The perennialists have influenced the curriculum of some small liberal arts colleges, notably St. John's College in Annapolis, but aside from registering dissatisfaction with the high-school curriculum, their attention generally has stopped at the level of higher education. The essentialists, however, have carried on a bitter defense of the traditional subject-matter curriculum. They have been led largely by professors in the colleges of liberal arts, who often complain about the high-school preparation of their students. Interestingly enough, the Council for Basic Education, whose publications urge schools to stress "liberal" in contrast with "vocational" courses, includes as its leaders many academic specialists, like the scientists and historians, whose disciplines were objected to in the nineteenth century as practical and utilitarian. Historians of the college curriculum need only look back to the Spencer and Huxley conflicts with the classicists to observe how some of the current defenders of the liberal arts had to fight to have their courses admitted to the curriculum of the secondary schools and colleges. Now they roundly condemn the "fads and frills" of commercial and vocational courses, as well as such leisure and recreational activities as band, physical education, and craft work. Too, they overlook the fact that the originators of the liberal arts, the ancient Athenians, considered music and gymnastics two of the most appropriate arts for the free—or liberal—man.

The rate of change in today's society makes it quite impossible for anyone to be sure about what children will need to know when they become adults. Consequently, the progressive looks to a concern with method and attitude about learning rather than the acquisition of subject matter. The essentialist would orient the school curriculum around present absorption of knowledge developed in the past in the expectation that it would be useful in the future. The progressive in contrast seeks to develop in pupils those skills and attitudes that will be useful whatever the future may hold.

The difficulty in resolving this conflict between essentialists and progressives is that there is little basic agreement on principles. The fundamental philosophical issue of the absolutism of idealism and realism versus the relativism of pragmatism underlies the controversy, and in such philosophical disagreements there is no way to prove one side right and the other wrong.

Other Curriculum Controversies

The philosophical conflict is not the only factor in the issue of what our schools should teach. Many proposals are made for specific emphasis or particular courses to be included in the curriculum without regard to philosophical position. The safety councils and insurance companies urge that driver training be part of the high-school curriculum. Businessmen want commercial subjects taught to prospective secretaries and clerks. Industrial leaders expect schools to give boys basic tool skills for the factory. When the Russians launched a satellite earlier than the United States, political and military leaders jumped on the science and mathematics bandwagon. Parents who want upward social mobility for themselves and their children want the schools to teach the social graces. The need of the military forces for strong, healthy young men has resulted in more strenuous athletic programs, and recognition of the need for more leisure-time activities has put golf, tennis, and bait casting in physical education classes. The lessened influence of the church and the loosening of family ties have led to the demand that the curriculum include moral and religious teachings. "Patriotic" societies and veterans organizations call for legislation requiring schools to indoctrinate the "American way of life" and to demonstrate the dangers of Communism.

Other curriculum proposals are of the negative kind. Minority religious groups complain that their freedom of religion is infringed upon by religious experiences in the schools. Certain fundamentalists in religion still protest against science courses that teach evolutionary theories. Right-wing political groups bitterly assail social studies courses that mention the United Nations favorably and science classes in which fluoridation of water is approved. Academicians protest the "fads and frills," such as Stagecraft I and the mythical "underwater basketweaving."

Counselors of the juvenile courts argue that the "arbitrary academic requirements" for high-school graduation discriminate against children of the lower economic classes, resulting in dropouts and delinquency.

There are several techniques used to secure desired changes in the school curriculum. Sometimes strong lobbies can pressure legislation requiring all schools to teach a particular subject or making it an offense to teach some subject. Often the same goal is achieved indirectly by providing financial incentives through legislative or Congressional appropriations for specific programs or courses. Another political avenue is the local school board or the state department of education, both of which can often be persuaded to require, forbid, penalize, or reward the teaching of some parts of the curriculum. Teachers are offered free materials —movies, books, posters, slides, pamphlets, and so on—by various interest groups seeking to propagandize their point of view. Pupils are invited to enter contests with prizes awarded to those who best parrot the sponsor's interests. Textbooks are often tailored to be inoffensive to everyone in order to be generally salable.

Curriculum changes are often controversial and bitterly contested. For example, the problems of city slums and Appalachia have caught the attention of political and social leaders, and the "War on Poverty" of Presidents Kennedy and Johnson includes curricular reforms in schools attended by "culturally disadvantaged" children. Although these reforms have the weight of federal financing and the general approval of newspaper editors, there has been debate and opposition on every reform thus far suggested. Proponents of vocational training for potential dropouts claim that machine shops are very much out of date and need to be replaced, but the advocates of economy and academic schooling complain that machine shops are too costly for a public school program, and so it goes.

Financing and Control of Education

Between 1929–1930 and 1957–1958 the percentage of the nation's public school revenue raised locally dropped from 82.7 to 55.8, while the proportion raised by the states rose from 17 to 40.6. In four states the state provided more than 70 percent of the total public-school budget.

The degree of state control does not always increase at the same rate as state financing. Aside from certain minimum standards, many states have left administrative details up to local authorities. According to Johns and Morphet, "*the amount of state control is not determined as much by the amount of state support as by the procedures and policies followed by the state in providing the support.*"[2] It is somewhat ironical to observe the reactions of the most strenuous advocates of local support contradicting themselves on the segregation issues. A number of local communities in the South, particularly metropolitan areas like Miami and Atlanta, were willing to desegregate their schools in compliance with the 1954 Supreme Court decision, only to find their governors and state legislators raising all kinds of barriers to such local decisions. State support does not necessarily result in controls which restrict local authorities —and, conversely, some state legislatures have not waited to provide financial support before enacting controls inhibiting effective local administration of schools.

The failures of state and local officials in the control and support of education hold important implications for federal aid and control. Although there has been a steady increase of federal aid in recent years, control over curriculum and teaching has been left largely to state and local authorities. But experience has indicated that federal aid without some controls leads to ineffective use of the grants, and recent Congresses have required strict accounting of funds and restricted their use to particular parts of the educational program. Too, the mobility of our population and the interdependence of the regions of the nation have done much to make state sovereignty obsolete. The impoverished school system of one state may well produce the criminals and welfare problems of another—and the most uninformed electorate shares with the best educated in the election of our Congressmen and Presidents. The rest of the world does not look on racially segregated schools as a matter of state policies but as national discrimination against Negroes. Gradually people in the states which have provided superior schools are beginning to recognize their responsibility to states that have not been able to finance quality education—and the responsibility shared by all states to develop schools that do not cause problems outside their own borders.

The nineteenth-century struggles to remove inequalities of educational opportunities among school districts has not been completely won, for suburban communities often build for themselves schools far superior to those in the rural areas or the crowded city districts in the same state. The reluctance of some localities to provide adequate schools has led state legislatures to create "minimum foundation programs" and other devices to require local school boards to meet the educational needs of their children. Similarly, states which have refused or are unable

[2] Roe L. Johns and Edgar L. Morphet, *Financing the Public Schools* (Englewood Cliffs: Prentice-Hall, 1960), pp. 115, 238, 240.

to set up good schools may well bring about federal legislation insuring national minimum standards for schools.

Racial Integration of Schools

One issue that greatly complicates the problems of control and finance of schools, particularly when federal aid is involved, is the practice of segregating Negroes from whites in public schools. With the legal question of segregation apparently settled by *Plessy vs. Ferguson,* many states continued the development of "separate but equal" school systems. Unfortunately, there was very little equality for the separate schools attended by Negro children.

Separate But Unequal

The separation of the races was confirmed by Supreme Court decisions in 1908 and 1927. In Kentucky, Berea College had operated on an integrated basis in defiance of a state law making segregation mandatory. Although the Court ruled against the college on technical grounds, "the case was generally accepted as a reflection of the Court's feelings that segregation was a matter better left to the states."[3] In Mississippi a Chinese parent, Gong Lum, petitioned to permit his daughter to attend a white school rather than a Negro school, and in 1927 the Supreme Court upheld the Mississippi ruling that the Chinese were "colored" and that it was no violation of the Fourteenth Amendment for the authorities to require her to attend a "separate but equal" school.

The concept of "equality" of even the most easily measured aspects of schools was rendered farcical by many Northern communities as well as the entire South. Outside the South, segregation was common in large cities because of the effect of residential segregation, and in some communities boundaries of school districts were gerrymandered to insure maximum separation. Under such conditions, the differences between white and Negro schools were those frequently found between middle-class schools and those in slum sections of cities. Some states, such as Indiana, Kansas, New Mexico and Wyoming, permitted local authorities to segregate children by race, and Arizona required it at the grade-school level until a 1951 law made such separation optional.[4]

In the states of the Confederacy and the Border States, the injustice

[3] Harry S. Ashmore, *The Negro and the Schools* (Chapel Hill: U. of North Carolina Press, 1954), p. 22.
[4] *Ibid.*, pp. 67–68.

of separation was blatant even to the casual observer. In counties in which Negroes made up a large proportion of the population, the discrimination was greatest. For example, one such county in Mississippi spent $80.00 for each white child in 1907 and only $2.50 for each Negro child. "In general, the pattern established in Mississippi was common to all the Southern states."[5]

Court Rulings on Higher Education

The first successful attacks on the separate educational system came at the level best understood by the judges and courts—admission to law school. In 1935 Donald Murray was denied admission to the School of Law of the University of Maryland, and he filed complaints in the courts. The Court of Appeals of Maryland ordered the University to admit Murray on the grounds that the instruction at the Negro branch of the University in Princess Anne was "far from equitable and equal; and the out-of-state scholarships for Negroes would not suffice."[6] Within a few months Lloyd Gaines sued for admission to the law school of the University of Missouri, his case finally reaching the United States Supreme Court in 1938. The Court ruled that the state must furnish Gaines "within its borders facilities for legal education, substantially equal to those which the state has afforded for persons of the white race." In 1946 Ada Lois Sipuel sued for admission to the University of Oklahoma on the grounds that the state provided no law school for Negroes. The case took two years to reach the Supreme Court and the decision was that the state must provide the opportunity for a legal education. Oklahoma circumvented the ruling by establishing a law school with a faculty of three white lawyers and Miss Sipuel as its student body. She refused to register and the Court denied further relief on technical grounds. Before her new appeal could reach the Supreme Court, the University had been integrated by another Negro, G. W. McLaurin, and Miss Sipuel was finally admitted in 1949. In 1950, a further breach in the separate system of legal education was made by Heman Sweatt. When he applied for admission to the University of Texas Law School in 1946, the state court gave the University six months to set up a law school substantially equal to that of the University. Sweatt refused to enroll in the new school, and his appeal reached the

[5] Truman Pierce, *et al.*, *White & Negro Schools in the South: An Analysis of Biracial Education* (Englewood Cliffs: Prentice-Hall, 1955), p. 49.

[6] Virgil A. Clift, Archibald W. Anderson, and H. Gordon Hullfish, *Negro Education in America.* The Sixteenth Yearbook of the John Dewey Society (New York: Harper, 1962), p. 55.

Supreme Court in 1950, the decision being that the Negro law school was inferior in number of faculty and their reputation, variety of courses, library, position and influence of alumni, and other such qualities.[7] This ruling clearly outlawed segregated law schools, for no Negro school of the South could ever claim to be the equal of its white counterparts on such grounds.

The breach having been made in the law schools, where judges could clearly see the inequality of the intangible aspects of education, the way was made easier for breakthroughs in other fields. In Oklahoma, G. W. McLaurin applied for admission to the graduate school of education at the University of Oklahoma, and when a federal district court held that he was entitled to admission to the graduate courses which were offered only at the white state universities, the legislature permitted the university to admit him but stipulated that segregation should be maintained on the campus. McLaurin was to sit apart from white students in the classrooms, library, and dining areas. He protested, and his case was taken to the Supreme Court, which held that the restrictions "impair and inhibit his ability to study, to engage in discussions and exchange views with other students, and, in general, to learn his profession."[8] This decision was handed down the same day as the *Sweatt vs. Painter* decision, June 25, 1950.

Efforts at Equalization of Schools

Political leaders, both North and South, recognized that the segregation barriers were falling. Northern legislatures began enacting antisegregation legislation affecting schools as well as other social institutions. Southern legislatures, undoubtedly fearing that the integration movement might spread to the public schools, began to remove some of the inequalities from the segregated school system. The change in expenditures between 1940 and 1952 was a remarkable reflection of the practice of "too little and too late." Over the South in general, in 1940, $50.14 was spent for each white child for current operating costs of schools (excluding transportation) to only $21.54 for each Negro child. That was only forty-three cents per Negro child for each dollar spent per white child. In 1952, Negroes were receiving seventy cents for each dollar spent on whites ($115.08 and $164.83). In erecting new buildings, the change was even more dramatic. In 1940 eight Southern states spent $4.37 per white child in capital outlay compared with only $.99 per Negro child. In 1952 the expenditure was $29.58 per child for Negro

[7] Ashmore, pp. 33–36.
[8] 347 U.S. 483 (1954), p. 493.

schools compared with $36.25 for white schools. Mississippi, all but openly admitting the attempt to improve Negro schools enough to avoid suits on the basis of unequal facilities, spent 38 percent more for Negro schools than for white: $35.23 to $25.48.[9] But the gap between white and Negro schools had become so great over the decades that it would take more than matching expenditures to correct it. The South could not afford the kind of "crash" program needed to produce equality in physical facilities.

More than that, the Negroes had begun to recognize other kinds of inequalities in their schools. Their teachers, products of poor schools and poor colleges, were not as well educated as white teachers, even if they had the same or higher degrees. Then there was the whole immeasurable psychological effect of being segregated—effect on both white and Negro. Negro leaders were beginning to talk about the personality factors caused by separate school systems. At first recognized only by leaders in the integration movement, the effect of segregation on the character of Negro children became apparent to most Negroes. At the dedication of a new Negro high school in Gainesville, Florida, the featured speaker was Dr. Gilbert Porter, executive secretary of the Florida State Teachers Association (even professional associations have been segregated in the South, and until 1964 the Florida Education Association denied membership to Negroes). After the members of the county school board had boasted to the audience about the wonderful building, Dr. Porter talked about the importance of education in the modern world and how the new building would help the Negro in his struggle for self-improvement. The predominantly Negro audience responded in camp meeting style, seconding his sentiments with shouted "Amens." Then Dr. Porter turned to the school board and said, "If you had provided this building thirty years ago, we wouldn't be having the trouble we're having now!" And the audience chanted "Amen!" Then turning to the assemblage, he measured out his words slowly—"But it's too late now!" With one voice, the auditorium roared, "Hallelujah!" The handful of whites invited to attend knew then, if they hadn't known it before, that segregation in education was doomed.[10]

The 1954 Decisions

The change should have been no surprise, for the Supreme Court had already handed down its critical decision ruling separate schools inherently unequal. On May 17, 1954, the Supreme Court ruled unani-

[9] Ashmore, pp. 153–156.

[10] The author was one of the handful of whites present at this moving event, November 18, 1957.

mously on five cases involving segregated schools, four affecting state laws and one the practices in the District of Columbia. The decisions were handed down under *Brown et al. vs. Board of Education of Topeka.* In his decision for the Court, Chief Justice Earl Warren based his opinion partly on legal precedent and partly on "psychological knowledge."

> Today, education is perhaps the most important function of state and local governments. . . . In these days, it is doubtful that any child may reasonably be expected to succeed in life if he is denied the opportunity of an education. Such an opportunity, where the state has undertaken to provide it, is a right which must be made available to all on equal terms.
>
> We come then to the question presented: Does segregation of children in public schools solely on the basis of race, even though the physical facilities and other "tangible" factors may be equal, deprive the children of the minority group of equal educational opportunities? We believe that it does.
>
> In *Sweatt vs. Painter* . . . in finding that a segregated law school for Negroes could not provide them equal educational opportunities, this Court relied in large part on "those qualities which are incapable of objective measurement but which made for greatness in a law school." In *McLaurin vs. Oklahoma State Regents* . . . the Court, in requiring that a Negro admitted to a white graduate school be treated like all other students, again resorted to intangible considerations: ". . . his ability to study, to engage in discussions, and exchange views with other students, and, in general, to learn his profession." Such considerations apply with added force to children in grade and high schools. To separate them from others of similar age and qualifications solely because of their race generates a feeling of inferiority as to their status in the community that may affect their hearts and minds in a way unlikely ever to be undone. The effect of this separation on their educational opportunities was well stated by a finding in the Kansas case. . . .
>
>> "Segregation of white and colored children in public schools has a detrimental effect upon the colored children. The impact is greater when it has the sanction of the law; for the policy of separating the races is usually interpreted as denoting the inferiority of the Negro group. A sense of inferiority affects the motivation of a child to learn. Segregation with the sanction of law, therefore, has a tendency to [retard] the educational and mental development of Negro children and to deprive them of some of the benefits they would receive in a racial[ly] integrated school system."

> Whatever may have been the extent of psychological knowledge at the time of *Plessy vs. Ferguson*, this finding is amply supported by modern authority. Any language in *Plessy vs. Ferguson* contrary to this finding is rejected.
>
> We conclude that in the field of public education the doctrine of "separate but equal" has no place. Separate educational facilities are inherently unequal.[11]

Delays and Circumventions

But Southern politicians did not agree, and governors and legislators worked overtime trying to circumvent the decision, continuing segregation as a policy of Southern governments. A year after the 1954 decision, the Court delegated to the District Courts the task of implementing the decision "with all deliberate speed" by reviewing proposals of Southern officials for desegregating schools. And as fast as the politicians erected barriers to desegregation, Negro parents and the National Association for the Advancement of Colored People brought suit to attack the new laws and practices. One proposal was to turn the public schools over to private concerns, and Prince Edward County, Virginia, abolished its public school system entirely. South Carolina had already (1952) adopted a constitutional amendment permitting the legislature to abolish public education; Georgia and Mississippi followed suit in 1954. Louisiana adopted an amendment (1954) providing for separate schools for "white and colored children," basing the separation on the "state police power to promote public health, morals, better education and the peace and good order in the state, and not because of race." Mississippi made compliance with the 1954 decision a criminal offense, punishing those who attended or taught in a mixed school, and then went on to enact legislation prohibiting "the fomenting and agitation of litigation" to prevent the effective use of the courts in integration questions. As one example of coercing conformity and silencing dissent, the Georgia State Board of Education in 1955 ordered that "all teachers who support, condone or agree to the teaching of mixed classes will have their licenses removed."[12] A number of states adopted pupil placement laws, permitting local school authorities to place children according to a large number of social and psychological criteria, making it difficult for anyone to prove that segregation was being maintained on racial grounds. In the decade following the 1954 decision, the legislatures of the eleven

[11] 347 U.S. (1954), pp. 493–495.

[12] Herbert O. Reid, "The Supreme Court Decision & Interposition," *Journal of Negro Education*, 25 (Spring, 1956): 109–110.

states of the Deep South approved approximately 450 acts and resolutions related to segregation-desegregation, virtually all of them attempts to delay compliance with the order of the Supreme Court.[13] But in spite of all the clever circumlocution and indirection, the intent of all these laws is clearly to maintain segregation, and most lawyers, even in the South, concluded that they "are all believed to be unconstitutional."[14]

One last-ditch defense ignored the whole issue over which the Civil War had been fought. In 1956 several of the Southern states adopted resolutions affirming the principle that the federal government had no powers other than those delegated to it by the "sovereign States," and therefore could not impose authority on them. Thus it was the duty of the state to "interpose" its authority between the federal government and the schools, nullifying federal laws and orders, if necessary by force. The secession of the Southern States in 1861 had been an extension of the principles of interposition and nullification. Historians generally thought that the outcome of the Civil War had ended the issue, but nearly a century later, Southern governors attempted to interpose their authority between schools and federal laws, though without marked success. Perhaps their attempts contributed to the spirit of lawlessness that resulted in riots, murder, and other violence.

One case which attracted international attention was the attempt of Authurine Lucy to enter the University of Alabama. As a result of court orders, the University admitted her on February 3, 1956. Three days of riots and disorder ensued, after which the board of trustees "excluded" her from the campus "until further notice." When she criticized the action, she was expelled on February 29 for having made accusations against University officials "which were slanderous and groundless."[15] Most of the other Southern universities were integrated quietly, but both Mississippi and Alabama suffered continued violence as state officials interposed their office between the courts and the schools.

Thus progress toward desegregation was slow except in the Border states. In the Deep South change came only when courts ordered it. Most Negro parents feared to initiate suits; to do so was to subject themselves to economic threats and even physical attack. When local officials were forced to lower the barriers, Negro parents were reluctant to risk the children in what might be an extremely hostile environment. Those who did enter their children in the previously all-white schools

[13] *Southern School News*, 10, Section B (May, 1964): 1–B.

[14] Reid, p. 110.

[15] Lewis W. Jones, "Two Years of Desegregation in Alabama," *Journal of Negro Education*, 25 (Summer, 1956): 206.

often withdrew them because their children were so handicapped by poor early schooling that they could not keep up with their white classmates. In 1960 only 6 percent of the Negro elementary- and secondary-school pupils in the South were enrolled in schools with white pupils, and 98 percent of these were in the six Border states and the District of Columbia.[16] Even eleven years after the 1954 decision, progress in the Deep South was still only token. Of the 3,044 school districts having both whites and Negroes, only 1,476 had desegregated before or during the school year 1964–1965. Of the nearly three million Negro pupils in the Deep South, 1,422,112 were living in desegregated districts, but only 66,135 were attending schools with white children. Only 2.25 percent of the total number of Negro pupils were actually in integrated schools. Even in the Border states only 58.2 percent of the Negro pupils were attending schools with white children. Progress was somewhat better in colleges and universities. By 1965 all 83 colleges and universities in the six Border states had desegregated. In the eleven states of the Deep South, 161 out of the total of 220 had desegregated. Every state had at least one desegregated college, and all the colleges in Arkansas, Louisiana, North Carolina, Tennessee, and Texas were integrated.[17]

Prince Edward County Schools

One conflict of vital interest to the maintenance of our public-school system took place in Prince Edward County, Virginia. One of the cases covered by the 1954 *Brown vs. Board of Education* decision was brought by Negro parents of children in Prince Edward County. The District Court found the Negro school "inferior in physical plant, curricula, and transportation," but denied the plaintiffs relief while the schools were being equalized.[18] The local school authorities tried vainly to circumvent the Supreme Court decision that separate facilities were inherently unequal, and after exhausting all other techniques, the public schools of the county were closed in the spring of 1959. Tuition grants were given to pupils who attended private schools, and tax relief was given those who contributed to the support of private schools. The white community, having more wealth than the Negroes, provided for their children in a system of segregated, private schools, but the Negroes had no school from the fall of 1958 to the fall of 1963, when a privately financed school was set up for Negroes, to operate until 1964.

[16] Marvin Wall, "Events in Southern Education Since 1954," *Harvard Educational Review*, 30 (Summer, 1960): 209.
[17] *Southern School News*, 11 (June, 1965): 11.
[18] 347 U.S. 483 (1954), p. 487 fn.

Negro parents began the long legal process of suits and appeals. The district court enjoined the school authorities against making tuition payments as long as the public schools remained closed and held that "the schools of the county may not be closed to avoid the effect of the law of the land as interpreted by the Supreme Court, while the Commonwealth of Virginia permits other public schools to remain open at the expense of the taxpayers." An Appeals Court reversed this decision, and the case went to the Supreme Court, which upheld the District Court—just ten years and eight days after the momentous 1954 decision. The 1964 decision sharply criticized the delays in compliance with its 1955 order to proceed "with all deliberate speed."

> There has been entirely too much deliberation and not enough speed in enforcing the constitutional rights which we held in *Brown vs. Board of Education, supra,* had been denied Prince Edward County Negro children. . . . The time for mere "deliberate speed" has run out and that phrase can no longer justify denying these Prince Edward County children their constitutional rights to an education equal to that afforded by the public schools in other parts of Virginia.[19]

The district court was ordered "to enter a decree which will guarantee that these petitioners will get the kind of education that is given in the State's public schools."

But the segregationists were still reluctant to give in. When the public schools opened in the fall of 1964, about 1600 pupils registered. All but seven were Negro.[20] The rest of the white children remained in the private schools of the Prince Edward School Foundation.

Although the integration of Prince Edward County schools was not achieved, the Supreme Court ruled that children have a "constitutional right" to public education. The attitude of the Court seems to be that extremists who fear ignorance less than prejudice will not be permitted to destroy the public school system by closing the doors and turning children away.

Desegregation in the North

The problem of racial segregation has not been limited to the South; indeed many Northern cities have a more difficult problem in some respects than Southern communities. In large cities, housing segregation

[19] *Supreme Court Reporter*, 84 (June, 1964): 1232, 1235.
[20] *Southern School News*, 11 (Sept., 1964): 1.

has resulted in large pockets of racially homogeneous populations, and the schools which serve those neighborhoods are virtually, if not completely, made up of students and teachers of one race. Suburban schools, drawing from middle-class families, are predominantly white; downtown schools, drawing largely from slum and lower-class neighborhoods, are often overwhelmingly Negro. In some instances this separation has been heightened by unpublicized gerrymandering of school districts, but often the only immediate way to eliminate or reduce the *de facto* segregation is by transporting children away from their home neighborhoods to more distant schools.

This problem has been especially great in New York City. In 1954 the Public Education Association undertook a study of *de facto* segregation in the New York schools. Although there was no evidence of intentional racial segregation through gerrymandering, the Negro schools were found to have "serious and consistent inferiority of education and educational standards." The buildings were older and more crowded, had poorer equipment and plant maintenance, were staffed by less competent teachers, and had higher faculty turnover. As a result of the study, the Board of Education has been attempting to remedy some of the defects.[21] One effort has been to transport children to schools away from home to produce schools with a cross section of the population. Many white parents from middle-class neighborhoods have protested the removal of their children from new, well-equipped schools to inferior schools. The problem is one not only of racial segregation but of almost unbelievably poor schools for some parts of the community.

Despite the difficulties in both South and North, it is quite possible that racial desegregation will become as accepted in schools as the coeducation of the sexes. But improvement of economic opportunities for Negroes and the breakdown of restrictions on housing would seem to be prerequisites.

Influence of Federal Aid

Though most school support still comes from local and state sources, increasing federal participation seems probable for the foreseeable future, and even though this federal aid may entail few controls affecting curriculum and teaching methods, local and state officials must conform to the Supreme Court decisions if they are to share in the federal school moneys.

[21] John A. Morsell, "Schools, Courts, and the Negro's Future," *Harvard Educational Review*, 30 (Summer, 1960): 183.

The Civil Rights Act of 1964 contains several sections which directly affect the desegregation of schools. Section 601 specifies that "No person in the United States" shall be discriminated against on the basis of "race, color, or national origin" under any program of activity receiving federal financial assistance. Section 602 directs all federal agencies making grants to "effectuate the provision of Section 601."[22] The United States Office of Education issued an order requiring all colleges and school districts to sign a letter of agreement to comply with Section 601 or show evidence of a plan to desegregate before they could receive federal funds. Though the proportion of federal funds used in any school system is still small, few are willing to relinquish it and many can not continue to operate without it. In the spring of 1965, Office of Education officials met with school superintendents, particularly in the South, to explain the directive, and by June 1965, 89 percent of the school districts had agreed to comply with the desegregation order of Title VI.[23]

Title IV of the Civil Rights Act of 1964 authorizes the Commissioner of Education to grant funds to colleges and universities for short-term or regular session institutes providing special training for school personnel to enable them to "deal effectively with special educational problems occasioned by desegregation." The Commissioner is further authorized to grant funds to school boards to finance in-service training of teachers in "problems incident to desegregation" and to hire consultants to advise the boards on matters relating to desegregation. Title IV also authorizes the Attorney General to institute civil action "for and in the name of the United States" when he receives a complaint of racial discrimination in a public school or college.[24] Previously, these costly legal actions could be brought only by individuals, a handicap which precluded most suits.

Religion and the Schools

One issue likely to create controversy long after problems of racial desegregation have disappeared concerns the separation of church and state in the public schools. Because of the long relationship between religion and all the other institutions of our society, religious expression and concern for religious belief have become almost inextricably entwined with our political, social, and educational institutions. Whenever the school touches on religious subjects it is likely to find itself chal-

[22] *United States Statutes at Large*, Vol. 78, p. 252.
[23] *Southern School News*, II (June, 1965): 1.
[24] *Ibid.*, pp. 247–248.

lenged by some group, and yet when it does not include "enough religion," it is pressured to "put God back in the curriculum."

Actually, the general issue of religion and education covers many practices, from Bible reading to paying teachers' salaries. These practices have been challenged under two clauses in the First Amendment, the first denying government the power to establish religion and the second granting freedom of religious exercise. Although some issues often involve both establishment of religion and freedom of worship and affect both public and parochial schools, problems of religion and education can be grouped under two general heads: (1) those which affect religious exercises in public schools and (2) those which deal with state support of church-related schools.

Religious Exercises in Public Schools

Most if not all states have constitutional or legislative provisions prohibiting sectarian instruction in public schools, yet continually there are complaints and legal suits alleging that some activity of the schools is abridging the freedom of religion of certain individuals. Some of the most common and significant issues involve science teaching, released time for religious instruction, flag salutes, and prayer and Bible reading.

SCIENCE TEACHING Although objective studies such as science would seem to be relatively unaffected by religious differences, particularly bitter conflicts have arisen over science teaching that seems to contradict religious opinion. Shortly after World War I, evangelistic movements triggered a number of laws affecting science teaching in schools. Legislatures in several states specified that schools must teach lessons on the evils of alcohol and tobacco. Religious fundamentalists condemned history and archeology lessons which pointed to the great antiquity of the earth, on the grounds that Biblical evidence points to 4004 B.C. as the date of creation. In the early 1920's legislatures in several states passed laws and resolutions forbidding the teaching of evolutionary theories of creation.

Shortly after the school term closed on May 1, 1925, John T. Scopes, a biology teacher in Dayton, Tennessee, remarked to some friends that no one could teach out of the state-approved biology book without violating the law against teaching evolution. Out of this conversation Scopes was brought to trial for having violated the law. The case attracted immediate nationwide attention, and two imposing teams of lawyers met to do battle. On the side of the state were six men, including the Attorney General of Tennessee and William Jennings Bryan;

for the defense, the six were led by Clarence Darrow, Dudley Field Malone, and Arthur G. Hayes. Scopes as an individual was almost ignored: the trial and publicity centered around the conflict between religion and science. Bryan entered the case as a champion of fundamentalist religion and literal interpretation of the Bible. Darrow, Malone, and Hayes were concerned with the defense of academic freedom against the restrictions imposed by the anti-evolution law. Darrow and his associates admitted that Scopes had violated the law and attempted to have the case center about the constitutionality of the law, but the local judge refused to permit any testimony from either scientists or theologians on the question of evolution and overruled the defense's contention that the law was unconstitutional. When the judge fined Scopes $100, the teacher made his only statement of the trial, charging that he had been convicted under an "unjust statute" which he believed to be "in violation of my ideal of academic freedom—that is, to teach the truth as guaranteed in our constitution, of personal and religious freedom."[25] He appealed his case to the Tennessee Supreme Court, which ruled the law constitutional, but reversed the lower court's decision on a legal technicality, thus preventing an appeal to the United States Supreme Court, which would have tested the constitutionality of the act.

Many such religiously promoted laws affecting the curriculum are still on the books. In 1961 the Tennessee legislature killed a bill aimed at repealing its evolution law. Curiously, one of the arguments given by the representatives who voted to table the bill was that it was unnecessary, since it "is ignored by teachers throughout the state."[26] While it may be true that a law that is not enforced does not silence the conscientious teacher who is willing to risk his position to preserve his right to teach and the rights of his students to pursue the truth, the mere existence of such legislation is often enough to coerce the less courageous teacher into avoiding areas of controversy.

Although Tennessee has been the center of notoriety on evolution, a number of other states have similar laws. Arkansas is unique in having an anti-evolution law which was approved by the voters in a referendum 108,991 to 63,406 on October 6, 1928. On December 6, 1965, Mrs. Susan Epperson, a biology teacher in Little Rock's Central High School, filed suit contesting the constitutionality of the law as a violation of religious freedom. She was joined by a parent of a student at North Little Rock High School, so that the case is now referred to as the

[25] *The World's Most Famous Court Trial* (Cincinnati: National Book, 1925), p. 313.

[26] *The Nashville Tennessean*, Feb. 16, 1961, p. 4.

Epperson-Blanchard case. In June, 1966, Judge Murray O. Reed ruled the law unconstitutional in that it "tends to hinder the quest for knowledge, restrict the freedom to learn and restrain the freedom to teach." The Attorney General of Arkansas, who defended the law in court, announced that he would appeal to the Arkansas Supreme Court. Since Mrs. Epperson has left the state, the case will be followed up in the name of Blanchard.

FLAG SALUTE The morning exercises which open the school day have also resulted in bitter conflict over the separation of church and state in education. Prayer, Bible reading, and the salute to the flag have all been attacked as violations of the First Amendment.

Jehovah's Witnesses believe in a literal interpretation of the Commandment against the worship of "any graven image." Considering the flag a graven image, they refuse to salute it. In 1937 the children of Walter Gobitis were expelled from the public school in Minersville, Pennsylvania, for refusing to salute the flag. Their father sought an injunction against the school order, and the appeal eventually reached the United States Supreme Court. By an 8-to-1 decision the Court ruled that religious freedom is not unlimited.

> The mere possession of religious convictions which contradict the relevant concerns of a political society does not relieve the citizen from the discharge of political responsibilities. . . . National unity is the basis of national security.[27]

The decision, on June 3, 1940, brought criticism of the Court from many religious groups and theologians. It also apparently stimulated mob violence against Witness congregations: the United States Department of Justice received reports of "hundreds of physical attacks upon the Jehovah's Witnesses" between June 12 and June 20.[28] Perhaps it was this criticism and the fear of further religious violence which brought the Court to a change of mind just three years later.

In 1942 the West Virginia Board of Education adopted a "resolution containing recitals taken largely from the Court's *Gobitis* opinion and ordering that the salute to the flag become a regular part of the program of activities in the public schools." Walter Barnette and other Witnesses secured an injunction in the United States District Court restraining the Board from enforcing its salute requirement, and when the Board's appeal reached the Supreme Court in 1943, a 6 to 3 majority of the Court ruled in favor of the Witnesses. The opinion, written by Justice

[27] 310 U.S. 586 (1940), p. 595.
[28] Pfeffer, p. 523.

Jackson, held that no governmental agency, including boards of education, could violate the Constitutional freedoms of the Bill of Rights.

> That they are educating the young for citizenship is reason for scrupulous protection of Constitutional freedoms of the individual if we are not to strangle the free mind at its source and teach youth to discount important principles of our government as mere platitudes. . . . We can have intellectual individualism and the rich cultural diversities that we owe to exceptional minds only at the price of occasional eccentricity and abnormal attitudes. . . . If there is any fixed star in our constitutional constellation, it is that no official, high or petty, can prescribe what shall be orthodox in politics, nationalism, religion or other matters of opinion or force citizens to confess by word or act their faith therein.[29]

Since 1954 the words "under God" have been a part of the Pledge of Allegiance, and some non-believers have objected to the words as a violation of their religious freedom, particularly when the Pledge is included in the school program. In the *Engel vs. Vitale* decision on prayer in the school handed down in 1962, the Court distinguished between religious exercises and "patriotic or ceremonial occasions" during which incidental reference might be made to "God" in anthems or recitations.[30] In November, 1964, the Court refused to review a New York Court of Appeals decision that the "under God" phrase in the Pledge of Allegiance was not a violation of religious freedom.[31]

SCHOOL PRAYERS It has been traditional in the public schools to begin the day with the recitation of a prayer, and some version of the Lord's Prayer has been customary. With the growing awareness, however, of religious differences, school officials sometimes have substituted a "nondenominational" prayer. Such was the case in New York, where the State Board of Regents recommended the following prayer to be recited daily in the public schools:

> Almighty God, we acknowledge our dependence upon Thee, and we beg Thy blessings upon us, our parents, our teachers and our country.

The Board of Education of New Hyde Park directed the school principal to have this prayer said aloud by each class in the presence of a teacher

[29] 319 U.S. 624 (1943), pp. 626, 638, 642.
[30] 370 U.S. 421 (1962), p. 435, fn 21.
[31] *The United States Law Week*, 33 (Nov. 24, 1964): 3190.

at the beginning of each school day. Parents of ten pupils charged that so doing constituted an establishment of religion, and the Supreme Court in 1962 agreed with them. "It is no part of the business of government to compose official prayers for any group of the American people to recite as a part of a religious program carried on by government."[32]

This decision raised a storm of protest from patriotic and church groups, who claimed that the Court was "hostile to religion" and had "taken God out of the classroom." Others, including some ministers, applauded the decision, pointing out that if it was constitutional for government to authorize a "non-denominational" prayer, it would also be constitutional to authorize one that was clearly sectarian. If the educational effect of the perfunctory recitation of prayers were to be considered, perhaps even the fundamentalists in religion would agree that the Court had done them a favor. The school child who mumbled "Harold be thy name" for years certainly did not learn thereby to be religious! Indeed, he might well have learned to accept the mere show of prayer as being sufficient and really be non-religious in his application of the ideas contained in the prayer. But elected boards of education and legislators, ever sensitive to aroused public opinion, continue to seek ways of using the schools to indoctrinate the traditional views of the Protestant Christian majority of our society.

From the colonial days when the Bible was a reading textbook, public schools included Bible reading as a regular part of the school program. During the late nineteenth and early twentieth centuries the practice began to decline, but in the conservative reaction to World War I the religious conservatives succeeded in having legislatures in most of the states revive religion in the schools. By 1960, thirty-seven states required or permitted Bible readings in the schools; only eleven states considered Bible reading a kind of sectarian instruction.[33] Many state courts had ruled on the constitutionality of Bible reading, some favorably, some unfavorably.

In 1963 the United States Supreme Court ruled on two cases, the decision being based largely on the *School District of Abington Township, Pennsylvania, et al. vs. Schempp et al.* Pennsylvania law required that "at least ten verses from the Holy Bible shall be read, without comment, at the opening of each public school on each school day." Parents who did not wish their children to participate could have them excused by a written request. Edward Schempp, a Unitarian, protested that the

[32] 370 U.S. 421 (1962), pp. 422, 425.

[33] Donald E. Boles, *The Bible, Religion & the Public Schools* (Ames: Iowa State U. Press, 1963), pp. 273–274.

readings were contrary to his beliefs but that he did not want to have his children excused from the opening exercises for fear that his children might be labeled "oddballs" and "un-American" and might miss the school announcements which immediately followed the Bible reading. Schempp brought suit in a District Court to enjoin the school district from continuing the Bible readings. The District Court ruled that Bible reading, "even without sectarian comment, possesses a devotional and religious character and constitutes in effect a religious observance." They therefore concluded, and the Supreme Court concurred by an 8-to-1 vote, that Bible reading constitutes an establishment of religion contrary to the First Amendment.[34]

STUDY ABOUT RELIGION AND THE BIBLE Among the unsubstantial criticisms of the *Schempp* decision have been charges that the Court has cut off children from any knowledge of religion. The opinion rendered by Justice Clark for the Court emphasized the responsibility of the school for teaching *about* religion as a social institution and about the Bible as a source of literary allusion and historical information.

> One's education is not complete without a study of comparative religion or the history of religion and its relationship to the advancement of civilization. It certainly may be said that the Bible is worthy of study for its literary and historic qualities. Nothing we have said here indicates that such study of the Bible or of religion, when presented objectively as part of a secular program of education, may not be effected consistent with the First Amendment.[35]

RELEASED AND DISMISSED TIME In 1914 William Wirt introduced the practice of releasing children from school for religious instruction as part of the Gary Plan. Other communities have experimented with various forms of released time, but reliable statistics are difficult to compile, partly because "Such programs have a distressingly high mortality rate." One 1946 survey reported released-time programs in forty-six states. A 1949 survey estimated that approximately 5 percent, or a little over a million children, of the total public-school enrollment were attending released-time religious classes.[36]

In Champaign County, Illinois, where students were released from their regular classes for weekly religious lessons held in the school buildings, Mrs. Vashti McCollum objected to the religious classes in the

[34] 374 U.S. 203 (1963), pp. 208 fn. 3, 209–210.
[35] *Ibid.*, p. 225.
[36] Pfeffer, pp. 318–320.

school buildings as a violation of the separation of church and state. In 1948 the Supreme Court agreed with her appeal (8 to 1) on the grounds that the "State's tax-supported public school buildings" were used "for the dissemination of religious doctrines" and that the compulsory school attendance law afforded "sectarian groups an invaluable aid in that it helps to provide pupils for their religious classes." The Court concluded that the "First Amendment was intended to forbid . . . an impartial governmental assistance of all religions" as well as preference of one religion over another. The First Amendment "has erected a wall between Church and State which must be kept high and impregnable."[37]

In New York City children were excused from school to attend religious instruction off the school grounds. Children who did not wish to attend were kept in school, but witnesses charged that they were in effect punished for not attending the religious classes. "Teachers would not permit them to do their homework, . . . nothing was taught to them and they were not permitted to do educationally significant work."[38] Churches turned in attendance reports on those children who were in the religious classes, and truants were checked on by the school principal or other teachers. Tessim Zorach, an Episcopalian, and Esta Gluck, a Jew, challenged the law authorizing the released-time program, but the Supreme Court in 1952 ruled that the New York program was different from the Champaign practice and was not a violation of the First Amendment. Justice Douglas, writing the opinion for the majority of six, held that the government must be neutral in religious matters. It cannot force anyone to worship, attend church, observe religious holidays, or take religious instruction. But the school "can close its doors or suspend its operation as to those who want to repair to their religious sanctuary for worship or instruction. No more than that is undertaken here."

A minority opinion written by Justice Black disagreed sharply. He felt that there was coercion on the children to attend the religious instruction.

> The greater effectiveness of this system over voluntary attendance after school hours is due to the truant officer who, if the youngster fails to go to the Church school, dogs him back to the public schoolroom. Here schooling is more or less suspended during the "released time" so the nonreligious attendants will not forge ahead of the

[37] 333 U.S. 203 (1948), pp. 211–212.
[38] Pfeffer, p. 357.

> churchgoing absentees. But it serves as a temporary jail for a pupil who will not go to church. It takes more subtlety of mind than I possess to deny that this is governmental constraint in support of religion.[39]

One fact which appears to support Black's contention is that programs where all children are dismissed from school to make attendance at religious instruction strictly voluntary have not been successful and are not satisfactory to the proponents of religious instruction through the schools. It is apparent that the coercion of the schools' compulsory attendance laws is necessary for such programs to be effective. This fact alone would seem to cast strong doubt on the constitutionality of released-time programs.

OTHER ASPECTS OF RELIGION IN THE PUBLIC SCHOOLS Some predominantly Catholic communities have employed members of Catholic teaching orders in the public schools. Although their employment as teachers has not been held unconstitutional except in Missouri, several states have court ruling or legislation forbidding the wearing of distinctive religious garb in the public-school classroom. The custom of a baccalaureate service at graduation and the offering of invocations and benedictions at school ceremonies have also been challenged in various communities, with varying results.[40] The school calendar is related to the Christian tradition, with customary holidays at Christmas and Easter being accompanied by school activities related to the religious significance to these dates. The singing of Christmas carols, production of Christmas or Easter plays or pageants, decorating trees and eggs, and other religious manifestations in the school program have been challenged by non-Christians and non-believers. One solution has been to make the religious celebrations an occasion for teaching about religious traditions of different peoples. At Christmas time children learn about the Jewish Hanukah and at Easter the Passover is discussed. The center of the observance has moved toward the secular aspects of the holidays —more Santa Claus and Easter Bunny than Birth and Resurrection. At the University of Florida Christmas program in 1964, the president's sermon ("Born to Make Men Free"), the Bible reading of the Christmas story, and the singing of carols were conducted as usual, but there was no invocation or benediction at the service "to make it less religion oriented"—a ludicrously illogical subterfuge for conducting a religious service on a state university campus.[41]

[39] 343 U.S. 306 (1952), pp. 314, 324.
[40] Pfeffer, pp. 412–420.
[41] *The Florida Alligator*, 57 (Dec. 4, 1964): 1.

State Support for Church Schools

Since the 1840's all the states except Vermont have adopted constitutional provisions prohibiting the use of public-school funds for sectarian purposes.[42] Yet in many ways there has been and continues to be expenditure of public moneys for assisting the educational work of church-related schools and colleges.

INCORPORATION OF PAROCHIAL SCHOOLS INTO PUBLIC SYSTEMS Though the mainstream of education in the United States has been the development of public, tax-supported schools, the desire of many parents for schooling with a religious orientation has resulted in the establishment of church-related schools. Seventh-day Adventists, Lutherans, Mennonites, Reformed churches, and Episcopalians all have denominational schools, but by far the largest system of parochial schools is that maintained by the Roman Catholics. About 14 percent of all the nation's school children are enrolled in Catholic schools. Between 1940 and 1960 public-school enrollments increased 36 percent, but nonpublic-school enrollments increased 118 percent.[43] This spectacular rise was due almost entirely to the expansion of the Roman Catholic parochial schools, and the supporters of that system have pointed out that the sudden addition of their more than five million pupils into the public schools would create a severe burden on school budgets. Because they serve such a large segment of the public, the Catholics argue that their schools are entitled to a share of the tax money. Over this issue many bitter legislative and court fights have already been fought, and many more appear certain for the future.

One system of direct aid to parochial schools has been the practice of incorporating church schools into the public-school system, maintaining the religious teachers on the staff but paying them from tax funds. Commonly under such an arrangement classes in catechism are held before the regular school schedule begins. In 1937 there were at least 340 Catholic schools in the country operating under the name of public schools.[44] In predominantly Catholic communities such schools arouse little reaction, but in North College Hill, Ohio, it created a rift in the community.

In that Cincinnati suburb in 1940, the city school board incorporated the Catholic parochial school into the public school system. In the following school board election, the school became a major issue, with

[42] Boles, p. 43.
[43] R. Freeman Butts, "Public Funds for Parochial Schools? No!" *Teachers College Record*, 62 (October 1960): 58.
[44] Pfeffer, p. 450.

one slate pledged to return the school to the Church and another committed to keeping it a tax-supported school. The parish priest sent a letter to his parishioners backing the latter group, noting that the failure to elect them would result in "heavy losses" in the salary paid the nuns who taught in the school as well as the rent paid the Church for the school and the free textbooks received by the children. The election produced new board members with four Protestants and one Catholic, and the school was returned to the Church. In the 1945 election, the Catholics won a 3-to-2 majority on the board, and the school was again incorporated into the public system. When a conflict broke out between the Catholic members of the board and the city superintendent of schools, he was discharged. The teachers of the non-Catholic schools protested, and in March, 1947, "more than 90 percent of the 750 students in the three schools" (the other two schools in the system were the Catholic school and a Negro school) went on a strike which lasted two months. Citizens signed petitions protesting the ouster, and suit was brought contending that payments to the Church and the employment of nuns as teachers were unconstitutional. At an April meeting of the board, a fist fight broke out when protesting Protestants physically assaulted the Catholic board majority, and the police had to intervene. Twenty-nine of the thirty teachers in the three white, non-Catholic schools resigned, and the Ohio and National Education Associations urged members of the teaching profession not to take positions in the community. When the board could not hire new teachers, they resigned, turning the schools over to Probate Court. The Court renewed the superintendent's contract, rehired the old teachers, and appointed a new board of four Protestants and one Catholic. In November an all-Protestant board was elected, and the Catholic school was returned to the Church.

> One conclusion stands out from the North College Hill incident: an attempt to invoke state machinery in the aid of religion always carries with it the danger of acrimony and strife dividing the people along religious lines, and of bringing with it the very evils which the fathers of the Constitution sought to avoid by declaring the government to be without constitutional power to assume the responsibilities that belong to the Church.[45]

A similar situation developed in New Mexico, where a "large number" of communities used existing Catholic schools as public schools. In 1948

[45] *Ibid.*, p. 455.

in the town of Dixon a public school attended by the Protestant children was closed without notice and its pupils transferred to the Catholic school. The church school contained religious objects and symbols, and children were required to recite "Hail Mary" several times a day. Protestant children who did not attend confession and mass were punished. Protestant parents brought suit for an injunction, and the New Mexico Supreme Court ruled that the practice violated the principle of separation of church and state, specifically ruling against the adoption of sectarian textbooks and furnishing them to tax-supported schools, furnishing free textbooks to other than tax-supported schools, providing free school bus transportation to pupils of parochial schools, teaching sectarian doctrine in tax-supported schools, holding tax-supported schools in buildings which have religious emblems such as crosses, grottos, religious statuary, and religious pictures peculiar to a certain denomination, and holding tax-supported schools in church-owned buildings.[46]

FEDERAL AID AND RELIGION Since 1945 the National Catholic Welfare Conference has supported bills for federal aid to education which have provided that non-public schools would share in the grants. Protestant groups have opposed such bills, and the conflict between the two church interests has contributed largely to the failure of Congress to enact any bills providing general aid for schools. In 1949 Representative Graham A. Barden, a former school teacher, introduced a series of federal aid bills appropriating funds to be used for public schools. Cardinal Spellman attacked Barden in a speech at Fordham University as a "disciple of discrimination" and his bill as guilty of promoting an "irrational, un-American, discriminatory thesis that the Public School is the only true American school." A few days later Mrs. Eleanor Roosevelt, in her column "My Day," commented that no denominational school—"Catholic, Episcopalian, Presbyterian, Methodist, or whatever"—should "receive Federal funds; in fact, no tax funds of any kind." Although she mentioned Spellman only incidentally as having made a request for federal aid, the Cardinal wrote a public letter accusing her of making a personal attack on him, of having a "record of anti-Catholicism," and of producing "documents of discrimination unworthy of an American mother!" Barden later criticized Spellman for his attack on Mrs. Roosevelt, calling him a "cruel authoritarian."[47] The bitter conflict doomed the bill and sharpened the religious conflict.

Although there have been no bills providing aid for general operating

[46] *Ibid.*, pp. 460–461.
[47] *Ibid.*, pp. 487–492.

expenses of schools, a number of bills have been enacted providing specific kinds of aid, some of which have benefitted church-related schools and colleges. For example, the National Defense Education Act of 1958 provided "financial assistance for strengthening science, mathematics, and modern foreign language instruction" in "private nonprofit elementary and secondary schools."

It is apparent from discussion and testimony on the NDEA Bill that Congressmen assumed that those subjects would be free from sectarian influence. But examination of textbooks in some church-related schools in those subjects reveals strong doctrinal influences permeating the teaching.

FREE TEXTBOOKS In the areas of free textbooks, free school lunches, and free bus transportation for parochial school students, a different legal principle has been followed from that of direct grants to schools. In 1929 the Louisiana Supreme Court upheld the distribution of free secular textbooks provided by the state for children in parochial schools on the grounds that the books benefitted the pupil and not the school. In 1930 the United States Supreme Court accepted this argument in the case of *Cochran vs. Louisiana State Board of Education.*[48] In 1946 five states (Louisiana, Mississippi, New Mexico, Oregon, and West Virginia) provided free secular textbooks for children attending parochial schools.[49] New York (1922), South Dakota (1943), and Indiana (1943) had rulings by the courts or state attorney general that free textbooks could not be supplied by the state to parochial school children.[50]

FREE TRANSPORTATION In 1954 there were at least 18 states providing public transportation for parochial school pupils.[51] State courts in Delaware, Oklahoma, New York, Washington, New Mexico, and Iowa have ruled such free transportation unconstitutional, but courts in California, Kentucky, Maryland, and New Jersey have held the practice constitutional under the theory that the aid is for the benefit of the child and not the school or the Church.[52]

The New Jersey case (*Everson vs. Board of Education*) was appealed to the United States Supreme Court, which ruled in 1947 by a 5-to-4 majority that public funds might be used to transport children to parochial as well as public schools. The majority opinion held that providing

[48] 281 U.S. 370 (1930).
[49] Pfeffer, p. 499.
[50] "The State and Sectarian Education," N.E.A., *Research Bulletin,* 34 (Dec., 1954): 187.
[51] *Ibid.,* p. 36.
[52] Pfeffer, pp. 470, 643 fns. 14 and 15.

transportation is of the same nature as providing policemen to protect children at street crossings. The state must be neutral in its attitude toward religion, and therefore it "cannot exclude individual . . . members of any . . . faith, *because of their faith, or lack of it,* from receiving the benefits of public welfare legislation." Although the majority affirmed the "wall between church and state . . . must be kept high and impregnable," it decided that there had not been "the slightest breach." The four-judge minority disagreed that the provision of free transportation was not an aid to the school and thus to the Church. They held that "transportation . . . is as essential to education as any other segment."

> The feat is impossible to select so indispensable an item from the composite of total costs, and characterize it as not aiding, contributing to, promoting or sustaining the propagation of beliefs which it is the very end of all to bring about. . . . Payment of transportation is no more, nor is it any less essential to education, whether religious or secular, than payment for tuitions, for teachers' salaries, for buildings, equipment and necessary materials. Nor is it any the less directly related, in a school giving religious instruction, to the primary religious objective all those essential items of cost are intended to achieve.[53]

The two state courts (Washington in 1949 and New Mexico in 1951) to rule on the transportation issue since 1947 have agreed with the minority opinion in the Everson decision rather than following the majority ruling.[54] As with textbooks, the legal issue is still somewhat in doubt.

SHARED TIME As the Roman Catholic schools have multiplied, they have placed an increasing financial burden on the Church. There are far too few teaching sisters and brothers to staff the schools, necessitating higher salaries to attract enough lay teachers. Some Catholics have advocated concentrating on the education of children of secondary age. Others have proposed that parochial-school students take part of their work in public schools. In such a shared-time plan, Catholic students would study their religion, social studies, and similar courses in the Church-controlled school and take their science, mathematics, physical education, music, and vocational courses in the public schools. Since those courses which the Church leaders feel are most crucial are the least

[53] 330 U.S. 1 (1947), pp. 16, 18, 47–48.
[54] Pfeffer, pp. 478, 643 fn. 24.

expensive to operate, the shared-time plan would greatly reduce the cost of parochial schools.

In 1964 the N.E.A. reported that 183 public school systems had shared-time programs with parochial schools. Both secondary and elementary schools were involved in some systems, though the plan was more common at the secondary level. In the 183 systems, about 18,000 parochial school pupils were involved, approximately 2.2 percent of the total regular school enrollment in these systems. Shared-time plans were under operation in 26 states, though 134 of them were concentrated in six states: Illinois, Michigan, Minnesota, Ohio, Pennsylvania, and Wisconsin.[55]

Supporters of the shared-time plan argue that it will provide greater educational opportunity by permitting parochial schools to reduce their overcrowded classes to something comparable to those of the public schools. It will give students who want a religiously oriented schooling a chance to get courses which the parochial schools cannot afford to provide. Further, they argue, it would reduce the conflict between Catholics and non-Catholics over school issues, opening the door to passage of federal aid bills.

Opponents argue that not only is the plan unconstitutional but scheduling of classes would be difficult; public schools might well find their day upset by peak loads alternating with half-empty buildings. Transportation costs would mount. Classes already overloaded in the public schools are the very ones that would be in greatest demand by the parochial pupils. Splitting the pupil's work between two schools would increase the compartmentalization of learning instead of bringing a greater integration of studies, as most educators believe is necessary.

Many Protestant and Jewish organizations have expressed strong opposition to any shared-time plan as endangering the public school system. Some Catholics have been concerned that it might lead to dissolution of the parochial school system: once a child begins to attend the public school for part of his work, he may decide to stay there for all of it. Shared-time has often engendered more ill feeling than good will, as has happened with other forms of state aid to religious activities.

THE ELEMENTARY AND SECONDARY EDUCATION ACT OF 1965 President Johnson compromised on the religious issue in offering federal assistance to local school systems for the "education of children of low-income families." The Elementary and Secondary Education Act of 1965, which

[55] N.E.A. Research Report 1964-R 10, *Shared-Time Programs: An Exploratory Study*, p. 7.

was signed into law on April 11, 1965, provides federal funds for the purchase of textbooks and library resources for private as well as public schools. In recognition of the principle of the separation of church and state, however, the law specifies that the title to these materials shall be vested "only in a public agency" and that only such materials shall be purchased as "have been approved by an appropriate State or local educational authority or agency for use, or are used, in a public elementary or secondary school of that State." Since local authorities have frequently ignored the separation of religion and government, this leaves a considerable loophole for breaching the "wall of separation." Furthermore, although the concluding section of the law prohibits any payments "for religious worship or instruction," the law encourages shared-time plans by providing grants for "developing and conducting exemplary educational programs, including dual-enrollment programs."[56]

The religious issues raised by this law will not be overlooked. Even before President Johnson delivered his message to Congress outlining the proposal, an organization called "Protestants and Other Americans United for Separation of Church and State" had announced its opposition to any aid that might reach church-related schools from tax funds.[57]

Unresolved Conflict

Because the institutions of religion and education are so inextricably entangled, the problems of separation of church and state in education may never be fully solved. The United States faces the prospect of conflict far into the foreseeable future. Even though the Supreme Court has ruled on such matters as prayer in the schools, the issues are not completely dead. Senator Everett Dirkson is championing a constitutional amendment which would make it possible to reverse the Court's ruling on school prayers. Recent federal aid programs which permit "private nonprofit" institutions to participate in tax funded projects and use tax funds for buildings and library resources raise questions of establishment of religion. Religion is a highly emotional area of controversy and issues which are affected by religious belief are apt to be damaging to both public and parochial schools.

[56] Stat. 27, pp. 37–38, 58, 41.
[57] *U.S. News and World Report*, 57 (Jan. 25, 1965): 66–67.

17

Critical Issues in Education: II

Academic Freedom

The Enlightenment philosophers who provided intellectual leadership for the American revolution recognized the importance of protecting the rights of men to think and speak freely. Americans have been justly proud of these rights, but both in the periods of social unrest leading up to revolutionary crises and in the conservative reactions which follow there have been general and persistent attempts to stifle dissent. Since World War II the Communist threat has been used to punish almost any kind of non-conformity. Supporters of racial integration, water fluoridation, the United Nations, abstract art, abolition of prayer in the schools, jazz, federal aid to education, and almost numberless other causes and interests have been attacked as Communists, "pinkos," and "unwitting followers of the Commie line."

Schools and universities particularly have felt the threat from those who believe that schools should teach only socially approved ideas. Teachers have been required to sign loyalty oaths whose main purpose seems to be to frighten them into conformity rather than to eliminate Communists—who would have no hesitancy whatever in signing loyalty oaths. Self-appointed censors attempt to screen textbooks and prevent students from reading books which challenge conservative points of view.

What Is Academic Freedom?

Unlike freedom of speech, academic freedom "is not a right that professors or students have under the Constitution or under any law of the land." It can be protected "only by appealing to the conscience of individuals and groups in society."[1] The only recourse to law in even an indirect defense of academic freedom occurs when contractual arrangements have been broken, as when a professor or teacher with tenure has been dismissed.

Academic freedom is more than mere absence of governmental restraint on the speech and thoughts of teachers. To ensure the broadest search for truth, teachers and students must be positively encouraged "to study, to investigate, to present and interpret, and to discuss facts and ideas concerning men, human society, and the physical and biological world in all branches and fields of learning."[2]

The ultimate consideration in the defense of academic freedom is the student and the fundamental importance of his right to learn.

> If our students are to grow to political and social maturity, no step should be neglected which will habituate them to the free interchange of ideas—unpopular and strange ideas as well as those which are favored and familiar.
>
> These primary considerations demonstrate the need for maintaining in extracurricular activities a system analogous, so far as practicable, to the rights of free speech and assembly enjoyed by the community at large. This system should begin to operate in the early grades in matters consonant with the intellectual and general maturity level of the students and gradually broaden as high school years are reached.

Students should be permitted to have responsible student government. They should have freedom of association in political as well as social and athletic groups, as long as these groups have "proper and lawful purposes." "Student organizations should be as free as any other responsible group of citizens to invite speakers to address them on any subject."

The principle of academic freedom protects teachers from discharge and harassment for their out-of-school activities as well as assuring their right to teach and carry on research.

> In his private capacity the teacher should be as free as any other citizen to participate in political, religious, and social movements and organizations and in any other lawful activity, and to hold and

[1] Fritz Machlup, "On Some Misconceptions Concerning Academic Freedom," *American Association of University Professors Bulletin*, 41 (Winter, 1955): 755.

[2] American Civil Liberties Union, "Academic Freedom & Academic Responsibility," *AAUP Bulletin*, 42 (Autumn, 1956): 517–518.

> to express publicly his political, religious, economic, and other views. . . .
>
> The teacher should be as free as any other citizen to write on any subject which interests him. . . .
>
> Like any other professional or non-professional worker, the teacher should be free to organize with others to protect group interests, or to join existing unions or other organizations for such purposes. . . .
>
> Teachers should not be required to take any special oath of loyalty to government. We object to the irrelevance and futility of such special oaths and to their use as thought control devices.[3]

Attacks on Public Schools

Public education has never been without opponents. Thomas Jefferson was not able to defeat them, and Horace Mann had to struggle valiantly to improve schools over their objection. In the nineteenth century, the attacks were open and direct, but the popular acceptance of the public schools has forced the modern enemies of public education to make their attacks indirectly. Harold Benjamin, chairman of the National Commission for the Defense of Democracy Through Education, analyzed this opposition in 1950, attributing it to the "taxpayer of unusual type in this country," one who prefers low taxes to "improvement of education for his people's children." This opposition is not one of penuriousness, but of principle. Rarely does the enemy of public education openly admit his principle, however, and Benjamin commended an official lobbyist of the National Association of Real Estate Boards for being more forthright than the typical opponent of public schools.

> "I do not believe in democracy," Mr. Herbert V. Nelson wrote in a letter read at a Congressional hearing on April 19, 1950, and quoted by the United Press on that date. "I think it stinks. I believe in a republic operated by the elected representatives who are permitted to do the job, as the board of directors should."[4]

Most anti-school tax, anti-public education movements recently have masked their real motives behind the "patriotic" front of anti-subversive witch hunts.

In the late 1940's and early 1950's, one of the most strident voices against the public schools was Allen Zoll of the National Council for

[3] *Ibid.*, pp. 519–524.
[4] Ernest O. Melby and Morton Puner (eds.), *Freedom and Public Education* (New York: Praeger, 1953), p. 139.

American Education, an organization with a title obviously designed to impress the naive. An anti-Semite, pro-Nazi in the early years of World War II, Zoll came into prominence with a series of pamphlets on "Red-ucators." His widely circulated publications included "How Red Are the Schools?", "Progressive Education Increases Delinquency," "How Red Is The Federal Council of Churches?", and "Private Schools: The Solution to America's Educational Problem." The distribution of these pamphlets was apparently subsidized by gifts from wealthy conservatives whose views of democracy were like those of Herbert V. Nelson. Zoll used the title "Ph.D." after his name, but admitted that he had been granted the degree by Temple Hall College and Seminary, "a one-man diploma mill" operated by a convicted confidence man and forger named D. Scott Swain. It is hard to realize that Zoll and his few followers would be taken seriously by many Americans, yet as important a periodical as the *Saturday Evening Post* printed a 1951 guest editorial written by one of his associates.

American educators were badly shaken by the circumstances of the dismissal in 1951 of Willard Goslin, superintendent of schools at Pasadena, California. A school-tax election was opposed by a group called the School Development Council (S.D.C.). When the tax measure failed at the polls, the S.D.C. began an attack on Goslin and "subversion" in the schools. Zoll's pamphlets were an important part of the propaganda attack. The upshot was that the city Board of Education asked Goslin to resign. James B. Conant compared "the foolish action of a weak school board under heavy pressures with the action of the posse in *The Ox-Bow Incident*." A number of cases of dismissals of teachers and other educators during the McCarthy era received somewhat less publicity than did Goslin's case.

Although the number of actual dismissals were relatively few, the publicity and propaganda attacks severely damaged teacher morale over the nation and frightened many teachers into conformity and silence about controversial topics.

In the fall of 1950 Frederick G. Cartwright, a Wall Street investment businessman, and the Catholic War Veterans demanded an investigation into the "activities and possible Communist ties of some teachers in the Englewood public schools." A hearing before the Board of Education revealed that Cartwright's evidence was all hearsay. In examining Cartwright's claim that the textbooks were subversive, for instance, the Board found that he had never read them. However, in spite of the fact that his charges were found to be completely baseless, his wild attacks had done their damage.

> The teachers were jittery. They were afraid the healthy open discussions that had previously characterized their classes would somehow be misconstrued. Several teachers . . . were sure that some students, under instructions from their parents, were trying to trap them into making incriminating statements.[5]

Such attacks have not ended. Extreme conservative groups and so-called "patriotic" societies have continued to cast doubt on the loyalty and democratic principles of American public education. The philosophy of pragmatism has been equated with Communism, ignoring the fact that the absolutism of the Communist philosophy is at the opposite pole from the relativism of the pragmatist. John Dewey and William H. Kilpatrick have been branded as subversive, and the progressive movement in education has been blamed for all the ills of the nation. The 1964 Presidential campaign gave wide circulation to one such attack in *None Dare Call It Treason.*[6] This book is a typical example of faking scholarly research by the use of misleading footnotes, quotations taken out of context, and meanings distorted by the omission of words or sentences.

These attacks have resulted in the institution of special loyalty oaths for teachers and censorship of textbooks and library books. Between the close of World War II and 1951 legislatures in eleven states set up special committees to investigate charges of subversion in colleges, universities, and public schools. Although these investigations turned up few if any Communists, and little that could be called subversive by any reasonable definition, two of these legislative investigations (California and Illinois) resulted in state-prescribed loyalty oaths for teachers.

Loyalty Oaths

Loyalty oaths for teachers have appeared at other times of crisis in our history. During and immediately following the Civil War, a number of the Border states instituted teacher loyalty oaths, but all but Nevada and West Virginia repealed them. A second flurry of twelve states added oaths in the conservative reaction following World War I. The early 1930's brought at least ten teacher-oath laws, though some of the earlier ones were repealed during the same period. But the time of greatest hysteria came after World War II, particularly in 1949, when nineteen state legislatures considered loyalty oaths and other bills affecting

[5] *Ibid.*, pp. 173–174, 162, 150, 165–166, 168.

[6] John A. Stormer (Florissant, Missouri: Liberty Bell Press, 1964), Chapter 6, pp. 99–123.

"loyalty and alleged subversive activities of public school personnel." Ten enacted the bills into law, and in one other state the board of education adopted a resolution barring Communists from employment as teachers.[7] In addition, a number of large cities adopted similar measures, and most of them were in states that already prescribed loyalty oaths for teachers. This duplication of restriction gives edge to the complaint that such laws are not an attempt to screen out active Communists or real subversives but are actually subtle devices to coerce teachers into silence on controversial topics.

NEW YORK'S FEINBERG LAW Two high points in legislative attacks on academic freedom came in 1949 in New York and Maryland. The Feinberg Law directed the New York Board of Regents to make a list of "subversive" organizations, membership in which would "constitute prima facie evidence of disqualification" for any position "in the public schools of the state." Since legally "prima facie" evidence is not considered conclusive, the effect of this bill was to put the burden of proof on the accused, a reversal of the American tradition that a man is innocent until proved guilty. Educators pointed out, too, that the bill was an attempt to legalize guilt by association. They feared that the Board's authority "could be perverted to destroy organizations that were not Communist but only liberal and radical" and that the law would "deter teachers from joining legitimate groups whose activities ran counter to the wishes of a political administration."[8] The law was quickly challenged in the courts, but in 1951, the United States Supreme Court ruled six to three that the Feinberg Law was not unconstitutional.[9]

MARYLAND'S OBER ACT In Maryland the Ober Act was a composite of almost all the loyalty oaths adopted in other states. It not only included overt acts and direct advocacy of the overthrow of the government, but also anyone who "teaches by any means any person to commit, attempt to commit, or aid in the commission of any act intended to overthrow, destroy or alter" government by force. A teacher need not be convicted of any charge, but could be discharged on the basis of "reasonable grounds on all the evidence to believe that [the teacher] is a subversive person."[10] This could mean that the innocent, patriotic teacher who

[7] E. Edmund Reutter, *The School Administrator & Subversive Activities* (New York: Teachers College, Columbia U., 1951), pp. 9–10, 23, 31. Reutter names eleven states as enacting loyalty laws, but apparently he counted New Hampshire twice (see p. 10).

[8] *The New York Times,* Sunday, Sept. 18, 1949, p. 12E.

[9] Reutter, p. 58.

[10] *Laws of Maryland, 1949,* p. 103.

had his class study the Declaration of Independence might be discharged on the grounds of subversion, for that revolutionary document advocated the "right of the people to alter or abolish" any government which was destructive of the rights of men.

When the Ober Act was contested, Baltimore Circuit Court Justice Joseph Sherbow contended that the law was unconstitutional. He ruled that the law was invalid because it defined the crime "in vague and ambiguous terms." He questioned the language of the clause dealing with the person who advocates or teaches "by any means" anyone to engage or assist in the "alteration" of the government. He pointed out the dangers of guilt by association:

> If a member honestly believes he belongs to an organization that is not subversive, he may find himself facing severe, even harsh penalties, if that organization has been found to be subversive. . . . It is then too late to withdraw from membership. . . .
>
> An organization, legal when founded, may become subversive within the meaning of this law, as a result of acts by a small group of officers in control for a short time, and in spite of the violent opposition of the general membership.

Sherbow pointed out that under the law a teacher might be discharged "upon no evidence at all, but merely upon 'reasonable grounds.'" This made the law a Bill of Attainder, inflicting punishment "upon persons supposed to be guilty of an offense, without any conviction in the ordinary course of judicial proceedings." The law could be used against "any and all who differ from the generally accepted beliefs of those who happen to be in the majority at the moment."[11]

When the case reached the Maryland Court of Appeals, the ruling of Sherbow was overturned on a technicality without a decision on the constitutionality of the law. Thus the oath and the rest of the Ober Act remained to coerce teachers into silence on matters of controversy. Although the Ober Act and its oath has not yet revealed a Communist among Maryland teachers, it may have done untold damage to the ultimate safety of our nation in blocking free discussion.

In January, 1966, Dr. William W. Krause, a psychoanalyst hired by the University of Maryland to conduct group therapy for students, brought suit in Federal Court for back salary which had been denied him because he refused to sign the Ober Act loyalty oath. The case is still pending at

[11] *H. Carrington Lancaster, et al. vs. Hall Hammond, Attorney General of Maryland,* Circuit Court No. 2 of Baltimore City, No. 30021-A Docket 58A-184 (1949).

the time of this writing. In April, Maryland reworded the oath as a result of the Supreme Court overturning a similar law in Arizona.

ILLINOIS' BROYLES BILLS A startling example of how a few hysterical or unscrupulous zealots can pervert the truth and stampede a whole state into damaging its liberties took place in Illinois. In 1949, under the pressure of the American Legion, the Illinois legislature created the Subversive Activities Investigation Commission, better known as the Broyles Commission. Although it was empowered to investigate all kinds of subversion, from the Communist Party to the Ku Klux Klan, the Commission decided to concentrate on subversion in the schools and colleges. Most of its hearings were secret. The two chief investigators of the Commission, Benjamin Gitlow and J. B. Matthews, were admitted ex-Communist leaders. No specific accusations were made against any of the teachers or professors who were called to testify. Two openly registered Communist Party clubs of ten students each were found at the University of Chicago (enrollment 8,500) and Roosevelt College (enrollment 6,000), but no other Communists were turned up by all the investigation. Not a single faculty member was found who had ever made a "Communist utterance or writing."

The work of the Commission was opposed by the major Illinois newspapers, including the ultra-conservative Chicago *Tribune*, by the Chicago Bar Association, by the Chicago Federation of Labor, by the Illinois Congress of Parents and Teachers, and by many other reputable civic groups. California Congressman Richard Nixon, testifying before the Commission, warned that using the techniques of totalitarianism might destroy the very Constitution the Commission claimed to be protecting. Yet the Commission ignored its evidence (or lack of it), accused its opposition of being Communists, fellow travelers and dupes, and recommended legislation restricting the freedom of teaching, inquiry, speech, and assembly.

The published transcript of the hearings of the Commission reveal the crude kinds of hearsay evidence that enflamed those willing to destroy freedom to force social conformity. One non-Commission member who attended its secret sessions was the chairman of the Americanism Commission of the American Legion, Department of Illinois. Early in the hearings he urged that the Commission subpoena a Professor Pooche of the University of Chicago, whom he charged with being an "avowed Communist." Actually, there was no one by this name—or any similar name—at the University, nor had there ever been! This same Legionnaire also urged the subpoenaing of a "Bloggert" of the University of Illinois, "who had written a book on social science." That may have been

Ralph Blodgett, a professor of economics who was asked a year or so later to resign because of the extreme conservatism of his economic views.[12] It was on the basis of this kind of wild, unsubstantiated charge that the Commission recommended legislation known generally as the Broyles bills.

Although the Broyles bills were killed in the 1949, 1951, and 1953 sessions of the legislature, the loyalty oath, which was copied from the Ober Act and was one of the Broyles Bills, was finally passed in 1955.[13]

WASHINGTON'S SUBVERSIVE ACTIVITIES ACT In 1951, the state of Washington passed a "subversive activities act" patterned after Maryland's Ober Act, and in 1955 it instituted a loyalty oath. Two members of the University of Washington faculty, Max Savelle and Howard Nostrand, refused to sign the oath, commenting that "it represents a frightening assumption by the state for controlling and regulating thought." After a confusing course through the courts, the United States Supreme Court on January 22, 1964, ruled the loyalty oath unconstitutional. "The Court's opinion casts a cloud of doubt over the oath laws of 26 states which may now be caught in the decision's backwash."[14]

THE UNIVERSITY OF CALIFORNIA OATH Concrete evidence of the damage possible from the requirement of loyalty oaths can be seen in the effects on the campuses of the University of California between 1949 and 1951. In 1949 the Board of Regents prescribed an oath which required university faculty members to swear that they were not members of any organization that "believes in, advocates, or teaches the overthrow of the United States Government, by force or by any illegal or unconstitutional methods." A number of the faculty refused to sign the oath, on the grounds of constitutionality. Although the Regents admitted that Communism and subversion were no longer the issue, the non-signers were discharged, because, according to Governor Earl Warren, they were "recalcitrant and won't conform." The legislature adopted a loyalty oath for all state employees in 1950, and the Board of Regents dropped their own, thus ending the controversy.

But the damage had been done. In the end, 26 faculty members had been dismissed, 37 others had resigned in protest ("including some of the most distinguished members of the faculty"), and 47 prospective staff members made "pointed refusals of appointment." Because of the

[12] "*To take a copy from the Nazis*" (Chicago: American Civil Liberties Union, Chicago Division 1951), pp. 6–7.

[13] *Illinois Education*, 44 (Sept., 1955): 19.

[14] *AAUP Bulletin*, 50 (Autumn, 1964): 228, 221.

loss of staff, 55 courses were dropped from the curriculum.[15] Although most of the dismissed faculty were invited to return to the University, most of them refused.

> And from all this wreckage of reputation, morale and intellectual power were dredged exactly two people who could be labeled as Communists. One was a piano player employed in dancing classes. The other was a part-time graduate student working as a teaching assistant.
>
> In short, the action of the regents followed the pattern of hysteria-induced actions—it came dangerously close the destroying the thing it was supposed to save.[16]

EFFECT OF LOYALTY OATHS AND INVESTIGATIONS From the lack of evidence of subversion turned up by investigating committees, it seems questionable that there was ever any expectation that such investigations and oaths would fight Communism. It is very clear, however, that these violations of academic freedom did have a deleterious effect on the search for truth and the preparation of our youth to live realistically and wisely in a time of social conflict. In an earlier period of social conservatism, the 1920's, an Indiana study had found that investigations into teacher activity had uncovered few cases of disloyalty, but that "the great mass of public school teachers were conscious of the censorious eye fixed upon them." In commenting on this statement, Howard K. Beale noted: "Investigation or threat of investigation in a few cases was sufficient to frighten nearly all teachers into 'loyalty' of the current school-official brand."[17] As Governor Warren stated, teachers and professors have been disciplined when they refuse to "conform." The American Civil Liberties Union remarked in 1951: "As a consequence, teachers everywhere have been made less courageous and less independent in the pursuit of truth, more cautious and more subservient."

Because of these inhibitions on freedom of teaching, organizations such as the American Civil Liberties Union and the American Association of University Professors have continued their efforts to have these oaths repealed. In August of 1965, suit was brought by Georgia affiliates of these two associations in Federal District Court in Atlanta, asking for a temporary restraining order to prevent firing, or refusing to

[15] "Academic Freedom & Tenure in the Quest for National Security," *AAUP Bulletin*, 42 (Spring, 1956): 105–106.

[16] Dan Fowler, "How to Damage a University," *Look*, 16 (Jan. 29, 1952).

[17] *Are American Teachers Free?* (New York: Scribner's, 1936), pp. 64–65. Referring to Bessie L. Pierce, *Public Opinion & The Teaching of History in the United States*, pp. 128–129.

hire, professors who will not subscribe to controversial oaths. The suit also asked that the oaths be ruled unconstitutional, complaining that the oaths of 1935 and 1949 were so vaguely worded that teachers and professors

> are required to steer far wider of the unlawful zone and restrict their inquiries and discussions to areas which are unquestionably safe. The inevitable effect of this unwarranted inhibition is to chill that free play of spirit and open-minded inquiry which it is the responsibility of all teachers to cultivate and upon which our democracy ultimately rests.[18]

ARIZONA AND THE ELFBRANDT DECISION The attitude of the Supreme Court toward loyalty oaths seems to be changing. In the early 1950's the Court upheld loyalty oaths relating to public employees in Los Angeles, teachers in New York State, and candidates for office in Maryland. More recently it invalidated Oklahoma's oath for public employees, Arkansas' loyalty oath for teachers, Florida's oath for public employees, and the state of Washington's oath for public employees and teachers. The most recent test involved the Arizona loyalty oath.

In 1961, Vernon and Barbara Elfbrandt, teachers in Tucson, refused to sign the Arizona loyalty oath, but continued to teach without pay until the spring of 1966 while the case was making its slow passage through the involved judicial processes of our appeals system. On April 18, 1966, the United States Supreme Court finally declared the oath unconstitutional. Justice William O. Douglas, who wrote the decision for the 5-to-4 majority, write that the wording was vague and that a person could be convicted of swearing a false oath even if he did not know the groups he had joined were Communist dominated and even if he did not subscribe to the subversive aims of the groups.

Censorship of Books

Closely related to the censorship of teachers has been the censorship of textbooks and libraries. Many books have been banned on grounds of obscenity and pornography. In addition to the novels of Steinbeck, Dos Passos, Orwell, Huxley, and Faulkner, unexpurgated editions of the classics—Chaucer, Shakespeare, Boccaccio, Rabelais—have been among those considered unfit for the eyes of high-school adolescents. Biology books have been criticized for presenting facts about human physiology and discussions of reproduction. Occasionally these attacks have been

[18] Quoted in *School and Society*, 93 (October 16, 1965): 362 ff.

delightfully absurd. For example, one Miami housewife assailed a very popular high-school biology text because it was pornographic. Displaying silhouettes of an adolescent boy and girl on facing pages in the book, she said, "Look at these naked children! You close the book and. . . ." With a nod of her head, she left the members of the Florida Interim Legislative Committee on Education to imagine the gross immorality going on inside that closed book.[19] Unfortunately, few of the attacks are so easily laughed off.

Although sex and profanity have been the targets of much censorship, by far the most serious attacks on academic freedom have centered around history and social studies textbooks. In the period of conservative reaction following World War I a number of states, including Wisconsin, New York, Oregon, Oklahoma, and California, enacted legislation designed to censor texts in these areas. In 1927 and 1928, resolutions were introduced in Congress calling for a national investigation of history textbooks. In general the charges against the books were that they were "wanting in national and patriotic spirit."

One history textbook under frequent attack was David S. Muzzey's *American History*. One northern city banned it because the local high school was named for General Grant and Muzzey had drawn an "unfavorable picture of Grant." North Carolina banned the book when some of the Daughters of the American Revolution and the United Daughters of the Confederacy pointed out that Muzzey had cited slavery as the chief cause of the Civil War. In other states and cities the book was removed from schools because it discussed socialism or because it did not "give sufficiently patriotic account of the founders of the nation." When a Washington, D.C., group attempted to have Muzzey's text banned, the author was called on to defend himself. Against the charge that he was an Englishman spreading British propaganda, he replied that his English ancestors had come to America in 1680 and one had been buried on the field of the Battle of Lexington. Sentences which had been quoted by his opponents he put back into context. The censors were defeated. When Mayor William H. Thompson banned the Muzzey books from the Chicago schools, the author sued lawyer John J. Gorman for damages. Gorman's attacks on Muzzey's text led to the lawyer's disbarring. To have Muzzey's suit discontinued, Gorman wrote a letter of apology and retraction, admitting that he had not even read the textbook he had attacked.

[19] From an oral report of H. Phil Constans, Jr., President of the Florida Education Association, who attended the hearings of the Interim Committee from 1957–1959.

> A careful study of your textbooks discloses nothing which I would criticize and I consider the books well adapted to use in the public schools.[20]

But as usual in such matters, much damage had already been done. Muzzey and other historians introduced changes in their revisions which would not offend "patriotic" critics, although the quality of this history sometimes suffered.

During the 1930's favorite targets for the self-appointed censors were the social studies texts by Harold Rugg, and after World War II, there was a spate of bans against *Scholastic* and *The Nation* magazines and the *Building America* series of N.E.A.-developed social studies textbooks. As in the Muzzey conflicts, the critics grossly misrepresented the contents of the books by misquoting, taking material out of context, exaggerating minor details, and charging authors with disloyalty because they were or had been members of liberal organizations.[21] In spite of strenuous opposition from the N.E.A., the American Library Association, and many other educational and scholarly associations, states and communities were frightened into removing the offending books and magazines from their schools and libraries.

Defenses of Academic Freedom

Supporters of the principle of academic freedom have taken some steps to combat censorship, loyalty oaths, teacher dismissals, and other attacks on academic freedom. The most vigorous defender of academic freedom has been the American Association of University Professors, whose concern is limited, unfortunately, to teachers at the college level. In 1915 the AAUP formulated a statement on academic freedom and tenure which has been the basis of much of its active program ever since, with revisions in 1925 and 1940. The 1940 statement has been endorsed by other organizations, including the American Library Association, Association of American Colleges, Association of American Law Schools, American Political Science Association, American Association of Colleges for Teacher Education, Association for Higher Education (a department of the N.E.A.), and American Philosophical Association. The AAUP did not grow spectacularly until after World War II. It began with 867 members in 1915. In 1935 it had only 11,500 members; in 1945, only 16,910. But by 1950, at the height of the gravest attacks on academic

[20] Beale, pp. 262–264, 271–272, 300–302, 615–616, 280–281.
[21] Helen Luce, *The Right to Find Out* (San Bernardino: California Library Committee on Intellectual Freedom, 1948), pp. 2–3, 14.

freedom, the membership had grown to 37,524 and by January 1, 1966 it had reached 74,962, with active chapters at 936 colleges and universities.[22] This rapid growth was clearly in reaction to the threats to academic freedom. Between 1945 and 1950, the Association considered 227 cases involving attacks on academic freedom and during "the decade of the fifties, legislative investigations heavily taxed academic freedom."[23]

In cases where professors are discharged or contracts not renewed and there appears to be a violation of the rights of academic freedom or tenure, the AAUP investigates the case carefully, and if the evidence indicates a violation of those rights, the Association votes censure of the administration of the offending institution. Censured administrations are listed in each issue of the *Bulletin* until satisfactory adjustment is made in the institution's personnel procedures to assure the protection of academic freedom. Many professors refuse to accept appointments from and refuse to refer students to institutions whose administrations are on the censured list.

Not until the general public comes to an awareness of the dangers to democracy inherent in the loss of rights of free speech and free thought can there be any relaxing of the efforts to protect academic freedom. It is only through the untrammeled search for truth that a democratic society can progress effectively. Justice Black pointed that out very forcefully in his dissenting opinion in *Barenblatt vs. United States,* holding that

> the obloquy which results from investigations such as this prevents all but the most courageous from hazarding any views which might at some later time become disfavored. This result, whose importance cannot be overestimated, is doubly critical when it affects the universities, on which we must largely rely for the experimentation and development of new ideas essential to our country's welfare.[24]

Teacher Preparation and Certification

One of the most acrimonious debates in education has been over the kind of preparation appropriate for teachers and whether or not they should be required to take courses in pedagogical methodology. Professors of education, leaders of teacher organizations, and school administrators generally defend present practices. The critics come from both

[22] AAUP *Bulletin,* 51 (May, 1965): 110, 117; 52 (Spring, 1966): 72.
[23] AAUP *Bulletin,* 50 (Sept., 1964): 225.
[24] 360 United States 109 (1959), p. 144.

within and outside education itself, as is indicated by a listing of some spokesmen: history professor Arthur Bestor, atomic submarine admiral Hyman Rickover, free-lance writer John Keats, columnist Dorothy Thompson, and businessman Albert Lynd. Some of these critics have organized the Council for Basic Education to promote a return to the curriculum of "liberal arts" in the schools and the elimination of any pedagogical courses in the preparation of teachers.

Some of the criticism has been constructive and has resulted in intelligent changes to improve schools and teachers. But much of it has been based on ignorance of what schools and teachers colleges were actually doing. Some critics have seemed more interested in creating sensational reading material than in improving schools. Ridiculous assertions have been made for which there is little, if any, justification. For example, John Keats generalizes about all teachers from his own statements about a fictional "Fairly Normal" teachers college, supposedly in New York. The weaknesses of all teachers he attributes to the lack of attention to courses in subject matter required in teachers colleges.

> In teachers college, she spent far more time learning to ventilate a classroom than she spent learning anything she might be asked to teach. Then she was told she could teach students a foreign language without being able to read, write or pronounce it herself. . . . A lesson on "proper classroom ventilation," for instance, is not just a five-minute lecture, but a separate course, the gist of which is that classroom air should be kept fresh and at a constant temperature. I regret having to say I am serious.[25]

If indeed there is such a college offering such a course, it is certainly an exception rather than a rule, as Keats implies. The educators' reaction to this kind of criticism is often almost as bad; with their defense based on the best schools and colleges, they accuse the critics of ulterior motives and resort to name-calling.

Because of the furor, the N.E.A. Commission on Teacher Education and Professional Standards began a series of annual meetings of leading specialists in education and specialists in liberal arts to discuss teacher preparation and similar matters. At the first of these TEPS conferences in 1958, over a thousand participants joined in five days of discussions and reports leading to new important cooperation between education specialists and liberal arts professors in teacher-preparation programs,

[25] John Keats, "How Well Are Our Teachers Being Taught? Never Worse!" *Better Homes & Gardens*, 36 (May, 1958): 51, 52.

developing the idea that preparing teachers is a responsibility of the whole university, not merely that of the colleges of education.

In 1961 the Carnegie Corporation provided a grant for a study of teacher education and certification by James Bryant Conant, a former president of Harvard. Conant published his conclusions in 1963, making twenty-seven recommendations about teacher certification and preparation but putting the main responsibility on the colleges and universities to decide what a teacher needs to know in order to be able to teach.[26] Unfortunately, Conant apparently failed to take into account past experience in certifying teachers. It was precisely the lack of specified standards that created the extreme of teachers colleges in which methods courses proliferate and the values of a general cultural education are ignored, and of liberal arts colleges in which teachers are produced with some command of subject matter but little knowledge of children, the schools, or the kind of subject matter appropriate for school teaching. However, as with the TEPS conferences, the Conant study offered another basis for discussion of the problems of preparing and certifying teachers.

Teaching Methods

Associated with the issue of how teachers should be prepared is the question of what teaching methods should be used. Much of the controversy over methods is directly related to the conflicts over the philosophy and purposes of schools discussed in the preceding chapter. A great deal of it results from the fact that teachers do not use the best theory that they have been taught but rely on run-of-the-mill routines most teachers have limped along with for years. Part of the controversy comes from the ignorance of the general public about what actually goes on in schools. Some of it is the fault of enthusiasts for educational panaceas, propagandists who are convinced that they have the answer to all the problems of teaching—the Montessori method, the Initial Teaching Alphabet, new curriculum arrangements of mathematics or science, any of which may be useful but none of which is a complete solution. The development of teaching into a vocation of highly professional characteristics depends largely on improving the theory of how to teach and getting teachers to use the best theoretical knowledge in determining what methods to use with a particular class or individual student.

[26] *The Education of American Teachers* (New York: McGraw-Hill, 1963), pp. 210–217.

Audio-Visual Media

The oldest aids to learning are, of course, the teacher and the textbook. Teachers have helped youth learn from earliest recorded history: even early primitive societies delegated teaching responsibilities to parents and witch doctors. Books have been used ever since man has learned to write and particularly since printing was invented. The use of pictures in books dates back to the early fifteenth century, but the first important illustrated textbook was Comenius' *Orbis Pictus*, or *The World in Pictures*, published in 1658. Within thirty years America had its famous picture textbook, the *New England Primer*. Books and pictures still make up an important part of the teacher's arsenal against ignorance, but modern inventions have extended our teaching weapons so greatly that the teacher who uses only the textbook as a teaching medium is greatly limiting his fire power.

The range of teaching media has been expanding for over a century. Between 1838 and 1848 Horace Mann encouraged the use of blackboards, globes, maps, scientific demonstration kits, and other "school apparatus." The Columbia Exposition in Philadelphia resulted in the Commercial Museum, which began to distribute collections of objects and photographs to schools in 1900.[27] At the close of the 1905 Louisiana Purchase Exposition, St. Louis city school superintendent Louis Soldan persuaded exhibitors to leave parts of their displays to a school museum.[28] Chicago's audio-visual program developed from a "projection club" organized by the principals of the schools, each of whom contributed $25 toward a fund for the purchase of lantern slides, each school purchasing its own projector. In 1917 the city school board took over the equipment of the club and set up a visual education department.[29]

The romance of radio created considerable educational excitement during the early years of that medium. As early as 1919 WHA, the state-owned radio station of the University of Wisconsin, began a regularly scheduled program of broadcasts to schools. Some of the radio pioneers envisioned radio as the panacea for the nation's educational ills, with master teachers lecturing to the remotest classrooms while poorly trained child custodians maintained order and checked attendance. Even conservative educators found themselves caught in the wave of enthusiasm. In 1930 William C. Bagley predicted that the "educational talkie and

[27] James S. Kinder and F. Dean McClusky (eds.), *The Audio-Visual Reader* (Dubuque: Brown, 1954), p. 31.

[28] National Society for the Study of Education, 48th Yearbook, Part I, *Audio-visual Materials of Instruction* (Chicago: U. of Chicago Press, 1949), p. 128.

[29] Kinder and McClusky, pp. 32–33.

radio-television" would revolutionize classrooms all over America. Even the opening exercises would be conducted by specialists, who would lead the children in a song and the pledge of allegiance. By enabling "the very ablest teachers . . . to carry their work to millions of pupils," the cost of schooling would be reduced. One school superintendent claimed, "The expense of teaching pupils in the public schools by means of radio is much less than the cost of instruction by any other known means."[30]

The enthusiasm for radio as a teaching device was widespread. Of the 627 licensed broadcasting stations in the United States in 1930, 77 (12.3 percent) were owned and operated by educational institutions. Fifty-three of the educational stations were on the air an average of eight hours a week, and 280 commercial stations reported a weekly average of seven and a half hours of educational broadcasting. The Damrosch Music Appreciation Hour was said to be reaching 150,000 schools. On February 4, 1930, the Columbia Broadcasting System began "an educational program in history, literature, music and art, prepared under a corps of experts headed by Dr. William Chandler Bagley."[31] By 1936, broadcasting licenses had been granted 202 educational institutions.

But the enthusiasm quickly died down and by 1944 fewer than 25 noncommercial stations were still on the air.[32] The *Education Index* lists twelve columns of articles on radio, including eight columns on "Radio in Education," published between January 1929 and June 1932; for the period between July 1959 and June 1961, the *Index* lists less than one column of articles on radio. As with other panaceas, radio failed to solve all the educational ills, and unfortunately it is not used effectively in those areas in which it could contribute greatly to improve education in schools or in adult learning.

The motion picture also stimulated extravagant claims, but these too have come to little. In 1922 Thomas Edison said that the motion picture would "revolutionize our educational system, and . . . in a few years it will supplant largely, if not entirely, the use of textbooks in our schools." Edison saw the movies providing "one-hundred percent efficiency" as contrasted with "only about two percent efficiency" of school books.[33] Although a few educational films had been made prior to World War II, it was the training program of the armed forces that

[30] Earl Y. Poore, "Learning's New Tool: Radio & the Public Address System," *The Nation's Schools*, 7 (March, 1931): 58–59.

[31] H. G. Cisin, "Modernizing Educational Methods through Radio Instruction," *The Nation's Schools*, 8 (July, 1931): 31.

[32] NSSE 48th Yearbook, pp. 33–34.

[33] Quoted in Hugh Weir, "The Story of the Motion Picture," *McClure's Magazine*, 51 (Nov., 1922): 85.

revealed how effective the motion picture and other audio-visual media could be. The armed forces produced over 5,000 sound motion pictures and over 3,000 film strips. The example of the war-time training programs gave rise to the increased use of films in schools and colleges. In 1947 the *Educational Film Guide* analyzed 3,758 sound and silent films, including those appropriate for every level of school from the primary grades to university. The largest number of films were related to social studies, but other areas included science, industrial arts, health and physical education, art, music, mathematics, language arts, foreign language, and guidance. Unfortunately, many instructors relied on the movie to do the teaching, without sufficient preparation and follow-up. As a consequence, movies have not been the effective aid they can be in the repertoire of a master classroom teacher.

The possibilities of mass education through television has excited more public interest—and financial support—than any of the previously developed audio-visual media. As early as 1951, 56 colleges and universities, 4 medical schools, 19 public schools, and 2 public libraries were producing television programs. In 1952 the Federal Communications Commission set aside television channels for educational purposes, and in 1963 it established 31 channels in the 2500-2690 mc frequency band for exclusive educational use. These 2500 mc channels are intended for low-cost ($25,000), short-range (5 to 20 miles) stations. The federal government has encouraged educational television by financial grants and presently offers aid through provisions of the Educational Television Facilities Act (87-447), National Defense Education Act (85-864), Economic Opportunities Act (88-452), and the Elementary and Secondary Education Act of 1965 (89-10).

A unique experiment in educational television is the Midwest Project on Airborne Television Instruction (MPATI), which broadcasts 26 programs four days a week to over 2,000 schools in six states by means of transmitters in an airplane flying over Purdue University. Station WNDT, transmitting from the top of the Empire State Building in New York, reaches two million pupils in six thousand schools in three states. By the fall of 1965 there were 102 educational television stations broadcasting open-circuit programs in the United States and nearly 900 closed-circuit television systems instructing an estimated seven million students.[34]

It will be interesting to see whether educators have profited at all by their previous educational experiments with monitorial schools, radio

[34] C. Fred Kelley, "ETV—Today and Tomorrow," *American School and University*, 37 (August, 1965): 24–26. See also Walter Wittich, "What ETV Research Has Taught," *Nation's Schools*, 76 (October, 1965): 45–48.

teaching, and the educational movie. Will a panacea-like enthusiasm give way to disappointment in the face of classroom realities? Or will the experience of the past be useful in incorporating a potentially invaluable teaching aid into the arsenal against ignorance?

One of the causes for the failure of other audio-visual experiments has been the lack of teachers prepared to utilize the new media effectively. Before 1930, there were probably fewer than a dozen courses available in the nation to prospective teachers in the use of audio-visual materials. The number gradually increased in the 1930's, but in the following decade the course offerings increased rapidly, until by 1947 there were nearly four hundred such courses taught in the United States.[35] Now virtually every college preparing teachers offers some course work in "educational media."

Other Recent Innovations

The psychological experiments of B. F. Skinner have led to the creation of programed learning and the "teaching machine." The concept of programed learning holds great promise for improving teaching, partly through freeing teacher time from routine tasks for things which cannot yet be done by books and machines, partly by indicating ways in which the teacher can present material more effectively. During World War II the military forces used a number of electronic devices—such as the Link trainer—to facilitate the training of specialists. These too have become adapted to the work of schools, including mock automobiles for driver training and elaborate tape recording studios for foreign language instruction. The digital computer may be utilized effectively for more than assistance in record keeping and other administrative tasks. Combinations of computers, tape recorders, movie film and programed instruction may result in classrooms of the future which look like something from today's science fiction movies.

The specialization of knowledge has led to the recognition of the need for teams of teachers to help children draw effectively on several different bodies of knowledge and yet see the integrated application of knowledge to human problems. New schools are being built to permit the use of a greater range of methods and classroom organizations—large lecture rooms, small discussion rooms, individual conference rooms, laboratories, bigger libraries with equipment for microfilm readers, tape recorders, and slide and movie projectors, as well as expanded collections of books and maps, globes, and the other more traditional audio-visual media.

Contrary to the promises of the early supporters of these devices, none

[35] NSSE, 48th Yearbook, pp. 26, 95.

of them has yet provided inexpensive schooling; rather they have increased the cost. This certainly does not mean that such teaching media are unnecessary frills, for the United States cannot afford poor education, and if television, motion pictures, electronic devices, and programed learning can improve education, we must invest in them. The greatest problems of educational technology are our failure to develop a fully articulated theory of teaching that will utilize mechanized and electronic devices effectively and our failure to train teachers and administrators who understand and take advantage of the technology we already possess.

Educational Issues and the Professional Educator

Some of the problems we have discussed must be solved primarily by the members of the education profession, including some of those problems dealing with method and details of content and the curriculum. Some must be solved by the general public, including the questions of church and state, racial segregation, the overall purpose of schools, and academic freedom. But even in these latter questions the teacher has an important responsibility. In many cases the general public is not even aware that a problem exists. When it is made aware of the problem, it needs to have the issues explained, the alternatives outlined, the possible consequences of each alternative pointed out, and expert opinions made available. Here the perspective of history is invaluable. A knowledge of any problem as it has developed helps us to see what issues really are involved. The experience of the past suggests alternatives and gives clues at least as to what may be successful and what unsuccessful. The educator who knows no history—or who knows history only as a conglomeration of dates and names unrelated to present problems—will be gravely handicapped in carrying out his professional responsibility of participation in making intelligent educational policies.

RESEARCH PROJECT

Select one of the following topics and prepare a paper of no more than 25 pages, tracing its historical development. Relate it to the social context of both the past and the present, considering attempts to solve it, and present your own evaluation of the problem in the perspective of history. You should limit the scope of the paper so that you can give reasonable coverage to the program. For example, the problem of federal aid might be limited to a consideration of secondary schools or to a particular part of the curriculum.

a. Curriculum of the schools
b. Teaching methods
c. Federal aid to education
d. State support of parochial schools
e. Religious exercises in public schools
f. Teacher education
g. Teacher certification
h. Interferences with academic freedom
j. Racial integration in schools

SUGGESTED READINGS

Bartky, John A. (ed.). *Social Issues in Public Education.* Boston: Houghton Mifflin, 1963.

Ehlers, Henry, and Lee, Gordon C. (eds.). *Crucial Issues in Education.* New York: Holt, Rinehart and Winston, 1964.

Johnston, Bernard (ed.). *Issues in Education. An Anthology of Controversy.* Boston: Houghton Mifflin, 1964.

Scott, C. Winfield, Hill, Clyde M., and Burns, Hobert W. *The Great Debate: Our Schools in Crisis.* Englewood Cliffs: Prentice-Hall, 1963.

This chapter ends with the developments current at the time the material was ready for the printer. To fill in the gap between that date and the immediate present, you will find periodical literature your best source. If you have not yet discovered the *Education Index* and the *Readers' Guide to Periodical Literature,* now is the time to explore them. Many periodicals, such as the *New York Times* and the *N.E.A. Journal,* have their own annual indices. Controversial questions frequently invite topical books which may be located through the card files of a library. The reports of the U.S. Office of Education are invaluable for statistical information. Legislative records and court reports provide primary sources of information, and most large libraries have files of records of state legislatures and courts as well as the *Congressional Record* and the *U.S. Report* on the United States Supreme Court.

EPILOGUE

The Stream of American Education

The stream of American education has not been steady and untroubled. At times, as in the late seventeenth century, change was slight and growth was slow. At other times, including our own century, change has come rapidly, and the stream has burst from its banks, opening up new courses and involving many more pupils and teachers. Occasionally the forces of the *status quo* have attempted to dam the stream and even reverse its flow, but they have never been entirely successful; even during the Federalist period and the Gilded Age, the stream of American education continued to expand. The growth of American education is an achievement of which we have a right to be proud.

Schools and Social Change

Many philosophers have proposed theories of how change occurs in the universe. Some attribute all progress to God. Others attribute change to forces inherent in nature. Such cosmic theories leave little room for the influence of man over his future. But if all change occurs because of impersonal or non-human forces, what role do schools play except to teach men to accept whatever fate has in store?

Opposed to those theories of change are others which give man some responsibility for what happens in his world. One view postulates that change comes because men, individually and collectively, make choices when they are faced with problems. And because they choose one alternative rather than another, they determine the direction of change in the world. In all these choices, the wisdom of the decision depends on the intelligence freed and operating at the time of the decision-making

Such a theory of social change gives a meaningful purpose to schooling, that of helping individuals be more intelligent in solving their problems, whether problems they must solve for themselves or those they will solve in conjunction with others.

The United States is going through a period of rapid social change. If we are to progress peacefully and with greatest benefit to all, we must maintain agencies for communicating information, clarifying values, and conducting social planning. A democratic government is one of those agencies, but it can be effective only if it is supported by schools which teach children the attitudes, information, and skills necessary for democratic living. Whether or not American education will be permitted to play this vital role will be determined by the way we solve the controversial issues affecting education in our culture. American education demands an interpretation of American history and American culture. If there is justification in the assumption that we are a culture that has grown largely through revolution, we must examine our present and future with the lessons of past revolutions in mind. And there lies the great challenge for the teacher who hopes to be a professional educator, helping to guide the future of American education and American culture.

Revolution or Evolution?

Future historians may be able to look back at our present period and describe us as the dying embers of a great social revolution and the beginning of an era of conservative reaction. Or they may see us as the opening stage of another turbulent period of rapid social progress leading to a new revolution. There is evidence now to support either analysis, and only time can tell what the prevailing forces will be. How much better it would be, however, if we could avoid both reaction and revolution, if the historian yet unborn could describe us as a people who learned to make progress without the need of periodic revolutions, with their heartbreak and disappointing reactions. If any society can hope to achieve such a distinction, it would seem to be a democracy with an effective democratic school system. Whether we continue to build that school system depends in part on you.

List of Sources

The following list is for convenience in ascertaining bibliographic data abbreviated in footnotes. Since the full citation appears at the first reference to a source, those sources which are cited only once are not included here. This list does not include the additional readings suggested at the ends of Chapters unless they also appear in footnotes.

Among the most frequently used sources are the publications of the United States Office (Bureau) of Education, including *Biennial Surveys, Bulletins, Circulars of Information,* and *Reports. The Congressional Record* and its predecessor *The Congressional Globe* are sources for much of the debates on federal influence over education. Laws are generally taken from the various state codes or from the *U. S. Statutes at Large.* Court decisions and legal references follow the footnote form in law reporting and correspond to shelving practices of law libraries.

Among the frequently used non-governmental sources are the periodicals and yearbooks of education associations, including the American Association of University Professors, the National Education Association, the National Herbart Society, and the National Society for the Study of Education. They are cited by the initials of the associations, *e.g., NEA Proceedings* or *NSSE 13th Yearbook.*

The sources mentioned in the preceding paragraphs are generally not included in this *List of Sources.* Exceptions include those which are cited by author, such as Kilpatrick's study of the Dutch Schools of New Netherlands.

Aikin, Wilford M. *The Story of the Eight-Year Study.* New York: Harper, 1942.

American Civil Liberties Union. "Academic Freedom and Academic Responsibility," *American Association of University Professors Bulletin,* Vol. 42, No. 3 (Autumn, 1956).

Ashmore, Harry S. *The Negro and the Schools.* Chapel Hill: U. of North Carolina Press, 1954.

Axt, Richard G. *The Federal Government and Financing Higher Education.* New York: Columbia U. Press, 1952.

Barnard, Henry. *American Journal of Education.* Volumes published from 1855–1888.

Beale, Howard K. *Are American Teachers Free?* New York: Scribner's, 1936.

Bode, Boyd H. *Modern Educational Theories*. New York: Macmillan, 1927.
Boles, Donald E. *The Bible, Religion and the Public Schools*. Ames: Iowa State U. Press, 1963.
Bond, Horace Mann. *The Education of the Negro in the American Social Order*. New York: Prentice-Hall, 1934.
Bourne, Randolph S. *The Gary Schools*. Boston: Houghton Mifflin, 1916.
Bourne, William Oland. *History of the Public School Society of the City of New York*. New York: William Wood, 1870.
Brameld, Theodore. *Patterns of Educational Philosophy*. New York: World Book, 1950.
Brown, Elmer Ellsworth. "Secondary Education in the United States," *The School Review*, Vol. VII, No. 1 (January 1899).
______. *The Making of Our Middle Schools*. New York: Longmans, Green, 1902.
Brubacher, John S., and Rudy, Willis. *Higher Education in Transition*. New York: Harper and Row, 1958.
Butler, Nicholas Murray. *Education in the United States*. New York: American Book, 1910.
Carter, James Gordon. *Essays Upon Popular Education Containing a Particular Examination of the Schools of Massachusetts and an Outline of an Institution for the Education of Teachers*. Boston: Bowles and Dearborn, 1826.
Childs, John L. *American Pragmatism and Education*. New York: Holt, 1956.
Clews (Parsons), Elsie W. *Educational Legislation and Administration of the Colonial Government*. New York: Columbia U. Press, 1899.
Clift, Virgil A., Anderson, Archibald W., and Hullfish, H. Gordon. *Negro Education in America*. The Sixteenth Yearbook of the John Dewey Society. New York: Harper, 1962.
Commons, John R., *et al*. *A Documentary History of American Industrial Society*. Cleveland: Arthur H. Clark Co., 1910.
Cremin, Lawrence A. *The Transformation of the School*. New York: Knopf, 1961.
Cubberley, Ellwood P. *Readings in Public Education in the United States*. Boston: Houghton Mifflin, 1934.
______, and Elliot, Edward C. *State and County School Administration*. Vol. II, Source Book. New York: Macmillan, 1915.
Dabney, Charles William. *Universal Education in the South*. Chapel Hill: U. of North Carolina Press, 1936.
Davis, Sheldon Emmor. *Educational Periodicals During the Nineteenth Century*. U. S. Bureau of Education Bulletin, 1919, No. 28.
Dewey, John. *Democracy and Education*. New York: Macmillan, 1916.
______. "Progressive Education and the Science of Education," *Progressive Education*, Vol. V, No. 3 (July-August-September 1928).
______, and Dewey, Evelyn. *Schools of To-morrow*. New York: Dutton, 1915.
Eaton, John. "The Relation of the National Government to Public Education," *Proceedings of the National Teachers Association*, 1857–1870.

Educational Policies Commission. *Federal Activities in Education*. Washington: National Education Association, 1939.

Eliot, Charles W. *Educational Reform*. New York: Century, 1898.

Ellsbree, Willard S. *The American Teacher*. New York: American Book, 1939.

Farish, Hunter Dickinson. *Journal and Letters of Philip Vickers Fithian, 1773–1774*. Williamsburg: Colonial Williamsburg, 1943.

Finegan, Thomas E. *Free Schools: A Documentary History of the Free School Movement in New York State*. Albany: U. of the State of New York, 1921.

Fitzpatrick, John C. (ed.). *The Writings of George Washington*. Washington: Government Printing Office, 1939.

Flanders, Jesse K. *Legislative Control of the Elementary Curriculum*. New York: Teachers College, 1925.

Ford, Paul Leicester. *The Works of Thomas Jefferson*. New York: G. P. Putnam's Sons, 1905.

Hansen, Allen Oscar. *Liberalism and American Education in the Eighteenth Century*. New York: Macmillan, 1926.

Harper, Charles A. *A Century of Public Teacher Education*. Washington: American Association of Teachers Colleges, 1939.

Harris, William T. *Psychological Foundations of Education*. New York: D. Appleton, 1898.

Harrower, John. "Diary of John Harrower, 1773–1776," *The American Historical Review*, Vol. VI, No. 1 (October 1900).

Hening. *Statutes at Large of Virginia*.

Hinsdale, B. A. "Documents Illustrative of American Educational History." U. S. Office of Education Report, 1892–1893, Part II.

Hofstadter, Richard, and Smith, Wilson (editors). *American Higher Education, A Documentary History*. Chicago: U. of Chicago Press, 1961.

Honeywell, Roy J. *The Educational Work of Thomas Jefferson*. Cambridge: Harvard U. Press, 1931.

Hubbard, Lucius L. *University of Michigan: Its Origin, Growth and Principles of Government*. Ann Arbor: U. of Michigan Press, 1923.

Huxley, Thomas. *Science and Education*. New York: D. Appleton, 1898.

Jernigan, Marcus W. *Laboring and Dependent Classes in Colonial America 1607–1783*. Chicago: U. of Chicago Press, 1931.

Johns, R. L., and Morphet, Edgar L. *Financing the Public Schools*. Englewood Cliffs: Prentice-Hall, 1960.

Kandel, I. L. *History of Secondary Education*. Boston: Houghton Mifflin, 1930.

Kilpatrick, William H. *The Dutch School of New Netherlands and Colonial New York*. Washington: U. S. Bureau of Education, Bulletin, 1912, No. 12.

_______. "The Project Method," *Teachers College Record*, Vol. XIX, No. 4 (September 1918).

Kinder, James S., and McClusky, F. Dean (eds.). *The Audio-Visual Reader*. Dubuque: William C. Brown, 1954.

Knight, Edgar W. *A Documentary History of Education in the South Before 1860*. Chapel Hill: U. of North Carolina Press, 1949.

———. *Fifty Years of American Education*. New York: Ronald Press, 1952.
———. *Public Education in the South*. Boston: Ginn, 1922.
———. "The Story of Teacher Training," *High School Journal*, Vol. X, No. 8 (December, 1927).
———, and Hall, Clifton L. *Readings in American Educational History*. New York: Appleton-Century-Crofts, 1951.
Leavell, Ullin Whitney, *Philanthropy in Negro Education*. Nashville: George Peabody College for Teachers, 1930.
Lee, Gordon Canfield. *The Struggle for Federal Aid: First Phase*. New York: Teachers College, 1949.
Lipscomb, Andrew W. (ed.). *The Writings of Thomas Jefferson*. Washington: The Thomas Jefferson Memorial Association, 1903.
Lyman, Rollo La Verne. *English Grammar in American Schools Before 1850*. Chicago: U. of Chicago Libraries, 1922.
Machlup, Fritz. "On Some Misconceptions Concerning Academic Freedom," *American Association of University Professors Bulletin*. Vol. 41, No. 4 (Winter, 1955).
Madison, James. *Letters and Other Writings*. New York: R. Worthington, 1884.
Mann, Horace. *Annual Reports of the Board of Education*. Boston: Dutton and Wentworth, 1843–1855.
McCall, William A. *How to Measure in Education*. New York: Macmillan, 1922.
McHale, Kathryn. *Changes and Experiments in Liberal-Arts Education*, National Society for the Study of Education, Thirty-first Yearbook, Part II. Bloomington, Illinois: Public School Publishing Co., 1932.
Melby, Ernest O., and Puner, Morton (eds.). *Freedom and Public Education*. New York: Praeger, 1953.
Meriwether, Colyer. *History of Higher Education in South Carolina*. U. S. Bureau of Education, Circular of Information No. 3, 1888.
Monroe, Paul. *The Founding of the American Public School System*. Ann Arbor: University Microfilms, 1940. Vol. II.
Morton, Richard L. *Colonial Virginia*. Chapel Hill: U. of North Carolina Press, 1960.
Mulhern, James. *A History of Secondary Education in Pennsylvania*. Philadelphia: Published by the author, 1933.
New England's First Fruits. London, 1643. Massachusetts Historical Collection. 1792. Vol. I, pp. 242–246.
Nightingale, A. F. "The Claims of the Classics," N. E. A. *Proceedings*, 1887.
Parker, Francis W. *Notes on Talks on Teaching*. New York: E. L. Kellogg, 1884.
———. *Talks on Pedagogics*. New York: E. L. Kellogg, 1894.
Parkhurst, Helen. *Education on the Dalton Plan*. New York: E. P. Dutton, 1922.
Pennington, Edgar Legare. *The Reverend Thomas Bray*. Philadelphia: The Church Historical Society, 1934.
Pfeffer, Leo. *Church, State and Freedom*. Boston: Beacon Press, 1953.
Pierce, Truman, *et al*. *White and Negro Schools in the South: An Analysis of Biracial Education*. Englewood Cliffs: Prentice-Hall, 1955.

Poore, Ben. Perley. *The Federal and State Constitutions, Colonial Charters and Other Organic Laws of the United States.* Washington: Government Printing Office, 1877.

Reid, Herbert O. "The Supreme Court Decision and Interposition," *Journal of Negro Education*, Vol. XXV, No. 2 (Spring, 1956).

Reutter, E. Edmund. *The School Administrators and Subversive Activities.* New York: Teachers College, Columbia U., 1951.

Rice, Jesse Pearl. *J. L. M. Curry, Southerner, Statesman, and Educator.* New York: King's Crown Press, 1949.

Sagendorph, Kent. *Michigan.* New York: E. P. Dutton, 1948.

Seybolt, Robert F. *The Evening Schools of Colonial America.* Urbana: U. of Illinois, Bureau of Educational Research, Bulletin No. 24, 1925.

———. *The Private Schools of Colonial Boston.* Cambridge: Harvard U. Press, 1935.

———. *The Public Schools of Colonial Boston*, 1635–1775. Cambridge: Harvard U. Press, 1935.

———. *Source Studies in American Colonial Education:* The Private School. Urbana: U. of Illinois, Bulletin No. 28, Bureau of Educational Research, 1925.

Sheldon, Edward Austin. *Autobiography.* New York: Ives-Butler, 1911.

Shoemaker, Ervin C. *Noah Webster: Pioneer of Learning.* New York: Columbia U. Press, 1936.

Shurtleff, Nathaniel B. (ed.). *Records of the Governor and Company of the Massachusetts Bay in New England, Vol. II 1642–1649.* Boston: Press of William White, 1853.

Spencer, Herbert. "What Knowledge Is of Most Worth?" *Education: Intellectual, Moral, and Physical.* New York: D. Appleton, 1860.

Steiner, Bernard C. *History of Education in Maryland.* U. S. Bureau of Education, Circular of Information No. 2, 1894.

Stout, John Elbert. *The Development of High-School Curricula in the North Central States From 1860 to 1918.* Chicago: U. of Chicago Press, 1921.

Tewksbury, Donald G. *The Founding of American Colleges and Universities Before the Civil War.* New York: Teachers College, 1932.

Turner, Frederick Jackson, *The Frontier in American History.* New York: Holt, 1921.

Venable, W. H. *Beginnings of Literary Culture in the Ohio Valley.* New York: Peter Smith, 1949.

Washburne, Carleton W., and Marland, Sidney P. *Winnetka, The History and Significance of an Educational Experiment.* Englewood Cliff: Prentice-Hall, 1963.

Washington, Booker T. *Up From Slavery, An Autobiography.* New York: Doubleday, Doran, 1938.

Wickersham, J. P. A *History of Education in Pennsylvania.* Lancaster: Inquirer Press, 1886.

Wittich, Walter Arno, and Schuller, Charles Francis. *Audio-Visual Materials: Their Nature and Use.* New York: Harper, 1957.

Woody, Thomas. *A History of Women's Education in the United States.* New York: Science Press, 1929.

Index

This Index includes the birth and death dates of significant persons included in the text.